W9-ABG-485

MULTICULTURAL TEACHING

MULTICULTURAL TEACHING

A Handbook of Activities, Information, and Resources

FIFTH EDITION

Pamela L. Tiedt

University of California, Berkeley

Iris M. Tiedt

Dean of Education Emerita
Moorhead State University

Allyn and Bacon
Boston • London • Toronto • Sydney • Tokyo • Singapore

Series Editor: Frances Helland
Editorial Assistant: Bridget Keane
Editorial Production Administrator: Joe Sweeney
Editorial-Production Service: Walsh & Associates, Inc.
Composition Buyer: Linda Cox
Manufacturing Buyer: Suzanne Lareau
Cover Administrator: Linda Knowles

Copyright © 1999, 1995, 1990, 1986, 1979 by Allyn & Bacon
A Viacom Company
160 Gould Street
Needham Heights, MA 02494

Internet: www.abacon.com

Library of Congress Cataloging-in-Publication Data

Tiedt, Pamela L.
    Multicultural teaching : a handbook of activities, information,
and resources / Pamela L. Tiedt, Iris M. Tiedt.—5th ed.
      p. cm.
    Includes bibliographical references (p.   ) and index.
    ISBN 0-205-27528-1
    1. Multicultural education—United States.   2. Cross-cultural
orientation—United States.   3. Teaching—United States.
4. Education, Elementary—Activity programs—United States.
5. Teachers—Training of—United States.   I. Tiedt, Iris M.
II. Title.
LC1099.3.T54   1998
370.117'0973—dc21

                                 98-22408
                                     CIP

Printed in the United States of America
10 9 8 7 6 5 4 3 2 1   02 01 00 99 98

CONTENTS

TO THE READER

As with the previous editions, we dedicate *Multicultural Teaching* to teachers now in K-8 classrooms and to students in teacher education programs who will be our future teachers. Because multicultural education is integral to teaching and learning at all levels, it is essential that all teachers be well prepared to infuse multicultural education throughout the curriculum. We know that the goals of multicultural education will not be achieved unless teachers at every level assume responsibility for designing and carrying out an inclusive curriculum. No matter what the color of our skin or the language of our parents, we share a responsibility for seeing that all children learn how to "get along" with others in this gigantic American multiculture. The range of diversity represented in our society includes the young and old, male and female, the physically able and those who are less able, as well as those who can be grouped by language, national origin, race, or religious belief. A multicultural curriculum has to address this diversity in the United States and in the world.

As we have prepared each edition of this text, our writing has reflected shifting perspectives and controversial topics. Twenty years ago, *Multicultural Teaching* was the first comprehensive text to appear on multicultural education. We showed teachers that all students need multicultural education in order to learn about themselves and others. This text, exceptional for its time, presented a student-centered language arts-based approach to multicultural teaching and used literature to introduce multicultural concepts.

Subsequent editions increased the focus on multicultural teaching across the curriculum with chapters integrating multicultural teaching into reading, language arts, and social studies classes around themes in the self-contained elementary school classroom and cross-disciplinary planning in the middle school. Over the years, we also clarified many of the key concepts associated with multicultural education such as culture and race. To support growing awareness of the teacher's role in delivering the curriculum, we strengthened our emphasis on the knowledge base required for multicultural education. We also expanded our treatment of controversies within the rapidly growing field of multicultural education and encouraged teachers to reflect on their teaching and learning experiences in order to become better at addressing diversity in their classrooms.

In the present edition we feature the two major components of multicultural teaching: (1) a knowledge base for teaching multiculturally and (2) activities that provide equitable learning opportunities for diverse students. Throughout the text we provide readers with a rich store of instructional strategies and resources to enhance their teaching. Thus, we establish a strong foundation for a fully integrated multicultural curriculum that teachers can implement in K-8 classrooms. The multicultural education that we describe in this book is what we consider to be the best education for all students. The overall goals of this approach are (1) to strengthen the self-esteem of each student, (2) to teach empathy for others with whom we share the world, and (3) to provide equity for all learners who enter our schools.

Finally, multicultural education is one of the basics, like literacy and quantitative reasoning. Thus, it must be considered an integral part of the total curriculum, not just a separate course, a special unit of study in February, or a series of discrete activities added to a prescribed curriculum. Recognizing how our own cultural background and experiences affect our thinking is a crucial first step toward multicultural understanding. To commit yourself to multicultural teaching presupposes creating a climate in which the teacher is not the only expert and students can dare to question, take risks, and learn from each other. This approach to multicultural education will prepare students for a changing world in which learning is not limited to information presented within the covers of a textbook nor confined within the school walls.

Multicultural Teaching is designed as a text that can be used in a variety of courses, for example:

Multicultural Education	Foundations of Education
Introduction to Student Teaching	Principles of Teaching
Teaching Language Arts	Teaching Reading
Elementary School Curriculum	School Administration
Teaching Social Studies	Teaching Ethnic Studies

The text is also suitable for staff development with experienced teachers and administrators who want to become involved in multicultural education.

Multicultural Teaching stands out as a textbook that:

- Addresses the concerns of elementary and middle-school teachers as they work with diverse students.
- Shows teachers how to translate multicultural theory into practice in a classroom.
- Focuses on individualization of instruction to meet the special needs of all students.
- Presents varied thematic units that teachers can adapt to different grade levels.
- Incorporates up-to-date computer and other technologies into multicultural education.
- Explains how thinking about multicultural education has changed over the years.
- Promotes a student-centered curriculum and learning through participation.
- Infuses multicultural education throughout the curriculum.
- Demonstrates how children's literature can be used as an integral component of multicultural education in every subject area.
- Provides a base for teaching *multiculturally,* not just *about* multiculturalism.
- Includes extensive features with information, activities, and resources on such groups as African Americans, Native Americans, Latinos, and women.
- Discusses different kinds of diversity; e.g., age, gender, ability, religion, race, and language.

In honor of the twentieth birthday of *Multicultural Teaching,* we would like to share something about ourselves and how we came to write this book. We are a unique mother (Iris)/daughter (Pamela) writing team, bringing together teaching experience and expertise in linguistics, ESL, and reading/language arts instruction. The motivation for publishing a text on multicultural education developed out of our complementary backgrounds in the women's movement and anti-war politics of the 1970s. As educators, we saw the need to integrate these social/political concerns into schooling. Furthermore, we believed that working with teachers and students was a way to move toward achieving social justice. Since our text was first published in 1979, we have seen the ideas presented gain greater currency as multicultural teaching has come to be more widely recognized as "the best teaching for all students." We hope that we have been able to provide ideas in *Multicultural Teaching* that will encourage you to join in this challenging endeavor.

We wish to express our appreciation for the assistance of our editors and those who reviewed the text and suggested ways of strengthening the presentation; namely, Tonya Huber, Wichita State University; Nancy Witherell, Bridgewater State College; and Mary-Lou Breitborde, Salem State College.

Welcome
Bienvenidos
Hawn txais tos
Chào Qúy Vị
ԲԱՐԻ ԳԱԼՈՒՍՏ
歡迎
សូមស្វាគមន៍
Maligayang Pagdating
어서오십시요
ยินดีต้อนรับ
Bem Vindos
ПРИВЕТСТВИЕ

Part I

C H A P T E R

1

Exploring Our Unique American Multiculture

The population of the United States is comprised of an increasingly diverse complex of cultures. In 1990 the U.S. population was 76% Anglo, 12% Black, 9% Latino, and 3% Asian. By the year 2050, these percentages are projected to be: 52% Anglo, 16% Black, 22% Latino, and 10% Asian.[1] For that reason, we cannot identify one distinctive "American culture." Rather we have a constantly changing, inclusive *multiculture* that encompasses a diverse population related to all of the peoples and nations on the planet. The United States is a unique universal nation of people who are learning how to get along in an ever-changing world.

Despite the inclusion of a "Bill of Rights" in our Constitution, the people living in the United States have had to struggle with many controversial issues involved in sharing space and power with others. Persistent conflicts among groups in the United States have been associated with prejudice, exclusion, and discrimination as this country developed. Laws assuring the rights of diverse groups needing legal protection were passed only relatively recently, for example, civil rights (1957), desegregation of schools (1954), bilingual education (1968), and guaranteed equal access for the disabled (1975). Moreover, racist violence and abuse of human rights continue to be problems in all areas of the country today, threatening everyone's chance to live a fulfilling life. Learning to get along with persons of diverse backgrounds, needs, and expectations requires commitment and effort on the part of all of us.

Education holds the promise of teaching us how to co-exist peaceably in this giant multiculture. Teachers have a significant role to play in guiding children at all levels to recognize and respect diversity as they interact with other people in and out of school. The overall goal of multicultural teaching, the subject we explore in this text, is to support individual **self-esteem,** to teach **empathy** for others, and to provide **equity** for all learners in our schools. However, the schools alone cannot provide the total education needed by our

Note: The following languages appear in order on the opposite page: English, Spanish, Hmong, Vietnamese, Armenian, Chinese, Cambodian, Filipino (Tagalog), Korean, Laotian, Portuguese, Russian.

children. Individuals, communities, states, the nation—all must join together in this effort to educate young people who can lead the way toward multicultural awareness and understanding as we learn to live in harmony on this planet.

After reading this chapter, you should be able to:

- Describe the composition of the American multiculture.
- Explain the need for multicultural education.
- Discuss the evolution of thinking about cultural diversity in the United States.
- Write a definition of multicultural education.
- Compare metaphors that describe cultural diversity.
- Reflect on your experiences as a member of the American multiculture.

EVOLVING MULTICULTURAL THEORY

In this section we examine the evolution of multicultural thinking in the United States. We identify the historical developments that preceded the present focus on multiculturalism and the contemporary conditions that demand it. We also discuss the changing demography of the American population and of the classroom as we begin to define multicultural education.

How National Thinking Changed

Of course our thinking has changed in many respects since the first settlement of Jamestown in 1607. Historically, we can note the controversy among those first settlers, then largely from Europe, that led to the Revolutionary War and the early beginnings of the United States. Historically, too, we can trace the evolution of thinking that led to the freeing of the slaves. In this section, we will address the thinking that has moved us to the present conception of multicultural education that we advocate presenting in the schools today. We will also examine the legislation that led to our current position.

Rethinking the Melting-Pot Theory

The term *melting pot* comes from a play by that name written by Israel Zangwill in 1909. The following speech illustrates the prevailing nationalist perception of an ideal American living in a homogeneous culture:

> America is God's Crucible, the great Melting Pot where all the races of Europe are melting and reforming! Here you stand, good folk, think I, when I see them at Ellis Island, here you stand in your fifty hatreds and rivalries, but you won't be long like that, brothers, for these are the fires of God. A fig for your feuds and vendettas! Germans and Frenchmen, Irishmen and Englishmen, Jews and Russians—into the Crucible with you all! God is making the American . . . The real American has not yet arrived. He is only in the Crucible, I tell you—he will be the fusion of all races, the coming superman.[2]

During those years, the aim of the dominant group, light-skinned West European Americans, was to assimilate all immigrants into one culture, the "American" culture, as quickly as possible. Newcomers were expected to forget their native languages and to learn to speak and write English, the accepted language of the new nation, the language of business and society. Metaphorically, the United States was seen as a huge cauldron, a "melting pot," into which all diverse people were dumped in order to melt away their differences, thereby creating people who were much alike. At the time this was a powerful vision. Americans could move beyond petty factionalism and small-minded nationalism in a land of opportunity.

The melting pot ideology continued well into the twentieth century, and it is still often advocated as we move into the twenty-first century. However, we can question whether this vision ever accurately reflected conditions in this country. For example, immigrants from different countries settled into communities with their compatriots (Italians), sent their children to special schools to maintain the language of the home country (German), and published literature in their native languages (Yiddish). Native Americans were isolated, confined to reservations and poverty. African Americans were rigidly segregated—residentially, educationally, and economically. As the United States expanded its territory, suddenly large populations with different histories and cultures were incorporated into "America" (Louisiana, the Southwest). Various distinct components have always co-existed in the American multiculture. It is time to rethink the melting pot theory.

America Is a Tossed Salad!

The melting pot metaphor seems especially inappropriate today as population diversity increases rather than diminishes. Social and economic mobility means that groups once isolated in enclaves now participate more directly in the mainstream of American public life (disabled people). Refugees stream into the United States seeking freedom (Haiti). Furthermore, more and more people have come to recognize that acknowledging their ethnic and cultural roots are a strength, not a weakness.

Rather than the melting pot, a better image for this country is the "tossed salad," with various groups maintaining their distinctive identities while contributing to the quality of the whole society. Today we are proud of our diversity instead of ashamed of our differences. The metaphor we choose directly affects the school curriculum as we teach students to recognize the contributions made by each group to the composition and to the success of this nation.

CHRONOLOGY OF MULTICULTURAL THINKING

1909

"The Melting Pot" theory generally accepted but not really practiced.

Many community schools existed to teach a specific language, such as German. Saturday classes were common.

1918

World War I brought about reactions against Germany and a resurgence of patriotic feeling; use of "English only" in schools legislated in many states.

1945

World War II led to realization of need for knowledge of foreign languages; teaching of foreign languages in schools encouraged.

1953

UNESCO published a monograph advocating use of the mother tongue to teach students; not widely accepted in the United States.

1954

Brown v. *Topeka Board of Education*—Segregated schools declared unequal.

1957

U.S. Commission on Civil Rights established.

1958

Russian launching of Sputnik frightened U.S. leaders who turned to schools. National Defense Education Act (NDEA) passed to help U.S. schools keep up with Russian education. Aid given to promote key subject areas including teaching of foreign languages.

1963

Dade County, Florida, initiated bilingual program for Spanish-speaking Cuban children coming to Miami. Interest spread to other states.

1965

Elementary and Secondary Education Act (ESEA): Funds granted to schools to upgrade education in many areas including English instruction (modern grammar, linguistics).

1968

Bilingual Education Act: Title VII of ESEA promoted bilingual programs in schools.

1971

Massachusetts Bilingual Education Act: Massachusetts was first state to pass law mandating bilingual education for non-English-speaking (NES) children. Other states followed.

1972

Title IX amendment to Civil Rights Act—Sex cannot determine participation in education programs.

1973

Bilingual Education Reform Act: Updated 1968 law; mandated language instruction as well as study of history and culture in bilingual programs.

1974

U.S. Supreme Court Decision: *Lau* v. *Nichols*—NES students have a legal right to bilingual instruction as part of "equal educational opportunity." Aspira Consent Decree class action suit on behalf of Puerto Rican children resulted in New York City Board of Education agreeing to provide instruction in students' native languages.

1981

Senator S. I. Hayakawa first introduced a Constitutional Amendment to declare English the official language of the United States. (Defeated)

1984–85

Illinois, Indiana, Kentucky, Nebraska, and Virginia passed resolutions declaring English as their official state language.

1988

U.S. government apologizes for internment of Japanese Americans, offers monetary compensation.

1990

School recognition of linguistic knowledge as important prior knowledge on which to build. Government recognition of student language abilities as asset to international economy.

1992

Increasing public support for Gay Rights.

1994

Noticeable increase in discussion of racial matters in the media.

1995

Strong opposition to support for illegal immigrant families, especially in California and Texas; demand for strengthening border patrols.

1996

Cases of sexual harassment in priesthood and military (U.S. Navy, Tailhook); first woman flyer ousted from U.S. Air Force for unethical sexual behavior.

Much sentiment expressed against bilingual education; English for Our Children movement.

First Asian governor elected (Washington State).

First woman appointed Secretary of State (Madeline Albright).

Table continues

1997

Proposition 209 passed in California rescinding Affirmative Action.

First presidential address to Gay Rights national meeting.

President appoints national commission to study race and related issues.

Head of Republic of China visits the United States.

1998

Continued resistance of isolated groups to equalization of rights for minority cultures.

Latino groups grow steadily in size, approaching that of whites in California; increasing voting activity, presence in politics.

Continued discussion of racism and diversity in public forum.

Canadian government formally apologizes for past oppression of its indigenous peoples—Indian, Inuit, and Métis.

Emergence of Multicultural Thinking

Today there is a strong push toward multicultural approaches to teaching at all levels. Many laws and court decisions paved the way for the current trend toward multicultural education. If we examine legislation and court cases, we see an evolving philosophy regarding the rights of the individual, particularly as it relates to language.

What are the issues involved? Legal actions affecting the education of minorities, persons of varied cultural backgrounds, and the economically disadvantaged are all relevant. The chronology of such events might begin with the benchmark case of *Brown* v. *Topeka Board of Education.* In 1954 this Supreme Court decision stated that segregated schools are inherently unequal. State laws providing separate schools for black and white students were declared unconstitutional.

Following this decision came legislation establishing the U.S. Commission on Civil Rights in 1957. This independent, bipartisan agency was charged to "investigate complaints alleging denial of the right to vote by reason of race, color, religion, sex, or national origin, or by reason of fraudulent practices."

The commission published *A Better Chance to Learn: Bilingual-Bicultural Education,* a report designed for educators as a "means for equalizing educational opportunity for language minority students." This overview, published in 1975, summarizes efforts to help students in school who speak languages other than English. This agency sees language and culture as basic considerations in providing equal rights.

In 1968 the Bilingual Education Act (BEA) was passed as Title VII of the Elementary and Secondary Education Act. The intent of this law was clarified by President Lyndon B. Johnson:

> This bill authorizes a new effort to prevent dropouts; new programs for handicapped children; new planning help for rural schools. It also contains a special provision establishing bilingual education programs for children whose first language is not English. Thousands of children of Latin descent, young Indians, and others will get a better start—a better chance—in school . . .

Efforts to enforce such legislation also appeared. The Office of Civil Rights Guidelines, for example, indicated that affirmative efforts to give special training to non–English-speaking (NES) students were required as a condition to receiving federal aid to public schools in 1970. The text read:

> Where inability to speak and understand the English language excludes national origin minority group children from effective participation in the education program offered by a school district, the district must take affirmative steps to rectify the language deficiency in order to open its instructional program to these students.

A related issue is the treatment of women in the United States. In 1972, Title IX, an amendment to the Civil Rights Act, stated, "No person in the United States shall, on the basis of sex, be excluded from participation in, be denied the benefits of, or be subjected to discrimination under any education program or activity receiving federal financial assistance." One result of this law has been the opening of school sports to girls and college athletic scholarships for women.

The most significant case related to multicultural/bilingual education, however, is *Lau* v. *Nichols,* a Supreme Court case that requires all school districts to provide for linguistic and cultural diversity. In 1974 it charged a school district as follows:

> The failure of the San Francisco school system to provide English language instruction to approximately 1,800 students of Chinese ancestry who do not speak English, or to provide them with other adequate instructional procedures, denies them a meaningful opportunity to participate in the public educational program and thus violates . . . the Civil Rights Act of 1964. . . .

This class-action suit against the San Francisco Unified School District led to a decision that school districts must provide education in languages that meet the needs of students who attend the school. Thus began plans to teach students in their native language, whether it be Yupik or Tagalog, and to provide English as a second language programs specifically designed for each group.

These laws stressed human rights and the need for bilingual education. Out of this thrust came multicultural approaches to teaching that recognized the need for awareness of our culturally diverse society. Teachers in bilingual classrooms are asked to present both linguistic and cultural instruction. Social studies classes must today present multicultural perspectives of sociology and history. Language arts instructors are expected to enrich their classrooms with multicultural literature and language information.

Legislation and court decisions reflect the thinking of our times. It is important to realize, on the other hand, that laws alone do not effect change. What you do in your classroom may, however, serve to break down stereotypes, promote multicultural understanding, and make a crucial difference in the personal development of many individual students. This book is designed to provide activities, information, and resources that will aid you in reaching those goals.

Recap

The history of the United States reveals a struggle to provide civil rights. There has always been controversy around major decisions, and we now acknowledge grievous errors made in our past. However, over the years we can observe persistent efforts moving the country toward guaranteeing human rights for all. Concern for the individual remains a basic tenet of our collective philosophy. Such societal thinking should be reflected in the schools, directly affecting what and how we teach.

EXAMINING THE AMERICAN MULTICULTURE TODAY

As a result of the mobility within our society, the student mix in most classrooms in elementary schools throughout the United States has changed perceptibly in the past twenty to thirty years. Increasingly, even rural and small-town classrooms in the Midwest more closely reflect the diversity of the total population in the United States. Frequently, the cultural roots of the teacher and the children she or he teaches are very different. Therefore, all teachers must know how to provide an equitable education for students from a wide variety of cultural backgrounds.

Equality for All Americans

Whatever their race, sex, age, religion, social class, national origin, (dis)ability, or language, equality of opportunity is a major concern for all members of American society today. Efforts have been made to eliminate discriminatory practices in the workplace and to ensure equal pay for equal work. Women and members of minority groups hold responsible political positions. Yet we continue to face problems daily to ensure that every American can feel equally valued. These changing attitudes must have a direct effect on practice in the schools. If all students have a right to equality of education, then textbooks, the concepts presented, and teaching practices must change to reflect that goal.

Teachers need to understand the complexity of our diverse national population and how this diversity has evolved. The history of our pluralistic population begins with the heterogeneous Native American civilizations that flourished here before explorers from Europe encountered them on the North American continent. On the east coast, emigrants in the early years came from various European countries—England, France, Germany, Spain. At the same time, too, exploration was taking place along the west coast as Russian hunters ventured east into the vast territory that is now Alaska and south into California. Cortez and others moved through Mexico into the Southwest and north into California. Following the explorers, some settlers remained to begin farming and developing the land. People continued coming to the New World with many different goals—freedom of religion, the challenge of exploration, and the hope of wealth. In addition, millions were brought forcibly from Africa as slaves. Twentieth-century immigrants include Vietnamese, Haitians, Ethiopians, and Mexicans. The history of the United States clearly identifies the polyethnic roots of a wide and fascinating variety of peoples, ranging from Scots in Appalachia to Inuit in Alaska, from Polynesians in Hawaii to Portuguese in Boston. Therefore, we find it difficult to identify a single distinctive American culture but rather perceive the people who live in the United States as comprising a giant American *multiculture.*

This multiculture reflects more than our diverse geographic origins, however. We also differ in many other ways that influence how we interact within our democratic society. We have learned to recognize distinct gender differences and expectations, for example, in language variation and career development. We differ, too, in age, with all of us moving in turn from young to elderly, changing our perspectives and needs as we mature. Along the way we identify with many different groups based on family, language, national origin, race, and beliefs. In addition, we often group ourselves by choice to support our interests and concerns, belonging to a number of groups at any one time. Belonging to various groups helps to shape our identities and our ways of thinking as we clarify group needs and shared expectations. Multicultural education should assist us in better understanding the roles individuals and groups play within a diverse society.

Individual Differences

All of us are members of a society; yet each one of us remains a unique individual. Beginning with the accident of birth, we are shaped by the knowledge, experience, values, and attitudes that we encounter in the people with whom we live; we are socialized into a particular community, time, and place. However, out of all the diverse factors that influence our attitudes and values, each of us internalizes a unique self-identity from which we operate.

We teachers therefore need to remind ourselves constantly that the students who face us in a classroom are unique individuals. In our efforts to understand and to teach children from the many groups that make up our multiculture, we often seek to make generalizations about learners who are members of a specific culture. Understanding that respect for the family is a characteristic of the Latino culture justifies neither the assumption that all Latinos possess this characteristic nor the corollary that persons from other cultures do not. Likewise, in learning about Black English, we need to be aware that not all African Americans speak Black English; furthermore, many who can speak Black English readily may be bidialectal, easily switching from this highly informal form to standard English depending on the situation. To take another example, the "Dick and Jane" readers reflect a fantasy of a time that never truly existed, or at least not for everyone, when the idealized American family consisted of a father who went off to work every day; a mother who stayed at home and baked cookies; two children, one boy and one girl; plus a family dog. Now we recognize the range of "families" that children experience, from those affected by divorce and remarriage to those formed by single parents, adoption, and multiple generations. Teachers must plan carefully to accommodate individual characteristics, permitting children to remain different. We must consciously work to avoid stereotyped thinking about members of any one particular ethnic group; for example, the expectation that all Asian American children are mathematical whizzes. Such stereotyped expectations may exert undue pressure on children and be damaging to a young learner's self-esteem. We will discuss how teachers can deal with such individual differences in more detail in Chapter 4.

Accepting Diversity

Never has the need for multicultural education been more clearly evident. Desecration of Jewish cemeteries, ridicule of the mentally retarded, and harassment of homosexuals are not only occurrences of the past. Fear and ignorance still lead individuals or groups to commit "hate" crimes against other human beings. Beginning in their very early years, the young people who will become our country's adult citizens need to learn broad concepts of cultural difference and respect for the diversity of our population. This diversity can stem from gender, age, national origin, language background, sexual orientation, religious beliefs, politics, the work world, physical and mental abilities, and individual experiences. We can recognize and accept both the differences and the universal human needs we share as we strive to promote appreciation and empathy for the diverse people that live in this complex multiculture.

Cultural diversity is not new in the United States. It has always been a distinctive characteristic of the American multiculture, and it is increasing rather than diminishing. For example, in 1992 a total of 32 million Americans spoke a language other than English at home; that is one in seven people. This number represents a 34% increase between 1980 and 1990. The number of Chinese speakers doubled during that period, while approximately 17 million Americans spoke Spanish in their homes in 1993.[3]

Another indicator of the changing mix in our multiculture is the ethnic composition of persons entering the work force in the United States in 1988 compared with that projected for the year 2000. The following chart shows that the percentage of white American workers, especially males, entering the work force will slowly decrease, while the percentage of American men and women of color will increase so that each of the latter will represent approximately one-fifth of the people entering the work force in 2000:

PERSONS ENTERING THE WORK FORCE

	1988	*Projected for 2000*
Native-born white males	41%	9%
Native-born white females	33%	28%
Native-born males of color	10%	21%
Native-born females of color	9%	21%
Immigrant males	4%	12%
Immigrant females	3%	9%[4]

Of the total persons in the work force in 1990, native-born white males represented 42%. This percentage is projected to diminish slowly to 36% by 2010. During the same period the numbers of Asians and Hispanics will increase from 3% and 8% to 6% and 12% respectively. These figures give us an indication of the projected demography of the U.S. population. It is estimated that people of color will soon represent approximately one-third of the country's population.[5] Although the number of African Americans will remain fairly constant at 12%, the number of immigrants will slowly grow. Such statistics may be interpreted as a threat by the native-born white male population, which has been accustomed to being the dominant group in the United States.

Americans must also be prepared to live in a more closely interactive, interdependent world society. No longer is ethnocentrism viable. We must all learn to collaborate in a global, international setting that brings diverse peoples to the negotiating tables. The cultural diversity of the world population is even more pronounced than that of the United States. Of the more than 6 billion people on this planet, only one in six will be of Caucasian origins in the twenty-first century. Thus, persons with "white" skins may often find themselves in the minority on international committees and at business planning meetings. More than ever, to interact within the global village, all Americans must be educated multiculturally.

Recap

In general, national thinking, exemplified by legislation and judicial decision, has evolved over the years toward greater acceptance of all citizens as having equal worth. Educators value self-esteem—the bottom line for all students—and political leaders are trying to provide equity for all people in the United States. We need to continue to learn how best to accommodate our diverse population and how to "get along" in this country.

DEFINING MULTICULTURAL EDUCATION TODAY

The term multicultural education has been a source of controversy and confusion. Defined geographically, it has led to studies of other countries and the concept of the earth as a global village. Focus on ethnic studies has brought an awareness of literature and folklore specific to groups that speak the same language or share a religious belief. Concern for the needs of all people has expanded the term to include, for example, the disabled, homosexuals, and the elderly. Multicultural education must include these themes and many others.

Rooted in the thinking of the 1950s and 1960s with its focus on civil rights, *multicultural education* first appeared in the early 1970s with an emphasis on human relations. It continued to develop in the 1980s and 1990s. In this section we begin by defining the components of multicultural education. We then examine different approaches to multicultural theory and practice. Finally, we present the inclusive definition that we will use throughout this book.

Exploring Relevant Terms

As we strive to define multicultural education and multicultural teaching, we focus first on defining the root word *culture* and other related terms: *social class, ethnic group, identity group,* and *race*. We also review terminology for groups of people that will be appropriate to use.

Culture denotes a complex integrated system of values, beliefs, and behaviors common to a large group of people. A culture may include shared history and folklore, ideas about right and wrong, and specific communication styles—the "truths" accepted by members of the group. Members of a culture "speak the same language," so they understand the unspoken assumptions, and they have similar expectations of life.

Each of us is born into a culture. Our beliefs derive from these ethnic and family backgrounds, but they continue to be shaped by all of our experiences after birth. For the most part, family attitudes, language, and other behaviors are internalized without question. It is only when we encounter other cultures that we begin to observe differences, to wonder, and to ask questions.

Each of us can map the influences that have shaped our individual thinking—our families, the kids we went to school with, the various places we have lived in or traveled to, a person we married or lived with, people with whom we have worked. Your individual map reflects the culture of your family, but it is not identical to the map of any other member of that culture. As we examine these influences, we must consider the many groups to which we have belonged and the many people with whom we have interacted. Each of us can create a map similar to that completed here for Carlita:

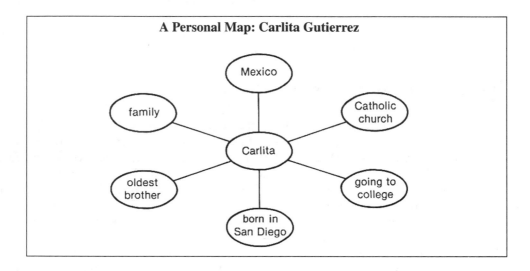

Notice that Carlita, a twenty-year-old college student in Athens, Ohio, is greatly influenced by her family, some of whom still live in Mexico. She acknowledges the influence particularly of her oldest brother, who serves as head of the family now that her father is dead. Carlita adheres to the tenets of the Catholic church as she has been taught since birth. However, education is causing her to question some basic assumptions of both family and church. She is the first member of her family to be born in the United States, and she is the first to go to college. She is moving ahead with career plans. We could predict that her individual values will continue to change as she encounters other career-oriented women and moves up the career ladder in her profession, encounters discrimination, or has children.

The influence of one's culture is powerful, but subtle. As members of a cultural group, we interact with the larger society, and we become aware of different ways of behaving, different expectations; we may gradually change our thinking individually or collectively. Thus, culture is dynamic, constantly changing in response to changing conditions.

In our discussion of multicultural education we use *culture* in an anthropological sense. We need to be aware, however, of other confusing connotations that have been associated with the word *culture*. This term has been attached to a number of different concepts, for example, "pop culture" or the "culture of poverty." A literary or elitist use assumes that wealthier, better-educated persons have more "culture" than do poor, uneducated people. This definition equates culture with knowledge of the arts and literature. In this text we acknowledge that all people have a culture, and we judge all cultures as being equally valid and having equal worth. All of us are acculturated or socialized to live appropriately within a particular culture from birth. Much of our learning is the result of socialization or cultural conditioning.

Social class, on the other hand, does refer to perceived status in the society, closely associated with socioeconomic status (SES). We sometimes think of the United States as a "classless" society because these strata are not clearly defined, and it is possible for persons to move from one class to another. Yet distinctions based on wealth, education, and occupation do affect people's access to scarce resources. There is an ever-widening gap between the upper middle class and those who live in poverty. As teachers, we need to be aware of class-based, stereotyped expectations and attitudes that may limit student potential, for example, that poor children who come to school in less attractive clothing are not as bright as well-dressed, more advantaged children and thus cannot learn more advanced thinking skills. An entire group, for example, Appalachians, may be stigmatized as "lower class."

Ethnicity is an umbrella term that includes varied groupings based on national or linguistic backgrounds. The origin of this term is the Greek *ethnos,* which means *nation.* This term is often used inaccurately to refer to members of all minority groups. The term *ethnocentrism* refers to dominance of a national group identity, that is, comparing all others against the group standards. Many Americans maintain strong ethnic ties, for example, Irish Americans, the Amish, or Korean Americans, while others of mixed heritage may not.

Identity groups are people who share interests, concerns, or roles and "speak the language" common to that group. Members share common concerns and work together toward a cause. They may share special skills and behaviors that bring them together on occasion. Identity groups may be based on vocational or professional roles. We all belong to many identity groups. The "Women's Movement" grew out of the needs of one identity group. The disabled are now speaking as a group to achieve equity and to fight discrimination. Identity groups do effect change.

Race is another term that has been inappropriately used and needs to be reconsidered. Race is not synonymous with nationality, a language spoken, or a culture. It is incorrect, therefore, to speak of the Jewish race, the English-speaking race, or the Negro race. For many years it was the practice to identify three races: European (white), African (black), and Asian (yellow). As scientific information grew, a number of major groups were identified, sometimes called geographical races:

1. African (Negroid)—Collection of related persons living south of the Sahara. Black Americans are mostly of this origin.
2. American Indian (Amerindian or American Mongoloid)—Related to the Asian geographical race; only group in the Western Hemisphere for many years.
3. Asian (Mongoloid)—Persons in continental Asia except for those in South Asia and the Middle East; includes China, Japan, Taiwan, the Philippines, and Indonesia.
4. Australian (Australian aborigine or Australoid)—A group of people in Australia.
5. European (Caucasoid)—Located in Europe, the Middle East, and north of the Sahara; includes persons living on other continents.
6. Indian—Persons in South Asia from the Himalayas to the Indian Ocean.
7. Melanesian (Melanesian-Papuan)—Dark-skinned persons living in New Britain, New Guinea, and the Solomon Islands.
8. Micronesian—Dark-skinned persons living on islands in the Pacific: Carolines, Gilberts, Marianas, and Marshalls.
9. Polynesian—Many persons living in the Pacific Islands such as Hawaii, Easter Island, and the Ellice Islands.

Group names have changed periodically. As changes have been made, there has been controversy about which terms are acceptable. Be aware that *race* categories are being questioned, particularly as the number of multiracial persons increases. See the discussion in Chapter 10. More militant members of ethnic groups have at times preferred one term while less militant members of the same group use another. Such terms as *Chicano, Mexican American,* and *Hispanic,* for example, are widely used today, and each has its own rationale.

We demonstrate our awareness of how thinking has changed by our own use of appropriate terms. The once common term *culturally disadvantaged,* for example, is no longer acceptable because many people are aware of its loaded implications. We recognize that all groups have cultures that are unique and at the same time have much in common. *Disadvantaged* is an evaluative term that assumes a standard against which all cultures are judged and has led to the assumption that minority groups do not have a culture of their own. Following is a brief discussion of terminology that may need clarification.

African Americans/Black Americans

The term *Negro*, the Spanish word for black, was acceptable in the past. Those who wish to stress their African origins prefer *African American.*

Asian Americans

When possible, use the more specific terms for example, *Chinese Americans* or *Japanese Americans,* because each group has a distinct history and identity. The use of *Oriental* has fallen into disrepute because it connotes stereotyped views and is considered a racist term.

Latinos/Hispanic Americans

Hispanic has been questioned because it includes many groups that differ greatly, for example, people who came from Spain (Hispania), those from Mexico, Puerto Rico, Cuba, and immigrants from the many Spanish-speaking Latin American countries. Also, it focuses more on the colonization by Spain and less on the Native American heritage. *Latino* is gaining acceptance because of its clear reference to common language roots. Labels such as *Chicano* (for Mexican Americans) emphasize the unique culture this group is developing in the United States based on Spanish and Native American roots.

Minority Group

"Minority" is being questioned when used in the sense of "minority group." Frequently, speakers equate "minority" (population size) with "subordinate" or "oppressed" (position or power). They refer to persons who have been underrepresented or discriminated against, for example, African Americans or Pacific Islanders, as "minorities." Identifying membership in "minority groups" is a typical aspect of hiring practices intended to achieve more equitable representation. However, as the percentage of such groups of people changes across the country, general use of the label "minority" may become confusing and inappropriate. In some neighborhoods, Asian Americans outnumber other groups. In California, for example, Caucasians are rapidly losing their numerical advantage. Teachers should be aware of the potential misuse of this term and should use it with care. "Minority" is often replaced with "people of color." Alternatives are "historically underrepresented groups" and "parallel cultures."

Native Americans

The terms *Indian* and *Native American* are both used. The problem with using *Native American* is that it is nonspecific, including Indian tribes as well as Eskimo and Aleut. If possible, designate a specific group, such as Hopi or Lakota. Some people object to *Native American* because they are natives of this country, too, and all our ancestors came from somewhere else.

People of Color

The term "people of color" has come into common usage in the 1990s, as an alternative to minority group. However, referring to people of color is confusing because in reality we are all "people of color." We prefer to use the names of specific groups wherever possible.

Current Theory and Informed Practice

For the most part, educators agree on defining the general parameters of multicultural education, as follows:

> An education that is multicultural is comprehensive and fundamental to all educational endeavors. Given an understanding of the nature of human differences and the realization that individuals approach concepts from their own perspectives, advocates of education that is multicultural are consistent in their belief that respect for diversity and individual difference is the concept's central ingredient.[6]

However, among educators there remain differences in interpretations of theory and how theory should inform practice. In 1986, Sleeter and Grant identified five discrete theoretical approaches to multicultural education: assimilation, human relations, focused group studies, integrated studies within the total curriculum, and social reconstructionism.[7] They critiqued each in turn, concluding that social reconstructionism was the most desirable basis for multicultural education.

In this text, we acknowledge the positive contributions of each historical approach as we develop our inclusive definition of multicultural education. We also would add a sixth consideration, that is, the influence of global and international studies.

Assimilation

Assimilation theory, which dominated the thinking of the early United States, assumes that all persons living in the United States should be acculturated to become *Americans*. According to this view, everyone should be culturally similar as in the "melting-pot" metaphor discussed previously. This theory lies behind the contemporary "English only" movement and is inherent in many of the questions related to immigration. The problem is that those who espouse assimilation may equate *difference* with *deficiency*. This stance can scarcely be termed multicultural, but it is a viewpoint that still appears in newspapers and is clearly lodged in the minds of many Americans who were educated to perceive assimilation and the melting-pot concept positively.

Aspects of assimilation theory that we continue to support, however, are related to work with English as a Second Language programs. We believe that children should always be encouraged to use their native oral languages as a way of learning and communicating. We also want to express value for knowing more than one language in today's world. However, we encourage students to learn English as a means for entering the privileged mainstream culture and preparing for a future career. It would be unrealistic for any teacher to pretend that learning standard English and cultural literacy, prestige knowledge, is not a desirable goal for any child in American schools today.

Human Relations and Ethnic Studies

The concern for human rights that characterized the civil rights movement of the 1960s led directly into the human relations movement in education with its emphasis on valuing the individual, nurturing individual self-esteem, and helping everyone succeed. In 1972, for example, the American Association of Colleges for Teacher Education (AACTE), defined multicultural education as follows:

> . . . education which values cultural pluralism. Multicultural education rejects the view that schools should seek to melt away cultural differences or the view that schools should merely tolerate cultural pluralism. Instead, multicultural education affirms that schools should be oriented toward the cultural enrichment of all children and youth through programs rooted in the presentation and extension of cultural alternatives. Multicultural education recognizes cultural diversity as a fact of life in American society, and it affirms that this cultural diversity is a valuable resource that should be preserved and extended. It affirms that major education institutions should strive to preserve and enhance cultural pluralism. Multicultural education programs for teachers are more than special courses or special learning experiences grafted onto the standard program. The commitment to cultural pluralism must permeate all areas of the educational experience provided for prospective teachers.[8]

At the same time, many states began incorporating elements of this widely accepted statement into teacher education requirements. In 1972, for example, Minnesota adopted a human relations requirement for the licensure of teachers, including courses in such areas as cultural pluralism, interpersonal communication, and ethnic studies. Anyone wishing to teach in the state today must meet that requirement.[9]

Note that part of this "human relations" requirement even then was—and still is—focused on studies of ethnic groups. Many universities created Black Studies or Chicano Studies programs at that time. Following this period into the 1980s, James Banks and others wrote books advocating ethnic studies and presenting methods for teaching ethnic studies, particularly at high school and university levels. Such focused ethnic studies courses emphasized pride in one's heritage, which is still an important goal of multicultural education. These programs also stressed interpersonal communication skills. Human relations programs remain an important tool for teaching how to get along in a culturally diverse society.

Integrated Multicultural Education

The broader term *multicultural education* was not widely used in educational literature until the late 1970s. It appeared for the first time in *Education Index* in 1978. In 1977, however, the National Council of Accreditation of Teacher Education rewrote its standards to include one on multicultural education. This text, *Multicultural Teaching,* which appeared in 1979, was the first comprehensive textbook to address multicultural education in the schools. In 1980, AACTE published *Multicultural Education: An Annotated Bibliography of Selected Resources* "to stimulate discussion, study, and experimentation of multicultural education among educators."[10]

Because the K–12 curriculum often lags behind current theory, however, it was not until 1988 that Minnesota's Board of Education adopted a ruling directing all school districts to develop and deliver a curriculum plan that emphasized: (1) the cultural diversity of the United States and the contributions made by diverse ethnic groups to the country's development, (2) the historical and contemporary contributions of both women and men to society, and (3) the historical and contemporary contributions to society by disabled (at that time termed handicapped) persons. The curriculum that is now being implemented is expected to be gender-fair and sensitive to the needs of the disabled.

Concern for the needs of all people now extends to include newly recognized groups, for example, the elderly, homosexuals, working women, people with AIDS, and disabled persons. Efforts to teach multicultural concepts and processes as an integral aspect of every subject area reach into all levels of education, including the preschool years. Multicultural education covers broad, inclusive themes touching on human relations, morality, values, and ethics; and it draws heavily on the study of pedagogy, for example, in its recognition of differing learning styles and individualization of instruction.

Global and International Education

Defined more broadly, thus, multicultural education connects the study of other countries, the concept of the world as a global village, and recognition of the need for everyone on this planet to collaborate to ensure clean air and preserve our resources. Focus on international studies brings an awareness of the shared concerns of nations around the world. It leads to a greater understanding of other people and the universal issues human beings face. Ecologically and economically, we will always be interdependent. Such studies engage us in reading the literature and becoming familiar with the folklore of specific groups around the world that may speak the same language or share a religious belief, thus helping to broaden studies across the total curriculum in the United States.

Social Activism

Active efforts to bring about a change in thinking and behavior have always been integral to our society—from the behavior of the eighteenth-century revolutionaries to contemporary efforts to challenge established views on such issues as abortion and the right to control one's own death. Activism, involvement rather than passive acceptance, is perhaps the newest approach to multicultural education. Refusing to be victimized, we all have a responsibility to speak out against injustice, discrimination, and prejudice and to work to assure that human rights are upheld for all. Individual involvement in this social reconstructivism will vary, but increasingly, educated Americans are intervening when unthinking individuals tell stories that insult certain ethnic groups or use insensitive language. Others join groups that work actively to achieve and maintain civil rights for specific groups. It is important to take a stance and to make our viewpoints known. Teachers have a special responsibility to manage classroom procedures and to plan the multicultural curriculum.

Our Definition for Multicultural Education

Any definition of multicultural education must recognize all of the above components and clearly demonstrate awareness of the changing thinking that has taken place in the United States. Such a definition must also include respect for the diversity that characterizes our American multiculture, and it must touch every individual. Multicultural education is justified on the following grounds: *Morality*—equality of all human beings; *Demography*—needs of a diverse student body; *Civics*—an educated citizenry required by a democracy; *Enhancement*—multiple cultural viewpoints that enrich knowledge; and *Politics*—empowerment for all students.[11]

To achieve these ends, we must design a multicultural curriculum that draws on a sound knowledge base. We must plan multicultural teaching that considers the needs of every student. This is a complex task.

In *Multicultural Teaching* we define multicultural education thus:

> Multicultural education is an inclusive teaching/learning process that engages all students in (1) developing a strong sense of self-*esteem*, (2) discovering *empathy* for persons of diverse cultural backgrounds, and (3) experiencing *equitable* opportunities to achieve to their fullest potential.

Defined thus, multicultural education is fundamental to all learning. It is an integral aspect of the discussions about fair behavior on the playground that might concern primary grade children. It underlies the dialogue of middle school youngsters as they respond to Maniac Magee's efforts to get along in a hostile society.[12] Multicultural education belongs in science, history, mathematics, language arts, and the fine arts. To be effective, multicultural education must be infused throughout any well-designed curriculum. It requires the efforts of committed teachers at all levels of education.

Recap

Defining multicultural education demands a review of historical thinking, for example, assimilation theory, and current theories, such as internationalization of education, that have influenced the development of multicultural education. A review of numerous components leads us to define a broadly inclusive approach to multicultural education that encompasses self-esteem, empathy, and equity for all learners.

PREPARING TO TEACH IN A MULTICULTURE

Everyone in the United States needs multicultural education, and we recognize that such learning must begin during the early years. If schools are to promote multicultural understanding, they need to begin by educating teachers. Both preservice and inservice education are necessary to prepare teachers to present multicultural concepts to K–12 students. Ideally, multicultural concepts will be interwoven throughout courses and experiences in a teacher education program. Multicultural education will appear in foundation courses, psychology and assessment coursework, and courses focusing on methods and materials of teaching. Field experiences should engage future teachers in volunteer work with both children and adults from diverse cultures, as well as student teaching at appropriate levels.

In the same way, teachers in the field will constantly learn new ways to thread multicultural concepts through the total K–12 curriculum. Students and teachers will learn together about the achievements of diverse members of our population. We all need continuing opportunities to extend our thinking beyond the two-dimensional stereotypes exemplified by "good-bad" or "right-wrong" distinctions. Learning to teach multiculturally is an ongoing process.

In the next section, we identify the outcomes expected from a multicultural program. We also summarize the assumptions that underlie the presentation of multicultural education in this text.

Desired Outcomes for Every Student

Just what are we trying to achieve with students during the time they spend in our classrooms? The outcomes we specify for multicultural teaching are often interpersonal; they include both cognitive and affective objectives. Teachers should strive to integrate the following outcomes into the expected achievements for any course or program.

If our multicultural curriculum is effectively taught, students will be able to:

- Identify a strong sense of their own self-esteem and express the need and right of all other persons to similar feelings of self-esteem.
- Describe their own individual cultures, recognizing the influences that have shaped their thinking and behavior.
- Identify racial, ethnic, and religious groups represented in our pluralistic society (e.g., African Americans, persons from Italian backgrounds, Jews).
- Discuss the history of immigration to the United States after its formation and the changing thinking about immigrants that evolved over the years.
- List identity groups to which each person belongs based on age, sex, or physical condition.
- List special interest groups to which each person belongs by choice (e.g., lawyers, feminists, swimmers, Republicans).
- Identify needs and concerns universal to people of all cultures (e.g., love, family, and health) and compare interesting cultural variations (e.g., food preparation, naming practices, or dance).
- Read and discuss literature by and about members of diverse cultures.
- Share folklore from different cultures, noting the common subjects and motifs that occur in folk literature.
- Discuss special gender-related concerns (e.g., sexual abuse, job discrimination based on sex, or the socialization of children).
- Discuss age-related concerns (e.g., rights of children, problems of the adolescent, or caring for the elderly).
- Discuss the needs of persons with disabilities (e.g., mainstreaming in school, parking facilities, special equipment).

- Identify examples of stereotyped thinking and prejudice in real life and in literature.
- Inquire multiculturally as they engage in broad thematic studies related to any field (e.g., science, history, or health).
- Discuss the negative impact of racism and discrimination on all groups.
- Demonstrate knowledge of such related topics as slavery, the United Nations, the history of the English language, or desegregation.
- Participate in community and school affairs as informed, empathetic young citizens who know and care about other people and recognize the enriching effect of having many cultures represented in our population.
- Continue to learn about cultural diversity as part of lifelong learning.

Such outcomes can be assessed through students' speaking or writing performances as well as observed in their body language or behavior. Students should discuss a list of expected outcomes for any study they undertake before the work begins. The outcomes listed above can be adapted for inclusion in the outcomes for a particular unit of study in any subject area, as we will discuss in the chapters that follow.

Basic Assumptions Underlying This Text

Based on our study of multicultural education over a period of time, we offer the following twelve basic assumptions or beliefs in support of a strong multicultural education program in K–8 classes throughout the United States. These assumptions undergird everything we present in the chapters that follow.

Multicultural education is for all of us. Just as we help preschoolers learn to play fair and to respect the toys of others, we continue to help students learn to value the opinions of others and to acknowledge human rights. We all need many opportunities to celebrate the diversity of which we are an essential part.

These broad assumptions are developed in more detail in the chapters that follow. They will shape curriculum development and help us select instructional strategies as we teach any subject at any level. They underscore the criteria for choosing literature and other materials to use in classrooms or to purchase for school libraries.

This We Believe . . .

1. In the United States we live in a multiculture, a society comprised of many diverse cultures. All of living, including schooling, involves contact between different cultures and is therefore multicultural. No one culture can be considered more American than any other.
2. The United States is gradually modifying its expressed goal of assimilation, or making everyone alike (the melting-pot metaphor), in favor of recognizing and appreciating the diversity in our society (the "tossed salad" metaphor). Educators play a role in disseminating this knowledge and acting on its implications.
3. Multicultural education is too complex and pervasive a topic to be encompassed in a single course for teacher educators. All of education must reflect

multicultural awareness, and curricula in the K–8 classrooms must therefore be designed to teach content about our multiculture and to provide equity for all learners in all subject areas.

4. We should not pretend or even aim to be creating teaching materials that are bias-free. Instead, we should guide students to recognize the biases from which they and all people operate.

5. We need to clarify our use of such terms as culture, ethnicity, and race. We also need to be aware of accepted labels for groups of people within our population, speaking out against insensitive usage whenever appropriate.

6. Although every child grows up within a given culture, he or she is shaped over the years by other influences, such as education and personal interactions with other people. Education can guide students to become more aware and appreciative of their individual culture and heritage. Children also can learn to become open to the cultural ideas shared by others so as to avoid ethnocentrism.

7. All children enter school with a store of prior knowledge, closely aligned with their individual cultural backgrounds, on which we can build.

8. Education can guide all students to become more aware and appreciative of the many cultures that have contributed to what is now the United States. Multicultural education prepares students to live in a democratic country and a world of diversity.

9. Teachers need to be aware of their own cultural backgrounds and biases. And they must recognize how these biases might influence their expectations of students and how they interact with others. Open dialogue with students will acknowledge these cultural influences as common to us all. Teachers and students can learn together about different ideas and ways of thinking.

10. Multicultural teaching is exciting but also scary because it is grounded in reality. Through active, constructivist learning strategies, students can become directly involved in their learning. At the same time, teachers may find such multicultural approaches more difficult because dialogue may include controversy and emotion. Open discussion may lead to expressions of anger or hostility, pain, and guilt. Since such discussions do not usually lead to identification of "right answers," the resulting ambiguity may cause students to feel unsettled. Parents may be confused about the intent of classroom activities.

11. Multicultural education, global studies, and internationalization of the curriculum are interrelated in their focus on human concerns. Thus, a study of universal needs suggests topics that overlap, so that the three are not completely separate areas to be added to the school curriculum.

12. Multicultural education deals with values and attitudes as well as knowledge. We can guide students to be aware of their own thinking and that of others. We guide them to make choices based on expressed reasoning, problem solving, and decision making. Changes in values and attitudes and the development of empathy take time, so that assessing such changes quickly is not possible.

An Overview of This Text

The presentation of *Multicultural Teaching* is organized in three major parts.

Part I is comprised of four chapters that establish the foundation for multicultural teaching: Chapter 1, "Exploring Our Unique American Multiculture," explains the rationale for multicultural education and provides an inclusive definition. Chapter 2, "Teaching for Diversity While Promoting Unity," expands the esteem/empathy/equity model on which multicultural teaching is based. Chapter 3, "Infusing Multicultural Concepts across the Curriculum," provides sample lessons and resources for art, language arts/reading, mathematics, music, physical education, science, and social studies. Chapter 4, "Organizing Interdisciplinary Studies," presents learning centers, thematic units, and modules as methods of individualizing multicultural instruction across the curriculum.

Part II is comprised of five chapters focusing on specific activities that further demonstrate how to carry out multicultural teaching. Chapter 5, "Learning about Ourselves," focuses on how a student-centered classroom can accommodate individual differences and the development of self-esteem. Chapter 6, "Building a Community of Learners," deals with making all students feel included in a classroom where their cultural diversity is accepted and appreciated. Chapter 7, "Enlarging Student Perspectives," treats the concerns of the larger community, demonstrating how teachers can help young learners to appreciate other people and understand how they are interconnected to the whole world. Chapter 8, "Exploring Language and Linguistic Diversity," guides teachers to celebrate language diversity in the classroom as children investigate their own languages, varieties of English, and the wealth of languages around the world. Chapter 9, "Celebrating Multiculturalism around the Year," more than a "heroes, heroines, and holidays" approach, provides materials for developing broad themes over a period of time.

Part III promotes reflection as part of the ongoing process of learning to teach multiculturally. Chapter 10, "Reflecting on Multicultural Teaching," provides an overview of controversial issues as well as promising practices, ending with a self-assessment designed to inspire further personal growth.

Throughout this text, we have integrated information about various groups in the United States. Special features about significant groups are included in the following chapters:

African Americans, Chapters 7, 9
The aged, Chapter 6
Chinese and Chinese Americans, Chapter 4
The Deaf, Chapter 8
Hawaii and Native Hawaiians, Chapter 9
Immigrants, Chapters 4, 7
Japanese and Japanese Americans, Chapters 3, 9
Jewish Americans, Chapters 7, 9
Latino/Hispanic Americans, Chapters 8, 9
Native Americans, Chapter 6
People with Disabilities, Chapter 6
Religions, Chapter 7
Women and girls, Chapter 5

An attempt has been made to include information about a variety of different cultures, but full attention could not be accorded every group represented in the United States. It is important that you and your students continue to investigate multicultural information because the discovery process is equal in importance to the content. The extensive listing of materials in the Appendix provides support for additional study.

Throughout *Multicultural Teaching* we have provided lists of suggested readings for students. Books especially suitable for primary grades are identified with an asterisk.

REFLECTIONS

This introductory chapter summarizes the evolution of multiculturalism in the United States and the changing ways of thinking that impact directly on the schools. It is essential that we teachers recognize our own ethnicity and cultural background as we learn to address the needs of our students. We begin with our own stories and then reach out to take in the stories of the students with whom we work. In this book we define multicultural education inclusively to take in the concerns of all of the diverse people that populate the United States.

A major focus in *Multicultural Teaching* also is education that provides esteem, empathy, and equity for all students. Educators need to lead the way in breaking down the stereotyped thinking that leads to dissension and violence. A humane approach to education threaded throughout the total curriculum presented in home and school over twelve or more years should prepare students to live peaceably in a democratic society and a diverse, interconnected world.

APPLICATIONS

In this part of each chapter, we present ideas and activities designed to challenge your thinking and to lead you toward greater understanding of the issues involved in multicultural education.

1. Form cooperative learning groups (CLGs) to work on activities presented thoughout this text. Groups of four to six people with similar interest in a grade level or subject area can work together to plan lessons. CLGs can be reformed to suit different needs and to increase interaction among diverse students. Findings of groups can be shared with the entire class.

2. Purchase a large three-ringed notebook in which to begin your Reflective Teaching Portfolio (RTP). This portfolio will summarize multicultural education and its impact on you as an individual, a teacher. To begin your portfolio, mark dividers to begin organizing the record of your progress toward becoming a multiculturally competent teacher. Include dividers for LEARNING LOG, INFORMATION, TEACHING IDEAS, and RESOURCES. Later, you may need to add other dividers. As the first entry in your portfolio, write several sentences about each of the twelve assumptions listed at the end of Chapter 1. These comments will provide a benchmark, summarizing your present position regarding multicultural education. Date this sheet and place it in your LEARNING LOG.

In addition to this notebook, you will need to begin a larger resource file (perhaps a heavy cardboard box with a lid) in which you can collect printed materials, including books, pictures, charts, and realia (artifacts representing different cultures). Purchase a packet of manila folders in which to store such resources as clippings, pictures, and book-lists. Your portfolio can be stored at the front of your resource file.

3. Find a shoebox that will hold 4" x 6" file cards. In this file you will begin your collection of MULTICULTURAL LITERATURE. Browse through the extensive bibliography of multicultural literature presented in the Appendix. Select several books that you would like to read. Begin your card file as you record the following information for each book that you read.

> Author
> Title
> Age level (Approximate)
> Short summary of plot or features included
> Ideas for using the book with a class

4. Many foreign-born parents want their children to be bilingual. They also want their children to remember their origins. A Korean parent in Chicago stated, "What I intend to say to my children is 'You're never going to be Americans . . . Even though you live here 100 years or 200 years, you're still Korean'." Discuss this issue in your CLG. As a teacher, what would you want to say to this father? Have someone from your group summarize your responses for the whole class.

5. Visit your local library to explore its multicultural offerings. Check the catalog to see what is listed under "Multicultural Education." Talk to the children's librarian to find out what resources are available in this field. Also peruse the audiovisual catalog to see if you can borrow films, videotapes, and other media from your library.

Referring to the extensive listing of books in the Appendix, select an ethnic group that interests you and scan through the titles to note several that you might like to read. When you finish reading a book, bring the book to your CLG to share the contents and the strengths of this piece of literature with your colleagues. Each member of the group can then make a card for the book you presented.

6. In 1993, the Association for Supervision and Curriculum Development passed a resolution focusing on equalizing educational opportunities, stating in part: "The widening gap between rich and poor results in disenfranchisement. This exclusion creates lifelong negative consequences for children, their families, and our global society. The gap is manifest in demonstrable differences in health care, school settings, access to information, learning environments, student expectations, and ultimately, in the academic, economic, and social success of students." How can teachers deal with this issue? Write your ideas in your LEARNING LOG. Think about what you need to learn in order to help students who may need support. What obstacles to learning do students face? What different factors can cause students to be "at risk" for school failure?

ENDNOTES

1. *Time Magazine.* Special Edition; Fall, 1993.
2. Israel Zangwill. *The Melting Pot* (play), 1909.
3. Associated Press, 1993.

4. Bureau of the Census. *Statistical Abstracts of the United States.* U.S. Government, 1991.

5. *Ibid.*

6. Carley H. Dodd. *Dynamics of Intercultural Communication.* Brown, 1987.

7. Christine Sleeter and Carl Grant. *Making Choices for Multicultural Education: Five Approaches to Race, Class and Gender.* Merrill, 1988.

8. AACTE Newsletter, 1972.

9. Minnesota Commissioner of Education. Ruling, 1988.

10. *An Annotated Bibliography.* American Association of Colleges of Teacher Education, 1972.

11. L. Border and N. Chism. *Teaching for Diversity.* San Francisco: Jossey-Bass, 1992, p. 1.

12. Jerry Spinelli. *Maniac Magee.* Viking, 1992.

EXPLORING FURTHER

At the end of each chapter we present books that will help you continue expanding your multicultural knowledge base.

James A. Banks, & Cherry A. Banks (Eds.) (1997). *Multicultural Education: Issues and Perspectives* (3rd ed.). Boston: Allyn & Bacon.

Mary E. Dilworth. (1992). *Diversity in Teacher Education: New Expectations.* San Francisco: Jossey-Bass.

Carl A. Grant. (1993). *Research & Multicultural Education.* Bristol, PA: Falmar.

Carl A. Grant (Ed.). (1992). *Toward Education That Is Multicultural: Proceedings from the First Annual Meeting of the National Association of Multicultural Education.* Morristown, NJ: Silver Burdett.

Patricia Ramsey. (1998). *Teaching and Learning in a Diverse World.* New York: Teachers College Press.

Christine Sleeter (Ed.). (1991). *Empowerment through Multicultural Education.* Albany, NY: State University of New York.

Joan T. Timm. (1996). *Four Perspectives in Multicultural Education.* Belmont, CA: Wadsworth.

Doris Walker-Dalhouse et al. "Attitudes of Preservice Teachers to Culturally Diverse Students." Albuquerque, NM: National Council of Teachers of English Convention, March 20, 1998.

Kenneth M. Zeichner. (1993). *Educating Teachers for Cultural Diversity.* East Lansing, MI: National Center for Research on Teacher Learning.

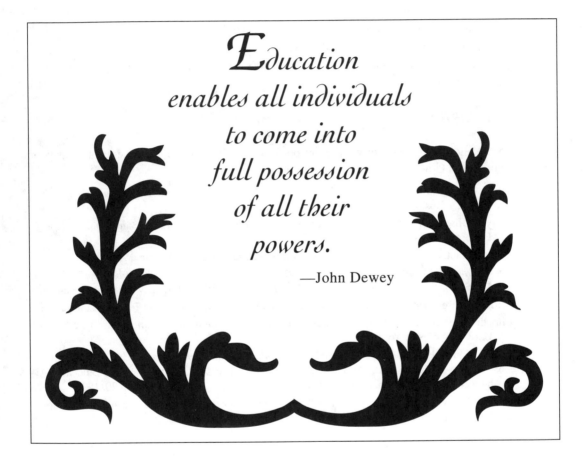

*Education
enables all individuals
to come into
full possession
of all their
powers.*

—John Dewey

2

Teaching for Diversity While Promoting Unity

As John Dewey wrote in 1902, "Education enables all individuals to come into full possession of all their powers."[1] Today most educators still agree that the aim of all good teaching should be to assist each student in reaching his or her fullest potential.

The emphasis in this text is not only on (1) accommodating individual differences but also on (2) teaching multicultural understandings to all students at all levels. In order to achieve this two-pronged goal, the teacher must plan with both the curriculum and the student constantly in mind. A multicultural curriculum must be carefully designed, beginning with an identified set of outcomes to address throughout the total elementary school curriculum. Then the multicultural curriculum must be effectively presented through what we call "multicultural teaching," that is, instruction that provides equitable opportunities for all students, accommodates cultural diversity in its full complexity, and addresses both process and product. Multicultural teaching can be described succinctly as "making the best teaching available for all students."

In this chapter we discuss the content to be taught, and we consider the needs of diverse student learners, including those who are most at risk of failing in school. Recognizing that students have different learning styles and abilities that are influenced by culturally diverse backgrounds will cause us to reflect further on the content to be taught: particularly when concepts will be introduced and how we will most effectively present content within a "spiraling curriculum."

After reading this chapter, you should be able to:

- Demonstrate learning and teaching processes that support the development of student self-esteem and empathy.
- Plan learning activities that offer equal opportunities for all children to learn.
- Design lessons that lead students to reflect on and to respond critically to what they observe, hear, or read about multicultural concepts and issues.

DEVELOPING A SPIRALING MULTICULTURAL CURRICULUM: OUTCOMES, GOALS, OBJECTIVES

In this section we explore the general content that needs to be presented in a multicultural curriculum. We begin by identifying the outcomes expected from implementing such a program and point out how multicultural objectives can be integrated into instruction across the curriculum. We discuss the spiraling nature of a well-developed curriculum as well as what is called the "hidden curriculum," unintended consequences or unplanned aspects of classroom learning.

Selecting Appropriate Outcomes

What are we trying to achieve? What should students be able to do? How will their thinking be affected? Before we select specific learning activities, we need to identify multicultural outcomes we expect to achieve in terms of student learning. In addition to concepts related to the traditional subject areas, for example, we might expect students to:

1. Identify their own cultural roots.
2. Define and use pertinent terminology appropriately.
3. Express concepts about diverse people that are accurate and free of stereotypes and bias.
4. Role play and empathize with the perspectives of different groups.
5. Respect and appreciate cultural diversity as a characteristic of the population of the United States and of the world.
6. Interact positively with diverse individuals inclusive of race, gender, and/or abilities.
7. Study literature that reflects all cultural groups.
8. Identify multicultural concepts related to all subject areas.
9. Apply evaluation and assessment measures that are equitable for diverse persons.
10. Assess their own experiences with cultural diversity.

Developing a scope and sequence for multicultural education begins with such outcomes that we expect students to achieve. Ongoing assessment of student performance continuously reminds us, and the students themselves, of the intent of the program and the progress they have made toward achieving the established objectives.

Major Goals for Multicultural Education

Throughout the curriculum we keep our major goals in mind. We want to increase not only the students' self-knowledge but also their understanding and appreciation of others who live in our country and in the world. We also want to provide equitable opportunities for all students to learn. Therefore, at all stages of development we will emphasize esteem, empathy, and equity—the key goals for multicultural education—as depicted in this diagram.

Identifying Objectives for the Multicultural Program

We need to consider both cognitive objectives and affective objectives as we design a multicultural education curriculum. Involving all faculty members in identifying competencies for the multicultural program will ensure that each person assumes responsibility for the

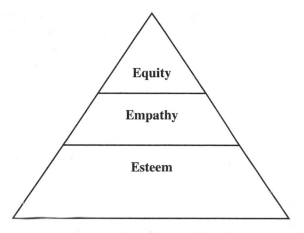

KEY GOALS FOR MULTICULTURAL EDUCATION

success of the program. Objectives must not only cross the total curriculum but also permeate deeply into the very practices that we use as we teach.

Objectives should be written in active terms that engage students in performing thinking tasks, for example:

acting out	deciding	inquiring	retelling
analyzing	defining	listing	solving
applying	describing	observing	stating
arguing	explaining	recalling	visualizing
comparing	identifying	reciting	writing

The process of discussing and identifying the essential competencies to be developed throughout the elementary and middle school is a critical step for all members of the staff in building a multicultural curriculum. Those who are engaged from the beginning will be committed to carrying out the program they plan together. We need to identify outcomes for each curriculum area—reading, oral and written language, mathematics, social studies, science, and so on. In teaching science, a teacher, for example, might include the following objectives for a study of animals:

Students will:

- Learn about people from different countries who have studied animals (expand horizons).
- Keep a learning log summarizing what they learn each day (reinforces learning; individualized).
- Identify stereotypes that we associate with specific animals (introduces multicultural concept in nonthreatening context).
- Compile information to support or disprove one specific stereotype (the scientific method).
- Define stereotyped thinking in general (transfer of knowledge).
- Demonstrate how to support generalizations with scientific facts (inquiry method; thinking skills).
- Explore the roles animals play in different cultures (cultural diversity).

Objectives designed specifically to promote self-esteem and the appreciation of others can be inserted into the list of behaviors expected for every instructional area. Consider how the following multicultural objectives could fit into a reading lesson or a social studies unit.

Students will:
- List their own strengths.
- Identify areas in which they need to grow.

Students will:
- Express positive feelings for other people.
- Work cooperatively in group situations to help each other.

Students will:
- Identify the many groups to which they belong.
- List ethnic groups in the community.
- Act out folktales from selected ethnic groups.

Students will:
- Describe the contributions made by diverse groups to our pluralistic society.
- Define such terms as *racism* and *sexism.*
- Discuss the importance of understanding among the people of the world in order to achieve world peace.

It is unlikely that any one of the objectives presented in this section will be fully achieved in one lesson, thus we need to think in terms of how each concept can be introduced and reinforced at different levels over a period of time. We need to begin defining a flexible curriculum that will grow with the students.

Building a Spiraling Multicultural Curriculum

A spiraling curriculum is a plan that moves upward and outward from the time a learner enters the classroom. Building on the knowledge and experience already possessed by each child, the curriculum is woven, concept by concept, over a period of time. Many ideas are first encountered in the primary grades through reading selected stories aloud, for example, Eve Bunting's *Cheyenne Again,* and talking about the story and the illustrations. Even young children should be introduced to many concepts related to multicultural education:

self-esteem	friendship	family
African Americans	Latinos	Asian Americans
stereotyping	racism	sexism
discrimination	disabled people	the elderly
civil rights	child abuse	prejudice
the United Nations	the global village	cultural pluralism
the right to vote	religious beliefs	world peace
empathy	equality and equity	humanity
poverty	immigration	democracy

Gradually students will learn about the demography of their community and of the nation. They will learn about the history and the geography of our continent and of the world. They will learn much about interpersonal interaction. More familiar themes—for example, friendship—will be absorbed by the 6-year-old and later will be built on as children progress through the upper grades. The subject of self-esteem will be addressed at each grade level. More explicit discussions may be part of the middle school curriculum following indirect attention to self-esteem through learning and assessment processes in the primary grades. Each concept will be expanded and extended as students develop. Through the spiraling multicultural curriculum, student knowledge grows recursively, developing with student maturity and experience.

Eubanks points out the "acute need . . . to assure that educational programs reflect the best knowledge available on education that is multicultural, and that this knowledge be ingrained throughout our educational programs" at all levels.[2] We perceive multicultural education as a thread that weaves throughout the total curriculum, not a single syllabus for a class taught in seventh grade or one unit of study presented in grades 3 and 6. Infusing multicultural concepts throughout the K–8 curriculum is admittedly more difficult than teaching a single class, but this spiraling incremental approach is more likely to be internalized by young learners.

Recognizing the Hidden Curriculum

We need to remember that curriculum consists of more than consciously planned messages presented in lectures and in textbooks. Children also learn through the hidden or covert curriculum that may not be recognized and is almost never assessed. Consider what students are learning from the attitudes, speech, and behavior of these teachers:

> *Motherly Mrs. McIntyre loves children and loves to teach first-grade reading. She always brags to the principal about the wonderful readers in her Great Books group and has one of them read aloud when he visits the classroom. (How do the less able students feel? What knowledge and attitudes are they internalizing?)*

> *Jim Melville loves to teach fourth-grade language arts. He reads aloud to his students and brings in piles of books from the library. He tells students that he always picks out books about boys because he knows boys hate stories about girls but girls enjoy the adventure stories about boys. (How might this practice affect the self-esteem of girls in this classroom? What are the boys and girls learning?)*

> *Eighth-grade history teacher, Donna Fosdick, has regular celebrations for Martin Luther King's birthday and Cinco de Mayo. She comments that she can't afford more time from the curriculum for extra observances. (Is there more to understanding other cultures than just observing these few holidays? What do students learn from hearing this attitude expressed? What are they failing to learn?)*

Children are very attentive to the hidden messages communicated by teacher behavior. We need to be aware of the stereotyped thinking that causes us to behave, for example, as if all children have the same advantages or disadvantages at home or that everyone in a class shares the same values. Beware of repeated evaluative statements such as "That's good" whenever students make a contribution. Students quickly learn to perform for teacher approval. We need to be aware of our role as the adult who not only chooses instructional content and strategies but also models respect and caring for students in the classroom.

Avoiding Pitfalls

In offering an inclusive educational program that serves the needs of all students, we want to refrain from:

Trivializing: Organizing activities only around holidays or only around food; involving parents only for holiday or cooking activities.

Tokenism: Displaying one black doll amidst many white dolls or having only one multicultural book among many others; any kind of minimal display in the classroom.

Disconnecting cultural diversity from daily classroom life: Reading multicultural books only for special occasions or teaching one unit related to cultural diversity and never addressing the topic again; for example, featuring African Americans only during Black History Month in February or talking about Native Americans only in relationship to November Thanksgiving celebration.

Marginalizing: Presenting people of color only in the context of the past or as victims.

Misrepresenting American ethnic groups: Using only books about Mexico, Japan, or African countries to teach about contemporary cultural groups in the United States. (We may be confusing Mexican Americans with Mexicans.)[3]

Jalongo (1992) cautions that the teacher must:

1. Be aware that multiculturalism must begin with adults.
2. Know the students and their cultural backgrounds.
3. Expect conflict and model conflict resolution.
4. Bring the outside world into the classroom and help parents see the value of learning, including play, firsthand.
5. Present modern concepts of families and occupations.
6. Use literature to enrich children's learning and understandings about cultural pluralism.[4]

As a future teacher, consider how you can carry out this author's recommendations.

Recap

We need to think of a multicultural curriculum as permeating the many disciplines that we teach. Goals, objectives, and expected outcomes in all subject areas should include both affective and cognitive aspects of learning and should result in active student performance. The spiraling multicultural curriculum introduces concepts, building on them at each level. The teacher plays a crucial role in selecting content and methods of instruction as well as modeling appropriate behaviors.

FOCUSING ON THE STUDENT LEARNER

Effective multicultural education must be student-centered if it is to be equitable. In learning to teach for diversity, we need to perceive students as individuals, being careful to avoid generalizations that lead to stereotyped thinking. Student-centered instruction recognizes student learning as the ultimate aim of education. We want students to be self-motivated learners, to inquire and to discover, and also to question established practices or assumptions. At the same time, students need to be aware of the responsibilities that are directly related to choice and decision making. In this section we look at several topics related to multicultural teaching and the student learner: student rights, primary grade schooling, students at risk, and the widening gap between teachers and students.

Student Rights

As we plan a multicultural program, we might begin by considering the rights of the students we teach. "Bill of Rights for Children: An Education Charter for the Decade of the Child" was drafted by Thomas Sobol, Commissioner of Education in New York State. Note that these rights tie in closely with the aims of multicultural education.

> *All children have the right to:*

- A healthy, secure, nurturing infancy and early childhood;
- A free, sound, basic education;
- An education appropriate for his or her needs;
- An education which respects each student's culture, race, socioeconomic background, and home language;
- Schools and educational programs which are effective;
- Educational programs which prepare them for jobs, for college, for family life, and for citizenship in a democracy;
- The resources needed to secure their educational rights;
- Education in school buildings which are clean, safe, and in good repair;
- Pursuance of their education without fear;
- An education which involves responsibilities as well as rights.[5]

Meeting these rights provides the foundation for multicultural teaching. Recognition of students' rights may call for rethinking the total curriculum and just how it is delivered, a topic worthy of consideration by the staff at a faculty meeting.

Primary Grade Schooling

During the 1980s and continuing into the 1990s, such efforts as Headstart have made a documented difference in providing equity in education for our youngest children. We must plan carefully to "ensure that young children experience transitional continuity in programming" as they move from preschool into kindergarten and the primary grades.[6] This collaborative effort involves diverse parents and community agencies in working closely with the schools.

Successful learning builds self-esteem. From the beginning all young children approach life eagerly, positively, no matter what their backgrounds. Self-confidently, they reach out to learn. They work hard to discover the complexities of language and how to function in their social environment—family, neighborhood, and school. They develop an "I Can" attitude.

What happens in school and in the home has a significant effect on the development of this natural potentiality to learn. School experience, peer attitudes, and teacher expectations directly influence children's performance. A six-year study of children from low-income homes by Virginia Shipman and others investigated "how home and school work together to influence the child's development."[7] Findings reveal that:

1. "Disadvantaged" and middle-class children enter school with the same average level of self-esteem.
2. After three years of schooling, children from low-income homes experience a significant drop in level of self-esteem compared to children from middle-class homes.
3. Although there is a loss of self-confidence, children from low-income homes still feel positive at this stage rather than negative about their ability to take care of themselves.

The Shipman study clarifies the characteristics of children from low-income homes, which may serve to dispel some stereotyped thinking. For example, based on more than 1000 diverse children from 1969–1975, the researcher found that these children:

1. Enter school with as broad a range of abilities as any other group.
2. Have as much self-esteem as children from other groups.
3. Come from homes containing the same range of positive and negative influences on learning as do middle-class children.

Her findings should help teachers rid themselves of the misconception that low socioeconomic status automatically means little family value for learning. They also point up the need for viewing each child as an individual. The implications of this study support caring, accepting classroom processes. Shipman notes, "It gets down to what happens in the classroom between the teacher and the child—how much encouragement that child is given, how much stimulation and warmth." Teachers who have low expectations for students may have a negative effect on children's performance.[8]

Teacher expectations based on income level or cultural background are not the only factors affecting student performance. Teachers need to consider the advantages the English-speaking child has on entering most U.S. schools compared to the Non-English Proficient (NEP) child.

English-Speaking Child	*Non-English Proficient Child*
1. Language used is familiar.	1. Language used is strange.
2. Teaching materials are presented in English, and the child learns to read English.	2. Child is expected to use materials presented in English; child may be illiterate in his or her native language.
3. Child's self-esteem is supported by successful experiences in school.	3. Child may feel unhappy, be unsuccessful in school, and cannot wait to go home.
4. He or she graduates from high school and may enter college.	4. He or she may drop out of school as soon as possible.[9]

While such summaries are valuable, note that they also tend to polarize characteristics in a way that may support stereotypes. We need to be aware, for example, that NEP students vary in the obstacles they face and how they overcome them, depending on the family social and economic status, the family background, and the individual's motivation. However, we do need to understand possible differences in how children may regard the school experience. The role of teachers should be to strengthen students' sense of belonging within the classroom community and providing support for successful learning.

Children who experience failure and frustration in their schooling may perceive themselves as having limited ability or little chance of success and may not even try a task before saying "I can't." Such children need an Individualized Education Plan (IEP) that provides positive experience from the beginning. Our task is not easy even if we begin working with a young child at the age of four or five; it becomes increasingly difficult as the child grows older. The earlier we begin planning for multicultural teaching, the better chance we have of counteracting negative influences.

Students at Risk

Many children are at risk of not succeeding in the schools today. We recognize that "school people did not create or cause most of the problems that confront young people today, nor can they solve the problems by themselves."[10] On the other hand, educators have a responsibility for not only alleviating but actively counteracting the conditions that place some students at risk and helping them overcome obstacles that impede successful achievement in school. As we identify any group, we must beware of overgeneralizing and equating "at risk" with minority or low SES students only. For too long we have failed to solve the problem of reaching diverse students, intervening in the early years, providing models with whom they can identify. For example, our teaching has often failed to recognize that "at-risk students need to learn higher order thinking such as problem solving, not just basic skills that may keep them dependent thinkers all their lives."[11] Multicultural approaches to education may offer all students something special as we deliberately select literature with which they can find a common bond and make a sincere effort to provide equitable opportunities for successful learning experiences, beginning in the primary grades.

Phi Delta Kappa, an educational honor society, sponsored extensive research of at-risk students. Begun in 1988, the study is based on reports from almost 22,000 elementary, middle school, and high school students, including about 30% African American, Latino, Native American, and Asian students. Researchers identified 34 indicators of risk, which were grouped into the following five categories or factors:

Personal pain (drugs, abuse, suspension, suicide)
Academic failure (low grades, failure, absences, low self-esteem)
Family tragedy (parent illness or death, health problems)
Family socioeconomic situation (low-level income, negativism, lack of education)
Family instability (moving, divorce)

Notice that these factors are not limited to so-called minority students, but appear across the whole group of students.

Researchers addressed four major questions:

1. Who is at risk? Only one in five of students interviewed had no risk factors; one out of four had three or more risk items evident. Older students are more at risk than younger; African Americans are more at risk than whites; Latinos are more at risk than Asians; and boys are more at risk than girls.
2. What factors put them at risk? "Most of the risk factors are beyond the sphere of influence of the school." If one risk factor is present, usually there are others. More than

half of students who were retained came from broken homes. One-third of them had low grades and 17% had fathers who had not graduated from high school.

3. What are schools doing to help these students? Nearly one-fourth of the 9700 teachers interviewed say they spend more than 50% of their time with at-risk students. Strategies used by more than 75% of teachers include: individualized scheduling, conferences with parents, more time on basic skills, emphasis on thinking skills, and notification of parents.

   The following practices were judged to be at least 75% effective: special teachers, smaller classes, special education, individualized scheduling, conferences with parents, more time on basic skills, peer tutoring, vocational courses (in high school), special study skills, emphasis on coping skills, emphasis on thinking skills, notification of parents, and teacher aides. In addition, "teachers and principals provide students who are at-risk with more instructional efforts than students who are not at-risk, and teachers are committed to and are concerned with helping students who have special problems, whatever those problems might be."

4. How effective are the schools' efforts? Although teachers and principals considered their efforts only 71 to 75% productive, principals reported that their schools had a great deal of influence over students' reading comprehension, math, writing, and listening skills; daily attendance, general behavior and attitude toward school; completion of homework, attention in class, and higher order thinking skills.[12]

From the findings of this study we can see that early assessment of students' backgrounds and abilities is essential in planning instruction designed specifically for students who are at risk. Teachers must recognize that, according to this study, these students may come from homes that lack literacy models and resources and read very little. They often have not mastered learning skills and may have a low school achievement record. However, we need to consider the strengths and weaknesses of each student as we plan individually for their growth. Just offering more drill work or lecturing will not solve their learning problems. On the other hand, teachers can do only so much; "the energy for learning comes from the student, and the responsibility for learning must be assumed by the student." Teachers can help children learn to assume this responsibility even early in their schooling. In summary, "understanding students, caring about them as individuals, nurturing the development of responsibility in them, and then emphasizing academic skills" holds some promise of helping at-risk students. These efforts must begin early in the school experience with continued support offered throughout the school years.

Yale professor James Comer, author of *Beyond Black and White,* supports these recommendations, noting: "Black children need somebody to care about them, first of all. They need somebody who wants them to learn, who believes they can learn, and who gives them the kind of experiences that enable them to learn. That's what all children need."[13] Comer has summarized what we envision as "teaching multiculturally."

The Widening Gap between Teacher and Students

In *Educating Teachers for Cultural Diversity,* Kenneth Zeichner addresses another key issue in teacher education: Teachers are becoming increasingly different from the students they teach. Furthermore, the number of teachers of color entering the teaching field is much too small to overcome the discrepancy between the teacher's cultural background and that of the culturally diverse group of students in most classrooms.[14]

It is essential, therefore, that all teachers acquire the appropriate attitudes, knowledge, and disposition needed to work effectively with students who come from varied cultural or class backgrounds. It is important to recognize, too, that not only will teacher and student be different, but also that in many classrooms students will also differ from one another. Multicultural education requires that teachers plan an inclusive classroom in which children learn about each other and learn to respect each other.

This may be a special challenge to those who come from middle-class Christian families of European origins that speak standard English. Can white monolingual teachers, members of the so-called dominant group, rise to the challenge of reaching out to ethnic and language-minority students? Can these teachers prepare themselves to work with children of color, children whose parents may have been born in a different country, who may still be preparing to be naturalized? Can they reach out to individual children and parents in the school community to bridge the gap? They can, if they believe that they can and if they are committed to teaching for diversity.

Research findings support our conviction that effective multicultural teaching is student-centered rather than teacher-dominated. The teacher does not abdicate his or her position but rather plans quality learning activities that engage students in active, hands-on experiences and builds on success to develop students' self-esteem. The teacher models appreciation for diversity by building on students' prior knowledge and setting clear, realistic expectations for each student's abilities. Learning experiences are designed to promote student interaction and to generate inquiry and thinking through both talking and writing. Such approaches benefit all students, but they are especially recommended for those who may be at risk.

Recap

Multicultural teaching is student-centered, addressing the needs of each individual student. In this section we examine the fundamental rights of all children that should influence the development of a multicultural program. We then address special concern for education in the primary grades when attitudes and patterns of learning are established. Following is a discussion of at-risk students and how we can help them succeed. The final discussion focuses on the problems caused by the gap that may exist between teachers and the students they teach.

DELIVERING THE CURRICULUM

Emphasizing learning processes, multicultural teaching attempts to facilitate the learning of every child, assisting each one to reach his or her highest potential. Multicultural education begins with clearly defined outcomes. However, attaining these outcomes requires us to select the best strategies—the delivery system—that will enable all children to learn. In this section we will focus on teaching for diversity, and just how we can achieve that goal.

Planning for Multicultural Teaching

Ernest Boyer states: "I'm convinced the time has come to . . . focus on the leadership of the principal, the renewal of the teachers, and above all, the dignity and potential of every student."[15] We need to make certain that teachers and administrators are well-informed and that their knowledge is accurate and up-to-date. Teachers also need to know how to use the best of teaching strategies—questioning, cooperative learning, engaging students in active hands-on learning activities. They need to select methods and materials that will involve students in thinking about real issues that affect their daily lives. Study after study reveals that the teacher is the key to the success or failure of any program, so what you do in your own classroom every day is of primary importance. From the moment students enter the classroom they begin learning. The climate of the room, the way you treat students, the language you speak all serve as models for student behavior. Fair evaluation, recognition of individual needs, a clear sense of liking projected to students as you work with them will demonstrate what you want to teach.

Teachers who respect students select teaching methods that treat students equitably. For example, good teachers do not need to use sarcasm as a way of putting students down nor do they use "teasing," which is often misunderstood by young people. Respect for students is shown in the acceptance of their needs as growing young people. The teacher should have realistic expectations of students and understand how to encourage their participation in school activities. Evaluation of student performance is a particularly sensitive aspect of teaching. As we consider "putting grades on report cards," we should be aware that students see us as "putting grades on them," which can be very threatening, indeed. As we plan for evaluation, keep the following alternative factors in mind:

1. *Grading.* Don't put grades on everything a student does. Have many short writing and speaking activities that are not graded, but shared with other students or perhaps placed in a class collection that students can read at their leisure.
2. *Writing in all subject areas.* Never grade the first draft of a student's writing. Periodically have students revise a selection that will be published in some way (on the bulletin board, in a class book, in the school newspaper). Tell the students that you will put a grade on this work after they have revised it to their satisfaction.
3. *Establishing criteria.* Always make your criteria clear for grades you give. What does a student have to do to receive an A, B, or C? Talk with students about the characteristics of outstanding work, average work, and poor work as you make a specific assignment, and show them examples.
4. *Self-evaluation.* As much as possible, have students check their own work. Provide answer sheets so they can discover mistakes immediately. Stress reading items over again as needed, and correcting errors. If you eliminate yourself from this kind of "grading," you cease to be the ogre who has all the "right" answers.
5. *Individual conferences.* Have a short conference, a conversation, with each student once a week, if possible. Five minutes of individual attention does a lot for children who need support. This is a good time for examining children's writing or talking about the library book they are currently reading. Focus on supporting the student's efforts, not "correcting errors" at this time.

6. *Send a commendation to parents.* Several times during the year, send a letter to each parent commending at least one thing their child has accomplished. Children will be glad to take a Good Work Letter home. Make an effort to write this letter in the language of the home, even if you have to prepare translations into several different languages.

7. *Accentuate the positive!* Focus on what students accomplish, not what they fail to achieve or the mistakes they make. Compare:

> Wow, you spelled thirteen words out of fifteen correctly!
> Too bad, you missed two words out of fifteen today.

According to Zeichner (1993), university students who intend to become teachers today must have the following key characteristics to be effective as multicultural teachers:

- A clear sense of their own ethnic and cultural identity.
- High expectations for student success.
- The expectation that all students can succeed and that they can help them succeed.
- Commitment to achieving equity for all students and knowledge about accommodating different learning styles and abilities.
- The ability to bond with students; genuine caring about young people and their welfare.
- A strong multicultural knowledge base that includes both depth and breadth regarding ethnic studies, gender concerns, and sensitivity to persons with special needs.[16]

Strategies and skills that the effective teacher needs to be able to use include:

- Planning meaningful learning tasks based on the curriculum.
- Engaging students in interactive and collaborative learning tasks.
- Challenging students to develop higher level thinking skills.
- Providing scaffolding (support) for students to ensure that they can succeed.
- Building on students' prior knowledge.
- Communicating to students the expectation that they can succeed and that you, the teacher, will help them.
- Explaining the culture of the school to students.
- Maintaining students' sense of ethnocultural pride and identity.
- Involving parents in their children's education.[17]

Reduce the distance between school and home by informing parents of the goals you expect to achieve and learning outcomes students are working toward in their classrooms. Engage parents as partners directly involved in their children's learning, providing encouraging support for school-initiated learning. You can suggest ways, too, that parents can extend their children's learning of content and skills. A short list of reasonable activities can be sent home, including taking children to the local library or just talking with their children and listening to their conversation with respect. Such practices support the child's development of self-esteem and a positive attitude toward learning.

Using a Sound Lesson Model

In planning any lesson it is important to think through the entire process. First of all, what are your objectives for teaching the lesson? What do you want students to be able to do?

Remember that objectives can, and should, be both affective and cognitive. The following lesson model begins with stating the expected outcomes.

Next, you begin thinking about how you can reach these outcomes. What procedures will you use? What materials—videos, books, pictures, software, objects—will help you stimulate student learning? Then determine what students will do in response to the stimulus. Plan an active, hands-on experience—something all students *can* do (realistic expectations). Next comes the follow-up. What do students do after participating in the learning activity? How do they share the results? Finally, how will you know they have met the objectives you specified? Evaluation techniques may range from acting out to telling to writing, resulting in a performance by the student.

By following this model, you will plan a theoretically sound learning experience for children. The acronym SAFE will help you remember to incorporate all four components required.

Stimulus
Activity
Follow-up
Evaluation

A SAMPLE LESSON FOLLOWING THE MODEL

SAFE Lesson 1: A Biographical Sketch

Level of Difficulty: Grades 7–8
Outcomes

Students will:

1. Read a short biographical sketch of a minority author.
2. Analyze the quality of the writing.
3. Identify the features of a biographical sketch.
4. Compose a biographical sketch following the model.
5. Expand knowledge about diverse authors and their writings.

Procedures

This lesson should be developed over a period of several days. Duplicate copies of the following biographical sketch of Alex Haley:

Introducing Alex Haley   Alex Palmer Haley is the well-known author of *Roots: The Saga of an American Family,* which was published in 1976 and made into a stirring film that was presented on television to millions of Americans. Born August 11, 1921, in Ithaca, New York, Alex Haley was the son of a professor.

Alex Haley served as a journalist in the U.S. Coast Guard. He tells of writing love letters for his fellow seamen who weren't particularly good at writing. He won their admiration and gratitude (and earned considerable money, too) by creating romantic letters that ensured that the men's sweethearts were waiting when they returned to port.

The *SAFE* Model Lesson Plan

Title of lesson: _____

Grade levels intended for: _____

Outcome(s): (What will students be able to do?)

1. _____
2. _____
3. _____

Brief description:

_____
_____
_____
_____
_____

Procedures:
STIMULUS (How do I use specific material?)

ACTIVITY (What will students do?)

FOLLOW-UP (Individual, pairs, small group, large group suggestions.)

EVALUATION (Performance criteria for success of lesson based on objective[s].)

Haley soon decided that he wanted to concentrate on writing full-time. After struggling for a number of years to earn a living as a writer, he finally succeeded by collaborating with Malcolm X, writing *The Autobiography of Malcolm X,* which appeared in 1965.

But it was *Roots* that brought Haley real acclaim. Recognizing this unique contribution to American literature, the noted author James Baldwin writes:

> *Roots* is a study of continuities, of consequence, of how a people perpetuate themselves, how each generation helps to doom, or helps to liberate, the coming one—the action of love, or the absence of love, in time. It suggests, with great power, how each of us, however unconsciously, can't but be the vehicle of history which has produced us. Well, we can perish in this vehicle, children, or we can move on up the road.

After twelve years of painstaking genealogical research, Haley collected the life story of seven generations of his family in the United States and several more generations in a village on the Gambia River in West Africa. He presents these facts in a fictionalized story, a form he calls "faction," a delicate combination of fact and fiction that allows him to flesh out these ancestral characters, to include their thoughts and emotions. The resulting novel has touched the lives of millions of readers in a way that a scholarly report would never have achieved. As Haley knows, "When you start talking about family, about lineage and ancestry, you are talking about every person on earth." Alex Haley died in 1992.

Stimulus

Have students read the sketch of Haley's life. Tell the students this form of writing is called a biographical sketch. Ask students to note and then discuss particular words they find interesting. Identify collectively and list on the board the features of a well-written biographical sketch, for example:

Tells where and when the person was born.
Makes clear why the person is known.
Uses a quotation about the person's work.

Tell students that they are going to write a biographical sketch about any minority (broadly interpreted) writer whose work they have read or want to read. (You may brainstorm a list of recommended authors on the board, such as Laurence Yep, Virginia Hamilton, Isaac B. Singer, Richard Wright, or Richard Rodriguez.) They may begin with an encyclopedia entry, but they are to use other resources, too. You may wish to specify that they locate at least two sources other than the encyclopedia.

Activity

Take students to the library where they can locate the encyclopedias, check out books by the author selected, use the computer, and locate other sources of information. Point out *Current Biography* and *Contemporary Authors*. Students should take notes from resources they cannot check out. For homework, they are to begin the first draft of the biographical sketch to present in class on the following day.

Followup

On the next day review the features of a biographical sketch and make any additions recommended. Then have students work in pairs as they read the first drafts of the sketches and check their writing together against the list of features. The partners should work cooperatively to suggest revisions that will strengthen each paper.

Evaluation

The aim is to communicate to an audience with clear expository prose that is interesting to read. Students can evaluate the finished products as Grabs Me! (5 points), So-So (3 points), and Not So Hot (1 point). Students should be permitted to improve their writing in order to gain more points. Cooperative learning techniques used in groups can assist each student in achieving the top score. Note that this teaching strategy aims to develop self-esteem by facilitating success. All students are learning to collaborate to reach a goal.

The polished biographical sketches are published in a class book entitled "Authors We Have Known." Students may refer to this book when they are selecting books to read. The collection can be further developed by including book reviews (see Chapter 3). Note that students are learning about the contributions of members of diverse cultures to what we call "American literature." They learn about these authors as people, and they are introduced to literature they may be motivated to read based on a classmate's recommendation.

Note that in planning any lesson it is essential to include a warm-up period that prepares students to succeed at the task they are to undertake. Directions must be clear and resources must be readily available. Students need adequate time and formative evaluation (ongoing throughout the process) to help them complete the task. Cooperative learning techniques enable students to learn from each other. With guidance, students can learn to work successfully with these peer-learning strategies. As students work in pairs and small groups, they have an opportunity to get acquainted and to help one another succeed. Such understandings and ways of behaving undergird multicultural teaching, but we recognize that they are essential components of all effective teaching.

Providing Support for Learning

Multicultural teaching calls for supporting students as they engage in a learning activity. Support can take many forms, for example, methods that break a task into manageable parts. Following are several recommended strategies that support successful student learning: Brainstorming, Reciprocal Teaching, SUCCESS FOR ALL, and Bibliotherapy.

Brainstorming Ideas about a Problem or Topic

Brainstorming is a good way of engaging all students in developing solutions to a problem. Make it clear that everyone's contributions are equally acceptable.

1. Ideas are suggested and listed without evaluation, critical analysis, or even comment.
2. Usually even wild ideas can be expected in the spontaneity that evolves when you suspend judgment. Practical considerations are not important at this point. The brainstorming process should stimulate creativity.
3. At this stage, the quantity of ideas counts, not quality. All ideas should be expressed, not screened out by any individual. The greater quantity of ideas will increase the likelihood of generating outstanding ones.

4. Encourage piggybacking, building on the ideas of other group members, whenever appropriate, thus pooling creativity. Students should be free to adapt ideas or to make interesting combinations of various suggestions.
5. Focus on a single problem or issue. Break a complex problem into parts or stages.
6. Establish a congenial, relaxed, cooperative climate.
7. Make sure that all members, no matter how shy and reluctant to contribute, get their ideas heard.
8. Record *all* ideas.

Write ideas on a chalkboard or large sheets of paper. After numerous ideas are generated, follow these procedures:

1. Review the list of ideas, selecting the top 5 or 10 (any appropriate number) to discuss further in terms of practicality. Have small groups discuss each one in detail. Have each group present the pros and cons of that idea for consideration.
2. Then vote on the top 2 or 3 ideas to try. Place them in order of priority according to your purpose or need.
3. Begin implementing the ideas in order.

Multicultural topics lend themselves to such brainstorming techniques. Invite students to suggest alternative solutions or ideas about such questions as:

• How might we help a student who is having trouble getting along with other students in school?
• Why should we be concerned about what is happening in Israel or Somalia?
• How have African Americans contributed to the development of the United States?
• What would be appropriate behavior if someone called you an insulting name?
• What might you do if you witnessed such behavior?

Brainstorming techniques can be used with groups or can be done individually before beginning to write or planning a presentation.

Reciprocal Teaching

Reciprocal teaching, an interesting group technique developed by Annemarie Palincsar and others, engages children in working with an adult who models techniques students can then use to teach each other. Reciprocal teaching provides scaffolding to help students develop literacy skills as well as content knowledge. Students are grouped in units of six to eight led by an adult who provides support until students learn to take the leadership role. For example, middle school students might read Katherine Paterson's *The Great Gilly Hopkins*, about the feelings and problems faced by a young girl who has been buffeted by a hostile world, in order to achieve empathy for another person and to recognize the common problems we may all face.

Following the reading of each chapter, the students, guided by the adult, take turns in leading a discussion about what has been read. Note that each student is involved and also assumes responsibility for his or her own learning. Following the discussion, the leader summarizes what has been said because "summarization is a comprehension monitoring strategy." The group helps adjust the accuracy of this summary, which can be recorded, providing a copy for each member of the group.

The intent of this strategy is to support/develop students' learning how to construct meaning from a text. In 1987, University of California researcher Ann Brown began a longitudinal study using this method.[18] She worked with 300 primary grade children and 300 junior high school students who were judged at risk. The older students were poor readers. The students were placed in "reciprocal teaching groups" and given daily comprehension tests. Eighty percent of the students were rated successful at the end of the study, having achieved at least 80% accuracy on five succeeding tests. Such collaborative learning activities lend themselves to theme or unit studies as described in Chapter 4.

SUCCESS FOR ALL—A Support Program for Literacy Learning

Led by Robert Slavin, the research team at the Center for Research on Elementary and Middle Schools (CREMS) attempts to provide support for children during the crucial preschool and primary grade years when the "die for failure is cast" for many children. Support is provided for children at risk through the use of certified teachers who serve as reading tutors. A tutor spends twenty minutes a day working one on-one with a child during nonreading class time. Assessment of performance is ongoing so that support is given only when need for help is indicated.

"Working one-on-one is a uniquely different situation from group teaching," reports Slavin. "There are no problems with student motivation; no management problems—you put your arm around a child and teach that child what he or she needs to know."[19] As Frank Smith phrases it, "You respond to what the child is trying to do."[20]

In SUCCESS FOR ALL the focus is on story. In larger groups children may listen to the teacher read an interesting book, for example, the fine translation of *The Crane Wife* by Katherine Paterson or John Steptoe's beautifully illustrated African tale, *Mufaro's Beautiful Daughters*. The children talk about the story, retelling especially interesting parts. Discussion includes questions and speculation about possible answers, thus stimulating thinking abilities. On subsequent days acting out activities are included with children playing roles and providing dialogue that fits the performance. The teacher may have cards on which paragraphs from the story are printed so that children can rearrange the cards to sequence events appropriately. As they handle the cards, children are rethinking and rereading the story. Thus, the story is told and retold in many ways without exhausting the children's interest. Throughout these activities, teachers are expanding children's language so that all children are immersed in new words used in context. Gradually, children move into more structured literacy activities with greater emphasis on reading literature and responding in writing. In individual tutorials a child may read this same text so that he or she receives help, as needed, and is assisted in participating in follow-up activities.

Bibliotherapy

Sharing a good book can be a way of stimulating discussions about needs that students have in common. Read books aloud for this purpose; for example, *North Town* by Lorenz Graham for grades 4 and up, or *Stevie* by John Steptoe for primary grades. These two books happen to be about black characters, but all children will identify with them as human beings who are experiencing emotions familiar to them. Other good books that reveal universal needs and feelings include the following:

Primary Grades

Jan Brett. *Fritz and the Beautiful Horses.* Houghton, 1981. A gentle pony is excluded from the in-group.

Susan Jeschke. *Perfect the Pig.* Holt, 1980. The runt of the litter wishes for wings.

Patricia Lakin. *Don't Touch My Room.* Little, Brown, 1985. Adjusting to a new baby.

Phil Mendez. *The Black Snowman.* Scholastic, 1989. Jacob learns to believe in himself.

Books for Older Students

Paula Fox. *Lily and the Lost Boy.* Orchard, 1987. Growing up.

Laura Nathanson. *The Trouble with Wednesdays.* Bantam, 1987. Sexual abuse.

Emily Neville. *It's Like This, Cat.* Harper and Row, 1963. Adolescent Dave Mitchell learns to get along with his father.

Cynthia Voigt. *Homecoming.* Atheneum, 1981. Growing up.

Children today need to be able to talk about varied problems that were not so freely discussed ten years ago. Death and divorce are two topics that we can talk about in the classroom as an aid to students who are faced with these events in their lives. Books can often serve to provide a realistic perspective as well as to open up controversial topics for students and teachers who may find it difficult to introduce such topics. Many fine books written for young people handle these subjects sensitively.

Divorce or Single-Parent Families
Primary Grades

Anne N. Baldwin. *Jenny's Revenge.* Four Winds, 1974.

Joan Lexau. *Me Day.* Dial, 1971.

Paul Zindel. *I Love My Mother.* Harper and Row, 1975.

Upper Elementary and Middle Grades

Charlotte Anker. *Last Night I Saw Andromeda.* Walck, 1975.

Patricia MacLachlan. *Sarah, Plain and Tall.* Harper, 1985.

Mary Mahoney. *The Hurry-Up Summer.* Putnam, 1987.

Death and Relationships with Aged People
Primary Grades

Jennifer Bartoli. *Nonna.* Harvey House, 1975.

John Burningham. *Grandpa.* Crown, 1985.

Helen Oxenburg. *Grandma and Grandpa.* Dial, 1984.

Upper Elementary and Middle Grades

Vera and Bill Cleaver. *Where the Lilies Bloom.* Lippincott, 1969.

Virginia Hamilton. *Cousins.* Philomel, 1990.

Doris B. Smith. *A Taste of Blackberries.* Crowell, 1973.

Recap

Teachers need to plan supportive strategies to ensure student success in completing a task. Providing scaffolding for students at all levels helps them succeed in the undertaking learning activities. Structured processes and rules for proceeding support children's attempts to complete given tasks, for example, reading a story. Bibliotherapy helps students in personal ways as they read about others who have similar problems.

SELECTING OUTSTANDING RESOURCES FOR TEACHING

An important responsibility of the teacher is to select not only effective methods but also outstanding resources to support instruction. In this section we recommend the use of excellent literature for young people with particular emphasis on quality multicultural texts. Then, we include a focus on the use of computers in the classroom as effective instructional tools that engage students in locating information as well as creating multimedia presentations.

Using Literature as a Rich Source of Ideas

Literature is a particularly fine resource for the development of a multicultural education curriculum. Select literature that:

> communicates the universality of human emotions,
> models prosocial behavior,
> gives children pride in their ethnic heritage,
> introduces children to contemporary families both alike and different from their own,
> reveals to children how it feels to be different,
> enables children to participate in another social era,
> shows a wide range of human characteristics and aspirations, and
> immerses children in another culture.[21]

Reading Literature Aloud to a Class

Reading aloud to students is an outstanding method of assuring that even less able readers have an opportunity to know good literature. Begin by presenting the book, short story, article, or poetry as writing done by another human being with whom students can enter into a transaction. The aim of the transaction is to construct meaning collaboratively. All we have are the words before us that an author wrote and our own ideas, so encourage students to ask questions about what the author might be saying and also about their responses to these ideas. (Avoid being the teacher who has all the "right" answers that you expect students to know.)

Use reading aloud as a method of engaging students at all levels and in all subject areas with the ideas presented in books. As you read a novel by Gary Soto, a picture book by Paul Goble, or the poetry of June Jordan, students are learning:

1. *What book language sounds like.* Remember that written language is different from the spoken language familiar to your students. More formal, usually representing the standard English dialect, book language is what they will gradually learn to write.

Before they can be expected to produce this written form, they need to hear it, to begin acquiring the structures and conventions of English in much the same manner that they earlier acquired the ability to speak their home language.

2. *Forms that writing can take.* As students listen to language or read it, they also gain knowledge of the forms (genres) through which they can express their ideas. Through listening to novels or short stories, for example, students are developing a "sense of story." They are learning how an author engages characters in dialogue and how character traits are revealed through behavior. They are introduced to such concepts as theme, setting, and plot development. Sharing other forms—haiku, song lyrics, an editorial, a letter of complaint—helps students learn how to write those forms.

3. *Grammatical structures.* As students listen to good writing, they hear a variety of sentence structures. They hear sentences composed of varied combinations of clauses, phrases, and strings of words, adding to and reinforcing their knowledge of English grammar. Listen to the opening sentences that William Saroyan wrote for *The Human Comedy:*

> The little boy named Ulysses Macauley one day stood over the new gopher hole in the backyard of his house on Santa Clara Avenue in Ithaca, California. The gopher of this hole pushed up fresh moist dirt and peeked out at the boy, who was certainly a stranger but perhaps not an enemy. Before this miracle had been fully enjoyed by the boy, one of the birds of Ithaca flew into the old walnut tree in the backyard and after settling itself on a branch broke into rapture, moving the boy's fascination from the earth to the tree.

4. *Feelings, ideas, content.* A good book presents interesting content, vicarious experiences, and ideas that students can talk and write about. The characters share emotions with which they can identify. Students gain insight into the lives of others and begin to understand the concepts of diversity and universality applied to the people with whom they inhabit the earth.

5. *The sound of fluent reading—intonation.* As you read, students hear what fluent reading sounds like. They hear the accents and pauses, the intonation that a good reader uses automatically. They can talk about the meaning that intonation adds to language.

6. *The joy of reading; what books have to offer.* Less able readers may be hearing a book that they could not read independently whereas able readers are often motivated to read for themselves a book that you have shared. All enjoy the experience of sharing an exciting story or laughing together. They are learning to enjoy reading and talking about good books together. The students are developing positive attitudes toward reading through your enthusiastic sharing.

Every piece of literature—every example of writing—that we share through reading aloud teaches students more about language and literature. Your reading aloud, however, offers additional assets as a teaching strategy of which you should be aware. One important advantage is that reading an article, a short story, or the chapter of a book means that *the whole class has a body of shared content that all can respond to immediately.* Your teaching is not hampered by students who have not read the assignment or completed their homework. Nor do you have to locate a class set of books. Reading aloud is *efficient and economical.*

Furthermore, reading aloud is very enjoyable. A sense of *camaraderie* develops through this shared experience—a *rapport* between you and your students that benefits the total learning program you present.

Choosing multicultural literature that supports instruction in the subject you are teaching adds the opportunity to deal with breaking down stereotypes and adding to student knowledge of people from diverse cultures. The following are representative of the multicultural fiction and nonfiction you might choose to read aloud and to talk about:

Grades K–3

Taro Yashima. *Crow Boy.* Viking, 1955. A boy who is different comes to be accepted.

Rosa Guy. *Billy the Great.* Delacorte, 1992. Perspective on prejudice; friendship.

Gary Paulsen. *The Tortilla Factory.* Harcourt, 1995. How tortillas are made from corn.

Grades 4–6

Harriette Robinet. *Washington Is Burning.* Holt, 1997. American history from a slave's viewpoint.

Laurence Yep. *Dragonwings.* Harper, 1976. Historical novel about a young Chinese American boy.

Malka Drucker. *Grandma's Latkes.* Harcourt, 1992. Grandmother passes the Jewish family's traditions to Molly.

Gary Soto. *The Skirt.* Delacorte, 1992. A picture of a Mexican American family in California.

Grades 7–8

Mary E. Lyons. *Letters from a Slave Girl: The Story of Harriet Jacobs.* Scribner, 1992. Historical fiction told through letters from a woman abolitionist.

Ofelia Lachtman. *The Girl from Playa Blanca.* Piñata Books, 1995. Children from Mexican village come to Los Angeles to search for their father.

Brenda Seabrooke. *The Bridges of Summer.* Cobblehill, 1992. Friendship between two girls across racial divisions in South Carolina.

Frances Temple. *Tonight by the Sea.* Orchard, 1995. A Haitian girl escapes military dictatorship.

Using Computers as Instructional Tools

As we move into the twenty-first century, much of our lives revolves around computers. Computer skills are essential in almost any line of work. We use the computer to locate a book in the library, our groceries are checked out by computerized pricing, and we use computers to write a report. Education, too, is fast moving toward greater use of the computer as whole schools are wired, equipment is acquired, and teachers learn how best to utilize computers in their classrooms and in laboratories.

Computers have much to offer to multicultural teaching. In this section we first address general techniques for using the computer with special multicultural applications, and then we list a number of Internet connections that fit with a multicultural program.

Wordprocessing

The most common use of computers is for all forms of writing. Encourage students to use computers to produce writing described in lessons in Chapter 3—for example, poetry, book reviews, reports. The computer facilitates revision thus encouraging students to write more, and the printer permits students to create an attractive copy of what they have written.

CD-ROM Programs

Computers enable students to use a wide range of interesting multimedia programs presented on CD-ROMs that support integrated reading, social studies, and science lessons. Virtual field trips provide sound, pictures, and text, integrating reading with geography and history knowledge and engaging students in challenging activities that stimulate thinking. One of the first to be published was *The Oregon Trail* (MECC), which takes students along the route of Lewis and Clark, led by Sacajawea, including encounters with Native American tribes. They have to solve problems and make decisions as they meet the challenges of the trail. (A number of other programs are described in Chapter 3.)

Tips for Using Computers Effectively

Following are a few suggestions that you may find helpful:

1. If you have only one computer in your classroom, maximize its use by providing a sign-up sheet where students can "make appointments" for 15- to 30-minute blocks of time. Encourage collaborative groups of 2–3 to gather around the computer to suggest ideas as members of the group take turns looking for or recording information for a study they are undertaking.
2. Teach a specific skill that students may find helpful each time students begin individual work in the computer lab. You might, for example, show them how to center a title or introduce them to spell-check. Don't be afraid to ask for help in teaching these skills from another teacher or even your students.
3. Give each student (or have them purchase) an initialized disk on which they can work using whatever program you have available. After students print their names on the disks, they can be filed alphabetically in a box in the classroom ready for use when needed.

Using the Internet

Now available in many schools and libraries, access to the Internet has opened up many possibilities to add to multicultural studies. Students can obtain information and, even more exciting, participate directly in the exchange of ideas and expression of their opinions with people around the world. Following are a few Internet sites that support aims of multicultural education; namely, (1) developing esteem and empathy and (2) exploring the world.[22]

Developing Esteem and Empathy

The Diary Project. <http://www.well.com/user/diary/>
    Suitable for grades 4 through 8, this project was inspired by Zlata Filipovic's diary, *Zlata's Diary: A Child's Life in Sarajevo* (Viking, 1994). Sponsored by the adult discussion forum, The Well, the project intends to record the voices of children from all over the world.

KIDLINK. <http://www.kidlink.org/>
    Suitable for grades 5 through 10, this site connects almost 100,000 children from more than 100 countries in both open and focused online discussions.

Make New Friends. <http://www.kidscom.com/orakc/newfriends.html>

Suitable for grades 1 through 10, this site presents electronic Graffiti Walls, one for students under age 11 and another for students aged 12–15. Students share their comments about pertinent topics.

Exploring the World

Children's Express. <http://www.ce.org/>

Suitable for grades 2 through 12. Sponsored by the Coalition for America's Children, this project won both an Emmy and the George Peabody Award. A news service run by children for children, it features public opinion on such topics as racial discrimination.

MayaQuest. <http://www.mecc.com/internet/maya/maya.html>

Suitable for grades 3 through 6, this site offers a six-week trip into Mayan lands in Mexico, Guatemala, and Belize. Sponsored by Apple Computer with materials provided by the Minnesota Educational Computing Corporation's The Learning Company, the site invites students to share their ideas.

Student Ambassador Project. <http://www.gsn.org/gsn/sa/program.html>

Suitable for grades 1 through 12, this site permits students to participate online as ambassadors for educational technology using e-mail. Sponsored by the Global Schoolhouse Project, it links students, teachers, and community members around the world.

Voices of Youth—UNICEF <http://www.unicef.org/voy/>

Suitable for grades 5 through 12, this site enables students to voice their opinions online about such issues as poverty, discrimination, and world peace.

Recap

A major responsibility of the teacher is to know about a variety of resources for use in the teaching/learning process. For example, reading good literature provides an inexhaustible source of ideas and information for both teacher and students, and reading selected literature aloud is a highly effective method of engaging students with literature. Using the computer as an instructional tool is essential today, and introducing students to the Internet as a resource opens doors and stimulates learning in a new way. Resources for teaching must move beyond a single textbook.

REFLECTIONS

Teaching multiculturally is not the easiest way to teach. It requires a teacher who is committed to the welfare of students. It requires a teacher who is willing to accept a challenge. The rewards lie in seeing students succeed.

Teaching for multicultural understanding begins with a well-planned curriculum based on expected outcomes. The teacher's role in delivering this curriculum is to guide student inquiries and to serve as facilitator and resource person. The student learner also plays an active part in initiating avenues of inquiry in conjunction with a group of fellow researchers. The best of methodologies and resources must be selected as we develop an integrated humanistic study that furthers multicultural understanding.

A sound multicultural education program depends on careful planning across levels and across subject areas. The major quality indicators of an effective program include:

Teachers who recognize the need for multicultural education, who are involved in the planning, and who are willing to learn with their students.

Students who are self-motivated learners concerned about their own rights as well as the rights of others.

Content that makes interdisciplinary and multicultural connections.

When we successfully bring these three components together, we will have an outstanding multicultural education program. All children will learn.

APPLICATIONS

1. Work with a group of fellow students to plan lessons for the primary grades. Locate appropriate books to use as stimuli for exciting learning activities. You might begin with these that focus on intergenerational understanding:

Cynthia Rylant. *The Old Woman Who Named Things.* Harcourt, 1996.

> This Appalachian woman names only things she will outlive until she falls in love with a shy little dog, whom she names Lucky.

Diane Wolkstein. *White Wave: A Chinese Tale.* Harcourt, 1996.

> "When the old men died, the shell was lost. . . .All that remained was the story."
> This folktale provides insight into coping with death.

2. Label a section of your portfolio "My Ethnic and Cultural Identity." Find out where your parents and grandparents were born, what languages they spoke, and how you happened to come to live in your present community. How did your parents meet? Think about what values are important to your family, how you celebrate rituals or holidays, and what kinds of foods you enjoy together. Refer to the personal map in Chapter 1. Discuss your findings with others in your Cooperative Learning Group. You might bring pictures to show each other or plan to share some foods. Think about what you are learning from this kind of sharing and how you might help young students engage in this type of sharing, too.

3. In your CLG discuss some of the following questions:

a. What is the difference between equality and equity?

b. How might you introduce the subject of racism to children of different age levels?

c. What can you do to create a climate of acceptance that supports each student's self-esteem?

Brainstorm other topics that your group would like to discuss or problems that they need help with.

ENDNOTES

1. John Dewey. *The Child and the Curriculum.* University of Chicago Press, 1902.
2. Eugene E. Eubanks, president, American Association of Colleges of Teacher Education. Speech, February, 1989.
3. Mary Jalongo in Edwina B. Vold. *Multicultural Education in Early Childhood Classrooms.* National Education Association, 1992, pp. 56–62.
4. *Ibid.*
5. Thomas Sobol, Commissioner of Education, New York State Department of Education. Undated.

6. Association for Supervision and Curriculum Development. *1993 Resolutions*, The Assn., 1993, p. 1.
7. Virginia Shipman et al. *Young Children and Their First School Experiences.* Educational Testing Service, 1976.
8. *Ibid.*
9. *Ibid.*
10. Jack Frymier. *Growing up Is Risky Business, and Schools Are Not to Blame*, Phi Delta Kappa, 1992. Copies of this final report may be obtained for $.50 each from Phi Delta Kappa, Box 789, Bloomington, IN 47402–0789.
11. Louise Derman-Sparks. *Anti-Bias Curriculum: Tools for Empowering Young Children.* National Association for the Education of Young Children, 1989.
12. James Frymier, *ibid.*
13. James Comer. "Dr. James Comer's Plan for Ensuring the Future." *Black Issues, 10,* 6:46, May 20, 1993.
14. Kenneth Zeichner. *Educating Teachers for Cultural Diversity.* Michigan State University, National Center for Research on Teacher Learning, 1993.
15. Ernest Boyer. "On the High School Curriculum: A Conversation with Ernest Boyer." *Educational Leadership, 46,* 1 (September 1988): 4–9.
16. Zeichner, p. 23.
17. *Ibid.*
18. Ann Brown and Annemarie Palincsar. "Interactive Teaching to Promote Independent Learning from Text." *The Reading Teacher,* 39:770–77, 1986.
19. Robert Slavin. Wisconsin Center for Education Research. *WCER Highlights, 3,* 1(Fall, 1990): 1–2.
20. Frank Smith. *Understanding Reading.* Holt, 1973.
21. Mary Jalongo, *ibid.,* pp. 62–63.
22. Eliza Dresang. "Developing Student Voices on the Internet." *Book Links* (September, 1997): 10–15.

EXPLORING FURTHER

Robert D. Barr, & William H. Parrett. (1995). *Hope at Last for At-Risk Youth.* Boston: Allyn & Bacon.

Laura Border, & Nancy Chism. (1992). *Teaching for Diversity.* New Directions for Teaching and Learning Series. San Francisco: Jossey-Bass.

Children's Defense Fund. (1991). *The State of America's Children.* Washington, DC: The Children's Defense Fund.

Robert W. Cole. (1995). *Educating Everybody's Children: Diverse Teaching Strategies for Diverse Learners.* Association of Supervision and Curriculum Development.

Allan A. Glatthorn. (1994). *Developing a Quality Curriculum.* Alexandria, VA: Association for Supervision and Curriculum Development.

Frances E. Kendall. (1996). *Diversity in the Classroom: New Approaches to the Education of Young Children.* (2nd ed.). New York: Teachers College Press.

Jonathan Kozol. (1991). *Savage Inequalities: Children in America's Schools.* New York: Crown.

M. Lee Manning, & Leroy G. Baruth. (1995). *Students at Risk.* Boston: Allyn & Bacon.

Gary Marcuse. (1995). *The Mind of a Child: Working with Children Affected by Poverty, Racism, and War.* Face-to-Face Media. (Video)

Theresa Perry, & James Fraser (Eds.). (1993). *Freedom's Plow: Teaching in the Multicultural Classroom.* London: Routledge.

Chris Stevenson, & Judy Carr (Eds.). (1993). *Integrated Studies in the Middle Grades: "Dancing through Walls."* New York: Teachers College.

Kenneth Zeichner. (1993). *Educating Teachers for Cultural Diversity.* East Lansing, MI: Michigan State University. National Center for Research on Teacher Learning.

FRIENDSHIP FOREVER

CHAPTER 3

Infusing Multicultural Concepts across the Curriculum

The Japanese characters on the opposite page present a powerful multicultural message: "Friendship Forever." Multicultural concepts and attitudes must be infused over time into learning activities across the curriculum if they are to have full effect. Both multicultural content and equitable teaching/learning processes can be included in lesson plans for any subject at any level.

A basic assumption in this book is that multicultural education should not be presented in a single class apart from other instruction. Multicultural concepts should permeate all teaching. For example, a first-grade teacher might choose to read Mary Hoffman's *Amazing Grace,* a story about a young black child who loves make-believe. Following the reading, the class acts out some of her activities and writes a collaborative story about her imaginary adventures and her success as Peter Pan in a school play. Students will learn that Grace and they have much in common, but discussion of the book will also demonstrate the need to overcome stereotyped thinking.

A middle or junior high school history teacher might develop a unit of study around the shared reading of *The Good Earth* by Pearl Buck. Students read other novels by the same author. They study the geography and history of China—a vast country that is just opening up to the outside world. They collect clippings from the newspaper and record current linkages between China and the United States. Connecting literature and contemporary events with history instruction gives the study a reality that is missing from many history textbooks.

Notice that the examples above promote multicultural understandings while developing language and literacy skills as well as content and skills in other areas of study. In this chapter we examine ways of integrating multicultural concepts and attitudes into all instruction. We present lessons and other learning activities from the perspective of each of the subjects taught; namely, art, language arts and reading, mathematics, music, physical education, science, and social studies.

After reading this chapter, you should be able to:

- Demonstrate methods for integrating multicultural concepts into instruction in varied subject areas.
- Utilize reading and writing processes to address multicultural issues across the curriculum.
- Plan multicultural lessons for individual and group study across the curriculum.

FOCUSING ON MULTICULTURAL CONCEPTS IN ART

Art enhances our lives. Defined more broadly than the European tradition of fine art, art includes the universal human need to create beauty and express emotions about the human condition. We can lead students to discover the role art has played in human development over the years—the pictographs of the cave dwellers, the art of the Native Americans, Asian calligraphy, American folk art, and so on. We can help them recognize the contributions of artists from diverse cultures, particularly within the United States.

In this section we present multicultural learning activities that involve students in producing art as well as in studying art around them. As is true throughout this chapter, the arts and crafts activities engage students in content that reaches into subject areas other than art itself.

A SAMPLE MULTICULTURAL ART LESSON: BEAUTIFUL WRITING

Grades 4–8

Outcomes

Students will:

1. Learn an interesting art form.
2. Select quotations from diverse cultures.
3. Create an attractive display.

Procedures

Collect examples of quotations presented in calligraphy. Many are presented in this text. Bring in books of quotations that students can use as resources. (Check the index.)

Stimulus

Show students examples of quotations presented in calligraphy. Explain the history of calligraphy. Teach students the rudiments of italic calligraphy, which is not unlike the manuscript or D'Nelian handwriting that they may have used in primary grades.

Activity

Have students select and print a quotation or saying they like from a specific culture.

Follow-up

Have each student frame the quotation. Framing can be done by mounting the quotation on a sheet of 9" × 12" red construction paper, or you may prefer to frame the quotations in simple black wooden frames that can be made or purchased. Older students may explore Chinese calligraphy following this experience.

Evaluation

Students should display their work in the classroom, the library, or another more public place where other students can view the art and the wise words depicted. No grades should be assigned for this project. Give credit or no credit for completing the task.

A SAMPLE MULTICULTURAL ART LESSON: MAKING A PARFLECHE

Grades 4–6

Outcomes

Students will:

1. Read books about the Plains Indians.
2. Observe the colorful art of the various tribes.
3. Create a small paper or cloth *parfleche* (a container for carrying dried buffalo meat).

Procedures

Take students to the library to locate books about the Plains Indians. Pay particular attention to the picture books that contain colored illustrations, for example, those of Paul Goble. Obtain a copy of one of his newer books, *The Return of the Buffalo* (National Geographic Society, 1996). This book includes directions for constructing a model *parfleche,* as shown in the figure on the next page. Enlarge the model provided..

Stimulus

Read *The Return of the Buffalo* aloud. This Lakota myth tells of a famine that ends when a mysterious woman brings the buffaloes out of Wind Cave in the Black Hills of South Dakota. "In your mind's eye when you visit this spot today," writes Goble, "you can see them surging up out of the cave, rushing down the ravines in clouds of dust and thunder of hooves, and out the hills through the 'Doorway of the Buffaloes,' Pte Tatiopa, called Buffalo Gap on modern maps." Share Goble's beautiful art with the students and discuss the use of a *parfleche* for carrying dried buffalo meat. Students should observe and discuss the Indian's relationship to the buffalo.

Activity

Students will follow directions for making and decorating small *parfleches.*

Follow-up

Prepare a large map to show the location of the Plains Indians. Students can display the completed *parfleches* around the map.

Evaluation

Students will receive credit or no credit based on their completing the task.

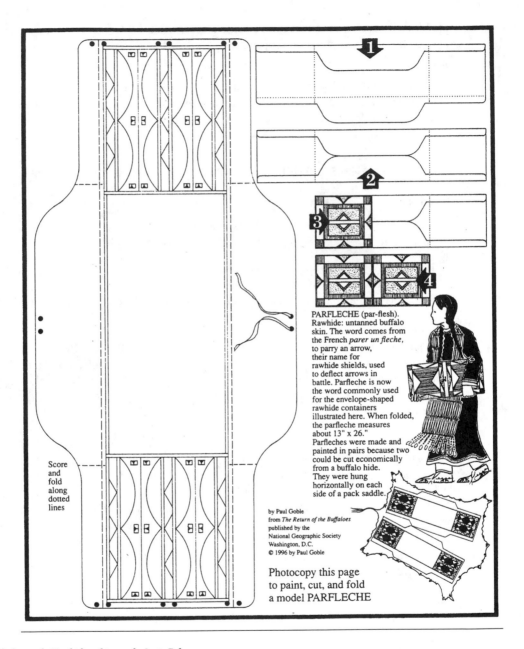

1

2

3

4

PARFLECHE (par-flesh).
Rawhide: untanned buffalo
skin. The word comes from
the French *parer un fleche*,
to parry an arrow,
their name for
rawhide shields, used
to deflect arrows in
battle. Parfleche is now
the word commonly used
for the envelope-shaped
rawhide containers
illustrated here. When folded,
the parfleche measures
about 13" x 26."
Parfleches were made and
painted in pairs because two
could be cut economically
from a buffalo hide.
They were hung
horizontally on each
side of a pack saddle.

by Paul Goble
from *The Return of the Buffaloes*
published by the
National Geographic Society
Washington, D.C.
© 1996 by Paul Goble

Photocopy this page
to paint, cut, and fold
a model PARFLECHE

Score
and
fold
along
dotted
lines

Additional Multicultural Art Ideas

Illustrated Children's Literature

Children's books offer a special art form in the illustrations, which are commonly created by highly talented artists. The variety of the art presented is truly amazing. Look for some of the following:

Mitsumasa Anno. *Anno's U.S.A.* Japanese artist; many books.

Lulu Delacre. *Vezigante Masguerader.* Puerto Rican illustrator.

Yumi Heo. *Father's Rubber Boots.* Korean story and artist.

Holly Keeler. *Grandfather's Dream.* Vietnamese story about saving the cranes.

Jacob Lawrence. *The Great Migration.* Noted African American artist depicts history.

Jerry Pinkney. *Talking Easter Eggs.* Popular African American illustrator.

Allen Say. *Stranger in the Mirror.* Japanese American author/illustrator.

Maurice Sendak. *Outside over There.* Jewish author/illustrator; this book won the Caldecott Medal in 1987.

These illustrators may serve to inspire students to emulate their techniques.

Origami

Children will enjoy creating attractive folded-paper animals, for example, the popular crane, a turtle, or an elephant. This traditional Japanese art form is described in *Classic Origami* by P. D. Tuyen (Sterling, 1995), which contains detailed instructions. Making origami fits well with writing such Japanese forms of poetry as haiku. (See the sample multicultural social studies lesson in this chapter.)

A touching Japanese story that all people can appreciate is *Sadako* by Eleanor Coerr and illustrated by Ed Young (Putnam, 1993). According to Japanese legend, anyone who is ill will become well if they make one thousand origami cranes. Sadako died of leukemia, as a result of the bombing of Hiroshima, before completing the cranes. Every year on Hiroshima Day (August 6) children around the world make origami cranes in memory of Sadako.

Filmed Documentaries

The video, *Oaxaca: Valley of Myth and Magic* (Crizmac, 1995), recommended for grades 4 through 12, provides an overview of art in this region of Mexico. It includes historical background, a local myth, and a map-making activity as well as an introduction to the kind of weaving for which Oaxaca is famous. Check your school district catalog to determine what kinds of films about art they have to offer along this line.

ABC Books

The ABC book continues to be used widely in primary grades. However, these books often present mature concepts and art that can provide interesting instructional ideas for older students, too. A new ABC book that combines art and multicultural concepts is *Gathering the Sun: An Alphabet in Spanish and English* by Alma Flor Ada (Lothrop, 1997). On each page is a short poem presented in both English and Spanish. Illustrated by Simon Silva with a hot palette of bold gouache, the book literally "glows." He depicts farm produce with mouth-watering reality and farm laborers with strength and sympathy. The book is dedicated to César Chávez.

A second type of ABC book offers information about a specific topic. Tanis Jordan's *Amazon Alphabet* (Kingfisher, 1996) is an attractive example that connects art with science and social science. Illustrated by skilled artist Martin Jordan, the book includes illustrated letters in the glossary where information about each animal is presented. Such ABC books provide models for students who are creating their own original children's books on a multicultural theme.

Chinese Papercutting

Show children how to create a butterfly or a dragon by following directions provided in Margaret Bateson-Hill's *Lao Lao of Dragon Mountain* (De Agostini, 1996; distributed by Stuart, Tabori, and Chang). This ancient art goes back to 618 A.D. Mounted on contrasting construction paper, cut paper figures make an attractive gift for parents. (This activity can be added to the module on Chinese Americans in Chapter 4.)

Art as a Theme in Children's Fiction

Occasionally authors write fiction that includes art as a theme. In *In Summer Light,* for instance, Zibby Oneal writes about a girl who wants to be a painter (Viking, 1985). Newbury Award-winner *I, Juan de Pareja* by Elizabeth De Trevino (Farrar, 1966) is narrated by a slave in the household of Spanish painter Velasquez. In *Meiko and the Fifth Treasure* (Putnam, 1993) Eleanor Coerr tells of a 10-year-old artist whose hand was injured in the Nagasaki bombing and how she began to draw again. This book also presents attractive calligraphy by Cecil Uyehara. The beautiful Hmong stitchery in *The Whispering Cloth: A Refugee's Story* by Pegi Shea (Boyds Mills, 1995) accompanies the story of Mai's life in a Thai refugee camp. See also the section in quilting in Chapter 6.

Reading about Real Artists

Students who are particularly interested in art may choose one of these autobiographies or biographies to review for a social studies report:

G. Everett. *Children of Promise.* Atheneum, 1992. Black artists.

Milton Meltzer. *Dorothea Lange: Life through the Camera.* Viking, 1985. Photography.

Philip Sendak. *In Grandpa's House.* Harper, 1985. Illustrated by Maurice Sendak, son of the author of this autobiography.

Kathleen Krull. *Lives of the Artists: Masterpieces, Messes (and What the Neighbors Thought).* Audio Bookshelf, 1996; 2 cassettes. An audio presentation suitable for grades 4–9. Read by John C. Brown and Melissa Hughes are minibiographies of 20 noted artists from da Vinci to Warhol. Students will enjoy the amusing, gossipy style that makes history and art come alive. Small groups of students could listen to these tapes at a Listening Center.

Check the index for books about Native American, African American, Latino, and women artists.

A Virtual Fieldtrip

For students in the United States, *The Louvre* (Voyager, 1996; Windows and Macintosh), a CD-ROM for all ages, provides the experience of going to this famous museum in Paris and viewing more than 150 representations of the art displayed there. The program is user-friendly and includes games and activities to help reinforce learning. (See also *With Open Eyes,* a similar visit to Chicago's Art Institute.) Virginia Walker suggests the following Book Connections:[1]

Elaine Konigsburg's classic, *From the Mixed-up Files of Mrs. Basil E. Frankweiler.* Atheneum, 1967. Favorite story set in the Metropolitan Museum of Art.

Peggy Thomson. *The Nine-Ton Cat: Behind the Scenes at an Art Museum.* Houghton, 1997. Information about backstage work at the National Gallery of Art.

Internet connections include:

Fine Arts Museums of San Francisco. <http://www.thinker.org/index.shtml> Virtual visits to the DeYoung and the Legion of Honor; includes 60,000 item database.

WebMuseum. <http://watt.emf.net/louvre//> A stunning collection of famous paintings, including some items too fragile to be viewed in person.

Suggest artists that students might research, for example: Diego Rivera, Frida Kahlo, R. C. Gorman, Maya Lin, and Faith Ringgold. Also suggest questions to guide their research, for instance, "Which women artists are included?" or "What kinds of art are presented?"

FOCUSING ON MULTICULTURAL CONCEPTS IN LANGUAGE ARTS (INCLUDING READING)

Language and literacy processes are fundamental to learning across the curriculum. Oral language enables even young children to express their thinking, which later can be expressed in writing. Reading written language opens the door to independent encounters with literature, both fiction and nonfiction, as students explore their world. Learning to listen, speak, think, read, and write effectively is an essential part of education related to any subject area at any level.

In this section we present ideas for multicultural learning activities in the language arts and reading curricula. As with all of the activities presented in this chapter, the language arts and reading activities spill over into other subject areas as well.

A SAMPLE MULTICULTURAL LANGUAGE ARTS LESSON: THE UNIVERSAL NEED FOR FRIENDSHIP

Grades 5–7

Outcomes

Students will:

1. Discuss the need for friends.
2. Identify problems that occur between friends.
3. Suggest solutions to problems that arise.

After listening to the teacher's reading of *Always and Forever Friends,* students discuss Wendy's search for a friend. Through discussion they identify the need for friendship as a universal need that they share with all other human beings. In small groups they discuss problems that can arise between friends and possible solutions. Enlarge the quotation at the beginning of this chapter to display and discuss.

Procedures

Obtain a copy of *Always and Forever Friends* by C. S. Adler (Houghton Mifflin, 1988) about a friendship between a white girl and a black girl.* Read the story aloud to the whole

---

* See also Joyce Hansen's *The Gift-Giver* (Clarion, 1997) about two fifth-graders in the Bronx. Other books on friendship are listed in Chapter 6.

class, chapter by chapter, over a two-week period. Give students a chance to talk about the events depicted in each chapter following the reading. This lesson is designed to follow the completion of the whole book. It requires at least two class periods.

Stimulus

Present the following quotation from the book on a transparency:

> "The way I look at it," Honor continued earnestly, "you don't wind yourself around a friend like a strangler vine, and you don't expect friendship to be always and forever."
>
> "But Honor, if it doesn't last, what good is it?"
>
> "I didn't say it *wouldn't* last. All I'm saying is, we shouldn't expect it to because life's sure to change us, you and me. In high school, we'll be different people, and boys will come in the picture—for you anyway. I don't know if I'll have time for them if I'm going to be a lawyer. And if boys don't do us in, then after high school we'll go our separate ways, and that'll make it hard."

Ask students to state Wendy's view of friendship. Then ask someone to restate what Honor is saying.

Activity

Have students number off from 1 to 6 to form six cooperative learning groups. (Adjust these numbers to produce groups of four to six students.) Assign a Leader and a Recorder for each group, and give everyone copies of the following sheet. Give the recorder an extra copy.

---

1. Could you live without having friends?
2. Can boys and girls be friends?
3. What are problems that make finding friends difficult?
4. What problems might break up a friendship?
5. What can we do to make a friendship last?

Take a few minutes for each person to read the questions and to write at least one response to each question.

Then discuss each question in turn. Each person should read one answer to the first question. Talk about the answers that were shared and agree on a response for the whole group. After the Recorder has written the group answer on the Group Answer Sheet, go to question 2, and so on.

Discuss the poster written in Japanese, "Friendship Forever," at the beginning of this chapter.

Follow-up

Working with the full class, have one person share the group response to each question in turn. After ideas have been shared, have each student write a paragraph about the importance of friendship in his or her life.

Evaluation

Have students meet in the same groups to share their paragraphs. After the group listens to a student's paragraph, group members in turn will identify one aspect of the writing they especially like. Then each student will make one suggestion for improving the writing of the paragraph.

Students will then rewrite their first drafts. The revised copies will be placed in a three-ringed notebook entitled *Friendship Forever.* After class members have had ample time to read it, place this class publication in the school library.

A SAMPLE MULTICULTURAL LANGUAGE ARTS LESSON: WRITING A BOOK REVIEW

Grades 5–8

Outcomes

Students will:

1. Read a book review.
2. Identify characteristic features of this form.
3. Write a book review that includes these features.

Procedures

Locate the review of a book that you would like students to know or perhaps an author you would like to introduce. Duplicate a class set of copies of the review. (You can write one yourself following the model presented here.) This lesson requires at least two class periods.

Book Review: *Where the Red Fern Grows*

Wilson Rawls was a country boy from the Ozarks. He spent much of his time roaming the hills with a blue tick hound, hunting and fishing, enjoying the out of doors.

It was natural, then, for him to write a book about a boy who wanted hunting hounds, a boy who also roamed the hills and river bottoms of the Cherokee country so familiar to Rawls. He describes the setting, thus:

> Our home was in a beautiful valley far back in the rugged Ozarks. The country was new and sparsely settled. The land we lived on was Cherokee land, allotted to my mother because of the Cherokee blood that flowed in her veins.
>
> It lay in a strip from the foothills of the mountains to the banks of the Illinois River in northwestern Oklahoma.

Where the Red Fern Grows is a story of love for family, for animals, and for this country. It is also a story of adventure as Billy achieves his greatest dreams.

Ten-year-old Billy wanted a pair of coon dogs, but hounds cost more money than the family could possibly afford. Determined, Billy began saving his money, storing it in an old K. C. Baking Powder can. After almost two years, he had fifty dollars, enough to buy the two redbone coon hound pups that would change his entire existence.

Billy, Dan, and Little Ann spent their lives together from the time he brought them home. As he said:

> It was wonderful indeed how I could have heart-to-heart talks with my dogs and they always seemed to understand. Each question I asked was answered in their own doggish way.

Although they couldn't talk in my terms, they had a language of their own that was easy to understand. Sometimes I would see the answer in their eyes, and again it would be in the friendly wagging of their tails. Other times I could hear the answer in a low whine or feel it in the soft caress of a warm flicking tongue. In some way, they would always answer. (p. 68)

The high point of the book is Billy's winning the gold championship cup in the annual coon-hunting contest. With the cup came a large cash prize that answered his mother's prayers for a new house.

Billy continued to hunt with his dogs until one night they met the "devil cat of the Ozarks, the mountain lion." His brave little dogs tried to save Billy from the lion whose "yellow slitted eyes burned with hate." Although Billy finally killed the huge animal with an ax, the dogs were badly wounded. Old Dan died from his injuries, and Little Ann soon died, too, of heartbreak at losing her hunting companion. Billy sadly buried the two dogs in a beautiful spot on the hillside.

As the family was leaving the Ozarks the following spring, Billy ran to this grave for one last farewell. It was then that he saw the beautiful red fern that had sprung up above the graves of the little dogs. He remembered the old Indian legend that "only an angel could plant the seeds of a red fern, and that they never died; where one grew, that spot was sacred." As they drove away, the family could see the red fern "in all its wild beauty, a waving red banner in a carpet of green."

Fast action, human interest, and believable characters make this a book for readers of all ages. A master storyteller, Wilson Rawls has shared a piece of himself.

—by Iris M. Tiedt

Stimulus (Prewriting)

Give students copies of the book review you have selected. Read the book review aloud slowly as students read their copies. (This is especially helpful for less able readers and ESL students, and it helps keep the class together for the purposes of the lesson.) Then have students return to the beginning of the review and direct them to identify the kinds of information the author included in the review.

Features of a Book Review
1. Includes quotations from the book
2. Comments about the content presented by the author
3. Tells something about the author, biography
4. Expresses personal reaction to the book
5. Includes the title and author of the book

Direct the students to bring a book that they have already read to class the next day.

Activity (Writing)

See that each student has a book to review. Display the Features of a Book Review list that the class compiled. Go through the features one by one with the class as students take notes based on the books they are reviewing. Tell students to complete the first draft of the new book review they have begun as homework.

Follow-up (Postwriting)

On the next day students should have the first drafts of their book reviews and copies of the book to be reviewed. Have students work in cooperative learning groups of three to five students. Each student is to read his or her book review aloud as the others listen to see if all features on the list have been included. After listening to a review, each member of the group should answer the following two questions for that writer:

1. What one aspect of this review was especially well written?
2. What one recommendation would help improve the writing?

The next day revised versions of the book reviews can again be shared in the same editing groups. Each writer should point out exactly what changes were made from the first draft. Any further changes should be made, as needed.

Evaluation

Before completing the final draft of the book reviews, students should work as a class to determine just how these reviews will be evaluated, for example:

A Simple Rubric or Standard (some recognition for excellence)
10 Uses excellent detailed description
    Shows clear personal involvement
    Includes important biographical information
    Speaks clearly to the audience
    Includes all features listed, very well presented
5 Presents all features adequately
    Needs further revision
2 Presents most features, very weak writing
    Needs extensive revision

Students who are involved in determining evaluation measures for their own work are assuming responsibility for their work, and they can help each other so that potentially everyone in each group can get the top score. Students learn much about writing by reading and evaluating each other's writing.

When book reviews are fully revised, they can be published instantly in a three-ringed notebook that bears the title: Books We Recommend. Have someone decorate the cover. This collection, containing something by everyone in the class, should be available for reading in the classroom and, later, in the library.

Additional Multicultural Language Arts Ideas

Here are a number of other language arts and reading activities that support multicultural education.

Conducting Meaningful Discussions

We often allude to discussion as part of classroom instruction. However, studies show that what is called discussion is often teacher-dominated, that is, the teacher asks questions to which students respond one by one. The percentage of student involvement revealing real thinking remains very low.[2]

Focusing on multicultural understanding offers an opportunity to deal with meaty concerns, matters of consequence. Introducing controversial topics that are presented in fiction is a safe way to open up what we identify as "philosophical discussions," the kind of talk in which informed adults frequently engage. Depending on the content of a particular book, a worthwhile discussion might involve students in talking about "experiences all children have had, such as being embarrassed by not knowing an answer. By discussing what happens to the characters in a novel, they can talk about things in the third person: Somebody else is the one involved."[3] An excellent selection to share in grades 4 to 6 is *The New One* by Jacqueline Turner, a novel about Jury, an African American boy, and his friends, that introduces issues of racism and prejudice.

Reading Aloud

Reading books aloud to a class has many benefits (see Chapter 2). Select multicultural titles by talented authors, for example, Virginia Hamilton, a prolific African American writer. Her book, *Cousins,* is a complex realistic novel that provides many interesting multicultural topics to discuss and to write about, such as the elderly, relations with family, and personal responsibility. Other noted authors who present multicultural themes include:

Katherine Paterson	Rose Blue
Laurence Yep	Eloise Greenfield
Gary Soto	Elaine Konigsburg
Pat Mora	Mildred Taylor
Milton Meltzer	Yoshiko Uchida
Scott O'Dell	Allen Say

International Pen Pals

Your students might like to write a letter to the editor of a major newspaper in such a city as Buenos Aires, Prague, London, and so on. Research in your public library will produce addresses for newspapers around the world. Here is a letter that appeared in the San Jose (California) *Mercury News* in August, 1997:

Dear Editor:

We are children who live in Israel and we like to collect stamps and trade stamps with people around the world. We really like stamps with animal pictures. When we get stamps from different places, we learn about your country, and we learn about you.

We are a girl and a boy, ages 13 and 10. If you print this letter, maybe people will send us stamps and we will send them our stamps. Our address is 9 Lotham Street, Efrat, Israel.

Thank you,

Rivka Bedein
Elchanan Bedein

Your class might begin by writing to these young people. The Internet is a great source of pen pal contacts.

Role-Playing

Role-playing is a versatile oral activity that allows students to express their opinions in a realistic situation. They can literally stand in someone else's shoes as they speak in the role they have assumed. Ideas for role-playing come from all areas of the curriculum, for instance:

- A group of parents discussing a city problem.
- Children greeting a new student from Vietnam.
- A Japanese American family preparing to go to an internment camp.
- The Abenaki tribe holding a feast in 1700.

Role-playing may be performed by a group of three to five students as the others observe and take notes. After the performance, class discussion focuses on the strengths and weaknesses of the performance, for example, the language used and the appropriateness of the topics discussed. After this analysis, another group can perform with the same roles and situation.

At other times, the whole class can role-play a situation, such as plantation life in 1800. Before beginning this activity, of course, students need to study to determine what the various roles would be. Group activities in specific areas of the room might focus on the slave quarters, the barn where horses are shod, or a group of runaways in the woods. Simple costuming lends interest to this dramatic play.

Role-playing can lead to formal debate as students discuss the pros and cons of an issue. After arguing informally in role-play, students may be stimulated to search out more information to be presented in a panel discussion or debate. These oral activities lend interest to learning, and they provide a firm foundation for writing to express opinions. They also teach advanced thinking skills.

Using All Language Processes across the Curriculum

Following are suggestions for strengthening specific language arts skills while teaching multicultural concepts:

Listening
- Retell a folktale the teacher has read aloud, for example, "Clever Gretel."
- Act out an Indian trickster tale after hearing it at the Listening Center, for example, "Raven the Trickster."
- Summarize the life of a writer after listening to *The Lives of Writers* (Audio Bookshelf, 1995).

Speaking
- Discuss the problems that Karana faced in *Island of the Blue Dolphins* by Scott O'Dell.
- Tell a "flannel board story" to younger children, for example, *John Henry*.

Reading
- Read a poem by Langston Hughes aloud as part of a class presentation on poetry.

- Review a book about someone who lives in another country, for example, *Winding Valley Farm: Annie's Story* (Poland).

Writing
- Keep a process journal while reading a book about the Japanese American internment, for example, *Journey to Topaz* by Yoshiko Uchida.
- Use mapping to outline the life of a famous woman leader, such as Indira Gandhi or Mother Teresa.

Thinking
- Compare their lives with that of Lisa in *Lisa and Her Soundless World* by Edna Levine.
- Write questions to ask Katherine Paterson after reading *Come, Sing, Jimmy Jo* (Appalachia).

FOCUSING ON MULTICULTURAL CONCEPTS IN MATHEMATICS

The use of numbers and mathematical concepts represents yet another universal language that we share around the globe. Students can study variations in applied mathematics in different countries, for example:

Monetary systems—compare the worth of coins
The abacus and its use
Metric system compared with U.S. weights and measures
Computer use around the world
Calendars (see Chapter 9)
Economic systems

Help students make connections between mathematics and other subjects or areas of interest. For example, how does math relate to art and music? What are the many relationships between math and the sciences? How are mathematical concepts displayed in nature, for example, Fibonacci numbers (patterns in pine cones)?

A SAMPLE MULTICULTURAL MATH LESSON: MONEY AROUND THE WORLD

Grades 6–8

Outcomes
Students will:

1. Learn that different kinds of money are used in various countries.
2. Compare the value of money in other countries to the U.S. dollar.
3. Work at a Learning Center focusing on Money around the World.

Procedures

Order a class set of newspapers from a major local paper. Be sure that it carries the daily business report and contains a chart of currency values. Set up a Learning Center—MONEY AROUND THE WORLD—that includes laminated copies of the Task Card. We suggest that you enlarge each part of the card, placing the questions on one side and the currency chart on the other. (See Chapter 4 for suggestions about creating a Learning Center.) Collect a few coins from different countries.

Stimulus

Distribute newspapers (at least one per two students). Ask the students to browse through the newspaper to see how many different uses of mathematics they can discover. List these on a large sheet of paper mounted on the wall. The stock prices (fractions) and foreign money values (percents) should be one of the items listed.

Activity

Point out the daily currency chart. Ask the students what this chart tells us (the value of world coins compared to the U.S. dollar). Show the students a few coins or bills from different countries, telling them the name of each—franc, peso, or krone. Ask them if they have traveled to other countries where they used different coins. Invite them to bring samples to show the class.

Ask students to tell you how many whole francs you would get for one U.S. dollar. Explain that when traveling in Paris, for example, you need to quickly translate a price into dollars, so that you know approximately how much you are paying for an item. If you saw a beret on sale for 24 francs, for instance, about how many dollars would you need to buy it? Show the students how to figure the amount exactly through long division.

Follow-up

Introduce the Learning Center you have set up entitled MONEY AROUND THE WORLD. Explain the activities at the center, which they will visit in small groups as assigned. Post assigned times at the center.

Each day bring in the newspaper for this center so students can compare the changing values of certain coins, for example, Mexico's peso.

Notice that this math activity challenges student thinking and involves them in reading as well as the use of math processes. Students might make cardboard francs or deutschmarks to use in role-playing purchases made in Paris or Berlin. Encourage students to use a few German or French words in their conversation, such as *Bonjour* or *Auf wiedersehn.*

Evaluation

Select several mathematically adept students to serve as consultants to assist students. The activity is graded Credit/No Credit based on a student's completing the questions on the Task Card (even with help). Students may receive extra credit by following the changing values of a specific coin for two weeks and reporting their findings to the class.

Additional Multicultural Mathematics Ideas

Recommended Resources

Material is constantly being published to help teachers connect math and multicultural education. A good resource book is *The Multicultural Math Classroom: Bringing in the World* by Claudia Zaslavsky (Heinemann, 1996). It presents a short history of mathematics, then suggests activities for grades K–8, beginning with finger counting and simple games and moving to geometry in architecture and art, data analysis, and probability theory.

Math across Cultures is a 50-page publication available from the San Francisco Exploratorium Order Dept., 3601 Lyon St., San Francisco CA 94123 (Phone: 800-359-9899). Appropriate for grades 4 through 12, it includes many multicultural activities and resources. A small group of students might, for example, follow directions for unraveling and counting the Incan Quipu knots and then present a report and demonstration to the class. Another group could learn to play Madagascar solitaire, offering to teach others who were interested.

A similar book is available for younger children: Cynthia Manthey's *Pre-K Math: Concepts from Global Sources* (Humanics Learning ISBN 0-89334-240-8). Appropriate for ages 2 to 5, this 160-page book helps children learn to count in different languages and play number games. Sketches and detailed instructions help teachers share ideas from such countries as Brazil, Congo, Cuba, India, and Thailand.

A Mathematical Word Search

Have students prepare a display of terms appropriate to their level of mathematical understanding. Include the etymology of the terms. Students will be surprised to discover the origins of such words in math as *algebra* and *algorithm.* Discuss the contributions of the Arab civilization to modern math.

Women in Mathematics

Students can focus a special unit of study on the achievements of women in mathematics. Invite female mathematicians to visit your classroom. Discuss math anxiety and how students can overcome it. Have students search the Internet for information about women mathematicians. Teri Perl presents a summary of women's achievements in *Math Equals: Biographies of Women Mathematicians* (Addison Wesley) which students might update.

Using the Computer

Software can help engage students with math across cultures, too. *Maya Math,* for example, a CD-ROM program, was designed by Bank Street College of Education and published by Sunburst Communications (Box 100, Pleasantville NY 10570; Phone: 800/321-7511). Appropriate for grades 4 through 8, it helps students discover the importance of place value and zero by deciphering the Maya base-20 number system. They learn to convert Maya dates to contemporary dates.

The above program has been integrated with social studies in *The Second Voyage of Mimi.* This program engages students in discovering a lost Mayan city.

Math in Thematic Studies

Mathematics will be part of any thematic study, as described in Chapter 4. Students can prepare different kinds of graphs to present their findings. They can report percentages of people involved and compare sizes in studies related to topography of the land. They can deal with time differences and mileages that affect travel plans. Students need to learn that math is very much a part of everyone's daily life and that it is far more than just 9×7 or $8 + 3$.

FOCUSING ON MULTICULTURAL CONCEPTS IN MUSIC

Music is an important part of every culture. Students should experience a variety of music, either live or recorded—the blues, folk, classical—by members of many cultures. Introduce them to many fine musicians, singers, and songwriters who have contributed to the world's musical heritage, for example, Ravi Shankar, Duke Ellington, Kiri Te Kanawa, and Pete

Have you ever heard of a guilder?

In which country would you find this coin?

(Look at the chart on the other side of this card.)

How much is a guilder worth compared with our dollar?

Do other countries use dollars besides the United States?

Which countries use dollars?

Are these "dollars" worth the same amount?

Which "dollar" is worth the most?

Every day this list of currencies appears in the newspaper. See if you can find it in the financial or business section. Compare the values for each coin to see how it has changed since this list was published.

Why might values of coins or bills go up or down?

See if you can find information about what determines the value of a piece of currency.

Pretend you are traveling to several different countries. As you enter each country, you exchange $10 for the currency of that country.

How many pesos would you get in Mexico?

How many francs would you get in France?

How many pounds would you get in Great Britain?

How many rands would you get in South Africa?

Find pictures of some of these coins. Perhaps someone you know has money from different countries.

Country	Currency	Worth in dollars*
Argentina	peso	1.0014
Australia	dollar	.7043
Austria	schilling	.0825
Belgium	franc	.0282
Brazil	cruzeiro	.9101
Great Britain	pound	1.6844
Canada	dollar	.7141
Chile	peso	.002389
China	yuan	.1203
Colombia	peso	.000791
Denmark	krone	.1528
Ecuador	sucre	.000236
Egypt	pound	.2939
France	franc	.1733
Germany	deutschmark	.5805
Hong Kong	dollar	.1293
Israel	shekel	.2832
Italy	lira	.00059
Japan	yen	.008187
Mexico	peso	.122699
Netherlands	guilder	.5156
Norway	krone	.1425
Peru	sol	.3709
Portugal	escudo	.005695
Russia	ruble	.000173
South Africa	rand	.2076
Spain	peseta	.006885
Sweden	krone	.1329
Switzerland	franc	.7124
Uruguay	peso	.1018
Venezuela	bolívar	.0020

*November 8, 1997.

Seeger. Students are intrigued by the varied musical instruments used in different countries and less familiar musical scales. See also the special feature on jazz in Chapter 9.

A SAMPLE MULTICULTURAL MUSIC LESSON: AMERICAN MUSIC FROM EVERY REGION

Grades 3–8

Outcomes

Students will:

1. Identify folk songs representative of different regions in the United States.
2. Integrate music into social studies activities.
3. Present a program for other classes in the school.

Procedures

This lesson ties in with studies of individual states and/or regions of the United States. It also fits with studies of different groups that live in this country, and it could be adapted to studies of other countries.

Check the catalogs of your school district or the public library to locate recordings of regional folk music. Songbooks may also include examples that you can use. Begin playing a song or two each day to students. Share the information provided about each song. Teach them the words to some of the songs to add to their singing repertoire.

Stimulus

Teach the class the following Pennsylvania Dutch folksong:

Johnny Schmoker

Pennsylvania Dutch Folk Song

John-ny   Schmo-ker,   John-ny   Schmo-ker

Can   you   sing?---   Can you   play?---
Kannst   du   sing-en?   Kannst du   spiel-en?

I   can   play up-   on   my   drum----------
Ich kann   spiel-en   auf   mein   trom-mel.

Rub-a-dub-a- dub, this   is   my   drum--------
Rub-a-dub-a- dub, das   ist   mein   trom-mel.

Explain that this song (with words in German) was sung by people of German ancestry who settled in what is now Pennsylvania. These people were called Pennsylvania Dutch because their name *Deutsch* (German) sounded like *Dutch.* You might also like to show students examples or pictures of their distinctive art. Then suggest that each group find a song that is typical of the state or region that they are researching. They should plan to incorporate the song into their report. They might plan to teach the song to the rest of the class.

Activity

Each group will plan to participate in an assembly to be attended by other classes. Each group will first point out on a large map the location of the area they studied. Group members will contribute to the presentation with information about the people who live there, how they live, and any distinctive contributions they have made.

Follow-up

Each group will submit a brief description of what they plan to contribute to the assembly. Two volunteers will prepare a printed program to send to the classes who are invited to attend their assembly. The groups will practice their presentations. The class will present the assembly.

Evaluation

The success of the total project will be assessed by each group. They will look at their individual presentations to decide what was particularly effective and also how it might have been improved. The responses from the other classes will add to the assessment process.

Additional Multicultural Music Ideas

Music should be an integral dimension of any unit of study that focuses on a group or country. Students should become aware of music as a universal language that all can share. They can create their own music to express their ideas and emotions.

Creating a MUSIC WORD WALL

Most of us enjoy music in one form or another. Students might brainstorm all the words and ideas they associate with music, just to assess what the class, as a group, knows about music. Write these words on a large sheet of paper to create a MUSIC WORD WALL, for example:

dancing	ballads	bagpipes
singing	country western	opera
notes	jazz	birds
lyrics	guitar	runing water
piano	flamenco	samba
humming	church	symphony
rhythm	choir	

Keep adding words to this list as students think of other ideas—names of performers, titles of songs, kinds of dancing, and so on. You might link related words. Encourage students to bring in pictures to illustrate this wall as you create a collage of words and pictures. After the wall seems to be pretty well completed, ask students to study the collage and to state observations. They should note the great variety in the kinds of music and the groups of people represented. They might categorize the words. They might conclude that music is an important element of any culture. They could then study the music of specific cultures in cooperative learning groups.

Children's Books Depict Songs

Individual songs have often been presented with illustrations as picture books for children—for example, *She'll Be Comin' around the Mountain* and *Lift Ev'ry Voice and Sing*. Children will be interested in observing the artist's illustrations and may be motivated to create a book or a poster featuring a favorite folksong.

Reading about Music in the Lives of Young People

Students may be interested in reading stories that tell of young people who have musical talent. Some examples include:

Bruce Brooks. *Midnight Hour Encores*. Harper, 1986. Cellist.

Gillian Cross. *Chartbreaker*. Holiday, 1987. Rock band.

Amy Littlesugar. *Marie in Fourth Position*. Philomel, 1996. Ballet.

Suzanne Newton. *I Will Call It Georgie's Blues*. Viking, 1983. Jazz piano.

Reading about Real Musicians

Students may select autobiographies, biographies, or fiction for reports required in the social studies, for example:

Pete Fornatale. *The Story of Rock 'n' Roll*. Morrow, 1987.

Robert Love. *Elvis Presley*. Watts, 1986.

Susan Saunders. *Dolly Parton: Country Goin' to Town*. Viking, 1985.

Catherine Scheader. *Contributions of Women: Music*. Dillon, 1985. Beverly Sills and four other women.

Challenge students to locate additional information about diverse persons who have made a contribution to the musical world.

An audio presentation, *Lives of the Musicians* (Audio Bookshelf, 1996), presents interesting facts about the lives of well-known musicians. Recommended for grades 4 through 8, the information is well-read and amusing.

Songbooks

The following collections of songs are particularly appropriate for supporting multicultural studies:

Lulu Delacre, ed., *Las Navidades: Popular Christmas Songs from Latin America*. Scholastic, 1990.

John Langstaff, ed. *What a Morning! The Christmas Story in Black Spirituals*. McElderry, 1987. Singing plus piano accompaniment.

Nicki Weiss. *If You're Happy and You Know It*. Greenwillow, 1987. Picture book includes eighteen songs to sing together.

FOCUSING ON MULTICULTURAL CONCEPTS
IN PHYSICAL EDUCATION

Today there is much interest in health and fitness. Around the world, eyes watch the performance of the Olympic contestants who represent their countries proudly. All share the emotion as each national anthem is played for the gold medalist. Physical performance, the power and the grace, is another universal language we all understand. We can help students become aware of the diverse cultures these athletes represent.

In the schools physical education focuses more directly on activities in which all individuals can participate—walking, running, dancing, exercising. Physical education is often associated with health emphasizing nutrition, cleanliness, and general well-being.

A SAMPLE MULTICULTURAL PHYSICAL EDUCATION LESSON:
MAKING A SPORTS COLLAGE

Grades 4–8

Outcomes

Students will:

1. Select one sport to research.
2. Collect information about this sport and the players.
3. Create a collage depicting the sport.
4. Report on the sport and display the collage.

Procedures

Brainstorm a list of sports played around the world. Students will choose one sport to study, working individually or in groups of two to three students. All students will be encouraged to contribute information or clippings that other students can use. Representative players of different sports will be invited to the classroom to be interviewed by class members. Students will create collages and report on their study.

Stimulus

Challenge students to see how many different sports they can name. Print their contributions on a large sheet of paper where they can remain for a few weeks. Tell students to talk with their parents or siblings about this list to see if they can suggest additional sports. You may need to define games versus sports.

Activity

Have students choose one sport to research, for example, soccer, lacrosse, lawn bowling, or bocce ball. Students can work individually or in small groups, if several are interested in the same sport. Limit the number studying one sport to three so that more sports will receive attention. Students will visit the library to locate informative nonfiction or biographies, for example:

Crystal Bowman. *Ivan and the Dynamos*. Eerdmans Books, 1997. Fiction; hockey.

Stew Thornley. *Deion Sanders: Prime Time Player.* Lerner, 1997. Biography; football.
Kristin S. Fehr. *Monica Seles: Returning Champion.* Lerner, 1997. Biography; tennis.

Students can also invite high school or college players to come to the school for interviews and to demonstrate aspects of their sport. Have students bring in newspapers and magazines to use for information and to clip as they collect material for their collages. Criteria for making reports and creating an effective collage should be discussed in order for students to do a good job.

Follow-up

A few at a time, students will present their studies and their collages to the class.

Evaluation

Reports and collages will be judged based on the criteria established. Five students can be selected as the judges to place ribbons on the collages: Blue for Outstanding; Red for Good; White for Incomplete. The class can select the best five collages to be displayed in the hall near the principal's office where they can be seen by parents and other students.

Additional Multicultural Physical Education Ideas

Reports on Diseases or Disabilities

Have students research information about specific diseases or disabilities. Each study should include an interview and a telephone investigation as methods of research. Completed reports should be presented to the class and then included in a publication that can be placed in the library.

Researching Games Played in Different Cultures

There are many different kinds of games played around the world that are not usually thought of as "sports." Encourage gifted students to undertake a special study to see what they can find out. Working collaboratively, they can plan their strategies, beginning by talking to a librarian about their research. Challenge them to see how many different resources they can use to locate information.

Issues Related to Sports and Physical Education

Brainstorm questions and concerns students have about their topics, for example: What are requirements for physical education in the schools? Why do famous athletes earn so much money? What are the opportunities for women in sports? Why is there increased concern about fitness and good nutrition in the United States? How has race been a factor in sports? How do disabled people overcome barriers to sports and physical education? Have students discuss these questions, researching the answers, as needed.

Games and Sports Originating with the Native Americans

A number of books contain information about Indian children's games, for example: *My Indian Boyhood* by Luther Standing Bear (University of Nebraska Press, 1959); *Whispers from the First Californians: A Story of California's First People* by Gail Faber and Michelle

Lasagna (Magpie Publications, 1994); and *American Indian Games* by Joy Miller (Childrens Press, 1996).

Many of the sports we know today originated in games the Native Americans first played. They played shinny, a game with a puck, similar to ice hockey. Native American children played such games as hide and seek, follow-the-leader, crack-the-whip, prisoner's base, and blindman's bluff. They also had games not unlike hopscotch, marbles, and jack straws.

For more information about Native American sports and how to play them, look for *Sports & Games the Indians Gave Us* by Alex Whitney (McKay, 1977). This author shows children how to make equipment for use in the games described. Stick dice are easy to make, for example. Use a stick about one-half inch wide and four inches long. With a knife round off the ends of the stick. Paint one side red and paint a multicolor design on the other side. With the red side counting as one point and the design as two, see who can get twenty points first.

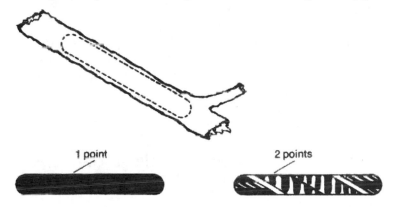

1 point   2 points

Sports and Fitness Themes in Fiction for Young People

Authors sometimes use a sports theme in fiction, which may add to the attraction of reading multicultural literature for some students. Suggest the following:

Lucy Bledsoe. *The Big Bike Race.* Holiday, 1995. Biking.

Matt Christopher. *Red-Hot Hightops.* Little, Brown, 1987. Basketball.

Wendy Hartman. *All the Magic in the World.* Children's Books, 1993. Physical abilities.

Jeffrey Kelly. *The Baseball Club.* Houghton Mifflin, 1987. Baseball.

R. R. Knudson. *Rinehart Shouts.* Farrar, 1987. Racing shell.

Doris B. Smith. *Karate Dancer.* Putnam, 1987. Karate.

Mary Stolz. *Coco Grimes.* Harper, 1994. Black baseball.

Cynthia Voigt. *The Runner.* Atheneum, 1985. Running.

Reading Nonfiction about Sports, Sports Stars, and Fitness

Writers for young people have written autobiographies and biographies about diverse sports figures as well as other nonfiction about sports and fitness. Students might choose one of these books to review:

Maury Allen. *Jackie Robinson: A Life Remembered.* Watts, 1987.

R. R. Knudson. *Babe Didrikson: Athlete of the Century.* Viking, 1985.

Robert Lipsyte. *Jim Thorpe, 20th Century Jock.* Harcourt, 1993.

Richard Rambeck. *Oksana Baiul.* Child's World, 1996.

Jeff Savage. *Tiger Woods: King of the Course.* Lerner, 1997.

Herma Silverstein. *Mary Lou Retton and the New Gymnasts.* Watts, 1985.

Dave Anderson. *The Story of Football.* Morrow, 1985.

Charles Cooms. *All-Terrain Bicycling.* Holt, 1987.

Edward F. Dolan. *Drugs in Sports.* Watts, 1986.

Jill Krementz. *How It Feels to Live with a Disability.* Simon & Schuster, 1992.

Margaret Ryan. *Figure Skating.* Watts, 1987.

FOCUSING ON MULTICULTURAL CONCEPTS IN SCIENCE AND TECHNOLOGY

Science has become increasingly important around the world. As we become more aware of our interdependence, nations are uniting to address problems related to maintaining the planet. Everyone is excited about the possibilities of exploring space and the new findings in astronomy. The United States plays a leading role in science and has lent its vocabulary to the world so that Chinese and Italians alike use English in guiding air traffic or talking about computer technology. Science, too, is developing a universal language.

A SAMPLE MULTICULTURAL SCIENCE LESSON: DEALING WITH STEREOTYPED THINKING

Grades 4–8

Outcomes

Students will:

1. Listen to a novel read aloud by the teacher.
2. Discuss the issues presented by the author.
3. Analyze the stereotyped thinking presented.
4. Discuss stereotyped thinking and how it can change.

Procedures

Read *There's an Owl in the Shower* by Jean Craighead George (HarperCollins, 1995) to the class over a period of a week or two. This short novel introduces the topic of stereotyped thinking and how it can be changed. Students will investigate this topic.

Stimulus

Read *There's an Owl in the Shower* to the class chapter by chapter. The plot can be summarized, as follows:

> One day Borden finds a young owlet blown out of a tree by an unexpected gust of wind. Because the owlet is still white, Borden thinks he must be a barred owl, not the protected spotted owl which depends for its existence on the old growth forest in northern California. Loggers like Borden hate the spotted owls that prevent them from cutting the big trees. They display

such bumper stickers as: "I like spotted owls fried" or "The only good owl is a dead owl." The community is divided: the loggers vs. the environmentalists. At a community meeting there is a fistfight between Borden's father, Leon, and his science teacher, who is sympathetic to the plight of the spotted owls.

Borden's father decides to care for the little owl Borden brings home in order to impress the judge when he appears for a hearing. He builds a box shelter and hunts mice to feed him, even cutting them up to feed this cute elfin baby which they name Bardy. Feeding the funny little bird 9–10 mice a day, Leon gets hooked on Bardy even making him a beautiful perch from a redwood sprout, and Bardy imprints on big Leon. The whole family comes to love Bardy, and then Borden notices the spots on Bardy's new feathers. Leon agrees to let Bardy go free when he realizes it is illegal to keep any endangered animal in captivity. He helps the other loggers realize that the owl has told them that they aren't managing the forests right. As Borden notes:

He came right into our midst and turned us all around. I'll never be able to look at an owl the same way again.

Jean George has presented a perfect example of how stereotyped thinking can be changed when we get to know an individual.

Activity

Encourage students to discuss events as they occur in the book. After completing this story, guide students to analyze the thinking exemplified by the various characters created by Jean George. Introduce the concept of "stereotyped thinking." Invite students to identify examples of this kind of thinking that they may have observed.

Ask students to complete the following phrases with the name of an animal:

as fast as a _____
as quiet as a _____
as busy as a _____
as sly as a _____

Point out that these phrases have been used so frequently that they have lost their freshness. They focus on only one characteristic of the animal rather than describing the animal in specific detail. Ask students what would happen if we did this to people.

Another theme in this book that could be developed is that of conflicting interests, in this case, logging as a source of jobs and company income versus the needs of an endangered species. Students could investigate similar situations that involve different issues.

Follow-up

Have students work in groups to discover more about animals for which we have stereotyped ideas, for example, wolves, rats, and pigs. They can search out both fiction and nonfiction to provide greater insight into the characteristics of these animals. Each group will then give a class presentation, noting their conclusions about the animal studies. This lesson can also lead to a study of humans, for example, children around the world.

Evaluation

Students receive grades of Credit/No Credit based on their participation in a group study and presentation.

Additional Multicultural Science Ideas

Talk with students about what science is. Bring out the understanding that science is very important to life in the United States and in the world. Have them suggest appropriate activities to enlarge their knowledge about multiculturalism and science.

Science in the News

Have students bring in copies of the daily newspaper. Working in pairs, they can search out news about science around the world. This news may be in a special section; however, it may also be on the Home Page or in the Business section. Have each pair present one finding to the group until all have been covered. Comment on the different kinds of science represented. Note how our planet depends on science and how interdependent we all are.

Science and ESL Students

Judith Rosenthal's *Teaching Science to Language Minority Students* (Taylor & Francis, 1996) presents linguistically modified methods of science instruction. The author discusses such topics as diversity of learning styles among LEP students, the many cultures of the science classroom, and pedagogical issues. This book can be ordered from Multilingual Matters Ltd., 1900 Frost Rd., #101; Bristol PA 19007.

Women and Science

Considerable effort has been expended to increase girls' interest in science during the early years with the hope that they will continue with careers in science. Providing experience with science in industry and meeting women scientists who serve as role models are some of the methods used nationwide. The following filmed resources are recommended:

Discovering Women: Six Remarkable Women Scientists (*VHS,* color, 6 1-hour videos). This outstanding series chronicles the stories of contemporary women scientists and their efforts to overcome prejudices in male-dominated fields. The scientists include a physicist, an archaeologist, a molecular biologist, a computational neuroscientist, a geophysicist, and a chemist. Encourage your library to order the set from: Films for the Humanities and Sciences, Box 2053, Princeton NJ 08543.

Jane Goodall: A Life in the Wild (VHS, color, 31 min.). Fascinating story of Goodall's life and work studying the chimpanzee. Films for the Humanities and Sciences, 1996, address above.

Evelyn Fox Keller: Science and Gender (VHS, color, 30 min.). Keller's life as a theoretical physicist working in mathematical biology and gender issues throughout the history of science. Films for the Humanities and Sciences, 1996, address above.

A Virtual Fieldtrip

The Africa Trail. (CD-ROM for Macintosh and Windows, Teacher's Guide with Educational Version) By the makers of *The Oregon Trail,* this complex simulation program takes students on a bike trek through Africa from Tunisia to South Africa. Although real problems (starvation, ethnic conflicts) and obstacles (rough roads) arise to be solved, the focus is on the people of the continent. The program presents the rich diversity of Africa today. Recommended for Grades 6–12. Published by MECC, 1995. (See also *The Amazon Trail.*)

Virginia Walker suggests the following Book Connections:[4]

Nancy Farmer. *A Girl Named Disaster.* Orchard, 1996. Eleven-year-old Nhamo escapes from betrothal to a cruel old man by undertaking a dangerous trek across Mozambique and Zimbabwe.

Beverley Naidoo. *No Turning Back: A Novel of South Africa.* HarperCollins, 1997. A story of homeless young blacks struggling to live in post-apartheid Johannesburg.

Internet Connections

Kruger National Park. <http://www.pix.za/Kruger_Park/> The Park Warden takes you on a safari through the game reserve in South Africa.

South African National Gallery. <http://www.gem.co.za/sang/index.html> Touring the collections in this Capetown museum.

Reading about Real Scientists

Autobiography and biography about scientists is becoming more available for students of all levels. Here are a few titles:

Steve Parker. *Marie Curie and Radium.* HarperCollins, 1992.

Andrea Davis Pinkney. *Dear Benjamin Baneker.* Gulliver Books, 1994.

Wendy Towle. *The Real McCoy: The Life of an African American Inventor.* Scholastic, 1993.

Ethlie Ann Vare. *Adventurous Spirit: A Story about Ellen Swallow Richards.* Carolrhoda, 1992.

Nonfiction about Science

Children's literature and that for young adults presents much informational material about science. Introduce students to the following:

Robert Cattoche. *Computers for the Disabled.* Watts, 1986.

Anne Ehrlich and Paul Ehrlich. *Earth.* Watts, 1987.

Noel Simon. *Vanishing Habitats.* Gloucester, 1987.

Bernie Zubrowski. *Mirrors.* Morrow, 1992.

Science Themes in Fiction

Encourage students to explore the many novels that have science backgrounds, for example:

Richard Albert. *Alejandro's Gift.* Chronicle Books, 1994. Desert irrigation.

Midas Dekkers. *Arctic Adventure.* Orchard, 1987. Whales.

Jean G. Howard. *Bound by the Sea: A Summer Diary.* Tidal Press, 1986. Science diary.

Betsy James. *The Mud Family.* Putnam, 1994. Drought, rainfall, flood.

Suggest that students share what they are reading in small groups. Such sharing offers a splendid opportunity for peer recommendations that stimulate further student reading. As students read such novels, they learn science concepts that expand their knowledge and may lead to further investigation.

FOCUSING ON MULTICULTURAL CONCEPTS IN SOCIAL STUDIES

Social studies instruction has typically focused heavily on student knowledge of geography and history. This area of study has often been poorly taught and, therefore, it has not been a favorite subject for students. The integration of multicultural education with its emphasis on people into the social studies curriculum should enliven the curriculum and make it more appealing to students. Thematic studies suggested in Chapter 4 are recommended for integrating multicultural concepts into the social studies classes. Focus units in Chapters 5 through 8 suggest additional activities and resources.

The study of geography provides a sense of place—where we are in relation to others and how we fit into the huge global village. Familiarity with maps and mapping techniques can begin with the earliest years as children develop a sense of the layout of a classroom, the setting of a story, the streets in the community. Using globes should clarify their understanding of the location of the United States, its immediate neighbors, the relative distances between our country and the areas from which our ancestors came, and the location of countries that are currently in the news.

The hope of history instruction is that "education can help us to see that not all problems have solutions, to live with tentative answers, to accept compromise, to embrace responsibilities as well as rights—to understand that democracy is a way of living, not a settled destination."[5]

A SAMPLE MULTICULTURAL SOCIAL SCIENCE LESSON: A READERS' THEATER PRESENTATION—REMEMBERING THE JAPANESE AMERICAN INTERNMENT

(Grades 4–7)

Outcomes

Students will:

1. Read a story about the Japanese American internment.
2. Discuss the implications of this governmental act.
3. Plan and present a program celebrating the contributions of Japanese Americans to the United States.

Procedures

Obtain a class set of *Journey to Topaz* by Yoshiko Uchida. (If a set is not available, plan to read the book aloud, chapter by chapter.) Students will discuss events in the book. They will then plan a Readers' Theater presentation to share with other classes.

Stimulus

Introduce students to the author, Yoshiko Uchida. Read the first chapter of *Journey to Topaz* aloud to the class. Discuss the beginning of the story, summarizing what has happened and what students think will happen next. Have students begin a log that they will keep during this project, writing in it at the end of each chapter of the book.

Activities

Students will continue reading the book, chapter by chapter, and writing in their logs as homework. Classtime will focus on discussion of what has happened in the story. As students express empathy for these displaced persons, suggest the preparation of a program that will show appreciation for what the Japanese Americans have contributed to their country—the United States.

Plan a Readers' Theater presentation following these directions. Be aware that there are various methods of working with Readers' Theater; we have selected one that engages students in thinking as well as in improving their reading skills.

Directions for Readers' Theater

Readers' Theater should involve students in reading various kinds of literature that is related to a selected theme. Several weeks are required for planning, searching for material, and giving the presentation to an audience. Follow these steps:

Step 1: Planning.   Talk with students about the idea of a reader's theater presentation. Explain that the presentation is read, not acted out. The presenters sit on stools or chairs and read their assigned parts. Discuss the kinds of materials that might be used, for example:

- short stories (fables, myths, etc.) and excerpts from novels
- sayings, proverbs, quotations, poetry, song lyrics
- factual statements

Step 2: Searching for Material.   Plan a visit to the library as the groups search for material related to the selected theme. If you notify the librarian ahead of time, she or he will be able to locate appropriate sources for class use. The material does not have to be written in play form for this kind of presentation, as you will see in the next step.

Step 3: Preparing the Script.   Duplicate copies of folktales or poems that students plan to use. These copies can then be marked and revised as the group deems appropriate. There may be three or four roles to read plus one or more narrators who read the descriptive passages. Students can supply dialogue to add interest and to develop a character.

Step 4: Rehearsing.   One student should be the director to signal the group when to stand and to sit. This person listens during rehearsals, ensures that students read clearly and effectively, makes suggestions for timing, and so on. Poetry and nonfiction can be divided in various sections or verses. One or more persons may read to provide variety.

Step 5: The Presentation.   Select an audience for whom to perform the finished production. The audience may be the rest of the class, another class that is studying the same topic, or the whole school in an assembly. A Reader's Theater presentation can be given to the Parent Teachers' Association meeting to show parents what students are studying. A study of Japanese Americans and contemporary Japan might culminate with a Reader's Theater presentation based on selections from books such as the following:

Sumiko Yagawa (translated by Katherine Paterson). *The Crane Wife.* Morrow, 1981.
Toshi Maruki. *Hiroshima No Pika.* Lothrop, 1982.
Nancy Luenn. *The Dragon Kite.* Harcourt, 1982.
Yoshiko Uchida. *The Dancing Kettle and Other Japanese Folktales.* Scribners, 1972.

Follow-up

To enhance a presentation for their audience, students could add songs or dances. Pictures could be displayed with original student haiku. A sharing time for both adults and children might be planned for May 5th, Children's Day in Japan.

Evaluation

Discuss with students appropriate criteria for rating the logs they are keeping, for example,

3 Outstanding writing: Clear, free from error, at least one page per chapter.
2 Good writing: Interesting comments, just a few errors, more than ½ page per chapter.
1 Acceptable writing: Appropriate comments, a number of errors, less than ½ page for more than one chapter.
0 Unacceptable writing: Missing or very short entries.

Evaluation for the Readers' Theater presentation will be Credit/No Credit based on participation with a group.

A SAMPLE MULTICULTURAL SOCIAL STUDIES LESSON: READING AND WRITING POETRY

Grades 3–8

Outcomes

Students will:

1. Read examples of haiku poetry.
2. Write original haiku.
3. Publish a collection of haiku.

Procedures

Collect books of poetry related to social studies to read aloud to students. Students will write haiku poems about selected social studies topics. They will then contribute their best haiku to a class publication.

Stimulus

Poetry is especially suitable for enhancing a social studies lesson. Your own enthusiasm will be contagious as students listen to you read (or recite) a favorite poem related to the current study. A wonderful collection of poems about people in history is *The Book of Americans* by Rosemary and Stephen Vincent Benet. *Bronzeville Boys and Girls* is a collection by Pulitzer Prizewinner Gwendolyn Brooks. Sample the work of a black poet, Langston

Hughes; the composer of outstanding free verse, Carl Sandburg; and the well-polished haiku written by Japanese poets of the thirteenth century.

Activities

Writing poetry is a way for students to express their ideas and feelings. Have students write haiku as part of a study of Japan. Here are two examples of haiku translated from the original Japanese:

First cold showers fall.
Even little monkey wants
A wee coat of straw
  —*Bashō*

All sky disappears
The earth's land has gone away;
Still the snowflakes fall.
  —*Hashin*

An excellent source of information for the teacher who wants to know more about haiku is *An Introduction to Haiku* by Harold Anderson (Doubleday). Children are most successful with this brief verse form if emphasis is rightly placed on the thoughts they are expressing rather than on the confining form, for example:

The sun shines brightly.
With its glowing flames shooting
It goes down at night.
  —*Ricky*

The old cypress tree,
So beautiful by the rocks,
Has been there for years.
  —*Marjorie*

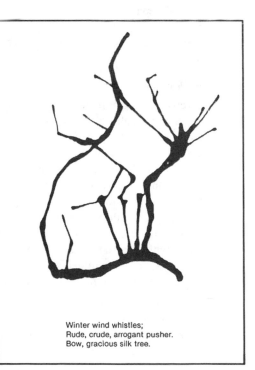

Winter wind whistles;
Rude, crude, arrogant pusher.
Bow, gracious silk tree.

Folded slightly overlapping . . .
. . . tied with ribbon

After first thinking about an idea they wish to express, the students are encouraged to write it on paper. They can then examine their own written thought to determine how it can be divided into three parts. Experimentation with word arrangement, imagery, changing the order of the lines, and choice of words used should be encouraged as the poem is developed.

Japanese poetry reflects the seasons, such as spring. Use a twig of any flowering fruit tree to prepare an attractive display to motivate the writing of haiku. Print out haiku written by a class with a computer using two long columns so that the folded sheets will produce two long, slim pages. Cut the sheets to form pages of an attractive booklet, and make a decorative cover (see p. 85).

Follow-up

A rewarding art experience that correlates well with the writing of haiku is blowing ink with a straw. Washable black ink is applied in a swath near the bottom of an unlined file card (or any nonabsorbent paper). The wet ink is then blown with a straw to direct the ink in the desired direction. Blowing across the ink causes it to branch attractively. When the ink is dry, tiny dabs of bright tempera may be applied with a toothpick to add spring blossoms to the bare branch. The student then writes a haiku on the card below the flowering branch, and the card is used for display or as a gift for parents.

For an authentic presentation of haiku use rice paper (or thin onion skin or tissue paper) mounted inside colored paper. The poem is written (a felt pen will write on thin paper) along with a Japanese design—reeds, moon over water, flowering branch—and the author's name. The cover is folded so that the front flaps overlap slightly, as in the sketch. A ribbon is then tied around the folder, which is ready for presentation as a gift.

Evaluation

Students will receive grades of Credit/No Credit based on their completing at least one haiku. Each student will have one haiku included in the class publication.

Additional Multicultural Social Studies Ideas

The social studies offer a wide range of topics to address. Almost any recommended multicultural instructional strategy fits with the social studies curriculum. In this section we present a few specific activities.

Discussion Topics

Children can study and discuss topics like the following: Why do we use the term *global village* today? Why has the history of Israel been full of conflict? Middle-grade students might read the novel, *The Boy from over There* by Tamar Bergman (translation from the Hebrew by Hillel Halkin, Houghton Mifflin, 1988).

Timely topics in this field can be debated. More advanced students need to be involved in thinking about the pro and con positions about real concerns as they learn to be active, informed citizens living in a global village. Contemporary history, for example, suggests the following topics related to learning to get along with the diverse people in the world:

1. Democracy's solutions for war-related problems at home and abroad and the strains on democracy produced by them.
2. The tragedy of Bosnia.
3. Problems faced by Africans today.

Mapping the Origins of the Members of the Class

Create a large outline map of the world by enlarging a map from a text with the opaque projector. Have students interview their parents to ascertain general information about where grandparents and earlier ancestors came from. Students can then locate these places and outline the trail of their individual origins on the map with colored pens. Each student can then tell his or her story and show the trail on the map.

Social Studies Themes in Literature

Social studies concepts can scarcely be separated from literature study. Here are a few books, however, that include a clear multicultural theme:

*Kathleen Allan-Meyer. *I Have a New Friend.* Barron's, 1995. A Japanese friend.

Paula Fox. *The Moonlight Man.* Bradbury, 1986. Nova Scotia.

*Jan Gilchrist. *Indigo and Moonlight Gold.* Black Butterfly Children's Books, 1993. African American mother and child.

Patricia Polacco. *Pink and Say.* Philomel, 1994. Interracial friendship; Civil War.

Gary Soto. *The Pool Party.* Dell, 1993. Social class tensions; Latino.

Yoko Kawashima Watkins. *So Far from the Bamboo Grove.* Lothrop, 1986. Korea; autobiographical.

Have students work in CLGs to act out parts of a book they have read together as a way of sharing information and encouraging other students to read the book presented.

Nonfiction about Multicultural History

Many fine books written for young people explain topics that are related to both multicultural education and social studies, for example:

S. Beth Atkin. *Voices from the Fields: Children of Migrant Farmworkers Tell Their Stories.* Little, 1993.

David M. Brownstone. *The Jewish-American Heritage.* Facts on File, 1988. Part of America's Ethnic Heritage series.

Richard Sobol. *One More Elephant: The Fight to Save Wildlife in Uganda.* Cobblehill, 1995.

Ted Wood with Wambli Numpa Afraid of Hawk. *A Boy Becomes a Man at Wounded Knee.* Walker, 1992.

Have students write book reviews of nonfiction they have read. Share the reviews orally, and publish them so other students can read them.

Reading about Real People

Both autobiography and biography provide information about history in action. Students will enjoy reading books about the lives of people who have clearly influenced world history, for example:

Linda Atkinson. *In Kindling Flame: The Story of Hannah Senesh, 1921–1944.* Lothrop, 1985. Hungary.

Carol Greene. *Mary McLeod Bethune: Champion for Education.* Children's Press, 1993.

William Sanford. *Chief Joseph: Nez Percé Warrior.* Enslow, 1994. United States.

Anne Schraff. *Women of Peace: Nobel Peace Prize Winners.* Enslow, 1994. International.

Have students make timelines for the lives of people they read about. Display the charts and have each student tell about the person featured in his or her timeline.

Analyzing and Comparing: Using the Venn Diagram

Developed by John Venn in the nineteenth century, the Venn diagram is used in mathematics to compare two sets. This method can be used to compare two concepts or books in an effective social studies lesson. After each student has read a novel about young people living in another land, ask each one to complete a Venn diagram that compares his or her life with that of the book character, thus:

Title and author of the book: *Seven Daughters and Seven Sons* by Barbara Cohen (Atheneum, 1982).

Brief description: This book is based on an Iraqi folktale that demonstrates the worth of daughters. Buran disguises herself as a man to help her family, and all kinds of adventures follow. It's really an exciting story.

In sections 1 and 2 of the Venn diagram unique characteristics are listed for each person. In section 3, the student lists adjectives that describe both, showing how they are alike. After completing the Venn diagram, each student writes a five-paragraph essay following this pattern:

Paragraph 1: Introduction
Paragraph 2: Description of herself or himself
Paragraph 3: Description of the book character
Paragraph 4: Summary of how the two are alike
Paragraph 5: Concluding paragraph

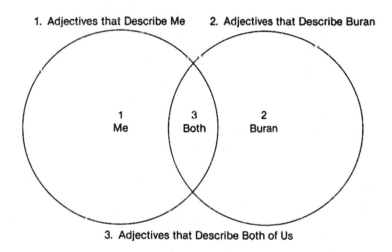

1. Adjectives that Describe Me   2. Adjectives that Describe Buran

1
Me

3
Both

2
Buran

3. Adjectives that Describe Both of Us

This exercise may lead students to observe that people are more alike than different, particularly when they consider their personal characteristics and problems. Once students know how to use this diagram, they can use it to guide comparisons of more complex topics, for example, two ethnic groups, two religions, or two forms of government.

Computers and Social Studies

Working with the Internet opens doors to a great variety of social studies information. Many fine software programs are available that engage students in simulations and problem solving. Here are a few more items to add to our list of resources.

U.S. Geography: An Overview. CD-ROM for Windows and Macintosh. This program presents more than geography, focusing also on history and people. Recommended for grades 5 through 12, the program gives students a multicultural overview of American history. It includes complete U.S. census data, a concise encyclopedia, and an index as well as audiotapes from famous speeches.

Where in the WORLD, USA, EUROPE Is Carmen Sandiego? Software Series, 3 packages; Macintosh and Windows. Recommended for grades 4 through 9, this series is supported with *Carmen Sandiego Day Kit; Carmen Sandiego Party Packet;* tapes, lab packs (including *Teacher's Guide, World Almanac, Fodor's USA Travel Guide, Rand McNally's Concise Atlas of Europe*). This software is available in French. An interesting article by Maureen Robinson and Annette T. Schonborn, "Three Instructional Approaches to *Carmen Sandiego* Software Series," appeared in *Social Education,* October 1991, pp. 353–354. These authors suggest three approaches to working with this software series:

> Teacher Directed Grouping—a two-week focus embedded within an already established curriculum.
>
> Curriculum Integration—a one-week lesson designed for a departmentalized setting where teachers team to work across subject areas.
>
> Isolated Lessons—selected lessons on geography, problem solving, decision making, and data analysis based on appropriate screens, ignoring the game as a whole.

Eco East Africa. CD-ROM for Windows; IVI Publishing, 1995, edited by Lee Barnes and Christopher Thompson. Recommended for the advanced student, this program enables players to experience some of the variables of overseas employment, e.g., as a Game Warden. The software focuses on issues of managing Ethemba, a game park in Tanzania.

The Amazon Trail. CD-ROM, Macintosh and Windows; MECC, 1994. This program does an excellent job of presenting the cultures of the rainforest and the interactions among the indigenous peoples, outside explorers, and other Brazilians who have made their living from the forest. (See also *The Oregon Trail* from the same publisher and *The Africa Trail* described in the section on science.)

Up to the Himalayas: Kingdoms in the Clouds. CD-ROM, Macintosh and Windows, DNA Multimedia, 1997. Recommended for grades 5 through 12, this outstanding program takes students on an interactive fieldtrip to Sikkim, India, and its capital city, Gantok.

California Mission Series. Lerner Publications, 1996. Organized regionally into six volumes, this series provides a balanced account of the establishment of the missions, their impact on existing cultures, and their influence on the growth and development of the state of California. Recommended for grades 4 through 7, the books contain full-color and black-and-white photographs, illustrations, maps, charts, and time lines.

Gumshoe Geography: Exploring the Cultural, Physical, Sociological, and Biological Characteristics of Our Planet by Richard Jones. Zephyr Press, 1997. This text will intrigue advanced students with a game format that encourages them to learn more about our planet. 176 reproducible activities send students on missions to gather information about other cultures and places in the world. Teacher's Guide with each activity.

REFLECTIONS

Although multicultural education fits well into the total curriculum, teachers need to confer as a faculty to determine just how they can best promote the understanding of diversity in any particular school. If each teacher agrees to present multicultural literature or to use a lesson that teaches a multicultural concept at least once a month, student understanding will gradually grow, reinforced by instruction in all classrooms. Teachers in self-contained classrooms can readily plan integrated units of study that incorporate multicultural studies in all areas of the curriculum.

APPLICATIONS

1. Working with your CLG, choose one country or group of people to investigate as you develop a unit of study with other CLGs on "New Americans." Begin by examining children's books you can use. For example, if your group focuses on the Vietnamese as a subject, you might locate the following:

Brent Ashabranner and Melissa Ashabranner. *Into a Strange Land: Unaccompanied Refugee Youth in America.* New York: Dodd, 1987.
Alexandra Bandon. *Vietnamese Americans.* New Discovery Books, 1994.
Janet Bode. *New Kids on the Block: Oral Histories of Immigrant Teens.* New York: Watts, 1989.
Tricia Brown. *Lee Ann: The Story of a Vietnamese Girl.* New York: Putnam, 1991.
Sherry Garland. *Shadow of the Dragon.* Harcourt, 1993.
Jeremy Schmidt and Ted Wood. *Two Lands, One Heart: An American Boy's Journey to His Mother's Vietnam.* Walker, 1995.

Read these books as a starting point to supply basic information and to suggest other avenues of research. Don't forget the local community as a resource. See the Appendix for more ideas.

2. Motivated by interest in the North American Free Trade Agreement (NAFTA), begin collecting information about our neighbors, Canada and Mexico, and consider how you can integrate such information into interdisciplinary instruction. Find an up-to-date reference for each country to obtain general information and maps, at the library or through the Internet. Locate such children's literature titles as: *The Land and People of Canada* by Andrew Malcolm (HarperCollins, 1991). Another resource is *Children's Literature in Canada* by Elizabeth Waterston (Twayne Publishers 1992).

3. Choose one state to study in detail. Think chiefly about the people who now live in that part of our country. Find out their backgrounds and how they came to settle there. As you focus on the people, you will discover how they make their living, the cities and towns in which they live, and the issues that concern them. Use the library as a resource, but also watch the daily newspaper and talk with people who have lived in that state.

Begin a file of books that you or your students might read in a cross-curriculum study. If you choose Hawaii, for example, you might list the following:

Marcia Brown. *Backbone of the King: The Story of Paka and His Son Ku.* Scribner's, 1966. Middle-grade students will enjoy this classic story written by an outstanding author.

Georgia Gulack. *Luka's Quilt.* Greenwillow, 1994. This intergenerational story focuses on tradition and the importance of communicating.

Eleanor Nordyke. *The People of Hawaii.* The University of Hawaii Press, 1981. This book tells about the multiethnic population on the islands.

Graham Salisbury. *Under the Blood-Red Sun.* Yearling, 1994. A Japanese American teenager in Hawaii in 1941.

Ruth Tabrah. *Hawaii: A Bicentennial History.* Norton, 1980. Written for the bicentennial, here is a good overview of Hawaiian history.

ENDNOTES

1. Virginia Walker, "Books and Bytes: Digital Connections." *Booklinks* (November, 1997), pp. 10–14.
2. Paul Gagnon. "Why Study History?" *Atlantic Monthly.* (November, 1988): 43.
3. *Ibid.,* p. 64.
4. Walker, *ibid.*
5. Gagnon, *ibid.,* p. 45.

EXPLORING FURTHER

Rosalinda B. Barrera et al. (Eds.). (1997). *Kaleidoscope: A Multicultural Booklist for Grades K–8* (2nd ed.). Urbana, IL: National Council of Teachers of English. (See also the first edition.)

Bette Bosna, & Nancy Guth. (Eds.). (1995). *Children's Literature in an Integrated Curriculum: The Authentic Voice.* New York: Teacher's College.

Lenora Cook, & Helen Lodge. (1995). *Voices in English Classrooms: Honoring Diversity and Change.* Urbana, IL: National Council of Teachers of English.

Deborah Eldridge. (1998). *Teacher Talk: Multicultural Lesson Plans for the Elementary Classroom.* Boston: Allyn and Bacon.

Evelyn B. Freeman, & Diane G. Person. (1992). *Using Nonfiction Trade Books in the Elementary Classroom from Ants to Zeppelins.* Urbana, IL: National Council of Teachers of English.

Violet J. Harris. (1992). *Teaching Multicultural Literature in Grades K–8.* Norwood, MA: Christopher-Gordon.

Mildred K. Laughlin, & Patricia P. Laughlin. (1991). *Literature-Based Social Studies: Children's Books & Activities to Enrich the K–5 Curriculum.* Phoenix, AZ: Oryx Press.

Sylvia Marantz, & Kenneth Marantz. (1994). *Multicultural Picture Books: Art for Understanding Others.* Publication and Growth Series. Decatur, GA: Linworth Publishing Company.

Theresa Rogers, & Anna O. Soter. (Eds.). (1997). *Reading across Cultures: Teaching Literature in a Diverse Society.* New York: Teacher's College Press and NCTE.

Marcia K. Rudman. (1993). *Children's Literature: Resource for the Classroom.* Norwood, MA: Christopher-Gordon.

Michael Schiro. (1997). *Integrating Children's Literature and Mathematics in the Classroom: Children as Meaning Makers, Problem Solvers, and Literary Critics.* New York: Teacher's College Press.

Marilou Sorensen, & Barbara Lehman. (1995). *Teaching with Children's Books; Paths to Literature-Based Instruction.* Urbana, IL: National Council of Teachers of English.

Helen E. Williams. (1991). *Books by African-American Authors and Illustrators.* Chicago: American Library Association.

...*In spite of everything, I still believe that people are really good at heart*

– Anne Frank –

4

CHAPTER

Organizing Interdisciplinary Studies

Anne Frank's statement provides an appropriate theme for multicultural studies as we continue to focus on esteem, empathy, and equity.

In this chapter we address three ways of organizing integrated multicultural studies that cross the curriculum. These methods allow for individualization of instruction by permitting students to move at their own pace and level while working, for example, at teacher-designed Learning Centers. Thematic units encourage small group work as well as individual pursuits, and they allow for a wide range of abilities and interests. The multicultural module can be constructed to support a textbook approach, as one of the major activities at a learning center, and/or within a broad thematic study.

After reading this chapter, you should be able to:

- Create a learning center that focuses on a specific topic.
- Organize a unit of study that begins with a novel or a broad theme.
- Develop a module to guide students' study of a given topic or theme.

USING LEARNING CENTERS

A learning center is a portion of the classroom, large or small, devoted to the study of a specific topic or set of skills. For example, you might have a language center, a United Nations center, a center for the study of Native Americans, or a center for the study of prejudice. Here are collected books, pictures, and other items related to the center focus. Here, too, teaching materials and equipment are placed to aid students working in the center as they engage in varied learning experiences. The learning center permits individual students to work at their own pace.

How to Develop a Center

Plan with your students. First, decide what kind of center is needed. This depends, of course, on the focus of study in your classroom. Give the center a name that can be printed on a large sign above the space allocated for this learning center. You may have several centers operating at any one time.

Use your ingenuity to create a suitable place in which to focus activities. A reading table can be used to collect materials together. You may have students construct a kind of cubicle. The bottom and sides of a large carton, placed on a table, form the back of the center; varied shapes and sizes of tables are appropriate. Feature any types of information pertinent to the study. A corner of the room is easily transformed into a center focusing on Alaska as shown below. In this case you might include a map of Alaska, the number of people living in Alaska, and other information. Check the index for additional resources.

Invite students to participate in collecting all kinds of pertinent information and materials that might be useful—clothing, postcards, magazine articles. Brainstorm possible activities, people to contact, and places to visit as you develop the study together. Provide paper, pencils, and other materials that may be needed as students engage in work at the center. Depending on the type of study being developed, you might consider the following materials and equipment for the center:

- Tape recorders
- Typewriter
- Stapler
- Scissors
- Rulers
- Various papers: lined and unlined, drawing paper, colored construction paper, cardboard, posterboard, and corrugated cardboard for construction
- Computers

In addition to pictures and information displayed to make the center attractive and inviting, there will be a variety of individualized activities. Planned activities should range from easy to more difficult as well as involve using varied skills—listening, speaking, read-

A Cozy Corner

ing, and writing. Included, too, can be activities that draw from different subject areas and those that stimulate student creativity in music and art. In the following sections of this chapter we will explain how to produce two useful kinds of teaching materials for the learning center—the task card and the learning module.

How to Use the Learning Center

After you and your students have created one or more learning centers, you need to talk about using them. Discuss how many students can work at each center at any one time. The number of seats provided is a good way to indicate how many can work at a center. As a seat is vacated, someone else may come to the center. Students may need to sign up for a particular center.

A good way to begin work at learning centers is to post a schedule giving each stu-

Name	M	T	W	TH	F	M	T	W	TH	F
Felipe	1	1	2	2	L	3	3	4	4	L
James	1	1	2	2	L	3	3	4	4	L
Kentu	1	1	2	2	L	3	3	4	4	L
Sandra	2	2	L	3	3	4	4	L	1	1
Hope	2	2	L	3	3	4	4	L	1	1
Harold	2	2	L	3	3	4	4	L	1	1
Marisa	3	3	4	4	L	1	1	2	2	L

dent a specific assignment for the day. You can prepare the schedule for a week, two weeks, or a month, depending on how long the study will take and how many centers are available. Working in the library could be one center activity that would accommodate a number of students. Your schedule for ten days might look like this:

Enlarging specific centers to provide more activities and seating space will permit additional students to participate. Sometimes, activities can be completed at the student's desk. Adding other learning centers also expands the capacity.

Keeping track of materials at each center is another important part of planning. Here are several tips that may help you.

1. Package all the parts of a game in one large envelope. Label the envelope in big print, thus:

2. Color-code everything that belongs at one center. If the center on France is blue, then mark games, task cards, modules, and so on, with a blue felt pen. Students soon learn to replace task cards or games at the appropriate center.
3. Hang activities in envelopes or plastic bags on the wall where they are visible. Pegboard is ideal for this purpose, but you can improvise with cork bulletin boards or strips of wood in which hooks can be placed. If you have a specially marked hook for each item, you can quickly tell when something is missing at the end of the day.

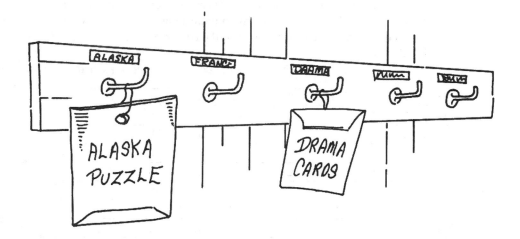

Whenever there are problems regarding classroom operations, have a class meeting to thrash out the problems and possible solutions. If students decide on the solution, their decision is more likely to carry weight, and they will enforce it, not you!

As teacher, your role in working with learning centers is to help students organize their work toward a goal and specific objectives. You facilitate and guide the learning experiences and serve as a resource, a person to be consulted when help is needed. You guide the students in assessing their own growth and learning as well as in checking their own work. Avoid playing the undesirable role of corrector or grader. Instead, use your talents and expertise to respond to student needs, to plan strategies for stimulating further learning, and to explore new resources and materials that come your way.

Creating Task Cards

The task card is one of the most useful and versatile forms of presenting learning activities. Especially appropriate for the learning centers and individualized instruction described in the preceding section, task cards can also be used in conjunction with whole class presentations. Developing sets of cards is well worth the time invested, for the cards can be used repeatedly and in various ways. Task cards are sometimes called job cards or activity cards. They come in various sizes, from small (about 3" × 5") to large (about 8½" × 11"). The size you choose depends on the age of the students who will use the cards (young children can handle large cards more easily) and on your instructional purpose.

Making Small Cards

Small cards work well for "idea files" to which older students refer individually, for example:

- *Acting Out.*   On each card a problem situation is described that calls for role-playing. Activities could be for small groups.
- *Books to Read.*   Each card lists the title and author of a book as well as a short synopsis of the story. Students use this file as they are searching for a book to read about Mexico, living in New York City, or any other topic you want to include.

Have students themselves develop these sets of cards. Each person can prepare a card, for example, about the book he or she has read. This activity serves a dual purpose—the students have a purpose for reading, and they create a set of cards about books other students will find interesting. Preparing "acting out" situations gives students a purpose for writing a short paragraph.

Making Large Cards

Large cards are usually constructed of sturdy poster board, so they are stiff and durable. These cards are used to present an activity that one or more students will undertake at different times. Directions must be clear if students are to work independently.

A task card for upper-grade students that focuses on the money used in various countries is presented in Chapter 3. When material is prepared for you like this, simply copy the material presented. Use larger type sizes on the computer to facilitate reading. If directions are short, printing with a felt pen is effective. Throughout this book you will find informative material and activities that can be presented in similar fashion on task cards.

Make these cards more durable by covering them with clear contact paper or laminating them. This kind of coating makes it possible to have students write on a card with a grease pencil. The writing can later be wiped off.

Designing a Specific Learning Center: Focusing on French Origins

Create a center that focuses on whatever aspect of this study you wish to emphasize, for example, Traveling in Québec, Flying to France! or Parlez-Vous Français? Display a map of the area, pictures, postcards, and/or items from the newspaper. Students can add to the display as the study progresses.

Making Cards for a Center about France

Make cards that direct students to discover facts about France or the French language, as shown in this example:

FACTS ABOUT FRANCE

1. List as many things as you can that you already know about France.
2. List any words you know that we have borrowed from the French language.
3. Find the answers to these questions:
   How big is France?
   Which other countries touch its borders?
   For what products is France best known?
   (Add more questions to guide student research.)

Display a map of France on the bulletin board to aid students in drawing their own maps as directed on the following card. Divide the map in fourths to assist them.

TRAVELING THROUGH FRANCE

As you prepare to take a trip to France, draw your own map. Use a large sheet of paper.

Step 1: Draw light pencil lines to divide your paper in fourths. This will help you make the map the right size. Then draw the outline of France; notice the harbors and seaports.

Step 2: Locate the larger cities and rivers. Try to place them accurately. The pencil lines will help you.

Step 3: Print in the names of the countries and bodies of water that touch France on all sides. Locate the mountains.

Now choose one of the cities on your map to investigate. Find out as much as possible about it. You may be able to find a book that takes place there. Be ready to tell something about your city. We will record each person's talk on a cassette.

Create a set of small cards that will help students learn French-English vocabulary. Begin with basic vocabulary such as numbers, objects around the room, expressions students can use, for example:

Numbers

1	un	*uhn*
2	deux	*duh*
3	trois	*twah*
4	quatre	*kat truh*
5	cinq	*sank*
6	six	*sees*
7	sept	*set*
8	huit	*weet*
9	neuf	*nuhf*
10	dix	*dees*

Colors

red	rouge	roozh
yellow	jaune	zh$\bar{o}$ne
blue	bleu	bloo
green	vert	vair
white	blanc	blahnk
black	noir	nwahr

Family

mother	mère	*mehr*
father	père	*pehr*
sister	soeur	*suhr*
brother	trère	*frehr*

Expressions

hello	bonjour	*bohn zhoor*
good-bye	au revoir	*oh ruh vwahr*
thank you	merci	*mair see*
please	s'il vous plaît	*seel voo pleh*

Any standard high school French book will provide an ample vocabulary to introduce to your students. Note that the suggested pronunciations are only approximate. Find a French teacher, or perhaps a parent who can pronounce the words on a tape for you and your students if you do not know French yourself.

Students can use these cards in numerous ways. They will enjoy just using them as flash cards to test each other. For this purpose prepare the cards with the French word or words on one side and the translation in English on the other, as shown here:

maison (may *zohn*)	house

To encourage students to use these vocabulary cards, construct a gameboard. To give the gameboard a French motif, glue pictures from travel brochures around the board. Spaces are colored with alternate colors such as blue and white. Cover the board with clear contact paper or have it laminated. Use a die to determine the number of moves a student is to make. If the student lands on blue, he or she draws a card from the French pile (French words are on top, and the student must supply the English). If the player lands on a white space, he or she draws from the English pile (English words are up, and the player must supply the French word). Students who are unable to answer correctly move back three spaces. Before they move, however, they read the correct answer, and the card is placed at the bottom of the pile.

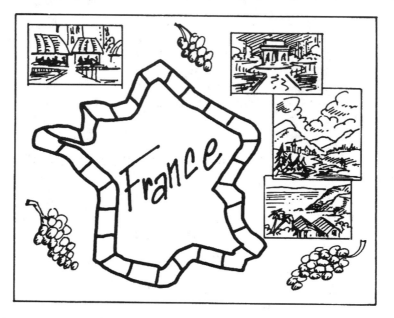

Focus a learning center on the Canadian province of Québec, which touches our states of Maine, New Hampshire, Vermont, and New York. The largest of the provinces, its capital is Québec City. Québec is especially interesting because 80% of its population is French Canadian. You might develop task cards that involve students in the following activities:

- Draw a map of Québec. Identify its cities and waterways.
- Reproduce Québec's flag on paper or cloth.
- Write letters to obtain information about such places of interest as Montréal, the Gaspé Peninsula, the Citadel in Québec City, the St. Lawrence River. (Address: Canadian Government Travel Bureau, Ottawa, Ontario, Canada KIA OH6).
- Make a poster featuring facts about Québec—the provincial tree, the flower, coat of arms, flag, and so on.
- Develop a class time line showing the history of Québec beginning with its discovery by Jacques Cartier in 1534.
- Read a book set in some part of Québec.

Have a number of books available for student use during this study. Following is a list of recommended titles:

Fiction

C. Marius Barbeau. *The Golden Phoenix and Other French-Canadian Fairy Tales.* Retold by Michael Hornyansky. Walck, 1958.

Natalie S. Carlson. *Jean-Claude's Island.* Harper and Row, 1963.

Nonfiction

Hazel Boswell. *French Canada: Pictures and Stories of Old Québec.* Atheneum, 1967.

Anne F. Rockwell, ed. *Savez-Vous Planter les Choux? and Other French Songs.* World, 1969.

William Toye. *Cartier Discovers the St. Lawrence.* Oxford, 1970; Walck, 1970.

A study of French-speaking Americans or those who have French backgrounds could also include a Louisiana learning center. Another center might focus on French in our language—the many English words borrowed from French (*ballet, adroit*), place names that are French, or French expressions that we use (R.S.V.P.). In this truly interdisciplinary approach to teaching, students study concepts from social studies, mathematics, and literature and develop such skills as reading, writing, painting, and singing.

Recap

Learning centers offer a versatile method for engaging students in varied activities focusing on studies that cross the curriculum. Students enjoy the change from the more common textbook approach to instruction, including the opportunity to move around the classroom. Because students proceed at their own speed, individual differences are more readily accommodated. Gifted students should have challenges that extend the study in new directions. These students might design a learning center that others in the class could use.

DEVELOPING THEMATIC UNITS

Focusing units of study on broad themes provides perhaps the best way of integrating factual knowledge with the multicultural understandings we want to promote. Integrated studies include opportunities for students of all abilities and interests to contribute and to learn from each other. Thematic units are best planned with the students. However, before introducing a proposed study to the students, teachers do need to explore the broad parameters of a theme along the following lines:

1. Selecting and introducing the theme
2. Planning a broad integrated study
3. Locating resources to investigate
4. Sharing what students have learned

Selecting and Introducing the Theme

Selecting a theme that reflects the outcomes to be achieved will probably be influenced by the established curriculum for the grade or class. After selecting the theme, teachers have a variety of possibilities to explore for introducing and engaging students with the study.

Selecting a Theme

Thematic units can be planned around a variety of topics that achieve multicultural outcomes. The best topics are sufficiently broad so as to include a spectrum of peoples from different cultures, for example:

celebrations

courage

families

friendship

growing up

heroes and heroines

homes around the world

overcoming obstacles

sports around the world

walls

Introducing the Theme

The purpose of the introduction is to engage student interest in the theme you plan to undertake. You might choose an approach that begins with:

Reading a novel aloud (*The Sign of the Beaver; Sounder*)

Discussing a current news event (Conflict in Rwanda; Native American rights)

Displaying a picture (poverty in Peru; the plight of the elderly in New York City)

Sharing picture books (*Don't You Know There's a War on?; The Butter Battle Book*)

Interviewing a guest (a Japanese American; a rabbi; a woman politician)

To introduce the theme, persecution, read Lois Lowry's Newbery Award-winning *Number the Stars* (Houghton Mifflin, 1989), a novel set in Copenhagen in 1943, when Nazi soldiers were rounding up Danish Jews. Then, invite students to list all the ideas that were presented in the book.

List the words and phrases quickly on the chalkboard, linking those that are related. Notice how the ideas develop into clusters. Label these concepts or categories.

Reading the novel may lead to a broader study of Jewish beliefs, the wholesale persecution of Jews during World War II by the Nazis, or the life of Jews in the United States today. A novel motivates students to become involved with the characters and the action described. They will want to know why the German soldiers behaved as they did and why the Jews in particular were threatened. They can depict scenes on a large floor map as they follow events in the story. Small groups can research the history and geography related to this novel. Through this study, students should gain insight into the plight of the Jewish people during the Holocaust, the historical significance of World War II. This thematic study is an excellent example of how to align an international focus with ethnic studies in the United States.

Students may also be stimulated to read other fiction and nonfiction about Jewish people and the horrors they have experienced as they have tried to survive, for example: *Letters from Rifka* by Karen Hesse (Holt, 1992) or *Memories of Anne Frank* by Alison Leslie Gold (Scholastic, 1997).

Planning a Broad Integrated Study

The purpose of planning at this stage is for students to identify the tasks they need to undertake. They should identify, for example:

What We Know
What We Need to Find Out

Students can work in small groups to assess this kind of information. Using Cooperative Learning Groups encourages greater participation by all students and provides the opportunity to get acquainted with individual students. Working as part of a team also gives students a sense of belonging that supports their self-esteem. After making lists, the class will work together to create a Wall of Information that can stay up while the study is ongoing.

The tasks listed under "What We Need to Find Out" will be assigned, perhaps by a drawing, to each of the learning groups. Group planning will then address the next stage of development of the study, locating resources. Later, they will need to plan how they will share the information gained.

Locating Resources to Investigate

Enlist the aid of the librarians in your area. They will be happy to supply a collection of materials related to the study you plan. Students can visit a library as a class or in their learning groups to find information specific to their portion of the assigned task. The librarian can help them locate books, newspapers, articles in magazines and journals, and other print material. Libraries will also be a source of multimedia materials such as videotapes, audio presentations, and computer software.

Schedule the computer lab for several periods where all students can use pertinent software and visit the Internet. Students should also use other means of finding information, for example, the telephone, personal interviews, and writing letters, faxes, or e-mail.

Note that, periodically, you will need to plan lessons on specific skills, for example, notetaking, interviewing, and accessing the Internet.

Sharing What Students Have Learned

Students will plan again to decide how they can share what they have learned through this study. If they have been actively involved, they will consider what they have learned as valuable information that everyone should know and they will want to communicate the information to others. Have students brainstorm methods they might use, for example:

Creating a class book to put in the library
Producing a schoolwide assembly
Inviting another class to visit them to see what they have accomplished
Preparing a multimedia presentation

Following is an example of a multicultural thematic study.

A SAMPLE THEMATIC STUDY: A NATION OF IMMIGRANTS

Almost all of the people who now live in the United States are immigrants or children of immigrants. Native Americans were the only ones here to greet Christopher Columbus, and even they may have emigrated from Asia. (While African Americans did not emigrate, they did come from another country.) Immigration is a particularly timely topic as issues at state and national levels are receiving media attention. This thematic study might be developed following these steps.

Step I: Introduction   Reading a book about an immigrant is a good way to engage students with the human as well as political and social issues that are involved in a discussion of immigration. For example, *Grandfather's Journey,* Allen Say's Caldecott Award-winning picture book, tells how the author's grandfather, a Japanese man, came to the New World, which he learned to love. He married a Japanese woman and brought her to California where they had a baby daughter, Allen's mother. His grandfather was happy in the United States, but he missed his homeland so much that he and his family returned to Japan to live. His mother remained in Japan and married there, so Allen was born in Japan. Later, he, too, emigrated to California where he learned to understand his grandfather's love for both countries.

This sensitive cross-cultural account may provide insight into the feelings that immigrants share as they become naturalized citizens and pledge allegiance to their new country, the United States, saying:

. . . I will support and defend the Constitution and laws
of the United States of America against all enemies,
foreign and domestic . . .
    Oath of Allegiance required of Naturalized Citizens

Other picture books that support this theme include:

Amy Hest. *When Jessica Came across the Sea.* Candlewick Press, 1997.
Liz Rosenberg. *Grandmother and the Runaway Shadow.* Harcourt, 1996.

Step II: Planning an Integrated Study   Talk about the three generations represented in *Grandfather's Journey.* Discuss the conflicting feelings they had about Japan and the United States and how difficult the decision must have been to leave one country for the other. Use the world map to point out the great distance between the two countries. Ask if students know anyone who has immigrated from another country (perhaps the students themselves, their parents, or grandparents).

Then let students join with you in planning a study called: A NATION OF IMMI-GRANTS. You might begin an information wall on which to collect facts related to the topic. Label sections on which to place information in various categories; for example:

Where Our Ancestors Came From (make a big map)
Who Lives In Our Community
What We'd Like to Find Out
    How do you become a citizen?
    What is the INS? Where is its nearest office?

Brainstorm for a while, but expect to keep adding information to this wall. Then, form CLGs to begin locating information on different aspects of this study, for instance:

Emigrating to the New World
Laws regarding immigration
What immigrants contribute to life in this country
The question of language differences

Step III: Locating Resources to Share   Take students to the school library and then to the local public library for a Treasure Hunt. The librarian can suggest various ways of searching for information: the card catalog, books on the shelves, the computer, and so on. Have students make a card for each discovery, which will go in a class Resource File. Include such books as the following:

Brent Ashabranner. *Still a Nation of Immigrants.* Dutton, 1993. A factual discussion of immigration.

*Elisa Bartone. *American Too.* Lothrop, 1996. Rosina sails into New York Harbor just after World War I. She wants to be American, but everyone she knows is Italian.

*Eve Bunting. *Going Home.* HarperCollins, 1996. Children come to understand their parents' love for Mexico and their families there although the parents chose to move to the United States.

Anne Galicich. *The German Americans.* Chelsea House, 1992. This book is one in an excellent series of more than 50 books, *The Peoples of North America.*

Jim Murphy. *Across America on an Emigrant Train.* Clarion Books, 1994. The story of immigrants who migrated west.

Claire A. Nivola. *Elisabeth.* HarperCollins, 1997. A Jewish child's memories of the flight from Nazi Germany.

Jeanette Winter. *Keana's New World*. Knopf, 1992. A Swedish girl emigrates from Sweden to Minnesota in the 1800s.

Step IV: Sharing What Students Have Learned   Help students plan ways of sharing what they have learned with each other first and then with other classes, or perhaps the whole school. Following are a few suggestions:

Teaching a Lesson. Each CLG can prepare a lesson to present to other members of their class. One teaching team might, for example, engage students in role-playing situations that occur as diverse people interact: WHAT WOULD YOU DO?

A Readers' Theater Presentation. The whole class could plan a presentation to be given before one or more classes of their peers. The readings could vary from a short play to poetry or a series of quotations. The presentation should follow a clear theme, for example, COMING TO A NEW HOME.

A School Assembly. The class could plan an assembly perhaps titled: NEW CITIZENS. This presentation could also be given at a PTA meeting as a way of spreading this information throughout the community.

Recap

Broad encompassing thematic units include something for every student. Beginning with an event, a short book read aloud, or the study of an ethnic group, such units can be as short as a week or two, but they might extend over a full semester or even a year. The thematic study reaches into every content area as students probe the depths and breadth of a topic or issue. The results of these broad studies can be shared with other classes through publications, a multimedia presentation, or a school assembly.

CREATING A MULTICULTURAL MODULE

In this section we focus on creating focused booklets of activities—modules—that students can use as they work individually or in small groups to study a portion of a broad theme. The module presented here is meant to be used as part of a study: Getting to Know Our Neighbors at Home and Abroad. This broad theme may be developed over a year in one class, or several classes may address the theme at one time, each choosing to focus on one part of the theme, that is, one group of neighbors.

This module, titled: "Getting to Know China and Chinese Americans," is intended to be used as only one part of a larger study. The study is outlined briefly here in order to provide the context for using a module appropriately.

Introducing the Larger Study

Begin with a preassessment exercise by having students *cluster* around the word *China*. Each student writes all the words he or she associates with China, connecting words that are related. The individual clusters may look something like the one below. Save this preassessment activity for examination later after the students learn more about this country and its peoples. Comparison should show growth and perhaps changed viewpoints.

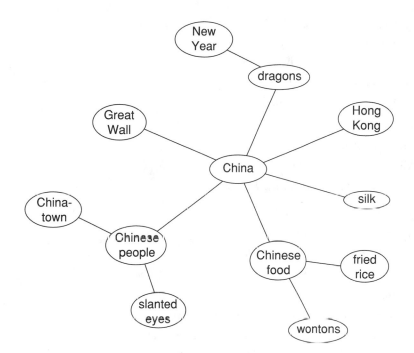

You might begin this study by reading a folktale from China, for example, *Tikki Tikki Tembo,* the story of a little boy who had such a long name that he almost drowned because his little brother had so much trouble repeating the name. This book won the Caldecott Award for illustrations by Blair Lent. A film of the tale is available from Weston Woods, Weston CT 06880.

Retold by Arlene Mosel, this story is a good example of a *pourquoi* tale, a story that explains why something happened, in this case why the Chinese have such short names. After hearing this story, students of all ages can write humorous pourquoi (the French word for *why*) tales to explain, for example:

- Why our clock has twelve numbers.
- Why cherries have pits.
- Why we have stoplights on city streets.

After students have written their pourquoi tales, have them collected in a book entitled: *Pourquoi? ¿Porqué? Why?* Place the book on the reading table where everyone can read it.

Collecting Resources

Explore your library as well as the computer to see what kinds of resources are available. To accommodate a wide range of reading abilities, include both easy and more difficult fiction. Also bring in the China entries from several encyclopedias, as well as other nonfiction written for young people. Here is a selection of titles to look for.

Fiction

Easy Books

Eve Bunting. *The Happy Funeral.*

Thomas Handforth. *Mei Li.*

Kurt Wiese. *Fish in the Air.*

Short Stories and Myths

Arthur Chrisman. *Shen of the Sea.*

Alice Ritchie. *The Treasure of Li-Po.*

Laurence Yep. *Dragon of the Lost Sea.*

Books for Older Students

Adrienne Jones. *Ride the Far Wind.*

Jean Merrill. *The Superlative Horse.*

Katherine Paterson. *Rebels of the Heavenly Kingdom.*

Nonfiction

Cornelia Spencer. *The Land and People of China.*

Cornelia Spencer. *The Yangtze, China's River Highway.*

Betty Lee Sung. *The Chinese in America.*

Creating a Learning Center

Create a learning center like the one shown here to serve as a focus for the study of China and Chinese Americans. Have students help develop the center.

You can feature any pertinent information to add interest to the center. Here we have presented facts designed to pique student curiosity, such as the fact that millions of people speak Chinese or that China is the third largest country in the world. The gameboard, Challenge the Dragon, can be presented as part of the module or as a separate activity with the directions displayed where students can read them easily. Place the modules, varied supplies, and numerous resources such as books at this work center.

Preparing a Module for Students

We find it helpful to prepare learning modules that guide students through a study, stressing activities that are stimulating and informative. A learning module is a booklet, usually 8" × 11", that focuses on a single topic. Rather short, five to twenty pages, the module is designed to teach two to three objectives that are part of an overall goal. The module begins with a simple pretest and concludes with a culminating activity that aids student self-evaluation. The learning module is self-contained and speaks directly to the student. A teacher's guide is included with suggestions for use and such teaching aids as test answers, additional enrichment activities, and recommended resources. Read through the sample that follows so that you have a clearer picture of how a module can be used.

The U.S. Bicentennial, 1976, was the "year of the dragon," as was 1988; the dragon comes again every twelve years. The title of the module could be modified according to the year in which you plan to present this unit to provide a more contemporary flavor. The dragon, however, is always a useful motif for the gameboard at any time.

Enlarge drawings by projecting them with a projector or copy machine. Prepare a simple construction paper cover that bears the title and perhaps the head of the dragon. Or the cover might be decorated with a Chinese ideograph (a symbol used for a word or idea).

THE YEAR OF THE DRAGON—2000

THE YEAR OF THE DRAGON: A STUDY OF CHINA AND CHINESE AMERICANS

美

The Cover of the Module

Module Activity 1: Gifts from China

The chart opposite shows that we have received many gifts from China. China's civilization developed long before that of the United States. Our country is an infant compared to such countries that trace their history back thousands of years.

Since China existed so many years before we did, naturally many things we take for granted today came originally from China. Can you name three things that we use today that were gifts from China?

1. _____

2. _____

3. _____

Module Activity 2: Your Own Book about China

Begin a book about China. You can put everything you do in this study in your book. Choose a title for the book. Select a piece of colored construction paper to use as the cover. Use a brush and black tempera paint to create a Chinese ideograph to decorate the cover. You may find some ideas in your encyclopedia or other books about China. Follow the directions given in Module Activity 3. Make a page for the table of contents. You can add titles to this page gradually as you make new pages for your book. Make a page now about Gifts We Received from China. You can make a chart like the one here or you can simply list the things we received from China. Perhaps you would like to include a picture from a magazine, a newspaper clipping, or some of your own illustrations.

Module Activity 3: Chinese Brush Painting

Try your hand at the beautiful figures used in classic Chinese writing. Use white art paper (9" × 12"), a brush, and black tempera to create the words shown here. For instructions, find *You Can Write Chinese* by Kurt Wiese in your library.

man   **beautiful**   **country**

CHINA'S GIFTS TO THE WEST

China*		The West*
Silk, about 1300		
Folding umbrella (?)	—300 B.C.—	
Lodestone, 240	—200 B.C.—	
	—100 B.C.—	
Shadow figures (?)	Birth of Christ	
	—A.D. 100—	
Lacquer Paper, 105		Peach and apricot
	—200—	
Tea, 264–273	—300—	
Word for porcelain first used		
Sedan chair	—400—	
	—500—	
Kite, 549	—600—	Silk, 552–554
Playing cards, Dominoes	—700—	
Gunpowder (?)	—800—	
Porcelain described, 851		
First printed book, 868	—900—	
	—1000—	
Movable type, 1041–1049		Orange
Compass	—1100—	
Zinc in coins, 1094–1098		Paper, 1150
Explosives, 1161	—1200—	Compass, 1190
	—1300—	Gunpowder and cannon, 1330
	—1400—	Playing cards, 1377
Chaulmoogra oil and ephedrine		Block printing, 1423
described, 1552–1578		Gutenberg's Bible, 1456
	—1500—	Zinc described
		Kite, 1589
	—1600—	Sedan chair, tea, folding umbrella, 1688
	—1700—	Wallpaper manufactured,
The use of the following also		Porcelain, 1709
originated in China in early times,		Lacquer produced, 1730
but cannot be accurately dated:		Zinc in industrial production, 1740
peach, orange, apricot, lemon,	—1800—	"German silver" production
pomelo, chrysanthemum, tea rose,		Chrysanthemum, tea rose,
camellia, azalea, China aster,		camellia, azalea, China aster,
gingko, "German silver,"	—1900—	grapefruit, shadow figures, gingko,
wallpaper, goldfish.		tung oil, soy bean, ephedrine,
		chaulmoogra oil

*Dates in the "China" column indicate approximate date of origin; "The West" column indicates the approximate date of receiving item described.

Source: From Derk Bode, *China's Gifts to the West,* American Council on Education, Washington, D.C., 1978.

Module Activity 4: Exploring China

Find articles about China in an encyclopedia, newspapers, or magazines. See what you can find out about: the people of China; the land—its boundaries, size comparison with the United States, mountains and rivers; China's government; the languages of China.

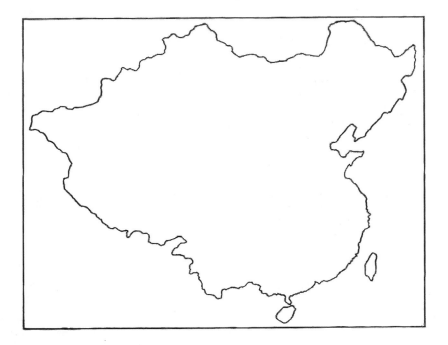

Study the map of China. Make an outline of this country like the one above. First divide your paper in fourths with light pencil lines. This helps you draw the map in proper proportion. The lines can be erased later.

Locate provinces, major cities, and rivers. Print the names of countries that border China. Identify the bodies of water that touch China.

Module Activity 5: The Puzzling Pagoda—Chinese Crossword Puzzle*

After reading about China and drawing a map of this country, you should be able to complete the crossword puzzle. If you can't think of an answer, refer again to the encyclopedia.

Definitions

Across

1. The capital of China (old name)
4. People's _____ of China

Down

2. Tallest mountain
3. Common cereal grain

---

* *Sources* for the Pagoda Puzzle were *China,* edited by Thomas W. Chinn, and *California, A Syllabus.* The Chinese Historical Society of America, 17 Adler Place, San Francisco, CA 94133.

8. Chinese philosopher and scholar
9. Jewel
10. Luxurious cloth
11. Basic Chinese coin
13. Largest city in China
14. Useful cloth produced
16. Famous leader: _____ En-lai
18. Unique building

5. Kind of government
6. Fishing boat
7. Country larger than China
12. Large woody plant
14. Common fish eaten
15. Prized lumber
17. Precious stone

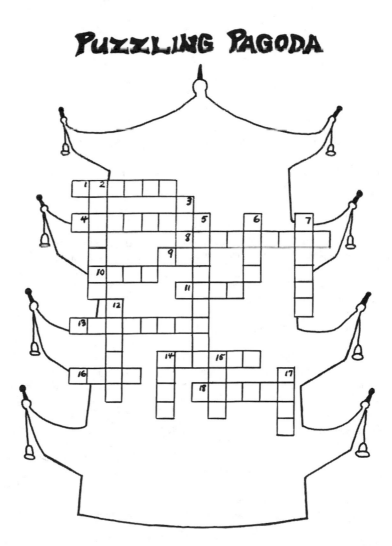

PUZZLING PAGODA

Answers to the Pagoda Puzzle

Across	Down
1. Peking	2. Everest
4. Republic	3. Rice
8. Confucius	5. Communist
9. Gem	6. Junk
10. Silk	7. Russia
11. Yuan	12. Bamboo
13. Shanghai	14. Carp
14. Cotton	15. Teak
16. Chou	17. Jade
18. Pagoda	

IN WHICH YEAR WERE YOU BORN?

Ox (1961, 1973, 1985, 1997) You have a calm patient nature. Friends turn to you because you are that rarest of creatures—a good listener. Love bewilders you so many people wrongly consider you cold.

Tiger (1962, 1974, 1986, 1998) You are a person of great extremes, a sympathetic and considerate friend, a powerful and dangerous enemy. In your career you are both a deep thinker and a careful planner.

Hare (1963, 1975, 1987, 1999) You are blessed with extraordinary good fortune and will inevitably provide financial success. This luck of yours not only extends to your business interests, but also to games of chance.

Dragon (1964, 1976, 1988, 2000) Your reputation as a fire-eater is based on your outward show of stubbornness, bluster, and short temper. But underneath you are really gentle, sensitive, and soft-hearted.

Serpent (1965, 1977, 1989, 2001) You Snake people have more than your share of the world's gifts, including basic wisdom. You are likely to be handsome, well-formed men and graceful, beautiful women.

Horse (1966, 1978, 1990, 2002) Your cheerful disposition and flattering ways make you a popular favorite. Great mental agility will keep you in the upper income.

Ram (1967, 1979, 1991, 2003) You are a sensitive, refined, aesthetic type with considerable talent in all the arts. Indeed success or failure will depend upon whether you can shepherd your ability and energy into a single field.

Monkey (1968, 1980, 1992, 2004) In today's parlance you are a swinger. And because of your flair for decision making and sure-footed feel for finance, you are certain to climb to the top.

Rooster (1969, 1981, 1993, 2005) You either score heavily or lay a large egg. Although outspoken and not shy in groups, you are basically a loner who doesn't trust most people. Yet you are capable of attracting close and loyal friends.

Dog (1970, 1982, 1994, 2006) You are loyal and honest with a deep sense of duty and justice. You can always be trusted to guard the secrets of others.

Boar (1971, 1983, 1995, 2007) The quiet inner strength of your character is outwardly reflected by courtesy and breeding. Your driving ambition will lead you to success.

Rat (1972, 1984, 1996, 2008) You have been blessed with great personal charm, a taste for the better things in life, and considerable self-control that restrains your quick temper.

Module Activity 6: The Chinese Calendar

The Chinese calendar is quite different from the one we usually refer to. It is based on ancient traditions. An animal symbol is identified for each year, and persons born in that year are supposed to have characteristics associated with the animal. Twelve symbols are repeated continuously. Examine this chart showing the meaning of each symbol. What is your symbol? Do you think the characteristics listed fit you?

Module Activity 7: Chinese Become Americans

People of Chinese origins have made major contributions to the development of the United States. Many are doctors, college professors, and business executives. As immigrants, however, their life was difficult.

Read this list of events that are significant in the history of Chinese Americans from the first immigration to the present.

1785 First record of Chinese in the United States. Three Chinese seamen from the ship *Pallas* were left stranded in Baltimore.

1815 First record of a Chinese in California. Ah Nam, a cook for Governor de Sola, was baptized as a Christian on October 27, 1815. (California was not yet a part of the United States.)

1849 In the year of the gold rush, Chinese in San Francisco recorded as 54; in 1850 there were 787 men and 2 women. First anti-Chinese riot at Chinese camp, Tuolumne County, California.

1850 First laundry business begun in San Francisco by a Chinese person.

1852 First Chinese opera performed in San Francisco. First Chinese theater built in San Francisco. Columbia Resolution expelled Chinese from gold mines in Tuolumne County; followed by a similar action in other counties.

1854 First Chinese newspaper in America, *Gold Hill News.*

1869 Completion of Transcontinental Railway. Chinese labor used by Central Pacific. Chinatown established in Deadwood, South Dakota, with discovery of gold. Chinese followed development of the mining industry as well as agriculture, and fishing; resentment by whites.

1871 Chinese massacre in Los Angeles.

1877 Special Report by Joint Committee of Congress investigated the "Chinese Question." Labor agitation; anti-Chinese movement.

1879 California Constitution contained anti-Chinese legislation prohibiting employment of Chinese by corporations and government agencies.

1882   Chinese Exclusion Act passed by U.S. Congress; ten-year ban on immigration; anti-Chinese riots.

1892   Geary Act extended exclusion for another ten years; required aliens to register.

1893   Anti-Chinese riots grew numerous; Fresno, Napa, Redlands, Tulare, Visalia, Ukiah (California).

1894   Vacaville, California, riot; Chinese driven to cities where they formed Chinese ghettos, called Chinatowns.

1902   Exclusion laws extended indefinitely.

1907   Vancouver, British Columbia, riot.

1943   Repeal of Chinese Exclusion Act: Chinese aliens in United States may become citizens. Chinese immigration quota set at 105 per year.

1965   Quota system repealed. Permits up to 20,000 Chinese to enter United States each year.

Work with others in your class to prepare a time line on a long strip of paper that looks something like this:

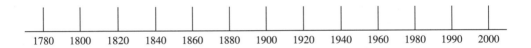

Add illustrations and other information related to the history of Chinese immigration into the United States.

Module Activity 8: Making a Game—Challenge the Dragon

Preparing the Gameboard.   If you choose to prepare the gameboard yourself as a stimulating extra activity for this study, begin by enlarging the drawing with an opaque projector or copier. Have other students help you as much as possible. Examine this part of the module again before reading the following directions so you will understand the instructions.

Duplicate or copy the directions to the student (below). Mount these directions on a heavy piece of colored cardboard. Cover the directions with a sheet of clear contact paper to protect the sheet as it is used repeatedly. Pressing the direction board (covered with a sheet of clean paper) with a warm iron will make the protective sheet adhere well.

Have a student construct the Curious Cube on the page that follows. Have several other students finish the Cardinal Cards. You will need to prepare additional cards similar to the examples given if a number of students wish to play at once.

Directions to the Student.   Here is a fiery dragon whose breath can destroy you or bring you fortune. Which will it be?

This dragon guards a Treasure Chest that you can reach only by performing the many tasks required by the fearsome beast.

At each step roll the dragon's Curious Cube to see how many tasks you must perform. To learn what the tasks will be, draw forth a Cardinal Card for each task. If you perform the required tasks, the dragon will permit you to move to the next perilous step. If you fail even one of the tasks, you must slide back to the previous step.

You have only a limited time to perform each task. As you complete each task, place the Cardinal Card under the great pile of Arduous Tasks. That task may be assigned to another unlucky challenger who dares to challenge the dragon.

Making the Curious Cube.   Copy the pattern shown here to make the cube that will tell how many of the Arduous Tasks you must perform. After cutting the cube pattern from heavy red paper, print the numbers indicated with a felt pen. Then fold the pattern on each line, folding in the same direction each time. Form the six-sided figure and tuck the flaps in after applying glue on each.

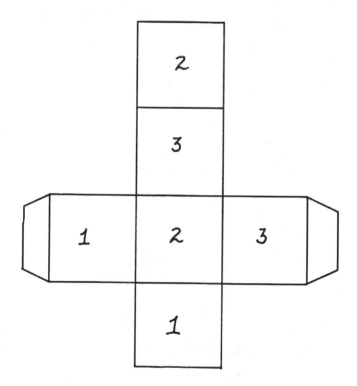

Preparing the Arduous Task Cards.   Cut the cards apart. Mount each one on red (cardinal) construction paper that is 3" × 4" so the color frames the card.

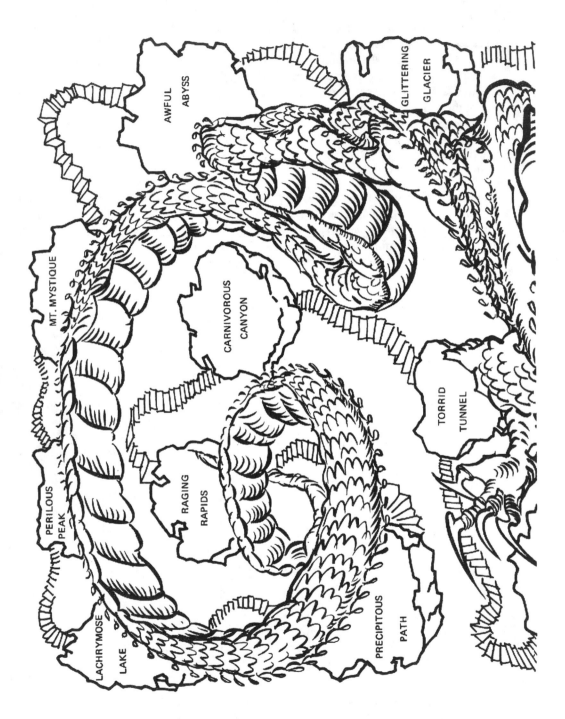

AWFUL ABYSS

GLITTERING GLACIER

MT. MYSTIQUE

CARNIVOROUS CANYON

TORRID TUNNEL

PERILOUS PEAK

RAGING RAPIDS

PRECIPITOUS PATH

LACHRYMOSE LAKE

1. About how many people live in China?	6. Name the tallest mountain in China.

2. Name the 3 largest countries in the world.	7. Identify the following:
	  a. pagoda
	  b. junk
	  c. carp

3. What kind of cloth was a gift from China?	8. Where did Chinese immigrants first settle in the United States?
4. What is the old name of the city that is the capital of China?	9. Which of these names is likely to be Chinese? Martin Chang Yomura
5. Which city is the largest in China?	10. Name two countries that border China.

Answers to Cardinal Cards:

1. 600 million
2. Russia, Canada, China
3. silk
4. Peking
5. Shanghai
6. Mt. Everest
7. a. special kind of building
   b. Chinese boat
   c. kind of fish

8. California
9. Chang
10. Russia   Bhutan
    North Korea   Sikkim
    North Vietnam   Pakistan
    Vietnam   Afghanistan
    Laos   Mongolia
    Myanmar
    India

Playing the Game Alone.   This is a good game to play individually as you challenge the dragon alone. You may need a person to serve as Timer and Checker to see if your answers are acceptable. Use any means to discover the correct answer within the time limit, for instance, a dictionary.

Playing the Game with a Friend.   You may wish to play this game with a friend or two. In this case do not wait for each person to finish the tasks assigned. If one player finishes a task in a short time, he or she can move to the next step, throw the Curious Cube, draw the Cardinal Cards, and work on the tasks assigned. In this way, each person moves ahead individually depending on the number of tasks received each time and how quickly they are completed. You will want to hurry, of course, if you are to reach the Treasure before someone else gets it away from the Dragon!

Module Activity 9: Exploring Your Community

What do you know about Chinese Americans in your own community? Begin a survey by turning to your local telephone book to answer the following questions:

- How many persons are listed under several common Chinese names such as Wong, Chang, or Yee? What other names might you try?
- How many listings begin with the word *Chinese,* for example, Chinese Alliance Church?
- How many Chinese restaurants are listed in the yellow pages under *Restaurants?*
- How many doctors under the entry *Physicians and Surgeons* in the yellow pages have Chinese names?

Write a summary of your findings. Then write a paragraph explaining your conclusions about the Chinese in your community.

Do your findings surprise you? How can you find out more about Chinese Americans in your community?

Module Activity 10: A Writing Lesson*

SAMPLE LESSON: DICTATION

Level of Difficulty: Grades 1–8 (Adapt materials selected.)

Outcomes

Students will:

1. Listen to sentences read aloud.
2. Write each sentence dictated.
3. Discuss spelling and conventions.

Procedures

Select a paragraph from a good book that students have already heard or one that you would like to introduce. Choose a paragraph that includes interesting sentence structures, varied uses of punctuation and capitalization, and new vocabulary. (Choose a less complex paragraph for the first experience with dictation.) In this lesson we use a paragraph from *Dragonwings* by Laurence Yep (Harper), a story of the Chinese in California during the early twentieth century.

Stimulus

Introduce the book and author to your class, for example:

> *Dragonwings* was written by a California author, Laurence Yep, who was inspired by the account of a Chinese immigrant who built a flying machine in 1909. This is how the story begins:
>
> "Ever since I can remember, I had wanted to know about the Land of the Golden Mountain, but my mother had never wanted to talk about it."

Invite students to conjecture about what the Land of the Golden Mountain is. Tell them that the main character, Moon Shadow, lives in China with his mother and grandmother, but his father, Windrider, lives in San Francisco's Chinatown.

Then share the interesting paragraph you have selected for the dictation exercise, for example:

---

* This activity is teacher directed. You may omit teacher directions in the student module, including only the title and a lined page for writing the dictated paragraph.

Mother had talked quite a bit about him and so had Grandmother; but that too was not the same. They were speaking about a young man who had lived in the Middle Kingdom, not a man who had endured the hardships and loneliness of living in the demon land. I knew he made kites; but as marvelous as his kites were, he and I could not spend the rest of our lives flying kites. I was afraid of the Golden Mountain, and yet my father, who lives there, wanted me to join him. I only knew that there was a certain rightness in life—the feeling you got when you did something the way you knew you should. I owed it to Father to obey him in everything—even if it meant going to such a fearful place as the Golden Mountain. And really, how really frightening could it be if Hand Clap wanted to go back? I turned to Mother and Grandmother. "I want to go," I said.

Talk about the passage the students have heard. Ask them questions such as the following:

1. Who is talking?
2. What characters are mentioned in this paragraph?
3. Who is Hand Clap?
4. What is this fearful place, The Golden Mountain? Where is it? How did it get that name?
5. Why was Moon Shadow afraid? Why did he decide to go?

Activity

Tell the students that you are going to dictate this paragraph to them, sentence by sentence. You will read each sentence only twice: The first time they are to listen without writing; the second time will be after they have begun writing. Challenge them to write each sentence as well as they can without help.

Follow-Up

After you have completed the dictation exercise, have students correct any errors together. Ask two students to write the first sentence on the chalkboard. Ask if any changes need to be made in spelling, punctuation, or capitalization. Tell students to correct any mistakes they made on their own papers.

Students should study this passage in preparation for writing the same passage again on the next day.

Evaluation

Have students compare the results of the two dictations. Have each one write several sentences summarizing what they learned from doing this exercise.

Module Activity 11: What Do You Know Now?

Write three things that you know about China or Chinese Americans now that you did not know before you began this study:

1. _____

2. _____

3. _____

Examine the answers you gave to the questions on the first page of this module. Would you change any of them now?

Choose one of the following activities to complete your work on this study:

- Write a poem or story about a person from China.
- Act out a story set in China that you have read. (You may work with several students on this task.)
- Plan a Reader's Theater presentation of a folktale from China. (Work with several students.)
- Make a diorama of a scene from China.
- Make a table-size relief map of China. (Work with another student.)

Additional Activities   As students are working on the module, you might wish to interject additional interesting activities that can involve the whole group or may be designed for small group interaction. Here are a few suggestions:

- Invite a parent who was born in China to visit your class to tell about China as they remember it, childhood experiences, coming to the United States, what his or her life here is like.
- Prepare a simple Chinese meal of rice and a combination of vegetables. See *Eating and Cooking Around the World; Fingers before Forks* by Erich Berry.
- Read a version of "Cinderella" that comes from China. See *Favorite Children's Stories from China and Tibet* by Lotta C. Hume.
- Write a Chinese play or produce one that is available in the library. See *7 Plays and How to Produce Them* by Moyne R. Smith.
- Learn how the Chinese New Year is celebrated. See *Holidays Around the World* by Joseph Gaer.
- Explore Chinese poetry. See *Chinese Mother Goose Rhymes* edited by Robert Wyndham; *The Moment of Wonder* edited by Richard Lewis.
- Read stories aloud that are set in China. You might choose, for example, *Seven Magic Orders: An Original Chinese Folktale,* beautifully illustrated by Y. T. Mui.

Chinese Children in Your Classroom   Presenting a study related to the country of origin for students in your class gives them a good feeling of belonging. They can often contribute special information and personal experiences. Their parents may be willing to share in the study, too. The students will learn as they participate in the study. Students who may have arrived recently from China or Hong Kong will be very much interested in finding out about Chinese Americans in the community and in the United States.

Recap

Multicultural modules can be developed to support the study of specific topics at a learning center or to fit within broad thematic units. A group of teachers can work together to create several modules used at one grade level. If one to three modules are created each year, the team will soon have a number of such resources from which to choose. The module permits individuals to progress at their own level of ability.

REFLECTIONS

Students respond positively to individualized instruction that challenges them to progress as quickly as possible. Learning centers, broad thematic studies, and prepared modules offer stimulating methods of presenting flexible learning activities for students of all abilities. Varied kinds of resources, instructional tools, and support groups can be provided to help slower readers, thus ensuring that they can succeed. Gifted students can be challenged to extend and expand their skills and knowledge. Using such approaches to instruction is especially appropriate for integrating multicultural concepts into the curriculum.

Throughout the rest of this text, you will discover additional suggestions for multicultural studies that focus on specific subjects or groups, for example, gender studies in Chapter 5 and an African American feature in Chapter 7. Remember, however, that in addition to these focused themes and units you plan, you need to consciously infuse multicultural concepts into all other instruction as well, always selecting strategies that reflect the ideas behind "multicultural teaching."

Since the individualized methods of instruction presented in this chapter do not follow a single textbook, the teaching materials are largely teacher-made. Thus, it is wise for teachers to work as teams in preparing multicultural learning center materials, including modules on selected multicultural topics or themes. Teachers can also plan collaboratively to develop certain broad themes as they brainstorm activities and collect resources that their classes can share. Such planning is wonderful curriculum development worth supporting during the summer by the school district.

APPLICATIONS

1. Develop a unit of study about one of the lesser known cultural groups in the United States. Begin by discovering as many books and other forms of literature as you can. You might, for example, initiate your exploration of Appalachia and the people who have lived in that region, by searching for picture books by Cynthia Rylant, who comes from West Virginia. Look for:

When I Was Young in the Mountains. Harcourt, 1983.
Appalachia: The Voices of Sleeping Birds. Harcourt, 1991.
Best Wishes. Owen, 1992.
Silver Packages. Orchard, 1997.

2. Working in a CLG, read a book appropriate for middle school students. Discuss the multicultural concepts presented and how you might develop a class study based on reading this book aloud together. You might consider studying such titles as:

Michael Dorris. *Guests.* Hyperion, 1994. Moss, a Native American boy, resents his father's inviting the "strange white men" to join their harvest feast.
Sherry Garland. *Song of the Buffalo Boy.* Harcourt, 1992. The story of a Vietnamese girl whose father was an American soldier (For more mature students).

Carol Matas. *The Garden.* Simon & Schuster, 1997. Sequel to *After the War.* Both deal with World War II and its atrocities.

Claudia Mills. *Dinah for President.* New York: Macmillan, 1992. A middle school girl runs for president of the sixth grade; humorous.

Patricia Beatty. *Jayhawker.* New York: Morrow, 1991. A young Kansas abolitionist plays a dangerous role in fighting slavery.

Keep a journal as you read the book selected, recording questions, teachable moments, and so on. Compare your notes with those of others in your CLG.

3. Design a module for use in teaching a specific unit of study. Plan an integrated study that will last for three to four weeks. Draw from the entire text of *Multicultural Teaching* for ideas that fit your topic. Modules can be produced for any subject area and can focus on groups of people, geographic areas, or broad concepts related to multilingual/multicultural studies. Examples of good topics for presentation are prejudice in America, Native Americans today, Americans from Puerto Rico, and breaking down stereotypes.

4. Brainstorm possible themes to develop with middle school age students. Then find at least one book or other resource that might introduce each theme, for example:

The Contributions of Native Americans to Our State
Native American Art Gallery—http://www.info1.com/NAAG/index.html
National Museum of the American Indian—http://www.si.edu/organiza/museums/amerind
American Indian Athletic Hall of Fame: Hashell Indian Junior College; Lawrence KS 66044.

EXPLORING FURTHER

Amy McClure, & Janice V. Kristo. (Eds.). (1996). *Books That Invite Talk, Wonder, and Play.* Urbana, IL: National Council of Teachers of English.

Elizabeth G. Cohen. (1994). *Designing Groupwork: Stategies for the Heterogeneous Classroom.* New York: Teachers College Press.

Elizabeth P. Pate et al. (1997). *Making Integrated Curriculum Work: Teachers, Students, and the Quest for Coherent Curriculum.* New York: Teachers College Press.

Chris Stevenson, & Judy F. Carr. (Eds.). (1993). *Integrated Studies in the Middle Grades: "Dancing through the Walls."* New York: Teachers College Press.

Wendy K. Sutton. (Ed.). (1997). *Adventuring with Books: A Booklist for Pre-K–Grade 6.* Urbana, IL: National Council of Teachers of English. New edition.

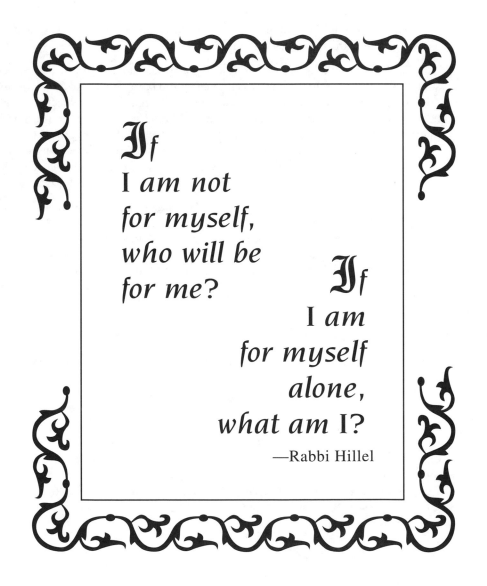

If
I *am not*
for myself,
who will be
for me?

If
I am
for myself
alone,
what am I?

—Rabbi Hillel

5

Learning about Ourselves

In Part I we examined multicultural teaching from different perspectives. Now, in each of the chapters in Part II, we adopt a particular lens through which to view the process of multicultural learning. In this chapter, the lens is the individual student as we teach students respect for individual identity. This lens directs our attention to the need for self-knowledge as well as knowledge of others. When we reflect on ourselves—who we are, where we come from, and what we believe—we can learn to see others more clearly and to appreciate how we are both similar and different. And the process of understanding works in reverse. As we explore the full range of diversity, we learn more about what makes each of us an individual.

Examining multicultural learning from the perspective of respect for individual identity means looking at students as "active" learners, constructing identity through interaction with others, absorbing messages from family, friends, community, and school, and translating cultural information into a unique self. When we ask students to look at where they come from, we bring students' culture into the classroom as more than just a topic of historical interest. Instead, we encourage students to become thoughtful participants in a tradition rather than inheritors of a cultural straitjacket. Although each individual encounters different circumstances and is exposed to a variety of influences, every student is also a part of the continuing development and redefinition of their cultural heritage.

How do you, the teacher, help develop active student learners? Because learning takes place as students build on prior knowledge and make connections to new information and experience, you must provide rich environments of activity and discussion, where students reflect on the relationships and patterns they discover. Because students are eager to teach and learn from other students, you will want to structure multiple opportunities for students to test their ideas against others through talk and small group work. And because students learn, not by smoothly and steadily accumulating knowledge, but by taking small steps and giant leaps, often in unexpected directions, you can't know how much your students are capable of unless you listen to them carefully. All students, no matter what their ethnicity, language, or family background, have the potential to succeed in school.

After reading this chapter you should be able to:
- Help students explore who they are and where they come from.
- Develop activities that relate personal knowledge and multicultural perspectives.
- Plan a thematic unit around food.
- Teach for equity between boys and girls in the classroom.

GETTING ACQUAINTED

As students learn about themselves, they prepare to learn about each other. They are engaged in the developmental tasks of developing empathy and learning to see the world from another's point of view; they begin to separate who they are from who others may be. Teachers can help to bridge the transition from home to school by making the school environment less foreign. Encourage students to bring important parts of themselves to school to share with others.

Special Days

Students' birthdays offer an opportunity to recognize students as individuals. On your class calendar, list the birthdays that will occur each month. Let the birthday student do something special that day, for example:

- Wear a special hat.
- Choose a game for everyone to play.
- Teach the class a poem.
- Distribute papers or books for the teacher.
- Use a favorite color on the bulletin board.

Another way of recognizing a student is to have the rest of the class brainstorm what they like about that person. These comments can be written down and collected in a book for the student to take home. The students can also make up a song about that person and sing it, perhaps to the tune of "Happy Birthday."

Decide how to schedule students with summer birthdays. You might ask students to select from open dates. An alternative would be to celebrate "unbirthdays."

Ask students how birthdays are celebrated in their families. Do they have any special customs or ceremonies? Suggest that there are many different ways to honor people on their special day.

Although many students enjoy being the center of attention for a day, others may be shy or embarrassed by the publicity. Monitor your birthday activities to make sure that the student feels like an important part of the class and not singled out for uncomfortable attention.

Some books to share about birthdays are:

Elisa Kleven. *Hooray, a Piñata!* Dutton, 1996. Clara chooses a dog piñata for her birthday party but can't face breaking him. Her friend Samson helps solve the dilemma. Multiethnic neighborhood, detailed illustrations.

Eve Feldman. *Birthdays, Birthdays, Birthdays! Celebrating Life Around the World.* Bridgewater, 1996.

The "Me" Collage

Collage comes from the French word "coller," meaning to glue together. When you make a collage, you assemble many different elements, often overlapping, to create an image.

Have students clip words and pictures from magazines or other sources and prepare a collage that tells something about their lives. Talk about the things they might include, for example:

- Hobbies
- Birthplace—picture, part of a map
- Baby pictures
- Things they like—food, sports
- Their family—people, pets
- Where they have lived or traveled

Letters as well as pictures can be included to add variety to the collage. Clippings are pasted on a large piece of colored construction paper or cardboard. A frame can be attached after the collage is completed.

Have students write a brief biographical description that can be attached to the collage or read aloud to the class. Feature a different student's collage every week.

These collages make interesting displays for Open House when parents visit the school. Record each student's presentation of the biographical sketch that accompanies his or her collage. Play the tape continuously as parents visit the classroom. Post an order of the presentations on the board so people can tell when their child will be heard.

Leaves on a Tree

Read the following story to the students.

There's Nobody Like You!

The French poet Jean Cocteau found out early in life why diversity is better than uniformity.

As a young man, M. Cocteau was designing a stage set which required a tree as background. He spent night after night in the theater basement cutting out individual leaves for his creation.

Then a wealthy friend, whose father owned a factory, approached him with another idea.

"Give me the design of that leaf," he said, "and in three days you will have thousands of them here."

After his friend's return, they pasted the multitude of identical leaves onto the branches.

The result, M. Cocteau recalled, was "the most boring package of flat, uninteresting forms one can see."

At last he understood why each leaf of a tree and each man in the world are different from any other.

— *Christopher News Notes,* no. 187, May 1971

Provide students with green paper and have them cut their own leaves. Students can sign their leaves. Mount the leaves on a paper tree on the bulletin board. Point out how the leaves vary in size and shape, just as human beings vary.

How Does It Feel to be Different?

Students of all ages often feel the pressure to be the same as everyone else. Open discussion of this sensitive issue by reading aloud *The Straight Line Wonder* by Mem Fox, illustrated by Marc Rosenthal (Mondo, 1997). This short book tells the story of a "straight line" whose desires to dance, jump, and twirl aren't understood by the other "straight lines." The humorous message will appeal to preschoolers and teenagers. Students can role play or write their responses to the story, taking on the perspective of the different characters.

Everyone Has Fears

Introduce the subject of being afraid by reading a book such as *There's a Nightmare in My Closet* by Mercer Mayer (Dial, 1987). Then ask the students to write a sentence or two about something of which they are really afraid. You participate, too. With no names attached, each paper is folded up tight and put in a box. You might say:

> Now that you have your fear written on paper, I want you to fold it up tight and put it in this box. (Collect everyone's fears.) Here we have everybody's fears collected in a box. Sometimes the things we're afraid of are only fearsome because we can't talk about them. We keep them hidden inside us. Today we're going to bring some of these fears out in the sunshine where we can look at them. I'm going to ask somebody to pick up one of these fears and read it out loud. If the one that's drawn is yours, you don't have to tell anyone because your name isn't on the paper.

Discuss the fear that is drawn from the box: "How many of you have been afraid of the dark when you go to bed? What did you do about it?" Repeat this activity as long as the group is interested. Then set the box aside for further discussion at irregular intervals.

Another sensitive presentation of a common concern is *Ira Sleeps Over* by Bernard Waber (Houghton Mifflin, 1972). Ira is worried about going to a friend's house to sleep for the first time. His sister tells him that his friend will laugh at him if he sleeps with his teddy bear. Read this book aloud to the class, pausing at each page to have students predict what will happen next and to recommend ways to handle Ira's concerns.

Personal Writing

An excellent way to promote writing that supports student self-discovery is to encourage freewriting in a journal. Journals can be spiral-bound notebooks or sheets of composition paper stapled together. Students can personalize the cover with drawings or a collage. Schedule a specific time for writing in student journals, and continue this writing for at least three weeks. The journals should be kept in the classroom so that all students have their journals on hand at the scheduled time. We recommend that you, too, write in a journal, both to demonstrate the value of the activity and to share entries periodically. Journal writing should never be graded or corrected. Students may select an entry to share, but the option of privacy must be assured.

At all times, students should feel free to write about something important to them. However, you may want to provide a stimulus each day for those who need an idea. Use some of the following topics for journal writing:

- Friends are important.
- I felt sad when . . .
- Some of my favorite activities are . . .

- If you were a superhero, what power would you have?
- What's the bravest thing you ever did?
- What one characteristic would you like to change about yourself?

Before you embark on this activity, recognize that students may write about painful or intimate topics. Decide in advance how you might handle some unpleasant or upsetting discussions. If you share writing with the class or in small groups, don't force reluctant students to contribute.

Here are some recommended resources to help you introduce journal writing in the classroom:

Lucy Calkins and Shelley Harwayne. *Living between the Lines.* Heinemann, 1991.

Lorraine M. Dahlstrom. *Writing down the Days: 365 Creative Journaling Ideas for Young People.* Free Spirit, 1990.

James Moffett and Betty Wagner. *Student-Centered Language Arts: K–12,* 4th ed. Heinemann, 1991.

Donald Murray. *Write to Learn,* 3rd ed. Holt, Rinehart, and Winston, 1990.

J. A. Senn. *325 Creative Prompts for Personal Journals.* Scholastic, 1992.

My Lifeline

Have students draw a series of mountain peaks across a sheet of paper. Tell them that this line represents their life. What are the big peaks in their life? What are the smaller peaks? What are the valleys? Have them label the peaks and valleys that they have experienced in their lifetime so far.

Older students can make this a timeline by adding the years and sequencing the events in chronological order. This idea can be extended by describing their usual daily existence across the base of the mountains. A few fantasies can be added on clouds: "Someday I'd like to. . . ."

Animal Metaphors

A metaphor is a comparison between two things, usually unexpected and often expanding our awareness of the object of the metaphor. For example, "the sun is a golden earring" (Natalie Belting). A simile is also a comparison but includes "like" or "as," such as "My Daddy smells like tobacco and books" (Christopher Morley).

Have students create animal metaphors (or similes) to describe themselves. They can write a short description explaining why they chose that animal.

> Jesús: I'm a jaguar because I like to run and climb.
> Tanisha: I'm like a rabbit because I'm shy.
> Vincent: My mother says I'm a busy bee. I'm always running around and getting in her way.

Primary students can draw pictures of themselves as these animals. Older students can read more about their selected animals and report to the class on the animals' characteristics. Students can also write on the topic "I'd like to be a (animal) because . . . "

Personality Prints

Another way to feature students as individuals is to make handprints. Have students place their hand on a piece of paper and draw around it with a thick colored pen. Then they write something about themselves on each finger. For example, they can write their name on the thumb, an adjective describing themselves on the next finger, then a favorite activity, a favorite color, and finally a favorite book. Post these on the wall to admire the students' diverse personalities.

When I Graduate

Have students imagine that it is the future and they are about to graduate from high school or college. The following questions will stimulate their thinking.

> How old are they?
> What year is it?
> How do they feel looking back on their education?
> What do they expect to do next?

After this discussion, they can put themselves in the shoes of their future selves and each write a first person account of his or her life and hopes at that time. This exercise will make it easier for all students to envision themselves as finishing high school or pursuing a college degree.

If I Were in Charge of the World

Read students examples from *If I Were in Charge of the World and Other Worries,* by Judith Viorst (Macmillan, 1981). Ask each student to complete the sentence:

If I were in charge of the world, . . .

Have students share their suggestions. This would make an excellent bulletin board display. This activity could also be completed by several classes at different grade levels so that the responses could be compared.

Students can invent variations on this pattern:

If I were in charge of this school, . . .
If I were in charge of the universe, . . .

NAMING OURSELVES

Names are one of our most personal possessions, representing individual identity as well as our connection with family and heritage. As a teacher, consider carefully how you respond to students' names. Care in pronouncing and spelling a name correctly translates into respect for the person. As appreciation of diversity increases, people are more and more proud of the distinctive first and last names that reflect their culture of origin. Students can learn how their own names are related to historical and cultural factors.

Choosing Names

Ask children about their first names. How do they feel about their names? Are they named after someone, perhaps an aunt or grandfather? Perhaps they have a family name, like Jamison, or an invented name composed of both parents' names, such as Rayella. Have them write on one of these topics:

- My parent named me _____ because _____.
- I like my first name because_____.
- I wish I could change my first name because _____.
- If I could choose a name for myself, it would be _____ because _____.
- If I had a child, I would name the baby _____ because _____.

Discuss *Chrysanthemum* by Kevin Henkes (Greenwillow, 1991), which tells the story of a young mouse who loves her unusual name until she starts school. Then the others make fun of her, saying her name is too long and not appropriate for a mouse. But one of her teachers helps her learn that her name is as special as she is.

Explore naming customs. Catholic children choose a saint's name when they are confirmed. Alex Haley describes an African naming custom at the beginning of this classic book *Roots*. Do students know of other naming customs?

What's Your Name? From Ariel to Zoe by Eve Sanders (Holiday House, 1995) presents history and stories about names from many cultures.

My Name Design

Because students like to see their names, have them make designs based on their first names. Fold a piece of paper in half lengthwise. With the fold on the bottom, write the name, making sure that each letter touches the fold. Letters that extend below the line can be raised so they fit on the same level. Now hold the folded paper up to the light and trace the name in reverse on the other side. Open up the paper to find an abstract design. This can be colored in or decorated to make an imaginary figure. Display these on the bulletin or use them to make covers for collections of student writing.

Popular Names

Some first names become fashionable and show up in packs in elementary classrooms while others have become unfashionable. The following chart shows the most popular names given to babies.

Girls		Boys	
1991	*1997*	*1991*	*1997*
Ashley	Brittany	Michael	Michael
Amanda	Ashley	Christopher	Christopher
Jessica	Jessica	Matthew	Matthew
Samantha	Amanda	Joseph	Joshua
Stephanie	Sarah	Daniel	Andrew

For girls, Samantha and Stephanie have moved to eighth and ninth place on the list for 1997. For boys, Joseph and Daniel have dropped below the top ten. Does your class roster look like this list? Or is it full of names like Marklon, Donte, Tanisha, T'Keyah, Hakeem? Or Lourdes, Felizardo, Cristeta, Amarnath, Ceizhar, and Keila?

Have students study the distribution of first names in the school or in one grade. Depending on their math skills, they can list the ten most common names and the ten least common, or they can calculate the percentage of frequency. Compare the list for your school to the list of baby names given above.

Name Acrostic

Use student names in puzzles or wordplay. A creative activity is to develop an acrostic based on students' names. Students write their name vertically down the left side of a page.

Then they fill in the acrostic with adjectives (or phrases) describing themselves, beginning with each letter of their name.

K ind
H elpful
A miable
L ight-hearted
I ntelligent
D aring

You can vary the difficulty of the game by allowing students to start to the left of their letter. This increases the number of words they can use.

b L ack
A mbitious
a M azing
pr E tty
L ively
Friend L y
Hon E st

Students with short names can include their middle or last name to make the acrostic more interesting. Students with long names can choose a short version. You may want to award points for the number of letters to the right of the name, or for the most unusual words chosen.

Encourage students to check the dictionary to find interesting word choices and expand their vocabulary.

How to Translate Your Name

Students will be interested, also, to discover that the same name is used in many languages. One illustration is the name John, which can be found in a variety of languages:

Yohanna (Arabic)	Jannis (Greek)	Johan (Norwegian)
Iban (Basque)	Yohanan (Hebrew)	Ivan (Russian)
John (English)	Sean (Irish)	Ian (Scots)
Jean (French)	Shane (Irish)	Juan (Spanish)
Hans (German)	Giovanni (Italian)	Evan (Welsh)
Johannes (German)	Jan (Northern European, Dutch)	

Many English names can be translated into Spanish and vice versa. See if the students can discover the equivalent in other languages of such names as Peter, James, David, William, Mary, Rose, and Helen. What names do not translate easily?

Family Names

Whether Greek (Stephanopoulos), Belgian (Van Der Mensbrugghe), Georgian (Shalikashvili), Laotian (Khammoungkhoune), or Indian (Umamaheswaran), many American family names are megasyllabic—and people are learning to spell and pronounce a greater diversity of names. Discuss family names (surnames). Why do we need them? Where do they come from? Have children state their surnames as you write them on the chalkboard. Observe the variety of names in the classroom. Some have only one syllable (Wong) and others contain several syllables (Asakura, Rodríguez, Anderson).

Use surnames in classroom learning experiences. Have students line up alphabetically for lunch. Younger students can line up according to the first letter only, while older students can check the second and third letters as needed for more precise order.

Discuss the characteristics of surnames. "Mc" and "Mac" names originated in Ireland and Scotland, for example. Let students make generalizations about the names represented in their classroom:

- We have many Spanish names: Castañeda, Chávez, Feliciano, Vásquez.
- Chinese names are short: Wang, Lee, Ching.
- Many Vietnamese people have the same last name, but aren't related: Nguyen, Ng, Huynh.

Family Names in Different Cultures

Different cultures have different rules for family names, or last names. In English-speaking countries, most children take the last name of the father. Some countries use both the mother's and father's names. In other countries, parents give different forms of the father's first and last names to male and female children.

In Spanish, for example, a person's surname consists of the father's family name followed by the mother's family name.

Teresa   Pérez   Gutiérrez
            (father)   (mother)

Sometimes the word *y* (and) is inserted between the surnames of the father and mother, for example; Juan López y Benavente. Juan would be called Señor López, however, and his name would be under L in the telephone directory. Likewise, Teresa and Carlos would be listed as follows:

Pérez Gutiérrez, Teresa

Russian names include a "patronymic" (father + name) in the middle. For example:

Tanya Ivanovna Kuznetsova (daughter of Ivan)
Sasha Ivanovitch Kuznetsov (son of Ivan)

In addition, the-*a* is added to the last name for women.

In traditional Vietnamese style, the last name is given first. When reading a Vietnamese name, it may be difficult to determine whether the Vietnamese or American order is being used.

Many children today have hyphenated names, to include the last names of both parents. School records can become confused, as when Rachel Vogel-Abrams is listed sometimes under V, sometimes under A.

Other students carry the last name of their father only and not the mother's, such as Matthew Peterson, son of Keith Peterson and Catherine McDonald. Children in "blended" families (formed by divorce and remarriage) may have surnames different from either parent, further complicating school records. As the teacher, you can't predict child-adult relationships by surnames.

Origins of Names

Family names are interesting to children when they discover the meanings that lie behind them. They can easily see that those names that have -*son* or -*sen* at the end carry the meaning "son of"; for example, Anderson and Williamson. One of the most common names is Johnson, son of John. Endings that mean *son of* in other languages include -*ez* or -*es* (Spanish), -*tse* (Chinese), -*wicz* (Polish), and -*ov* (Russian and other Slavic languages).

Up through the early Middle Ages, only first names were used in England. After that time, family names began to distinguish people who had the same first name.

Many last names were associated with a person's line of work; for instance, Carpenter, Smith, and Cooper. Challenge students: What does a smith do? What does a cooper do? Characteristics of a person often led to other names, such as Young, White, and Little. Another source for last names was the place where someone lived: Hall, Street, Wood.

Surnames can also represent a painful history. Africans brought to the United States as slaves were taken away from their families and their names. Slaves had no last name of their own; instead, they were given their owner's family name. When we talk about surnames indicating pride in one's heritage, it is also important to recognize that African American surnames can preserve the memory of slavery. Leaders such as Malcolm X chose to cast off these humiliating reminders.

For names of foreign origin, try a dictionary for that language. Set out on a discovery trip in which all can participate as they help each other find the origins of their family names.

Pennames, Stagenames, and Pseudonyms

Sometimes people decide to change their name. This may be because they don't like the sound or image conveyed by their name. Or they may want to create a new identity. Writers and actors often change their name because they prefer a simpler name or a name more suited to their profession. Sojourner Truth chose her name because she planned to travel from place to place and to tell the truth about slavery. Writer David Wallechinsky's family name had been changed to Wallace by officials at Ellis Island. He changed it back.

We know many writers more familiarly by their pennames than their real names. Do students know:

Who wrote *The Cat in the Hat?*	Theodor Seuss Geisel	(Dr. Seuss)
Who wrote *Alice in Wonderland?*	Charles Dodgson	(Lewis Carroll)
Who wrote *Tom Sawyer?*	Samuel Clemens	(Mark Twain)
Who wrote *1984?*	Eric Blair	(George Orwell)

Invite students to select a penname to use for their writing. They can imagine themselves in different roles as they try on different names, perhaps borrowed from someone they admire. You might set aside one week for pseudonyms so that students could try out a new name every day.

Names for Math

Use student names for math exercises. Have students count the letters in the names in the class (either first or last names) and develop a chart to show the results. They might produce a bar graph, such as the following.

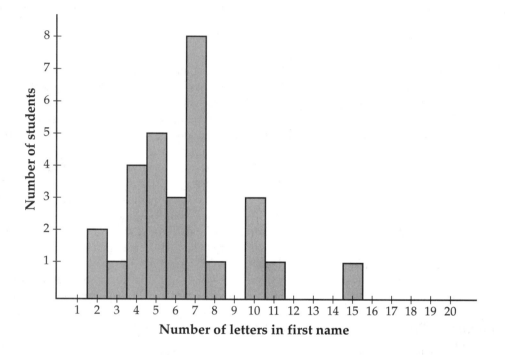

Challenge students to come up with alternative ways of displaying the same information.

Study of Names

Students might want to begin a more extensive study of names. This topic is called onomastics. Look for the following books that provide information about the meanings of common names and their origins:

Patrick Hanks and Flavia Hodges. *A Dictionary of First Names.* Oxford University Press, 1990.

Justin Kaplan and Anne Bernays. *The Language of Names.* Simon and Schuster, 1997.

Eloise Lambert and Mario Pei. *Our Names: Where They Came from and What They Mean.* Lothrop, 1960.

Milton Meltzer. *A Book about Names.* Crowell, 1985.

*Mary Lee and Richard Lee, *Last Names First—and Some First Names Too.* Westminster Press, 1985.

FAMILY TIES

As students begin to look at who they are, they also begin to discover where they came from. Learning about their family history and customs can help them find their place in the world. They can learn that everyone has a family but families can be very different.

A Family Tree

Begin a discussion with primary students by talking about the family tree. Who are the members of their family? What relatives do they have? Students can draw a tree and write the names that they know in circles around the tree.

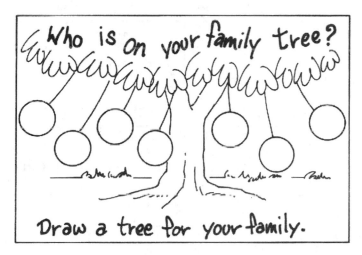

What Is Genealogy?

Introduce the big word *genealogy* (notice the spelling), which means the study of lineage, family history. Many people trace their family history as a matter of pride. Today there are societies focusing on such study.

Students can ask their families about family history and write the information on a chart, such as the diagram on the next page. They can interview their parents and any other relatives to assemble as much information as possible.

When introducing this kind of activity, be aware that parents may be sensitive to this potential invasion of privacy. Therefore, it is important to discuss the project in the classroom first so that children have a clear sense of your intent, namely, developing *pride in the family,* the importance of remembering our ancestors, our *roots.* You might, for example, tell the group something of your own origins.

Books to help students explore their family roots are:

Kay Cooper. *Where Did You Get Those Eyes? A Guide to Discovering Your Family History.* Walker, 1988.

Lila Perl. *The Great Ancestor Hunt.* Clarion, 1989.

Younger students will enjoy *Rosy Cole Discovers America!* by Sheila Greenwald (Little, Brown, 1992) in which Rosy, disappointed in her ordinary immigrant ancestors, invents a royal past for herself.

Older students can take advantage of the Internet resources to trace their family. Check out these sites to get started:

Computerized Ancestor	www.montana.com/yates/
Gendex	www.gendex.com
Roots Web	www.rootsweb.com

The Family Tree of Juana Fuentes

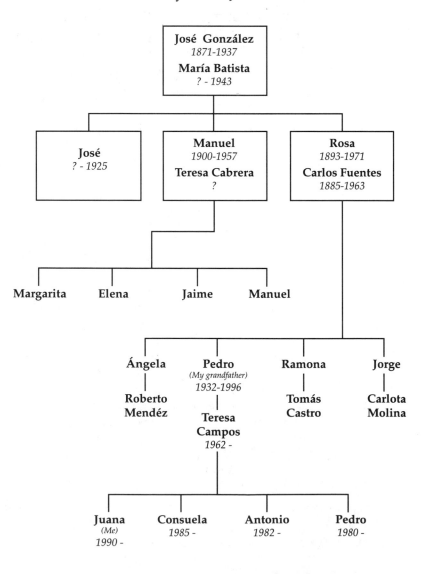

Families Differ

Discuss the topic: What is a typical family? Students will probably arrive at the stereotyped perception of a family as a mother, father, and two children, even if their family is not like this.

Is this what families are really like? How many families represented in the classroom consist of two parents and two children? What other arrangements do the children know about? List them on the chalkboard.

Father Mother One Child
Father Mother More than Two Children
Mother One Child
Grandmother Three Children
Father Two Children
Father Mother One Child Grandfather

The point of this discussion is to show children that families differ. It also opens up an opportunity for students to talk about their own families, something about which they may have felt uncomfortable. It helps to know that other parents have been divorced or that someone else's parent has died.

Related topics that can be discussed without evaluation include the following:

- Some mothers work outside the home and some do not.
- Sometimes relatives live together.
- Some children have a mother, a father, a stepmother, and a stepfather.
- Some children have half-brothers and half-sisters.
- Some children are adopted.

Defining a Family

With so many different arrangements of families, how do we know what a family is? Invite students to offer their definition of a family. Is a family a group of people who live together? What about when parents are divorced and a child may have more than one home? If you are adopted, are you part of a family? When you raise these topics, it shows students that it is okay for them to wonder about such questions.

Cultural background also affects how we define family. Some students may think of a family as composed of parents and children, known as a "nuclear" family. Others' conception may include several generations, with aunts, uncles, and cousins as well. This is called an "extended" family. Have students draw a picture of their "family." They can explain their drawing to the class. Some students may include their pets.

Family Responsibilities

In every family, different people have different jobs to do. Everyone has something to contribute to the family, even the smallest child. Ask students what they do to help out. They may set the table, fold the laundry, watch a baby brother or sister, prepare food, go shopping, or help a parent by translating something into English. If parents work at home, students may even participate in the family business. Discuss how each of these tasks is important to the family. Point out how necessary even these small chores are in order for everyone to be able to live.

The following books show that in families, everyone is important.

Muriel Stanek. *I Speak English for My Mom.* Whitman, 1989. Lupe has to help her mother who doesn't speak English.

Eve Bunting. *The Wednesday Surprise.* Clarion, 1989. A young girl secretly teaches her grandmother to read.

Diane Hoyt-Goldsmith. *Arctic Hunter.* Holiday, 1992. The photographs in this book show how much is expected of each family member, including 10-year-old Reggie, when they go to their fishing camp each spring.

Ruth Yaffe Radin. *All Joseph Wanted.* Macmillan, 1991. Joseph loves his mother, but her illiteracy is hard on him. Finally, Joseph convinces his mother to go to an adult literacy class.

Alice Schertle. *Down the Road.* Harcourt, 1995. Hetty's parents ask her to go to the store alone to buy eggs. She feels grown up because of the responsibility but the eggs get broken. Too ashamed to go home, she is relieved when her parents find her and assure her of their love and understanding.

Family Routines

All families have different daily routines and special rituals for marking celebrations. Students can compare their routine for waking up and preparing for the day with that of the girl in Jan Ormerod's *Sunshine.* (Lothrop, 1981) Use student examples to practice sequencing skills. What do you do first? What happens next? What do you do last?

Share Byrd Baylor's classic *The Way to Start a Day,* (Macmillan, 1978) a Caldecott Honor Book illustrated by Peter Parnall, to stimulate discussion of different ways to greet the dawn. Students can add more examples to this exploration of how different cultures celebrate the sun. Have them describe how they would plan to celebrate the sun's rising. How would they celebrate the sunset?

Two Mothers or Two Fathers

Most discussions of families presume the existence of a mother and a father, even when only one parent lives at home. However, there are children whose family consists of two Moms or two Dads. These children go to school like any other children. In addition, students may know of such families in the community. Classroom discussion of families headed by same-sex partners requires considerable sensitivity, yet open and careful discussion can allow children to feel more comfortable without exposing them to public humiliation and thoughtless ridicule by other children.

In your discussion, you can help students move from the stereotype of the nuclear family to the concept that a family can be built in many different ways and is held together by bonds of love and responsibility. Homophobia, fear of or discrimination against people because of their homosexual orientation, is based on an intolerance for differences, just like prejudices such as racism and anti-Semitism. And just as with these other prejudices, the fear of differences correlates closely with labeling others inferior or disgusting, and making them a target for violence. Your goal is for children to learn how to treat each other with respect, regardless of what beliefs they bring to school.

A book such as Christina Salat's *Living in Secret* (Bantam, 1993), written for intermediate students, is useful for raising these issues in class. It presents the story of a girl who has to lie about her life with her mother and her mother's "girlfriend" and the effects that this concealment has on her.

Other books that present aspects of this sensitive situation are:

Susanne Bosche. *Jenny Lives with Eric and Martin*. Gay Men's Press, 1983. Set in London, Jenny deals with prejudice, describes her feelings.

Rosamund Elwin and Michele Paulse. *Asha's Mums*. Illustrated by Dawn Lee. Women's Press, 1990. Asha's teacher doesn't understand about her two mums so they visit the class. Shows a diverse classroom in Toronto.

Leslea Newman. *Saturday Is Pattyday*. Illustrated by Annette Hegel. New Victoria Publishers, 1993. When lesbian mothers separate, Frannie is worried about losing a mom.

Johnny Valentine. *One Dad, Two Dads, Brown Dad, Blue Dads*. Illustrated by Melody Sarecky. Alyson Publishers, 1994. Lou has to answer questions about his dads. His friends discover that blue dads are like other dads.

Michael Willhoite. *Daddy's Roommate*. Alyson, 1990. When his parents divorce, a boy learns that his father is gay. Being gay means another way to love someone.

Jacqueline Woodson. *From the Notebooks of Melanin Sun*. Scholastic, 1995. Thirteen-year-old African American boy is upset when he finds out his mother is in love with a white woman.

Families Then and Now

Have students complete a comparison chart to examine family life in one historical period with family life today. After reading book such as *Sarah Morton's Day,* or *Samuel Easton's Day,* by Kate Waters, photo essays from Plimoth Plantation that recreate everyday life for Pilgrims in 1627, ask students to list some of the features of family life:

> Toys, recreation
> Chores
> Living conditions
> Clothing

Write the headings THEN and NOW on the board. Under THEN, students can contribute what they have learned about Pilgrim life. Draw a vertical line to separate the two categories and have students draw on their own life for examples of NOW. Afterwards, students can write their own statements, comparing aspects of Pilgrim life with life today.

Books about Different Family Arrangements

Children's books are helpful in exposing children to different family arrangements. It is helpful for all children to have a broadened perspective of this institution as it is rapidly changing in our society. Here are a few titles that you might want for your library:

Primary Grades

Karen Hess. *Lavender.* Holt, 1993. Codie's aunt is having a baby, and Codie wonders if her aunt will still have time for her.

David Kherdian. *A Song for Uncle Harry.* Illustrated by Nonny Hogrogian. Philomel, 1989. Set in the 1930s, this story describes the special relationship between Pete and Uncle Harry.

Anne Herbert Scott. *Sam.* Illustrated by Symeon Shimin. Philomel, 1992. Reissue of an old favorite. Sam's family don't seem to want him around. Finally they realize he needs a job of his own.

Camille Yarbrough. *Cornrows.* Illustrated by Carole Byard. Coward, 1979. As the girls have their hair braided into cornrows, Grammaw and Mama entertain them with stories of their African origins.

Lucille Clifton. *Everett Anderson's Nine Months Long.* Holt, 1987. Everett's mother has remarried and is going to have a baby. Look for other stories about Everett, an African American boy.

Nina Pellegrini. *Families Are Different.* Holiday House, 1991. Nico, an adopted Korean girl, is unhappy because she doesn't look like her parents. She learns that families come in all colors and sizes.

Catherine Bunin and Sherry Bunin. *Is That Your Sister? A True Story of Adoption.* Our Child Press, 1992. An adopted six-year-old girl and her sister tell their story.

Jeanette Franklin Caines. *Daddy.* Harper and Row, 1977. An African American father and his daughter make a family.

Roslyn Banish. *A Forever Family.* HarperCollins, 1992. Eight-year-old Jennifer is adopted after several foster homes. Shows multiracial families.

Allen Say. *Allison.* Houghton Mifflin, 1997. Allison is angry because she looks like her Asian doll, not like her Caucasian parents. A story of the search for belonging.

Karen Katz. *Over the Moon.* Holt, 1997. North Americans fly south of the border to pick up their adopted daughter.

Upper Elementary Grades

Brenda Wilkinson. *Ludell.* Harper and Row, 1975. Grandmother and fifth-grade girl; unwed mother does not live with them.

Zilpha K. Snyder. *The Witches of Worm.* Atheneum, 1972. Twelve-year-old girl and divorced mother.

Charlotte Anker. *Last Night I Saw Andromeda.* Walck, 1975. Eleven-year-old girl and mother; father visits.

Melrose Cooper. *Life Riddles.* Holt, 1993. With Daddy gone and the family on welfare, mother tries to keep the family together.

Candy Dawson Boyd. *Chevrolet Saturdays.* Macmillan, 1993. Joey, a fifth grader, can't accept his mother's remarriage, but his family understands him.

Marc Talbert. *The Purple Heart.* HarperCollins, 1992. Luke's picture of his dad as a war hero doesn't match the man who comes home.

Patricia MacLachlan. *Journey.* Delacorte, 1991. Journey's mother leaves him when he is eleven. He has to learn to accept her for what she is.

Fred Rogers. *Let's Talk About It: Stepfamilies.* Photos by Jim Judkis. Putnam, 1997. A multiethnic cast talks about issues such as anger, difficulties to overcome, and step-sibling relations.

Susan Beth Pfeffer. *Make Believe.* Holt, 1993. Carrie and Jill's friendship is affected by Jill's parents' divorce.

Harriet Langsam Sobol. *We Don't Look Like Our Mom and Dad.* Coward, 1984. This is the story, in photographs, of two Korean boys adopted by an American couple. The boys learn to develop pride in being both Korean and American.

When you read such stories as part of your regular time for reading aloud to the class, you help students feel comfortable knowing that there are other young people like themselves; and you provide a safe environment for discussing potentially difficult topics.

FOOD—A THEMATIC UNIT

A significant part of students' cultural identity is the food that they eat. And sharing food with others is a positive and non-threatening experience. You can begin a study of food with the food habits of students as individuals and lead the class to an understanding of larger cultural patterns as they explore food facts around the world. This unit can be used to develop these concepts:

> Everyone has the same nutritional needs but different groups eat different foods to satisfy them.
> Eating customs vary around the world.
> The food we eat comes from different places.
> We depend on others to supply our food.

In this section we provide some sample activities to stimulate your development of a thematic unit based on food.

Favorite Foods

Ask students what their favorite foods are. List responses on the board. Have students write descriptions of their favorite foods and read them to the class. Do all students like the same foods? Or do some students' favorites inspire groans from others? Talk about these differences of opinion. Is it possible for different people to have different likes and dislikes?

Food Diary

Have students keep a log for one day of what they eat for breakfast, lunch, and dinner, including snacks. Ask them what they learned from this record. Are they surprised by the variety, the quantity, the specific items? Students can use this information to make a chart for the class showing the most common foods eaten and the least common. Challenge them to decide the best way to depict these results.

Discuss with students the influences on what they eat. Some influences they might suggest are:

Convenience
Borrowed idea from a friend
Parent makes lunch
Parent does the food shopping
Cultural/ethnic background
Personal preferences

Classifying Foods

Food can be divided into three groups: proteins, carbohydrates, and fats. We need to eat food from each group in order to live. Prepare a large poster for each of these categories and have students decide where to place the foods they eat. They will have to do some research to determine what the foods are made of. Also, some foods will fit into more than one category.

Protein	Carbohydrate (Includes starches, grains, fruits, and vegetables)	Fat
hamburger	bread	lard
tunafish	potato chips	butter
eggs	tortillas	peanuts
tofu	rice	olives
cheese	bok choy	oil
milk	eggplant	ice cream
yogurt	nopales	avocado

Analyze this poster with students and point out the variety of foods we eat to satisfy our needs. Not everyone eats meat or fish. Some people eat tofu (soybean curd) as a source of protein. People eat many different kinds of beans, bread, fruits, and vegetables. Different groups use different kinds of fat for cooking, including lard, butter, and olive oil. While advertising promotes the slogan "everybody needs milk," people from many racial or ethnic groups (such as Native Americans, Asians, East European Jews) are allergic to dairy products and eat soy-based foods instead.

This poster, produced from student experience, can provide a basis for comparison as students expand their study of food around the world.

Food around the World

Every culture around the world prepares some kind of bread, rice, pasta, or other starch. What kinds of bread do students eat? What other kinds of bread do students know? Provide students with a chance to generate questions about food in different cultures, based on their own interests. For example:

Are the breads that people in India eat different from or similar to the bread familiar
to our community?

Where do bagels come from?

How do you make sopaipillas?

In *Everybody Bakes Bread,* by Norah Dooley (Carolrhoda, 1996), a girl explores her
neighborhood and discovers how bread varies according to the country each family comes
from. Recipes are included. Another resource is *Bread, Bread, Bread* by Ann Morris
(Lothrop, Lee, Shepard, 1989), which is a photographic tour of bread throughout the
world's cultures. Students will enjoy selecting an unfamiliar type and experimenting with
making and eating their own bread.

Sharing Food

Some of our most treasured moments may be of food shared with members of our family.
Cultural heritage is passed down along with memories. Use the following books to stimulate student reflection, research, and writing about the meaning of food in their family.

Amy Córdova. *Abuelita's Heart.* Simon and Schuster, 1997. A grandmother passes on stories of her ancestors to a young girl as they prepare "la comida." Includes recipe.

Meredith Hooper. *A Cow, a Bee, a Cookie, and Me.* Kingfisher, 1997. Ben's grandmother
teaches him how to make honey cookies and explains the origin of each ingredient. Includes recipe.

Class Recipe Book

Collect recipes to be duplicated and made into a collection for each student to take home.
Students can bring in recipes for their favorite foods or a special dish from their family or
culture. Each student can explain his or her recipe and talk about the preparation and ingredients. If possible, invite a parent or a member of the family to come to the class and
show everyone how to make one of these dishes. (You might even ask students to bring in
samples of their favorite foods.)

Class work with recipes leads naturally to a study of measurement (weight, mass) and
the mathematics of conversion. Students can practice measuring with different instruments
and multiplying quantities for larger groups. Students may also want to investigate the scientific questions of cooking; for example, how food changes from raw to cooked.

Holiday Food

People in every culture celebrate special holidays and most holidays have special foods associated with them. Ask students what foods mean holiday to them. Perhaps latkes (potato
pancakes) are a special treat for Hanukkah, or their grandmother prepares an elaborate traditional feast for Chinese New Year. Some may hold a family reunion where everyone
brings familiar food like corn on the cob and watermelon. What are students' favorite holiday foods?

Read one of these books aloud to stimulate student sharing.

Jama Kim Rattizan. *Dumpling Soup.* Little Brown, 1993. Multiracial family in Hawaii prepare special soup for New Year's.

Gina Macaluso Rodríguez. *Green Corn Tamales/Tamales de elote.* Hispanic Books Distributors, 1994. In bilingual, predictable book, family prepares Labor Day meal.

Students can write a description of a holiday meal. Discuss what makes descriptive writing effective. Talk about specific words that appeal to the senses. Generate examples of adjectives and other vocabulary to make students' writing more powerful.

International Grocery

Send students on a scavenger hunt. Have them take a notebook to the grocery store to do research. What foods come from other countries? How many different countries are represented in the grocery store? Students can read labels on cans or check the origin of fruits and vegetables in the produce section. What does the presence of food from other countries tell them? Who might buy this food? Discuss how to organize and present the data they collect. What generalizations can they make about their findings?

A Multicultural Menu

After studying food around the world, students can present what they have learned with a Multicultural Food Day. Groups of students can prepare food to represent the range of food found across the five continents of Europe, Asia, Africa, the Americas, and Oceania. Invite parents or other classes to share in your findings. Have students create posters to explain what each food is, who eats it, and where they live.

Food History

Ask students what food they consider typically "American." They might list pizza, hotdogs, hamburgers, tuna sandwiches, macaroni salad. Have them investigate the origins of these foods. What country did they come from? What foods come originally from the Americas? (Tomato, potato, chocolate) Where did noodles come from? (China) What did Italians eat before they had what we think of as Italian food—tomato sauce and noodles? What foods did students' ancestors eat? Each student can choose a food to research and report back to the class.

Another area to investigate is regional food history. Are there foods that are particular to your area? Recipes for chili (or chile) vary depending on the region. There are many foods found primarily in the South, such as grits or hush puppies. Where do they come from? Students will be interested to discover that some foods they take for granted are unfamiliar in the rest of the country.

Eating Customs

How people eat varies along with what people eat. What implements do people eat with other than knife, fork, and spoon? Do any of your students eat with chopsticks? Bring chopsticks to class and have these students demonstrate how to pick up food. Some groups eat with their fingers. Hawaiians scoop up poi (a kind of mush) in their hands. Ethiopians use injera (bread) as a plate and tear off pieces to wrap up their food. When people with different eating customs meet, each may consider the other's habits awkward or impolite.

Ina Friedman's *How My Parents Learned to Eat* (Houghton, 1984) tells how two people, one from Japan and one from the United States, overcame this hurdle.

Sources for Further Study

The following books will help you plan this study:

Patricia C. Marden and Suzanne I. Barchers. *Cooking Up World History: Multicultural Recipes and Resources.* Teacher Ideas Press, 1994. The book surveys cookery in more than twenty countries and regions, providing recipes and information to help students make the connection between culture, food, and history.

Milton Meltzer. *The Amazing Potato.* HarperCollins, 1992. This book for young people tells the incredible history of the potato, weaving in stories of the Incas, European conquerors, wars, and immigrants.

Raymond Sokolov. *Why We Eat What We Eat: How the Encounter between the New World and the Old Changed the Way Everyone on the Planet Eats.* Summit, 1991. Essays and references on food provide a humorous exploration of the post-Columbus migration of ingredients and ideas from the New World to the Old and back again.

See also the following books for children.

Kaur Sharon. *Food in India.* Rourke, 1989.

Virginia McLean. *Pastatively Italy.* Redbird, 1996.

Vijay Madavan. *Cooking the Indian Way.* Lerner, 1985.

Norah Dooley. *Everybody Cooks Rice.* Carolrhoda, 1991.

Deanna F. Cook. *The Kid's Multicultural Cookbook: Food and Fun Around the World.* Illustrated by Michael Kline. Williamson, 1996. Easy recipes from all six continents with illustrations and photographs of children.

Linda Illsley. *A Taste of Mexico.* Thomas Learning, 1994. Food presented in context of history and geography.

Fran Osseo-Asare. *A Good Soup Attracts Chairs: A First African Cookbook for American Kids.* Pelican, 1993. Recipes from Ghana and West Africa, includes resources.

FOCUS ON GENDER: SEARCHING FOR EQUITY

Male and female stereotyping is a particularly significant area of concern in multicultural teaching. Although women make up more than half the population, they have much in common with other groups that experience discrimination and limited opportunities. Despite the increasing number of women with college degrees, women earned only 71% of men's wages in 1994 (compared to 59% in 1970). In the classroom, the attitude that "boys will be boys and girls will be responsible" still predominates. Teachers continue to call on boys more than girls and spend more time responding and interacting with boys than girls. Stereotyped media messages overwhelm young people. From children's books to television programs, advertising to magazine articles, girls and women are shown to be more concerned with their appearance and romance than with working or going to school.

The lives of boys and girls do not have to be channeled into stereotyped roles; there is a range of lifepaths they can follow. Even as women are still rarely found in positions of power and men who choose to stay home and raise children are unusual, the socially imposed limitations on men's and women's lives are decreasing. Students can learn to question the images, attitudes, and assumptions of sex-role stereotyping. Through multicultural teaching, we can make sure that all students learn that girls are not lesser human beings just because they are female.

A Gender-Fair Curriculum

How can we reduce sexism and promote gender equity in our classrooms? A gender-fair curriculum, claims Gretchen Wilbur, quoted in the AAUW report *How Schools Shortchange Girls* (p. 64) would:

1. Acknowledge and affirm variation among students.
2. Be inclusive of all students.
3. Present accurate information.
4. Affirm differences in values.
5. Represent multiple perspectives.
6. Be integrated, weaving in males and females.

Research shows that one teacher can make a difference for students. In your selection of materials, in your discussions, in your responses to students, you can communicate the message that both boys and girls should speak up, that all students need to learn how to work together, and that girls are just as capable in math and science as boys.

Beginning a Unit on Sex Equity

Begin a study of gender issues with an assessment of what students know. Ask students to make a list of ten famous men and ten famous women, not including people from television or music. After allowing time for students to complete the task, discuss what they have learned from the experience. Was it more difficult to think of famous women? Could everyone come up with ten names? Write on the board some of the women's names that students thought of. Are the same few women repeated many times? Ask students to come up with possible explanations for these results. What gaps in student knowledge of women's accomplishments show up in this exercise? Use this discussion to stimulate further study as students themselves identify areas they need to explore. Save these lists for comparison at the end of this unit.

Sex-Role Stereotypes

Ask students to make individual lists of characteristics of men and women. After each has had time to write a number of items, ask each one to contribute something to add to a class compilation of these characteristics. The list may include items like this:

Men can	Women can
play sports	cook dinner
fix things around the house	go shopping
go to work	wear makeup
be firemen	be nurses

Discuss the items on each list. Do women play sports too? Can men cook dinner too? Have students respond from their experience.

To encourage them to expand their ideas of possible roles for men and women, turn their examples into sentences such as:

Men can play sports, and women can too.

Women can cook dinner, and men can too.

Sexual Harassment

Because we tend to associate this problem with adults, we may neglect the issue of sexual harassment among young people. Although we as teachers may not want to acknowledge the presence of sexual behavior and talk in the elementary school, part of making the classroom fair for boys and girls is raising everyone's awareness of behaviors that we consider unacceptable.

Begin a discussion of this sort by defining sexual harassment: creating a hostile environment through unwelcomed sexual behavior or talk. This may include activities such as calling girls or boys sexual names, public humiliation of girls or boys by referring to their body parts, and touching or grabbing others in inappropriate places. Ask if anyone has noticed this kind of behavior. How would they feel if it happened to them? What could they do about it? Brainstorm suggestions to resolve such incidents if they occur in the future. Have students set standards or rules for dealing with teasing and taunting. Establish the students' right to complain to someone in authority if this happens to them or if they see someone else involved. Help them decide what to do if their personal space is infringed.

Many students are confused about how to approach other students, particularly of the opposite sex. Talk with them about positive strategies to get to know another person. Develop a list of approaches students recommend if someone wants to become friends with them. This kind of discussion in a safe environment, with the teacher as mediator, may defuse some of the tension surrounding friendships between boys and girls at any stage.

What's "A Woman's Job"?

Many students are convinced that doctors must be men and nursing is a woman's job, even if there are examples in their lives that show them otherwise. These sex-role expectations are examples of stereotyping because they limit students' choice of occupation. Discuss sex-role stereotyping. A stereotype is a belief that a certain group has specific characteristics, often negative, shared by all members of that group. Show students how sex-typed stereotypes about jobs are limiting because they don't allow for individual differences in interests and abilities.

Help students overcome these stereotypes by featuring books about men and women in all kinds of jobs.

Virginia Meachum. *Jane Goodall.* Enslow, 1997.

Carole Ann Camp. *Sally Ride.* Enslow, 1997. Two volumes in the *People to Know* series.

Andrea Davis Pinkney. *Alvin Ailey.* Illustrated by Brian Pinkney. Hyperion, 1993. Picture book biography of African American man who became a dancer and choreographer, eventually leading his own company and revolutionizing modern dance through African American influences.

Corinne Szabo. *Sky Pioneer.* National Geographic, 1997. A photobiography of Amelia Earhart, pioneer aviator, who was brought up to be "inventive, independent, and imaginative."

Vicki Van Meter and Dan Gutman. *Taking Flight.* Dutton, 1995. Based on diaries of 14 year-old Van Meter's flight across the Atlantic in 1994. When she was 12, she was the youngest pilot to fly across the United States.

Kathryn Lasky. *The Most Beautiful Roof in the World: Exploring the Rainforest Canopy.* Photos by Christopher G. Knight. Harcourt Brace, 1997. The story of field scientist Meg Lowman who works in Belize, Central America.

Laurence Pringle. *Elephant Woman: Cynthia Moss Explores the World of Elephants.* Photos by Cynthia Moss. Atheneum, 1997. Book shows biologist's work with elephants.

Emily Keller. *Margaret Bourke-White.* Lerner, 1996. Profiles life of photojournalist who worked for *Life* magazine and was a war correspondent.

Sue Macy. *Winning Ways.* Holt, 1996. This black-and-white photohistory shows how American women have changed the men-only status of sports, from bicycling in 1870 to baseball in 1990.

Penny Colman. *Rosie the Riveter: Working Women on the Home Front in WWII.* Crown, 1997. Nonfiction account of women in non-traditional jobs, for middle school students.

Take Our Daughters to Work Day

Since April 28, 1993, many companies have participated in a program sponsored by the Ms. Foundation to introduce girls aged nine to fifteen to opportunities for women in the workplace. In your classroom, support these efforts to build girls' self-esteem by planning to expose them to a greater variety of careers. Contact companies associated with your school and invite women who hold different positions to speak to the class. Survey parents and friends for suggestions of women who have interesting jobs. Feature photographs, news articles, and biographies of diverse women with a variety of careers. Use students' stereotypes as starting points for discussion. They probably know that girls can be secretaries, but do they know that girls can be financial planners? Extend their awareness of the possibilities. Is baseball only for boys? Pose questions that connect careers with early education and training. What skills do you need to be a maintenance supervisor?

If the girls are absent from class in order to visit job sites, will the boys feel left out? How will you handle this teaching challenge? Both boys and girls can benefit from increased awareness of career possibilities. Plan to use this day to discuss opportunities for men and women.

Contact the Ms. Foundation on the Web to find out what others are planning in your area: www.ms.foundation.org.

Women's Hall of Fame

Women have been left out of most accounts of history. They are rarely seen as developers of ideas, initiators of events, or inventors of technology.

The National Women's Hall of Fame, located in Seneca Falls, New York (76 Fall Street, Seneca NY 13148) conducted a survey of more than three hundred historians and scholars to determine who were considered the most influential American women of the twentieth century. The following are the top ten names. How many of these women are familiar to students?

1. Eleanor Roosevelt
2. Jane Addams
3. Rosa Parks
4. Margaret Sanger
5. Margaret Mead
6. Charlotte Perkins Gilman
7. Betty Friedan
8. Barbara Jordan
9. Helen Keller
10. Alice Paul

Use this list as a starting point for a discussion of women's achievements. Groups of students can research each woman's life and accomplishments to determine why she was voted into the Women's Hall of Fame.

This list includes two African American women but there are no Asian, Latina, or Native American women. Challenge students to develop their own list: Who do they think belongs in the Women's Hall of Fame?

Offer students biographies that illustrate the range of women's roles, from politics to science to sports.

Who Are These Women?

Stimulate students to investigate the lives of influential women, past and present. Have students select an individual by drawing a name out of a hat. They can prepare a report on that person's life and present it to the class so that all students learn more about these people. Students can write a diary entry for a significant day in the person's life. They can prepare artifacts, or appropriate objects, to accompany their presentation, such as eye goggles, a compass, and a map for Amelia Earhart. The following names provide a representative selection of different ethnic groups with which to start. You can also include names of local community interest.

Ruth Bader Ginsburg	Bessie Coleman	Sojourner Truth
Kristi Yamaguchi	Bonnie Blair	Barbara Jordan
Rosa Parks	Golda Meir	Indira Gandhi
Althea Gibson	Wilma Rudolph	Florence Griffith Joyner
Susan Butcher	Nancy Lopez	Sally Ride
Toni Morrison	Rita Dove	Gwendolyn Brooks
Zora Neale Hurston	Elizabeth Blackwell	Eleanor Roosevelt
Amelia Earhart	Marian Anderson	Mary McLeod Bethune
Judith Jamison	Wilma Mankiller	Elizabeth Cady Stanton
Joan of Arc	Margaret Thatcher	Maria Tallchief
Hillary Clinton	Katherine Dunham	Harriet Beecher Stowe
Sacagawea	Abigail Adams	Joan Baez
Maya Angelou	Amy Tan	Olga Korbut
Georgia O'Keeffe	Frida Kahlo	Faith Ringgold

These books will help students begin their study:

Nancy Kline. *Elizabeth Blackwell: A Doctor's Triumph.* Conari Press, 1997. Biography of first woman doctor in United States. Finally admitted to medical school in 1847, she struggled all her life to be accepted as a doctor, fought for public health, and advocated better health education for women.

Barbara Kramer. *Amy Tan: Author of the Joy Luck Club.* Enslow, 1996. One in a series of biographies for older students, this book looks at the Chinese American author's childhood and her struggle to get published.

Elaine Slivinski Lisandrelli. *Maya Angelou: More than a Poet.* Enslow, 1996. This biography for older students covers the famous African American's life from a troubled childhood to success as an artist and writer.

Reeve Lindbergh. *Nobody Owns the Sky.* Illustrated by Pamela Paparone. Candlewick Press, 1996. A picture book biography of Bessie Coleman, first licensed African American aviator.

Kathleen Krull, *Wilma Unlimited: How Wilma Rudolph Became the World's Fastest Woman.* Illustrated by David Diaz. Harcourt Brace, 1996. A biography of African American athlete who overcame physical disabilities, for primary grades.

Paul Lang. *Maria Tallchief.* Enslow, 1997. Biography of Native American ballet dancer, for middle school.

Shiobhan Donohue. *Kristi Yamaguchi: Artist on Ice.* Lerner, 1994. Description of skater's life and career with photos, for intermediate to middle school students.

Russell Freedman. *Eleanor Roosevelt: A Life of Discovery.* Clarion, 1993. Shows how Roosevelt overcame lack of support from her family, who considered her an ugly duckling, and her own shyness to create a new role as First Lady. She established herself as an individual, not just a politician's wife, and continued to make significant contributions after her husband's death.

Patricia McKissack. *Sojourner Truth: Ain't I a Woman?* Scholastic, 1992. A biography for intermediate students presents the life of the extraordinary woman who was born a slave in 1797 and died in 1883. Although she couldn't read or write, she became an eloquent speaker for the abolition of slavery.

Tonya Bolden. *And Not Afraid to Dare: Stories of Ten African American Women.* Scholastic, 1998. Women from Ellen Craft to Toni Morrison are included, for middle school students.

Role Models

Who can girls (and boys) look to for role models in today's world? In 1997, the Ms. Foundation published a list of ten women whose "achievements create new opportunities for today's girls." Discuss these women and their accomplishments with students.

- Madeleine Albright, Secretary of State
- General Claudia Kennedy, first female Army three-star general
- Dee Kantner and Violet Palmer, first female referees for National Basketball Association

- Jody Williams, Nobel Peace Prize winner for campaign to ban land mines
- Phile Chionescu, organizer of the Million Woman March
- Ellen DeGeneres, actress who brought lesbian issues to popular TV show when she came out
- Oprah Winfrey, talk show host organized on-air book club.
- Kira Colvin, eight-year-old science whiz in National Science Olympiad
- Christy Haubbeger, founder of *Latina,* a magazine for Hispanic women

Older students can plan their own project on role models, perhaps including men as well as women. After discussing the qualities that they would look for in a role model, they can begin to collect information about potential role models from books and magazines over a period of time. After students develop a list of candidates, they can report on their nominees and the class can vote on its list of *Role Models of the Year.*

Women's Suffrage

When did women get the right to vote? Not until 1920, after black men and before Native Americans. Why did it take so long? Investigate the history of rights for women, from "suffrage" to the Equal Rights Amendment.

Books to start with are:

Gwenyth Swain. *The Road to Seneca Falls: A Story about Elizabeth Cady Stanton.* Carolrhoda, 1996. How Stanton and Lucretia Mott organized the women's rights convention in 1848.

Jean Fritz. *You Want Women to Vote, Lizzie Stanton?* Putnam, 1995. For intermediate students, an account by noted historical writer.

Women in Folklore

Positive models and stories of successful women can help us persevere, overcoming obstacles and others' lack of faith. Folktales, a traditional source of community wisdom, often reflect stereotypical roles for men and women. However, alternative models do exist. Present tales of strong women to counteract popular folklore images, such as Cinderella and Sleeping Beauty, of passive women who need a man to rescue them.

Robert San Souci. *Cut from the Same Cloth: American Women of Myth, Legend and Tall Tale.* Illustrated by Brian Pinkney. Philomel, 1993. Less well known tales of strong and determined women, including African and Native American traditions.

Ethel Johnston Phelps. *The Maid of the North: Feminist Folk Tales from around the World.* Holt, 1981. Stories with interesting and clever heroines; a good resource for storytelling.

Suzanne I. Barchers. *Wise Women: Folk and Fairy Tales from around the World.* Teacher Ideas Press, 1990. Collection of stories and teaching ideas.

Aaron Shepard. *Savitri: A Tale of Ancient India.* Whitman, 1992. A strong-woman story from the Mahabharata.

Virginia Hamilton. *Her Stories: African American Folktales, Fairy Tales, and True Tales.* Illustrated by Leo and Diane Dillon. Scholastic, 1995. This collection of 19 tales includes captivating stories and legends.

Verna Aardema. *Borreguita and the Coyote.* Knopf, 1991. In a tale from Mexico, a clever ewe lamb outwits Coyote.

Peter Asbjornsen. *The Squire's Bride.* Illustrated by Marcia Sewall. Atheneum, 1975. In this Norwegian tale, the farmer's daughter escapes an undesirable suitor.

Walter de la Mare. *Molly Whuppie.* Farrar, 1983. Traditional English folktale of the youngest daughter who outwits a giant.

Anne Isaacs. *Swamp Angel.* Illustrated by Paul Zelinsky. Dutton, 1994. Tall tale about the feats of Angelica Longrider, the greatest woodswoman of Tennessee.

Patricia McKissack. *Flossie and the Fox.* Dial, 1986. African American girl outwits a clever fox.

Featuring Women Artists

Show students that art is not the sole property of dead, white, European males. The following books will broaden students' ideas about art and may inspire some to follow in the footsteps of these famous women.

Leslie Sills. *Visions: Stories about Women Artists.* Whitman, 1993. This collection features Mary Cassatt, Leonora Carrington, Betye Saar, and Mary Frank. Although they came from different backgrounds and lived at different times, they all had to overcome similar obstacles to pursue their careers as artists.

Leslie Sills. *Inspirations: Stories about Women Artists.* Whitman, 1989. An introduction to four diverse women artists (Georgia O'Keeffe, Frida Kahlo, Alice Neel, Faith Ringgold) with brief biographies and generous color reproductions of their works.

Peggy Roalf. *Self-Portraits.* Hyperion, 1993.

Peggy Roalf. *Children.* Hyperion, 1993. These books show how different artists have treated the same theme. The artists selected include women and men of diverse backgrounds. *Self-Portraits* features Frida Kahlo on the cover; *Children* features Mary Cassatt.

Linda Lowery. *Georgia O'Keeffe.* Carolrhoda, 1996. Biography of artist known for her paintings of American Southwest.

Robyn Montana Turner. *Frida Kahlo.* Little Brown, 1993. From the series Portraits of Women Artists for Children. Other books in the series include *Rosa Bonheur, Georgia O'Keeffe, Mary Cassatt,* and *Faith Ringgold.*

(For more information on women artists, contact The National Museum of Women in the Arts, 1250 New York Ave, NW, Washington DC 20005–3920.)

Countering Sex Stereotypes in Children's Literature

Frequently you will encounter examples of stereotyped thinking and behavior in books that you use with students in the classroom. Over 75% of the characters in children's books are male. In addition, the male characters tend to take action, while the female characters stand on the sidelines. Stereotypes weaken the value of these books because they result in cardboard characters and predictable plots. However, you cannot eliminate all examples of stereotyping. Instead, help students practice critical thinking skills by identifying stereotypes and evaluating sexism in the books they read. An example of such stereotyping is *Sylvester and the Magic Pebble* by William Steig (Simon and Schuster, 1969). Although the characters are drawn as donkeys, they conform to stereotyped sex roles. The mother donkey wears an apron and acts "helpless," the father donkey sits smoking his pipe and reading the newspaper while his wife sweeps under his feet. Discuss with students the message communicated by these illustrations and accompanying text.

Select a well-known children's book such as Maurice Sendak's *Where the Wild Things Are* (Harper, 1963). Have students retell the story, changing the main character Max into Maxine. Can Maxine have the same adventures as Max? Discuss the changes with students. An alternative is to tell the story from another character's point of view.

Traditional folktales can be revised to reflect a different attitude towards men and women. For example, in *Rumpelstiltskin's Daughter,* by Diane Stanley (Morrow, 1997), the miller's daughter refuses to marry the king as expected and instead chooses Rumpelstiltskin. Students can write their own versions of familiar tales, changing the characters or changing the endings.

Analyzing Sexism in Children's Books

Students can begin to look critically at the material that they read in light of class discussion of sex-role stereotypes. Involve them in analyzing and collecting data. Students can count the number of male and female characters in books and categorize what kinds of activities these characters participate in. What do the characters say? Do they comment negatively on the abilities of boys or girls? Students can also look closely at the illustrations. How are the characters pictured? What effect does this have on the reader?

Have students assemble their data and prepare a report of what they have found. What conclusions do they draw based on their results? They can share this with other classes in the school or send it to the local newspaper.

Sex-Typed Play

Even children's toys and games perpetuate ideas of sex-role stereotypes. Ask students to list examples of boys' toys and girls' toys. What kinds of toys are considered suitable for boys? For girls? Might girls want to play with games that are supposed to be for boys? Or boys play with girls' games? What would happen? (Who has the most interesting, inventive games?) This discussion should result in increased options for boys' and girls' play and decreased negative response to behavior that does not fit sex-role stereotypes.

Students can also investigate use of sex-role stereotypes in the marketing of toys and games. Look at television commercials, packaging, and names. Can you tell whether they are directed at boys or girls? Why would manufacturers choose to do this? If students study examples of stereotyping, they may want to write letters to the companies, explaining their investigation and their findings. They can also make recommendations for changes.

Positive Models in Books for Children

We know that books transmit values to children, particularly when the messages are subtle. As much as possible, choose books that portray males and females in nonstereotyped roles and in multicultural settings. Share with students old favorites such as *Madeline* by Ludwig Bemelmans and *Pippi Lonstocking* by Astrid Lindgren. Here are some more recent books that you will enjoy.

Especially for the Primary Grades

Jay Williams. *Petronella*. Parents, 1974. This king's daughter does not want to play the passive princess.

Camille Yarbrough. *The Shimmershine Queens*. Putnam, 1989. Self-esteem and achievement counter the negative image of sexism and racism that face black girls.

Allen Say. *Emma's Rug*. Houghton Mifflin, 1996. Portrays the creative process from a little girl's point of view.

Barbara Cooney. *Miss Rumphius*. Viking, 1982. Alice Rumphius leads an exciting life but when she retires, she finds a way to make the world more beautiful.

Emily Arnold McCully. *Mirette on the High Wire*. Putnam, 1992. After Mirette learns tightrope walking, she helps her teacher conquer his fears.

Carole Lexa Schaefer. *The Squiggle*. Illustrated by Pierr Morgan. Crown, 1996. Story of the importance of imagination, illustrations feature a Chinese girl.

For Older Students

Patricia Wrede. *Dealing with Dragons*. Harcourt, Brace, Jovanovich, 1990. Princess Cimorene is not going to wait around for someone to rescue her. Look for more books about Cimorene's adventures.

Jerry Spinelli. *There's a Girl in My Hammerlock*. Simon and Schuster, 1991. Maisie faces opposition from her family and friends when she chooses wrestling.

Carol Ann Duffy. *I Wouldn't Thank You for a Valentine: Poems for Young Feminists*. Illustrated by Trisha Rafferty. Holt, 1994. Woman poets from many cultures and backgrounds tell of ways in which women are phenomenal.

Tryntje Van Ness Seymour. *The Gift of Changing Woman*. Holt, 1993. When an Apache girl comes of age, there is a special ceremony to teach her the story of creation and her place in the world.

Marilyn Levy. *Run For Your Life*. Houghton Mifflin, 1996. Based on the true story of the Oakland (CA) Acorn Track Team, shows how teamwork changed the lives of poor black girls.

Astrid Lindgren. *The Adventures of Pippi Longstocking*. Illustrated by Michael Chesworth. Viking, 1997. All of Pippi's adventures are collected in this new edition.

Sources of Information for Teaching about Gender: Searching for Equity

Myself and Women Heroes in My World; Women at Work, Home and School; Women as Members of Groups; and *Women as Members of Communities*. These integrated social studies/language arts elementary curriculum units are available from National Women's History Project, 7738 Bell Road, Windsor, CA 95492–8518. They include both famous (Harriet Tubman) and not-so-famous (Dolores Huerta) women of the past and the present.

Carol Burgoa and Barbara Tomin. *Multicultural Women's History Curriculum Unit.* Available from NWHP (see address above). A variety of cross-curricular activities for intermediate grades cover five women of different ethnic backgrounds and time periods: Mary Shadd Cary, abolitionist; Tye Leung Schulze, immigration officer at Angel Island (CA); Frances Willard, leader of the WCTU; Felisa Rincón de Gautier, former mayor of San Juan, Puerto Rico; and Ada Deer, Native American rights activist.

National Women's History Project. *Women's History Resources.* Updated regularly. This book contains state and national lists of information, people, and publishers as well as annotated lists of resources for Native American, Asian, Hispanic, and African American women. Also see www.nwhp.org/.

Edward T. James and Janet Wilson James, eds. *Notable American Women 1607–1950.* 3 vols. Short biographies of 1,359 women who influenced their time and society, including many from diverse ethnic backgrounds about whom little is known.

Barbara Sicherman and Carol Hurd Green. *Notable American Women: The Modern Period.* A companion to the earlier work includes 442 biographies of historically significant women who died between 1951 and 1975.

Edith Blicksilver. *The Ethnic American Woman: Problems, Protests, Lifestyle.* The voices of women, both historical and contemporary, representing twenty-five different ethnic groups.

Connecting the Past into the Future: Women in Mathematics and Science. Videos and print material on Ada Lovelace, Mary Somerville. Dale Seymour Press.

Emma Hahn. *16 Extraordinary American Women.* J. Weston Walch, 1996. Two-page biographies of famous women, including Cherokee leader Wilma Mankiller, black singer Ella Fitzgerald, Hawaiian princess Ka'iulani, black Congressperson Barbara Jordan, and black poet Nikki Giovanni. For intermediate students, includes comprehension questions.

Profiles of Women Past and Present: Women's History Monologues for Group Presentations. Thousand Oaks Branch of the American Association of University Women, PO Box 4223, Thousand Oaks CA 91359–1223. 1996. Monologues based on the lives of fifteen famous American women. One set is for primary grades, another for intermediate students, along with instructions for performing them.

Nell Irvin Painter. *Sojourner Truth: A Life, A Symbol.* Norton, 1996. Sojourner Truth's role as a symbol has obscured the facts of her life. This adult biography shows her as even more of a heroine.

Women of Hope: Poster Portfolios. Bread and Roses Cultural Project, Local 1199. 330 West 42nd St., 4th floor, New York NY 10036. One set of 12 posters honors Latinas, the other 12 honor African American women. Women chosen, mostly contemporary, represent a range of occupations and have in common their commitment to equity and justice. Includes a study guide with biographical information.

Martha Wheelock. *Madeleine L'Engle: Star Gazer.* Videotape available from Ishtar Films. PO Box 51, Patterson NY 12563 or 6253 Hollywood Blvd, Suite 623, Hollywood CA 90028. Biography of noted author, discusses her ideas and life story.

Kathleen Krull. *Lives of Athletes: Thrills, Spills, and What the Neighbors Thought.* Harcourt, 1997. Short biographies of famous athletes, women as well as men.

Darleene Stille, *Extraordinary Women Scientists.* Children's Press, 1995. Fifty short biographies, from Maire Curie to Rosalind Franklin. Intermediate to middle school students.

Mavis Jukes. *It's a Girl Thing: How to Stay Healthy, Safe, and in Charge.* Knopf, 1996.

Catherine Dee. *The Girl's Guide to Life.* Little Brown, 1997.

REFLECTIONS

Students need to reflect on who they are and what forces have influenced them. As teachers, we offer them that opportunity by bringing their own background into the classroom. We offer books and activities that help them recognize themselves. We value what they have to bring to the classroom instead of making them over in one image. We model learning as a process of integrating and connecting who we are with what we know.

APPLICATIONS

1. In your learning journal, write a response to the Hillel quote that opens this chapter. Many approaches to cross-cultural learning have focused on learning about "the other." In what ways might learning about yourself strengthen your learning about others? In your experience, what has helped you to understand people from other groups?

2. How do you plan to organize your classroom and your curriculum to promote equity for both sexes? Plan a unit on sex-role stereotyping. What materials and activities will you use? How will you assess student learning? How will you evaluate sex-role stereotyping in children's literature? Develop your own form for evaluation. How will you rate text, illustrations, format? Presence or absence of positive and negative features? Characters' behavior, language, roles? Select five books to evaluate using this form, perhaps Caldecott (picture books) or Newbery (chapter books) Medal winners. Report your findings to the class.

3. In your CLG, explore how you learned about *difference* as a young child. When and how did you learn that other people were different from you? What differences were the most salient to you as a child—sex, age, race, social class? What messages did you absorb from your family, friends, community about the "Other" group that were defined as "not like Us"? When you went to school, did you find that the classroom "mirrored" your experience? Or was it foreign to you? Discuss how this affected you.

EXPLORING FURTHER

The AAUW Report. (1992). *How Schools Shortchange Girls.* Washington, DC: AAUW and NEA.

Mary Field Belenky, et al. (1986). *Women's Ways of Knowing: The Development of Self, Voice and Mind.* New York Basic Books.

Janet Mancini Billson. (1995). *Keepers of the Culture: The Power of Traditions in Women's Lives.* Columbus, OH: Lexington Books.

Lyn Mikel Brown, & Carol Gilligan. (1993). *Meeting at the Crossroads.* New York: Ballantine.

Susan Bullard. (1996). *Teaching Tolerance: Raising Open-Minded, Empathetic Children.* New York: Doubleday.

California State Department of Education. (1986). *Beyond Language: Social and Cultural Factors in Schooling Language Minority Students.* Sacramento CA: Author.

Jack Canfield, & Harold Wells. (1994). *100 Ways to Enhance Self-Concept in the Classroom* (2nd ed.). Boston: Allyn & Bacon.

Louise Derman-Sparks, & Carol Brunson Phillips. (1997). *Teaching/Learning Anti-Racism: A Developmental Approach.* New York: Teachers College Press.

Karen Gallas. (1998). *"Sometimes I Can Be Anything": Power, Gender, and Identity in a Primary Classroom.* New York: Teachers College Press.

Carol Gilligan. (1982). *In a Different Voice: Psychological Theory and Women's Development.* Camridge, MA: Harvard University Press.

Mary Pipher. (1994). *Reviving Ophelia.* New York: Putnam.

Patricia Ramsey. (1987). *Teaching and Learning in a Diverse World: Multicultural Education for Younger Children.* New York: Teachers College Press.

Virginia Beane Rutter. (1996). *Celebrating Girls: Nurturing and Empowering Our Daughters.* Emeryville, CA: Conari.

Myra & David Sadker. (1994). *Failing at Fairness: How America's Schools Cheat Girls.* New York: Macmillan.

Robert Slavin, Nancy Karweit, & Barbara Wasik. (1994). *Preventing Early School Failure: Research on Effective Strategies.* Boston: Allyn & Bacon.

Peter Smagorinsky. (1991). *Expression: Multiple Intelligences in the English Class.* Urbana, IL: National Council of Teachers of English TRIP booklet.

Barbara Thomson. (1993). *Words Can Hurt You: Beginning a Program of Anti-Bias Education.* Reading, MA: Addison-Wesley.

D. R. Walling, ed. (1996). *Open Lives, Safe Schools.* Bloomington, IN: Phi Delta Kappa Educational Foundation.

e

pluribus

unum

6

Building a Community of Learners

All children come to school as members of specific cultural groups. Along with their native language, they learned a particular way of being in the world; they were socialized into their culture. And they come to school carrying their parents' hopes for the future.

In this chapter we consider multicultural learning through the lens of culture. The Brazilian educator Paulo Freire defines culture as anything that humans make. This broad definition serves to distinguish things cultural from things natural. Culture is what we elaborate on the basic biological framework that we are given. Less effort is required to focus on its visible, concrete aspects: food, shelter, music, clothing, art. However, on a deeper level, culture is invisible. We may be unaware of how our culture shapes our interpretation of the world, our perception of reality, our sense of what is normal. But the omnipresence of culture is expressed in the remark, "That's just the ways things are done around here."

From family and community members, children unconsciously absorb standards of behavior, attitudes towards authority, patterns of speaking, and spiritual values. But when they enter school, they are exposed to another set of values and expectations, called "school culture." In school, for example, students are expected to work independently and often competitively. They are called on to show off in front of others or to expose their imperfect reading. Rewards are given for speed and uniformity. How can we provide a bridge between students' home culture and the school? How can we keep students from feeling excluded? Today's multicultural classroom requires teaching that incorporates and responds to the many cultural influences affecting students' ability to learn.

The process of becoming a culturally responsive teacher has three facets. First, you have to learn about your own cultural background. Because so much of one's culture is taken for granted, this process entails making the unseen visible. Otherwise, you may unconsciously assume that the way you live is the only way to live (provincialism) or that your own cultural system is superior to others (ethnocentrism). Instead of glossing over the differences in the way people think and act, we want to draw conscious attention to them. The more we understand why we make the judgments we do, the more we will be able to accept how other people can reach different conclusions.

The second facet of culturally responsive teaching involves learning about your students. Your students may, for example, know a language that you don't, practice a religious philosophy that is considerably older than your own, have made life-or-death choices that you hope never to face. A little humility, some admitted ignorance, and a willingness to learn more about others will help you cope with potentially overwhelming differences in culture.

The third facet of culturally responsive teaching requires you to share your own culture, your customs and beliefs, with the students. By doing so, you model respect for others and demonstrate how culture is important in everyone's life. This reciprocity makes it easier for students to inquire and explore: What does it mean when someone . . . ? A culturally responsive teacher can be a valuable translator and guide for students, helping them bridge the gap between the familiar and the unknown.

After reading this chapter, you should be able to:

- Provide a welcoming environment in the classroom for all students.
- Develop a positive classroom climate and community.
- Plan lessons that expose stereotyping and prejudice.
- Teach a unit based on quilts to help students understand the importance of diversity.
- Introduce students to aspects of Native American history and contemporary culture.

INCLUDING ALL STUDENTS

The first step in learning to work well together is getting to know one another. In today's schools, the students may not all come from the same community, so they may not be aware of backgrounds or experiences that they share with other students. In addition, a teacher who comes from a background different from that of the students must make an extra effort to get to know the students' community. Teachers can create unity among diverse students by helping students get to know one another, breaking down barriers of ignorance and suspicion, and providing the shared experience that creates group cohesiveness. The goal is to build an atmosphere of trust in the classroom. In order to learn, students need to feel comfortable taking risks and exposing themselves to the possibility of failure.

Welcoming Students

Challenge a group of older students to organize a "Welcome Club" that would assume responsibility for personally welcoming newcomers to the school. Students of all levels could be part of this team effort. Encourage students to brainstorm possibilities for making students feel at home in their new surroundings. They might ask themselves, "What would make me feel good about coming to a new school?" Here are some ideas.

- Introduce the student to several children who live near him or her.
- Meet the child at the principal's office to express a welcome and to introduce him or her to the classroom teacher.

- Give the newcomer a small gift, such as a welcome card made by students or a flower to pin on (if everyone knows this symbol, they can be encouraged to smile their own welcome or to say hello).
- Assign a buddy in the class to help the newcomer with classroom routines.

Getting to Know Each Other

An activity for the beginning of the year is to ask each student to write ten things about himself or herself. Students can list anything, for example:

Alice Hafoka
I get up at 5:30 each morning to deliver papers.
I live next to Julio and Uriel.
My favorite food is groundnut stew.

Students can exchange their lists. Working in small groups, each person then introduces the student whose paper he or she received. The student introducing Alice might say:

I'd like you to meet Alice Hafoka. She gets up at 5:30 every morning and makes breakfast for her brothers and sisters. I'm impressed—my mother won't let me cook anything on the stove. Her favorite food is groundnut stew. That's an African dish. Groundnuts are also called peanuts.

A Class Directory

Type a list of the students' names to give to the children in your room. You may include their addresses, birthdays, or other information that might interest the children as they become acquainted. They will be highly motivated to read this directory even though names of students and streets may be difficult.

Have students introduce themselves according to this listing. They may simply say, "I am Takasoto Watanabe. I live on Fairglen Avenue." Or they might add other information, such as what they like to do on Saturdays or where they were born. Ask the students what they would like to know about each other and what each is willing to share.

If you ask students to include information about their hobbies and what they like to do in their free time, they can identify other students who might share their interests. This is an easy way to break down barriers and help students become friends with people from different groups.

How We Differ, How We Are the Same

Discuss with students some of the ways in which they differ from one another. They are different sizes, and they wear different clothes. Some of them have straight hair, some curly. They come from different families; some of them have older or younger brothers and sisters, and some do not; their parents have different kinds of jobs. Extend this discussion to explore the multitude of factors that make up individual identity:

We live in different places (house, apartment, farm).
We were born in different places.
We enjoy different recreational activities.
We are good at different skills and activities.

Are there advantages to being different from each other? What can we learn from these differences?

Now look at the other side. Discuss with students the ways in which they are similar. Make a list of factors that make up the experience of community:

We are about the same age.
We live in the same area.
We are in the same grade.
We are all learning new things.

Students can make a chart for their class comparing these differences and similarities. They will notice the relative insignificance of the differences in light of the similarities.

Mapping Our Origins

Because students are curious about one another, use a map to show where students were born and where their families come from. Mark locations with pins and name tags. Connect the pins to the classroom location with yarn. Which students have come the farthest? How many students were born outside the United States? How many were born in a different state? Where have students traveled? Have any of them visited other countries?

What languages do the students speak? If you include the languages their parents speak, how many languages are represented in the classroom? Consider ways to use these differences as assets. Have students teach others a few words in another language. Ask students to tell the class about life in a different region. Was the weather different? Did they play different games? Ask newcomers what they found particularly different or hard to get used to in their new environment.

Children's Lore

Engage students in the study of children's folklore: riddle games, jump-rope rhymes, numbering chants, and so on. Children who come from different regions or different ethnolinguistic backgrounds can compare their versions. Are the same rhymes used by children from different parts of the United States? The class can make a collection of the stories and verses that they collect. They may be surprised to learn that adult scholars study children's folklore.

For a description of the origins of this field, see Iona and Peter Opie, *The Lore and Language of Schoolchildren* (Clarendon Press, 1960). This work reports an extensive study of children in Britain. Students can compare the folklore that they collected with the British versions.

A classic American collection is *A Rocket in My Pocket: The Rhymes and Chants of Young Americans* by Carl Withers (Holt, 1988), which includes over four hundred verses.

Cooperation

Talk about ways we depend on other people. What would we do without people in the helping professions—firefighters, police, nurses, doctors? Bring an article from the newspaper about people helping one another to share with the class.

Students also help each other. Discuss the importance of assisting other people in school or at home. Have students answer the following questions:

- How do you help your family?
- How do your family and neighbors help each other?
- How does a friend help you?
- How can students help each other at school?

Differences in answers may reveal some of the cultural diversity in what is considered *acceptable* helping behavior. Sometimes, "helping" someone can get you into trouble, like helping with the answers on a test. Students can discuss these differences and develop a list of acceptable helping behaviors for the classroom.

Using the information on the list, prepare a chart for the classroom so that all students understand the rules and new students will be able to fit in easily.

Cooperative Learning

Many teachers are implementing plans for small-group learning that are cooperatively rather than competitively based. In cooperative learning, students are assigned to teams containing heterogeneous skills and ability levels. All the members of the team are rewarded or recognized for the work done by the team. At the same time, students are accountable for their own work.

A cooperative classroom is not just a place where students work collaboratively and share materials but a structure in which students are rewarded as a group for collective behavior. Developing student interaction skills requires careful, ongoing feedback from the teacher. You can enlist your students' help in finding ways to work together effectively without giving in to the problem of domination by the few or pressure to conform.

In cooperative learning, students will learn to appreciate the different skills of others and the value of these skills. Because they are assigned to work with students they may not know, they will learn about people from different backgrounds. They will learn how to depend on others, learn from others, stand up for themselves, and handle disagreements. The following books provide examples and support for building a cooperative learning environment in your classroom.

Eliot Aronson, *Jigsaw Classroom*. Sage, 1987.

Shlomo Sharan et al. (Eds). *Cooperative Learning in the Classroom*. Erlbaum, 1984.

Susan Ellis and Susan Whalen. *Cooperative Learning: Getting Started*. Scholastic, 1990.

David Johnson and Roger Johnson. *Learning Together and Alone: Cooperative, Competitive, and Individualistic Learning*. 4th ed. Allyn & Bacon, 1994.

Robert Slavin. *Cooperative Learning: Theory, Research, and Practice*. 2nd ed. Allyn & Bacon, 1995.

Y. Sharan and Shlomo Sharan. *Expanding Cooperative Learning Through Group Investigation*. Teachers College Press, 1992.

Friendship

What is a friend? Why do we need friends? Read poems to students from the collection *I Like You, If You Like Me: Poems of Friendship* edited by Myra Cohn Livingston (McElderry, 1987). These capsules of the special emotion called friendship can serve as springboards for discussion of this topic, which is so important to children. Provide opportunities for students to reflect on what friendship means to them by writing a story, creating a poem, or drawing a picture. Publish their efforts in a class book called *Friendship Is. . . .* This book can be shared with other classes. Older students can read their stories or poetry to primary-grade students.

How does it come about that friends can make us feel better about ourselves? Discuss the qualities of friendship with students to start them thinking about similarities and differences. Do we expect our friends to be just like ourselves? Why or why not? How are our relationships with our friends different from our relations with our brothers and sisters? Explore the dimensions of friendship through books that talk about how far we should go for the sake of a friend, or books honoring friendships that cross boundaries such as race, sex, or age.

Patricia Polacco. *Chicken Sunday.* Philomel, 1992. Two African American boys and a friend (the author as a girl) try to earn enough money to buy the boy's grandmother an Easter hat from a Jewish shopkeeper.

Judith Nigna. *Black Like Kyra, White Like Me.* Whitman, 1996. Two little girls learn first hand about prejudice.

Lucille Clifton. *Everett Anderson's Friend.* Holt, 1976. Everett is disappointed in his new neighbor because she's a girl. But it turns out all right when he finds she can run and play ball.

Marcia Savin. *The Moon Bridge.* Scholastic, 1992. The friendship of two fifth-grade girls survives the hatred and prejudice of World War II, even when Mitzi Fujimoto, a Japanese American, is sent to an internment camp.

Mildred Taylor. *The Friendship.* Bantam, 1989. Two friends are divided by racial prejudice.

Dirlie Herlihy. *Ludie's Song.* Puffin, 1990. In Georgia in the 1950s, Marty goes against community prejudice by making friends with a black family.

Jean Little. *Different Dragons.* Viking, 1986. This story by a Canadian writer features a boy who has a secret fear. When he makes friends with a neighborhood girl, he learns that everyone has different dragons to overcome.

Bruce Coville. *Jeremy Thatcher, Dragon Hatcher.* Harcourt Brace Jovanovich, 1991. At first, Jeremy is embarrassed that Mary Lou is the only one who understands him.

Jerry Spinelli. *Maniac Magee.* Scholastic, 1990. An extraordinary boy brings racially divided communities together.

Yoshiko Uchida. *The Bracelet.* Philomel, 1993. Before Japanese American Emi and her family are taken to the relocation center, her friend Laurie gives her a bracelet as a symbol of their friendship.

Kevin Henkes. *Words of Stone.* Greenwillow, 1992. Two motherless children, Blaze and Joselle, find comfort in each other.

Additional Resources

From the Heart: Books and Activities about Friends by Jan Irving and Robin Currie (Teacher Ideas Press, 1993) includes literature-based programs and units, games, and speaking and writing activities for friendship-related themes in the primary grades. Books featured include *The Wednesday Surprise, Chester's Way, Frog and Toad Are Friends, Jessica, Won't Somebody Play with Me?,* and *Henry and Mudge.*

BREAKING DOWN PREJUDICE AND STEREOTYPES

Students bring unquestioned stereotypes and expectations to the classroom that they have picked up from their own family, the media, and their experiences outside of school. In order to work together, students have to learn how to bring these out into the open and examine them through discussion. Students already know about bias and fair and unfair approaches to life. Teachers can help them see how to generalize from their individual experiences with prejudice to a positive approach to diversity.

Establishing a Baseline

Stereotypes are often based on lack of information. Before beginning a unit of study, take time to find out what students know or think they know about the subject. Brainstorm ideas, phrases, sentences, and feelings with the class and keep a record of what the students produce. This simple preassessment can be used to design exercises or activities based on student misconceptions or ignorance. It can also serve to test what students have learned by the end of the unit. You can use the same brainstorming technique and compare the two lists, or you can present the first list as a question-and-answer or true-false exercise to assess change.

Stereotypes of Animals

Many people have developed rigid ideas about specific animals, and children learn this when quite young. Have students verbalize these stereotypes by describing the following animals in one or two words: mouse, fox, deer. Where do these ideas come from? Have they ever seen one of these animals? If a student has had a mouse as a pet, he or she may give specific examples to contradict the general statements made by others.

Focus on one animal, such as the wolf. Have students describe this animal. Record what they say in writing or on a cassette. Then read a story that portrays a sympathetic picture of the wolf, such as *The Friendly Wolf* by Dorothy and Paul Goble, *Mowgli and His Brothers* by Rudyard Kipling, or *Julie and the Wolves* by Jean Craighead George.

After completing the story, ask students to comment on what wolves are like. Record this session also. Play the first recording for the class. Has there been a change of opinion? Why?

Recent studies of wolf behavior in the wild have demonstrated that the wolf's reputation for being a "rapacious killer" is unfounded. In fact, wolves seem to possess many of the qualities associated with dogs, including sociability, lack of aggression, and family loyalty. Yet the negative image from "Little Red Riding Hood" remains. Challenge this picture by having students rewrite the story from the wolf's point of view. All we know is Little

Red Riding Hood's side. What if she were wrong? What might have happened, according to the wolf? Or students could write the grandmother's experience. What really happened to her? Discuss several different solutions offered, stressing the idea that there is not one "correct" answer.

If White *Means Good, Then* Black *Means . . .*

Children quickly learn to make the association that *white* = good and *black* = evil, and to transfer this association to people. The many references in our society that represent black as evil or bad serve to reinforce this association. To help students become more aware of how their attitudes are conditioned, discuss expressions that include black. List examples given by students. How many of them are positive, how many negative?

blackmail	black lie	black magic	black market
black rage	blackout	black sheep	black humor
Black Death	in black and white	blacken	in the black

What does *black* mean in each of these expressions? What does *black* mean when we are talking about a person's skin color? Does the word *black* used in the expressions Black Power and "Black is beautiful" have any connection with the expressions listed? These are important questions for students to discuss in order to confront the stereotype of *black*.

Point out that despite the overwhelming number of negative associations, we can still find some affirmative meanings for the color *black*. Consider the circumstances in which wearing black signals respect, for example, at funerals, for ministers, for formal occasions.

Defining Stereotype

Now that students have seen for themselves examples of stereotypes and how they color our thinking, you can talk about the term itself and what it means. Do they know *stereo* from *stereophonic?* Or *stereoscopic?* They probably associate *stereo* with two (speakers, pictures) but actually it refers to the three-dimensional quality obtained by using two speakers for sound or two pictures for vision. How is this related to *stereotype?* Have students look up the word, preferably in different dictionaries, and compare definitions. Can they see the connection between *stereo* and *stereotype?* (A stereotype reduces the complex, multidimensional nature of human beings, or other things, to a single statement, image, or attitude.)

After completing a unit on stereotypes, have students write their own definitions of *stereotype.* Collect these in a book and discuss.

Images of Native Americans

Students are surrounded by negative and inaccurate images of Native Americans or Indians. Many materials used in schools reinforce these and are demeaning. Talk about the ideas students have about Native Americans. Brainstorm a list on the board or on a chart of all the information students can think of. They will probably reflect the common stereotypes of Native Americans as savages, fighters, or primitives. They may mention rain dances or tom-tom drums. Many may think the Native Americans had no language other than grunts or gestures.

Use this list to investigate the reality and rich variation of Native American life. Look at the Native American groups that used to live in your area. What happened to them? What were they like? Research the present situation for Native Americans. Check the stereotypes against the facts. How would students feel if someone used these stereotypes about them? Would they be insulted? How might Native American children feel when students play "Cowboys and Indians"?

Discuss the stereotypes that students had. Do they still think these are true? Talk about where they got their stereotyped information and compare it to their current study. Why do most people still hold the same old inaccurate, insulting ideas?

Use this technique to deal with stereotypes about any group represented in the classroom. The best way to handle omnipresent stereotyping is to confront it directly, identify it as stereotyping, present facts that contradict the stereotypes, and model recognition and acceptance of diversity. Because stereotypes are subtle and pervasive, you will need to remind students of these understandings and reinforce them again and again.

Evaluating Books for Children

How can you evaluate literature for use in the classroom? We need to examine books in terms of (1) realistic portrayals of members of ethnic groups, (2) inclusion of a fair representation of persons that make up our society, and (3) an honest attempt to break down existing stereotypes and prejudices.

You can design your own checklist especially to fit your purposes. You can also guide students in developing a checklist and in applying this instrument. A simple checklist might look something like this:

Book Title _____

Author _____ Publisher _____ Year _____

Illustrator _____ Pages _____

Positive images: Negative images:

Story | *Art*   *Story* | *Art*

_____|_____ women   _____|_____ women

_____|_____ men   _____|_____ men

_____|_____ aged persons   _____|_____ aged persons

_____|_____ ethnic groups   _____|_____ ethnic groups
               (list below)   (list below)

This checklist notes only what is present. The lack of checkmarks means, therefore, that there was nothing offensive, but that neither was there a positive effort to combat stereotypes.

Comparing Evaluations of Books

Students can compare their evaluation of specific books with evaluations that have been published. The Council on Interracial Books for Children, for example, has published

Guidelines for Selecting Bias-Free Textbooks and Storybooks (1994), which analyzes contemporary books. Older students could easily read this report and discuss the evaluation. Here are two sample evaluations, one for *Ludell,* a book ranked outstanding, and the second for *Three Fools and a Horse,* a book that was severely criticized.

Ludell

Brenda Wilkinson. Harper and Row, 1975. Grades 5 and up.

In this sensitive and powerful novel, the positive and the negative sides of growing up in a rural southern Black community are revealed through the eyes of fifth-grader Ludell. The place is Waycross, Georgia, in the 1950s where Ludell Wilson lives with her grandmother ("Mama"). Next door is the Johnson crew: Mrs. Johnson, sixteen-year-old Mattie and her child, Ruthie Mae (Ludell's best friend), Willie, Hawk, and Cathy.

Ludell's keen perceptions expose the harsh underside of life in Waycross—the poverty, the selfishness and unconcern of her teachers in the segregated school she attends, the constant reminders that both Mama and Mrs. Johnson work as maids in white people's homes. Whenever racism and oppression are manifest, it is commented upon and clearly defined.

Each experience, whether humorous or tragic, contributes to Ludell's growing awareness of herself and of others. The reader can sense that one day her aspirations will lead her to seek a life outside of Waycross and to exercise more control over her destiny.

Author Wilkinson effectively captures the subtle nuances of Black southern dialect and draws readers inside the Black experience. In addition she provides a truly positive role model for young Black readers. Ludell has a keen sense of who she is, shares with those less fortunate than herself and is shown overcoming adversities in her life.

	Art	Words		Art	Words			Art	Words	N.A.
anti-Racist		✓	non-Racist			Racist	Omission			
							Commission			
anti-Sexist			non-Sexist		✓	Sexist				
anti-Elitist		✓	non-Elitist			Elitist				
anti-Materialist			non-Materialist		✓	Materialist				
anti-Individualist		✓	non-Individualist			Individualist				
anti-Ageist			non-Ageist		✓	Ageist				
anti-Conformist			non-Conformist		✓	Conformist				
anti-Escapist		✓	non-Escapist			Escapist				
Builds positive image of females/ minorities		✓	Builds negative image of females/ minorities				Excellent	Good	Fair	Poor
						Literary quality		✓		
Inspires action vs. oppression			Culturally authentic		✓	Art quality				

Three Fools and a Horse

Betty Baker. Illustrated by Glen Rounds. Macmillan. Grades 3 and up.

The Foolish People were an imaginary group invented by the Apaches as an object of humor. *Three Fools and a Horse* chronicles the misadventures of three of the Foolish People of Two Dog Mountain—Little Fool, Fat Fool, and Fool About. The trio decide they must have one of the horses of the "flat land men" (Plains Indians) in order to be "big men, the biggest men of the Foolish People." Little Fool challenges one of the flat land men to a horse race (Little Fool has no horse). Surprisingly, he wins the race and the horse. Unexpected consequences follow from the Fools' attempt to ride horseback.

Native American folk stories should be told by Native Americans, not appropriated from "folklore and anthropology magazines" and then vulgarized by whites. Ms. Baker has no business writing about the Foolish People if their stories are going to be, as they have been in this book, "combined, slightly changed and much elaborated. . . ." The Apache's Foolish People stories are entertaining in their own context, and their misrepresentation here is unethical and racist. Both the Fools (portrayed as ugly and self-seeking) and the Plains Indians (equally ugly and ridiculous) are maligned. The flat land people are differentiated in looks from the Fools only by the addition of leggings, braids, feathers and hook noses.

Though the author claims these stories taught moral lessons to Apache children, her book strongly reinforces the "heap dumb Injun" stereotype.

	Art	Words		Art	Words			Art	Words	N.A.
anti-Racist			non-Racist			Racist	Omission			
							Commission	✓	✓	
anti-Sexist			non-Sexist			Sexist				✓
anti-Elitist			non-Elitist	✓	✓	Elitist				
anti-Materialist			non-Materialist	✓	✓	Materialist				
anti-Individualist			non-Individualist	✓	✓	Individualist				
anti-Ageist			non-Ageist			Ageist				✓
anti-Conformist			non-Conformist	✓	✓	Conformist				
anti-Escapist			non-Escapist	✓	✓	Escapist				
Builds positive image of females/minorities			Builds negative image of females/minorities	✓	✓					
Inspires action vs. oppression			Culturally authentic							

	Excellent	Good	Fair	Poor
Literary quality		✓		
Art quality		✓		

Source: Adapted from *Human Values in Children's Books.* Council on Interracial Books for Children, Inc., 1841 Broadway, New York, NY.

Types of Stereotypes

Discuss the categories listed in the preceding evaluation. Ask students to think of an example of each of the types: Racist, Sexist, Elitist, Materialist, Individualist, Ageist, Conformist, Escapist. Can students define these terms? Why would we want to rate books along these lines? What do these terms have in common? Have students bring in their own books and talk about the presence or absence of these features. Discuss with the class what "N.A." means (not applicable—used on the preceding checklist).

Disability

One in ten of all American adults, 26 million people, are severely disabled, according to a 1994 survey. About 1.8 million Americans over age 6 use a wheelchair. Despite the frequent association of the terms "disabled" and "handicapped" with wheelchairs, people in wheelchairs make up only one part of the disabled population. More numerous are those with less visible disabilities: people who cannot walk a short distance, lift light objects, read normal print, or hear normal sound levels. When talking about diversity, be sure to include the children in your classroom who have invisible disabilities due to chronic illnesses, those whose mother or father uses a wheelchair because of multiple sclerosis, and those with family members or friends with cerebral palsy or Down's syndrome. There will be few families in the community who have not been touched by disability in some form, whether temporary or permanent, visible or invisible.

Although people are familiar with blue handicapped parking signs, the term "handicapped" has negative connotations, signaling inferior, less-than-human status. "Disabled" is preferred, but most disabled people would like to be treated as ordinary individuals who happen to lack a specific physical capability, not as people deprived of all their ability to function. Introduce models of disabled people to overcome student ignorance and embarrassment, provide an opportunity to respond to student curiosity, and develop student empathy with others.(See Chapter 8 for a discussion of American Sign Language.)

Michelle Edwards. *Alef-Bet: A Hebrew Alphabet Book.* Lothrop, Lee and Shepard, 1992. While the focus of this ABC book is on the Hebrew language, the illustrations feature warm family scenes with three children, the oldest in a wheelchair with spina bifida.

Nancy Hope Wilson. *Bringing Nettie Back.* Macmillan, 1992. Eleven-year-old Raz and Nettie are best friends until Nettie has a stroke and suffers brain damage. Raz has to accept that Nettie will never be the same.

Sally H. Alexander. *Mom's Best Friend.* Photographs by George Ancona. Macmillan, 1992. This is the author's second book about a mother who is blind. The book focuses on the extensive training of guide dogs for the blind and the period of adjustment required for both to work well together.

Jill Krementz. *How It Feels to Live with a Physical Disability.* Simon and Schuster, 1992. This is a good source for information about a particular disability. It includes photographs of twelve children, representing common disabilities, who tell their own stories.

Paula Fox. *Radiance Descending.* DK Ink, 1997. Paul resents his younger brother who has Down's syndrome.

Lori Wiener, Aprille Best, and Phillip A. Pizzo. *Be a Friend: Children Who Live with HIV Speak.* Albert Whitman, 1994. Children tell how it feels to be different and how they face rejection when people learn they are sick.

E. L. Konigsburg. *The View from Saturday.* Atheneum, 1996. Story of four 6th grade students. Their teacher is paraplegic. Newbery Medal winner.

B. Mikaelsen. *Stranded.* Hyperion, 1995. A twelve-year-old girl is self-conscious about her severed leg and must prove her self-reliance.

M. Thompson. *Andy and His Yellow Frisbee.* Woodbine House, 1996. Illustrates empathy and acceptance of a child with autism.

*E. Watson. *Talking to Angels.* Harcourt Brace, 1996. Author tells of experience with a sister who is autistic.

*P. McMahon. *Listen for the Bus: David's Story.* BoydMills, 1995. A blind and deaf boy's first day at kindergarten as well as life with his family, nonfiction.

*V. Fleming. *Be Good to Eddie Lee.* Illustrated by Floyd Cooper. Philomel, 1996. A boy with Down's syndrome seems a pest but he has something to contribute.

*J. S. Rheingrover. *Veronica's First Year.* Whitman, 1996. A brother's love for his baby sister with Down's syndrome.

*S. Kline. *Mary Marony Hides out.* Putnam, 1993. A second-grader is self-conscious about her stuttering.

How Does It Feel?

Have students go on a "blind walk" to experience the world in a different way. Each student in turn is blindfolded and led around the room and outdoors for a few minutes. After this exercise, discuss how students felt. What might it be like to be blind forever? What did they learn about the difficulties facing blind people? What adaptations would make the world more accessible for blind people? Perhaps students have noticed audio crosswalk signals or a seeing-eye dog. If students know anyone who is blind, have them share their experiences. How should students help someone who is blind?

Other exercises students can try include riding in a wheelchair and muffling their hearing. How do these conditions affect what they can or cannot do?

Students will learn that blind people, people in wheelchairs, and deaf people are still people like themselves. They can understand better the importance of "access" for the disabled, so that all people can participate fully in life.

Read more about the history of education for the blind.

Russell Freedman. *Out of Darkness: The Story of Louis Braille.* Illustrated by Kate Kiesler. Clarion, 1997. This biography for intermediate readers shows the generally bleak conditions for blind people in nineteenth century France. (A free Braille alphabet card is available from the American Foundation for the Blind, 15 West 16th Street, New York, NY 10011.)

Including Students with Special Needs

After sharing some of these fiction and nonfiction books about disabilities, involve students in studying their own community. They can develop empathy as they read, do research, and conduct interviews, in order to learn about the difficulties faced by their fellow students with disabilities as well as the contributions that these students can make to the classroom community. The Westridge Young Writers Workshop has provided a model that your students can follow in their *Kids Explore the Gifts of Children with Special Needs* (John Muir, 1994), a collaboration between elementary school students and ten special needs students who tell their stories.

Intergenerational Relations

1999 is the international year of the elderly, sponsored by the United Nations. Ask students if they know anyone who is "older." Perhaps a grandparent or other older relative is living with their family. What do we call these people? Labels that have been used include *senior citizen, aged, mature adult, retirees, third agers*. Which would students rather be called when they are old?

Relationships with people from another generation provide multiple opportunities for children. They can have relationships with adults who have time for them, grandparents and other older adults can tell them stories about the past and their childhood, and they can learn to see the world through the eyes of another person. The following books are useful for starting discussions and enriching a unit on families. They can also motivate students to investigate the treatment of older people in our society. Students may choose to visit a nursing home or to write letters to elderly people who have no family.

Some of the most stirring books in this category are picture books. These books will provoke thought when read aloud at any grade level.

Karen Ackerman. *The Song and Dance Man.* Knopf, 1988. The children are the audience as Grandpa transforms himself into the vaudeville performer he once was. Caldecott medal.

Eve Bunting. *The Wednesday Surprise.* Clarion, 1992. Anna helps her grandmother learn to read.

Judith Caseley. *Dear Annie.* Greenwillow, 1991. Annie has been receiving mail from her grandfather since she was born. At first her mother answers, but as she gets older, she responds on her own. She takes the collection of letters to school for show and tell. As a result, the class decides to begin a pen pal program.

Donald Crews. *BigMama's.* Greenwillow, 1991. Young Donald is pleased to find that everything is still the same on his annual summer visit to his grandmother's house. African American family. *Shortcut* is the sequel.

Arthur Dorros. *Abuela.* Dutton, 1991. Young Rosalba and her grandmother imagine wonderful flying adventures as they travel through New York.

Ana Sisnett. *Grannie Jus' Come!* Children's Book Press, 1997. A girl eagerly anticipates her beloved grandmother's weekly visit. Set in Panama, includes Caribbean English dialect.

Bettye Stroud. *Down Home at Miss Dessa's.* Illustrated by Felicia Marshall. Lee and Low, 1996. In the rural South, an elderly neighbor looks after children. They help each other. African American family.

Mem Fox. *Wilfred Gordon McDonald Partridge.* Kane/Miller, 1989. Wilfred lives next door to a nursing home. When Miss Nancy loses her memory, he asks the other people where to find it.

Gloria Houston. *My Great-Aunt Arizona.* HarperCollins, 1992. Arizona comes from Appalachia and grows up to become a teacher who influences generations of children.

Jeanne Lee. *Ba-Nam.* Holt, 1987. A young Vietnamese girl visiting her ancestors' graves finds the caretaker helpful.

Carmen Santiago Nodar. *Abuelita's Paradise.* Whitman, 1992. Marita listens to her grandmother's stories of growing up in Puerto Rico, a paradise.

Patricia Polacco. *Mrs. Katz and Tush.* Bantam, 1992. A special friendship develops between Mrs. Katz, an elderly Jewish widow, and Larnel, a young African American.

Books for Independent Readers

John Chech. *My Grandmother's Journey.* Bradbury, 1991. A Russian grandmother tells of her early life and how she came to the United States.

Eth Clifford. *The Remembering Box.* Houghton Mifflin, 1985. Nine-year-old Joshua learns about his family history from his grandmother when he visits her every Jewish Sabbath. The memories help him cope when she dies.

Kathryn Lasky. *The Night Journey.* Puffin, 1981. At first, thirteen-year-old Rachel finds her visits to her great-grandmother boring. But soon Rachel is caught up in Sashie's tales of the czar's armies, pogroms, and the time the nine-year-old Sashie planned her family's escape.

Patricia MacLachlan. *Journey.* Delacorte, 1991. Journey and Cat are dumped on their grandparents by their mother. In trying to overcome his feelings of abandonment, Journey develops a closer relationship with his grandparents.

Sharon Bell Mathis. *The Hundred Penny Box.* Scholastic, 1975. Michael's 100-year-old great-great-aunt has a special box filled with a penny for each year of her life.

Cynthia Rylant. *An Angel for Solomon Singer.* Orchard, 1992. An old man living in a residential hotel dreams of what he can't have, but a friendly waiter in a cafe gives him a kind of home.

COPING WITH CONFLICT AND CHANGE

Shared experiences through the year help bring students together. Remind students of past events and activities and help them reflect on the process of learning as it takes place. Students need guidance to find out how much they are alike underneath superficial differences. Set guidelines for dealing with conflict in advance. Organize students to resolve disagreements as a group.

Managing Conflict

What do people argue or fight about? Ask students to suggest areas where children and parents might disagree. Is it ever possible that both sides could be right? Does the biggest (or oldest or strongest) person always win?

Develop an analogy with a baseball game. Have students describe an argument and a baseball game. Write the characteristics on the board. Then ask students: "How is an argument like a baseball game?" Possible answers include the following:

- You make points off each other.
- One side wins.
- People get more and more involved.

Then ask them: "How is an argument different from a baseball game?" Possible answers include the following:

- You're not always on the same side.
- There's no umpire to make sure you fight fair.
- Both sides aren't evenly matched.

Although students may take time to warm up, they will enjoy this challenge as long as you reinforce the idea that there are no right or wrong answers.

After discussing situations that can lead to conflict, students may want to write their own examples of problems. These can be used for a finish-the-story activity (other students write an ending), creative drama (students act out the situation for the class to watch and comment on), or role-play (students take on the roles involved and develop them out of their own experience).

Playing a Part

Through role-play, students can experience potential sources of conflict and ways to reach an agreement in a nonthreatening way. Have the class generate a list of topics or situations. Even the shyest students will participate and contribute when they lose themselves in acting out the part of another person. The following are some guidelines to setting up a successful role-play.

1. Use props such as hats or masks to help students assume their roles.
2. Set a time limit. Keep role-plays short at first.
3. Assign students to partners or groups so that they don't always work with friends.
4. Give them an explicit, detailed situation or explanation to get started. Or have them draw the plot elements (who? what? where?) out of a box.
5. Start with focused sessions before you try open-ended, more complex situations.
6. Consider the best arrangement of the classroom and decide in advance where to place students.
7. Encourage all communication and praise originality.

Sample Topics for Role-Play

Role-play offers students a chance to think about and identify with the point of view of another person. Here are some topics that will stimulate heated discussion and involvement.

- Would you tell on a friend if you saw her break something but she told the teacher she didn't do it?
- All the other kids get a larger allowance than you do. Could you convince your parents to raise it?
- If you're at a friend's house and you forget the time and you get home really late, what would your parents (mother, father, guardian) say?
- Your parents only allow you to watch television at certain hours but you want to watch a particular program outside that time. Could you persuade them to change the rules, even if it is a school night?
- What if you borrow your friend's bike and then someone steals it? What should you say or do?
- All the other kids are calling the new student names. Would you join in? What would you do?
- The teacher asked each student to bring $4 for the class picnic. Your mother says she can't afford it but you're too embarrassed to tell the teacher. What should you do?

Facing Problems

Read books aloud occasionally about students who have problems. Talk about the characters and their problems with the group. You might use some of the following books:

Primary Grades

Joseph Kraus. *Leo, the Late Bloomer.* Windmill, 1971. A little tiger is slow about doing things, but he finally "blooms."

John Steptoe. *Stevie.* Harper and Row, 1969. A young black boy resents having Stevie in his home but misses him when he is gone.

Brinton Turkel. *The Adventures of Obadiah.* Viking, 1972. A young Quaker boy living in colonial Nantucket faces the problem of lying; see other books about Obadiah.

Diane Stanley. *The Conversation Club.* Macmillan, 1983. Peter Fieldmouse is welcomed to a new neighborhood.

Kevin Henkes. *Owen.* Greenwillow, 1993. The question of whether a tattered security blanket should go to school creates a family crisis for a young mouse.

Upper Elementary Grades

Maia Wojciechowska. *Shadow of a Bull.* Atheneum, 1964. The son of a great Spanish bullfighter fears being a coward.

Jean Little. *Kate.* Harper and Row, 1971. In this sequel to *Look through My Window,* Kate learns to value her Jewish heritage.

Joseph Krumgold. *And Now Miguel.* Crowell, 1953. This is a moving story of New Mexican sheepherders and Miguel's problems of growing up.

Janet Lunn. *The Root Cellar.* Scribner's, 1983. An unhappy orphan discovers an exciting fantasy world.

Death and Grieving

Well-written literature can help children learn how to manage the emotional and practical aspects of loss. Reading about other children who have gone through similar experiences, from the upheaval of moving to the loss of a loved one, will provide models of coping strategies, language to organize and process their experience, and a safe setting in which to express their emotions. Select stories that demonstrate the variety of approaches people have used to confront these problems.

Paul Goble. *Beyond the Ridge.* Aladdin, 1993. This picture book shows an old woman confronting death according to the beliefs of the Plains Indians. For her, dying is like climbing up a difficult slope toward a high ridge. Beyond the ridge, she can see the Spirit World. Death may seem like an end but it is not.

Rylant, Cynthia. *Missing May.* Orchard, 1992. In this extraordinarily sensitive novel, winner of the Newbery Award, twelve-year-old Summer grieves for her Aunt May, who took her in when no one else in the family wanted her.

Lucille Clifton. *Everett Anderson's Goodbye.* Holt, 1983. In one of many picture books about Everett Anderson, an African American boy, his father dies.

Tomie de Paola. *Nana Upstairs and Nana Downstairs.* Puffin, 1973. Tommy loves to visit his grandmother (who is "Nana Downstairs") and his great-grandmother ("Nana Upstairs"). When Nana Upstairs dies, he seeks reassurance from his family.

Judith Viorst. *The Tenth Good Thing about Barney.* Aladdin, 1975. Grieving for his cat, Barney, a young boy is encouraged to think of ten good things about him.

Mavis Jukes. *I'll See You in My Dreams.* Knopf, 1993. A young girl finds an outlet for her grief over her dying uncle by dreaming of writing a message in the sky.

Eve Bunting. *The Happy Funeral.* Illustrated by Mai Vo-Dinh. Harper and Row, 1982. Chinese American girl's grandfather dies.

Bruce Coville. *My Grandfather's House.* Illustrated by Henri Sorenson. Bridgewater, 1996. A boy can't understand where his grandfather has gone when he dies.

Kevin Henkes. *Sun and Spoon.* Greenwillow, 1997. A 10-year-old boy lists 52 special things about his late grandmother.

Life in a Relocation Camp

Fear of Japanese Americans and prejudice against them because of their heritage led to the evacuation of Japanese Americans from their homes in World War II, when the United States was at war with Japan. They were imprisoned behind barbed wire in relocation camps in remote areas. How did they manage to survive? Several books describe the horror of life in a relocation camp, where large groups of families were imprisoned for years, and the effect that this period had on children and the Japanese American community.

Ken Mochizuki. *Baseball Saved Us.* Lee and Low, 1993. Baseball provided a distraction and helped children endure the hardships of camp life.

Jeanne Houston. *Farewell to Manzanar: A True Story of Japanese American Experience during and after the World War II Internment.* Houghton Mifflin, 1973. Describes how the author's family was uprooted and how she coped with being imprisoned as a child.

Daniel Davis. *Behind Barbed Wire: The Imprisonment of Japanese Americans during World War II.* Dutton, 1982.

Yoshiko Uchida. *Journey to Topaz: The Story of the Japanese American Evacuation.* Scribner's, 1971. This fictional account is based on Uchida's own life. A young girl, Yuki, is interned in Utah. The sequel is *Journey Home.*

Steven A. Chin. *When Justice Failed: The Fred Korematsu Story.* Steck-Vaughn, 1993. Constitutional case in 1944 tested the legality of the Japanese American internment.

Ellen Levine. *A Fence Away from Freedom: Japanese Americans and World War II.* Putnam, 1995. Based on interviews with Japanese Americans who were young people at the time.

Read passages from one of these books to the class. If you have time, read the whole book. Afterwards, discuss the students' reactions to the book. They can discuss how they would feel going to a camp, what the people guarding the camp thought about their prisoners, whether this could happen again today, or what the people thought about the United States when they were released from the camp.

Have students write a letter to a friend, as if they lived in one of the camps, describing their life in the camp, or write a diary entry, telling what they do every day and how they feel.

People Make a Difference

In World War II, the German government rounded up Jewish people and other groups they considered undesirable. In a short period, six million Jews were taken to concentration camps and killed. Many people cooperated with the authorities in this plan; others looked the other way. Yet, a few people stood up to prejudice and helped Jewish people survive. What kind of people would risk their lives to help others? Have students investigate this period of hate and fear and those who helped others under frightening circumstances.

Maxine Rosenberg. *Hiding to Survive: Stories of Jewish Children Rescued from the Holocaust.* Clarion, 1994.

Jo Hoestlandt. *Star of Fear, Star of Hope.* Illustrated by Johanna Kang. Walker, 1995. Helen grew up with Lydia, a Jewish girl, in France and now regrets her lack of understanding when Lydia's family faced arrest.

David Adler. *Child of the Warsaw Ghetto.* Holiday, 1995.

Eleanor Ayer. *The Holocaust: America Keeps the Memory Alive.* Silver Burdett, 1994.

Lila Perl and Marian Lagan. *Four Perfect Pebbles: A Holocaust Story.* Greenwillow, 1996.

Otto H. Frank and Mirjam Pressler. *Anne Frank: The Diary of a Young Girl, the Definitive Edition.* Anchor, 1995. Anne Frank and her family hid in a small room in an Amsterdam apartment.

Alison Leslie Gold. *Memories of Anne Frank.* Scholastic, 1997. A friend of Anne's recalls that time. Nonfiction.

Rian Verhoeven and Ruud van der Rol. *Anne Frank.* Viking, 1993. A photographic remembrance of the family shows they weren't just passive victims.

Jane Yolen. *The Devil's Arithmetic.* Puffin, 1988. Hannah has always complained about her family's Holocaust stories but she is suddenly transported to a Polish village in the 1940s.

Ken Mochizuki. *Passage to Freedom: The Sugihara Story.* Lee and Low, 1997. The Japanese consul to Lithuania defied his own government and issued visas to Jewish refugees. Up to 10,000 people survived as a result of his work.

Livia Bitton-Jackson. *I Have Lived a Thousand Years.* Simon and Schuster, 1997. A memoir of the Hungarian ghetto and concentration camp.

Ask students if they think an individual can make a difference. Can they think of times when someone said or did something that could cause harm? What would they do? What can any of us do about prejudice? Help students discuss the positive aspects of standing up to prejudice.

QUILTS AS A METAPHOR FOR AMERICAN LIFE

Seeing the United States as a quilt is the opposite of the "melting pot" metaphor. In a quilt, separate elements are assembled, without losing the beauty of the many-colored pieces, into a whole composition that is beautiful as well. Early in the history of the United States, groups of people often got together to accomplish what was too difficult to do separately, such as building a barn. Women assembled regularly in quilting bees to work together on stitching large quilts. The metaphor of quilting recalls the historical image of separate individuals who come together to make a pattern, providing a way to create a sense of commonality without a loss of distinctive identity.

Quilts also represent shelter, comfort, and family. This caring handiwork communicates across generations. In addition, the modern recognition of folk art, or functional objects made by ordinary people, as worthy of study is a belated tribute to these craftspeople, often anonymous. There are many different traditions of quilting in the United States, from Kentucky pioneers to Hawaiian natives. Other cultural groups in the world also have similar traditions of needlework. But most of all, quilts tell us about ourselves. We are like the varied scraps of material assembled into a warm covering that can endure for many years. Use quilting as a theme to incorporate activities that cross the curriculum. Quilting can be the base for math work on symmetry, fractions, and geometric figures; the study of periods in history or different groups; language arts activities; and the science of color, dyeing, flowers, and animals.

What's in a Quilt?

A quilt is a three-layer sandwich, composed of a top (pieced or appliqué), a filling or batting (for warmth), and a back (sometimes pieced as well). There are three distinct processes usually referred to by the term "quilting." *Patchwork* traditionally incorporates leftover scraps of material or pieces of old clothing. The scraps are pieced together into special patterns, with attention to color and design, and then sewn together to make a block. These blocks often have colorful names, such as Rocky Road to Kansas or Jacob's Ladder. A special kind of patchwork is the crazy quilt. In this version, special pieces of fabric (often velvet or silk) are sewn together in a pleasing fashion but without a fixed pattern. In *appliqué,* a design (often floral) is cut out from material and sewn onto background fabric in blocks or for a whole quilt. *Quilting* itself refers to the stitching (done by hand or machine) that holds the three layers together. Sometimes the quilting stitches create a design in themselves. Quilts may also be held together by knots tied at intervals.

What are some of the names for patchwork patterns? Where do the names come from? Students can learn about the different patterns and investigate what they mean by reading Ann Whitford Paul's *Eight Hands Round: A Patchwork Alphabet,* illustrated by Jeanette Winter. (HarperCollins, 1991) This ABC book explains the origin of the interesting names for patterns (Flying Geese, Monkey Wrench), shows the different designs, and tells the story of the people behind the quilts.

Quilts in History

Quilts kept log cabins warm, went along in wagon trains, and preserved the memory of friends and relatives. Women used their needles to make quilts that reflected passages in their lives. There are many books that tell stories of these early quilts and provide examples of quilt blocks.

Raymond Bial. *With Needle and Thread: A Book about Quilts.* Houghton Mifflin, 1996. A social history of quilting.

Ann Whitford Paul. *The Seasons Sewn: A Year in Patchwork.* Harcourt, 1996.

Mary Cobb. *The Quilt Block History of Pioneer Days.* Millbrook Press, 1995. Examples of projects for children using paper and cut magazines.

Jane Bolton. *My Grandmother's Patchwork Quilt: A Book and Portfolio of Patchwork Pieces.* Doubleday, 1994.

Patricia Polacco. *The Keeping Quilt.* Simon and Schuster, 1988. Polacco traces her family's Jewish heritage through a quilt made from relatives' clothing and passed down through generations to celebrate births, marriages, and deaths. In each shape she can see the stories she's been told of her family.

Valerie Flournoy. *The Patchwork Quilt.* Illustrated by Jerry Pinkney. Dial, 1985. When Tanya's grandmother gets too sick to work on her quilt, telling stories of family history, Tanya decides to help her finish it. African American family.

Ellen Howard. *The Log Cabin Quilt.* Holiday, 1996. Quilt scraps warm a family by providing chinking for their new cabin in Michigan.

Eleanor Coerr. *The Josefina Story Quilt.* Harper, 1989. When Faith's family sets out for California in 1850, she brings along the old hen Josefina. After Josefina rescues them from trouble, Faith sews a quilt to commemorate the trip. Also available in Spanish.

Deborah Hopkinson. *Sweet Clara and the Freedom Quilt.* Illustrated by James Ransome. Knopf, 1993. As a slave, Clara is not allowed to read or write, so she carefully stitches into a quilt the information she needs for her escape.

Ask students if they have any quilts. Who made these quilts? What designs were used? What do these quilts mean to them? Share books with students that reflect how quilts can preserve people's heritage and help them remember.

Amish Quilts

The Amish, a religious group living in small communities in Pennsylvania, are known for their quilts featuring solid colors and strong, simple, symmetrical designs. These quilts are representative of the Amish culture and beliefs, which include plain clothing, farming without machinery, and horse-driven buggies for transportation. Use a study of Amish quilts as a point of entry into this interesting culture and the choices that Amish people have made to live a simple religious life.

Patricia Polacco. *Just Plain Fancy.* Bantam, 1990. A story about the Amish in Lancaster County, PA.

Doris Faber. *The Amish.* Illustrated by Michael Erkel. Doubleday, 1991. Nonfiction.

African American Quilts

There is a distinct tradition of quilts passed along by African Americans. They have used a kind of scrap piecing, similar to the European piecing yet influenced by African woven strip designs. These quilts are characterized by bright, contrasting colors, large designs, assembly into long strips, asymmetry, and improvisation on set patterns. If students have any examples of these quilts, encourage them to show them to the class. For more information, consult these references:

Roland Freeman. *A Communion of the Spirits: African American Quilters, Preservers, and Their Stories.* Rutledge Hill Press, 211 7th Ave N., Nashville TN 37219, 1996.

Eli Leon. *Who'd a Thought It: Improvisation in African-American Quilting.* San Francisco Craft and Folk Museum, 1990. Shows the connections between contemporary quilting and African traditions.

Hawaiian Quilts

Hawaiians are another groups with a distinctive regional tradition. The native Hawaiians sewed tapa before the European arrival. When they began to make quilts, they adapted many of the same techniques to sewing cotton. Traditional Hawaiian quilts are made of a single large appliqué design (based on local flowers, trees, animals, or birds) sewn onto a solid background of a contrasting color. While in traditional European quilting everyone uses the same patterns to make very different quilts, Hawaiian quilters believe that every quilter should make her own pattern and not borrow another's without permission.

Students can experience the effect of a Hawaiian-style quilt by folding a square piece of paper into eighths (like a snowflake design). Cut out a design, making sure that they keep the paper connected along the folded side. Students may want to plan their design on paper first. They can draw designs based on animals, plants, or other familiar objects. When they unfold their design, notice how symmetrical it appears. Point out the axes of symmetry—vertical, horizontal, other.

Nine-Patch Math

A nine-patch square is the basis for many quilt designs. Provide students with an 8- or 9-inch square. Have them divide it into thirds along each side, making 9 equal spaces. Then ask them to divide some of those spaces in half. What are some different ways to do this? Can they divide the spaces into thirds or quarters? What different patterns can they make in their squares? Have students color in their designs. Show them how the same pattern can come out looking different depending on the arrangement of colors.

The illustration below shows two examples of nine-patch patterns. Have students color one of these designs. Assemble the student squares into a paper quilt. Are there alternative ways to put the quilt blocks together? Can students see larger patterns in the class quilt?

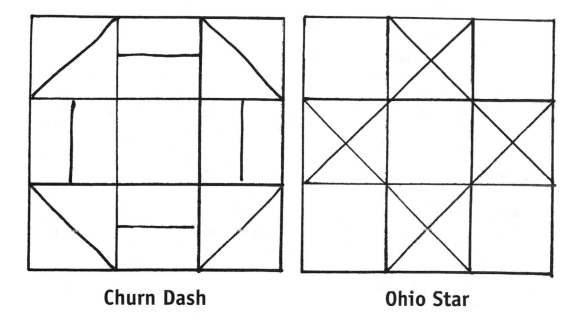

Churn Dash   **Ohio Star**

Quilt Quotes

Feature quotes about quilting as you discuss social studies, history, art, or other topics. Place quotes on the bulletin board for students to read. Students can write responses to these quotes. What do these quotes tell us about people's lives? About the importance of beauty in utilitarian objects?

> My husband tells about the time he got sick with the measles. He was six years old. His mother set him to piecing a quilt and every other block he set in red polka-dot pattern. Said it was his measles quilt. (Patricia Cooper and Norma Bradley Allen. *The Quilters: Women and Domestic Art.* Anchor, 1989, p. 39)

> It's nothin' about makin' it a little different. It's still the same pattern. You just added somethin' of your own to it. (Odessa Derby, in Eli Leon, *Who'd a Thought It,* p. 22.)

> In the summers we'd put up the frame on the screened porch, and when the work was done, Mama would say, "O.K., girls, let's go to it." That was the signal for good times and laughin'. We'd pull up our chairs around the frame and anyone that dropped in would do the same, even if they couldn't stitch straight. Course we'd take out their stitches later if they was really bad. But it was for talking and visiting that we put in quilts in the summer. (Patricia Cooper and Norma Bradley Allen. *The Quilters: Women and Domestic Art.* Anchor, 1989, p. 76)

> You can give the same kind of pieces to two persons, and one'll make a "nine-patch" and one'll make a "wild goose chase," and there'll be two quilts made out of the same kind of pieces, and just as different as they can be. And that's just the way with the living. The Lord sends us the pieces, but we can cut them out and put them together pretty much to suit ourselves, and there's a heap more in the cutting out and the sewing than there is in the calico. (*A Quilter's Wisdom:*

Conversations with Aunt Jane, based on a text by Eliza Calvert Hall. Chronicle, 1994, pp. 37–38)

I plan my quilts just like I used to plan a house. Folks say, "How come you quilt so good?" I say, "If you make careful plans, it will come out right." (Patricia Cooper and Norma Bradley Allen. *The Quilters: Women and Domestic Art.* Anchor, 1989, p. 90)

Everyone put their hand to piecing in the winter. All my boys pieced right along with the girls. It was work that had to be done. (Patricia Cooper and Norma Bradley Allen. *The Quilters: Women and Domestic Art.* Anchor, 1989, p. 154)

Story Quilts

Sometimes quilts are used to tell a story. The story quilts of Faith Ringgold, an African American artist, are an example of stitched work based on a theme of pride in one's heritage. Her works assemble words and images in fabric to create a narrative through a kind of collage. Investigate her work with students to show them how a person's own life and experience can be reflected in art. Look at examples of her books and read about her life.

Faith Ringgold. *Tar Beach.* Crown, 1991. This story of a girl's dreams as she lies on her city rooftop is framed by pieces of Ringgold's story quilts.

Robyn Montana Turner. *Faith Ringgold.* Little, Brown, 1993. From her childhood in Harlem in the 1930s to her status as an artist today, this detailed biography follows Ringgold's life and development, setting it in the context of African American experience.

Faith Ringgold. *The Last Story Quilt.* Video, 1991. Ringgold talks about her life and shows her artwork.

Faith Ringgold's work has been an inspiration to many people. In 1997, Booklinks/Hyperion Books for Children held a Faith Ringgold Story Quilt Contest in honor of preserving history through art. The winning quilt, called "Guns and Arrows," was made by fifth graders at Wyngate Elementary School, Bethesda MD. Making a story quilt as a class is something all students can participate in.

Another famous story quilter is Harriet Powers, who worked in the nineteenth century. Her work links the quilting traditions of slaves with that of contemporary artists. Read about her surprisingly modern images in:

Mary E. Lyons. *Stitching the Stars: The Story Quilts of Harriet Powers.* Scribner's, 1993. African American artist's Bible-based quilts.

Students Make Friendship Quilts

Students may be motivated to make quilts to express their creativity, to distribute to the homeless, or to raise money. For example, they can select one of the many attractive Amish designs to cut out and sew, using solid colors. The drafting of the patterns for cutting will involve use of basic geometric shapes. Students in fourth grade and up can handle a sewing machine or a needle and thread with some adult assistance. Students can also make a crazy quilt, using donated scraps of fabric. Have each student assemble the odd-sized pieces on a foundation block of a fixed size so that the quilt can be assembled easily. Another popular theme for student quilts is "Our Neighborhood." Each student can make a block representing a house, embellishing each house differently with trim and buttons. Or they can make individual blocks for particular features of the community—special buildings, sights, people. Students can also make an international quilt, showing children from many different countries and different backgrounds.

Primary students can draw on fabric with fabric crayons that become permanent after ironing. One kindergarten class made an alphabet quilt. For students who were unable to draw a letter, the teacher outlined large letters and the students colored them in. Students tied knots to hold the quilt together.

Students can also adapt quilt techniques to paper. Collect supplies of colorful paper such as wrapping paper, magazines, or catalogs. Have students cut long strips of equal width. They can sew or glue these strips together lengthwise to make a band of 6 inches. Then cut across the strips every 6 inches so that you have squares. These squares can be assembled into the Rail Fence pattern. Encourage students to experiment with different possibilities for arranging their squares in a pleasing pattern.

Other Traditions

Investigate other quilting-like traditions with students. Perhaps students know of the Hmong stitchery, called pa'ndau (story cloth). These intricate designs are passed on through generations. Show students examples in books such as:

Pegi Deitz Shea. *The Whispering Cloth: A Refugee's Story.* Illustrated by Anita Riggio, stitched by Yon Yang. Boyds Mill, 1995. A Hmong family in a refugee camp in Thailand makes story cloths to earn money.

Dia Cha. *Dia's Story Cloth: The Hmong People's Journey of Freedom.* Stitched by Chue and Nhia Thao Cha. Lee and Low, 1996. This story cloth, made by the author's aunt and uncle, chronicles Hmong life, past and present.

FOCUS ON NATIVE AMERICANS, YESTERDAY AND TODAY

When white explorers and settlers encountered the native population in North America, they tended to see the Native Americans as simple primitives, a view that justified paternalistic treatment and genocide. This was succeeded by the Noble Savage, a romanticized image of a lost tradition. Such stereotypes of Native Americans fix them in the past, making it difficult for young Native Americans to develop a cultural identity suitable for the twentieth century.

Native Americans haven't been absent from the school curriculum as much as they have been reduced to cardboard figures, all wearing headdresses and saying "How." Young Native American students may cope by hiding behind apparent Latino or Black ancestry rather than risking humiliation and embarrassment. Life outside the reservation brings economic opportunities but cultural starvation. Teachers can help support young Native Americans in their search for identity and a place in the world. Teachers can also make sure that all students learn more about Native American life, historical and modern. We also need to broaden our perspective of Native Americans to include such groups as the Mayas and Aztecs in Latin America and the Inuit (Eskimos) and Aleuts in Alaska.

Planning Your Study

Before beginning a study of Native Americans in the United States, use some means of assessing student information and attitudes. This will provide an interesting and instructive comparison at the end of the study. Try some of these ideas:

* Have each student draw a picture of a Native American engaged in some activity.
* Ask students to complete this sentence at least three times: A Native American . . .
* Ask students to list as many Native American tribes as they can.

Put these sheets away until the study is completed. After the study you might have the students repeat the same activities. Then compare the results.

Native American Tribes

Draw a large outline map of the United States on which to locate the various groups of Indian tribes. They can be grouped as follows according to similar modes of living:

Eastern Woodland Area   Algonquin Delaware, Iroquois, Massachuset, Mohawk, Mohegan, Narraganset, Onandaga, Penobscot, Powhatan, Tuscarora, Passamaquoddy, Pawtuket, Tippecanoe, Wampanoag, Wyandot

Great Lakes Woodland Area   Chippewa/Ojibwa, Huron, Illinois, Kickapoo, Miami, Oneida, Ottawa, Potawatomi, Sac and Fox, Seneca, Shawnee, Winnebago

Southeastern Area   Catawba, Cherokee, Creek, Lumbi, Natchez, Seminole, Yuchi

North Central Plains Area   Arapaho, Arikara, Assiniboine, Blackfeet, Cheyenne, Cree, Crow, Gros Ventre, Mandan, Pawnee, Shoshone, Sioux/Dakota

South Central Plains Area   Caddo, Chickasaw, Choctaw, Comanche, Iowa, Kaw/Kansa, Kiowa, Omaha, Osage, Ponca, Quapaw

Southwest Area   Apache, Hopi, Maricopa, Navajo, Papago, Pima, Pueblo, Zuñi

California Area   Chumash, Hoopa, Maidu, Mission, Modoc, Mohave, Mono, Pit River, Pomo, Tule River, Wailaki, Yahi, Yokuts, Yuma, Yurok

Northwestern Plateau Area   Bannock, Cayuse, Coeur D'Alene, Colville, Flathead, Kalispel, Klamath, Kootenai, Nez Percé, Nisqually, Paiute, Puyallup, Spokane, Ute, Walla-walla, Wasco, Washoe, Yakima

Northwest Pacific Coast Area   Aleuts, Eskimo (Inuit), Haida, Lummi, Makah, Muckleshoot, Nootka, Quinault, Salish, Shoalwater, Snohomish, Suquamish, Tlingit

Native American Reservations

The following chart shows states with reservations, the population of those states, and the names of the tribes or nations.

FEDERAL NATIVE AMERICAN RESERVATIONS AND TRUST LANDS

State	No. of Reser.	No. of persons	Major tribes and/or nations
Alabama	1	16,504	Poarch Creek
Alaska	1	85,698	Aleut, Eskimo, Athabascan
Arkansas	1	—	unknown
Arizona	23	203,527	Navajo, Apache, Papago, Hopi, Yavapai, Pima
California	96	242,164	Hoopa, Paiute, Yurok, Karok, Mission Bands
Colorado	2	27,776	Ute
Connecticut	1	6,654	Mashantucket, Pequot
Florida	4	36,335	Seminole, Miccosukee
Idaho	4	13,780	Shoshone, Bannock, Nez Percé
Iowa	1	7,349	Sac and Fox
Kansas	4	21,965	Potawatomi, Kickapoo, Iowa
Louisiana	3	18,541	Chitimacha, Coushatta, Tunica-Biloxi
Maine	3	5,998	Passamaquoddy, Penobscot, Maliseet
Massachusetts	1	—	Wampanoag
Michigan	8	55,638	Chippewa, Potawatomi, Ottawa
Minnesota	14	49,909	Chippewa, Sioux
Mississippi	1	8,825	Choctaw
Missouri	1	—	unknown
Montana	7	47,679	Blackfeet, Crow, Sioux, Assiniboine, Cheyenne
Nebraska	3	12,410	Omaha, Winnebago, Santee Sioux
Nevada	19	19,637	Paiute, Shoshone, Washoe
New Mexico	25	134,355	Zuñi, Apache, Navajo
New York	8	62,651	Seneca, Mohawk, Onondaga, Oneida
North Carolina	1	80,155	Cherokee
North Dakota	3	25,917	Sioux, Chippewa, Mandan, Arikara, Hidatsa
Oklahoma	1	252,420	Cherokee, Creek, Choctaw, Chickasaw, Osage, Cheyenne, Arapahoe, Kiowa, Comanche
Oregon	7	38,496	Warm Springs, Wasco, Paiute, Umatilla, Siletz
Rhode Island	1	4,071	Narragansett
South Dakota	9	50,573	Sioux
Texas	3	65,877	Alabama-Coushatta, Tiwa, Kickapoo
Utah	4	24,283	Ute, Goshute, Southern Paiute
Washington	27	81,483	Yakima, Lummi, Quinault
Wisconsin	11	39,387	Chippewa, Oneida, Winnebago
Wyoming	1	9,479	Shoshone, Arapahoe

Source: Bureau of Indian Affairs, U.S. Dept. of the Interior (data as of 1990).

Which states have the most reservations? Which have the largest Native American populations? How many states do not have reservations?

Native groups in Canada include Indians, Inuit, and Métis (people of mixed heritage). Tribes in Mexico include the Maya, Nahuatl, Huichol, Purepecha, Tarahumar, Mazateco, Zapoteco, Nahua, Cora, Tzeltal, Otomi, and Mixteco. Students can investigate historical and contemporary Native groups in Latin America.

English Words from Native American Languages

Words borrowed into English show how much the first settlers owed the Native Americans they encountered. Most words come from the Algonquin languages, spoken along the East Coast. Can students guess the English equivalent? Develop a chart to show the relationship.

chitmunk	(chipmunk)	pawcohiccora	(hickory)
aroughcoun	(raccoon)	paccan	(pecan)
squnk	(skunk)	pasimenan	(persimmon)
ochek	(woodchuck)	msickquatash	(succotash)
musquash	(muskrat)	askootasquash	(squash)
moos	(moose)	tamahak	(tomahawk)
aposoun	(opossum)	mohkussin	(moccasin)

Other Gifts from the Native Americans

Students will be interested in learning of the many things we gained from the Native Americans. They knew the best trails and ways of traveling across the country by canoe and by snowshoe. They invented hammocks. The Native Americans were the first, too, to grow and use tobacco and rubber. They introduced white settlers to the following foods that we use today:

corn	tomatoes	cranberries	maple sugar
potatoes	vanilla	chicle (for chewing gum)	artichokes
chilies	avocados	beans	hominy
pineapples	peanuts	chocolate	popcorn

Have several students prepare an illustrated chart of these foods. You may experiment with hominy or dishes that are easy to make in the classroom.

Of course, Native American contributions were not limited to food supplies. The following books suggest areas that advanced students can explore:

Jack Weatherford. *Native Roots: How the Indians Enriched America.* Fawcett, 1991.

Jack Weatherford. *Indian Givers: How the Indians of the Americas Transformed the World.* Fawcett, 1989.

Native American Place Names

Many state names, such as Massachusetts, originated in Native American languages. Names of many rivers, such as the Ohio and Mississippi, and cities, such as Pontiac, Michigan, and Chicago, Illinois, also originated from Native American languages.

Look for evidence of specific tribes. For example, there are many Abenaki place names in Maine, Vermont, and New Hampshire.

Androscoggin	place where fish are cured
Connecticut	the long river
Katahdin	the principal mountain
Kennebec	long water without rapids
Merrimack	at the deep place
Nashua	between streams

For more information on where names come from, see *Indian Place Names of New England* by John C. Huden (Museum of the American Indian, New York: Heye Foundation, 1962).

Prepare a map on which to locate Native American names. Include a chart to explain what the names mean and where they come from.

The "New World" in 1492

What did the world of the Native Americans look like when the European explorers arrived, beginning with Columbus in 1492? Students may be surprised to learn that there were no horses (dogs and turkeys were the only domestic animals). It is impossible to know how many people lived on the North American continent at the time, but there were a number of complex cultures, based in different regions, and trading with others.

Dennis Fradin's historical biography *Hiawatha: Messenger of Peace* (McElderry, 1993) provides much background information about the Iroquois. Although Hiawatha lived five hundred years ago, she made significant contributions to American history. As a leader in her tribe, she helped set up the Iroquois Confederacy, the most politically complex group in 1492. Iroquois customs and beliefs eventually influenced the development of the U.S. Constitution. Also see volumes on the Iroquois and the Mohawk in the Chelsea House series *Indians of North America* for historical data.

For more information on life in 1492, see the following:

Jean Fritz, Jamake Highwater, Margaret Mahy, Patricia and Fredrick McKissack, and Katherine Paterson. *The World in 1492.* Holt, 1992. Provides a detailed description of each part of the world—Africa, Asia, Europe, Australia, the Americas—and how the people there lived at that time.

What Happened to the Native Americans after 1492?

After setting the stage with a picture of the Native Americans before the European conquest, continue the story and explore how the Native Americans were affected by it. Several books deal with specific tribes in specific regions.

Florida

Eva Costabel. *The Early People of Florida.* Atheneum, 1993. Presents the history of tribal groups such as Calusa and Tequesta present in 1492. First the Spanish and the French fought over their lands, then the British came.

Kathleen Kudlenski. *Night Bird: A Story of the Seminole Indians.* Illustrated by James Watling. Viking, 1993. Eleven-year-old Seminole girl must leave Florida Everglades in 1840 to move to Oklahoma.

Colorado

Albert Marrin. *Cowboys, Indians, and Gunfighters: The Story of the Cattle Kingdom.* Atheneum, 1993. Outlines the destruction of the Plains Indians' way of life, from 1521 when the first cattle arrived from Hispaniola to the killing off of the buffalo.

Plains

Paul Goble. *Death of the Iron Horse.* Aladdin, 1993. This picture book tells the true story of the Cheyenne's struggle to preserve their way of life after soldiers and settlers invade their territory with the steam locomotive.

North Dakota

Russell Freedman. *An Indian Winter.* Paintings and drawings by Karl Bodmer. Holiday House, 1992. Journal of a German prince and scenes painted by a Swiss artist who spent a winter with the Mandans in 1833–1834 in today's North Dakota. Afterwards, the Mandan and Hidatsa were devastated by smallpox and their traditional way of life vanished. The detail of this text and pictures bring to life the vanished customs of the people.

Native American Life Today

Balance historical information with contemporary accounts that show real people living in today's world. Bring your historical account of Native American life up to the present. Students may be surprised to realize there are modern Native American children like themselves, not just characters out of history. Young Native Americans face many of the same issues concerning growing up that all children face. In addition, they may struggle to learn more about their heritage and the history of their people. They may wonder why people are prejudiced against them or their people. And they face the question of how to maintain their culture in a hostile world. Look for a variety of children's books to show students what it feels like to be a Native American today.

Fiction

Russ Kendall. *Eskimo Boy: Life in an Inupiaq Village.* Scholastic, 1992. Photographs of seven-year-old Norman, who lives in a remote village off the northwest coast of Alaska.

Jean Craighead George. *Water Sky.* Harper, 1987. Lincoln Noah Stonewright goes from Boston to Barrow, Alaska, to stay with an Eskimo family and learn what happened to his uncle, who had wanted to stop the Eskimo whaling there.

Ron Hirschi. *Seya's Song.* Illustrated by Constance Bergum. Sasquatch Books, 1992. A S'Klallam grandmother and grandfather pass on their language and stories to a young girl. Includes many S'Klallam words and incorporates information on the life and customs of these people, who live in Washington and British Columbia.

Monty Roessel. *Kinaaldá: A Navajo Girl Grows Up.* Lerner, 1993. In recent years, Navajos have adapted an ancient coming-of-age ceremony for thirteen-year-old girls to modern days. Photographs by the author.

Susan Braine. *Drumbeat . . . Heartbeat: A Celebration of the Powwow.* Lerner, 1995. Traditions from the Northern Cheyenne reservation in Montana. Photographs by the author.

Sandra King. *Shannon: An Ojibway Dancer.* Lerner, 1993. A thirteen-year-old girl's life combines tradition and modern customs as she prepares to dance in a powwow in Minnesota. Photographs by Catherine Whipple. From *We Are Still Here* series.

George Ancona. *Powwow.* Harcourt Brace, 1993. The Montana Crow Fair is the largest powwow in the country. Photographs by the author.

Robert Crum. *Eagle Drum: On the Powwow Trail with a Young Grass Dancer.* FourWinds, 1994. Shows nine-year-old Louis and his family. Photographs by the author.

Diane Hoyt-Goldsmith. *Apache Rodeo.* Holiday House, 1995. Ten-year-old Felicita, living in Arizona, reflects on her history and traditions as she prepares for the rodeo.

Joseph Bruchac. *Eagle Song.* Dial, 1997. Fourth-grade Mohawk boy is teased for being Indian; his father tells class the real story of Hiawatha, the Iroquois leader who sought peace.

Craig Kee Strete. *The World in Grandfather's Hands.* Clarion, 1995. An eleven-year-old Cherokee boy who loses his father and moves to the city feels uprooted.

Normee Ekoomiak. *Arctic Memories.* Holt, 1990. A picture book of an Inuit childhood in Quebec illustrates a way of life that is almost extinct. Text in Inuktitut and English.

Tryntje Van Seymour Ness. *The Gift of Changing Woman.* Holt, 1993. When an Apache girl comes of age, she goes through a ceremony to teach her the story of creation and her place in the world. Includes pictures by Apache artists and words of the Apache people.

David Morrison and George Hebert Germain. *The Inuit: Glimpses of an Arctic Past.* University of Washington Press, 1996. A young girl tells the history of the Copper Inuit culture.

Laurie O'Neill. *The Shawnees: People of the Eastern Woodlands.* Millbrook Press, 1995. Part of a series: Native Americans; see also *The Inuit: People of the Arctic.*

Virginia Driving Hawk Sneve. *The Hopis: A First Americans Book.* Holiday, 1995. Abundant pictures of traditional Hopi life.

Marcia Keegan. *Pueblo Boy: Growing Up in Two Worlds.* Cobblehill, 1991. Tells of ten-year-old boy's life; many photos.

Diane Hoyt-Goldsmith. *Pueblo Storyteller.* Holiday, 1991. The life of a young Cochiti Pueblo girl.

Rina Swentzell. *Children of Clay: A Family of Pueblo Potters.* Lerner, 1992. Story of a Tewa family in New Mexico.

Gordon Regguinti. *The Sacred Harvest: Ojibway Wild Rice Gathering.* Lerner, 1992. Color photographs; informative text about processing the rice.

Barbara Mitchell. *Red Bird.* Illustrated by Todd Doney. Lothrop, 1996. Powwows of the Eastern Indians; notes multiracial aspects of tribes.

Monty Rossel. *Songs from the Loom.* Lerner, 1996. Photo essay of a young girl learning to weave.

Linda Yamane. *Weaving a California Tradition.* Illustrated by Dugan Aguilar. Lerner, 1997. Follows eleven-year-old Western Mono girl's life; shows full process of weaving a basket and entering it in a basketweaver's showcase; photographs of California Indians.

Native American Stories and Folktales

Folklore from the various Native American tribes is an excellent source for learning more about culture and for storytelling activities. Older students can learn one of these tales to present to students in the primary grades. All of these stories adapt well to other modes of oral presentation, such as Reader's Theater. In addition, when you read one of the teaching stories to the class, students can respond to the moral by drawing a picture and discussing what it means to them.

When selecting folktales for use with students, consider carefully the image presented of the people in the group. Many authors have written versions of Native American tales without respect for their authentic cultural background. Contrast these with books by writers such as Paul Goble and Gerald McDermott, who are scrupulous in citing the sources of their stories and in presenting appropriate cultural context in their illustrations. Also look for books by Native American authors, which have become more available as individuals and tribal organizations promote culturally sensitive materials. For example, a booklist of recommended works is available from Oyate, 2702 Mathews Street, Berkeley, CA 94702.

Retold by Tony Hillerman. *The Boy Who Made Dragonfly.* University of New Mexico Press, 1986. Retelling of a Zuni myth about how a young boy and his sister gain the wisdom to become the leaders of their people.

Gerald McDermott. *Raven: A Trickster Tale from the Pacific Northwest.* Harcourt Brace Jovanovich, 1993. How the raven steals the sun from the Sky Chief so that the people can have light.

Paul Goble. *Crow Chief.* Orchard, 1992. A combination of several Plains Indian tales explains why crows are black.

Shonto Begay. *Ma'ii and Cousin Horned Toad.* Scholastic, 1992. This Navajo teaching tale includes text in Navajo. Coyote is hungry but is too lazy to get his own food.

Retold by Jonathan London with Lanny Pinola. *Fire Race.* Illustrated by Sylvia Long. Chronicle Books, 1993. The tale of what happens when Coyote steals fire from yellow jackets.

Leanne Hinton. (trans.). *Ishi's Tale of Lizard.* Farrar Straus Giroux, 1992. Recent translation of a Yahi tale. Ishi, the sole survivor of the Yahi people, emerged from hiding in 1911.

Clifford Trafzer, ed. *Blue Down, Red Earth.* Archer 1996. New Native American storytellers.

Howard Norman. *The Girl Who Dreamed Only Geese and Other Tales of the Far North.* . . . Illustrated by Leo and Diane Dillon. Harcourt, 1997.

Bruce Hucko. *A Rainbow at Night: The World in Words and Pictures by Navajo Children.* Chronicle, 1997.

Carol Purdy. *Nesuya's Basket.* Roberts Rinehart, 1997.

Mary-Joan Gerson. *People of Corn: A Mayan Story.* Illustrated by Carla Golembe. Little, 1995. A creation story.

C. Shana Greger, retold. *The Fifth and Final Sun.* Houghton, 1994. An Aztec story tells of the origin of the sun.

John Bierhorst. *The Hungry Woman: Myths and Legends of the Aztecs.* Morrow, 1993.

Tom Pohrt, retold. *Coyote Goes Walking.* Farrar, 1995. Four brief stories, including a creation myth.

Joseph Bruchac and Gayle Ross, retold. *The Story of the Milky Way: A Cherokee Tale.* Illustrated by Virginia A. Stroud. Dial, 1995.

Janet Stevens, retold. *Coyote Steals the Blanket: A Ute Tale.* Holiday House, 1993.

Ekkehart Malotki, retold. *The Mouse Couple: A Hopi Folktale.* Illustrated by Michael Lacapa. Northland, 1988.

Paul Goble. *Death of the Iron Horse.* Bradbury, 1987. A historical event, the coming of the railroad, as a folktale.

Paul Goble. *The Return of the Buffaloes: A Plains Indian Story about Famine and Renewal of the Earth.* National Geographic Society, 1996. Based on Lakota myth.

Harriet Peck Taylor, retold. *Coyote and the Laughing Butterflies.* Macmillan, 1995. A tale from the Tewa Pueblo.

Mary Helen Pelton and Jacqueline DiGennaro. *Images of a People: Tlingit Myths and Legends.* Illustrated by Jennifer Brady-Morales. Libraries Unlimited, 1994. Description of the culture accompanied by tales.

Gayle Ross, retold. *How Turtle's Back Was Cracked: A Traditional Cherokee Tale.* Illustrated by Murv Jacob. Dial, 1995.

Rafe Martin. *The Eagle's Gift.* Illustrated by Tatsuro Kiuchi. Putnam, 1997. In this Inuit tale, a boy brings joy to his people.

Joseph Bruchac. *Between Earth and Sky: Legends of Native American Sacred Places.* Illustrated by Thomas Locker. Harcourt, 1996. Describes the seven sacred directions that represent the unity of life and our oneness with the natural world, seen and unseen.

Michael Lacapa. *Antelope Woman: An Apache Folktale.* Northland, 1992.

Jerrie Oughton. *How the Stars Fell into the Sky: A Navajo Legend.* Illustrated by Lisa Desimini. Houghton Mifflin, 1992.

Margaret Shaw-MacKinnon. *Tiktala.* Illustrated by Liszlo Gal. Holiday, 1996. Wonderful art; realistic portrayal of Inuit.

Gail Haley. *Two Bad Boys: A Very Old Cherokee Tale.* Dutton, 1996. A pourquoi tale—why people have to hunt for their own meat and plant vegetables to survive.

Russell Freedman. *Buffalo Hunt.* Holiday House, 1988. Lore and daily life of Plains Indians; hunting and the use of total animal killed.

When studying Native American folklore with students, encourage them to look for patterns. Can they find several examples of a "trickster" tale? Compare some trickster tales in other cultures, such as Anansi stories in African traditions. Are there several versions of one tale? How do the versions differ? In folklore, stories are transmitted orally, so several different written versions may all be authentic. What values do these stories teach?

Other teaching ideas can be found in this collection:

Michael Caduto and Joseph Bruchac. *Keepers of the Animals: Native American Stories and Wildlife Activities for Children.* Fulcrum, 1991. A teacher's guide was published in 1992. Look for Bruchac reading and telling Abenaki stories on audiocassette.

Making Navajo Fry Bread

Create a learning center at which children can take turns making a semiauthentic version of fry bread. (Teacher supervision is necessary for this activity.)

Directions

Fill the electric skillet half full of oil. Turn on high to heat.
Measure into bowl:

4 c. flour	1 tsp. salt
3 tsp. baking powder	1½ c. water

Gradually add the water as you stir.

Knead the dough until it does not stick to your hands. Add a little more flour as needed. Divide the dough into small balls. Then flatten them until thin and make a hole in the center like a doughnut. Slide into hot oil. Fry on each side until light brown. Remove and drain on layer of paper towels. Eat while warm.

Studying Native American Masks

Begin a study of masks by showing the excellent film, *The Loon's Necklace* (Britannica Films, 11 minutes), a legend told by the artful filming of authentic masks from the Pacific Northwest. Have students explore fiction and nonfiction about Native Americans to learn about the importance of masks in Native cultures. Following are a few resources to use:

Yvonne Y. Merrill. *Hands on Alaska: Art Activities for All Ages.* K/ITS, 1994. (8115 Jewell Lake Road; Anchorage, AK 99502.) Beautiful book includes pictures of artifacts and instruction showing students how to replicate original Native American crafts. Highly recommended.

Indian Handicrafts Catalog. Southwest Indian Foundation; Box 86; Gallup, NM 87302–0001. A wide range of dolls, pottery, drums, and so on of interest to children and adults.

California Indian Arts—1997. A full-color calendar of California Indian art. Heyday Books; Box 9145; Berkeley, CA 94709.

Students can create their own masks from heavy cardboard. Folding the cardboard in half makes it fit the child's face more closely. A piece of elastic holds it securely in place.

The shape of the mask and the way the eyes are developed serve to suggest the person or animal. It is not necessary, however, to be overly realistic. Masks can then be used to tell folktales, perhaps pourquoi tales the children have written.

Native American Poetry

Share these poems with the children in your room. Display the following poem over an outline of the intriguing Kokopelli figure included below. Kokopelli is the hunchbacked flute player (and water sprinkler) found throughout the Southwest.

May I Walk

On the trail marked with pollen may I walk,
With grasshoppers about my feet may I walk,
With dew about my feet may I walk,
With beauty may I walk,
With beauty before me, may I walk,
With beauty behind me, may I walk,
With beauty above me, may I walk,
With beauty under me, may I walk,
With beauty all around me, may I walk,
In old age wandering on a trail of beauty, lively, may I walk,
In old age wandering on a trail of beauty, living again, may I walk,
It is finished in beauty.
—*Navajo*

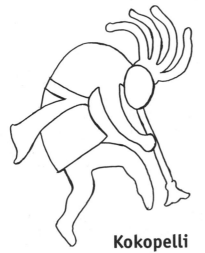

Kokopelli

Reading poetry written by people from another culture is an excellent way of learning about shared values and cultural differences. Feature examples from the following excellent collections.

Hettie Jones. *The Trees Stand Shining: Poetry of the North American Indians.* Illustrated by Robert Andrew Parker. Dial, 1993. These oral tradition poems are really folk chants and songs, preserved for generations and only written down and translated in the nineteenth century. Each is short, identified by tribe, and grouped by similar topic.

Joseph Bruchac and Jonathan London. *Thirteen Moons on Turtle's Back: A Native American Year of Moons.* Illustrated by Thomas Locker. Philomel, 1992. Poems about the moon, representing traditions from different tribes, such as Pomo, Cree, and Abenaki. These poems transmit respect for the power and wisdom of the natural world.

Joseph Bruchac, ed. *New Voices from the Longhouse: An Anthology of Contemporary Iroquois Writing.* Greenfield Review Press, 1989. Poems and short prose represent thirty contemporary adult writers. The book includes photographs, brief biographies of the poets, and a map of Iroquois settlements.

Shonto Begay. *Navajo: Visions and Voices across the Mesa.* Scholastic, 1995. Art and poetry illustrate the struggle for balance and harmony in contemporary Native life.

Neil Philip, ed. *Songs Are Thoughts: Poems of the Inuit.* Illustrated by Maryclare Foa. Orchard, 1995. Originally collected by Danish ethnologist in 1920s, these poems are meant to be sung. Includes information on cultural context.

Arlene Hirschfelder and Beverly Singer, eds. *Rising Voices: Writings of Young Native Americans.* Scribner's, 1992. Poems and short prose by middle and high school students represent a variety of tribes and regions. The poems were chosen to reflect concerns about identity, education, and harsh realities.

After reading some of these examples, students can choose to write poems based on similar themes of nature or identity. Students can also write poems as a response to the unit on Native Americans, to show their reactions to what they have learned.

A Mural of Native American Life

After students have gained information through reading and discussing topics related to Native American life, have them plan a large mural to which each one can contribute. The space of the mural might be considered similar to the map of the United States. Roughly, then, space could be allocated to activities associated with the Plains Indians, those of the Southwest, the Pacific Northwest, and so on. Sketch this plan on the chalkboard.

Bring in books with pictures that suggest scenes to be included. Crayons can be used for the figures, and the background can be painted in with pale brown or light green, as appropriate. When the mural is completed, display it in the school hall or a room where all can see it.

A Culminating All-School Assembly

Plan a school assembly to share the results of your study. Let students discuss various ways they can present an informative and entertaining program. Consider some of the following activities:

- An introduction (the purpose of your study and some of the things you learned).
- Presentation of the mural with an explanation of the many Native American tribes in what is now the United States.
- Reader's Theater presentation of folklore from the tribe native to your area, which might include music.
- Demonstration of Native American sports, dances, and so on.
- Creative dramatization of a Native American story.
- An invitation to visit your room to see the things you have made.

Sources of Information for Teaching about Native Americans: Yesterday and Today

Beverly Slapin and Doris Seale, eds. *Through Indian Eyes: The Native Experience in Books for Children.* New Society Publishers, 1992. Includes guidelines for evaluating treatment of Native Americans in curriculum materials.

The American Indian Museum of Natural History, Central Park West and 79th Street, New York, NY 10024.

Bureau of Indian Affairs, Department of Interior, Washington, D.C. 20242. Ask for their list of penpals.

Museum of the American Indian, Broadway at 155th St., New York, NY 10032.

The Earth Is Our Mother: A Guide to the Indians of California, Their Locales & Historic Sites. Trees Company Press, 1996. Historical coverage; lists museums and calendar of annual events.

Jane Katz, ed. *Messengers of the Wind: Native American Women Tell Their Life Stories.* Ballantine, 1995. Interesting collection for teacher resource.

Nunatsiaq News (www.nunanet.com/~nunat/). Serves the Inuit people of Canada's Northwest; good resource with a Photo Gallery, Kid's Page.

Creation's Journey: Native American Music. CD or cassette. Smithsonian/Folkways/National Museum of the American Indian. Includes many tribes.

Carolyn Meyer. *In a Different Light: Growing Up in a Yu'pik Eskimo Village in Alaska.* Simon & Schuster, 1996. Month by month presentation of activities and family life.

500 Nations: Stories of the North American Indian Experience. CD-ROM. Microsoft, 1995. Best CD-ROM available on history of Native Americans; includes wonderful music, photographs, interviews of contemporary Native Americans; for Windows.

Barbara J. Kuipers. *American Indian Reference and Resource Books for Children and Young Adults.* Libraries Unlimited, 1995. Extensive annotated list of recommended books; how to incorporate into curriculum.

Women of Hope: Native Americans/Hawaiian. 1997. Bread and Roses Cultural Project, Local 1199, 330 W. 42nd St., 4th floor, New York NY 10036. Twelve posters of women and a study guide with biographies and information about the issues.

Westridge Young Writers Workshop. *Kids Explore the Heritage of Western Native Americans.* John Muir, 1995. Information collected and reported by elementary students.

REFLECTIONS

Students bring their cultural backgrounds with them to school. Because culture is usually invisible, it is often difficult to recognize its effects. As teachers, you cannot resolve all the social issues that beset children's lives, but you can make a difference through effective teaching. Student-centered teaching involves students in a partnership, as everyone contributes to learning.

APPLICATIONS

1. How influential is our language in creating and maintaining stereotypes and prejudices? Pick a group that you belong to, for example:

parent	blonde
athlete	wears glasses

What phrases or descriptions are associated with the group you selected? Do they carry positive or negative connotations? How do they make you feel when somebody uses them? What effect might these words have on children's ideas about you? Discuss your results in small groups. Would you want to change some of the language used?

2. Begin to collect a picture file. Look for pictures of men, women, boys, and girls who represent a variety of ethnic and racial backgrounds and who are engaged in both common and unusual activities. Mount them on cardboard with a plastic overlay for protection, then group them according to subject or possible use. Is it easy to find pictorial representations of all groups in our society (or in the world), in all occupations? Which groups are rarely depicted? What impression do students receive who seldom see pictures of people like themselves or their family? Write two lesson plans using your picture file.

3. Using the evaluation form given in the chapter (or one of your own), select ten children's books (fiction and nonfiction) to evaluate for race, age, sex, or other stereotypes. Decide how you would use each book to promote awareness and acceptance of diversity. What would you do with such books as *Huckleberry Finn* or *Little House in the Big Woods,* which some have condemned for their racism? How could you use each book to discuss the destructiveness of stereotyping? Select books that have been criticized for stereotyped language or images and develop two lesson plans that teach critical thinking.

EXPLORING FURTHER

James Banks. (1997). *Educating Citizens in a Multicultural Society.* New York: Teachers College Press.

Deborah Byrnes. (1988). *"Teacher, They Called Me a _____!" Prejudice and Discrimination in the Classroom.* Anti-Defamation League of B'nai B'rith. (823 United Nations Plaza, New York, NY 10017.)

Paul Christiansen, & Michelle Young. (1997). *Yesterday, Today, and Tomorrow: Meeting the Challenge of Our Multicultural America and Beyond.* San Francisco, CA: Caddo Gap Press.

Linda Miller Cleary, & Thomas D. Peacock. (1998). *Collected Wisdom: American Indian Education.* Boston, MA: Longwood.

James Cummins. (1995). Power and Pedagogy in the Education of Culturally Diverse Students. In J. Frederickson, ed. *Reclaiming Our Voices,* pp. 99–138. Ontario, CA: California Association of Bilingual Education.

Interracial Books for Children Bulletin. The Council on Interracial Books for Children.

Alvin Josephy, ed. (1993). *America in 1492.* New York: Knopf.

Peter Nabakov, ed. *Native American Testimony: A Chronicle of Indian-White Relations from Prophecy to the Present, 1492–1992.* New York: Viking.

Maynard Reynolds, ed. (1989). *Knowledge Base for the Beginning Teacher.* New York: AACTE/ Pergamon.

Evelyn Wolfson. (1988). *From Abenaki to Zuni: A Dictionary of Native American Tribes.* New York Walker.

It takes
a whole village
to raise a child.

—African Proverb

CHAPTER 7

Enlarging Student Perspectives

One of our primary tasks as teachers is to prepare students to live in the wider world. Because we cannot know exactly what they will face, we try to give them the adaptability and self-confidence to make their way under any circumstances. Because we are all part of a community, we cannot separate the interests of some people from the interests of the rest, the success of some students from the success of all. Every one of us has a stake in the task of educating our children for the future.

The lens through which we view multicultural education in this chapter is that of power. Although discussion of power may conflict with the American ideology of democracy, equal opportunity, and achievement through individual effort, we can see the effects of the unequal allocation of social resources in our students and the schools. When students walk through the door on the first day of school, experienced teachers can sort them into groups: those who have absorbed the belief that the world belongs to them and those who have learned that the world is not set up for people like them. Early experiences of privilege or marginalization based on skin color, language, or culture are powerful forces in the maintenance of the social status quo.

Multicultural education is often equated with support services for "minority" students. But the term "minority" is misleading because it focuses attention on the relative size of a group rather than its lack of access to power. Consider societies such as South Africa in which the apartheid system enabled the white minority to maintain control. "Historically disadvantaged" may be a more accurate term, reflecting long-standing policies of social, economic, and legal exclusion. For example, women are still struggling to achieve parity with men in many spheres. However, multicultural education must include any group whose members have been denied access to the full human rights enjoyed by others. In this chapter, we open students' eyes to the full range of the human community.

By 2050, half of all Americans will probably be non-white. Our definitions will have to change: who is an "American," who has control over increasingly scarce resources, whose history is studied in books, whose culture is represented in school. These shifts are reflected in the problems facing teachers today. Schools are institutions that preserve and transmit fixed knowledge, yet teachers are expected to prepare students for the future. How will this affect your teaching and your relations with students?

After reading this chapter, you should be able to:
- Direct students' attention to problems and issues in their community.
- Develop students' skills for living in a larger world.
- Increase students' understanding of the diversity of cultures in the United States through the study of folklore.
- Incorporate information about the history and accomplishments of African Americans throughout the curriculum.

EXPLORING YOUR COMMUNITY

Most students today live in urban settings. They are familiar with violence, poverty, and the increasing breakdown of traditional social support systems. Focus attention on the nature of their community and the factors that influence its condition. Show students that school can be a place to talk about what is most important in their lives. At the same time, expect them to learn how to analyze and think critically about their circumstances.

The Neighborhood

Explore the concept of a neighborhood with your students. Does the area where your school is located have a name? Do all students live in the same neighborhood? Talk about the neighborhood. What are the most significant spots to students? (church, school, park, ice cream store, etc.) Bring a city map and have the students mark where they live. You can show students that a word such as *neighborhood* is a *concept,* an idea in people's minds, rather than a physical object, so that there may be more than one definition of the neighborhood.

Have students write a description of their neighborhood. How do they feel about it? What are some of the people and places in it? What sights, sounds, smells do they think of?

For another writing activity have students complete these sentences.

My favorite place in the neighborhood is _____.

I like it because _____.

The most important thing that ever happened to me in the neighborhood was _____.

When I think of my neighborhood, I think of _____.

Students' responses to these prompts can be collected into an illustrated book entitled *Thoughts about Our Neighborhood.*

Have students compare their neighborhood to the one pictured in *A Street Called Home* by Aminah Brenda Lynn Robinson (Harcourt Brace, 1997). This accordion-style fold-out book portrays an African American neighborhood in Ohio in the 1940s.

A Neighborhood Map

Talk about maps with students. What are different kinds of maps? What goes into a map? What can maps be used for? In discussions about the neighborhood, students have talked about places and people of importance to them. Now each student can propose a list of elements to be included on a map of the neighborhood.

Construct a class map on a large sheet of butcher paper. Depending on the level of the students, you may decide to represent only one or two main streets, an interpretation of a larger area (not to scale), or a standard grid map with scale and/or cardinal directions. Students will enjoy developing symbols to use on the map (explained in the *key*) and illustrating or landscaping the map as much as they choose. A more elaborate project would be to create a relief map or three-dimensional model from clay, plaster, or similar material. Such a project will give students a different perspective of the place where all of them live.

Comparing Perspectives

Maps give you a different view of the world. Have students compare their own maps with maps prepared by other organizations. A street map of their neighborhood will show different relationships between areas. Aerial maps show features not visible from the ground. Many maps show political boundaries that are not physical features. Finally, all maps represent a particular perspective. Mapmakers tend to put themselves at the center and locate others based on that perspective. Students may be surprised to see that world maps published in other countries do not put North America at the center.

Source for maps are:

State tourist offices, community Chambers of Commerce (see addresses in the Appendix)

Federal government: Contact the Government Printing Office or the Superintendent of Documents, GPO, Washington, DC 20402

U.S. Geological Survey, Earth Sciences Information Center, 507 National Center, Reston, VA 22092

National Aeronautics and Space Administration (NASA), 400 Maryland Ave SE, Washington, DC 20546

Joel Makower, ed. *The Map Catalog*. Random House.

A Neighborhood Collage

Have students make a collage to represent their neighborhood. They can do this individually or prepare a class collage for a wall mural. Have them collect pictures and objects that portray their neighborhood. Think about:

What do I see in my neighborhood?
Who lives here?
What do people do in the neighborhood?
What kinds of buildings are found in the neighborhood?

A Place to Live

One issue that has become critical in many neighborhoods is the homeless. Perhaps as many as seven million Americans were homeless at some point in the late 1980s. Students may be aware of this problem through family and friends, or through the growing presence of people on the streets in their neighborhood. Talk with students about the importance of having a place to live. All people, all living things need shelter.

A good introduction to the concept of shelter for primary-grade students is Mary Ann Hoberman's *A House Is a House for Me,* illustrated by Betty Fraser (Viking, 1978). This pattern book lists shelters for many animals in rhyme. The final line is "the earth is a house for us all."

Another book, *Houses and Homes* by Ann Morris (Lothrop, Lee, and Shepard, 1992), offers a global approach, with photographs of people and their homes from around the world. Also look at Michael Rosen's *Home: A Collaboration of 300 Distinguished Authors and Illustrators to Aid the Homeless* (HarperCollins, 1992), which includes fifteen works that show the special meaning of home.

Enlist students in some form of action, to express their concerns about homelessness, such as writing to organizations that support better services, especially for homeless children. Share books such as Judith Berck's *No Place to Be: Voices of Homeless Children* (Houghton Mifflin, 1991), which includes quotations, photographs, and statistics about the causes and conditions of homelessness. Other books you can read with the class include the following:

Stephanie Tolan. *Sophie and the Sidewalk Man.* Four Winds, 1992. Sophie is saving money to buy a stuffed animal, but when she sees a homeless man sitting on the sidewalk she decides to give him half of her savings.

Paula Fox. *Monkey Island.* Orchard, 1991. Clay's mother has disappeared, leaving him in a welfare hotel. He takes to the streets, where he makes friends; but they're attacked, and Clay ends up in the hospital with pneumonia.

A Community Guidebook

What do students know about their community? How would they describe it to visitors? What do they think visitors might want to know about it?

Talk about the different elements that make up the community, such as people, services, places, history, and customs. Who might arrive in the community and need information? Have any students recently moved into the area? What did they have to find out? Talk about different types of visitors (including new arrivals), their reasons for coming, and the kind of information they would require. For example, if a family with young children moved into the area, they would want to know about schools, playgrounds, inexpensive family restaurants, and so on.

Decide what to include in your guidebook by determining who could benefit most from it. If there are other guidebooks to your area, examine them to discover what they have and have not included.

Divide students into small groups. Each group can take responsibility for a section of the book. They must decide among themselves how best to present this information (a list, description, story, illustration, etc.). Each student should have the opportunity to contribute something. Include other work done by students related to the community, such as the maps suggested in a previous activity.

When the groups have finished, their efforts can be assembled into a book that everyone will be proud of. You can have it duplicated for the parents, or even consider having it reproduced professionally and distributed by a group such as the local chamber of commerce.

Languages in Our Community

Do students know what languages are spoken in their area? Begin with local names. What languages have influenced local names? Ask families. What languages are spoken in the students' families? Do students know people who speak different languages?

Make a map or chart of the area on which to record the information students find. Have them research local history to see what the earliest languages were. Were there any Native American groups living nearby? What language did they speak and what happened to them? What do names of local places mean in these languages? Ask who the first European settlers were and what languages they brought with them. Trace the language history down to the present time. Students should be able to discover what the major local language groups are and how long their speakers have been in the area.

Once the major languages are identified, they can become an important resource for further study. Plan lessons around examples from these languages. Bring in people who speak various languages so that students can hear what the languages sound like.

Community History

Each community has its own history, reflecting the contributions of the various groups that comprise it. The history of the development of the community may reflect a mini-history of the state, or it may represent idiosyncratic development. In either case, students can learn a lot about the forces that formed this country by studying the example of their own community.

What is history? Talk about the idea of history. More than just a list of past presidents, history deals with events and their consequences, change, and the influence of the past on the present. Ask students why we would want to study history. Have them brainstorm a list of reasons and objectives for studying local history. What do they want to find out? The students might pose some of the following questions:

- Who was here first?
- What happened to them?
- Why did they come?
- What traces have they left behind?
- What did this area look like then?
- How did people live?

Next, talk about where the students would go to find the information they are seeking. Have students suggest as many different sources as possible. They might mention the following:

- Visit the local library.
- Interview people who have lived there a long time.

- Read old newspapers.
- Review city records (archives)—maybe old maps.
- Search the Internet.

The results of student research can be compiled in a booklet that is organized according to the questions the students asked and the answers they found. Share this information with the community.

If your students are interested in continuing their study, consult David Weitzman's *My Backyard History Book* (Little, Brown, 1975). This classic book, written by kids and teachers, is full of practical and creative ways to learn about the past and other people.

Interviewing: An Oral History Project

Investigating your community's history can turn into a yearlong project if students decide to find out more information by interviewing people about their past. As students define questions they would like to have answered, they can begin to create a list of people who might know the answers. Brainstorm a list of possible interviewees. Have students tell everyone they know about this oral history project in order to identify more people to interview. They might ask the following questions:

- How long have you lived here?
- What was this town like when you first came?
- Where did you live when you were a child about my age?
- What was school like for you at that time?

Discuss what an interview is. What does the interviewer do? What is the interviewee supposed to do? Decide what questions you want to ask. Decide how you will record the information (tape recorder, notes on paper?). Prepare an interview schedule.

The most important aspect of this activity is the process that students go through, so the task should be carefully adapted to suit the level of the students. Students will come into contact with a different group of people (older people) and they will learn about people who are similar to and yet different from themselves. Children not only gain information related to social studies through this technique, they also increase language abilities. Both oral and written skills are developed as they conduct the interview, report back to the class, and record the results for a class book.

An English teacher in an Appalachian community developed the study of oral history to such an extent that his students have published several collections of their writings, starting with *The Foxfire Book* in 1972. There are now nine Foxfire books, edited by Eliot Wigginton and published by Doubleday Anchor Books. Information about the Foxfire Teacher Networks is available from Foxfire Teacher Outreach, PO Box 541, Mountain City, GA 30562.

Another example of oral history is *Cracked Corn and Snow Ice Cream: A Family Almanac* (Harcourt Brace, 1997), by Nancy Willard—recollections of rural relatives in Iowa and Wisconsin.

A Community Time Line

A time line can help students organize the information they have discovered about their community. Make a list of all the various dates, events, and historical periods that are important to your study of the community. Transfer this list, in chronological order, to a line drawn across several sheets of butcher paper. This can become a class mural as students add to the time line and update it. You can also have students draw or cut out illustrations for significant historical events.

Personalizing History

When students compare their own lives with the history of their community, they can begin to see the connections between historical events and what has happened to them. What was happening in the community when they were born? Have them ask their parents or other relatives what they remember from that time. Students also can look up the front page of the local newspaper for their birthdate to see what people were thinking and talking about. Then they can report to the class on the significant events of the day that was most significant to them.

What has happened in the community and the world since the students were born? Using the time line they developed for their community and researching important inventions and world events, they can construct a list of the most significant happenings of the past ten years, more or less. (Opinions on what to include may vary among the students.) Now have students discuss and write about how these events affected them and their family. How has the world changed since they were born? How is it the same?

Community Issues

Students are members of a community and the problems of that community affect them, too. What do they think are the major issues facing their community today? Some responses may be:

Drugs
Graffiti
Gang violence
Traffic

How do these issues affect them? Often the opinions of young people are ignored in discussions. What would students like to say? They can make their voices heard by writing a letter to the editor of the local newspaper. Have students compose a letter in their cooperative learning groups or as a whole class.

CONTRIBUTIONS OF DIFFERENT GROUPS

As we look at the variety of groups in the United States, we can see that the melting pot model is an illusion. Immigrants from different countries were glad to achieve greater freedom and economic opportunities, but they never completely lost awareness of their distinct heritages. For many of these groups, schooling has been a double-edged sword. It has provided the necessary access to prestige, knowledge, and skills; yet at the same time it has acted as a mechanism to reduce the uniqueness of local identities and traditional cultures. The tension between assimilation or acculturation and maintenance of one's culture is an important issue in education today. Today, as we shift our perspective to look at diversity as an asset, schools can welcome many cultures that were not acknowledged before.

Writing an "Autobiography"

As students find out more about the history of their community and their origins, they can personalize their study by researching and writing an autobiography of an imagined ancestor. Tell the class to choose a period and decide what their ancestors might have been doing then—arriving in America, pioneering the West, struggling in a city or on a farm. Students will need to read books, both fiction and nonfiction, to supply information on how people lived, as well as the position or treatment of groups in that period. Their autobiographies can take the form of a day in their character's life, several journal entries, or a description of the influences on that person. They can also illustrate their account and read it to the class.

We All Belong to Many Groups

Ask students to list on a sheet of paper all the groups they belong to. After they have had time to write a number of ideas, ask each person to tell one group they belong to; encourage them to share different ideas as much as possible. As new ideas are suggested, have students add to their individual lists. Then ask children to draw pictures of themselves and to list all the groups they belong to. Display these pictures on the wall. They can then be bound in a class book: Room 15, the Class of 1999.

Sue Wong is . . .
a girl
a daughter
a member of the Wong family
a Californian
a member of this class
a twelve-year-old
a Chinese American
a U.S. citizen
an athlete

Immigrants and Refugees

Most of the population of the United States arrived here through immigration, but many people whose families have been here several generations don't know what it means to be an immigrant and to struggle for survival. Nearly half the current population of the United States can trace their ancestors back to Ellis Island, the famous threshold of arrival in New York. In the peak years of immigration (from 1900 to 1914), the Ellis Island immigration station processed five thousand people a day. *Ellis Island: Gateway to the New World* by Leonard Fisher (Holiday House, 1986) contains photographs and stories of immigrants. See also *Ellis Island and Beyond* by Wendy Wilson and Jack Papadonis (Lerner, 1996).

Now both legal and illegal immigration are topics in the news as people from non-European countries arrive in increasing numbers. Students can explore this topic in terms of family history (When did their ancestors immigrate? Where did they arrive? How were they treated when they arrived?), as a human issue (How does it feel to leave your country? What factors make people take this risk?), and as a source of social questions (Can we accommodate all people, including families, from different countries?). By reading some of the following books, students can take the first steps toward understanding and empathizing with immigrants of previous generations and of today.

Bette Bao Lord. *In the Year of the Boar and Jackie Robinson.* Harper, 1984. The accomplishments of Jackie Robinson, black baseball star, help Shirley Temple Wong make the adjustment from China to America.

Russell Freedman. *Immigrant Kids.* Dutton, 1980. Photographs and stories of immigrants to New York, from the late nineteenth to the early twentieth century, focus on children's experiences.

Margy Burns Knight. *Who Belongs Here: An American Story.* Illustrated by Anne Sibley O'Brien. Tilbury, 1993. The story of Nary, a Cambodian refugee, who encounters racism and distrust of immigrants in the United States. The book asks who would be left if all the immigrants had to go back to their home countries. The book also introduces people working to help immigrants succeed. Although a picture book, the ideas will be provocative for students at all levels.

Karen Hesse. *Letters from Rifka.* Holt, 1992. The journey of a Jewish family from Russia to the United States, told in letters from a young girl, reveals courage and perseverance.

Frances Temple. *Grab Hands and Run.* Orchard, 1993. Twelve-year-old Felipe is a political refugee. His father has disappeared in El Salvador. Only his mother remains to lead the family to a safe haven in Canada.

Susan Kuklin. *How My Family Lives in America.* Bradbury, 1992. This book presents pictures of today's "American" families. Sanu's father comes from Senegal, Eric's family is from Puerto Rico, and April's family comes from Taiwan.

Sybella Wilkes. *One Day We Had to Run: Refugee Children Tell Their Stories in Words and Paintings.* Millbrook, 1995. Powerful images, mostly children from Sudan, Somalia, Ethiopia. Includes information on conflict in Rwanda, suggestions for use by teachers.

Keith Elliot Greenberg. *An Armenian Family.* Lerner, 1997. Describes a family that left the former Russian republic to escape ethnic conflict.

Stephen Chicoine. *A Liberian Family.* Lerner, 1997. A family flees war-torn Liberia for Houston, from *Journey between Two Worlds* series.

Julia Pferdehirt. *One Nation, Many Peoples: Immigration in the United States.* Knowledge Unlimited, 1997. Useful background and other information.

Exploring Regions and Cultures

Throughout our country there are small pockets of people who share a unique culture. Challenge students to discover such groups as the following: Amish, Mennonites, Cajuns. In addition there are groups such as the Gypsies, whose presence is less recognized. What distinctive groups are found in your state? How do these groups resist pressures to assimilate and manage to preserve their distinct identity?

We Are All Americans

Focus attention not only on heroes and heroines, the people whose names are well known, but also on ordinary people of different ethnic groups who make up this country. Prepare a display, for example, based on Walt Whitman's well-known poem, "I Hear America Singing," from his collection *Leaves of Grass*. Use the title of the poem as a caption.

Around the poem display pictures of Americans at work. Include members of different ethnic groups as well as people performing nonstereotyped jobs, such as a woman working on lines for the telephone company or a black father caring for his children.

Have students draw pictures of diverse Americans, people that they know, people they have studied, people in their class. This would be a good theme for a class quilt.

Recognizing Contributions of Others

Focus on broad topics that make it possible to observe the contributions of people from many ethnic groups. Consider such subjects as art through the ages, housing and shelter, foods of the world, and the urban environment. Within such studies students will learn that cultures have their distinctive qualities and contributions. Students will discover the universals of human needs such as eating and the problems of living together. See the unit on folklore in this chapter for an example.

Varied Religions

Help your students recognize that there are many religions represented in the United States.

Dominant Religions in the U.S. and Canada (1995):

Christians (including Roman Catholic, Protestant, Orthodox, and Anglican)	237.3 million
Nonreligious	25.3 million
Jews	7.0 million
Muslims	2.6 million
Others	5.7 million

What do students know about these religions? There are also less well-known religious groups, such as Quakers and Mormons, that have rich traditions of service to the community and support for equality of all peoples. Encourage students to become familiar with the diversity of religious belief. The following books will help:

Debbie Holsclaw Birdseye and Tom Birdseye. *What I Believe: Kids Talk about Faith.* Holiday, 1996. Six students talk about their religious beliefs, including Hindu, Buddhist, Jew, Christian, Muslim, and Native American.

*Jane Yolen. *O Jerusalem.* Illustrated by John Thompson. Blue Sky Press, 1996. This holy place for Jews, Christians, and Muslims is 3000 years old.

Catherine Chambers. *Sikh.* Children's Press, 1996. This introduction includes beliefs, activities, and a glossary.

*Demi. *Buddha.* Holt, 1996. A picture book about this religious figure.

Anita Ganeri. *What Do We Know about Hinduism?* Peter Bedrick, 1996. Shows how Hinduism affects people's daily lives.

Betsy Maestro. *Story of Religion.* Illustrated by Giulio Maestro. Clarion, 1997. Basic introduction to Judaism, Christianity, Islam, Buddhism, Hinduism, and Chinese religions for young readers.

Lisa Sita. *Worlds of Belief.* Black Birch, 1995. More in-depth coverage of major religions of the world, including leaders and rituals.

Susan Meredith. *Usborne Book of World Religions.* Usborne, 1996. Development, history, and practices of major religions.

William Jay Jacobs. *World Religions: Great Lives.* Atheneum, 1996. From the ancient world to the modern, profiles of religious leaders. Less familiar names are Baha'u'llah (founder of Baha'i), Ann Hutchinson (championed religious freedom in 1638), and Mary Baker Eddy (founder of Christian Science).

What Others Believe: Religions

Invite students to share with the class some of their religious beliefs, if any. Since stereotypes and prejudice are fed by ignorance, open discussion will aid in accepting and understanding different beliefs. Almost every Jewish child has seen a Christmas tree but how many non-Jewish children have seen a *dreidl?* Mormon children are sometimes taunted by those outside their faith because of misconceptions about Mormonism.

WORLD RELIGIONS

Christians (total)	1,928 million
Roman Catholic	968 million
Protestant	396 million
Orthodox	218 million
Anglican	71 million
other	276 million
Baha'i	6 million
Buddhist	324 million
Chinese folk religions	225 million
Confucians (Korea)	5 million
Hindus	781 million
Jain	5 million
Jew	14 million
Muslim	1,100 million
Sikh	19 million
Shinto	3 million

Source: *Encyclopedia Britannica* 1996.

Invite guests to the classroom—a rabbi, a priest, a Protestant minister (a woman?)—to talk briefly about a specific religion. It may be difficult to find information about religions such as Voodoo, Santería, Native American, or charismatic Christianity but these are important religions as well.

Asian Americans: A Diverse Group

"Hate Crimes on Rise Against Asian Americans" and "American Beats Kwan" (when American skater Tara Lipinski beat American skater Michelle Kwan at the 1998 Olympics): headlines such as these indicate the problems that Asian American children face, despite their reputation for performing well in schools. Use children's books to stimulate student discussion of these issues. What special obstacles do Asian American children encounter? How do the lives of Chinese Americans, Japanese Americans, Vietnamese Americans, and Filipino Americans differ, for example? Share books such as these:

Milly Lee. *Nim and the War Effort.* Illustrated by Yangsook Choi. Farrar, 1997. Autobiographical account of growing up in San Francisco's Chinatown, shows the tension between two worlds.

Yoshiko Uchida. *The Invisible Thread.* Simon and Schuster, 1995. First volume of this Japanese American writer's autobiography about growing up in California.

Check the Appendix for more examples.

Jewish Americans

The Jews are a different kind of grouping. Though often ethnically and racially homogenous, they are defined primarily by their religion. Yet there are many differences within this group. Black people can be Jewish. There are many Jews from Ethiopia, for example. Some Jews come from Eastern Europe (called Ashkenazi) and others from Spain, Portugal, and North Africa (called Sephardim). These groups bring different traditions with them despite a shared religion. In addition, there are distinct groups within the Jewish faith, such as Hasidic Jews.

Discuss with students the prejudice against Jews, called anti-Semitism. According to the Anti-Defamation League of the B'nai B'rith, anti-Semitic incidents declined in 1996 but an apparent increase in anti-Semitic postings on the Internet is worrying. Although spoken slurs may be declining, negative stereotypes of Jews still persist. Help students confront these ideas and attitudes by presenting information about Jewish people to the class. Offer books on history, Jewish folklore, and the contemporary experience of Jewish children.

Eric A. Kimmel. *The Adventures of Hershel of Ostropol.* Holiday, 1995. Stories of a folk hero in nineteenth century Ukraine.

Howard Schwartz. *Next Year in Jerusalem: 3,000 Years of Stories.* Viking, 1996. Folktales and historical lore from the center of Jewish culture.

Maxine Rose Schur. *Sacred Shadows.* Dial, 1997. A girl living in a German area that was retaken by Poland experiences anti-Semitism in the years before Hitler.

Nina Jaffe. *The Mysterious Visitor.* Illustrated by Elivia Savadier. Scholastic, 1997. Real-life settings for eight magical Jewish tales about the prophet Elijah, heaven's messenger of peace.

Racial Identity: The Census

In the year 2000 census of the U.S. population, for the first time people will be able to check off more than one category in the question about race. People whose parents are of different races will no longer have to choose the race of one parent over the other. At one time, a single drop of African American blood, if anyone knew about it, was enough to place the person in the category of African American. Today, people are more conscious of mixed racial identity. The NAACP estimates that 70% of African Americans are of mixed racial heritage. The example of Tiger Woods, young golf champion, points out the difficulty of assigning a single racial label to someone who has Caucasian, Black, Native American, and Asian ancestry. In addition, Latinos may be Caucasian, Native American, African American, or any combination of these groups. In 1990, two million children had parents of different races, and this number is expected to increase.

Have students conduct a "census" (counting) of the class according to the 1990 census categories and then according to the 2000 census categories.

1990 (check one)	*2000 (check all that apply)*
_____ Black	_____ American Indian/Alaskan Native
_____ White	_____ Asian
_____ Asian/Pacific Islander	_____ Black/African
_____ Native American	_____ Native Hawaiian/Pacific Islander
_____ Alaska Native	_____ White
_____ Other (ethnic)	_____ (ethnic) Hispanic/Latino

Compare the results. Are the totals for each group different depending on which form is used? Which do students believe is more accurate in reflecting the composition of the class? This survey can be extended to a larger group, including other classes or members of the community. Note that all responses must be anonymous.

Students can discuss the implications of the 2000 census and its categories. Why does the government conduct a census? The results are used in planning many programs, particularly social services. What might happen if the figures for the African American population are smaller than expected?

Interracial Relations

Literature can provide case studies of prejudice and conflict in the relationships between members of different races. Students from interracial families may feel that they belong in neither camp. Use these examples to stimulate student problem solving. How would they resolve these identity conflicts? Is it possible to be friends with someone from another race?

Mildred D. Taylor. *The Friendship and the Gold Cadillac*. Bantam, 1989. Two stories of prejudice, one told by Cassie Logan, about a neighbor who thought he had a special relationship with a white man, and another about an African American family from Ohio who travel south to Mississippi and are frightened by the racial hostility they experience.

Arnold Adoff. *All the Colors of the Race*. Illustrated by John Steptoe. Lothrop, Lee and Shepard, 1982. "All the colors of the race are in my face," begins the poetic expression of a young girl's experience in an interracial family. (Adoff is married to Virginia

Hamilton.) The poems express with poignancy how hard it is to cope with other people's expectations of being one or the other, black or white.

Pat Costa Viglucci. *Sun Dance at Turtle Rock.* Stone Pine Books, 1996. Cody Spain, a biracial boy, visits his white relatives in a small town in Pennsylvania. His grandfather has never accepted Cody's African American heritage.

Faith Ringgold. *Bonjour, Lonnie.* Hyperion, 1993. A boy of mixed race lives in Paris.

*Toyomi Igus. *Two Mrs. Gibsons.* Illustrated by Daryl Wells. Children's Book Press, 1996. A young girl pays tribute to her grandmothers, one Japanese and one African American.

Patricia McKissack. *Run Away Home.* Scholastic, 1997. In Alabama, 1888, an African American sharecropper family takes in a fugitive Apache boy.

*Kathryn Lasky. *Marven of the Great North Woods.* Illustrated by Kevin Hawkes, Harcourt Brace, 1997. During the 1918 flu epidemic, a Jewish family in Minnesota sends their son to a camp of French Canadians.

Paul Fleischman. *Seedfolks.* HarperCollins, 1997. A childless Korean widow and a pregnant Mexican American teen come together in an ethnically diverse Cleveland neighborhood to plant a garden.

City Life

Urban living is a broad topic that encompasses many subjects of interest to those who live in the city as well as those who live in suburban or rural settings. As the subject of city living is explored, an important element to consider is the multiethnic population. Explore books such as the following about people living in the city:

Langston Hughes. *The Block.* Collage by Romare Bearden. Metropolitan Museum of Art/Viking, 1995. A city block in Harlem, New York.

Rachel Isadora. *City Seen from A to Z.* Greenwillow, 1983.

*Patricia Casy. *Beep! Beep! Oink! Oink!* Animals in the City. Candlewick, 1997.

Share poems about city living as another way of exploring this topic. A useful collection for younger children is *A Song in Stone: City Poems,* compiled by Lee Bennett Hopkins (Crowell, 1983). A collection for upper elementary and junior high level is *On City Streets,* selected by Nancy Larrick (Bantam, 1969).

Children can write city poems, too. Begin with the words, *A city is.* . . . Collectively or individually, children can add phrases like this to form a list poem:

A city is . . .
   Horns honking—
   Red lights,
   Green lights—
   Traffic on the go!

A city is . . .
   People walking—
   Down the street,
   Up the street—
   In sun or rain or snow.

HOW WE LIVE IN A GLOBAL VILLAGE

It has become increasingly obvious that the way we live affects people in other countries and that what they do affects us here. From the clearing of the rain forests in the Amazon, to an oil spill in Alaska, human actions can upset the earth's elaborately balanced ecological system. Political events also spill over national boundaries. The overthrow of apartheid in South Africa and the dismemberment of the former Soviet Union have consequences for people in many other countries. Your teaching must prepare students to live in a world that is becoming increasingly interdependent. More than ever before, students need to know about their peers in other countries and to understand how people think and live in other parts of the world.

Topic for Thought: From Right to Peace

Discuss the Chinese proverb below. Have students notice the progression from *right* to *peace*. Students can discuss the importance of peace and how it can be brought about.

> If there is right in the soul,
> There will be beauty in the person;
> If there is beauty in the person,
> There will be harmony in the home;
> If there is harmony in the home,
> There will be order in the nation;
> If there is order in the nation,
> There will be peace in the world.
>
> Chinese Proverb

This poetic presentation can also be used as a model for student writing. They can follow this pattern:

If there is _____ ,

There will be _____ .

Two-line free verse poems can be produced like this:

If there is prejudice anywhere,
There will be unhappiness.

Repeating this pattern produces additional verses. The verses could be rhymed, thus:

> If there is one friend in your life,
> There will be singing.
> If there is love in your life,
> There will be joy-bells ringing.

Living in Other Countries

One of the best ways for students to experience what it is like to live in different countries is to read books about children of their own age who have traveled to a different country or who are growing up in another country. Here are some books you can suggest:

Books about Childhood in Another Country

Africa: Lyall Watson. *Warriors, Warthogs, and Wisdom: Growing Up in Africa.* Kingfisher, 1997.

Egypt: Betsy Byars. *The 18th Emergency.* Viking, 1973.

England: Mabel Alan. *A Dream of Hunger Moss.* Dodd, 1983.

Greece: William Mayne. *The Glass Ball.* Dutton, 1962.

Netherlands: Meindert DeJong. *The Wheel on the School.* Harper and Row, 1954.

Spain: Maia Wojciechowska. *Shadow of a Bull.* Atheneum, 1964.

General: Maya Ajmera and Anna Rhesa Versola. *Children from Australia to Zimbabwe: A Photographic Journey around the World.* Charlesbridge, 1997.

Books about American Children Living in Other Countries

Tobago: Caroline Binch. *Gregory Cool.* Dial, 1994.

China: Jean Fritz. *Homesick: My Own Story.* Putnam, 1982.

Lebanon: Belle D. Rugh. *Crystal Mountain.* Houghton Mifflin, 1955.

Making Sense out of Population Figures

How many people live in the world today? Have students guess and write their estimates on the board. Did anyone come close to 6 billion? (Source: Population Reference Bureau 1998.) Such a large number has virtually no meaning to most of us unless we can express it in familiar terms. Research some comparative figures. How many people live in your city? How many live in the state? What's the population of the United States?

Have students predict what country has the largest population and what country has the greatest land area. They may be surprised to learn that China has the largest population of any country in the world: over 1.2 billion inhabitants, 21 percent of the world's population. India is second with 968 million people; its population is expected to reach 1 billion by the end of the decade. The United States is next, with a population of only 270 million, followed by Indonesia, Brazil, Russia, Pakistan, Japan, Bangladesh, and Nigeria. Russia has the largest land area, over 6.5 million square miles, followed by Canada, China, the United States, and Brazil.

Explore different strategies to represent the relative sizes of the population of the United States and the world. Students can make pie charts or block graphs. Another technique is to choose a small object such as a book, pencil, or apple to represent a fixed number (1000, for example). How many books would it take to show the population of your city, state, country, or the world? Demonstrations like this help students to understand and visualize large numbers and the relation between thousands, millions, and billions.

Studying Population: Demography

Ask students if they know what a demographer does. Can they figure it out on the basis of the roots *demo* and *graph?* (Think of other words that have these roots in them.) Reward the first student who uses the meanings of the roots to come up with a definition close to "one who measures population and its characteristics."

Challenge students to become *demographers* and find out how fast the population is growing. Has the rate of growth changed over time? Compare the growth rate in this century with the past century. What does this growth rate predict for the next ten years? Twenty years? Some areas are growing at different rates. How will the composition of the world change in the next ten years? Twenty years? What about age? How will the percentage of old and young people change over the next ten years? Why will this change? What effects might this have on all of us?

How do we count population figures? Is it really possible to count everyone living in the country on one day? What factors might affect the accuracy of this figure? Are there specific groups that might be "undercounted" or "overcounted"?

Dealing with Social Injustice and Global Conflict

As you talk with students about issues such as prejudice, racism, and the homeless, recognize their desire to take some action based on their beliefs. Although these large social questions will not be solved simply, do not discourage students from wanting to be involved. Despite their young age and lack of power in society, students have strong feelings about injustice. In discussing books and topics that raise troublesome questions, guide student responses into productive channels. What can students do? They can publicize problems, write letters, organize people, talk to others, invite people to speak, and publish their efforts. In *It's Our World, Too!* (Little, Brown, 1993), Phillip Hoose describes young activists who have taken a stand on sensitive issues such as sexism, racism, and the homeless and shows the power of people of any age to make a difference. Older students will appreciate *Finding Solutions to Hunger: Kids Can Make a Difference* by Stephanie Kempf (World Hunger Year, 1997). This book discusses both roots and solutions of hunger issues, from world famine to the working poor to colonialism.

One topic that concerns young people very much is war, or any violent conflict, and its impact on people. The following books will stimulate discussion of student fears and how these issues affect them:

Elizabeth Laird. *Kiss the Dust.* Dutton, 1992. Tara, thirteen, and her family are Kurds who are forced to flee Iraq during the 1984 war. They face a harsh existence in refugee camps.

*Yukio Tsuchiya. *Faithful Elephants: A True Story of Animals, People and War.* Translated by Tomoko Tsuchiya Dykes. Illustrated by Ted Lewin. Houghton Mifflin, 1988. The story of what happened to the elephants in the Tokyo zoo at the end of World War II, when there was no more food. This story has been read aloud in Japan for twenty years to mark the anniversary of the end of the war and as a reminder of the uselessness of war.

*Florence Heide. *Sami and the Time of the Troubles.* Clarion, 1992. A picture book about Sami, a ten-year-old Lebanese boy who spends his life in the basement bomb shelter hoping for peace.

Gaye Hicyilmaz. *Against the Storm.* Dell, 1993. This novel for older students is set in contemporary Turkey and focuses on the plight of displaced people and the strategies they use to survive.

Laurie Dolphin. *Neve Shalom/Wahat Al-Salam: Oasis of Peace.* Scholastic, 1993. Describes a unique village near Jerusalem where Israeli Arabs and Jews choose to live and work together. Although the Arab and Jewish families maintain separate cultures, they meet in the bilingual, bicultural school setting.

*Eve Bunting. *Smokey Night.* Illustrated by David Diaz. Harcourt, 1995. Conflict sets a city afire, from a child's perspective.

Marybeth Lorbiecki. *My Palace of Leaves in Sarajevo.* Dial, 1997. Girl's letters show the impact of ethnic conflict in Bosnia.

Dance—A Universal Language

Dance is something that is shared and understood around the world. Demonstrate the universality of dance and its themes by showing films of dancing performed by different cultures. Here are a few examples:

African Rhythms. 13 minutes, color. Associated Film, Inc., 1621 Dragon St., Dallas, TX 75207.

The Strollers. 6 minutes, color. The Moiseyev Dance Company in a Russian folk dance.

Dancer's World. 30 minutes. NET. Martha Graham discusses dancing as her students dance the emotions of hope, fear, joy, and love.

Students can learn some simple folk dances to perform.

International Folk Dancing, a book by Betty Casey. Doubleday, 1981. Includes directions and pictures of costumes for students.

Rhythms for Movement

Encourage students to move to various rhythms by playing recordings of music from different countries around the world. Representative records available include the following:

Authentic Afro-Rhythms. LP 6060, Kimbo Educational, P.O. Box 246, Deal, NJ 07723. Rhythms from Africa, Cuba, Haiti, Brazil, Trinidad, and Puerto Rico.

Authentic Indian Dances and Folklore. Kimbo Educational. Drumming and storytelling by Michigan Chippewa chiefs who narrate history of dances.

Authentic Music of the American Indians. 3 records. Everest. Chesterfield Music Shops, Inc., 12 Warren St., New York, NY 10007.

Folk Music from around the World

Folk songs from other countries offer immediate enjoyment through their patterned verses and easy-to-learn choruses.

Kathleen Krull. *Gonna Sing My Head Off!* Knopf, 1992. Folk music accompanied by energetic artwork.

Grace Hallworth. *Down by the River: AfroCaribbean Rhymes, Games, and Songs for Children.* Illustrated by Caroline Binch. Scholastic, 1996. Based on memories of growing up in Trinidad.

Songs for Singing Children with John Langstaff. CD/cassette.

John and Nancy Langstaff, comp. *Sally Go Round the Moon. Revels Songs and Singing Games for Young Children.* Revels, Inc., One Kendall Square, Bldg 600, Cambridge MA 02139.

The following are some of the recordings available in different formats:

Children's Songs and Games from Ecuador, Mexico, and Puerto Rico. Folkways FC 7854.

Sing Children Sing: Songs of Mexico. Caedmon TC 1654.

Alerta Sings Children's Songs in Spanish and English from Latin American, the Caribbean, and the United States. Folkways FH 7830.

Lírica Infantil con José-Luís Orozco. Hispanic Children's Folklore. Arco Iris Records, P.O. Box 7428, Berkeley CA 94707.

Suni Paz. *Canciones para el recreo: Children's Songs for the Playground.* Smithsonian Folkways. Catalog from Folkways, Office of Folklife Programs, 955 L'Enfant Plaza, Suite 2600, Smithsonian Institution, Washington DC, 20560. Or order from Rounder Records, One Camp Street, Cambridge MA 02140.

Ella Jenkins. *African American Folk Rhythms.* Smithsonian Folkways.

Sports and Games in Other Countries

Sports and games are of universal interest. Offer students the opportunity to learn about different games from other cultures. Students may already be aware of significant sports figures from other countries. In an Olympic year, plan activities related to the widespread interest in these sports and the countries represented.

Richard Lyttle. *The Games They Played: Sports in History.* Atheneum, 1982. Includes games from Greek, Roman, Egyptian, Spanish, Eskimo, and Mayan cultures.

The Olympics: An Educational Opportunity Enrichment Unit. 1750 East Boulder St., Colorado Springs, CO 80909. Curriculum materials for all grade levels, based on the Olympian theme.

David Wallechinsky. *The Complete Book of the Olympics.* Penguin, updated after each Olympiad. History and statistics of the Olympic Games.

Sarah Pooley. *Jump the World: Stories, Poems, and Things to Make and Do from around the World.* Dutton, 1997. A collection for ages 4–10.

Mary D. Lankford. *Jacks around the World.* Illustrated by Karen Dugan. Morrow, 1996. Fourteen variants of this favorite game. See also *Hopscotch around the World.*

Strategy Challenges. Collection 1: Around the World (includes Mancala, Nine Men's Morris, and Go-Moku). *Collection 2: In the Wild* (Surakarta [Java], Tablut [Lapland], and Jungle Chess), CD-ROM from Edmark, 1995. For ages 8 and up.

Human Needs

Looking at other cultures can help students learn more about themselves and their culture. After you have been studying a particular group of people or reading tales from several cultures, ask students to list the most basic needs they think are common to all cultures. Focus on the fundamental human needs for love, food, and shelter. Relate these to students' lives. How are these provided for in their lives? How do different groups satisfy them?

Students can brainstorm examples of how different people respond to one need, such as *love.* Then they can write personal responses, completing the sentence "Love is . . . " and illustrating their ideas. As a class, students can prepare a collage for the bulletin board, showing how different needs are met in different cultures, based on their own illustrations or examples they have found.

For a graphic representation of the global family, see *Material World: A Global Family Portrait* by Peter Menzel (Sierra Club, 1995). Thirty families, from countries such as Bosnia, Mali, Haiti, India, and Japan, were asked to display all their possessions and tell how they live. The striking disparities as well as similarities among the families will stimulate student interest and discussion.

STUDYING FOLKLORE WITH CHILDREN

Folklore refers to knowledge and stories passed on through an oral tradition. As they are retold, they are changed and adapted by their many anonymous tellers. Because the simple content of these tales is often confused with simplistic, folktales have become misidentified as stories for children. Instead, these stories are ways of passing on the elements of a culture. Often they are teaching stories intended for all members of a culture. The stories teach what is right and what is wrong and why members of the culture do what they do.

There are many types of folktales that express universal themes, such as creation stories, wonder stories, and tall tales. Many different groups possess distinctive folklore—stories, legends, traditions. They range from regional (such as Appalachian), and ethnic/racial groupings (Jewish, Hawaiian, Mexican American) to stories from other countries (Japan, Ireland), urban folklore (legends often passed on as true), and children's folklore (passed directly from child to child).

In order to work with students and folklore, it is important to choose the best examples in an area where the quality varies greatly. Consider the following criteria, adapted from the American Folklore Society:

- The use of folklore should be central to the book's content and, if appropriate, to its illustrations.
- The folklore, as presented in the book, should accurately present or reflect the cultural worldview of the people whose folklore is the focus of the book.
- The readers' understanding of the folklore should be enhanced by its appearance in the book, as should the book be enhanced by the presence of the folklore.
- The book should reflect the high artistic standards of the best of children's literature and should have strong appeal to the child reader.
- Folklore sources should be fully acknowledged and annotations referenced within the bound contents of the publication.

Through introducing students to folklore, you should expect to:

- Teach students about world cultures.
- Help them understand others through learning about the history, values, and traditions of another culture.
- Motivate students to explore the roots of their own heritage.

Incorporating Western Folklore into the Classroom

Introduce all students to the joys of Hans Christian Andersen, the Grimm Brothers, Charles Perrault, Aesop, and so on. It may seem strange to include Western folklore in a book on multicultural teaching but all students need to know where these stories come from. We cannot assume that all students have heard of the Greek and Roman myths that are part of our common culture, for example. No matter what their background, students can benefit from exploring these tales together. Once students are familiar with some of the stories, they can compare different versions. Have them analyze the language of the text and the details in the illustrations. Students can make generalizations to explain these differences. Start students with these retellings:

Neil Philip, retold. *The Adventures of Odysseus.* Illustrated by Peter Malone. Orchard, 1997. A version to introduce young people to this ancient tale.

Neil Philip, retold. *Fairy Tales of the Brothers Grimm.* Illustrated by Isabelle Brent. Viking, 1997. This collection sets the stories in the context of the scholarship of the time.

Writing from Folklore Models

When you have a mixed group of students, some of whom are familiar with a set of folktales and others are not, you need to teach folklore so that no one is left out. One way to do this is to treat these stories as models. Students can choose a story and write a different version of it, called a parody.

Show students some examples. Read students the conventional story of Rumpelstiltskin, in which the girl is rewarded with the king's hand in marriage for completing her spinning task. Ask them what would happen if the miller's daughter refused to marry the king. Here's how one author answered this question. Share Diane Stanley's *Rumpelstiltskin's Daughter* (Morrow 1997), where she marries Rumpelstiltskin instead.

Have students work in cooperative learning groups and study the original version closely so that they can write their own versions of traditional stories. Here are some suggestions for changes:

Make it contemporary.
Change the setting.
Tell what happened next.

The following examples will stimulate student ideas.

Gail Carson Levine. *Ella Enchanted.* HarperCollins, 1997. Here is a feminist version of the traditional Cinderella.

Janet and Allan Ahlberg. *The Jolly Postman, or Other People's Letters.* Little, Brown, 1986. This spirited look into the world of Mother Goose rhymes features the correspondence of familiar names such as the Wicked Witch, Cinderella, and Jack and the Beanstalk. Students who know the stories will enjoy retelling them to the class. Older students will appreciate the level of detail in the samples of letters that are included.

William Brooke. *Untold Tales.* HarperCollins, 1992. These are wacky versions of familiar folktales that will spark student interest in writing their own.

Jon Scieszka. *The Stinky Cheese Man.* 1992. Nine parodies of well-known folk tales are narrated by Jack (of Beanstalk fame).

Jon Scieszka. *The Frog Prince Continued.* Viking 1991. This version tells what happened after the popular ending "and they lived happily ever after." Students can make up their own endings for traditional tales.

Babette Cole. *Prince Cinders.* Putnam, 1987. This rewrite features a boy in the role of Cinderella. Imagine how the story would be changed.

Ed Young. *Seven Blind Mice.* Philomel, 1992. Noted illustrator's interpretation of a traditional story about the blind men and the elephant.

Steven Kellogg. *The Three Little Pigs.* Morrow, 1997. Mama Pig leaves the business to her three children when she retires but she has to return to rescue them from the wolf.

Susan Lowell. *The Bootmaker and the Elves.* Illustrated by Tom Curry. Orchard, 1997. Familiar story translated to a western setting.

Folklore from Different Cultures

When studying folklore with students, provide examples of the different types. *Creation* stories are powerful religious stories to be treated with care. These stories represent beliefs that are a central part of people's lives. When you talk about people's gods, take them as seriously as commonly acknowledged religious traditions such as the Bible and the Koran. Another popular type is the *pourquoi* story, which explains how something came to be. Students particularly enjoy *trickster* tales, such as Brer Rabbit in the African American tradition, Anansi the Spider in Africa, and Juan Bobo in Puerto Rico. In these stories, a character who is small or overlooked gets the better of someone more powerful or bigger. Share some of these folktales with students. Ask students if they know of any folktales. They can ask their parents or other people. Students can retell the stories they collect, write them down or record them, and illustrate them.

Robert San Souci, retold. *The Hired Hand: An African American Folktale.* Illustrated by Jerry Pinkney. Dial, 1997. Set in Virginia, this is a story of free blacks in the days before the Emancipation Proclamation.

Alma Flor Ada, retold. *Medio Pollito/Half-Chicken.* Illustrated by Kim Howard. Doubleday, 1995. A pourquoi tale in English and Spanish of why there's a chicken atop the weathervane.

Ellin Greene. *Ling-Li and the Phoenix Fairy: A Chinese Folktale.* Illustrated by Zong-Zhou Wang. Clarion, 1996. Ling-Li is an active heroine who does not shrink from obstacles.

Carol Ann Williams. *Tsubu, the Little Snail.* Illustrated by Tatsuro Kiuchi. Simon and Schuster, 1995. A childless couple are granted a son, a little snail. This story is based on Shintoism, one of the religions of Japan.

Joseph Bruchac, retold. *The Boy Who Lived with the Bears, and Other Iroquois Stories.* Illustrated by Murv Jacob. HarperCollins, 1996. Six traditional tales crafted for storytelling.

Judith Ernst, retold and illustrated. *The Golden Goose King: A Tale Told by the Buddha.* Parvardigar Press, 1995. This picture book can be used through high school to show the moral teachings, art, and culture of India. The illustrations are based on famous Buddhist wall paintings.

J. J. Reneaux. *Cajun Fairy Tales.* August House, 1996. Stories from a Cajun storyteller. Five of the stories are available on audiocassette, performed by Reneaux and accompanied by fiddle music.

Jeannette L. Faurot, ed. *Asian-Pacific Folktales and Legends.* Simon and Schuster, 1995. A variety of types of tales (creation, animals, magic gifts) from many lands (China, Japan, Philippines, Thailand).

Judy Sierra, retold. *Wiley and the Hairy Man.* Illustrated by Brian Pinkney. Lodestar, 1996. Here is a famous folktale from Alabama about the Hairy Man, part European devil, part African ogre, part Southern conjure doctor. Perfect for storytelling.

Sally Bahous. *Sitti and the Cats: A Tale of Friendship.* Illustrated by Nancy Malick. Roberts Rinehart, 1993. This Palestinian folktale introduces different words and a special culture.

Paul Goble. *Remaking the Earth: A Creation Story from the Great Plains of North America.* Orchard Books, 1996. From the well-known writer, based on Algonquin stories.

Jessica Souhami. *Rama and the Demonking: An Ancient Tale from India.* 1997. This classic story has illustrations based on shadow puppets and Indian paintings.

Minfong Ho and Saphan Ros. *The Two Brothers.* Illustrated by Jean and Mousien Tseng. Lothrop, 1995. This Cambodian story shows the importance of predestination as two brothers follow different paths in life.

Kavita Ram Shrestha and Sarah Lamstein. *From the Mango Tree and Other Folktales from Nepal.* Libraries Unlimited, 1997. Fifteen stories serve as an introduction to the history and culture of this country.

Norma J. Livo and Dia Cha. *Folk Stories of the Hmong: Peoples of Laos, Thailand, and Vietnam.* Libraries Unlimited, 1996. Twenty-seven tales accompanied by photos of Hmong dress and needlework.

Supaporn Vathanaprida, retold. (Margaret Read MacDonald, ed.) *Thai Tales: Folktales of Thailand.* Libraries Unlimited, 1995. Stories set in Buddhist traditions.

Audrey Burie Kirchner and Margaret R. Tassia. *In Days Gone By: Folklore and Traditions of the Pennsylvania Dutch.* Libraries Unlimited, 1996. Includes history and legends.

Rafe Martin. *Mysterious Tales of Japan.* Illustrated by Tatsuro Kiuchi. Putnam, 1996.

Margaret Mayo, retold. *When the World Was Young: Creation and Pourquoi Tales.* Illustrated by Louise Brierley. Simon and Schuster, 1995.

Jama Kim Rattigan, retold. *The Woman in the Moon: A Story from Hawai'i.* Illustrated by Carla Golembe. Little Brown, 1996.

Aaron Shepard, retold. *The Maiden of Northland: A Hero Tale of Finland.* Illustrated by Carol Schwartz. Simon and Schuster, 1996.

Nikki Siegen-Smith, comp. *Songs for Survival: Songs and Chants from Tribal Peoples around the World.* Illustrated by Bernard Lodge. Dutton, 1995.

Judy Sierra, retold. *Nursery Tales around the World.* Illustrated by Stefano Vitale. Clarion, 1996.

Laurence Yep. *The Butterfly Boy.* Illustrated by Jeanne Lee. Farrar Straus Giroux, 1993. A boy thinks he's a butterfly in this southern Chinese folktale. (Note that most Chinese Americans come from southern China but Chinese folktale collections reflect the culture of northern China.)

Jane Yolen. *Dream Weaver.* Illustrated by Michael Hague. Philomel, 1989. One of many collections of a respected folklorist's stories, reflecting universal themes. Great for reading aloud or learning for storytelling because of the exceptional quality of the language.

Yoko Kawashima Watkins. *Tales from the Bamboo Grove.* Bradbury, 1992. The author's parents kept their Japanese culture alive in Korea by telling these folktales.

Virginia Hamilton. *A Ring of Tricksters: Animal Tales from America, the West Indies, and Africa.* Illustrated by Barry Moser. Scholastic, 1997. An excellent collection of stories to compare similar ideas in different settings.

What Is a Folklorist?

After exploring the folklore from different cultures, regions, and groups, students will begin to realize that the stories they have grown up with are also worthy of attention. Show them how professional folklorists work.

"Folklore is the art of the people before they find out that there is any such thing as art" wrote Zora Neale Hurston (1891–1960). In Hurston's time, the value of African American tales was not yet recognized. She studied anthropology but realized that what people studied by going to distant islands and jungles could be applied to her own background and the stories she was surrounded by as a child. Hurston was born into a black community with an extensive oral tradition. She attended Harvard and Barnard but went back to her roots. She travelled to listen and collect stories heard in her childhood, particularly attending to the language used by the storytellers. Recent writers such as Alice Walker have been responsible for the rediscovery of Hurston's work. The following books will introduce students to this eminent folklorist:

*William Miller. *Zora Hurston and the Chinaberry Tree.* Illustrated by Cornelius Van Wright and Ying-Hwa Hu. Lee and Low, 1994. Tells the story of Hurston as a young girl, fascinated by stories. Her father said conform but her mother told her to imagine.

A. P. Porter. *Jump at de Sun: The Story of Zora Neale Hurston.* Carolrhoda, 1992. A biography for intermediate students.

Paul Witcover. *Zora Neale Hurston.* Chelsea, 1991. A more detailed look at her life for older students, puts her in the context of the Harlem Renaissance.

Della A. Yannuzzi. *Zora Neale Hurston: Southern Storyteller.* Enslow, 1996. Focuses on Hurston's early life and career and how she failed to achieve recognition in her lifetime.

Hurston's work is now back in print and is collected in two volumes: *Hurston: Novels and Stories,* and *Hurston: Folklore, Memoirs, and other Writings* (Library of America, 1995).

Another famous folklorist that students can investigate is Harold Courlander, known for collecting African tales. Find out what led him to become interested in this study by reading Nina Jaffe's *A Voice from the People: The Life and Work of Harold Courlander* (Holt, 1997).

Students Research Their Own Folklore

After discussion of folktales from different cultures, students will be encouraged to research stories from their own culture. Explain that very few folktales are ever written down. Although today folktales are often considered a part of children's literature and of interest only to children, in the past scholars often visited the elders of a cultural group and recorded the tales that they told. Why would anthropologists and folklorists be interested in stories from different, often obscure cultures?

Students can act as their own folklorists, to discover and preserve the valuable tales of their heritage. If no one asks to hear these stories or records them, the stories may be lost forever. Brainstorm with students ways to go about initiating this folklore investigation. Whom can they ask? What do they say if people claim they don't know any stories? Plan how to record the stories. Some students may have relatives who can write the stories in their original language. Students can translate the story and preserve both versions. In other cases, students can record the person telling the story and transcribe it later. If necessary, students can write the story down as the teller dictates it to them.

Students can choose one of the stories to present to the class. Students who speak the same language or share the same heritage can work together to develop a presentation that includes information about the culture and history of the tale.

For a model of teaching and learning about different folk traditions, share with students *In My Heart, I Am a Dancer* by Chamroeun Yin (Philadelphia Folklore Project, 1996). In this bilingual book (Cambodian/English), the author describes his life as a traditional Cambodian dancer. He also sews, gardens, and teaches.

A Multicultural Cinderella

The story of the valiant, loyal girl who is mistreated by her (step) sisters, but whose worth is finally recognized, is found in different versions in many cultures. To introduce this folktale to children, first read aloud a version that may be familiar to some of the children, for example, Marcia Brown's classic *Cinderella or The Little Glass Slipper* (Scribner's, 1954), which presents Charles Perrault's retelling. After discussing the plot of the story and the students' reactions to the behavior of the sisters, read aloud several versions of this tale from other cultures. Have students compare each version with others they have read. What features define this story as a Cinderella story? How is the text different from others? How do the illustrations differ? What choices have the reteller and illustrator made to emphasize certain points or to create different effects?

There are numerous versions of the Cinderella story. Ask your librarian to help you find additional books to use in a class study, for example:

Shirley Climo. *The Irish Cinderlad.* Illustrated by Loretta Krupinski. HarperCollins, 1996.

Charlotte Huck. *Princess Furball.* Illustrated by Anita Lobel. Greenwillow, 1989.

Ai-Ling Louie. *Yeh-Shen: A Cinderella Story from China.* Philomel, 1982.

Penny Pollock. *The Turkey Girl.* Illustrated by Ed Young. Little, 1996. A Zuni tale with an unexpected ending.

Robert San Souci. *Sootface: An Ojibwa Cinderella.* Doubleday, 1994.

Alan Schroeder. *Smoky Moutain Rose: An Appalachian Cinderella.* Illustrated by Brad Sneed. Dial, 1997. Includes examples of regional dialect.

Two interesting stories that are similar include Terri Cohlene's adaptation, *Little Firefly: An Algonquian Legend,* illustrated by Charles Reasoner (Rourke, 1990) and Rafe Martin's *The Rough-Face Girl,* illustrated by David Shannon (Putnam, 1992). Another tale that students might find engaging is Elizabeth Winthrop's *Vasilissa the Beautiful* (Harper-Collins, 1991), a Russian story that includes elements of Cinderella, Hansel and Gretel, and the wicked witch, Baba Yaga.

Show students how to compare two stories using the Venn diagram, as in Chapter 3:

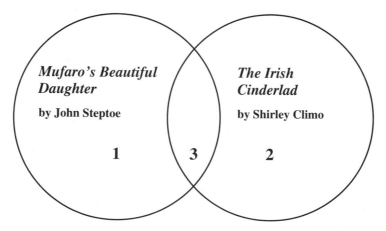

In Space 1 students note elements of the story that are unique to this tale, for example, set in Africa. In Space 2 students note elements that are unique to the Irish story, e.g., set in Ireland. In Space 3 students note elements that are common to both stories. After students have developed the Venn diagram individually, have them share their ideas in cooperative learning groups, making changes to their individual diagrams, as appropriate. Then, each student can write a short essay. With this kind of structure, each one can produce a reasonable piece of expository writing.

Students might also be inspired to write alternative versions of the Cinderella plot. Read Caralyn and Mark Buehner's *Fanny's Dream* (Dial, 1997) to suggest possible variations.

As a conclusion to this study, you might help students observe the stereotyped images presented in these tales, for example, the mean stepmother, the wicked stepsisters, and the magical fairy godmother. Discuss how these images have become part of our culture and also how they may be changed.

A practical resource for developing this study is *The Multicultural Cinderella* by Jean Rusting, which includes lesson plans for more than twenty versions of this tale (available from: Rusting Educational Services, 4523 Elinora Avenue; Oakland CA 94619).

Presenting Folktales Orally

Encourage students to choose stories to present within their small groups or to other classes. Folktales lend themselves particularly to storytelling. Even young children can learn to retell simple tales. Guide students to observe the familiar internal patterns, repeated phrases or rhymes that help the teller to remember a tale. The use of a few simple props, storyboards, and/or music will add interest to storytelling. Stories can also be told through the use of hand puppets or even the more elaborate puppet theater presentation. Students can write scripts for plays or prepare Readers' Theater presentations of tales. Following are resources to assist you in helping students with oral presentations:

Joseph Bruchac. *Tell Me a Tale: A Book about Storytelling.* Harcourt, 1997.

Anne Pellowski. *The Storytelling Handbook: A Young People's Collection of Unusual Tales and Helpful Hints on How to Tell Them.* Simon & Schuster, 1995.

Ramon Ross. *Storyteller.* August House, 1996.

J. Saldaña. *Drama of Color: Improvisation with Multiethnic Folklore.* Heineman, 1995.

Louise Thistle. *Dramatizing Myths and Tales: Creating Plays for Large Groups.* Dale Seymour, 1995.

Judy Sierra. *Fantastic Theater of Puppets: Puppets and Plays for Young Performers and Young Audiences.* Wilson, 1991.

For additional information contact The National Storytelling Association through its Web Page at http://members.aol.com/storypage/nsa.htm. Other Internet resources include:

Tejas Storytelling Resources: http://users.aol.com/storypage/jmaroon2:htm

Jewish Storytelling Coalition: http://www.ultranet.com/~jewish/story.html

The Old Alaska Storyteller: http://users.aol.com/darrow1806/oas1/oas.htsl

Talespinners Tavern: http://www.neca.com/~jester/tavern/

Storytellers: http://www.crocker.com/~gisland/story.html

Gifts of Story: http://www.swarthmore.edu/~sjohnson/stories/gos

Featuring Gerald McDermott

Gerald McDermott is a renowned reteller and illustrator of tales from many different ethnic and cultural groups. His work poses the question: "Can a non-native accurately and responsibly portray an account of a specific culture?" In his case, the answer is yes. In fact the Pueblo Indians use his book, *Arrow to the Sun: A Pueblo Indian Tale* (Viking, 1974), which won the Caldecott award for its illustrations, as a teaching resource in their schools. Inspired by Joseph Campbell, he delights in responding to the universal themes expressed in diverse cultures. As an artist, he immerses himself in each group's traditions in order to achieve a sense of story, color, theme, and place. Other titles by McDermott include:

Anansi the Spider: A Tale from the Ashanti. Holt, 1972.

The Stonecutter: A Japanese Folk Tale. HarBrace, 1995.

Papagayo: The Mischief Maker. HarBrace, 1992.

The Magic Tree. Holt, 1994.

Musicians of the Sun. Scholastic, 1994.

Zomo the Rabbit. HarBrace, 1992.

Coyote: A Trickster Tale from the Southwest. HarBrace, 1994.

The Voyage of Osiris: A Myth of Ancient Egypt. HarBrace, 1995.

Raven: A Trickster Tale from the Pacific Northwest. HarBrace, 1993.

Students might compare his Raven to other versions of this tale. They might also compare his style in the various works that he has produced.

Sources for Further Study

Following are a variety of resources that will aid you in developing this focus with your students.

Gloria Blatt. *Once upon a Folktale: Capturing the Folklore Process with Children.* Teachers College Press, 1993.

Jan Brunvand. *American Folklore: An Encyclopedia.* Garland, 1996.

Gail de Vos. *Tales, Rumors, and Gossip: Exploring Contemporary Folk Literature in Grades 7–12.* Libraries Unlimited, 1996.

Robert Ingpen and Barbara Hayes. *Folktales and Fables of the Middle East and Africa.* Chelsea, 1994.

Susan Milord. *Tales Alive.* Williamson, 1995. Ten multicultural folktales with activities.

R. L. Thomas. *Connecting Cultures: A Guide to Multicultural Literature for Children.* Bowker, 1995.

August House in Little Rock, Arkansas, has a World Storytelling series that presents nature tales from many cultures, including several Native American cultures. A recent title is by Pleasant De Spain; *Eleven Nature Tales: A Multicultural Journey* (August House, 1996).

Bulletin Blue Ribbon Storytelling. Annual review publication from the Bulletin of the Center for Children's Books, reviews storytelling audio and videotapes. Center for Children's Books, 51 Gerty Drive, Champaign IL 61820.

Grandfather Stories, a series of titles for grades K–3, presents stories about different cultures told by a grandfather. Classified as "Core Literature" in California's Recommended List; comes with teacher edition and video; ten books. (Educational Activities; 1937 Grand Avenue; Baldwin NY 11510.

Jan Irving and Robin Currie. *Straw into Gold: Books and Activities about Folktales.* Teacher Ideas Press, 1993. Intended for use with primary-grade students, this work includes story variations, activities, games, and plans for theme-related teaching.

FOCUS ON AFRICA AND AFRICAN AMERICANS: RECLAIMING TRADITIONS

When African Americans were slaves, the struggle just to learn to read and write despite legal prohibitions was the focus for education. Later, Booker T. Washington and W. E. B. Du Bois debated whether the appropriate education for African Americans would be a vocational track, because those were the jobs blacks were most likely to get, or a liberal arts degree, which might lead to aspirations that were less likely to be fulfilled. Today African Americans still experience the limited access to economic opportunities that sparked the original discussion. By birth, they enter what has been described as a "caste"; their prospects for health, work, and education are circumscribed by their race.

The Supreme Court decision of *Brown* v. *The Board of Education* in 1954 established that separate schools for blacks were inherently unequal. But inequality persists even as school districts try to plan for a more equitable distribution of blacks and students of other races. Meanwhile the notion of community is being questioned, as some educators propose separate schools for African Americans, or African American boys. How do we respond to this? What is required for African American students to receive the "best education any parents could want for their child"? As a teacher, you have to confront these issues that influence your attempts to build community among your students and to share African American history and culture with all students. All students need to learn that African Americans have a rich heritage of achievements and traditions.

Famous African Americans in History

Students need to hear about black men and women who have made contributions in areas other than sports and music. Challenge students to match these names with their contribution.

C	Matthew Henson	A. astronomer
A	Benjamin Banneker	B. first person killed in Boston Massacre (Revolutionary War)
D	Charles Drew	
B	Crispus Attucks	C. went to North Pole with Admiral Peary
G	Bill Pickett	D. invented blood transfusions
E	Phillis Wheatley	E. poet in colonial America
F	Harriet Tubman	F. led slaves to freedom
		G. black cowboy

Once students realize the number of blacks who have been recognized for their accomplishments, they will want to discover more names and find out more information about these people. Start a chart on the bulletin board where students can write the name of an achiever or someone they admire, and the reason. Students will be motivated to seek out names of historical figures, as well as people they know and respect today. *Come This Far to Freedom: A History of African Americans* by Angela Shelf Medearis and illustrated by Terea Shaffer (Atheneum, 1993) is a collection of short sketches to start you off.

Holidays and Heroes

Several holidays provide reminders of African American accomplishments. Kwanzaa, celebrated in December, acknowledges African cultural roots. Feature books about Kwanzaa and about Africa.

Angela Shelf Medearis. *The Seven Days of Kwanzaa; How to Celebrate Them.* Scholastic, 1994. A primer on African American pride and culture. Includes ideas for gifts and food plus stories of seven African Americans to celebrate, from Fanny Lou Hamer to James Van Der Zee.

Ella Grier. *Seven Days of Kwanzaa.* Illustrated by John Ward. Viking, 1997. This special book features a kente-cloth border.

Verna Aardema. *Misoso: Once Upon a Time: Tales from Africa.* Apple Soup, 1994. Collection of twelve fables and tales.

Another special day is Martin Luther King's birthday in January. On this day, provide opportunities to discuss King's work. What have we achieved in civil rights? How far do we still have to go?

Myra Cohn Livingston. *Let Freedom Ring: A Ballad of Martin Luther King, Jr.* Illustrated by Samuel Byrd. Holiday House, 1992. Livingston's verse incorporates quotations from King's speeches, reflects his voice.

Jean Marzollo. *Happy Birthday, Martin Luther King.* Illustrated by Brian Pinkney. Scholastic, 1993. A child asks his family why they celebrate King's birthday, and family members share their memories of King's accomplishments.

Another significant African American holiday is Juneteenth (June 19), commemorating the day that the slaves in Texas finally learned about the Emancipation Proclamation. This would be a good time to focus on black history, particularly the period of slavery.

African American History

The story of African Americans should be a part of the history that all of us learn. Unfortunately, presentations that focus on African Americans tend to occur in clumps in February and remain rare the rest of the year. Spread discussion of African American history throughout the curriculum with books that make black people more visible and help black students find their lives in history.

Jacob Lawrence. *The Great Migration: An American Story.* HarperCollins, 1993. Paintings by the famous artist Jacob Lawrence, accompanied by explanatory text, show the movement of blacks from the rural South to the urban North. Lawrence also painted sequences of the lives of Harriet Tubman and Frederick Douglass. The epilogue is a poem by Walter Dean Myers.

Walter Dean Myers. *Now Is Your Time: The African American Struggle for Freedom.* HarperCollins, 1991. The history of African Americans starts in 1619 (before the Mayflower arrived) and continues today. This book is significant in showing African Americans not as victims but taking action on their own behalf.

Faith Ringgold. *Dinner at Aunt Connie's House.* Hyperion, 1993. Another book by distinguished artist Ringgold, based on her African American story quilt/paintings. When the children visit Aunt Connie, her paintings come to life and the women tell their stories. Voices of Mary McLeod Bethune, Madame Walker, and others will encourage readers to discover more about significant black women.

Ayanna Hart and Earl Spangler. *Africans in America.* Lerner, 1995. This history shows the continuity of African traditions and values.

Dorothy Hoobler and Thomas Hoobler. *The African American Family Album.* Oxford University Press, 1995. This social and cultural history, part of the *American Family Album* series, is full of project ideas.

Slavery and the Civil War

The history of African Americans in the United States is overshadowed by their involuntary presence as slaves. A common misconception is that the slaves accepted their condition passively until they were freed by Abraham Lincoln. In fact, free blacks worked unceasingly to abolish slavery, while enslaved blacks exercised what resistance they could. Correct student misconceptions by telling stories of African American resistance to slavery. When studying the history of the United States up to the Civil War, make sure that the story of slavery is included.

Africans were first imported as slaves by Spanish landowners to work on sugar plantations in 1517. In the United States, twenty African slaves arrived in Virginia on a Dutch ship in 1619. From the beginning of the slave trade in the early 1500s until it was outlawed by the French in 1848, fifteen to twenty million Africans passed through the slave center on Goree Island in Senegal. By 1776, the black population in the United States was estimated at half a million. There were over 4 million blacks by the end of the Civil War.

Display a map of the United States to the class. Which were the slave states and which the free states? Have students trace the paths by which slaves could escape to freedom (to the North, frequently later to Canada, and also to the Bahamas, since they were British and, therefore, free). How far would slaves have to travel and how long would it take? What motivated people to risk such a long, difficult journey into unknown territory?

Research the history of the Underground Railroad in your area, if possible. Are there any remains or memories of stations where slaves were directed and hidden? Helping slaves escape was illegal and especially dangerous in the South, yet all kinds of people (northerners, southerners, Indians, Quakers, Canadians, British, free blacks, and other slaves) risked their own lives. Why would people do something for which they could be arrested or killed? Read biographies and historical accounts to understand the extraordinary people who fought against slavery.

Tom Feelings. *The Middle Passage: White Ships, Black Cargo.* Dial, 1995. With no text, only paintings, this book communicates the experience of Africans crossing the ocean to slavery.

Jeri Ferris. *Go Free or Die: A Story about Harriet Tubman.* Carolrhoda, 1988. Harriet Tubman, an escaped slave, returned to slaveholding territory nineteen times to rescue other slaves, despite a high bounty on her head. She lived long enough to see the end of the Civil War and the results of her efforts.

Jeri Ferris. *Walking the Road to Freedom: A Story of Sojourner Truth.* Carolrhoda, 1988. This northern-born slave became a sought-after speaker against slavery; she pleaded for the rights of blacks and women.

Virginia Hamilton. *Anthony Burns: The Defeat and Triumph of a Fugitive Slave.* Knopf, 1988. The federal government supported fugitive slaves but was forced to give way to slaveholding interests. Burns became a symbol of this struggle when he escaped to Boston and his return was sought by his owner.

Doreen Rappaport. *Escape from Slavery: Five Journeys to Freedom.* Illustrated by Charles Lilly. HarperCollins, 1991. Relates the escape stories of courageous African Americans who found freedom in the years before the Civil War.

Gwen Everett. *John Brown.* Paintings by Jacob Lawrence. Rizzoli, 1993. In this dramatic account, Annie Brown describes how her father led a "liberation army" in Virginia in 1859.

Patricia C. McKissack and Frederick L. McKissack. *Rebels Against Slavery: American Slave Revolts.* Scholastic, 1996. Chronicles 250 years of anti-slavery movements, including the famous uprisings of Nat Turner (1831), Joseph Cinque (1839), Denmark Vesey (1822), and Gabriel Prosser (1800).

Virginia Hamilton. *Many Thousand Gone: African-Americans from Slavery to Freedom.* Illustrated by Leo and Diane Dillon. Knopf, 1992. The stories of the many brave blacks who struggled against slavery, from Harriet Tubman and Nat Turner to others less well known. Rich language lends itself to reading aloud.

William Loren Katz. *Breaking the Chains: African-American Slave Resistance.* Atheneum, 1990. Written and oral history accounts document the defiance and resilience of slaves before emancipation.

Read fictional accounts to feel what it was like to live as a slave. The following books help students understand how hard it was to maintain stable families, to remember previous lives in Africa, and to accomplish something as simple as learning to read and write.

James Berry. *Ajeemah and His Son.* HarperCollins, 1992. Ajeemah and his son, in Ghana on their way to celebrate his marriage, are kidnapped and sold as slaves in Jamaica. Atu, the son, kills himself, but Ajeemah doesn't give up hope. An excellent starting point for discussing the degradation of slavery and the different ways in which people responded to it.

Jennifer Armstrong. *Steal Away.* Orchard, 1992. Forty-one years after they ran away, a black woman and a white woman relive the year 1855, when they were thirteen and went north seeking freedom. (A good companion book to *Sweet Clara and the Freedom Quilt.*)

Joyce Hansen. *Which Way Freedom?* Walker, 1986. After escaping from slavery, Obie serves in a black regiment and fights in the Civil War.

Delores Johnson. *Now Let Me Fly: The Story of a Slave Family.* Macmillan, 1993. Beginning with the capture of a young girl in Africa, the story follows her through harsh years of slavery as she works to help her family survive.

Jacob Lawrence. *Harriet and the Promised Land.* Simon and Schuster, 1993. Terse story of Harriet Tubman's life, dominated by dramatic paintings.

Mary Lyons. *Letters from a Slave Girl: The Story of Harriet Jacobs.* Scribner's, 1992. Fictionalized account of Jacobs's life. She tried to escape from North Carolina in 1842.

Mary Stolz. *Cezanne Pinto.* Knopf, 1994. Ex-slave Pinto, on his ninetieth birthday, looks back to his childhood on a Virginia plantation, his escape north, and his search for his mother.

Patricia C. McKissack and Frederick L. McKissack. *Christmas in the Big House, Christmas in the Quarters.* Illustrated by John Thompson. Scholastic, 1994. Contrasts the life of slaveholder family with that of slaves on a Virginia plantation in 1859, the last Christmas before the Civil War.

Gary Paulsen. *Nightjohn.* Delacorte, 1993. Sarny, a young female slave, risks her life in order to be taught to read and write by a mysterious escaped slave. Gripping short novel of the power of literacy and the drive to resist. *Sarny* (1997), the sequel, has her looking back on her 94 years of life.

Connie Porter. Addy Walker Series: *Meet Addy; Addy Learns a Lesson; Addy's Surprise.* American Girls Series. Pleasant Company, 1993. The life of a young African American girl growing up in the mid-1800s. The books start when Addy is a slave on a plantation in North Carolina. She and her mother run away to begin a new life in Philadelphia.

Paula Fox. *The Slave Dancer.* Dell, 1973. Winner of the Newbery Award, this story tells of a boy who is forced to play his fife to make the slaves dance on the voyage from Africa to the United States to be sold. Recounts in vivid, gruesome detail a story of survival.

Patricia Beatty. *Who Comes with Cannons?* Morrow, 1992. A young Quaker girl goes to live with her aunt, uncle, and cousins in North Carolina. Their home is also a station on the Underground Railroad. Explores why people risked their lives to help slaves reach freedom.

Michael J. Rosen. *A School for Pompey Walker.* Illustrated by Aminah Brenda Lynn Robinson. Harcourt Brace, 1995. Fiction based on true stories, the tale of a slave who, with the help of a white friend, had himself sold into slavery repeatedly and was able to save enough money to build a school for black children.

Virginia Hamilton. *The Mystery of Drear House.* Scholastic, 1997. Another story set in the house that was a stop on the Underground Railroad.

Kathryn Paterson. *Jip.* Lodestar, 1996. A boy in 1847 doesn't know who his parents are. When he finds he's the child of a slave, he must flee.

Kathryn Lasky. *True North: A Novel of the Underground Railroad.* Scholastic, 1996. In 1858, Afrika, a slave girl trying to escape, meets Lucy, a white Boston girl.

Lois Ruby. *Steal Away Home.* Simon and Schuster, 1994. Set in the present, children find a skeleton of a black woman. Flashbacks to 1856 show the difficulty of escaping slavery.

Civil Rights Movement

Sometimes students feel that all they hear about is African Americans and slavery. This focus can leave students feeling hopeless. Show students that there is more to the history of African Americans than slavery. The civil rights movement is important history in the immediate past, part of their parents' or relatives' memory.

Alice Faye Duncan. *The National Civil Rights Museum Celebrates Everyday People.* Bridgewater, 1995. Includes photos.

Patricia C. McKissack and Frederick L. McKissack. *The Civil Rights Movement in America: From 1865 to the Present.* Children's Press, 1991. A history for young people.

Ellen Levine. *Freedom's Children.* Putnam, 1993. Children share their experiences through stories and photos.

Richard C. Stein. *The Montgomery Bus Boycott.* Children's Press, 1993. The story of the people and events.

Leon Walter Tillage. *Leon's Story.* Illustrated by Susan L. Roth. Farrar, 1997. Leon was born the son of a sharecropper and grew up in the segregated South but his family sustained him.

Casey King and Linda Barrett Osborne. *Oh Freedom! Kids Talk about the Civil Rights Movement with the People Who Made It Happen.* Knopf, 1997. Includes 31 interviews that kids taped with family and friends, makes for a vivid documentary.

History of the Civil Rights Movement. Video, 1994. Includes historical base for civil rights.

Learning Pride in One's Culture

African American children are surrounded by negative images of their race and culture. They need to have many opportunities to take pride in their history and heritage, their nappy hair, and African looks. Books can reach across time and space to supply what may be lacking in their own community. The following books give students something to hold on to, to help them counterbalance negative stereotyping. After reading these books, have students share examples of family stories and customs.

Lucille Clifton. *All Us Come Cross the Water.* Illustrated by John Steptoe. Holt, 1973. Ujamaa is confused about his heritage until Old Tweezer tells him that the same boat—slavery—brought everyone here, making everyone brothers.

Anita Rodriquez. *Aunt Martha and the Golden Coin.* Clarkson-Potter, 1993. One of a series of books about Aunt Martha, who tells the children learning stories from her African American heritage. In this one, she has a magic coin that fends off a burglar. But is the coin really magic, or does Aunt Martha's own strength of mind save her?

Camille Yarbrough. *Cornrows.* Illustrated by Carole Byard. Sandcastle Books, 1991. Mama and Great-Grammaw pass on their African American heritage with pride as they braid cornrows in the children's hair, telling stories of the power and richness of African traditions.

Carolivia Herron. *Nappy Hair.* Illustrated by Joe Cepeda. Knopf, 1997. At the annual family picnic, uncle gives a call-and-response speech on the joys of Africanness.

Elizabeth Fitzgerald Howard. *Aunt Flossie's Hats (and Crab Cakes Later).* Illustrated by James Ransome. Clarion, 1991. Two African American girls visit Great Aunt Flossie. She has a story to tell with each hat they try on.

Wade Hudson and Cheryl Hudson, sel. *How Sweet the Sound: African-American Songs for Children.* Illustrated by Floyd Cooper. Scholastic, 1996. From traditional songs and street cries to spirituals and protest songs.

Kathleen Krull. *Bridges to Change: How Kids Live on a South Carolina Sea Island.* Lodestar, 1995. Two descendants of Gullah speakers and their efforts to maintain their culture. From *A World of My Own* series.

Belinda Rochelle. *Jewels.* Illustrated by Cornelius Van Wright and Ying-Hwa Hu. Lodestar, 1998. A girl's favorite time is spent with her grandparents as they tell stories about her ancestors, one freed by Harriet Tubman, another a Buffalo Soldier.

Cheryl Willis Hudson, comp. *Hold Christmas in Your Heart: African American Songs, Poems, and Stories for the Holidays.* Scholastic, 1995. Includes work by noted authors and illustrators.

African American Folklore

Some of the richest American folklore comes from the African American tradition. Read examples aloud to students to stimulate their interest in this oral tradition. Have students work in groups to present a tale to the class or for a schoolwide program. Students who may not do as well with written work have a chance to shine as performers. And all students have the opportunity to develop their speaking skills as they concentrate on delivering their dialogue with appropriate emotions.

Oral performance provides a context in which to talk about different ways of speaking. Students can have some of the characters speak formal English and others speak so-called Black English. How will students distinguish these ways of speaking? Because students have had different amounts of experience with formal English, encourage them to share their knowledge as they work in groups to decide how each character will talk.

Virginia Hamilton. *The People Could Fly: American Black Folktales.* Illustrated by Leo and Diane Dillon. Knopf, 1985. A rich, well-written collection.

Patricia McKissack. *The Dark Thirty: Southern Tales of the Supernatural.* Illustrated by Brian Pinkney. Knopf, 1992. Favorite scary stories. Students will probably recognize familiar tales.

Robert San Souci. *The Talking Eggs.* Illustrated by Jerry Pinkney. Dial, 1989. This retelling of a Creole folktale is set in the American South with African American characters. It is the story of two sisters, one good and one bad. The bad one has to learn that surface appearances are not always a guide to the quality inside.

Molly Bang. *Wiley and the Hairy Man.* Macmillan, 1976. Wiley and his mother must outwit the Hairy Man three times.

Julius Lester. *John Henry.* Dial, 1994. Can a steel-driving man work faster than a steam drill?

Priscilla Jaquith. *Bo Rabbit Be Smart for True.* Philomel, 1980. Humorous stories drawn from Gullah traditions, Sea Islands off the coast of South Carolina.

Share some audiocassette retellings of African American folktales with students.

Brer Rabbit and the Wonderful Tar Baby. Rabbit Ears, 1990. Narrated by Danny Glover, music by Taj Mahal.

John Henry. Rabbit Ears, 1992. Narrated by Denzel Washington, music by B. B. King.

Positive Images of Black Families in Literature

Students need to see realistic yet positive images of the lives of people like themselves. Well-written children's books can give students a mirror against which to measure themselves as well as a chance to imagine a better world. The following books acknowledge the problems and conflicts typical of African American children's lives and at the same time offer hope. In addition, the quality of the writing ensures that children from other racial backgrounds will appreciate the stories, too.

> Jacqueline Woodson. *Maizon at Blue Hill.* Delacorte, 1993. When Maizon is accepted at Blue Hill, an elite, mostly white boarding school, she has to leave behind her grandmother, her best friend, and her familiar neighborhood. She struggles to find her own place despite the barriers. Look for other stories about Maizon.

> *Lucille Clifton. *Some of the Days of Everett Anderson.* Illustrated by Evaline Ness. Henry Holt, 1970. The famous black poet has written a series of books about lively Everett, with warm pictures of family life in an apartment in the city.

> Mildred Taylor. *Roll of Thunder, Hear My Cry.* Bantam, 1976. Classic story of a southern black family maintaining its pride and its land despite the humiliations of racial prejudice. A Newbery Award winner, it is especially noteworthy for its acknowledgment of the complexity of black-white relations.

> *Faith Ringgold. *Tar Beach.* Crown, 1991. Cassie and BeBe in Brooklyn dream of flying away from the pressures of the world.

> *Phil Mendez. *The Black Snowman.* Illustrated by Carole Byard. Scholastic, 1989. Jacob learns pride and bravery from a snowman that he builds with his younger brother.

> Margaree King Mitchell. *Uncle Jed's Barbershop.* Illustrated by James Ransome. Simon and Schuster, 1993. A black man dreams of owning his own barbershop, not an easy goal in the 1920s.

> *Robert San Souci. *Sukey and the Mermaid.* Four Winds, 1992. Sukey finds comfort from a mermaid in her escape from her stepfather. Set in the Sea Islands, off the Carolina coast.

> *Sherley Williams. *Working Cotton.* Harcourt Brace Jovanovich, 1992. The story of an African American girl and her family's work in the cotton fields of central California. A Caldecott Medal book.

> *Mary Hoffman. *Amazing Grace.* Illustrated by Caroline Binch. Dial, 1991. Grace likes to act out characters from stories she reads. Her grandmother tells Grace she can be anyone she wants to be.

> *Gloria Pinkney. *Back Home.* Illustrated by Jerry Pinkney. Dial, 1992. Eight-year-old Ernestine from the city visits relatives on a farm in North Carolina. She's eager to fit in, but the country ways are different. This story of a black family presents universal themes of home, family, and belonging.

> *Karen English. *Big Wind Coming!* Albert Whitman, 1996. A Southern family's courage during a hurricane. Set in the 1940s.

> *Synthia Saint-James. *Sunday.* Albert Whitman, 1996. How a family celebrates a special day.

Poetry by Black Poets

How many students know the names of any black poets? Students may be surprised to learn that there are famous male and female black poets. Share with the class poems such as "Motto" by Langston Hughes and "We Real Cool" by Gwendolyn Brooks. Both of these poems make especially effective use of "street" language.

As you discuss the poems, ask students why the poets chose to use this kind of language. The poems don't read like conventional poetry—can we still call them poems? Are they written to be read silently or aloud? Using these poems as models, students will be motivated to write poems based on their experience, with familiar words and rhythms.

Collections of poetry by African Americans for children include the following:

*Joyce Carol Thomas. *Brown Honey in Broomwheat Tea.* Illustrated by Floyd Cooper. HarperCollins, 1993.

Deborah Slier, ed. *Make a Joyful Sound: Poems for Children by African American Poets.* Illustrated by Cornelius Van Wright and Ying-Hwa Hu. Checkerboard, 1991.

Tom Feelings. *Soul Looks Back in Wonder.* Dial, 1993. Feelings illustrated the book, then selected poems by thirteen African American poets, past (Langston Hughes) and present (Maya Angelou), to accompany them.

Wade Hudson, ed. *Pass It On: African-American Poetry for Children.* Illustrated by Floyd Cooper. Scholastic, 1993. Poems by Gwendolyn Brooks, Paul Dunbar, Nikki Giovanni, Langston Hughes, and Eloise Greenfield, with information about the poets.

Arnold Adoff, ed. *I Am the Darker Brother.* Simon and Schuster, 1997. A new edition of this book includes more recent poets, particularly women.

Eloise Greenfield. *Honey, I Love and Other Poems.* Illustrated by Jan Spivey Gilchrist. HarperFestival, 1995.

*Nikki Giovanni. *The Sun Is So Quiet.* Illustrated by Ashley Bryan. Holt, 1996. Short poems play with language in beautifully illustrated book for preschool to primary.

Davida Adedjouma, ed. *The Path of My Heart: Poetry by African American Children.* Illustrated by Gregory Christie. Lee and Low, 1996. Through writing workshops, inner-city children give voice to their concerns. These examples will motivate students to produce their own poetry.

Javaka Steptoe, ed. *In Daddy's Arms I Am Tall: African American Celebrating Fathers.* Lee and Low, 1997. These poems about a range of fathers are illustrated by Steptoe's unusual collages.

Labels

I have not labeled myself yet. I would like to call myself revolutionary, for I am always changing, and growing, it is hoped for the good of more black people. I do call myself black when it seem necessary to call myself anything.

—Alice Walker

What should we call the 30 million people (in 1990), 12% of the U.S. population and growing at more than twice the rate of whites, people who are the largest so-called minority group in the country? Different names have seemed appropriate at different points in time, as seen by the names of organizations such as the National Association for the Advancement of Colored People and the United Negro College Fund. More recently, discussion centers around the use of terms Black American or African American. Discuss with students the importance of labels. Does it matter what a group is called? What difference is there between these two labels? What would students prefer to be called? Interview people of different ages in the community. Survey people's preferences:

Black American
African American
No Preference
Other

Decide how to present these results. Consider a bar graph, a pie chart, or other method to illustrate the percentages.

Role Models

Students need the benefit of examples of others who have faced similar hardships and obstacles of prejudice or poverty and overcome them to go on to lead positive lives. Provide students with many illustrations of people who have overcome adversity, freed themselves from a limited environment, contributed to the world, and inspired others. What can we learn from these people's lives? How did they cope with the problems that confront all of us?

The Spingarn Medal has been awarded by the NAACP since 1915 for high achievement by an African American. How many of these names do students know?

James W. Johnson (1925)	Edward Kennedy Ellington (1959)
Carter G. Woodson (1926)	Kenneth B. Clark (1961)
Charles W. Chesnutt (1928)	Medgar W. Evers (1963)
Mary McLeod Bethune (1935)	Jacob Lawrence (1970)
Walter White (1937)	Gordon Parks (1972)
Richard Wright (1941)	Alvin Ailey (1976)
A. Philip Randolph (1942)	Coleman Young (1981)
Charles Drew (1944)	L. Douglas Wilder (1990)
Paul Robeson (1945)	Dorothy I. Height (1993)
Dr. Percy L. Julian (1947)	John Hope Franklin (1995)
Ralph J. Bunche (1949)	A. Leon Higginbotham (1996)

Biographies of African Americans

Familiarize yourself with the enormous number of excellent biographies of African Americans, from the useful series books to books written by top children's authors. Groups of students can select a period (the Harlem renaissance), a region (the West), or a field (science) to study. Help them collect biographies of people to study. Older students will benefit from comparing several biographies of the same person. There are many biographies of Harriet Tubman, for example. How do they differ in their approach to her life? Look carefully at what each writer chooses to include, what is not included, and how the writer presents the information. Are there disagreements about the facts of her history? Have students analyze critically the different interpretations in these historical accounts.

Here are a few of the current biographies to feature:

Lawrence S. Ritter. *Leagues Apart: The Men and Times of the Negro Baseball Leagues.* Illustrated by Richard Merkin. Morrow, 1995. For the elementary student, an introduction to the baseball players and the hardships they faced in the days of segregated sport.

Jack L. Roberts. *Booker T. Washington: Educator and Leader.* Millbrook Press, 1995. *Gateway Civil Rights* series. Explains his debate with W. E. B. DuBois and his founding of the Tuskegee Institute, for the elementary student.

James Earl Hardy. *Spike Lee: Filmmaker.* Chelsea House, 1995. *Black Americans of Achievement* series. Known for his film biography of Malcolm X, this book tells of Lee's family and analyzes his work in a white-dominated industry. For older students.

Libby Hughes. *Colin Powell: A Man of Destiny.* Dillon Press, 1996. *People in Focus* series. Sets his life in the context of the closely knit West Indian community in Harlem. For older students.

Barbara Kramer. *Alice Walker: Author of The Color Purple.* Enslow, 1995. *People to Know* series. This biography for young adults describes hardships faced by Walker and analyzes the themes of her work—racism, feminism, rape.

D. J. Herda. *Thurgood Marshall: Civil Rights Champion.* Enslow, 1995. *People to Know* series, for young adults, puts Marshall in the context of the civil rights movement.

Philip S. Hart. *Up in the Air: The Story of Bessie Coleman.* Carolrhoda, 1996. Coleman was the first African American to win a pilot's license. A book for middle school students. See also *Flying Free: America's First Black Aviators* by the same author.

Reeve Lindbergh. *Nobody Owns the Sky.* Illustrated by Pamela Paparone. Candlewick, 1996. A biography of Bessie Coleman for younger readers, this tells how she had to move to France in order to become a pilot.

*Andrea Davis Pinkney. *Bill Pickett.* Illustrated by Brian Pinkney. Pickett, the son of a slave, was the first black rodeo performer. He wrestled a steer when he was ten.

Patricia McKissack and Frederick McKissack. *Red-Tail Angels.* Walker, 1995. The Tuskegee airmen persevered against racism and indignities in World War II and proved their heroism.

*Eloise Greenfield. *Mary McLeod Bethune.* Illustrated by Jerry Pinkney. Harper Collins, 1994. A picture book about the Great Educator.

Robert Coles. *The Story of Ruby Bridges.* Illustrated by George Ford. Scholastic, 1995. Noted child psychiatrist tells how Ruby integrated an all-white school in New Orleans when she was six years old.

Ellen R. Butts and Joyce R. Schwartz. *May Chinn: The Best Medicine.* Freeman/Scientific America Books for Young Readers, 1995. Born in 1896, she faced prejudice at every turn yet managed to establish a medical practice in Harlem.

Jeanne Moutoussamy-Ashe. *Daddy and Me: A Photo Story of Arthur Ashe and His Daughter.* Knopf, 1993. Life of the tennis star who died from AIDS, seen by his daughter, a story for elementary students.

*David Adler. *A Picture Book of Sojourner Truth.* Illustrated by Gershom Griffith. Holiday, 1994. A book to introduce primary students to the life of this activist.

*Andrea Davis Pinkney. *Dear Benjamin Banneker.* Illustrated by Brian Pinkney. Harcourt Brace, 1994. Noted astronomer.

*Alan Schroeder. *Satchmo's Blues.* Illustrated by Floyd Cooper. Doubleday, 1996. A book to read aloud to primary students, based on the childhood of Louis Armstrong.

Kenneth Rudeen. *Jackie Robinson.* Illustrated by Michael Hays. HarperCollins, 1996. A chapter-book biography of the baseball player for elementary students.

Videos are also available based on Chelsea House's *Black Americans of Achievement* series. Some titles include *Jesse Owens: Champion Athlete, Marcus Garvey: Black-Nationalist Leader,* and *Matthew Henson: Explorer.*

Featuring African American Authors for Children

Talk about the authors of the books that you share with students. How many of them are African American? Make sure that students know who these people are, so that they recognize that African Americans can write books, too. Show them pictures of the authors and talk about the authors as real people. African American authors who have written many exceptional books for young people include Virginia Hamilton, Mildred Taylor, John Steptoe, and Julius Lester. Investigate books by some more recent authors, for example, Angela Johnson, Faith Ringgold, and Andrea Davis Pinkney.

Two major African American authors today are Patricia McKissack and Walter Dean Myers. Plan a special study around one of these authors. Have students analyze the author's style. What themes does this author prefer? Does the author use a particular style of language? What is the author's attitude toward his or her characters? Does the author favor a particular genre, or type of book, such as history or folklore? Find out more about the author's life. What led him or her to write for a young audience?

Patricia McKissack often writes books with her husband, Frederick McKissack. Here are some titles to look for:

Ma Dear's Aprons. Simon and Schuster, 1997.

Rebels against Slavery: American Slave Revolts. Scholastic, 1996. (with Frederick McKissack)

Christmas in the Big House, Christmas in the Quarters. Scholastic, 1994. (with Frederick McKissack)

Mirandy and Brother Wind. Knopf, 1988.

A Long Hard Journey: The Story of the Pullman Porter. Walker, 1989.

Red-Tail Angels: Tuskegee Airmen. Walker, 1995. (with Frederick McKissack)

The Civil Rights Movement in America. Children's Press, 1991. (with Frederick McKissack)

The Royal Kingdoms of Ghana, Mali, and Songhay. Holt, 1993. (with Frederick McKissack)

For more information about this author, see *Patricia McKissack: Can You Imagine?* (Richard C. Owen, 1997) in *Meet the Author* series.

An author who usually writes for a middle or high school audience is Walter Dean Myers, winner of the Newbery Honor Medal for *Scorpions* and the Coretta Scott King Award for *Fallen Angels*. In addition to these books about black teenagers, he has written poems, picture books, historical novels, and books about African American history and culture.

Harlem. Illustrated by his son, Christopher Myers. Scholastic, 1997.

One More River to Cross: An African American Photograph Album. Harcourt Brace, 1995.

Malcolm X: By Any Means Necessary. Scholastic, 1994.

Righteous Revenge of Artemis Bonner. HarperCollins, 1992.

Somewhere in the Darkness. Scholastic, 1992.

Now Is Your Time: The African American Struggle for Freedom. HarperCollins, 1991.

Amistad: A Long Road to Freedom. Dutton, 1997.

*How Mr. Monkey Saw the Whole World. Doubleday, 1996.

*Toussaint L'Ouverture: The Fight for Haiti's Freedom, Simon & Schuster, 1996.

Featuring African American Illustrators

There are many excellent African American illustrators working in the field of children's literature. Encourage students to become more aware of the people who illustrate the books that they read. Provide information and talk about the artists as real people. Analyze the artist's style. Does this person use the same techniques in each book? What are the distinctive features of this artist's style? Students will notice artists such as Tom Feelings, Floyd Cooper, and James Ransome.

Two excellent artists who have been working in this field for a long time are the husband and wife team of Leo and Diane Dillon. They won the Caldecott Award for "Why Mosquitoes Buzz in People's Ears" (by Verna Aardema). This interracial couple is known for their atmospheric illustrations often accompanying folk tales. Look for their work in these books:

Howard Norman. *The Girl Who Dreamed Only Geese: and Other Tales of the Far North.* Harcourt Brace, 1997.

Virginia Hamilton. *Her Stories: African American Folktales, Fairy Tales, and True Tales.* Scholastic, 1995.

Virginia Hamilton. *Many Thousand Gone: African Americans from Slavery to Freedom.* Knopf, 1992.

Margaret Musgrove. *Ashanti to Zulu.* Dial, 1976.

Mildred Pitts Walker. *Brother to the Wind.* Lothrop, Lee, Shepard, 1985.

Sharon Bell Mathis. *The Hundred Penny Box.* Viking, 1975.

Nancy White Carlstrom. *Northern Lullaby.* Philomel, 1992.

Nancy Willard. *Pish, Posh, Said Hieronymous Bosch.* Harcourt Brace, 1991.

Katherine Paterson. *The Tale of the Mandarin Ducks.* Lodestar, 1989.

Students can see a video presentation of the Dillons' work for "Why Mosquitoes Buzz in People's Ears" in the collection *Emperor's New Clothes and Other Folktales* (Weston Woods Video, 1991). *The Art of Leo and Diane Dillon* edited by Byron Preiss (Ballantine, 1981) provides background for further study of these artists.

Another well-known illustrator is Jerry Pinkney. Some of his books include:

Gloria Pinkney. *Back Home.* Dial, 1992.

Virginia Hamilton. *Drylongso.* Harcourt, 1992.

Robert San Souci. *The Talking Eggs.* Dial, 1989.

Rudyard Kipling. *Rikki-Tikki-Tavi.* Adapted and illustrated by Jerry Pinkney. Morrow, 1997.

Julius Lester. *Sam and the Tigers: A New Retelling of Little Black Sambo.* Dial, 1996.

Eloise Greenfield. *Mary McLeod Bethune.* HarperCollins, 1994.

Alan Schroeder. *Minty: The Story of Young Harriet Tubman.* Dial, 1996.

A video is available of "A Visit with Jerry Pinkney" from Penguin USA Author Videos.

For more information about the life and work of Leo and Diane Dillon, Jerry Pinkney, and other artists, see Pat Cummings, ed. *Talking with Artists* (Bradbury, 1992). Includes conversations with fourteen children's illustrators.

Exploring Africa

Africa still holds a special fascination due to its size, diversity, and long history. From Marcus Garvey to Nelson Mandela, Africa has exerted a powerful hold on the imaginations of American blacks. Bring Africa into the classroom through stories, music, games, and pictures.

Put a map of Africa on the board. Can students name any of the 53 countries? How big is it compared to the United States? To your state? What different languages are spoken on this continent? Why would some countries use English for their official language and others use French? These are languages they have to learn in school. Why don't they use the language they learn at home? Learn about Swahili, a language spoken in many countries.

Talk about the diversity of Africa. What do the people look like? Display pictures to show the population: Arabs, South African whites, Asians (Indians), different African tribes. Locate these groups on the map. A reference book that students can use is Yvonne Ayo, *Africa* (Random House, 1995). For intermediate students, this book covers the rich diversity of Africa, including topics such as houses, sports, religion, dress, and music.

Who is Nelson Mandela? Read about his life to find why he is an African leader respected around the world.

Benjamin Pogrund. *Nelson Mandela: Strength and Spirit of a Free South Africa.* Gareth Stevens, 1992.

*Floyd Cooper. *Mandela.* Philomel, 1997. A chronological overview of Mandela's life for primary students.

Learn what life is like in the different countries by listening to music, playing games, and making crafts.

Florence Temko. *Traditional Crafts from Africa.* Lerner, 1996. Using a variety of everyday materials, readers can make objects while learning about the role of crafts in African cultures.

Caedmon Records has collections of songs from different regions, such as *Songs of the Congo.*

Read stories about different tribes and countries in Africa to illustrate the diversity of this enormous continent.

*Ifeoma Onyefulu. *Chidi Only Likes Black.* Cobblehill, 1977. Photos show life in a Nigerian village.

Virginia Kroll. *Masai and I.* Illustrated by Nancy Carpenter. Four Winds, 1992. Linda, an African American city girl, learns about the Masai in East Africa. She wonders how her life would be different if she lived there.

Margaret Sacks. *Themba.* Illustrated by Wil Clay. Dutton, 1992. Themba's father is expected home from working in the gold mines near Johannesburg. When he doesn't return, Themba leaves his Xhosa village to look for him.

Gregory Scott Kreikemeier. *Come with Me to Africa: a Photographic Journey.* Golden, 1993. This account of a trip through each country in Africa includes numerous photographs of people, animals, the countryside, and descriptions of how people live. Shows how the different African tribes vary in appearance and culture.

*Catherine Stock. *Where Are You Going, Manyoni?* Morrow, 1993. The spectacular, detailed watercolors evoke the African veld of Zimbabwe showing a typical day in Manyoni's life as she gets up, walks through the countryside to the school, and plays with her friends. Illustrations have animals hidden in them to identify and show the homes, school, and children's games so that students can find similarities and differences.

*Ifeoma Onyefulu. *A Is for Africa.* Cobblehill, 1993. Photos from Nigeria (by an Igbo) illustrate African "universals" such as *D* is for Drums and *Y* is for Yams, encouraging a falsely homogeneous view of African tribal life and customs. Use this book to stimulate further exploration of different aspects of African culture and history.

Patricia and Fredrick McKissack. *The Royal Kingdoms of Ghana, Mali, and Songhay: Life in Medieval Africa.* Holt, 1993. The kingdoms of West Africa flourished from 500 A.D. to 1700. The great cities were centers for learning, medicine, and religion. Dispels the image of Africa as an empty, dark continent.

Jim Brandenburg. *Sand and Fog: Adventures in South Africa.* Walker, 1994. Set in Namibia, the most recently independent African country.

Isimeme Ibazebo. *Exploration into Africa.* New Discovery Books, 1995. Includes information on geography, maps, and the current political situation.

Robert Steven Bianchi. *The Nubians: People of the Ancient Nile.* Millbrook, 1994. These black Africans are less familiar than their neighbors the Egyptians. From *Beyond Museum Walls* series.

Jim Haskins and Joann Biondi. *From Afar to Zulu: A Dictionary of Cultures.* Walker, 1995. Explores 32 different groups with useful information for students.

African Tales

All students will enjoy reading stories from various traditional African cultures. They will learn about the lives and values of the major African groups, from Ashanti to Zulu, and compare these cultures with their own.

Most short tales reflect common human problems and traits and are easily adapted to storytelling or creative dramatics. A typical story is *The Vingananee and the Tree Toad,* a Liberian tale retold by Verna Aardema (Warne, 1983).

Or you can read a story aloud and have students illustrate the characters and incidents. A good place to start is *The Crest and the Hide and Other African Stories* by Harold Courlander (Coward McCann, 1982). The famed collector not only includes a variety of stories but also offers important background on sources and related tales.

Students can also investigate a particular genre of folktale, for example, the trickster tales exemplified by West African stories about Anansi the spider.

More African tales to read:

Verna Aardema. *Anansi Finds a Fool.* Dial, 1992. An Ashanti story, one of many about Anansi.

Barbara Knutson. *How the Guinea Fowl Got Her Spots: A Swahili Tale of Friendship.* Carolrhoda, 1990. When a guinea fowl saves a cow from a lion, the cow reciprocates by giving her camouflage spots.

Gerald McDermott. *Zomo the Rabbit: A Trickster Tale from West Africa.* Harcourt Brace Jovanovich, 1992. The ancestor of Brer Rabbit, an African trickster tale.

Sheron Williams. *And in the Beginning.* Atheneum, 1992. Retelling of the myth, how the first man was created from the dark earth of Mount Kilimanjaro.

John Steptoe. *Mufaro's Beautiful Daughters.* Lothrop, Lee, and Shepard, 1987. Based on a Shona folktale (Zimbabwe), this is a modern fable of two sisters, one proud and one humble.

Verna Aardema, retold. *The Lonely Lioness and the Ostrich Chicks: A Masai Tale.* Illustrated by Yumi Heo. Knopf, 1996. A story from Aardema's classic *Tales for the Third Ear,* now out of print.

I. Murphy Lewis. *Why Ostriches Don't Fly and Other Tales from the African Bush.* Libraries Unlimited, 1997. Portrait of the Bushmen culture with traditional tales and photographs.

Heather McNeil. *Hyena and the Moon: Stories to Tell from Kenya.* Libraries Unlimited, 1996. Representing the diverse ethnic groups of Kenya, this includes literal translations and versions for storytelling.

Doreen Rappaport. *The New King.* Illustrated by E. B. Lewis. Dial, 1995. A folktale from Madagascar about the impact of death on a child.

Angela Shelf Medearis. *Too Much Talk.* Illustrated by Stefano Vitale. Candlewick Press, 1995. This story from the Akan people (Ghana) is about a farmer who meets objects that talk.

Sources for Information for Teaching about Africa and African Americans: Reclaiming Traditions

Heritage of the Black West. National Geographic video. National Geographic Society, Washington DC 20036. Examines the history and contemporary presence of blacks in U.S. West with the contributions of men and women.

Henry L. Gates and Nellie Y. McKay, eds. *The Norton Anthology of African American Literature.* Norton, 1997. 120 authors from 1746 to present, a magnificent reference work for students and teachers. Includes examples of writing in Black English.

Toni Eubanks. *Passage to Womanhood: Journey Home.* Peoples Publishing, 1996. This novel tells of African Americans in the West. Accompanied by teacher's guide and student activities. For middle school.

Clifton Taulbert. *Once Upon a Time . . . When We Were Colored.* Council Oak Books, 1996. Shows the positive influence of his community in Mississippi on his childhood. Also made into a film.

Dianne Johnson-Feelings. *The Best of the Brownies' Book.* Oxford University Press, 1996. Collection from the magazine edited by W. E. B. DuBois, designed to instill pride in children.

Jane Beck and Wes Graff. *On My Own: The Traditions of Daisy Turner.* Vermont Folklife Center/University of Vermont. Video and audiocassette with study guide distributed by Multicultural Media, 1996. Turner, a native of Vermont, told the story of her life when she was 100. A classic work of oral history.

Ayanna Hart and Earl Spangler. *Africans in America.* Lerner, 1995. Overview of Africa and African American history for young people.

Muriel Miller Branch. *The Water Brought Us; The Story of the Gullah-Speaking People.* Cobblehill, 1995. A reference work on this regional black culture whose language is the source for much of Black English.

Venice Johnson, ed. *Voices of the Dream: African American Women Speak.* Chronicle, 1995.

William Loren Katz. *The Black West.* Simon and Schuster, 1996. New edition of work in this area, covers Buffalo soldiers, black cowboys, relations with Indians and Latinos.

African American Artists Series. Documentary videos from L&S Video Inc., 45 Stornowaye, Chappaqua, New York 10514. Features renowned artists such as Jacob Laurence, Faith Ringgold, Betye Saar, and Romare Bearden.

Cultural Contributions of Black Americans. 1996. Three parts—jazz, literature, and artists.

African American History: Heroism, Struggle, and Hope. 1996. Part One covers up to the Civil War.

Leading Black Americans. 1996. Biographies of Mary McLeod Bethune, George Washington Carver, Benjamin Banneker. All are CD-ROM for Macintosh and Windows, from the Society for Visual Education.

REFLECTIONS

We have been exploring ways to incorporate a global perspective on diversity in our teaching. Through looking carefully at conditions around them, students can develop an understanding of what it means to respect their heritage, to understand social forces of discrimination and prejudice, and yet to be free to be citizens of the world.

APPLICATIONS

1. Students identify with others of their own age. Begin to collect resources so that you can present a unit on childhood in other countries. You can include books that describe growing up in a particular country, names of possible speakers who could talk to your class about going to school in other countries, and examples of children's toys or games. (UNICEF is a good source of simple childhood games from different countries.) Identify suitable sources of information in the library or on the Internet so that older students can do their own research on this topic. Finish your unit by considering how you want students to present what they have learned from this study. Primary students could assemble a notebook of stories, letters, and pictures. Older grades might prepare a dramatization for other classes.

2. Read three to five folktales from a particular region or culture. What can they tell you about the people? Find out more about the history and culture of these people. What themes are repeated in the folktales? What basis do they have in the group's history? Develop a plan for teaching these tales to students. How are universal themes depicted? What cultural values are being promoted? Decide what you expect students to learn from studying these tales. Prepare a folktale for storytelling.

3. Develop a booklet of community resources for teaching about a local group. Many excellent sources of multicultural information are available right in your own community. Sometimes an organization has produced a list of possible contacts for materials, resources, or speakers. Your public library may have this information already compiled. If not, begin developing a list of your own. The best place to start is the telephone directory. Look for national organizations that have branches in a big city close to you. For example, names to look for include National Conference of Christians and Jews. Look also under group names to see what services are offered. Try Chicano, American Indian, Mexican American, Native American, La Raza, Black, African American, and so on.

Another important resource is the local college or university. Write or call them for information about possible ethnic studies departments or organizations for students of different ethnic backgrounds. Check the catalogs to see whether courses are taught in the history or culture of a particular group that might be of interest to your students. Sometimes the teachers of such courses can help locate more materials and information as well as perhaps provide contacts with other people in the community. They might also come to speak to the class.

EXPLORING FURTHER

Charlotte C. Anderson with Susan K. Nicklas and Agnes R. Crawford. (1994). *Global Understandings.* Alexandria VA: ASCD.

Kwame Anthony Appiah, & Henry Louis Gates, Jr., eds. (1997). *The Dictionary of Global Culture.* New York: Knopf.

Molefi K. Asante, & Mark T. Mattson. (1992). *Historical and Cultural Atlas of African Americans.* New York: Macmillan.

Andrew Billingsley. (1993). *Climbing Jacob's Ladder: The Enduring Legacy of African-American Families.* Simon & Schuster.

Children's Storybooks on the Arab World: An Annotated Bibliography. (1997). From the American-Arab Anti-Discrimination Committee, 4201 Connecticut Ave, NW, Suite 300, Washington DC 20008.

James Cummins, & Dennis Sayers. (1997). *Brave New Schools: Challenging Cultural Illiteracy through Global Learning Networks,* 2nd ed. New York: St. Martin's Press.

Merryl Goldberg. (1997). *Arts and Learning: An Integrated Approach to Teaching and Learning in Multicultural and Multilingual Settings.* White Plains, NY: Longman.

Darlene Clark Hine. (1993). *Black Women in America: An Historical Encyclopedia.* Brooklyn, NY: Carlson Publishing.

Kids Explore America's African American Heritage. (1993). Westridge Young Writers Workshop. Santa Fe, NM: Muir Publishing.

Michael Lerner, & Cornel West. *Jews and Blacks: A Dialogue on Race, Religion, and Culture in America.* Penguin, 1996. A paperback edition of intellectual dialogue, includes ideas on Simpson verdict and the Million Man March.

Theresa Perry, & Lisa Delpit, eds. (1998). *The Real Ebonics Debate: Power, Language, and the Education of African American Children.* Milwaukee, WI: Rethinking Schools Ltd.

John W. Pickering. (1997). *Comparing Cultures: A Cooperative Approach to a Multicultural World.* Portland ME: J. Weston Walch.

Katherine Ruggieri-Vande Putte. (1997). *Our Town: A Simulation of Contemporary Community Issues.* Tucson, AZ: Zephyr Press. (PO Box 66006, Tucson AZ 85728-6006.)

Ronald Takaki. (1994). *From Different Shores: Perspectives on Race and Ethnicity in America.* New York: Oxford University Press.

Beverly Daniel Tatum. (1997). *"Why Are All the Black Kids Sitting Together in the Cafeteria?" and other Conversations about Race.* New York: HarperCollins.

Stephen Thernstrom, Ann Orlove, & Oscar Handlin, eds. (1980). *Harvard Encyclopedia of American Ethnic Groups.* Cambridge, MA: Harvard University Press.

HAPPY BIRTHDAY

Feliz Cumpleaños

Bon Anniversaire

Χρονια Πολλα

Buon Compleanno

Geburtstagswünsche

STO LAT!

祝
生
日
快
樂

8

Exploring Language and Linguistic Diversity

Every generation claims that the English of its time is being degraded by slang and other forces of change. Few people, except linguists, have the historical perspective to see that English would not be the language that they wish to preserve unless it had changed substantially along the way. In fact, language changes are normal.

As you present the English language to students, remember that so-called standard English is the product of influences from many different people and languages. The English that exists today bears the imprint of factory workers as well as scientists, children playing in the street as well as English professors in schools; and it contains the particular speech patterns of people from different cultural and linguistic backgrounds—African, Jewish, Latino. The grammar rules that are carefully presented in textbooks are not etched in stone but describe what is generally considered effective communication for a specific place and time.

Your job is to help students cope with these issues by explaining clearly the conventions that govern the written and spoken English they encounter in school. Since students who speak English already know a lot about the structure of English (the grammar), they need fewer lists of rules and more examples of writing from real texts (literature) as a source for discussion and analysis of what makes good writing.

The increasing number of students in the classroom who speak languages other than English is an area of great concern and controversy today. All teachers need to know how to teach this population effectively. Unfortunately, the labels usually associated with these students, such as ESL (English as a second language), LEP (limited English speaking), and NES (non-English speaking), focus our attention on what students cannot do, leading to language deficiency models and remedial instruction. In addition, many people confuse an inability to express oneself fluently in English with an inability to think clearly, so that students needing assistance only with English language skills are denied access to the full academic content of their grade level. An alternative approach, which we advocate in this chapter, is to view the students' native language as an asset, both in helping them learn a new language and also as a benefit to all students. Instructional strategies, such as Sheltered English in which teachers modify their delivery of lesson content to make new information more comprehensible, serve to make all students feel included and promote the goal of teaching multiculturally.

After reading this chapter, you should be able to:
- Help students appreciate the rich variety of forms of English.
- Promote the learning of other languages as an asset.
- Support the English learning of students for whom English is not a first language.
- Describe the contributions of Latinos to American society.

VARIETIES OF ENGLISH

The English that we speak, read, and write varies according to systematic factors. One of the most obvious is regional variation. People who come from different regions tend to speak differently. When people move from one region to another, they sometimes maintain their former habits of speech, which makes for interesting mixes of vocabulary and pronunciation habits. Although everyone speaks a dialect, some regional dialects are considered more prestigious than others. In addition, there are "social" dialects. People who live in the same neighborhood but inhabit different social spheres will talk differently. The speech pattern called Black English is an example of a social dialect. Finally, speech varies according to social context, or register. We use language differently when speaking to an audience, to a close friend, to a baby, to a person in the street. All of these differences make up the rich variety of English in this country. Moreover, quite different varieties of English are spoken in other countries. The English of England, Australia, India, and Nigeria is acknowledged to be the same language, yet we may have to struggle to understand people from other English-speaking countries.

Exploring Regional Dialects

Many common objects have different names in different parts of the country. Early dialectologists (people who investigate regional differences in pronunciation and vocabulary) developed maps that showed the spread of words for particular objects. Conduct an experiment in dialectology and see how many different regional terms you can find. Ask students questions such as the following:

> What do you say to stop a game?
> (time out, times, pax, time, fins)
> What do you say you do if you don't come to school?
> (play hookey, ditch, bag school, bolt, lay out, play truant, skip class, cut school)
> What do you call someone from the country?
> (hayseed, rube, hick, yokel, hillbilly, moss back, cracker, redneck, sodbuster)
> What do you call a thick sandwich?
> (dagwood, hoagie, submarine, sub, grinder, hero, poor boy)

Have students ask their parents the same questions. Discuss the regional patterns you find. Do students from the same area use the same terms? Why or why not? Depending on how many different regions the students represent, can you divide the United States into several main dialect areas?

Students might be interested in seeing some of the dialect atlases that have been prepared for most areas of the United States. The *Dictionary of American Regional English,* edited by Federic Cassidy (Harvard University Press, 1985) explains the distribution of American dialects and represents an ongoing project. This comprehensive collection has only reached volume three and the letter O.

We All Speak Dialects

It is important for students to realize that we all speak different dialects. Have students try pronouncing the following words as they compare the varied ways of saying them:

greasy	here	car
bath	dog	get
aunt	because	idea

Keep in mind the wide variation in pronunciation and draw students' attention to it as you work together in the classroom. It is particularly evident as the teacher pronounces spelling words. For words that present obvious difficulty, you might have a student or two pronounce the same word aloud.

Consider particularly the vowels in *Mary, merry,* and *marry.* Some students may pronounce these as three different sounds. Other students say them as two homonyms or even as three homonyms. Remember to allow for student differences in pronunciation when teaching spelling and reading rules.

Listening to Regional Dialects

Practice listening for regional variation with the record *Our Changing Language* (McGraw-Hill) by Evelyn Gott and Raven I. McDavid, Jr. (available from The National Council of Teachers of English, 1111 W. Kenyon Road, Urbana, IL 61801). On one side of this record high school students read a story that contains many words that are pronounced differently. Each student is from a different city in the United States, and the speech variation is fascinating. Students who are from these geographic regions will identify their own speech characteristics as they listen.

To demonstrate the difference in speech in your own classroom, have a number of children record the same passage onto a tape. Then play the tape. Discuss what kinds of variations are noted. Which words are pronounced differently? Have students compare their pronunciations of the following words:

right	bath	were	here
house	child	fire	log
fit	Mary	park	sorry

British-American Differences

The English spoken in Britain differs from the English of the United States in interesting ways. For example, mix these words up and challenge students to match the British word on the left with the American equivalent. Do they recognize any of these words?

Food

biscuit	(cookie)
jelly	(jello)
tinned meat	(canned meat)
sweet	(candy)
tea	(light meal, supper)

Transport

pram	(baby stroller)
boot	(trunk of car)
lorry	(truck)
lift	(elevator)
underground, tube	(subway, metro)

Clothing

trainers	(sneakers)
vest	(undershirt)
jumper	(pullover sweater)

In many cases, the British words are familiar but less common. However, some words have very different meanings in Britain and the United States. A good example is football, which means soccer in Britain.

Spelling across the Atlantic

Write several of the following familiar words on the board for students to read and pronounce. Wait for students to notice something strange about these words. Tell them that these represent British rather than American spellings. Can they identify the differences?

theatre	colour	programme	civilise	tyres
kerb	practise	grey	behaviour	gaol

Discuss the use of spelling conventions with the students. Why do we insist that everyone spell the same way?

You can also point out that some words are spelled the same way in the two countries but pronounced differently. Examples are *schedule* (pronounced *sh*edule) and *clerk* (pronounced *clark*). What are some of the implications of these differences? (Learning to read or spell, writing poetry-rhymes, etc.)

British English in Books

Have students search for additional examples of British English. Reading books written by British authors will bring out more items. Suggest titles by these British authors to upper-grade students:

Lucy Boston
The Children of Green Knowe
A Stranger at Green Knowe

Joan Aiken
The Wolves of Willoughby Chase
Black Hearts in Battersea

Students could also investigate the language used in familiar books such as *Mother Goose.* Ask students what *curds and whey* and *pease porridge* mean. *The Annotated Mother Goose,* by Martin Gardner, is a useful source for the origin of many of these phrases.

Standardized Spelling

Dictionary Day, October 16, commemorates the birth of Noah Webster. Students may be surprised to learn that the spelling they have so much trouble with was standardized only relatively recently. When Noah Webster was preparing the first American dictionary, he wanted to emphasize that American English was distinct from British English and thus further the Revolutionary cause. He set a standard against which we could measure our spelling. Previously, well-educated people could spell words as they chose. Because of Webster, we write *civilize* and *theater,* not *civilise* and *theatre,* as they do in England.

Is there any reason to have everyone spell the same way? Discuss with students the advantages and disadvantages of standardized spelling. (Students might be comforted to know that many spelling demons are reminders of how words used to be pronounced; for example, *night* was once pronounced with a hard *g*.) Organize a debate on spelling reform: Resolved—the English language should be spelled the way it sounds.

The Language in the Dictionary

If we all speak different dialects, whose dialect is the one represented in dictionaries? Students may look on dictionaries as the ultimate authority on language, not realizing that the editors of dictionaries have to select carefully which words and specific pronunciations are included in their pages. As students might predict, some dialects are more likely to be represented than others. How is this decided? Are the most prestigious dialects the most likely to be included? (What are "the most prestigious" dialects?) Can you tell how to pronounce a word by looking it up in the dictionary? Should we have different entries for different dialects? Ask students to propose arguments on both sides.

Before the 1960s, dictionaries generally professed to set a standard for "good" English, so they did not include slang, swear words, or "street" (informal) vocabulary. More modern dictionaries represent a more inclusive definition of language, aiming to describe English in its actual form instead of a limited and idealized version of good English. If you have access to a fairly new dictionary, have students look up pronunciations. Do the entries match how they themselves pronounce these words? They can also look up slang words. Does this dictionary include slang words? Are there words that might not be included? Should dictionaries include all the words in English? After discussion, students may realize that this is impossible.

An excellent library resource for further investigation is the 1993 *New Shorter Oxford English Dictionary* (2 vols), a new edition of the famous guide to the English language. This edition includes new words from fields such as computers (laptop), physics (quark), politics (political correctness), music (grunge), and the street (dweeb). Have students brainstorm a list of contemporary words that should be in the dictionary. They can research these words and report back to the class. Have them argue in favor of including these words in the dictionary. Note that because this dictionary comes from England, it reflects a different view of the language than that of a dictionary published in the United States. Can students find any British American differences in this work?

English Borrowings

English is a mixture of many languages. Although English is historically related to German (see the Language Tree in the next section), it has been heavily influenced by French and has borrowed words from many of the other languages it has been in contact with. Words that were borrowed a long time ago are now considered part of English. Words borrowed recently usually show their foreign origins. When students look up word origins in the dictionary, point out that any word that does not come from Old English must have been borrowed into English at some time.

List a number of borrowed words for students. How many of the words do they know? Can they guess the language each word came from?

Language	*Word*
Malay	ketchup
Arabic	alcohol
German	kindergarten, sauerkraut
French	souvenir, menu, encore
Hindi	shampoo
Spanish	bonanza, mosquito
Dutch	cole slaw, sleigh
Native American	squash, raccoon
Italian	macaroni, piano
Yiddish	kosher
Japanese	kimono
Scandinavian	smorgasbord

Prepare a display showing the origins of the words. Use a map of the world pinned to the bulletin board with the words printed on cards placed near their country of origin. Or mount the Indo-European tree on the bulletin board and place the borrowed words on leaf shapes attached to the proper branches. Discuss how the display shows which languages have contributed most to the English language. Why are some languages represented more than others? Speculate on why these words might have been borrowed.

Why We Speak English

Although this country was settled by people from many different countries who spoke such languages as Spanish, French, and German, English became recognized as the national language. How did this happen? Discuss possible causes with the students and have them develop a list of hypotheses, such as the following:

- English speakers were the first settlers.
- England was the most powerful mother country.
- The settlers voted English the official language.

Students will be motivated to read and research further to determine the accuracy of their predictions. Once they have established the facts (there was no vote), they can come up with a more informed picture of what led to the acceptance of English.

Compare the development of the United States with that of Canada. How and why did Canada select two official languages (French and English)?

Students' Right to Their Own Language

The following is a statement prepared by the National Council of Teachers of English in response to the educational controversy over Black English and other dialects. Read this to the students and discuss it. Do they agree with the position expressed?

> We affirm the students' right to their own patterns and varieties of language—the dialects of their nurture or whatever dialects in which they find their own identity and style. Language scholars long ago denied that the myth of a standard American dialect has any validity. The claim that any one dialect is unacceptable amounts to an attempt of one social group to exert its dominance over another. Such a claim leads to false advice for speakers and writers, and immoral advice for humans. A nation proud of its diverse heritage and its cultural and racial variety will preserve its heritage of dialects. We affirm strongly that teachers must have the experiences and training that will enable them to respect diversity and uphold the right of students to their own language.[1]

Considering Black English

Black English is a dialect of English (sometimes referred to as *ebonics*) spoken by many people in the United States, primarily urban African Americans. It has many distinctive features of grammar and vocabulary, and it serves as a significant marker of African American identity. As with all dialects, speakers vary in the ease with which they can switch to more standard dialects of English. A lawsuit in 1977 brought public attention to Black English as an educational issue when parents in Ann Arbor, Michigan, claimed that their children were called learning disabled because they spoke Black English. Although the structure of Black English as a legitimate variant to English has been known for many years, some people still associate it with poor grammar and lack of learning skills. (Refer to the discussion of ebonics in Chapter 10.)

Speaking Black English (the black vernacular) doesn't prevent students from being able to learn in school. In fact, students' knowledge of black vernacular represents the same level of intellectual achievement as that of any child who has mastered the language of the home. At the same time, students speaking black vernacular will also benefit from access to the language of wider communication, in this case, standard English. Reassure students that they can learn to use standard English without losing the use of their familiar language that connects them to family and community.

Varied models for the teaching of standard English to speakers of black vernacular have included bilingual education and the teaching of (standard) English as a second language. We would like to suggest a model of code switching. All speakers switch among various registers of their language (or languages), using specific registers for different contexts. To be an effective communicator, a speaker of black vernacular needs to be able to use that form in casual talk with peers in the community but to switch to a more formal style when applying for a job.

What can teachers and students do to learn more about standard English and to master the skill of code switching?

Teachers can:

- Model standard English as part of formal speech in the classroom.
- Switch into Black English in specific situations of informal discussion.

Students can:

- Create a list of black vernacular expressions and translate them into standard English.
- Translate common phrases in standard English into black vernacular.
- Develop role-play exercises, setting up different situations that might require using different speech registers.
- Analyze the way black characters deliberately vary speech patterns on television programs.
- Read and retell stories in black vernacular and standard English.

Throughout these activities, establish shared goals with students. Your aim is to increase their exposure to standard English, to permit them to practice using standard English in safe, playful environments, and to direct their conscious attention to the differences between black vernacular and standard English.

Origins of Black English

Students may feel more pride in the way they speak if they investigate the origins of these speech differences. The source of Black English is disputed. Some linguists argue that it comes from Gullah, an early black creole still spoken by some people in the Sea Islands off the Carolina coast. Because the Africans brought to the United States as slaves spoke different languages, they needed to develop a way to communicate. The resulting language, called a creole, used English words as a base but followed a structure more similar to many African languages. Almost all of the distinctive features of Black English resemble Gullah. In communities where Gullah still exists, some teachers may be trying to eradicate traces of Black English in children's speech while linguists are carefully studying every word of the same speech from the elders. See *The Story of English* by Robert McCrum, William Cran, and Robert MacNeil (Viking, 1986) for more information about Gullah. A book about the speakers of Gullah is *The Water Brought Us* by Muriel Miller Branch (Cobble Hill, 1995).

Black English in Books

Many contemporary writers attempt to reproduce the sound of Black English in their books. Some just include black slang and others incorporate both vocabulary and grammatical features of Black English. Unfortunately, no written version can accurately portray spoken Black English, just as standard spoken English is very different from written English. However, these books have the advantage of sounding more familiar to speakers of Black English and may be easier for black students to read than standard English. They also are important for introducing other students to Black English, because the context makes the meaning of unfamiliar words and constructions clear.

Read passages from some of the following books to the class and discuss the language used. How do students feel? Does it sound realistic or familiar? Do they understand what the people are saying? Why would someone want to write like that?

Brenda Wilkinson. *Ludell.* Harper and Row, 1975.

Eloise Greenfield. *There She Come Bringing Me That Little Baby Girl.* Lippincott, 1974.

Virginia Hamilton. *Sweet Whispers, Brother Rush.* Philomel, 1982.

John Steptoe. *Train Ride.* Harper and Row, 1971.

Walter Dean Myers. *Fast Sam, Cool Clyde, and Stuff.* Puffin, 1975.

Patricia McKissack. *Mirandy and Brother Wind.* Knopf, 1988.

THE MANY LANGUAGES OF THE WORLD

English is only one of many languages in the world. Some languages, such as Spanish, Russian, and Hindi, are related to English because they share a common ancestor language; other languages, such as Vietnamese, Swahili, and Arabic are strikingly different. More than two hundred immigrant languages are represented in this country. Some were brought by recent refugees, some have been maintained as a part of cultural heritage for many generations, and some reflect early inhabitants of this country. Language diversity is great among Native Americans as well. Although only 1.9 million in number, they speak over two hundred languages, some as different from each other as English is from Chinese.

Linguistic Diversity in the United States

One in every fourteen U.S. residents over the age of five speaks a language other than English at home, according to the 1990 census. This represents a 35% increase over the figures for the 1980 census. Contrary to popular perception, however, 80% of these people speak English fluently as well. Not surprisingly, Spanish is the most common language next to English; 17.3 million people reported that they speak Spanish at home.

Spanish	17,339,172
French	1,702,176
German	1,547,099
Italian	1,308,648
Chinese	1,249,213
Tagalog	843,251
Polish	723,483
Korean	626,478
Vietnamese	507,069
Portuguese	429,860
Total	31,844,979

Determine what languages are represented in your classroom. Ask students not only what languages they speak but what languages their ancestors spoke. Students can learn about the history of this country as they find out what languages their families spoke before coming here and when their family started speaking English. Make a list of the languages represented and show on a map where they are spoken. Students can better understand the concept of ethnic diversity when they see how many of their parents and grandparents (and their friends' parents and grandparents) came from another country and had to learn to speak English when they arrived. Students will also identify more

LANGUAGE LOCATION

Location	Language
Arizona	Spanish, Uto-Aztecan
California	German, Italian, Spanish, Polish, Yiddish, French, Russian, Hungarian, Swedish, Greek, Norwegian, Dutch, Japanese, Chinese, Serbo-Croatian, Portuguese, Danish, Arabic, Tagalog, Armenian, Turkish, Persian, Malay (Indonesian), Scandinavian, Basque, Mandarin, Gypsy (Romani)
Florida	Spanish
Hawaii	Japanese, Tagalog, Polynesian
Idaho	Basque
Illinois	German, Italian, Spanish, Polish, Yiddish, Russian, Swedish, Greek, Norwegian, Slovak, Dutch, Ukrainian, Lithuanian, Czech, Serbo-Croatian, Danish, Balto-Slavic
Maine	French, Amerindian
Massachusetts	Italian, Polish, Yiddish, French, Swedish, Greek, Lithuanian, Portuguese, Celtic, Armenian, Albanian, Breton
Michigan	German, Polish, French, Hungarian, Dutch, Finnish, Arabic, Balto-Slavic, Near E. Arabic dialects, Amerindian, Iraqi, Algonquin, Gypsy (Romani)
Minnesota	Swedish, Norwegian, Finnish
Montana	Algonquin
New Hampshire	French
New Jersey	German, Italian, Polish, Yiddish, Russian, Hungarian, Slovak, Dutch, Ukrainian
New York	German, Italian, Spanish, Polish, Yiddish, French, Russian, Hungarian, Swedish, Greek, Norwegian, Slovak, Dutch, Ukrainian, Lithuanian, Czech, Chinese, Portuguese, Danish, Finnish, Arabic, Rumanian, Balto-Slavic, Celtic, Hebrew, Armenian, Near E. Arabic dialects, Turkish, Uralic, Albanian, Persian, Scandinavian, Amerindian, Dalmatian, Breton, Mandarin, Egyptian, Georgian, Gypsy (Romani), Athabascan
Ohio	German, Polish, Hungarian, Greek, Slovak, Czech, Serbo-Croatian, Slovenian
Pennsylvania	German, Italian, Polish, Yiddish, Russian, Hungarian, Greek, Slovak, Ukrainian, Lithuanian, Serbo-Croatian
Rhode Island	French, Portuguese
Texas	Spanish
Washington	Swedish, Norwegian, Scandinavian, Amerindian
Wisconsin	German

Source: Adapted from Theodore Andersson and Mildred Boyer, *Bilingual Schooling in the United States.* U.S. Office of Education, 1970, pp. 26–27.

with the problems of recent immigrants when they realize how recently their own families arrived.

Compare the languages of your class with the data on the chart below, showing the distribution of speakers of other languages. Which states have populations speaking the languages found in your classroom? Why do New York and California have the most languages listed? Which states have no non–English-speaking populations listed? Why? Students will have to apply facts and concepts learned in social studies in order to answer these questions and to understand the implications of this list.

Note that these languages represent stable populations of state residents. Recent groups of immigrants, such as Indochinese, are not shown here.

Discussing the Value of Knowing More than One Language

Open discussions about languages in our country will aid students in recognizing the issues involved. Discuss the following topics.

- List the advantages of knowing a second language. List the disadvantages.
- How many different languages are spoken in your area? Do you know someone who speaks more than one language?
- What languages would you like to learn? Why?

A Fable

In a house there was a cat, always ready to run after a mouse, but with no luck at all.

One day, in the usual chase the mouse found its way into a little hole and the cat was left with no alternative than to wait hopefully outside.

A few moments later the mouse heard a dog barking and automatically came to the conclusion that if there was a dog in the house, the cat would have to go. So he came out, only to fall in the cat's grasp.

"But where is the dog?"—asked the trembling mouse.

"There isn't any dog—it was only me imitating a barking dog," explained the happy cat, and after a pause added, "My dear fellow, if you don't speak at least two languages, you can't get anywhere nowadays."

Source: Reprinted from *BBC Modern English*, Vol. 2, No. 10, p. 34, December 1976.

The Language Tree

Prepare a bulletin board to provide information about the family of Indo-European languages, spoken by half the world's population, and the relationship of English to other languages. Construct a large tree out of construction paper, with eight branches representing the main groups:

- Albanian
- Armenian
- Balto-Slavic: Russian, Polish, Serbo-Croatian, Czech, Ukrainian, Bulgarian, Lithuanian
- Celtic: Irish, Scots, Gaelic, Welsh, Breton, Cornish
- Greek
- Indo-Iranian: Hindi, Urdu, Bengali, Persian
- Romance: French, Italian, Spanish, Portuguese, Rumanian
- Germanic: German, English, Dutch, Danish, Norwegian, Swedish
- Tocharian ⎫
- Hittite ⎭ extinct languages

Have students research what languages belong to each branch. Where does English fit in? Which are the most populous branches? In what countries are these languages spoken?

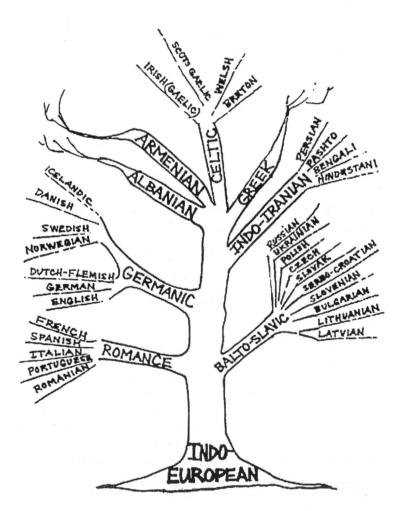

Exploring Different Languages

When the language tree is constructed and the branches labeled with the major languages, have students add life to the tree by discovering words in these different languages. Students can look up words or use words they have found in books. Provide "leaves" cut out of construction paper on which to write words to place on the tree according to the "branch" they belong to.

Exercises such as looking up the word for *ten* in many languages will help demonstrate to students the relationship among these languages, as well as their similarities and differences. Here are some examples to begin with:

English	ten	German	zehn
French	dix	Dutch	tien
Italian	dieci	Swedish	tio
Spanish	diez	Danish	ti
Portuguese	dez	Norwegian	ti
Rumanian	zece		

Other Language Families

Can students name languages that do not belong to the Indo-European language family? (Check names against the Indo-European family tree you constructed.) They may suggest some of the following names:

Language	Family
Chinese	Sino-Tibetan
Japanese	Japanese and Korean
Hebrew	Hamito-Semitic
Hungarian	Ural-Altaic

After the class has accumulated a list, have students look up the languages to find out which languages are related to one another. There are many language families besides the Indo-European, and some include languages with many speakers. Students may be surprised to learn that Chinese and Japanese are not related but belong to separate families. Many Native American languages belong to distinctly different language families as well. None of these families are as extensive or as well-studied as the Indo-European family.

So many different languages are spoken in Africa that it is difficult to classify all of them. Swahili, the best known, is the native language of some Africans but is learned by many others as a second language in order to communicate with neighbors.

English in Other Languages

Just as English has borrowed many words for new things, so other languages have borrowed words from English for objects or ideas that came from English-speaking people. Words that look or sound familiar to English speakers can be found in French, Japanese, Russian, Spanish, and many other languages. Ask students to guess what the following words mean.

le pique-nique	(French, picnic)
le coquetel	(French, cocktail)

el ampayer	(Spanish, umpire)
los jonroneros	(Spanish, homerun hitters)
gamu	(Japanese, chewing gum)
garu-furendo	(Japanese, girlfriend)
parken	(German, to park)
hitchhiken	(German, to hitchhike)

Languages in the World

Ask students if they know which language has the most speakers in the world. Write several guesses on the board. Have students research how many people speak each language. They can prepare a chart of the most widely spoken languages in the world. Figures can be obtained by counting the populations of countries that speak a particular language, or you can use information on what languages people learn as a second language. Check figures in almanacs and encyclopedias. Because the population of China is large, more people grow up speaking Chinese than any other language. English is the most widely used second language.

Compare how many people in the world speak English and how many speak Spanish. Which languages in the world would be the most useful to learn as second or third languages? Why?

Languages in the Classroom

Bring other languages into the classroom by giving students a chance to hear what different languages sound like. Folk songs are an easy way to introduce students to other languages. Talk about what the words mean and why they sound different. Use the languages that are represented in your classroom. Have students teach the rest of the class how to say *hello, good-bye, please,* and *thank you* in a language they know.

Animals Speak in Different Languages, Too

What does a rooster say, or a dog, or a cat? Students may be surprised to find out that different languages have different ideas about the sounds animals make. Ask students who speak other languages to contribute examples. Share the book *Cock-a-Doodle Doo! What Does It Sound Like to You: Learning Sounds in Other Languages* written by Marc Robinson and illustrated by Steve Jenkins (Stewart Tabori Chang, 1993), which contains examples from such diverse languages as Portuguese, Russian, Greek, Hindi, Chinese, and Hebrew. It also includes a map showing where these languages are spoken. *Animal Lingo* by Pam Conrad, illustrated by Barbara Bustetter Falk (Laura Gerringer, 1995), also provides examples of different names for animal sounds.

Esperanto

The following paragraph is written in Esperanto. Write it on the board and read it to the class. (It is pronounced approximately like Spanish). See how much students can understand.

La inteligenta persono lernas la interlingvon Esperanto rapide kaj facile. Esperanto estas la moderna, kultura lingvo por la internacia mondo. Simpla, flekselbla, praktika solvo de la problemo de universala interkompreno, Esperanto meritas vian seriozan konsideron. Lernu la interlingvon Esperanto!

Esperanto is an artificial language invented to be used as an international language. It is easy to learn and easy to understand because it is completely regular.

Bring books about Esperanto to the class. Students will enjoy practicing the new language and using it in interesting ways. They can write to each other in Esperanto and perform simple translation exercises. In addition, they will learn more about how their own language is constructed by comparing it with Esperanto.

Discuss why Esperanto was created. Is there a need for an international language? What are the advantages and disadvantages of Esperanto? Esperanto is only one of a large number of artificial international languages. Have students investigate the history of Esperanto and other artificial languages (Interlingua, for example).

A Language of Hands

Another special language is a silent language, the language of hands. This kind of language is used by deaf people and takes the place of speech. Although American Sign Language (ASL) uses signs that are equivalent to words, there are also signs for each letter (fingerspelling). Fingerspelling is sometimes called the manual alphabet. Anyone can quickly learn to fingerspell and the exercise helps practice English spelling. Students enjoy being able to signal each other secretly, across a noisy room, and without making a sound. Several books present fingerspelling for beginners. *Handtalk* by Remy Charlip, Mary Beth Ancona, and George Ancona (Parents Magazine Press, 1974) and *My First Book of Sign* by Pamela Baker (Gallaudet, 1986) include photographs of a person signing.

American Sign Language

Who uses ASL? Many people. Deaf people, their families, their friends, sign language interpreters, and deaf educators. Ask students if they or anyone they know uses sign language. Today sign language is the fourth most frequently used language in the United States, and the primary communication system for 300,000 deaf Americans.

Discuss differences between sign language and spoken language. What are the advantages of sign language? What are the advantages of spoken language? What language is best when you are eating? Under water? On the phone? Students may not know that sign language is a "real" language. Present some of the following information about sign.

Facts about Sign Language

There are different sign languages used in different countries, just as there are spoken languages. People who use ASL cannot understand people who use British Sign Language.

ASL is not a word-for-word translation of English. Signed English is used for simultaneous translation and matches spoken English more closely.

Children can learn ASL as a first language, similar to the way hearing children learn a spoken language. Signers (people who use sign) can express themselves as well in sign as hearing people can in a spoken language.

Provide books for students that dispel stereotypes, show how deaf people live, and enrich students' understanding of what diversity means.

S. Brearley. *Talk to Me.* A & C Black, 1996. With color photographs, shows children interacting and communicating in many different ways. Includes the finger alphabet.

D. Abbott and H. Kisor. *One TV Blasting and a Pig Outdoors.* Whitman, 1994. The story of life with a father who lost his hearing at an early age. Shows deaf culture, use of adaptive technology.

S. H. Collins. *Signing at School.* Garlic, 1992. One of a series of basic sign language books, this includes the finger alphabet and common question and answer signs used at school.

*P. Lakin. *Dad and Me in the Morning.* Whitman, 1994. A boy and his dad watch the sun rise. The boy is deaf.

*D. H. Levi. *A Very Special Friend.* Kendall Green, 1992. Two girls are friends; one is deaf.

*D. Slier. *Word Signs: A First Book of Sign Language* and *Animal Signs: A First Book of Signs.* Checkerboard, 1993. Designed to teach signs to young children.

*Aliki. *Communication.* Greenwillow, 1993. The comic-strip format includes facts about deaf people and sign language.

Exploring Sign

Approximately two million Americans are profoundly deaf. Invite a deaf or hearing person who knows sign language to speak to the class and demonstrate signing. (Try facilities for the deaf, teachers of sign language, and relatives of deaf people.) If students watch closely, they may be able to guess what some of the signs mean.

- Drink—fingers shaped around glass move to mouth
- See—two fingers move away from eyes
- Nose, Mouth—point to them on face

Find out what services are available for deaf people. Sometimes television news programs have simultaneous sign translations. Discuss with students why these services are necessary. Would printing the news on the screen as subtitles work? What does the "CC" on television programs mean? Can deaf people use telephones?

Deaf people are a neglected group in our discussion of the multicultural society. Too often included with the disabled, most deaf people do not want to be "fixed." They consider themselves a cultural and linguistic minority with their own heroes, history, and language. As with other language groups, deaf students can best be served by a bilingual education program. For more information on this educational controversy, see *The Mask of Benevolence* by Harlan Lane (Knopf, 1992) and *Seeing Voices: A Journey into the World of the Deaf* by Oliver Sacks (University of California Berkeley, 1989).

Different Writing Systems

There are three basic types of writing systems. Alphabetic systems use symbols to represent individual sounds. Syllabaries have separate symbols for consonant-vowel pairs. Pictographic or ideographic systems represent entire words or ideas with a single symbol.

Bring in examples of each type of writing (in print or handwritten) to show students how languages differ. Include some of the following:

- Alphabetic: *Roman,* used by English speakers. *Cyrillic,* used for Russian and other Slavic languages, based on the Greek alphabet. *Hebrew,* an alphabet without written vowels, similar to *Arabic.*
- Syllabary: *Japanese,* despite adoption of some Chinese characters, still primarily uses *Kana,* syllable-based.
- Pictographic: *Chinese,* with large numbers of distinct characters, is difficult to learn to write.

Discuss with students the implications of these different writing systems. Consider, for example, how dictionaries would be organized. How would Hebrew students read new words when they are written without the spoken vowels? The complex Chinese system works better for the Chinese than an alphabetic system. Speakers of different Chinese languages who cannot understand each other's spoken language can communicate through using the same writing system. How might these different writing systems make translation into English difficult? What would a keyboard look like in other writing systems?

Look for examples of Japanese writing, such as the illustration at the beginning of Chapter 3. A source for information about Japanese is the alphabet book *A to Zen* written by Ruth Wells and illustrated by Yoshi (Picture Book Studio, 1992). Note that this book reads from back to front, like books in Japanese.

Another interesting language to investigate is Hebrew, the national language of Israel. Although for many centuries Hebrew remained a purely religious language, today it is spoken on a daily basis by Jews, Arabs, and Christians living in Israel. A good introduction to Hebrew is *Alef-Bet: A Hebrew Alphabet Book* by Michelle Edwards (Lothrop, Lee and Shepard, 1992). Each page shows a letter in Hebrew, its Hebrew name, a Hebrew word, and the English pronunciation.

Bilingual books allow students to compare languages and writing systems directly. For example, show students Chamroeun Yin's *In My Heart I am a Dancer* (Philadelphia Folklore Project, 1996), written in Cambodian and English, to illustrate another alphabetic writing system.

Where does the word *alphabet* come from? *Alpha* and *beta* are the first two letters of the Greek alphabet. Look at the Greek alphabet. Does it look anything like the alphabet we use? Where did our letters come from? Have students research the history of the English alphabet, from its origins in Greek and Phoenician letters, through Gothic, to its present form.

In an alphabetic writing system, each sound is represented by a symbol. Is this always true of English? What individual sounds in English are represented by pairs of letters? (Examples are *ch, sh, th.*)

Although the Russian language is related to English, it looks very different as students can see in the chart of the Cyrillic alphabet. The Cyrillic alphabet comes from Greek. Cyrillic writing is used by many groups in Eastern Europe while others use the same words but write them in the Roman alphabet.

Students can learn more about language variation in *Who Talks Funny: A Book about Language for Kids* by Brenda Cox (Linnet, 1995). She explains dialects, writing systems, and features of languages around the world.

Cyrillic Alphabet

Letters	Names of Letters	Equivalent sounds in English
А, а	ah	*fa*ther
Б, б	beh	*b*et
В, в	veh	*v*at
Г, г	gheh	*g*o
Д, д	deh	*d*am
Е, е	yeh	*ye*t
Ё, ё	yoh	*yaw*n
Ж, ж	zheh	plea*s*ure
З, з	zeh	*z*one
И, и	ee	*ee*l
Й, й	ee KRAHT-koh-yeh	bo*y*
К, к	kah	*k*ick
Л, л	el	*l*ow
М, м	em	*m*et
Н, н	en	*n*et
О, о	oh	t*o*y, sp*o*rt
П, п	peh	*p*et
Р, р	er	d*r*ead (trilled *r*)
С, с	es	*s*ell
Т, т	teh	*t*ell
У, у	oo	m*oo*n
Ф, ф	ef	*f*un
Х, х	khah	lo*ch*, soft sound *H*ugo
Ц, ц	tseh	ca*ts*
Ч, ч	chah	*ch*urch
Ш, ш	shah	*sh*ip
Щ, щ	shchah	prolonged *sh* sound
ъ	tv'YOR-dee znahk	indicates hard stress on previous consonant
ы	yeh-REE	s*i*t
ь	m'YAH-kee znahk	no sound, indicates soft emphasis
Э, э	eh (oh-boh-ROHT-noh-yeh)	*pe*t
Ю, ю	yoo	*yu*le
Я, я	yah	*ya*rd

The Birth of Writing, by Robert Claiborne and the Editors of Time-Life Books, 1974, is an excellent resource for teachers on the origin of writing and the importance of knowing how to write.

Language Differences and Similarities: Background

One of the tasks of linguistics is to describe the structure of various languages. On the basis of language structure and history, languages are classified together into families. Examples of ways in which languages differ include the following:

1. Out of a limited number of possible sounds, no languages use precisely the same group of sounds. Some of these sounds do not occur in English and, therefore, sound strange to ears accustomed to English. On the other hand, the *th* sound in English is difficult for language learners because it does not occur in most languages.

2. Some languages have a system for classifying nouns. Often this is called gender. Objects are arbitrarily assigned to one of two groups, called masculine and feminine (as in Spanish), or to one of three groups: masculine, feminine, and neuter (as in German). This use of gender is not equivalent to the division of humans into male and female. For example, in German, *Mädchen* (maiden) and *Fräulein* (young woman) are both neuter. Different languages may assign the same object different genders. The word for table is *Tisch* in German (masculine) and *mesa* in Spanish (feminine). In languages with gender, pronouns usually agree in gender with the nouns to which they refer. In addition, adjectives usually have different endings depending on the gender and number (singular or plural) of the noun modified. Note this example in French:

ils	préfèrent	les	tasses	blanches
they	*prefer*	*the*	*cups*	*white*
(3rd person	(3rd person,	(plural)	(feminine,	(feminine,
masculine, plural)	plural)		plural)	plural)

In this sentence, the pronoun *ils* could refer to *les hommes* (men, masculine, plural) or to *les chats* (cats, masculine, plural) but not to *les femmes* (women, feminine, plural). Therefore, French speakers easily confuse the English he/she/it contrast and use he/she for inanimate objects. Examples of languages with a noun classification system not based on gender are the Bantu (African) languages. In these languages nouns are grouped into categories based primarily on the physical shape of the object; for example, long and thin, small and round.

3. The concept of *word* differs from language to language. The Japanese word *ikimasu,* for example, carries the potential meaning of these English words:

Japanese: ikimasu

$$
\text{English:} \quad \left. \begin{array}{l} \text{I} \\ \text{you} \\ \text{he} \\ \text{she} \\ \text{we} \\ \text{they} \end{array} \right\} \quad \left. \begin{array}{l} \text{am} \\ \text{is} \\ \text{are} \end{array} \right\} \quad \text{going}
$$

Japanese speakers decide who is going from the context of the conversation.

An example of the concept of *word* taken from the Yana Indian language in northern California is even more complicated:[2]

yābanaumawildjigummahánigi

ya = several people move
banauma = everybody
wil = across
dji = to the West
gumma = indeed
ha´ = let us
nigi = we

Try reading these definitions as a "sentence."

Even with the parts of the long word defined, we still do not understand it, because we arrange our thoughts differently and do not repeat words as the Yanas did. An English sentence that conveys the same meaning as the Yana word might go like this:

Let us each move to the West.

4. Word order differs in various languages. In English, adjectives usually precede the noun described. Compare these phrases in English and Spanish:

English	*Spanish*
the blue book	el libro azul
	(the book blue)

5. Word order affects meaning in English, as is clear in these sentences:

The dog bit the man.
The man bit the dog.

In other languages special endings carry meaning so the words can be arranged in any order. For example, this Latin sentence says "Peter (subject ending *us*) sees Paul (object ending *um*)" no matter what the order.

Pet*us* videt Paul*um*.
Paul*um* Petr*us* videt.
Videt Paul*um* Petr*us*.

While languages differ in vocabulary for cultural and historical reasons, all languages have the same expressive potential. There is no such thing as a primitive language, just as there is no such thing as a primitive people. All human languages and all human cultures are rich and complex and capable of adapting to different circumstances. A language may not express some concepts that are considered important in our society, but it can develop the vocabulary to express any of them if the speakers of the language consider it necessary. The use of formerly unwritten African languages to conduct all the affairs of law, government, and education is an example of the flexibility of language. Another example is Hebrew, a language that was revived for use as a national language in modern Israel. All languages possess the capacity to adapt to such new uses.

Languages All Around Us

Encourage students to begin a collection of different languages that they see in print. The newspapers and magazines often have examples of the languages in local communities.

Companies that serve the public frequently publish instructions in the languages people use in their service area. The following example, mailed in February 1997 to users of the local telephone services in a large California city reveals some interesting language characteristics. Students will note that the phone numbers are written the same way in all these languages.

Para obtener más información sobre los dos cargos adicionales nuevos en su factura, por favor llame al 1-800-573-7847 y oprima el número 1 en su teléfono de botones.

Muốn biết chi tiết về hai khoản bội phí mới trong hóa đơn của quý vị, xin gọi số 1-800-573-8828 và bấm số 1 trên điện thoại bấm số của quý vị.

有關您的帳單上兩項新的附加費之資料，請電1-800-570-8868（粵語），或1-800-303-8788（國語），並請在您的按鍵式電話上按1。

귀하의 전화 요금 청구서에 있는 두 가지의 새로운 부과세에 관한 정보를 원하시면 1-800-560-8878로 전화를 거신 다음, 터치톤 전화기 번호판에서 1번을 누르십시오.

Para sa impormasyon tungkol sa mga bagong surcharges sa inyong bill, tumawag sa 1-800-404-1212, pagkatapos ay pindutin ang number 1 sa inyong touch-tone phone.

SUPPORT FOR STUDENTS LEARNING ENGLISH AS A SECOND LANGUAGE

One of the most noticeable ways in which today's classrooms are heterogeneous is in the number of students who come from different language backgrounds and are learning English in school. Some of these children have parents who are working in this country for a limited time and expect to return to their home country. These parents often view learning English as an asset for their child and they continue to take responsibility for maintaining another language in the home. Other children may have been born in this country but grew up in communities where English was not a dominant language. Perhaps their parents do not speak English. In this case, teachers may encounter communication barriers that make it difficult to find out important information about the students. Another group of students are refugees. They may have undergone great hardships to come to this country and the student's family may be separated, making the position of parental responsibility unclear. In some cases, these students have not gone to school before, although they are older, and learning about school expectations may be the primary language task before they can participate in a class.

All of these situations place different demands on the teacher, who may lack specialized training in second language teaching. Nonetheless, we need to offer the best teaching we can to all students who are encountering English as an unfamiliar language. We can help students develop the oral fluency that provides a base for further language learning. We can also structure activities that help students attend to the elements of the English language. Reading, writing, and many word games support the essential vocabulary development for students. Oral language and literacy development in the student's first language provide significant support for English language learning. Finally, we can make sure that all students feel included in the class because they know they make an important contribution.

Developing a Literacy Base

Students who come to school with little or no English-speaking proficiency need a solid foundation in basic areas to achieve literacy in either or both of their languages. In any program that starts with the student's first language and gradually introduces English in order to develop literacy skills, the following points are fundamental to success.

1. *Read aloud to students.* Students need to hear the special kind of language used in books. Have them respond by writing in the language they choose.
2. *Give students time to write everyday.* Beginning writers need frequent practice to develop fluency. Invented spelling and grammatical mistakes are evidence that students are applying hypotheses about how each language works.
3. *Publish some student writing.* This gives students an incentive to polish some of their pieces. As they revise and edit, they learn the conventions of written language. Use teacher-student writing conferences to focus attention on aspects of form and content.
4. *Provide many books and printed materials, particularly in the language other than English.* Students can transfer their literacy skills from one language to another. The more they read, the more they will learn about language.

Choral Speaking

Many students learning English as a second language (ESL) respond well to choral activities because they are not singled out or embarrassed by their mistakes. The class can learn a short piece to recite together, or a group of students can prepare a passage to present to the class. Different parts can be spoken by different groups or parts of the class. Poems and prose with a strong rhyme and rhythm are easier to learn and more fun to recite. ESL students will learn oral skills such as pronunciation and intonation by participating.

In the following example, divide the class in half and ask each group to alternate lines.

If all the seas were one sea,
What a *great* sea that would be!
If all the trees were one tree,
What a *great* tree that would be!
And if all the axes were one ax,
What a *great* ax that would be!
And if all the men were one man,
What a *great* man that would be!
And if the *great* man took the great ax,
And cut down the *great* tree,
And let it fall into the *great* sea,
What a splish-splash that would be!
   (Old Nursery Rhyme)

For more examples, see *Presenting Reader's Theater: Plays and Poems to Read Aloud* by Caroline Bauer (Wilson, 1987).

Language Experience Stories

With this approach, even students with limited English vocabulary can write their own stories. Introduce students to the technique by composing a story as a group. After an experience shared by the class, begin writing about it on a chart. As students make comments, write down the sentences they contribute. Prompt them to include more information if necessary. After the story is completed, read it back to the class so that they can see it is *their* story. Save these stories for a class collection of Big Books. Or students can copy the class story and read it themselves.

The same technique can be used for individuals. Students can dictate a story to the teacher or an aide, or write it themselves, in their own fashion, to read back later. ESL students can dictate stories into a tape recorder. After these stories are transcribed and typed, they can be read back to the students, showing the relation between the spoken and written language.

Tape-Assisted Reading

Tape-record several stories from a class reading textbook or other literature book. Enlist parents, aides, or older students to help you with this, providing a variety of voices. ESL students can listen to the stories on cassette as they follow along in the book. If you use multiple headsets, a group of students can listen and read at the same time. They will enjoy listening to these stories over and over again, and in the process, they will begin to make the connection between sound and symbol.

Oral Practice

The following books provide models for developing oral language fluency, appropriate for all levels of English language learning, including native speakers. Repeated phrases and rhyming structure hold student interest, illustrations provide the context for understanding vocabulary. Students can respond as a group at first and then individually or in writing.

Alison Jackson. *I Know an Old Lady Who Swallowed a Pie.* Illustrated by Judith Byron Schachner. Dutton, 1997. This version of the familiar humorous verse tells of a woman who ate too much at Thanksgiving dinner—"perhaps she'll die."

Anne Miranda. *To Market, to Market.* Illustrated by Janet Stevens. Harcourt, 1997. Animals run wild in this updated rhyming tale of chaos at home.

Eloise Greenfield. *Honey I Love.* Illustrated by Jan Spivey Gilchrist. HarperFestival, 1995. Poet list things she loves.

Advanced students can write down their examples and create their own books based on these structures.

Pattern Books

ESL students of any age can learn about English grammar by reading primary/picture books that establish a syntactic pattern and then repeat it through many variations. For example, Wanda Gag's *Millions of Cats* provides excellent practice with number words and the plural ending. After the first couple of pages, students will have no trouble filling in the refrain: "Millions and millions of cats." *The Judge,* by Margot Zemach (Farrar, 1959), focuses attention on the -*s* ending as it repeats verbs in the third person singular. And Marjorie Flack's *Ask Mr. Bear* (Macmillan, 1958) is an excellent exercise for pronouns, especially the possessive adjective.

These books achieve their appeal through repetition, making them easy to memorize. Students learn the patterns quickly and practice important grammatical elements painlessly. Students will be motivated to "read" these books that they have memorized.

Traveling Sentences

Exercises that allow more than one right answer are especially important because they give the ESL student more chances to succeed. Begin by placing a simple sentence on the board and then go around the room, inviting students to add to it. Have them write the sentence on the board as it is revised. You can restrict the additions to one word each time, or you can require that each contribution make a complete sentence.

I	*II*
Manolo flew	Manolo flew.
Manolo flew kites	Manolo flew kites.
Manolo flew kites and	Manolo flew kites in the park.

Remind students that they can add words anywhere in the sentence, even in front.

Class Log

All students can participate in recording class activities and other information on a daily basis. They can make weather observations, write about special events, and note birthdays and other news. Students can take turns being secretary, making entries in a class log or diary by copying information off the board or from weather instruments. This is useful to refer to later and it is interesting to show to visitors as a record of the class year.

> *October 3*
>
> It was 76 degrees outside and partly cloudy at 10 A.M. Today a woman from the Police Department came to talk to us about bicycle safety. She gave us a list of rules and taught us how to lock up our bikes. We saw a film about life in the ocean. My favorite part was how the hermit crab lives in other shells.

Scrambler

Play word games such as scrambled words to teach ESL students possible letter combinations in English and develop their vocabulary. If you write scrambled words on cards with the answer on the back, students will enjoy playing this game alone or in pairs. You can even have students develop their own cards.

A version for older students is to present a sentence out of order. Can they arrange the words to form a correct sentence? Be careful—sometimes there's more than one right answer. This exercise gives students practice in English word order patterns, groups of words that go together, and how the beginning of a sentence constrains the ending.

Students can also arrange mixed-up sentences to form a paragraph. They will enjoy creating examples to challenge their classmates. The skills involved in sorting out this mixed-up paragraph reinforce those required for successful reading and writing.

Students Can Help

Your English-speaking students can help you enormously to integrate the student with limited English skills into the class. Assign a "buddy" to each student. This buddy can show the student where to go and what to do, as well as help explain what the teacher wants. Most significantly, the buddy, by speaking lots of English, provides important vocabulary and grammar input for the English language learner. And both participants in the pair receive rewards.

Peer tutoring, using a student in the same class, and cross-age tutoring, when a student in the upper grades helps a student in the lower grades, have proved helpful for language development of ESL students.

Guide for New Students

Encourage ESL students to prepare a guide to the school. It could include information useful for other ESL students as well as any new students. Have students take pictures of classrooms, student activities, and other important elements of school life. They can prepare captions ranging from a few words to a longer description of what is expected of a student. If you work with one particular language group, you might consider having the guide translated and sent out to incoming families as a bilingual introduction to the U.S. school system.

Older students can extend this project by preparing a guide to the community. It might include information about important resources for non–English-speaking families.

ABC Books

Challenge students to prepare their own ABC books. Limit the words to a certain category (animals or plants, for example) in order to stimulate a hunt for new words. ESL students will particularly benefit from this approach to vocabulary learning as they seek out dictionaries. Have students prepare "real" books writing one example for each letter per page, illustrating it, and stapling the pages together. Encourage students to pass their books around and share their unusual discoveries. They can choose their favorite word in each book. Here are some examples of alphabet books that are also useful for vocabulary work:

Stephen Kellogg. *Aster Aardvark's Alphabet Adventures. Morrow,* 1987.

Kate Duke. *The Guinea Pig ABC.* Dutton, 1986.

Marty Neumeier and Byron Glaser. *Action Alphabet.* Greenwillow, 1985.

Luci Tapahonso and Eleanor Schick. *Navajo ABC: A Diné Alphabet Book.* Simon & Schuster, 1995.

Juwanda Ford. *K Is for Kwanzaa: A Kwanzaa Alphabet Book.* Illustrated by Ken Wilson-Max. Scholastic, 1997.

Categories

Another vocabulary game that helps ESL students is the familiar "Categories." Most often used as a unit review, it consists of a word (the topic) written down the left side of a sheet and several categories across the top. Students fill in words under each category that begin with the letters of the topic word. For example, after discussing the subject of "space" for several days, give students this challenging exercise:

	Heavenly Bodies	*Colors*	*People/Professions*
S	Saturn	silver	scientist
P	Pluto	purple	pilot
A	Asteroid	azure	astronaut
C	Ceres	cocoa	chemist
E	Earth	emerald	engineer

This game works best if there is more than one possible answer. If you want to make it more difficult, you can give points for each letter and reward students who have the longest entries.

Individualized Dictionaries

Have primary-grade ESL students develop their own picture dictionaries. They can cut out or draw illustrations of all the new objects they encounter and copy the English word next to each one. Then students can refer to these dictionaries in class and even take them home for extra practice. Some older students may benefit from recording the pronunciation phonetically in their own language.

Intermediate and upper-grade students could construct a dictionary/notebook that focuses on signs and symbols. They could include examples such as the following:

Morphemes for Word Power

When you teach vocabulary, pay particular attention to teaching *morphemes*. (Morphemes are units of meaning that are put together to form words.) Demonstrate the power of morphemes by taking a familiar word such as *telephone* and exploring the meaning of each morpheme. *Tele* is a morpheme meaning *far,* and *phone* is another morpheme meaning *sound.* Ask students if they can list other words that contain one of these morphemes. Words they might know are *telegraph* and *phonograph.* They can look up more examples in the dictionary.

Based on the list, what do they think *graph* means? Did they guess it meant *write?* Once students learn that morphemes have meanings, independent of the words they are found in, and that they can be combined to form new words, students will be able to understand many more words.

Factors That Promote Language Learning: Summary

As you prepare your lessons for students learning English as a second language, keep the following points in mind:

1. Proficiency in English does not develop automatically.
2. Primary language literacy facilitates literacy development in English.
3. Teachers must understand the nature of the second language acquisition process.
4. Oral language development is the foundation for literacy development.
5. The primary purpose for assessing the language and literacy development of English language learners is to inform instruction.
6. No single instructional approach will meet the needs of all English language learners.
7. Meaningful reading instruction should integrate thinking, listening, speaking, reading, and writing.
8. Students should have access to literacy that includes a variety of genres, interests, levels, and cultural perspectives.[3]

FOCUS ON LATINOS: AN ETHNOLINGUISTIC GROUP

In the 1990 census, 22,354,059 people in the United States identified themselves as being of Hispanic origin. Of these, 13,495,938 were of Mexican origin, 2,727,754 were Puerto Rican, and 1,043,932 were Cuban. The category "of Hispanic origin" refers to ethnic identity and is independent of racial identity. This Hispanic/Latino ethnicity is closely tied to Spanish, the shared language of their origin.

With people of Hispanic origin making up 9% of the U.S. population, it is not surprising then that the most commonly spoken language in the United States, after English, is Spanish. In many classrooms, Spanish speakers are in a majority. But not all Americans who come from Spanish-speaking backgrounds speak Spanish themselves, and many who do speak Spanish also speak English. So the most appropriate label for this group may be "ethnolinguistic" minority, to reflect the fact that some people who identify with the culture do not necessarily speak the language. In addition, the label Latino includes people who come from different countries and speak different varieties of Spanish. Today, people from communities with roots dating back to the settlement of California and the Southwest in the 1700s may feel they have little in common with the recent immigrants from El Sálvador.

It is not surprising, then, that there is much confusion over what label to use to identify people (Latino, Hispanic, and Chicano have been some of the options). The Latino students that you have in the classroom may have lived in this country for a generation, immigrated from Mexico leaving many relatives still there, or arrived as war refugees with no option but permanent settlement in this country. These origins affect the extent to which the students have already learned English and also the family's desire to maintain Spanish at home.

We can serve all of our students best by exposing them to Latino culture and to Spanish as a significant language in this country and a language of both historical and international importance. In addition, students who are able to contribute to the discussion through their own knowledge of this language will be able to take pride in their heritage. Use the materials and activities in this unit to confront actively the stereotyped images of Latinos that surround students.

Spanish on the Map

The importance of Spanish-speaking people in the history of this country can be easily seen in the names on the map. Project a copy of a U.S. map on the wall so that all the students can see the names marked on the map. Have students find examples of Spanish place names. Talk about how you can tell whether a name is Spanish or not. If the first word is *San* or *Santa* the name is probably a Spanish saint name. What would these names be in English? (San Francisco/Saint Francis, San Antonio/Saint Anthony, for example.)

Look at different areas of the country separately. Students will notice that more Spanish names occur in certain areas. Which areas have more Spanish names, and why?

As students search for Spanish names, they will notice other groups of foreign names. There are a number of French names in Louisiana, for example. Why? Ask students if they can think why the names used on the map might reflect the history of a region. Does the presence of Spanish names in an area necessarily mean that there are Spanish-speaking people living there?

Comparing Phonemes and Graphemes

Show students the phonemes used in speaking Spanish, some of which are similar to English but none of which are exactly the same. Also show them corresponding graphemes for these phonemes. Here they will notice many differences between Spanish and English, as shown in the chart that follows.

Consonants	Spanish	English
b	también	ri<u>b</u>
	abrir	like <u>v,</u> but with lips almost touching
c	casa	<u>c</u>ase (before a, o, u)
	nación	<u>c</u>ent (before e, i)
ch	chico	<u>ch</u>urch
d	donde	<u>d</u>own
	madre	<u>th</u>e
f	familia	<u>f</u>amily
g	gente	like exaggerated <u>h</u> (before e, i)
	gordo	<u>g</u>ame
h	hacer	silent
j	jugar	like exaggerated <u>h</u>
k	kilómetro	<u>k</u>itchen
l	lástima	<u>l</u>ittle
ll	llena	<u>y</u>ellow
		mi<u>lli</u>on } (regional variation)
m	mañana	<u>m</u>orning
n	nada	<u>n</u>othing
ñ	niño	ca<u>ny</u>on
p	piña	su<u>pp</u>er
q	queso	<u>k</u>ey
r	pero	<u>r</u>ich
	rico	trilled <u>r</u>
rr	perro	trilled <u>r</u>
s	sala	<u>s</u>ad
t	trabajar	<u>t</u>ime
v	enviar	like <u>b</u> in también
	la vaca	like <u>b</u> in abrir
w	Wáshington	<u>w</u>ash
x	examen	e<u>x</u>am
	extranjero	<u>s</u>ound
	México	<u>h</u>it
y	yo	<u>y</u>es
z	zapato	<u>s</u>ave

Vowels	Spanish	English
a	padre	father
e	es	they
i	nida	police
o	poco	poem
u	luna	spoon
	querer	silent after q

Dipthongs	Spanish	English
ai, ay	traiga	nice
au	auto	mouse
ei, ey	aceituna	tray
eu	deuda	ay plus oo
ia, ya	hacia	yonder
ie, ye	nieve	yes
io, yo	dios	yolk
iu	ciudad	yule
oi, oy	soy	boy
ua	guante	wander
ue	vuelve	weight
y	y	even
ui, uy	muy	we
uo	cuota	woe

Spanish Words You Know

Students may be surprised to see how many Spanish words they know. If Spanish is frequently used in the community, students should have no trouble recalling words seen on signs and heard in conversations. Have students list words they know as you write them on the board. Do they know what the words mean? They might suggest the following words:

amigos	fiesta	siesta
adiós	tortilla	piñata

Do any stores in the community have signs in Spanish? Where do the children hear Spanish spoken? What does "Aquí se habla español" mean? ("Spanish is spoken here.") Are there any Spanish place names or street names in the community?

Spanish Borrowings

English has borrowed extensively from Spanish, particularly in the Southwest. List examples of borrowings on the board. Do students know what these words mean? What kinds of words have been borrowed? Discuss why borrowings might take place. The following are examples of borrowings from Spanish:

arroyo	burro	avocado	plaza
bronco	canyon	vanilla	stampede
rodeo	lasso	adobe	mesa
sombrero	chili	mustang	sierra

Have students research Spanish borrowings. What do the original Spanish words look like? What happens to the words when they enter English?

Indian Borrowings

The Spanish spoken in Latin America is distinctively different from the Spanish of Spain because of the influence of the Native American languages. Many words borrowed into English from Spanish come originally from these languages. *Chocolate* was borrowed from Nahuatl, the Aztec language, into Mexican Spanish and then into English. As students research Spanish borrowings, have them notice examples of Native American words. The following are examples of words borrowed from Guaraní, a language spoken in Paraguay, into English: *tapioca, maracas, jaguar, jacaranda, tapir,* and *toucan.*

Spanish spoken in our country differs from the rest of Latin America because it has continued to borrow from the Native American languages and it has also been influenced by English.

Learning about Latinos and Their Heritage

Many books can be used to show students how others live. Select books carefully to avoid stereotyping. The best books include culturally specific details and promote respect for the diversity of the people. The following books introduce students to the lives of young Latinos, along with information about their culture and language.

Susan Kuklin. *How My Family Lives in America.* Bradbury, 1992. The story of three families from different cultures. Eric's family comes from Puerto Rico.

Tricia Brown. *Hello, Amigos!* Holt. 1986. A picture book, with photos of a seven-year-old Mexican American boy who lives in San Francisco and is celebrating his birthday. Includes many Spanish words that students will understand from the context.

Joan Hewett. *Hector Lives in the United States Now: The Story of a Mexican American Child.* Lippincott, 1990. Ten-year-old Hector was born in Mexico but lives in Los Angeles. The book describes his parents' application for citizenship through the amnesty in 1986.

Muriel Stanek. *I Speak English for My Mom.* Whitman, 1989. Reflects a common experience for many children. Lupe's mother works in a factory, but she begins taking English classes to get a better job.

Gary Soto. *The Cat's Meow.* Strawberry Hill Press, 1987. Nicol is "part Mexican." She is fluent in English and understands some Spanish. Her cat Pip, however, speaks Spanish.

Arthur Dorros. *Tonight Is Carnaval.* Dutton, 1990. Describes the preparations for the festival in Peru. Features local crafts, culture.

Omar Castañeda. *Among the Volcanoes.* Lodestar, 1991. A Mayan girl, living in a village in Guatemala, has to take care of her sick mother. She wants to become a teacher.

David Nelson Blair. *Fear the Condor.* Lodestar, 1992. The story of an Aymara Indian girl in Bolivia, set in the 1930s during the Chaco War over Indian rights and land reform.

Fran Leeper Buss. *Journey of the Sparrows.* Lodestar, 1991. The struggle of three young people from El Sálvador to come to the United States.

Varieties of Spanish

The information on Spanish presented in this book is very general. There are many varieties of Spanish spoken in the United States, depending on where the speakers live, how long they have lived in this country, and where they came from originally. Spanish in the Southwest is different from Spanish in the Midwest (Chicago), the Northeast, and Florida. Even in New York City, there are important cultural and linguistic differences between persons from Puerto Rico, Cuba, the Dominican Republic, Colombia, Ecuador, Peru, Mexico, Venezuela, Bolivia, and other South American communities.

The differences in the Spanish of Latin America are primarily vocabulary and pronunciation. Some vocabulary differences are due to influence from local Indian languages, others are due to independent development of Spanish.

The following are examples of different words used in Latin America for *boy:*

Mexico	chamaco	Panama	chico
Cuba	chico	Colombia	pelado
Guatemala	patojo	Argentina	pibe
El Sálvador	cipote	Chile	cabro

Pronunciation also varies regionally. The following are some of the differences found:

- Syllable final *s* becomes *h* or disappears—*estos* is [éhtoh] or [éto]
- *ll* becomes same as *y*—*valla* and *vaya* are alike
- Syllable final *r* sounds like *l*—*puerta* is [pwelta], *comer* is [komel]

Introduce vocabulary specific to local Spanish-speaking groups by having a variety of children's books available. Many books, written about members of particular groups, take pride in presenting common Spanish words that are special to that group.

Books in Spanish and English

Bring books in Spanish into the classroom. Students will enjoy exploring bilingual books, where they can compare stories in Spanish and English, as well as books in Spanish alone. Perhaps children who read Spanish can tell the other students about these books. Show students that knowing another language, such as Spanish, can be an asset. The following list of books in Spanish includes many excellent children's books that have been translated into Spanish. Other books are available from publishing companies in Mexico, Latin America, and Spain.

Sylvia Cavazos Pena. *Kikiriki: Stories and Poems in English and Spanish for Children.* Arte Publico, 1987. This book includes a variety of stories, poems, and riddles written by Latinos. Some selections are in English, some in Spanish.

Alma Flor Ada. *Gathering the Sun.* Illustrated by Simon Silva. Lothrop, 1997. Bilingual poems in Spanish and English honor farm workers in this ABC book.

Jose-Luis Orozco, editor and translator. *Diez Deditos and Other Play Rhymes and Action Songs from Latin America.* Illustrated by Elisa Kleven. Viking, 1997. More than 30 songs and rhymes with directions and parts for voice, piano, and guitar.

Susan Middleton Elya. *Say Hola to Spanish Otra Vez (Again!)* Illustrated by Loretta Lopez. Lee and Low, 1997. Animals use verse to introduce 70 words. See first book, *Say Hello to Spanish.*

Ralfka Gonzalez and Ana Ruiz. *My First Book of Proverbs/Mi primer libro de dichos.* Children's Book Press, 1995. A celebration of Mexican-American culture; delightful art.

Gloria Anzaldúa. *Prietita and the Ghost Woman/Prietita y la llorona.* Illustrated by Christina Gonzalez. Children's Book Press, 1996. A fanciful journey of a young girl with the ghost woman on the King Ranch in Texas.

Pat Mora and Charles Berg. *The Gift of the Poinsettia/El regalo de la flor de nochebuena.* Illustrated by Daniel Lechón. Piñata Books Arte Publico Press, 1994. The loving relationship of Carlos and his aunt during *las posadas.*

Michael Rose Ramirez. *The Little Ant/La hormiga chiquita.* Illustrated by Linda D. Sawaya. Rizzoli International Publications, 1995. Based on a Mexican folktale that presents the theme of diversity.

Juan Felipe Herrera. *Calling the Doves/El canto de las palomas.* Illustrated by Elly Simmons. Children's Book Press, 1996. Story of a migrant farm worker's childhood.

Lois Ehlert. *Cuckoo/Cucú: A Mexican Folktale/Un cuento folklórico mexicano.* Harcourt, 1997. A bilingual tale illustrated with examples from Mexican folk art.

Angel Vigil. *The Corn Woman: Stories and Legends of the Hispanic Southwest.* Libraries Unlimited, 1995. Stories (cuentos) in Spanish and English representing the history and culture of the region.

Francisco Alarcón. *Laughing Tomatoes and Other Spring Poems/Jitomates risueños y otras poemas de primavera.* Illustrated by Maya Christina Gonzales. Children's Book Press, 1997. Twenty poems in Spanish and English in a colorful book for intermediate students.

Lucha Corpi. *Where Fireflies Dance/Ahí, donde bailan las luciernagas.* Illustrated by Mira Reisberg. Children's Book Press, 1997. Memories of growing up in Mexico.

Developing Pride in Latino History and Culture

Latino students need to see books that reflect their own lives and cultural experiences, just as children from any cultural background do. Choose books that represent a variety of regions and backgrounds, from Puerto Rico to Mexican Americans in the Southwest. These examples include rich cultural information and Spanish language in context.

Carmen Lomas Garza. *Family Pictures/Cuadros de familia.* Children's Book Press, 1990. The life of a young Mexican American girl who lives in south Texas. Excellent for details about Latino culture in the region.

Gary Soto. *Baseball in April.* Harcourt Brace Jovanovich, 1990. Short stories of growing up Chicano in central California, each featuring a different Mexican American child.

Pat Mora. *A Birthday Basket for Tía.* Macmillan, 1992. Cecilia wonders what to give her great aunt for her ninetieth birthday.

Arthur Dorros. *Abuela.* Dutton, 1991. A young girl imagines flying over the city of New York with her grandmother.

Denys Cazet. *Born in the Gravy.* Orchard, 1993. Margarita, born in Guadalajara, comes home from her first day in kindergarten in the United States and tells Papa all about it.

Ruth Sonneborn. *Friday Night Is Papa Night.* Puffin, 1987. A Puerto Rican family welcomes the hardworking father home on Friday night.

Lulu Delacre. *Vejigante/Masquerader.* Scholastic, 1993. In Puerto Rico, Ramón wants to sew a costume to march in the carnival parade and make his family proud. The book includes instructions so that students can make their own carnival masks. The text is in Spanish and English.

Gloria Anzaldúa. *Friends from the Other Side/Amigos del otro lado.* Children's Book Press, 1993. Joaquín and his mother fear *la migra,* the Immigration Service.

Richard García. *My Aunt Otilia's Spirits.* Children's Book Press, 1987. A young boy remembers his aunt's strange visits to New York from Puerto Rico.

Cruz Martel. *Yagua Days.* Dial, 1976. On his first visit to Puerto Rico, a boy learns how children use the large yagua leaves to slide down a hill after a rainstorm.

Nicholasa Mohr. *Going Home.* Dial, 1986. Eleven-year-old Felita goes "home" to Puerto Rico for the first time and finds she doesn't fit in.

Rudolfo Anaya. *The Farolitos of Christmas: A New Mexico Christmas Story.* New Mexico Magazine, 1987. Luz is worried because his grandfather won't be able to light the fires to guide the shepherds on Christmas Eve, but he solves the problem. Illustrates the language and customs of Latinos in New Mexico and how people began lighting lanterns for Christmas Eve.

Omar Castañeda. *Abuela's Weave.* Lee and Low, 1993. This picture book shows the importance of respecting elders and maintaining the folk arts.

George Ancona. *The Piñata Maker/El piñatero.* Harcourt Brace, 1994. Shows a dedicated craftsman in Mexico at work on a piñata, step by step.

Mary D. Lankford. *Quinceañera: A Latina's Journey to Womanhood.* Millbrook, 1994. Photographs tell the story of the significant ceremony for fifteen-year-old girls. Includes background information.

Valerie Tripp. *Meet Josefina: An American Girl,* Illustrated by Jean Paul Tibbles. Pleasant, 1997. Life in New Mexico on a rancho in 1824.

The Color Wheel

A Spanish color wheel is helpful to show students the names for colors they know. Make a large poster to display on the wall like that on the next page.

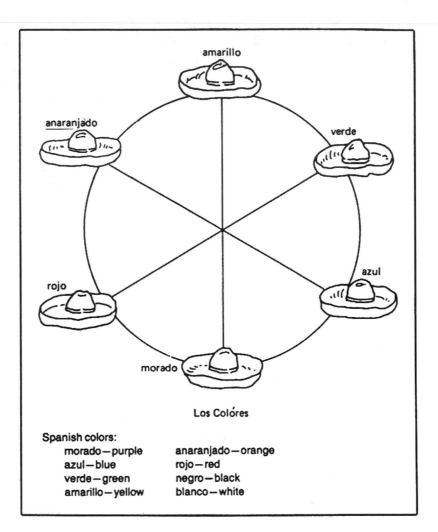

amarillo

anaranjàdo

verde

azul

rojo

morado

Los Colóres

Spanish colors:
morado—purple   anaranjado—orange
azul—blue   rojo—red
verde—green   negro—black
amarillo—yellow   blanco—white

This idea can be easily adapted for use with any language spoken by students in the class. With languages such as Tagalog and Navajo, it is often difficult to find printed materials for use with students. Prepare a variety of displays similar to the color wheel showing basic vocabulary. Include numbers, days of the week, and words used in the classroom.

Review Charts

Help students practice Spanish vocabulary they have learned or seen by preparing review charts. Construct a slip chart with common Spanish words written on the front. Students read the Spanish, say it aloud, give the English equivalent, and check their response by pulling the tab that shows the English word below each Spanish example. These are especially useful for practicing limited sets of words such as numbers and days of the week. (See example on the next page.)

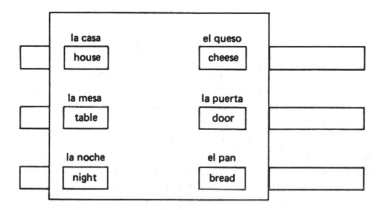

Charts can also be made with pictures of objects on the front. Students review by saying the name of the object in Spanish and then lifting the picture (attached at the top) to read the correct answer. Use these charts for independent student review or small group work. Both kinds of charts are useful for practicing English as a second language as well.

Famous Latinos

Help students break down stereotypes they may have about Latinos by sharing stories of famous people of Latino heritage. In addition, they will learn more about the diversity of people who have contributed to this country. Look for information about leaders in the local Latino community. Students will be encouraged to see examples of people who have become successful without giving up their Latino heritage.

Corinn Codye. *Vilma Martínez.* Raintree, 1990. This bilingual biography of the Mexican American attorney depicts her journey from poverty to leadership in the fight for Mexican American civil rights.

John Gillies. *Señor Alcalde: A Biography of Henry Cisneros.* Dillon, 1988. Students should know the name of Henry Cisneros, one of the most successful Latino politicians.

Janet Nomura Morey and Wendy Dunn. *Famous Mexican Americans.* Cobblehill, 1989. This collection covers the stories of nine men and five women, among them César Chávez, Edward James Olmos, and Vilma Martinez. They share a determination to succeed despite obstacles of poverty and prejudice.

Joan Anderson. *Spanish Pioneers of the Southwest.* Lodestar, 1989. A photographic essay focusing on the people and history of mid–eighteenth-century New Mexico.

Milton Meltzer. *The Hispanic Americans.* Crowell, 1982. An old but still useful source of information about this people and their history.

Dorothy Hoobler and Thomas Hoobler. *The Mexican American Family Album.* Oxford University Press, 1994. Covers the history, culture, and people of today.

Elizabeth Coonrod Martinez. *The Mexican American Experience.* Millbrook, 1995. From settlers to modern immigrants, part of *Coming to America* series.

Spanish Folklore

An important aspect of studying Spanish language and culture is Spanish folklore. This folklore reflects Spanish, English, and Indian influences and is unique to the Spanish-speaking culture as well as an important part of the American experience. Folklore includes stories (cuentos), sayings (dichos), songs, music, legends (leyendas), and drama. Special types of songs are corridos, mañanitas, and rancheros. Many legends center around La Bruja (the Witch) and La Curandera (the Healer).

Provide examples of different kinds of folklore and discuss the ritualized characteristics of each form. Encourage students to research more examples. Because all of the stories and songs are short, they are particularly suitable for presenting in front of the class. Several students can take turns telling stories that are spooky or humorous. You can also obtain records of traditional ballads and songs to play.

Folklore Books for Children

Pura Belpre. *Perez and Martina.* Viking, 1991. From the Puerto Rican storyteller, the tale of Perez the mouse and Martina the cockroach.

Gerald McDermott. *Papagayo the Mischief Maker.* Harcourt Brace Jovanovich, 1992. Papagayo the parrot is the traditional trickster hero of the Amazon rain forest.

Lulu Delacre. *Arroz con Leche: Popular Songs and Rhymes from Latin America.* Scholastic, 1989. This collection includes twelve verses in Spanish and English, along with music.

Latino Voices in Poetry

Writers often find poems the most suitable means through which to communicate issues of identity and conflict. Encourage students to listen to their own inner voices by sharing examples of poems from the books suggested here. These poems illustrate the wide range of themes that are possible and the rich language that can be used to describe experience.

Lori M. Carlson, ed. *Cool Salsa: Bilingual Poems on Growing up Latino in the United States.* Fawcett, 1994.

Carlos Cumpián. *Latino Rainbow: Poems about Latin America.* Illustrated by Richard Leonard. Children's Press, 1994. Includes history and biographies.

Pat Mora. *This Big Sky.* Illustrated by Steve Jenkins. Scholastic, 1998. Poems about the landscape of the Southwest by noted Latina writer.

Student Projects

Students can collect what they have learned and develop a book to share with other classes and schools. A model for this activity is *Kids Explore America's Hispanic Heritage* from the Westridge Young Writers Workshop (Muir Publishing, 1992). This book, written by students, includes information about and examples of dances, food, games, history, art, songs, and people.

Sources for Information for Teaching about Latinos: An Ethnolinguistic Group

Jerome R. Adams. *Latin American Heroes: Liberators and Patriots from 1500 to the Present.* Ballantine, 1993.

Nicholás Kanellos. *The Hispanic Almanac: From Columbus to Corporate America.* Visible Ink Press, 1994. (P.O. Box 33477, Detroit MI 48232-9852)

Frances Ann Day. *Latina and Latino Voices in Literature for Children and Teenagers.* Heinemann, 1997. Includes 38 writers, with extended biographies of 23, such as Gary Soto, Sandra Cisneros, Pat Mora, and Omar Castañeda. Also how to evaluate literature and connections to make to other literature.

Angel Vigel. *Teatro! Hispanic Plays for Young People.* Libraries Unlimited, 1996. Fourteen short scripts; folktales, fables, and holidays; from Mexico and the Southwest.

Milagros: Symbols of Hope/Simbolos de esperanza. Crizmac Video, 1996. Bilingual with teacher's guide. (P.O. Box 65928, Tucson AZ 85728-5928)

Southwest Organizing Project. *Chicano History Teaching Kit.* Bilingual, pictures, 500 years of Chicano history, teaching guide. *¡Viva la causa!: 500 Years of Chicano History.* 2-part video, English or Spanish. 211 10th Street, Albuquerque NM 87102.

REFLECTIONS

In school, students *learn* language, they learn *about* language, and they learn *through* language. As teachers, we need to recognize the central role that language plays in teaching and learning. For education that attempts to address multicultural issues of difference and diversity, language is the heart of the students' identity. We have the responsibility to bring language into the classroom in a way that acknowledges its importance in knowing who we are and what the world is about. We do this by reflecting on our own language, its history and variety, and by exploring other examples of languages and their uses.

APPLICATIONS

1. Investigate the children's literature available in the library and select several books that are based on patterns: refrains, repeated story lines, or questions and answers. Write lesson plans to show how you could use these books with students who need English as a second language support to help them develop oral fluency, to provide writing models, or to practice vocabulary.

2. Collect examples of writing in different languages. Try to find different scripts and different systems (pictographic, syllabary). Look for familiar children's books in different languages. Design a lesson plan to use these books to introduce children to different languages and their writing systems.

3. Look at different books that attempt to reproduce how people really talk (regional or social dialects, Black English). Are they accurate? What effect are they trying to produce? How would you read these aloud to students? Compare and analyze treatment of the same dialect in several books and make recommendations for the teaching of these books and the dialect.

4. Write a letter to parents explaining the language policy in your classroom. Describe the Students' Right to Their Own Language policy in this chapter and how you support it. Outline what actions you expect to take to help their children develop their language abilities.

ENDNOTES

1. *Students' Right to Their Own Language* (NCTE, 1976).
2. J. N. Hook, *The Story of American English* (Harcourt Brace Jovanovich, 1972), p. 2.
3. California Reading Association. *English Language Learners: Position Paper.* Adopted November 1997.

EXPLORING FURTHER

California Office of Bilingual-Bicultural Education. (1986). *Beyond Language: Social and Cultural Factors in Schooling Language and Minority Students.* Los Angeles, CA: Evaluation, Dissemination, and Assessment Center, Los Angeles.

California State Department of Education. (1988). *Schooling and Language Minority Students: A Theoretical Framework.* Sacramento, CA: Author.

Courtney Cazden. (1988). *Classroom Discourse: The Language for Teaching and Learning.* Portsmouth, NH: Heinemann.

David Crystal. (1987). *The Cambridge Encyclopedia of Language.* New York: Cambridge University Press.

Leslie Crawford. (1993). *Language and Literacy Learning in Multicultural Classrooms.* Boston: Allyn and Bacon.

J. L. Dillard. (1972). *Black English: Its History and Usage.* New York: Random House.

Alan Dundes, ed. (1973). *Mother Wit from the Laughing Barrel.* Upper Saddle River, NJ: Prentice-Hall.

Yvonne Freeman, & David Freeman. (1992). *Whole Language for Second Language Learners.* Portsmouth, NH: Heinemann.

Eugene Garcia. (1991). *The Education of Linguistically and Culturally Diverse Students: Effective Instructional Practices.* Santa Cruz, CA: National Center for Research on Cultural Diversity and Second Language Learning.

Shirley Brice Heath. (1983). *Ways with Words: Language, Life, and Work in Communities and Classrooms.* New York: Cambridge.

Shirley Brice Heath, & Leslie Mangiola. (1991). *Children of Promise: Literate Activity in Linguistically and Culturally Diverse Classrooms.* Washington, DC: NEA.

Robert McCrum, William Cran, & Robert MacNeil. (1986). *The Story of English.* New York: Viking. (See also the PBS video series of the same title.)

Suzanne Peregoy, & Owen Boyle. (1993). *Reading, Writing, and Learning in ESL.* White Plains, NY: Longman.

Pat Rigg, & Virginia Allen, eds. (1989). *When They Don't All Speak English: Integrating the ESL Student into the Regular Classroom.* Urbana, IL: NCTE.

Geneva Smitherman. (1977). *Talking and Testifying: The Language of Black America.* Boston, MA: Houghton.

Catherine Wallace. (1988). *Learning to Read in a Multicultural Society: Social Context of Second Language Literacy.* New York: Pergamon.

The World is my country, All mankind are my brethren. Thomas Paine... We dare not just look back to great yesterdays. We must look forward to great tomorrows. Adlai E. Stevenson... Beware, as long as you live, of judging people by appearances. La Fontaine ... If you have built castles in the air, your work need not be lost. Now put foundations under them. OSA Johnson... Until you have become really in actual fact, a brother to everyone, brotherhood will not come to pass. Fyodor Dostoyevsky... You must look into people as well as at them. Lord Chesterfield... True friendship is a plant of slow growth. George Washington... Coming together is a beginning; keeping together is progress; Working together is success. Henry Ford... He has a right to criticize who has a heart to help. Abraham Lincoln... Democracy is based upon the conviction that there are extraordinary possibilities in ordinary people. Henry Emerson Fosdick... While democracy must have its organization and controls, its vital breath is individual liberty. Charles Evans Hughes. Whoever seeks to set one race against another seeks to enslave all races. Franklin D. Roosevelt... Nothing happens unless first a dream. Carl Sandburg... No man is an Island, entire of itself. John Donne... Breathes there the man with soul so dead, Who never to himself hath said, "This is my own, my native land." Sir Walter Scott... Ask not what your country can do for you; ask what you can do for your country. John F. Kennedy... No man is good enough to govern another man without that others consent. Abraham Lincoln... Gently scan your brother man. Robert Burns...

Celebrating Multiculturalism around the Year

In Part I, we explained why and how multicultural understandings must permeate the school curriculum. The succeeding chapters provided further examples of multicultural topics and activities for use with students at all levels. In this chapter we look at opportunities to integrate multicultural concepts, events, and influences, based on the school year. In addition to infusing multicultural content and teaching throughout the curriculum, we expect teachers to take time to raise and discuss specific multicultural issues and ideas explicitly as well. Rather than an oversimplified "heroes and holidays" approach, we advocate that students be constantly involved in exploring the differences and similarities among people and the influence that the presence of many cultures has had on our identity.

In addition to a month-by-month presentation of information, activities, and resources on which you can build a Multicultural Calendar specific to your class, we present a special unit focusing on the study of cultures and time.

After reading this chapter, you should be able to:

- Incorporate multicultural perspectives into all content areas of your teaching.
- Build on student knowledge about different racial, ethnic, and other groups and the history of their treatment in this country.
- Stimulate student interest in and appreciation for the value of different perspectives.
- Encourage students' pride in and awareness of their own heritage.
- Help students understand the historical and cultural basis of calendars.

PREPARING THE CALENDAR

Challenge students to decide on the most effective way to prepare the calendar for the class. Have them brainstorm ideas and alternatives for displaying the months. Students can work in teams to construct a display. While some students mount a frame for the month, others can be researching and collecting quotations, pictures, and other items to supply background information. The materials collected for each month can be assembled in a class notebook for students to consult throughout the year as they work on other projects.

The Multicultural Calendar should always be the result of the effort and interest of the whole class. Although you may want to keep the materials developed from year to year, each class will need to create its own version, reflecting students' own perspectives and discoveries.

Displaying the Calendar

You can reproduce the calendar directly on a large bulletin board. Divide the display space into squares or rectangles using thick, colored yarn or strips of colored construction paper. Students can choose colors and pictures or designs appropriate for each month.

Make the spaces as large as possible. (Challenge several students to solve this measurement problem!) Cut large block letters for the days of the week and the names of the months. Cut a set of numbers from 1 to 31. Computer graphics give students different options for font style and size. Use colored paper for variety.

Developing the Calendar

Older students can type or print the names and dates on slips of colored construction paper or unlined file cards to mount in the appropriate block for each month. Be sure that they check the current calendar so that the number 1 is placed under the correct day of the week; the rest of the dates will then fall in place accordingly. Add events that occur locally or dates of personal interest to your students, such as birthdays. Include pictures and quotations wherever possible.

Quotations are of special interest for the multicultural calendar. Find as many as possible for people whose names appear for that month. Begin with the quotations presented throughout this book. Additional sources of quotations include the following:

Robert Andrews. *Famous Lines: The Columbia Dictionary of Familiar Quotations.* Columbia University Press, 1996.

Deborah Gillian Straub. *Voices of Multicultural America: Notable Speeches Delivered by African, Asian, Hispanic and Native Americans 1790–1995.* Gale, 1995.

Angela Partington. *The Oxford Dictionary of Quotations,* 4th ed. Oxford University Press, 1992.

Advanced readers will enjoy poring over these books, which they probably have not yet explored.

Pictures add a special dimension to the calendar. Let other teachers know that you are searching for multiethnic pictures for this purpose. Keep your eyes open as you look at the daily newspaper or magazines; it is surprising how many suitable pictures you will find. If you have a large bulletin board on which to display the calendar, you might place a ring of pictures around the calendar. Challenge students to identify the people and events pictured.

Encourage students to add to the calendar. As they read, they can take notes on information to include in the calendar. They can even do research in particular areas for this purpose as they search the newspapers, their textbooks, library reference books, and fiction. Students can become investigators as each one takes responsibility for exploring a specific topic.

Students can also decorate the bulletin board by adding appropriate designs, symbols, or illustrations. Snowflakes for the winter months, leaves for the fall, and flowers for the spring add interest and individuality to the calendar. Other popular seasonal motifs include pumpkins, kites, butterflies, and hearts. Avoid symbols associated with stereotypes, such as shamrocks or Indian headdresses.

Strategies for Using the Calendar

Sometimes a more extensive study is triggered by a single event or even a series of dates on the calendar. The following sample thematic units cross subject areas as well as periods of time and require students to use affective and cognitive abilities.

- Ethnic Groups in Our Community
- Seasons around the Country
- History of Asian Americans
- Religions of the World
- Holidays and Celebrations
- Women in Sports

Almost any topic that you study in the elementary and middle school classroom will lend itself to a multicultural approach. Point to the contributions of various groups—ethnic, religious, young and old, male and female—as a strength of our society.

Multimedia Presentation

Students can select a person or topic from the calendar to research. They will present their findings in a speech to the class, using notes and appropriate visual and/or auditory aids, such as graphics imported from CD-ROMs or the Internet, pertinent newspaper clippings mounted on posters, audio or video recordings of speeches, overhead transparencies for new vocabulary, a timeline displayed on the wall, and props or artifacts to share with the class.

Great Interviews

Students practice significant skills as they interview a personality from the past or present. Two or more students will need to develop this activity together as they plan the best questions and appropriate responses. Students can also interview several people, perhaps from different times. Encourage students to do the research needed to play these roles as realistically as possible.

The Time Machine

Ask students whom they would like to invite from the past to visit their community. For example, how would W. E. B. Dubois or Frederick Douglass react to the problems of people today? What would they think of your town? How would they react to meeting people such as U.S. Supreme Court Justices Clarence Thomas or Ruth Bader Ginsberg? Students can then write an imaginary diary entry for their visitor from the past, including an account of such reactions.

Letters

Encourage students to develop their ideas about people and issues in the form of letters. They can write letters to the local newspaper when there is an issue on which they have an opinion. They can also write letters to people from whom they would like information—members of Congress, authors of articles or books, leaders of groups or movements, and so on.

THE MONTHLY CALENDAR

In this section you will find ideas for celebrating multicultural understandings every day of the year. The activities presented in this section provide opportunities for students to ask and answer questions, to discuss fundamental issues such as race and identity, and to begin to develop the skills and information essential to live in a complex world.

The calendar includes:

- Birthdays of historical and contemporary Americans from major ethnic groups
- Important dates in the history of different groups
- Religious and cultural holidays and festivals

The individuals mentioned here are the exceptional few whose achievements have been recognized by history. We want to honor them without limiting ourselves to their example. Encourage students to come up with their own suggestions for notable entries. In every community there are people who have made significant contributions to the welfare of the group. One way to acknowledge and appreciate their efforts is to include them on the multicultural calendar.

Following each month is a short list of suggested activities for incorporating the calendar information into your everyday teaching.

To facilitate presentation, we have not prepared the calendar for one specific year. You will need to make slight adaptations to correct the dates accordingly. For each month, too, there are certain special weeks or holidays that occur on variable dates. July and August are included so that you can present this information during the rest of the school year.

September Activities

From September 15 to October 15 we recognize the contributions of Americans of Latino heritage. What events occur during September that are particularly associated with Latinos? Local celebrations of Latino Heritage Month give teachers an excellent opportunity to collect ideas and materials to be used in classrooms throughout the year. In addition, Chapter 8 includes an extensive feature on Spanish-speaking Americans.

September 8.   On International Literacy Day, focus student attention on the importance of reading. Ask students if they have library cards. Have they ever been to the library? Provide information for students who aren't familiar with the library.

Discuss "literacy" with students. What does it mean to be "literate"? Why is literacy important? Dictators traditionally control access to literacy, for fear that knowing how to read and write will encourage people to seek their freedom. Share with students powerful tales of the importance of literacy. When blacks were enslaved, it was illegal to teach them to read and write. A fictional account, *Nightjohn* by Gary Paulsen, describes the obstacles encountered by black slaves attempting to become literate. Read *Richard Wright and the Library Card* by William Miller, illustrated by Gregory Christie (Lee and Low, 1997) to learn more about Richard Wright and how he had to sneak books out of the library.

September 16.   Prepare the class for Mexican Independence Day by featuring Mexico in the classroom. Use all available materials to create an atmosphere of Mexico. Travel posters, clothes, and objects from Mexico will contribute a festive appearance. Display books about Mexico. Older students can write reports on different aspects of Mexico to put around the room. Use a map of Mexico as a focus for featuring facts about Mexico. Have students research information to construct a time line of significant events in Mexican history. Why is Mexican Independence Day important? What are other dates that are celebrated in Mexico? Make task cards such as the one shown below for individualized approaches.

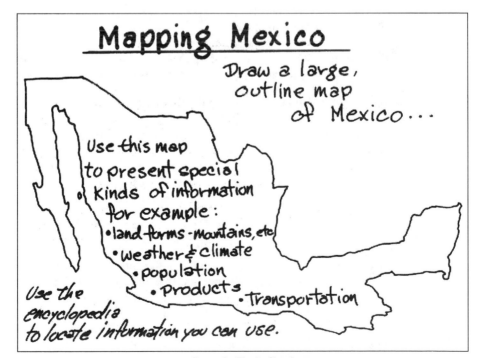

Sample Task Card

Read students the Mexican tale *The Woman Who Outshone the Sun/La mujer que brillaba aún más que el sol,* from a poem by Alejandro Cruz Martínez (Children's Book Press, 1987). Provide colored pens for students to illustrate the story. Students can also compare the English and Spanish texts in this bilingual book. Perhaps a Spanish speaker can read the Spanish version aloud or on audiotape so that all students can hear how it sounds. Another book to share with primary students is *Diego,* by Jonah Winter, illustrated by Jeanette Winter (Knopf, 1991), the story of Diego Rivera, Mexican artist. Older students will appreciate *The Tree Is Older Than You Are: A Bilingual Gathering of Poems and Stories from Mexico,* collected by the noted poet Naomi Shihab Nye and illustrated by Mexican artists (Simon and Schuster, 1995). Including works by children and adults, this book provides insight into contemporary Mexican culture, as well as universal themes.

September 17.   The importance of citizenship is recognized on the anniversary of the signing of the Constitution (1787). Do students know what it means to be a citizen of a country? While people who are born in the United States are automatically U.S. citizens, legal immigrants must pass a test to become citizens. Once they are citizens they gain the right to vote, to hold public office, and to serve on juries. This process is called naturalization. About 1 million aliens (people from other countries) applied for citizenship in 1996. Conditions for naturalization are:

- Living in the United States for five years
- No convictions for serious crimes
- Ability to read, write, and speak basic English
- Passing grade on U.S. history and civics test (answer questions such as How many stars are on the flag? What were the names of the first thirteen colonies?)

Discuss these requirements with students. Should all people who want to be citizens have to pass a test? Why do people want to become citizens? Invite an immigration lawyer or naturalization advisor to the class to explain the naturalization process. Discover what countries the new citizens come from.

Who Belongs Here: An Immigration Story, by Margy Burns Knight and Anne Sibley O'Brien (Tilbury House, 1993) will spark student discussion of the issues of immigration and citizenship. A teacher's guide is also available. For more information see the sample thematic unit on immigration in Chapter 4.

Fourth Week in September.   Banned Books Week is sponsored by the American Library Association. The goal of the program is to highlight the importance of the First Amendment and the power of literature and to celebrate the freedom to read. Ask students what they would do if someone took their books away. Why is reading important? Have each student complete the sentence: Reading is important to me because. . . . For more information on censorship and challenges to books, contact the ALA, 50 E. Huron, Chicago, IL 60611. They also publish *The Banned Books Resource Guide.*

SEPTEMBER

1	2	3	4	5	6	7
	Liliuokalani, 1838–1917, last sovereign of Hawaii	Prudence Crandall, 1803–?, first to admit black girls to her school	Richard Wright, 1908–1960, black author Geronimo surrenders 1886	Harriet E. Wilson published first novel by black American		
8 International Literacy Day	**9** Ellis Island Museum of Immigration opened 1990 Sarah Douglass 1806–1882, black teacher and abolitionist	**10** Alice Davis, 1852–1935. Seminole tribal leader	**11**	**12** Mae Jemison, first black woman in space, 1992	**13** Maria Baldwin, 1856–1922, black educator and civic leader Aloha Festivals, Hawaii	**14**
15 Porfirio Díaz, President of Mexico, 1830–1915 Latin American Independence Day, 1821	**16** Mexican Independence Day, 1821 Mayflower Day (Pilgrims left England, 1620)	**17** Citizenship Day International Day of Peace	**18** Quebec surrendered to English, 1759	**19** Lajos Kossuth, Hungarian patriot, 1802–1915 Booker T. Washington founded Tuskegee Institute, 1881	**20**	**21** Sandra Day O'Connor, first women confirmed as Supreme Court Justice, 1981
22 Religious Freedom Week Martha Corey hung for a witch, Salem, 1692 Banned Books Week	**23**	**24** Francis Watkins Harper, 1825–1911, black author and reformer Federal troops enforce desegregation Little Rock, 1957	**25** Balboa "discovered" Pacific Ocean, 1513 Columbus began second trip to America, 1493 Howard University founded, 1867, first all-black university	**26**	**27** Native American Day	**28** Confucius birthday (National holiday, Taiwan)
29 Bryant Gumbel 1948–	**30** Elie Wiesel 1928–					

My spirit was never in jail.
—*César Chávez*

October Activities

In October, instead of focusing on Christopher Columbus, the symbol of European exploration and exploitation, we aim for a balanced perspective by recognizing the substantial presence of Native Americans before the European arrival, the impact of colonization on the Native populations, and the prejudice they encounter today.

October 12.   Columbus Day commemorates the landing of Christopher Columbus at San Salvador in 1492. Locate San Salvador on the map. Trace Columbus's journey from Spain to the "New World."

Columbus may not have been the first European to land on the continent. There is evidence of Viking settlements and perhaps other voyagers landed here. Should we celebrate Viking Day instead? Discuss with students. Why has Columbus become the symbol of all European contact and colonization?

Encourage students to look at Columbus's voyages from different perspectives. How did the Native Americans perceive his arrival? Read *Encounter,* written by Jane Yolen and beautifully illustrated by David Shannon (Harcourt Brace Jovanovich, 1992), a book for primary students. This encounter with Columbus is told from the point of view of a Taino boy on San Salvador. An excellent book to read with older students is *Morning Girl* by Michael Dorris (Hyperion, 1992). An Arawak boy and girl tell of their life in the West Indies, little dreaming of how it will change with the arrival of the strange visitors. After studying the many rich civilizations of the Native Americans before First Contact, students can write their own accounts of how they might have reacted upon first meeting the European explorers with their strange skin, language, clothing, and customs.

Students can also imagine what it was like to travel with Christopher Columbus. Share the excitement and adventure through the following books:

Pam Conrad. *Pedro's Journal: A Voyage with Christopher Columbus: August 3, 1492– February 14, 1493.* Illustrated by Peter Koeppen. St. Martin's, 1991.

Susan Martin. *I Sailed with Columbus: The Adventures of a Ship's Boy.* Overlook Press, 1991.

Miriam Schlein. *I Sailed with Columbus.* HarperCollins, 1991.

Have students work together to plan their trip as they prepare to accompany Columbus on his expedition. They will need to research the period in order to decide what to bring along and what to expect during the trip. How long will they be gone? How will they react to the people whom they encounter? For more information, consult these nonfiction books for older readers.

Francine Jacobs. *The Tainos: The People Who Welcomed Columbus.* Putnam, 1992.

Kathy Pelta. *Discovering Christopher Columbus: How History Is Invented.* Lerner, 1991.

October 24.   United Nations Day was first observed in 1948, three years after the creation of the United Nations. Fifty countries signed the charter in 1945. Large numbers of countries joined in the 1950s and 1960s as African colonies became independent and in the 1980s and 1990s as the Soviet Union broke up. Some of the nations that do not belong include Switzerland and Taiwan. Have students look into the history of the United Nations and the League of Nations that preceded it. What are the advantages and disadvantages of such an organization? What power does the UN actually have? How are UN peacekeeping forces constituted and where are they sent? For more information, write the United Nations Information Center, 1889 F Street NW, Washington DC, 20006.

October 31—Halloween.   Popular customs for this time of year draw on many of the world's cultures. In ancient Egypt they used to set out oil lamps and delicacies in honor of Osiris, the god of the dead. The Romans established November 1 and 2 for similar rituals. October 31, All Hallows Eve, became a Christian holiday in 1006. In the British Isles, Samhain (the Celtic festival of the dead) meant candles lit in carved turnips. For the autumn festival of Bon, the Japanese dress up in disguise and hang paper lanterns to guide the spirits of their ancestors home. In Mexico, El día de los muertos (the Day of the Dead) is celebrated with special sweets to feed the spirits and with masks and skeletons to scare them away.

How is Halloween celebrated in different communities in the United States? Read about the Day of the Dead in George Ancona's *Fiesta USA* (Lodestar, 1995, also available in Spanish). His photos document the inclusive spirit of the ritual as celebrated by a Latino community in San Francisco. *Day of the Dead* by Diane Hoyt-Goldsmith, with photographs by Lawrence Migdale (Holiday House, 1996), shows a Mexican American family in Sacramento, California. How does this celebration compare with the one in your community?

Have students prepare favorite scary tales for reader's theater or storytelling to present to other classes. See Chapter 7 for folklore suggestions. A mysterious story to read aloud is *Celie and the Harvest Fiddler,* by Vanessa Flournoy and Valerie Flournoy, illustrated by James Ransome (Morrow, 1995). Set in the South in the 1870s, Celie wants to win a prize for the scariest costume at the All Hallow's Eve harvest festival.

National UNICEF Month.   Previously UNICEF Day, the U.S. Committee for UNICEF (the United Nations Children's Fund) has expanded its focus, working in partnership with schools and communities in order to understand global diversity better. For more information, write UNICEF, 331 East 38th Street, New York, NY 10016.

An excellent resource for introducing global diversity is *Children Just Like Me: A Unique Celebration of Children around the World,* by Barnabas Kindersley and Anabel Kindersley (Dorling Kindersley, in association with UNICEF, 1995). Included are pictures and information about individual children, ages 6 to 12, from a variety of backgrounds. Representing the United States are an Acoma Pueblo boy and a Yu'pik Eskimo boy. How are these children like the ones they know? How are they different? What more would they like to know about these children? Information about a penpal club is provided if students want to explore further.

November Activities

In November, we celebrate Native American Heritage Month. See Chapter 6 for a unit on Native Americans to feature this month. Also watch for opportunities to extend student understanding through media programs and information during this month.

1	2	3	4	5	6	7
Thurgood Marshall becomes first Black Supreme Court Justice, 1967 International Day for the Elderly James Meredith became first black student at UMiss, 1962	Mohandas K. Gandhi, 1869–1948 First Pan American Conference—Washington, DC, 1889		Tecumseh (Shawnee) died, 1813		Faith Ringgold, 1930– Fannie Lou Hamer 1917–1977, black Civil Rights leader	Imanu Amiri Baraka (LeRoi Jones), 1934– Marian Anderson, first black hired by Metropolitan Opera, 1954
8	9	10	11	12	13	14
Jesse Jackson 1941–	Leif Erikson Day Mary Shadd Cary, 1823–1893, black teacher, journalist, lawyer	Shawnees defeated in Battle of Point Pleasant (WV), 1774, ends Lord Dunmore's War Chinese Revolution began, 1911	Eleanor Roosevelt, 1884–1962 Casimir Pulaski Memorial Day	Columbus lands at San Salvador, 1492 Día de la Raza (Latin America)		Eamon de Valera, Irish president, 1882–1975 William Penn, 1644–1718
15	16	17	18	19	20	21
3rd Week, Black Poetry Week World Poetry Day	Sarah Winnemucca died, 1891, Paiute Indian leader Alaska Day Festival John Brown's Raid, 1859	Albert Einstein came to U.S., 1933	First Chinese opera performed in U.S.—San Francisco, 1852 Helen Hunt Jackson, 1831–1885, author of *Ramona*			Alfred Nobel, 1833–1896
22	23	24	25	26	27	28
4th Week, United Nations Week	Hungarian Freedom Day, 1956 Pélé, Brazilian Soccer star, born, 1940	United Nations Day Kweisi Mfume, 1948–		Mahalia Jackson, 1911–1972	Ah Nam, first Chinese in California, baptized, 1815	Statue of Liberty Day, dedicated 1886
29	30	31				
		Black Hawk died, 1838, Sauk Indian leader Roberta Lawson, 1878–1940, Delaware civic leader				

National UNICEF Month

There is a sufficiency in the world for man's need but not for man's greed.

—*Mohandas Gandhi*

While November has traditionally been the month for activities featuring Pilgrims and Indians, we now understand the one-sidedness of that perspective. For Native Americans, Thanksgiving is a national day of mourning. Help students understand the native perspective by reading Marcia Sewall's *People of the Breaking Day* (Atheneum, 1990) about the Wampanoag, a tribe in Massachusetts, and their life when the Pilgrims arrived. Students can use their imagination to speculate on what will happen in *Guests* by Michael Dorris (Hyperion, 1994), when Moss is confused by the strange white visitors that his father invites to the tribe's feast. Instead of reinforcing the stereotype of the first Thanksgiving, consider ways to promote multicultural understanding. Celebrate the season with a harvest festival, featuring the food of cultures from around the world, to learn about the sources of our food as well as issues of hunger and famine. For example, why do we have turkey at this time of year? Do other people eat turkey as well? The turkey we eat comes originally from Mexico, where the Aztecs called it *uexolotl,* and it was brought to Europe in the 1500s. What are some of the dishes at your holiday feast? Where do they come from? For a thematic unit on food, see Chapter 5.

November 5, 8.   Edward Brooke was elected to the Senate in 1966 and Shirley Chisholm to the House of Representatives in 1968. They were the first blacks in Congress since Reconstruction. Have students investigate and discuss these questions. How many African American men and women serve in the U.S. Congress now? Are there any African Americans (or women or people from other historically underrepresented groups) in your state legislature? What about city mayors or state governors? What factors, such as racial prejudice or lack of financial support, affect the presence of African Americans in politics today? Why should minority groups be represented among our lawmakers? Shirley Chisholm ran for the presidential nomination in 1972. Discuss the following quote:

> I don't want to be remembered necessarily as the first black woman to have made a bid for the presidency. Or even the first black woman elected to the U.S. Congress. I would rather be remembered as a daring, determined woman who happened to be black and was a catalyst for change in the 20th century.

Thanksgiving: A Celebration of Arrival.   Because we all, including Native Americans, came from some other place, make Thanksgiving a holiday of arrival, a day to honor the many immigrants to this country. How and why did the students, their parents, or their ancestors come to this country? By choice, by force, or by migration? To seek better jobs, to flee religious or political persecution, for educational opportunities? How has each group of newcomers been treated by the previous inhabitants of this country?

Read *Coming to America,* by Eve Bunting, a book for primary-grade children about a family forced to flee their country for the United States and freedom. When they arrive, they find that everyone is celebrating Thanksgiving and they join in gratefully. As Eve Bunting notes, whether you arrive by boat or by airplane, you share the pain of leaving the familiar and the challenge of making a home in the new land.

Molly's Pilgrim by Barbara Cohen, a book for intermediate-level students, teaches everyone a lesson about diversity. A simple Thanksgiving assignment to dress a doll like a Pilgrim has unexpected consequences. Molly's mother doesn't know about the Pilgrims,

1	2	3	4	5	6	7
Sholem Asch, 1880–1957 Seminole War began FL, 1835	Haile Selassie crowned Emperor of Ethiopia, 1930			Shirley Chisholm, first black woman elected to House of Representatives (NY), 1968 Guy Fawkes Day (Canada)		L. Douglas Wilder, 1st black governor since Reconstruction (VA) elected 1989 William Harrison defeated the Shawnee Prophet at Tippecanoe (IN), 1811 Marie Curie 1867–1934
8	**9**	**10**	**11**	**12**	**13**	**14**
Edward Brooke, first black U.S. senator in 85 years, elected (MA), 1966 First Women's College, Mt. Holyoke, 1837	Krystalnacht, 1938 W. C. Handy, 1873–1958 Benjamin Banneker, 1731–1806 Berlin Wall torn down, 1989	Martin Luther, 1483–1546	Remembrance Day (Canada)	Dr. Sun Yat-sen, 1866–1925 Baha'u'llah birthday, 1817, founder of Baha'i faith	Supreme Court upheld segregated buses illegal, 1956	Freedom for Philippines, 1935 Jawaharlal Nehru, 1889–1964
15	**16**	**17**	**18**	**19**	**20**	**21**
	Louis Riel hanged (Canada) 1885 Chinua Achebe, 1930– Brother and Sister Day (India, Nepal) W. C. Handy, father of the blues, 1873–1958	Opening of Suez Canal, 1869	First Thanksgiving, Pilgrims and Massasoit, chief of Wampanoags, 1777	Indira Gandhi, 1917–1984 Christopher Columbus landed, Puerto Rico, 1493	Atahualpa, Inca of Peru, filled room with gold for Pizarro, 1532	
22	**23**	**24**	**25**	**26**	**27**	**28**
Nation of Islam founded, 1930			St. Catherine's Day (Canada) Religious Liberty Day	Sojourner Truth died, 1883		
29	**30**					
	Shirley Chisholm, 1924–					

To understand is hard. Once one understands, action is easy.

—*Sun Yat-sen*

but she does understand religious freedom and she dresses the doll to represent herself, a Russian Jewish immigrant woman. At first, Molly is embarrassed in front of her classmates because her doll looks "different." But the teacher explains how Molly's "Pilgrim" fits the meaning of Thanksgiving.

November 26.   In 1851, Sojourner Truth said:

> The man over there says women need to be helped into carriages and lifted over ditches, and to have the best place everywhere. Nobody ever helps me into carriages or over puddles or gives me the best place . . . ain't I a woman? Look at my arm! I have ploughed and planted and gathered into barns and no man could head me—ain't I a woman? I could work as much and eat as much as a man—when I could get it—and bear the lash as well! And ain't I a woman? I have born 13 children and seen most of 'em sold into slavery, and when I cried out with my mother's grief, none but Jesus heard me . . . and ain't I a woman?

Who was Sojourner Truth? Investigate her life with the class. She was born a slave in the late 1790s and won her freedom in 1827 when all the slaves in New York were freed. Look for information on the life of women and of African Americans at that time. Why did Sojourner Truth fight for the women's movement and women's right to vote? What might she say to women today? A biography for young students is *A Picture Book of Sojourner Truth* by David Adler and illustrated by Gershom Griffith (Holiday House, 1994).

Older students will appreciate *Sojourner Truth: Ain't I a Woman* by the award-winning African American author, Patricia McKissack. Also available is a video called *Sojourner Truth* (Schlessinger, 1992).

December Activities

Many cultures, ancient and modern, celebrate the end of darkness and the return of the sun, or the winter solstice, on December 21. Instead of restricting December festivities to Christmas and Santa Claus, which can exclude some students, a multicultural approach to this month would be to study the variety of winter celebrations around the world and the origin of specific customs such as lighting candles, burning the Yule log, and decorating a tree. Students can learn the Hanukkah dreidl song, reenact the Posadas, interpret the seven principles of Kwanzaa, make snowflakes, and write their updated version of *Twas the Night before Christmas.* (See *Twas the Night b'fore Christmas,* by Melodye Rosales, published by Scholastic in 1996, for a Southern African American retelling.)

Include books in your classroom that reflect diverse perspectives on this time of year, such as the following:

Mary Hoffman. *An Angel Just Like Me.* Illustrated by Cornelius Van Wright and Ying-Hwa Hu. Dial, 1997. Tyler's African American family looks for an angel that represents them.

Cynthia Rylant. *Silver Packages.* Illustrated by Chris K. Soentpiet. Orchard, 1997. A rich man tosses packages to poor children in Appalachia for Christmas.

Lulu Delacre. *Las Navidades: Popular Christmas Songs from Latin America* Scholastic, 1990. This collection of songs and music for Christmas to Epiphany includes information on the origins of the songs and descriptions of the traditions.

December 10, 15.   Human Rights Day celebrates the proclamation of the Universal Declaration of Human Rights by the United Nations (1948). Ask each student to complete this sentence: Every human being has the right to . . .

Related to human rights is the Bill of Rights, the first ten amendments to the U.S. Constitution. A group of students can present the Bill of Rights as a series of short skits, acting out the meaning of each amendment.

A resource for more information is *You Decide! Applying the Bill of Rights to Real Cases* by George Bundy Smith and Alene L. Smith (Critical Thinking Books and Software, PO Box 448, Pacific Grove, CA 93950). This book for middle-grade students includes activities that show the difference between applying the law and personal opinions.

December 16.   Latino communities hold several distinctive celebrations at this time of year. Las Posadas, a nine-day ritual commemorating the journey of the Holy Family in search of lodging, and the lighting of luminarias are customs characteristic of New Mexico. Two books to share with the class, both for primary grades, are:

Rudolfo Anaya. *The Farolitos of Christmas.* Illustrated by Edward Gonzales. Hyperion, 1995.

Jean Clavonne. *Carlos, Light the Farolito.* Clarion, 1995.

In Spanish Catholic tradition, children receive their gifts from the Three Kings on January 6, El Día de los Reyes. This custom is maintained by parades in communities such as Puerto Ricans in New York City. George Ancona's book *Fiesta USA* (Lodestar, 1995) includes photographs of the festive Puerto Rican parade as well as Las Posadas in Albuquerque, New Mexico.

December 18.   The ratification of the Thirteenth Amendment meant the official end of slavery. Begin reading a book such as *The Slave Dancer* by Paula Fox (Bradbury, 1973), which won the Newbery Award in 1974, an excellent historical novel for grades 5–9.

> Neither slavery nor involuntary servitude, except as a punishment for crime whereof the party shall have been duly convicted, shall exist within the United States, or any place subject to their jurisdiction.

A book for younger students, *The Freedom Riddle* by Angela Shelf Medearis and illustrated by John Ward (Lodestar, 1995), tells the story of a slave named Jim who composes a riddle in order to win his freedom one Christmas.

> Mr. Lincoln had told our race we were free, but mentally we were still enslaved.
> —*Mary McLeod Bethune*

Discuss this quote. What does *mentally enslaved* mean? Is it possible to change people's thinking by passing a law? What factors made it difficult to change? (education, jobs)

December 26–January 1.   Begun in 1966, Kwanzaa (Swahili for "first fruits of the harvest") is a nonreligious celebration of African American culture, community, and family that lasts seven days. Each day participants light a candle and discuss one of the seven

UNITED STATES BILL OF RIGHTS

Amendment 1
Congress shall make no law respecting an establishment of religion, or prohibiting the free exercise thereof; or abridging the freedom of speech, or of the press; or the right of the people peaceably to assemble, and to petition the government for a redress of grievances.

Amendment 2
A well-regulated militia being necessary to the security of a free State, the right of the people to keep and bear arms shall not be infringed.

Amendment 3
No soldier shall, in time of peace, be quartered in any house without the consent of the owner; nor in time of war but in a manner to be prescribed by law.

Amendment 4
The right of the people to be secure in their prisons, houses, papers and effects, against unreasonable searches and seizures, shall not be violated, and no warrants shall issue but upon probable cause, supported by oath or affirmation, and particularly described the place to be searched, and the persons or things to be seized.

Amendment 5
No person shall be held to answer for a capital or otherwise infamous crime, unless on a presentment or indictment of a grand jury, except in cases arising in the land or naval forces, or in the militia, when in actual service in time of war or public danger; nor shall any person be subject for the same offense to be twice put in jeopardy of life or limb; nor shall be compelled in any criminal case to be witness against himself, nor be deprived of life, liberty, or property, without due process of law; nor shall private property be taken for public use, without just compensation.

Amendment 6
In all criminal prosecutions the accused shall enjoy the right to a speedy and public trial, by an impartial jury of the State and district wherein the crime shall have been committed, which district shall have been previously ascertained by law, and to be informed of the nature and cause of the accusation; to be confronted with the witnesses against him; to have compulsory process for obtaining witnesses in his favor, and to have the assistance of counsel for his defense.

Amendment 7
In suits at common law, where the value in controversy shall exceed twenty dollars, the right of trial by jury shall be preserved, and no fact tried by a jury shall be otherwise reexamined in any court of the United States than according to the rules of the common law.

Amendment 8
Excessive bail shall not be required, nor excessive fines imposed, nor cruel and unusual punishments inflicted.

Amendment 9
The enumeration in the Constitution of certain rights shall not be construed to deny or disparage others retained by the people.

Amendment 10
The powers not delegated to the United States by the Constitution, nor prohibited by it to the States, are reserved to the States respectively, or to the people.

DECEMBER

1	2	3	4	5	6	7
Rosa Parks arrested, 1955, refused to give up seat on bus	Monroe Doctrine, 1823	Myrtilla Miner opened first Colored Girls School, Washington DC, 1851 International Day of Disabled Persons	Phillis Wheatley died, 1784, black poet		Feast of St. Nicholas Columbus discovered Haiti, 1492	Bombing of Pearl Harbor by Japanese, 1941
8	**9**	**10**	**11**	**12**	**13**	**14**
2nd Week, Human Rights Week Diego Rivera, 1886–1957		Red Cloud died, 1909 U.S. acquired Cuba, Guam, Puerto Rico, Philippines, 1898 Human Rights Day, Universal Declaration of Human Rights ratified, 1948	Aleksandr Solzhenitsyn, 1918–		Yehudi Menuhin makes NY debut, 1927	
15	**16**	**17**	**18**	**19**	**20**	**21**
Bill of Rights day, Bill of Rights ratified, 1791 Sitting Bull killed, 1890	Las Posadas begin	Maria Stewart died, 1879, black teacher and lecturer	Ratification of 13th Amendment ended slavery, 1865	Bernice Pauahi Bishop, 1831–1884, Hawaiian leader	Cherokees forced off their land in Georgia because of gold strike, 1835 Sacajawea died, 1812, Shoshoni interpreter	María Cadilla de Martinez, 1886– , early Puerto Rican feminist Pilgrims landed at Plymouth (MA), 1620
22	**23**	**24**	**25**	**26**	**27**	**28**
Teresa Carreño, 1853–1917, Venezuelan American concert pianist	First Chinese theater built, San Francisco, 1852 Madame C. J. Walker, 1867–1919, black businesswoman		Christmas Day	Kwanzaa begins		
29	**30**	**31**				
Wounded Knee massacre 1890	Pocahontas rescued Captain John Smith, 1607 Gadsden Purchase signed with Mexico, 1853					

We didn't have any of what they called Civil Rights back then. It was just a matter of survival—existing from day to day.

—*Rosa Parks*

principles to live by all year: Umoja (unity), Kujichagulia (self-determination), Ujima (collective work and responsibility), Ujamma (cooperative economics), Nia (purpose), Kuumba (creativity), and Imani (faith).

The Seven Days of Kwanzaa: How to Celebrate Them, by Angela Shelf Medearis (Scholastic, 1994) includes all the instructions students need for this holiday, such as ideas for gifts to make, African foods, and stories of inspirational African Americans. Another rich source of information is *Celebrating Kwanzaa* by Diane Hoyt-Goldsmith (Holiday, 1993), with photographs and text showing how thirteen-year-old Andiey's family celebrates African American history and traditions.

Books for primary students are:

Denise Burden-Patmon. *Imani's Gift at Kwanzaa.* Illustrated by Floyd Cooper. Simon and Schuster, 1992.

Andrea Davis Pinkney. *Seven Candles for Kwanzaa.* Illustrated by Brian Pinkney. Dial, 1993.

Donna L. Washington. *The Story of Kwanzaa.* Illustrated by Stephen Taylor. HarperCollins, 1996.

January Activities

The name of this month comes from the Roman god Janus, who had two faces and looked back into the past and forward into the future. Janus was the spirit of doorways and the god of beginnings, also represented as two sides of the same coin. It is very appropriate, therefore, to take time now to consider where we have been and where we are going. Talk with the class about the history of this country. Have them list ways in which the country has changed: inventions, attitudes, and people. Then ask them to face forward and think about what might change in the future. What would they like to see happen in their lifetime? Use the excitement of speculating about the future to show the importance of finding the roots of the future in the past.

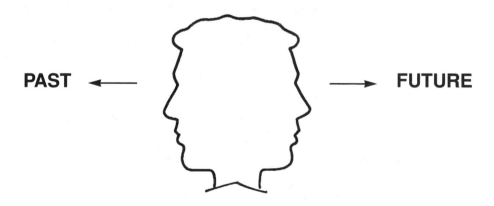

PAST ←   → **FUTURE**

January 1.   Although the Emancipation Proclamation was supposed to free the slaves, it had little impact in the South since the Confederate States would not be bound by it until the war was over. It did, however, enable blacks to join the Union forces. The Massachusetts

54th Colored Infantry was the first officially sanctioned regiment of black soldiers. These heroic soldiers fought in the front lines despite knowing that, if captured by the Confederate forces, they would be treated as slaves and not military prisoners. For more information on this regiment, see *Undying Glory* by Clinton Cox (Scholastic, 1991) or the video *Glory* (RCA/Columbia Home Video, 1990). Have students investigate the word "emancipation." What does it mean? What other words contain the root word "manu"? How many synonyms for "emancipation" can students list?

January 15.   Discuss with students the quotation by Martin Luther King, Jr. featured on the calendar. What does lynching mean? Martin Luther King, Jr. is known as a leader in the civil rights movement for African Americans. What are civil rights? In 1964, he received the Nobel Prize for Peace, an international award in recognition of his work for human relations. Why would people in other countries think that his work was important?

Happy Birthday, Dr. King, written by Kathryn Jones and illustrated by Floyd Cooper (Simon and Schuster, 1994), features a boy puzzled by a school assignment to celebrate King's birthday. But after talking with his family, he learns about the civil rights movement and King's achievements.

Ask students what they would do if they wanted to change someone's behavior or opinion. What methods work best, and when? Do any laws protect them from other people? What about classroom rules—do they protect anyone? Discuss problems the students might have with a bully or a liar. Have them write and act out possible strategies to resolve the conflict.

Students can find out more about Martin Luther King, Jr.'s life and work in these books:

Margaret Davidson. *I Have a Dream, the Story of Martin Luther King.* Scholastic, 1991.

Rosemary Bray. *Martin Luther King, Jr.* Greenwillow, 1995.

King was only 39 when he was assassinated in 1968, yet his influence continues to be felt. His birthday became a national holiday in 1986. Martin Luther King, Jr.'s vision of an inclusive society is an inspiration for all Americans, not only African Americans. How should we celebrate this holiday? Involve students in planning and carrying out an appropriate celebration. They might read excerpts from his speeches or prepare a skit dramatizing an important event in his life. Check your library for audio or videotapes to illustrate the power of King's words. Other resources are:

Peter J. Albert and Ronald Hoffman. *We Shall Overcome: Martin Luther King and the Black Freedom Struggle.* Da Capo, 1993.

Taylor Branch. *Parting the Waters: America in the King Years, 1954–1963.* Simon and Schuster, 1988.

Martin Luther King, Jr. *Wisdom of Martin Luther King, Jr.* Meridian, 1993.

I Have a Dream: Dr. Martin Luther King. An Illustrated Edition. Scholastic, 1997. The text of King's speech, given August 28, 1963 in Washington, DC, is accompanied by paintings from noted children's book artists such as Leo and Diane Dillon, Floyd

1	2	3	4	5	6	7
Emancipation Proclamation, 1863 Commonwealth of Australia established, 1901 Ellis Island opened, 1892	Emma, 1836–1885, Queen of Hawaii Zora Neale Hurston, 1891–1960		Louis Braille, 1809–1852 Selena Sloan Butler, 1872, founded first black PTA in country	Sissieretta Jones, 1869–1933, black singer	Celebration of King's Day—Pueblo Dances Lucy Laney, school for Negro children, 1886	Harlem Globetrotters played first game (Illinois), 1927
8	**9**	**10**	**11**	**12**	**13**	**14**
	Joan Baez, 1941– , Latina singer	League of Nations founded, 1920, Geneva George Washington Carver, 1864–1943, black scientist	Eugenio de Hostos, 1839–1903, Puerto Rican patriot	Adah Thomas, 1863–1943, black nursing leader	Charlotte Ray, 1850–1911, first black woman lawyer First black Cabinet member, Robert Weaver, becomes Secretary of HUD, 1966	Carlos Romulo, Philippine leader, 1901–? Albert Schweitzer, 1875–1965
15	**16**	**17**	**18**	**19**	**20**	**21**
Martin Luther King, Jr., 1929–1968, black minister and civil rights leader Human Relations Day	Religious Freedom Day				Martin Luther King holiday began 1986	Fanny Jackson-Coppin died, 1913, black educator Eliza Snow (Smith), 1804–1887, "Mother of Mormonism"
22	**23**	**24**	**25**	**26**	**27**	**28**
Sam Cooke, 1932–1964	24th Amendment barred poll tax in federal elections, 1964 Amanda Smith, 1837–1915, black evangelist Elizabeth Blackwell, first woman to receive U.S. medical degree, 1849	Eva del Vakis Bowles, 1875–1943, black youth group leader	Florence Mills, 1895–1927, black singer and dancer	Bessie Coleman, 1892–1926, black aviator	Vietnam War ended, 1973	Louis Brandeis, first appointment of American Jew for U.S. Supreme Court, 1916
29	**30**	**31**				
	Mohandas Gandhi (India) assassinated, 1948	Jackie Robinson, 1919–1972				

It may be true that the law cannot make a man love me, but it can keep him from lynching me, and I think that's pretty important....
—*Martin Luther King, Jr.*

Cooper, James Ransome, Jan Spivey Gilchrist, Brian Pinkney, Jerry Pinkney, and Tom Feelings.

January 30.   Although Gandhi lived in another country, students should know something about his life and his ideas because he influenced so many people around the world, from Martin Luther King to Nelson Mandela. Feature several quotations from Gandhi:

Ahimsa ("harmlessness" or nonviolence) means the largest love. It is the supreme law. By it alone can mankind be saved. He who believes in nonviolence believes in a living God.

All humanity is one undivided and indivisible family, and each one of us is responsible for the misdeeds of all the others. I cannot detach myself from the wickedest soul.

All amassing of wealth or hoarding of wealth above and beyond one's legitimate needs is theft. There would be no occasion for theft and no thieves if there were wise regulations of wealth and social justice.

My nationalism is intense internationalism. I am sick of the strife between nations or religions.

A biography to share with students is John Severance's *Gandhi: Great Soul* (Clarion, 1997).

February Activities

February is African American History Month so you can look forward to programs, articles, speeches, and discussions about the history and current status of African Americans. Formerly Black History Week, this celebration is sponsored by the Association for the Study of AfroAmerican Life and History, founded by historian Carter G. Woodson. The week was first observed in 1926 and it included the birthdays of Abraham Lincoln (12) and Frederick Douglass (14). However, the whole month is rich in the birthdays of exceptional African Americans. Request from the association a publication list of materials to be used at this time: 1407 14th Street NW, Washington, DC 20005.

As the calendar quotation illustrates, Carter G. Woodson was concerned about promoting the history of underrepresented groups. The National Council for the Social Studies presents the Carter G. Woodson Book Award annually for the most distinguished social studies book for young readers that depicts ethnicity in the United States, to encourage writers and readers of literature that treats multicultural subjects sensitively and accurately. The 1996 winner was *Songs from the Loom—A Navajo Girl Learns to Weave,* by Monty Roessel (Lerner, 1996).

Students can learn James Weldon Johnson's song "Lift Ev'ry Voice and Sing," also known as the African American National Anthem, presented in *Lift Ev'ry Voice and Sing* (Scholastic, 1995) and illustrated by Jan Spivey Gilchrist. James Weldon Johnson, a school principal, wrote the poem and his brother, J. Rosamond Johnson, composed the music in 1900 to celebrate Abraham Lincoln's birthday. James Weldon Johnson also became the first African American director of the NAACP in 1920. Feature the activity "Celebrating African Americans." You can also challenge students to create their own acrostics with historical or contemporary African Americans.

Celebrating African Americans

Fill in the last names of these famous twentieth century African Americans to solve this puzzle. Their occupation is given as a clue.

_ _ B _ _ _ _ _	baseball player
_ _ _ _ L _	retired general
_ _ _ _ _ A _	children's advocate
_ _ C _ _ _ _	ran for president
_ _ _ K _ _	author
H _ _ _ _	poet
_ I _ _ _ _ _	talk show host
_ S _ _	tennis champion
_ _ T _ _ _ _	educator
_ _ _ _ _ O _ _	artist, quilter
_ _ R _ _ _ _ _	former Supreme Court justice
_ _ _ _ Y	comedian, actor
M _ _ _ _ _ _ _	won Nobel Literature Prize
_ _ _ _ O _ _	astronaut
_ N _ _ _ _ _	writer, poet, dancer
_ _ _ _ T _ _	writer, folklorist
_ _ _ _ _ _ H	Olympic star runner

1. Choose one name and find out why that person is famous.
2. List five other famous African Americans in the same field.

Answers to "Celebrating African Americans": Jackie Robinson, Colin Powell, Marian Wright Edelman, Jesse Jackson, Alice Walker, Langston Hughes, Oprah Winfrey, Arthur Ashe, Mary McLeod Bethune, Faith Ringgold, Thurgood Marshall, Bill Cosby, Toni Morrison, Guion Bluford, Maya Angelou, Zora Neale Hurston, Wilma Rudolph.

February 1. Feature the poetry of Langston Hughes. An attractive collection is *The Dreamkeepers and Other Poems,* illustrated by Brian Pinkney (Knopf, 1994). Langston Hughes's poetry lends itself to graphic presentation. Have students create posters featuring a selection from a poem. Encourage them to use calligraphy and art on the poster in order to celebrate the poem. *The Collected Poems of Langston Hughes* is available from Knopf (1994). Play the recording *Langston Hughes Reads and Talks about His Poems* for students (Spoken Arts). Read aloud Floyd Cooper's biography for younger students, *Coming Home: From the Life of Langston Hughes* (Philomel, 1994).

FEBRUARY

1	2	3	4	5	6	7
Langston Hughes, 1902–1967 National Freedom Day Treaty of Guadalupe Hidalgo, 1848	Candlemas Day	15th Amendment (right to vote) ratified, 1870	Liberia founded, 1822 home for freed slaves Apache Wars begin, 1861 Rosa Parks, 1913–	Constitution Day (Mexico)	Senate ratified treaty ending Spanish-American War, 1899	
8	9	10	11	12	13	14
	Alice Walker, 1944–	Leontyne Price, 1927– End of French and Indian War, 1763	Nelson Mandela released from prison, 1990 Vermont abolished slavery, 1777	NAACP begun, 1909 Fannie Williams, 1855–1944, black lecturer, civic leader Thaddeus Kosciusko, Polish patriot, 1746–1817 Abraham Lincoln, 1809–1865 Chinese Republic, 1912		Frederick Douglass, 1817–1895 Valentine's Day
15	16	17	18	19	20	21
Galileo Galilei, 1564–1642 Susan B. Anthony, 1820–1906		Chaim Potok, 1929–	Toni Morrison, 1931–	Amy Tan, 1952– Executive Order signed, 1942, Japanese-Americans sent to camps	Buffy Saint-Marie, 1942–	Malcolm X Day, assassinated, 1925–1965 Barbara Jordan, 1931–1996
22	23	24	25	26	27	28
Gertrude Bonnin, 1876–1938, Sioux author and reformer Ishmael Reed, 1938–	W.E.B. Du Bois, 1868–1963		First black in Congress, Hiram Revels (MS), 1870 José de San Martín (the great liberator), 1778–1850		Marian Anderson, 1902–1993	
29						
Emmeline Wells, 1828–1921, Mormon leader and feminist Mother Ann Lee, 1736–1784, Founder of the Shakers	Week of 3rd Monday: **Brotherhood/Sisterhood Week, sponsored by National Conference of Christians and Jews, 71 Fifth Avenue, New York, NY 10003**			If a race has no history, if it has no worthwhile tradition, it becomes a negligible factor in the thoughts of the world and it stands in danger of being exterminated. *—Carter G. Woodson*		

Students can learn a poem or tell a story. "Thank You, Ma'am," a short story by Langston Hughes, is included in *Jump up and Say! A Collection of Black Storytelling* (Linda Goss and Clay Goss, Simon and Schuster, 1995). *The Sweet and Sour Animal Book* is an alphabet book of poems by Langston Hughes illustrated by students from the Harlem School of the Arts (Oxford University Press, 1994). Students will enjoy these humorous poems that offer playful language.

February 12.   Have students prepare a bulletin board display about Abraham Lincoln, a president who has become a folk hero. He symbolizes the poor boy who rose to leadership, the president who freed the slaves. Feature quotations by Lincoln around his picture, for instance:

> The ballot is stronger than the bullet.

> Any people anywhere, being inclined and having the power, have the right to rise up and shake off the existing government, and form a new one that suits them better. This is the most valuable, a most sacred right—a right which we hope and believe is to liberate the world.

> A house divided against itself cannot stand. I believe this government cannot endure, permanently half *slave* and half *free.*

> As I would not be a *slave,* so I would not be a *master.* This expresses my idea of democracy. Whatever differs from this, to the extent of the difference, is no democracy.

A group of students can prepare "The Gettysburg Address" for choric speaking. Plan a short program using this address, quotations, and poetry about Lincoln. One or two students might tell a story about Abe.

Of the People, by the People, for the People (Columbia University Press, 1996) is a collection of quotations from Abraham Lincoln. For an easy biography, see *Honest Abe* by Edith Kunhardt, illustrated by Malcah Zeldis (Greenwillow, 1993). It includes the Gettysburg Address.

March Activities

Women's history is celebrated this month, in honor of March 8, International Women's Day. This holiday commemorates the beginning of a strike by women garment workers in New York City in 1908, which resulted in the eight-hour work day.

As you collect materials for use in the classroom this month and throughout the year, aim for a diverse perspective: women of the past and women of today, women who represent different ethnic and other groups, stories of both women and men who have actively combated stereotypes about both sexes. The National Women's History Project (7738 Bell Road, Windsor, CA 95492-8518) offers books, posters, and other resources for the classroom. See Chapter 5 for activities and information to feature this month.

March 10.   Harriet Tubman led an active and dangerous life. Although she could not read or write, she was able to escape slavery and flee to the North where she was free. Instead of remaining safe in the North, she returned to slave holding territory many times to guide other slaves to freedom. Read about her exploits and have students choose several crucial

MARCH

1	2	3	4	5	6	7
Ralph Ellison, 1914–1994, black author; Peace Corps est., 1961; St. David's Day (Wales)	Texas declares independence from Mexico, 1836; Puerto Rico became territory, 1917	Doll Festival (Japan); Indian Appropriations Act, 1885	Knute Rockne, 1888–1931	Crispus Attucks Day	Fall of the Alamo, 1836	Thomás Masaryk (Czech patriot), 1850–1937; First Selma (Alabama) civil rights march, 1965—Bloody Sunday

8	9	10	11	12	13	14
International Women's Day; Women garment workers began strike, New York, 1908	Amerigo Vespucci, 1451–1512, Italian navigator; Antonia Novello, first woman, first Latino surgeon general, 1990	Harriet Tubman's death, 1913; Hallie Q. Brown, 1850–1949, Black teacher and women's leader		Gabriele d'Annunzio, 1863–1938		Albert Einstein, 1879–1955

15	16	17	18	19	20	21
Eugene Marino, first black Archbishop, appointed 1988; Ruth Bader Ginsburg 1933	Freedom's Journal, first black newspaper in U.S., 1827	St. Patrick's Day; Myrlie Evers-Williams, 1933–	Hawaii admitted to Union, 1959 (50th state)	St. Joseph's Day (Italy)	Harriet Beecher Stowe's *Uncle Tom's Cabin* published, 1852; Spike Lee, 1957–	Benito Juárez, Mexican leader, 1806–1872; Namibia became independent, 1990; New Year (India)

22	23	24	25	26	27	28
Emancipation Day (Puerto Rico)		Canada gives blacks right to vote, 1837	Seward's Day (Alaska)	Kuhio Day (Hawaii)	Marconi sends first international wireless message, 1899; First Mormon temple dedicated, 1836	

29	30	31				
	U.S. purchased Alaska from Russia, 1867	First treaty U.S.–Japan, 1854; U.S. took possession of Virgin Islands from Denmark, 1917; César Chávez, 1927–1993				

All novels are about certain minorities: the individual is a minority.

—*Ralph Ellison*

events to dramatize. They can prepare a play by writing dialogue and narration and using a few props. This play can be presented for other classes to watch. There are many biographies of Harriet Tubman. A book for primary students is *Minty: The Story of Young Harriet Tubman* by Alan Schroeder and illustrated by Jerry Pinkney (Dial, 1996). This fictionalized account focuses on her childhood.

Harriet Tubman is not just a figure in the past but a symbol of liberation and strength for today. In Faith Ringgold's book, *Aunt Harriet's Underground Railroad in the Sky,* Harriet is the conductor for a fantasy trip through the skies of New York.

March 17. March is also Irish American Heritage Month. Although highly stereotyped, St. Patrick's Day offers an opportunity to recognize Irish Americans and their history. Two books provide accurate information on Irish and Irish immigrants.

Eve Bunting. *St. Patrick's Day in the Morning.* Clarion, 1993. Set in Ireland, a boy wants to prove he is big enough to march in the parade.

Steven Kroll. *Mary McLean and the St. Patrick's Day Parade.* Illustrated by Michael Dooling. Scholastic, 1991. Story of recent Irish immigrants in New York in 1850. Includes information on Irish traditions and St. Patrick.

What Irish customs or symbols can students name? If a shamrock or a leprechaun is all they know, then have students look into Irish folklore and historical traditions. They can report their findings to the class.

Read aloud Irish tales such as the following:

Shirley Climo, *The Irish Cinderlad.* Illustrated by Loretta Krupinski. HarperCollins, 1996.

Padraic Colum. *The King of Ireland's Son.* McGraw-Hill, 1966.

Virginia Haviland (retold by). *Favorite Fairy Tales Told in Ireland.* Little, Brown, 1961.

Have students prepare stories for dramatization, assigning parts and rewriting the dialogue.

March 22. Emancipation Day. Puerto Rico is a part of the United States but it is not a state. As a result, Puerto Ricans cannot vote for representation in Congress. Have students research the history of Puerto Rico's relationship to the United States. What is Puerto Rico like? Explore Puerto Rico through its traditional folklore.

Nicholasa Mohr and Antonio Martorell. *The Song of El Coquí: And Other Tales of Puerto Rico.* Viking, 1995. This collection includes stories from the three strands of Puerto Rican heritage—Taino (native), African, and Spanish. A good resource for storytelling, includes Spanish vocabulary in context and a glossary.

*Nicholasa Mohr. *Old Letivia and the Mountain of Sorrows.* Illustrated by Rudy Gutierrez. Viking Penguin, 1996. This tale to read aloud features a curandera (healer) in the Puerto Rican rain forest.

Jan Mike. *Juan Bobo and the Horse of Seven Colors: A Puerto Rican Legend.* Troll, 1995. A traditional tale with a foolish folk hero, includes information about Puerto Rico.

A nonfiction source for further information is Joyce Johnston's *Puerto Rico* (Lerner, 1994). Also contact the Puerto Rico Tourism Corporation, 575 Fifth Avenue, 23rd floor, New York, NY 10017.

April Activities

Because April includes many birthdays of jazz (and blues) musicians such as Duke Ellington and Ella Fitzgerald, you might choose to focus this month on jazz, America's classical music. Jazz, with its roots in African rhythms and the black church, and influenced by Latin musical traditions, has become an international language. Introduce students to the history of jazz through these books:

Tony Esposito, ed. *Greatest Little Jazz Book.* Belwin, 1995.

Morgan Monceaux. *Jazz.* Knopf, 1994.

Stephen Longstreet. *Magic Trumpets: The Story of Jazz for Young People.* Zephyr Press, 1989.

Students can also consult the *History of Jazz,* a CD-ROM program (Clearvue/eav, 6465 N. Avondale Avenue, Chicago IL 60631, 1996) that shows how different influences combined to develop this art form. Includes profiles of jazz musicians.

Have students select a jazz musician or singer for research. They can pick an instrument that they are interested in or a period to investigate. What did this person contribute to the development of jazz? Accompany the presentation with pictures and music. Here are some books to get them started:

Leslie Gourse. *Dizzy Gillespie and the Birth of Bebop.* Atheneum, 1994.

Wendie Old. *Duke Ellington: Giant of Jazz.* Enslow, 1996.

*George David Weiss and Bob Thiele. *What a Wonderful World.* Illustrated by Ashley Bryan. Story of Louis Armstrong, goodwill ambassador.

*Angela Shelf Medearis. *Little Louis and the Jazz Band: Story of Louis "Satchmo" Armstrong.* Illustrated by Anna Rich. Lodestar, 1994. (*Rainbow Biography* series)

*Roxann Orgill. *If I Only Had a Horn.* Illustrated by Leonard Jenkins. Houghton, 1997. Louis Armstrong and New Orleans in 1910.

*Chris Raschka. *Mysterious Thelonious.* Orchard, 1997. Unusual biography links Thelonious Monk's music to tones of diatonic music scale and values of the color wheel.

April 14—Pan American Day.   On this day, we remember that America includes many countries besides the United States. James Blaine, the U.S. Secretary of State under President Benjamin Harrison, called for an international conference of North and South American countries. The group met April 14, 1890 to form the Pan American Union, now the Organization of American States. In recognition, President Hoover established Pan American Day in 1931.

Display a map of North, Central, and South America, showing the names of the countries and their capitals. Illustrate it with the flags of the different countries. Discuss what these countries have in common. For example, all the countries of the Americas have great ethnic, linguistic, and racial diversity, as well as substantial immigrant populations. Note that the people in these countries are "Americans" too.

April 15.   On this date in 1947, Jackie Robinson broke the colorline. He became the first black big league baseball player. Before this date, blacks played in the Negro Baseball League and whites played in the major leagues. Why was Jackie Robinson's achievement significant? Today many more blacks are successful in sports.

Students can investigate the position of black athletes then and now. Read about Jackie Robinson, the problems he faced, and how he handled them.

Peter Golenbock. *Teammates.* Harcourt Brace Jovanovich, 1990.

Kenneth Rudeen. *Jackie Robinson.* HarperCollins, 1996.

Interview adults who remember Jackie Robinson's career. How did they feel about his success? Compare Jackie Robinson to the black athletes of today. How do they continue to struggle against racial stereotypes and prejudice?

After learning about Jackie Robinson's experience, students will be able to formulate more complex questions about the historical context for his achievements. Have them brainstorm a list of questions raised by their study, such as:

What was it like playing in the segregated leagues?
Were there other players as good as Jackie Robinson?
Would black players prefer to play in the major leagues?
Who supported these changes?

They can find out more about the Negro Baseball Leagues in the following books.

William Brashler. *The Story of Negro League Baseball.* Ticknor and Fields, 1994.

David K. Fremon. *The Negro Baseball Leagues.* New Discovery Books, 1994. *American Events* series.

Patricia McKissack and Frederick McKissack. *Black Diamond: The Story of the Negro Baseball Leagues.* Scholastic, 1994.

April 22.   The U.S. Holocaust Memorial Museum in Washington, DC opened on this date in 1993, keeps alive public awareness of the immensity of this tragedy in which 6 million men, women, and children were killed simply because they were Jewish. What does the word "holocaust" mean? Talk about genocide. Analyze the parts of this word. Can students apply this understanding to similar words such as suicide, patricide, fratricide, homicide? What other words does the morpheme *gen-* appear in?

Many people believe that this tragedy could never happen again. Yet large groups of people around the world are still being killed because of their religion, ethnic background,

Sunday	Monday	Tuesday	Wednesday	Thursday	Friday	Saturday
1 Spring Corn Dances (Pueblos); Telugu New Year (India)	**2** Ponce de León landed in Florida, 1513; International Children's Book Day; Hans Christian Andersen, born 1805, Denmark	**3**	**4** Martin Luther King, Jr., assassinated, 1968; Henry Cisneros elected mayor of San Antonio, 1981, first Hispanic mayor large city	**5** Booker T. Washington, 1856–1915; Pocahontas married John Rolfe, 1614; Colin Powell, 1937–	**6** Peary and Henson reached North Pole, 1909; John Smith founded Mormon Church, 1830; Alexander Herzen, 1812–1870	**7** Billie Holiday, 1915–1959
8 First synagogue in America founded in NYC, 1730; Buddha's birthday (Japan), 563–483 BC	**9** Civil War ended, Treaty of Appomattox, 1865; African Methodist Episcopal Church established, 1816	**10** Joseph Pulitzer, 1847–1911; Dolores Huerta, 1940–; Buchenwald Liberation Day, 1945	**11**	**12** Civil War began, 1861, Ft. Sumter; Yuri Gagarin, cosmonaut, became first person to orbit earth, 1961	**13** Lucy Laney, 1854–1933, black educator; Tamil New Year	**14** Pan American Day; Abraham Lincoln assassinated, 1865; Carlos Romulo, Philippine leader, 1899–1985; First U.S. abolition society (PA), 1775
15 Bessie Smith, 1894–1937, black blues singer; Jackie Robinson played for Brooklyn Dodgers, 1947	**16** Mary Eliza Mahoney, 1845–1926, first black nurse	**17** World Health Day; Giovanni Verrazano, NY harbor, 1524	**18**	**19** Revolutionary War began, 1775	**20**	**21** Spanish-American War began, 1898
22 Earth Day; U.S. Holocaust Memorial Museum opened, 1993	**23**	**24**	**25** Ella Fitzgerald, 1918–1996; UN founded, 1945	**26** Gertrude (Ma) Rainey, 1886–1939, black blues singer; Syngman Rhee, 1875–1965; First democratic elections South Africa, 1994	**27** Coretta Scott King, 1927–; Eritrea becomes independent from Ethiopia, 1993; August Wilson, 1945–	**28** Canada/US Goodwill treaty signed, 1817
29 Emperor's birthday (Japan); Duke Ellington, 1899–1974; St. Catherine (Italy)	**30** Louisiana Territory purchased, 1803; Loyalists and blacks attacked Shrewsbury, NJ, 1780					

You can't hold a man down without staying down with him.

—*Booker T. Washington*

or race. Why should we remember the Holocaust? How can students respond to the genocide occurring today? Discuss the following quotes:

> Forgiveness is the key to action and freedom.
> —Hannah Arendt

> The motto should not be: Forgive one another; rather, Understand one another.
> —Emma Goldman

The Holocaust Day of Remembrance (Yom Hashoah) is celebrated on the 27th day of Nissan according to the Jewish calendar and falls in March, April, or May.

April 26.   In 1994, the black majority population in South Africa was able to vote for the first time. Locate South Africa on the map. Who lives here? The population includes colonial groups of English and Boer (Dutch) settlers and varied African tribal groups such as Xhosa. Sanctions, or penalties, by many nations against the white government for its system of apartheid (racial separation) helped force South Africa to hold democratic elections.

Who is Nelson Mandela, the former political prisoner who was elected President in this first free election? Share this biography with students.

Jack L. Roberts. *Nelson Mandela: Determined to Be Free.* Millbrook, 1995. *Gateway Biography* series.

How did it feel to vote for the first time? Find out by reading:

Elinor Batezat Sisulu. *The Day Gogo Went to Vote: South Africa, April 1994.* Illustrated by Sharon Wilson. Little Brown, 1996. A six-year-old Thembi girl accompanies her 100-year-old grandmother who is determined to vote for the first time.

How would students feel if their families were not allowed to vote? Why is being able to vote important, especially for oppressed groups? When did African Americans receive the right to vote? When were women allowed to vote? Compare these dates to 1924, when Native Americans were granted citizenship. What is required in order to vote in the United States today? The last major change in voting requirements was the lowering of the age limit from twenty-one to eighteen. Should teenagers be allowed to vote?

May Activities

This month has been selected to recognize the contributions made by people of Asian and Pacific Islander heritage. During this month, we can acknowledge the diversity of Asian and Pacific Island immigrants, and the rich cultural and linguistic heritage that they hope to maintain.

How many groups of Asian and Pacific Islanders can students name? Which groups are represented in your class? In your community? Locate their place of origin on the map. Note that this category includes such diverse groups as Koreans, Hmong, Pakistanis, Samoans, and Filipinos. See the Appendix for teaching resources for each group.

May 5.   Today, Japanese children fly carp kites. Students can make their own gaily decorated fish to hang like streamers. Each student can draw their own, or you can provide one for everyone to trace onto construction paper. (Enlarge model below.) They should have two fish shapes, one right side and one reversed. After the children color and cut out the fish, they glue the two pieces together around the edges (except for the mouth) and gently stuff with tissue paper for a three-dimensional effect. These fish can be hung around the room with thread tied to the back, or attached to a stick (fishing pole) by the mouth. If you have Japanese-speaking children in the class, this is a good opportunity to have them teach the class how to count in Japanese.

ichi—one	san—three	go—five	shichi—seven	ku—nine
ni—two	shi—four	roku—six	hachi—eight	ju—ten

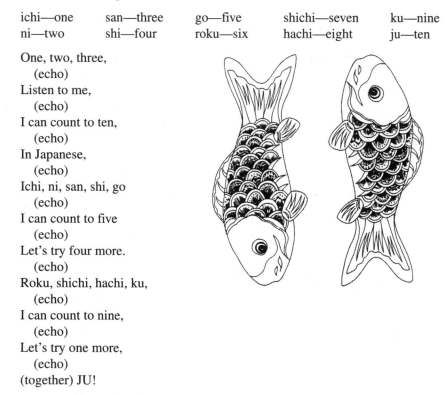

One, two, three,
    (echo)
Listen to me,
    (echo)
I can count to ten,
    (echo)
In Japanese,
    (echo)
Ichi, ni, san, shi, go
    (echo)
I can count to five
    (echo)
Let's try four more.
    (echo)
Roku, shichi, hachi, ku,
    (echo)
I can count to nine,
    (echo)
Let's try one more,
    (echo)
(together) JU!

Count Your Way through Japan by Jim Haskins (Carolrhoda, 1987) is a good book for students, with numbers in Japanese accompanied by pictures of the country. Provide a variety of other books on Japan so that students can explore this country.

John Langone. *In the Shogun's Shadow: Understanding a Changing Japan* Little Brown, 1994. Covers history and culture, including information on United States–Japan relations.

Richard Tames. *Exploration into Japan.* New Discovery Books, 1995.

May 5.   Cinco de Mayo marks the victory of Mexican forces over the French at Puebla, Mexico, on May 5, 1862. It is celebrated today in Mexican American communities in the United States as the occasion for a fiesta, with a parade, dancing, and other activities. You can hold a fiesta in your room. Bring recording of Mexican popular music, folk songs, or Mexican Indian music. Let the students prepare food such as tortillas, guacamole, or

MAY

1
Lei Day (Hawaii)
Agrippa Hull, free black, began six years of army service, 1777

2

3
Golda Meir, 1898–1978
World Press Freedom Day

4

5
Children's Festival (Japan)
Gwendolyn Brooks won Pulitzer Prize for Poetry, 1950
Cinco de Mayo

6
Chinese Exclusion Act passed, 1882
Rudolph Valentino, 1895–1926

7
Rabindranath Tagore, 1861–1941

8
Joan of Arc Day (France)

9

10
Chinese labor helped complete Transcontinental Railroad, Utah, 1869
Nelson Mandela inaugurated president of South Africa, 1994

11

12

13
Jou Louis, 1914–1972
Congress declared war on Mexico, 1846

14
Jamestown established, 1607

15

16

17
Supreme Court declared racial segregation in schools unconstitutional, 1954, Brown v. Topeka

18
Hispanic Society of America founded, 1904
Supreme Court affirmed separate but equal laws, 1896, Plessy v. Ferguson

19
Malcolm X, 1925–1965
Lorraine Hansberry, 1930–1965

20
Cher, 1945–

21
Amelia Earhart completed solo flight across Atlantic, 1932

22

23
Emilio Aguinaldo, Philippine independence leader, captured, 1901

24
Ynés Mexia, 1870–1938, Mexican-American botanical explorer

25
African Freedom Day

26
Susette LaFlesche Tibbles died, 1903, Omaha Indian rights advocate

27
Victoria Matthews 1861–1907, black author and social worker
Buddha's birthday (China)

28
Jim Thorpe, 1888–1953

29
Baha'u'llah Ascension Day

30
Hernando de Soto landed in Florida, 1539
Countee Cullen, 1903–1946

What other countries have taken three hundred years or more to achieve, a once dependent territory must try to accomplish in a generation if it is to survive.

—*Kwame Nkrumah (Ghana)*

buñelos. Students can decorate the room appropriately by using poster paint or felt pens to create murals that evoke Mexico and Mexican American life. Possible subjects include food, sports, clothing, arts and crafts, and historical figures.

Create a learning center on Mexico. (Let students contribute ideas.) Explore your library for nonfiction and fiction about Mexico as well as stories about Mexican Americans or Chicanos, for example, *Viva Chicano* by Frank Bonham (Dutton, 1970) and *Graciela: A Mexican-American Child Tells Her Story* by Joe Molnar (Watts, 1972).

Develop task cards that focus on Mexico for reading in the content areas. Use a biography such as *¡Viva México! A Story of Benito Juárez and Cinco de Mayo* by Argentina Palacios and illustrated by Howard Berelson (Raintree Steck-Vaughn, 1993). This volume in the *Stones of America* series tells of the Mexican hero, born a poor Zapotec Indian in Oaxaca, who grew up to be compared to Abraham Lincoln.

May 25.   African Freedom Day offers an opportunity to discuss the origins of African Americans. Explore books such as the following:

Primary Grades

Muriel Feelings. *Jambo Means Hello; Swahili Alphabet Book.* Dial, 1974.

Xan Hopcraft and Carol C. Hopcraft. *How It Was Done with Dooms: A True Story of Africa.* McElderry, 1997.

Ifeoma Onyefulu. *Emeka's Gift: An African Counting Story.* Cobblehill, 1995.

Upper Grades

Ashley Bryan. *Lion and the Ostrich Chicks, and Other African Tales.* Atheneum, 1986.

John Chiasson. *African Journey.* Bradbury, 1987.

Eric Campbell. *The Story of the Leopard Song.* Harcourt, 1992.

Jason Laure. *Botswana.* Children's Press, 1993. *Enchantment of the World* series.

Beverly Naidoo. *No Turning Back.* Harper, 1997.

June Activities

The theme for this month is immigration. In this month we feature Alaska and Hawai'i, both states that illustrate how this is a country of immigrants. The Juneteenth celebrations mark another kind of migration, the emancipation of African slaves. Talk with students about immigration as a historical event and as a contemporary issue. See the unit in Chapter 4 for resources for teaching about immigration. For more information, write to Ellis Island Museum, Statue of Liberty/Ellis Island Foundation, 52 Vanderbilt Avenue, New York, NY 10017-3898.

June 11.   Discover Hawai'i, the fiftieth state, with your students. One of the state's assets is its multicultural, multilingual heritage. Investigate the history of Hawai'i. How and when did it become a state? People from many different countries are represented in Hawai'i. What are some of them? Who are the native Hawaiians?

Ask students to find examples of unusual words used in Hawai'i, for example, words for different foods. Here are a few words used commonly in Hawai'i:

ae	(eye)	yes
aloha	(ah *loh* hah)	hello/goodbye
haole	(*how* lay)	foreigner (white person)
hula	(*hoo* lah)	dance
lani	(*lah* nee)	sky
lei	(lay)	wreath
luau	(loo ah oo)	feast
mahalo	(mah *hah* loh)	thanks
mauna	(*mou* nah)	mountain
moana	(moh *ah* nah)	ocean

The following are examples of books about the multicultural heritage of Hawai'i:

Stephanie Feeney. *Hawai'i Is A Rainbow.* University of Hawaii Press, 1985.

Julie Stewart Williams. *Maui Goes Fishing.* University of Hawaii Press, 1991. Another tale of Maui and how the Hawaiian Islands came to be.

Roy Kakulu Alameida. *Stories of Old Hawai'i.* The Bess Press, 1997. Author has adapted 45 traditional tales for intermediate students, includes a glossary.

Write to this address for more resources: Hawai'i Visitors Bureau, 2270 Kalakaua Avenue, #801, Honolulu, HI 96815.

June 14—Flag Day. On this day in 1777, the U.S. flag was adopted. In 1877, Congress declared the flag should be flown on this day. In 1916, President Woodrow Wilson proclaimed Flag Day. The first flag, "Old Glory," had 13 stars and 13 stripes. How is today's flag different? A flag is a symbol. Ask students what symbols represent the United States to them. What would they put on an American flag if they designed a new one? Students can discuss different kinds of flags and banners—for countries, states, organizations—and work together on creating a banner to represent their classroom or school.

June 19—Juneteenth. News of the 1863 Emancipation Proclamation freeing the slaves did not reach African Americans in Texas until June 1865, more than two months after the end of the Civil War. Juneteenth (June 19) has become a community celebration of African American heritage, featuring picnics and music.

In Carole Boston Weatherford's *Juneteenth Jamboree,* illustrated by Yvonne Buchanan (Lee Low, 1995), Cassandra, who has just moved to Texas, learns about the history of this celebration and the end of slavery.

June 20. Investigate Alaska, the forty-ninth state. Only a little more than half a million people (603,617 in 1995) inhabit this huge area (656,424 square miles). That's about one person for every square mile. Alaska is the first of the fifty states in size but 48th in population. Only Vermont and Wyoming have fewer inhabitants. Compare Alaska's population

1 Brigham Young, 1801–1877 International Children's Day	**2** Congress granted American Indians citizenship, 1924	**3** DeSoto claimed Florida for Spain, 1539 Roland Hayes, 1887–1977	**4**	**5** English colonists massacre Pequot village in Pequot War, 1637 Kaahumanu died, 1832, Hawaiian ruler	**6** Marian Wright Edelman, 1939– Evacuation of Japanese Americans into concentration camps completed, 1942 Sarah Remond, 1826–1887?, black lecturer and physician	**7** Gwendolyn Brooks, 1917–, black poet Nikki Giovanni, 1943–
8	**9**	**10**	**11** Kamehameha Day (Hawaii) Addie W. Hunton, 1875–1943, black youth group leader Henry Cisneros, 1947–	**12** Philippine Independence Day Anne Frank Day Girls allowed to play Little League baseball, 1974	**13** St. Anthony (Portugal, Brazil)	**14** Hawaii organized as territory, 1900 Harriet Beecher Stowe, 1811–1896 Flag Day
15	**16** Flight of Valentina Tereshkova (first woman in space), 1963 Soweto Day	**17** Susan LaFlesche Picotte, 1865–1915, Omaha physician James Weldon Johnson, 1871–1938 Sweden-America Day	**18** War of 1812 declared against Great Britain, 1812 Sally Ride, first U.S. woman in space, 1983	**19** Statue of Liberty arrived in New York Harbor, 1885 Juneteenth—Emancipation reaches Texas, 1865	**20** Start of French Revolution, 1789 Announced purchase of Alaska from Russia, 1867	**21**
22 Slavery abolished in Great Britain, 1772 Joe Louis (Brown Bomber) defeated Max Schmeling, 1938	**23** William Penn signed treaty with Indians, 1683 Wilma Rudolph, 1940–1994	**24** San Juan Day (Puerto Rico)	**25** Crazy Horse (Sioux) defeated Custer–Battle of the Little Bighorn, 1876	**26** Pearl S. Buck, 1892–1973 UN Charter signed, 1945	**27** Paul Dunbar, 1872–1906, black writer Joseph Smith, Mormon prophet, killed, 1844 Helen Keller, 1880–1968 Stonewall Inn fight, 1969	**28** Treaty of Versailles ended World War I
29 First African church in the U.S. (Philadelphia), 1794 Azalia Hackley, 1867–1922, black singer José Rizal, 1861–1896	**30** Korean War began 1950					

. . . We could never learn to be brave and patient, if there were only joy in the world.

—*Helen Keller*

326

and area to that of Hawai'i, which had 1,186,815 people in 1995 in only 10,932 square miles. How do these figures compare with your state? Have students calculate how many times their state would fit inside Alaska's area. How many times would Alaska's population fit into their state's population?

Who lives in Alaska? Read about this unusual land in the following books:

Ruth Crisman. *Running the Iditarod Trail.* Silver Burdett, 1993.

Michael Prince. *The Totems of Seldovia.* Sundog Publications, 1994.

Daniel Cohen. *The Alaska Purchase.* Millbrook, 1995.

Carolyn Meyer. *In a Different Light: Growing Up in a Yu'pik Eskimo Village in Alaska.* Simon and Schuster, 1996.

Barthe De Clements. *The Bite of the Gold Rush: A Story of the Alaskan Gold Rush.* Viking, 1992.

Ulli Steltzer. *Building an Igloo.* Firefly, 1991.

For more information, contact the Alaska Division of Tourism, PO Box 110801, Juneau AK 99811-0801.

July Activities

In this month we celebrate independence with the Fourth of July and Canada Day on July 1. Plan a program in which all students can participate. Have students portray the multicultural heritage and contemporary diversity of this country.

July 1, 3. Recognize Canada on Canada Day, celebrating the Confederation in 1867. Display its symbol, the maple leaf, with pictures of Canada from travel folders. (See Chapter 4 for ideas specific to Québec.) Can students name some famous Canadians? Display a map of Canada. Look at the names of the provinces. What do they indicate about the ethnic influences on Canada and where the early settlers came from? How is the history of Canada different from that of the United States? How is it similar?

Ted Harrison. *O Canada.* Tickner and Fields, 1993. Based on national anthem.

Barbara Greenwood. *A Pioneer Story: The Daily Life of a Canadian Family in 1840.* Tickner and Fields, 1995.

Suzanne LeVert. *Alberta* (Chelsea House, 1991) and *Newfoundland* (Chelsea House, 1992). *Let's Discover Canada* series.

Donna Bailey. *Canada.* Steck-Vaughan, 1992. *Where We Live* series.

Or write for information to the Canadian Embassy, 501 Pennsylvania Ave NW, Washington DC 10001.

Include books set in Canada in your library such as the following:

James Heneghan. *Torn Away.* Viking, 1994.

Jonathan London. *The Sugaring-Off Party.* Dutton, 1995.

1	2	3	4	5	6	7
Canada Day	Thurgood Marshall, 1908–1993 Civil Rights Act of 1964 Voting Rights Act became law, 1964	Champlain founded Québec, 1608	Edmonia Lewis, 1845–?, black-Cherokee sculptor Lucy Stowe, 1885–1937, black teacher and administrator Giuseppe Garibaldi, 1807–1882		Cecil Poole, first black U.S. attorney, 1961	
8	9	10	11	12	13	14
	Dr. Daniel Hale Williams, black doctor, performed first open heart surgery, 1893	Mary McLeod Bethune, 1875–1955 Arthur Ashe, 1943–1993			Wole Soyinka, 1934–	Bastille Day (France), 1789 George Washington Carver monument dedicated, 1951
15	16	17	18	19	20	21
Maggie Walker, 1867–1934, black insurance and banking executive Ch'iu Chin died, 1875–1907	Ida Barnett-Wells 1862–1931, black journalist and civic leader Mary Baker Eddy, 1821–1910, founder, Christian Science	Spain transferred Florida to U.S., 1821 S. Y. Agnon, 1888–1970	Miguel Hidalgo, 1753–1811, Father of Mexican independence	Alice Dunbar Nelson, 1875–1935, black author, teacher	Seneca Falls Convention (NY) launched women's suffrage movement, 1848	First daily black newspaper, New Orleans Tribune, 1864 National Women's Hall of Fame dedicated, 1979
22	23	24	25	26	27	28
	Pham Tuan, first non-Caucasian in space, 1980	Simón Bolívar, 1783–1830 Mormons settled Salt Lake City, 1847 Pioneer Day	Puerto Rico became a commonwealth, 1952 (Constitution Day) Saint James (Spain)	Americans with Disabilities Act signed, 1990	Korean War ended, 1953	Senator Hiram Fong (HI) and Rep. Daniel Inouye (HI) first Asian American in Congress, 1959
29	30	31				
		Sarah Garnet, 1831–1911, black educator and civic worker				

I did not equate my self-worth with my wins and losses.
—*Arthur Ashe*

July 4—Independence Day.　Independence Day for the United States can be recognized in many ways. Prepare a program that includes poetry and prose representing the many voices of America—people of different colors, languages, and religions yet united in their celebration of U.S. independence. *Celebrating America: A Collection of Poems and Images of the American Spirit,* poetry compiled by Laura Whipple and art from the Art Institute of Chicago (Philomel, 1994) is an excellent example of just such a multicultural sampler.

A book to share with students is *Celebration*! by Jane Resh Thomas, illustrated by Raul Colon (Hyperion, 1997). An African American extended family gathers to celebrate the Fourth of July with a picnic. Rich with description of food and games, this story will stimulate student discussion of their family get-togethers. They can compare the foods they eat and the activities they engage in with those described in this book.

Younger students can talk about words associated with the Fourth of July, such as democracy, independence, equality, liberty, and fraternity.

July 10.　Who was Mary McLeod Bethune? Known as The Great Educator, she was born in South Carolina and grew up working in the cotton fields. In an age when the education of black children was not considered terribly important, she graduated from college and became a teacher. When she heard that the town of Daytona Beach in Florida didn't have a school for blacks, she established one for young black women that is now the Bethune-Cookman College. She also founded the National Council of Negro Women. In 1935, President Franklin Roosevelt appointed her administrator of the new Office of Minority Affairs.

Challenge students to find out more about this amazing woman. Read a biography such as *Mary McLeod Bethune* by noted poet Eloise Greenfield, illustrated by Jerry Pinkney (HarperCollins, 1994) or *Mary McLeod Bethune* by Patricia McKissack (Children's Press, 1985).

Discuss the following quote:

> I am my mother's daughter, and the drums of Africa still beat in my heart. They will not let me rest while there is a single Negro boy or girl without a chance to prove his worth.
> —Mary McLeod Bethune

August Activities

In this month of Hiroshima and Nagasaki, the fall of the Aztec and Incan Empires to the Spanish conquerors, and the violence accompanying Indian and Pakistani independence, we focus on the need for world peace and justice. Talk with students about the need to resolve differences peacefully, without resorting to violence, on a personal level as well as an international level.

First Sunday in August—Celebration of Peace Day.　How can we help students appreciate peace without their having to endure the horrors of war? Stories of what people have experienced in war and how they survived offer students an opportunity to empathize yet not be overwhelmed. Two books for young children tell war-time stories set in Vietnam and Korea:

*Rosemary Breckler. *Sweet Dried Apples: A Vietnamese Wartime Childhood.* Illustrated by Deborah Kogan Ray. Houghton Mifflin, 1996. Two children living in the countryside are forced out of their village by the war.

Haemi Balgassi. *Peacebound Trains.* Illustrated by Chris K. Soentpiet. Clarion, 1996. A young girl's grandmother tells her of life during the Korean War. Although she was forced to flee Seoul by train with her children, someday the trains will bring people home from war.

August 6—Hiroshima Day.   Hiroshima Day marks the anniversary of the dropping of the atomic bomb on Japan, resulting in Japan's surrender, ending World War II. Although the war was over, the effects of radiation from the bomb lingered long afterward. Explore the impact of the bomb on the Japanese people and motivation for world peace.

Eleanor Coerr's *Sadako,* illlustrated by Ed Young (Putnam, 1993) is a picture book rewrite, suitable for older students, of the author's famous earlier book, *Sadako and the Thousand Cranes,* the true story of a Japanese girl who suffered from radiation poisoning. Sadako attempts to ward off death by folding a thousand origami cranes. Although she was not successful, schoolchildren still fold paper cranes in her memory, united in their desire for world peace. Today, a statue of Sadako holding a golden crane in outstretched hands stands in Hiroshima Peace Park. Inscribed below are the words: "This is our cry, this is our prayer: Peace in the world."

Other books to support student study of this period are:

Tatsuharu Kodama. *Shin's Tricycle.* Illustrated by Noriyuki Ando. Translated by Kazuko Hokumen-Jones. Walker, 1995. Shin dreamed of having a tricycle but war meant metal was scarce. He never enjoyed the tricycle he received for his fourth birthday because he was killed in Hiroshima. His tricycle is displayed at the Hiroshima Peace Museum.

Laurence Yep. *Hiroshima.* Scholastic, 1995. This book juxtaposes the flight of the Enola Gay delivering the bomb with the story of two Japanese sisters taking a walk in their city. Includes accounts of survivors.

August 7.

> I was offered the ambassadorship of Liberia once, when the post was earmarked for a Negro. I told them I wouldn't take a Jim Crow job.
> —Ralph Bunche

Ralph Bunche was a famous diplomat and the first African American to win the Nobel Peace Prize in 1950. Ask students whether they know what a "Jim Crow" job is. Can they guess? Why would the ambassador to Liberia be expected to be black?

Martin Luther King, Jr. was also awarded a Nobel Peace Prize. What other famous people have received this award? How are the recipients chosen? Students can investigate the lives and achievements of the following men and women from diverse

AUGUST

1 Maria Mitchell, 1818–1889, astronomer	**2** James Baldwin, 1924–1987	**3** Columbus started first voyage, 1492	**4** Anne Frank captured, 1944 Freedom of the Press Day Zwenger acquitted 1735	**5**	**6** Hiroshima Day (U.S. bombed Hiroshima, Japan, 1945) President Johnson signed Voting Rights Act, 1965	**7** Ralph Bunche, 1904–1971 Congress authorized Vietnam War, 1964
8 Roberto Clemente, 1934–1973	**9** Janie Porter Barrett, 1865–1948, black social welfare leader U.S. bombed Nagasaki, Japan, 1945	**10**	**11** Alex Haley, 1921–1992 Watts Riots (CA), 1965	**12** U.S. annexed Hawaii, 1898 King Philip's War ended, first Indian War, 1676	**13** Cortez conquered Aztecs, 1521	**14** Japan surrendered, World War II, 1945 Pakistan became independent, 1947
15 India became independent, 1947	**16** Carol Moseley-Braun, 1947–	**17** Charlotte Forten (Grimke), 1837–1914, black teacher and author V. S. Naipaul, 1932–	**18** 19th Amendment ratified 1920, women right to vote	**19** Mammy Pleasant, 1814–1904, black California pioneer	**20** Bernardo O'Higgins Chilean patriot, 1778–1842 First African slaves arrived in U.S., 1619	**21**
22	**23** Parsi New Year Sacco and Vanzetti electrocuted, 1927	**24** Lucy Moten died, 1933, black educator Amelia Earhart flew non-stop across U.S., 1932	**25**	**26** Women's Equality Day Women's Suffrage 19th Amendment certified, 1920	**27** Rose McClendon, 1884–1936, black actress	**28** Martin Luther King, Jr. gave "I have a dream" speech, Washington, DC, 1963
29	**30** Guion Bluford, first black astronaut, flew 1983 Saint Rose of Lima (Americas)	**31** Josephine Ruffin, 1842–1924, black leader				

The wonder is not that so many Negro boys and girls are ruined but that so many survive.

—James Baldwin

backgrounds who have won this international recognition for their efforts on behalf of peace and justice.

1994	Yasir Arafat (Palestine), Shimon Peres, and Yitzhak Rabin (Israel)
1993	Frederik de Klerk, Nelson Mandela (South Africa)
1992	Rigoberta Menchú (Guatemala)
1991	Aung San Suu Kyi (Myanmar, formerly Burma)
1990	Mikhail Gorbachev (Russian Federation)
1989	Dalai Lama (Tibet)
1984	Bishop Desmond Tutu (South Africa)

Read a biography to students such as the following:

Caroline Lazo. *Rigoberta Menchú.* Dillon, 1994. Tells how a poor Mayan Indian woman from Guatemala came to world attention for her philosophy of nonviolence and her ability to bring groups together. Part of the *Peacemakers* series.

August 13.   Who were the Aztecs and how did the Spanish conquer them? Pose such questions to the students and have them search for the answers. The Aztec civilization is particularly interesting because it was so advanced, and yet we know very little about it because the Spanish destroyed most of the records. Investigate the Spanish treatment of the Aztecs. (See information on the Aztec calendar in Chapter 9.)

The following books are a starting point for student research.

John Bierhorst. *The Hungry Woman: Myths and Legends of the Aztecs.* Morrow, 1993.

Johanna Defrates. *What Do We Know about the Aztecs?* Bedrick Books, 1993.

Andrea Guardiano. *Azteca: The Story of a Jaguar Warrior.* Rinehart, 1992.

Variable Dates

Listed here are holidays or events that fall on different dates each year. Add them to the appropriate months.

United States Holidays or Special Days

Note that many holidays are celebrated on a Monday or Friday to provide a holiday weekend.

Commonwealth Day (Canada)	second Monday in March
Memorial Day	last Monday in May
Labor Day	first Monday in September
Canadian Thanksgiving	second Monday in October
Election Day	first Tuesday after first Monday in November
Veterans' Day	fourth Monday in October
Thanksgiving Day	fourth Thursday in November

Jewish Feasts and Festivals

Because the Jewish calendar (described in the next section) is lunar, the dates of Jewish holidays vary each year. The following chart gives the names and dates for the holidays by year and shows the corresponding Jewish calendar year under Rosh Hashanah, when the new year begins. Note that each holiday actually begins at sundown on the preceding day.

Year	Purim (Feast of Lots)	Pesach (Festival of Freedom)	Shavuot (Feast of Weeks)	Rosh Hashanah (New Year)	Yom Kippur (Day of Atonement)	Succot (Feast of Tabernacles)	Hanukkah (Feast of Dedication)
1998	March 12	April 11	May 31	Sept. 21 (5759)	Sept. 30	Oct. 5	Dec. 14
1999	March 2	April 1	May 21	Sept. 11 (5760)	Sept. 20	Sept. 25	Dec. 4
2000	March 21	April 20	June 9	Sept. 30 (5761)	Oct. 9	Oct. 14	Dec. 22

Islamic Holidays

The chart below shows the dates of the major Islamic celebrations. See the next section for more information on the Islamic calendar.

New Year: Muharram 1	Ashura: Muharram 10	Mawlid: Rabi'l 12	Ramadan: Ramadan 1	Eid al-Fitr: Shawwal	al-Adha: Zulhijjan 10
1998 April 27 (1419)	May 6	July 6	Dec. 20	Jan. 19	March 28
1999 April 17 (1420)	April 26	June 26	Dec. 9	Jan. 8	March 16
2000 April 6 (1421)	April 15	June 14	Nov. 27	Dec. 27	March 5

Variable Holidays—Activities

Divali

Divali, the Hindu New Year celebration, lasts five days. Like Hanukkah, Divali is known as the Festival of Lights, because South Asians light oil lamps and set off fireworks, symbolizing the triumph of good over evil. Divali has become a chance to celebrate Hindu culture as well as religion. At this time of year, Hindus give thanks for life's bounty with special foods, gifts, and cleaning house. The holiday commemorates the return of Lord Rama after fourteen years of exile and his victory over Ravan, the demon king. See the following books:

Dianne M. MacMillan. *Divali: Hindu Festival of Lights.* Enslow, 1997. Shows celebrations of South Asians in United States and Canada with photographs. Includes a glossary.

Rachna Gilmore. *Lights for Gita.* Illustrated by Alice Priestley. Tilbury House, 1995. Gita, a recent immigrant from New Delhi, is looking forward to celebrating Divali in Canada, her new country. At first disappointed because the weather is not like in India, she learns the true meaning of the holiday.

Asian New Year

According to the lunar calendar used by Chinese, Koreans, Vietnamese, Tibetans, and Hmong, the New Year falls in January or February. For many Asian Americans, this is the biggest holiday of the year. Chinese American families give children red (lucky) envelopes with money and hold large family banquets. Firecrackers and a parade also herald the New Year. Korean Americans pay homage to their ancestors and feast on special dishes. The Vietnamese Americans celebrate with firecrackers, incense, food, and an exchange of gifts. Tet, the Vietnamese New Year, is also the advent of spring. Ask Asian American students in your class to describe how their families plan to celebrate the holiday. Share the following book with your students to dispel misinformation and introduce students to the Chinese New Year celebrations:

Karen Chinn. *Sam and the Lucky Money.* Illustrated by Cornelius Van Wright. Lee and Low, 1995. After receiving his lucky money envelope, Sam and his mother go to Chinatown (New York) to spend it. The book shows Chinatown alive with preparations for the holidays—the reader sees firecrackers, red lanterns, bakery tarts, and a Chinese lion dancing in the street.

Happy New Year (Chinese)

Ramadan

Muslims throughout the world celebrate God's delivery of the Koran, Islam's holy book, to Muhammed by fasting for the month of Ramadan. For 29 or 30 days, Muslims are forbidden to eat, drink, or smoke from sunrise to sunset. The fast ends with the three-day feast of Eid al-Fitr. Because many students are unaware of Muslim observances or have stereotyped preconceptions, share books such as the following:

Suhaib Hamid Ghazi. *Ramadan.* Illustrated by Omar Rayyan. Holiday House, 1996. Hakeem, an elementary school student, shows how Muslims celebrate Ramadan. Includes information on Islamic history and customs.

Hanukkah—The Festival of Lights

On this eight-night Jewish holiday, candles are lit in a menorah to commemorate the survival of the Jews in the second century B.C. Non-Jewish students may have heard about Hanukkah but be confused about the meaning of this holiday. Books to help primary students understand the holiday are:

Linda Glaser. *The Borrowed Hanukkah Latkes.* Illustrated by Nancy Cole. Whitman, 1997.

Fran Manushkin. *Latkes and Applesauce: A Hanukkah Story.* Illustrated by Robin Spowart. Scholastic, 1990.

Intermediate students will appreciate *Celebrating Hanukkah* by Diane Hoyt-Goldsmith, with photos by Lawrence Migdale (Holiday House, 1996). This book explains and illustrates the distinctive features of the holiday. It also includes instructions for playing the dreidl (a top to spin), a recipe for making latkes (potato pancakes), and information about the Hebrew calendar.

The Christmas Menorahs: How a Town Fought Hate (by Janice Cohn, illustrated by Bill Farnsworth, Whitman, 1996) tells how the people in one town were able to resist attempts to divide Christians and Jews. Another book for this season that breaks down the barriers between groups is *Elijah's Angel: A Story for Chanukah and Christmas,* written by Michael Rosen and illustrated by Aminah Brenda Lynn Robinson (Harcourt Brace, 1992).

FOCUS ON CULTURES AND TIME

The calendar itself is an object of interest in the multicultural classroom. Although students may assume that the calendar and the way people count time has always been the same, you can introduce the idea of cultural diversity in time measurement as you work with the Multicultural Calendar. In addition, the calendar has changed over time, due to political as well as scientific considerations. And once students begin to look at the calendar as an object of study, they will be interested to learn the origins of the names of the months and the days of the week. Students will enjoy discovering the amazing diversity of contemporary and historical methods of telling time.

Marking Time

What is a day? One idea of day is a 24-hour period that includes both light and darkness. Is it not strange that we count a day from the middle of a night to the middle of the next night? In some cultures there is no word that means just that. Many ancient cultures recognized a single event such as dawn, the rising of the sun, and spoke of so many dawns or suns. Other cultures used the night and spoke of "sleeps." Gradually the light period was broken up with terms related to the sun: daybreak, sunrise, noon, afternoon, twilight, and sunset. The crowing of cocks, the yoking of oxen, and the siesta are other examples of ways of marking the time of day. For some peoples day begins with dawn, but, for example, Hebrew days begin at sundown. Dividing the day into hours is a modern concept brought about by industrialization.

Beginning the day at midnight and having two sets of times designated one to twelve are arbitrary decisions that are not always followed. Many students will have heard of 24-hour clocks, which are used in many countries and in some cases (such as military organizations) in the United States. They might not know, however, that astronomers begin their day at twelve noon in order to use the same date for observations made at night.

Why is the day divided into 12 or 24 hours rather than 10, or 25, for example? Students can research the historical basis for these choices. What would happen if we counted only the daylight hours? People living in the North, beyond the Arctic Circle, experience long hours of sunlight and only a few hours of twilight in the summer (and the reverse in the winter). How is their day different from your day?

Many countries use metric (decimal-based) measurements. Why don't we use metric time? At one time, in France in 1793, revolutionaries attempted to create a more rational calendar, in a move to reduce the power of the church. Each month had 30 days (3 "decades" of 10), days were divided into 10 hours, hours into 100 minutes, and minutes into 100 seconds. However, people preferred the Gregorian system and it was restored by Napoleon in 1805. What would students prefer? What are the advantages and disadvantages of each system?

Weeks and Months

The idea of months is based on the cycle of the moon, which is 29 ½ days long. Early societies noted the phases of the moon and measured time from new moon to full moon. The moon is still the basis for many calendars. In school, however, we use a calendar that divides the year into months of 28 to 31 days to fit the solar year, so the phases of the moon occur at different times of the various months.

The seven-day week began when people who were trading needed some regular arrangement. A week, as the interval between trading or market days, has varied from four to ten days. It is thought that the selection of seven days has to do with the significance of the number *seven*. This hypothesis is supported by our use of Norse gods and goddesses to name the days of the week.

However, it is difficult to mesh a lunar (moon-based) calendar with the solar year (the time it takes the earth to go around the sun). Have students calculate the differences between a lunar calendar and a solar calendar. Why are they different? Why do we need to make adjustments to keep the calendar accurate?

Folklore provides a wealth of information related to these concepts of time. Encourage students to search out such ideas. They might begin with expressions or beliefs related to time, for example, Friday is a bad day, and Friday the thirteenth is the worst of all days! *Blue Monday and Friday the Thirteenth* by Lila Perl (Clarion, 1986) explores the origins of many beliefs. Students can pursue the study of cultural beliefs and superstitions in such books as *Cross Your Fingers, Spit in Your Hat* by Alvin Schwartz (Lippincott, 1974).

Counting Years

Gradually, people found a need for longer designations of time than market days or lunar months. This need was chiefly to count the ages of people and to compare these ages. Some of the following measures were used:

- Family generations
- Momentous events—plague, famine, war
- Reigns of monarchs or chiefs
- Cycles of seasons or weather

How Calendars Developed

Encourage students to investigate the history of calendars. They can learn, for example, the origins of the word, which goes back to the Latin *calendarium,* which means *account book.* Calendars are associated, therefore, with the payment of debts, marking times when payments were due. A calendar, as generally used, is a system for recording the passage of time. Congress, for example, has a calendar, or schedule of events.

The first calendars, created by the Babylonians, were based on moons. Twelve moons make a 354-day year. When it was observed that every four years the year needed an adjustment to make the calendar fit the seasons, the Babylonians added another moon, or month. This calendar was adapted by the Egyptians, Semites, and Greeks.

The Egyptians modified this calendar by basing their calculations on the regular rising of the Nile River, which occurred each year just after Sirius, the Dog Star, appeared. They developed a calendar that more nearly matched the solar year, using 365 days, which was still a little off from the 365¼ days we now consider accurate. Considering that they created this system around 4000 B.C., however, they were amazingly exact. They worked with 12 months of 30 days each and simply added 5 days at the end of the year.

Plot some of these different calendars on a timeline. Show students what calendars were in use in different parts of the world at the same time.

Gregorian Calendar

The Gregorian calendar, the most common in the Western world, developed out of the one used by the Romans. Their calendar, introduced around 700 B.C., was derived from that used in Greece. The Romans had ten months: Martius, Aprilis, Maius, Junius, Quintilis, Sextilis, September, October, November, and December. The names of the last six months correspond to the Latin numbers—five, six, seven, eight, nine, and ten. One king, who wanted to collect more taxes, added two more months, Januarius and Februarius. Needless to say, the calendar soon became very confused and did not correspond with the solar year.

Then came the Julian calendar, which Julius Caesar created in 46 B.C. to correct this inaccuracy. He divided the year into 12 months of 30 and 31 days except for February which he gave 28 days plus one every fourth year, so his year was a few minutes longer than the solar year. He changed the beginning of the year to January 1st instead of March 1st and renamed the month of Sextilis August, after Emperor Augustus. The month Quintilis was renamed Julius in his honor. Thus, we have the origins of our names for the twelve months. The Julian calendar was used for more than 1500 years.

The Gregorian calendar was created to correct the error in the Julian calendar, which was off by ten days in 1580. Pope Gregory reformed the calendar so that October 5, 1582 became October 15. England adopted this reform in 1752, Russia and Greece after World War I.

Students might investigate and report on further efforts to reform the calendar. The thirteen-month calendar would contain thirteen months of equal length. The perpetual calendar is another topic to explore.

Adjustments to the Calendar

Students may have heard of leap years, which occur every fourth year, when February has an extra day. But that doesn't provide sufficient accuracy for the calendar to match the Earth's trip around the sun. In fact, century years that are not evenly divisible by 400 will not be leap years. Have students calculate which century years are leap years and which are not. Will February in 2000 have 28 days or 29 days? (29)

Even this adjustment is not enough. About every year, scientists add a "leap second" to their atomic clock, the most accurate measurement of time. This is necessary because the Earth's spin is slowing slightly, not enough for us to notice, but enough to make a difference between the day as measured by the atomic clock and the day as measured by the sun in the sky.

In addition, most of the United States changes the clocks twice a year, in spring and fall, for Daylight Savings Time. The idea of daylight savings was first suggested by Benjamin Franklin. However, it was not put into practice until World War I, when England, the United States, and some other countries tried it out to save fuel by not turning on lights. In World War II, clocks in the United States were set ahead one hour for the duration of the war, from February 1942 to September 1945. Since 1986, daylight savings in the United States has begun the first Sunday in April. Most European countries change their clocks the last Sunday in March. However, Arizona, Hawai'i, and much of Indiana do not observe Daylight Savings Time. Neither do Puerto Rico, the U.S. Virgin Islands, or American Samoa.

B.C. and A.D.

Students may have noticed that dates in history are expressed as B.C. and A.D. What does this mean? B.C. stands for Before Christ and A.D. for Anno Domini, or the year of our Lord. Where do these phrases come from? Many other European languages use the simpler form Before Christ and After Christ. A.D., first used in the twelfth century, may be a holdover from religious texts. Some people would prefer to replace B.C. and A.D. with the more secular B.C.E. (before the common era) and C.E. (common era). Why do we need these forms?

The present year-numbering system for the Gregorian calendar was devised by Dionysius Exiguus in the sixth century A.D. Previously, years had been counted A.U.C. (from the founding of Rome). Dionysius starting counting from January 1,753 A.U.C., choosing that as the year of Christ's birth, making it 1 A.D. However, historians do not agree on the exact year for Christ's birth, dating years from 1 A.D. (or C.E.) is really a cultural convention.

The Millenium

When does the new millenium begin? Talk with students about the significance of this major event. Whether we celebrate on January 1, 2000 or January 1, 2001, there is a special aura around this "rollover of the cosmic odometer." Why do we look ahead to the new century with both excitement and trepidation? What does the year 2000 symbolize to students? What are their hopes for the new century? How do students fell whose lives follow different calendars?

The Christian Church Calendar

On this Christian calendar there are certain fixed dates, such as December 25, Christmas, based on the solar year. Movable feast days include Easter and Palm Sunday, based on the lunar calendar.

Christian Holidays

	Ash Wednesday	Easter Sunday
1998	February 25	April 12
1999	February 17	April 4
2000	March 8	April 23

Easter falls on the first Sunday following the arbitrary Paschal Full Moon, which does not necessarily coincide with a real or astronomical full moon. The Paschal Full Moon is calculated by adding 1 to the remainder obtained by dividing the year by 19 and applying the following:

1—April 14	6—April 18	11—March 25	16—March 30
2—April 3	7—April 8	12—April 13	17—April 17
3—March 23	8—March 28	13—April 2	18—April 7
4—April 11	9—April 16	14—March 22	19—March 27
5—March 31	10—April 5	15—April 10	

Thus, for the year 2000 the key is 6, or April 18. Since April 18 in the year 2000 is a Tuesday, Easter Sunday is April 23. *Caution*—If the Paschal Full Moon falls on a Sunday, Easter is the following Sunday. The earliest Easter can fall is March 23 and the latest is April 25.

Orthodox Christians—such as Greeks, Syrians, Ethiopians, Eritreans, Bulgarians, Russians, and Serbs—celebrate Easter and other holidays according to a different formula.

The Hebrew Calendar

Another calendar that is widely used today is the Hebrew, or Jewish, calendar, based on the Creation, which preceded the birth of Christ by 3760 years and 3 months. The Hebrew year begins in September rather than January. From the fall of 1998 to the fall of 1999, therefore, the Hebrew year will be 5759.

Based on the moon, the Hebrew year usually contains twelve months, alternately 30 and 29 days long. Seven times during every 19-year period, an extra month of 29 days is inserted to adjust this calendar, as shown here:

Months in the Hebrew Calendar

Tishri	Nisan
Heshvan	Iyar
Kislev	Sivan
Tevet	Tammuz
Shevat	Av
Adar	Elul

(Veadar added in leap years
  and one day added to Adar)

The Jewish New Year, Rosh Hashanah, begins on the first day of Tishri. Students can learn more about the Jewish calendar from books like *Annie's Shabbat* by Sarah Marwil Lamstein, illlustrated by Cecily Lang (Albert Whitman, 1997) and *Milk and Honey: A Year of Jewish Holidays* by Jane Yolen, illustrated by Louise Anjust (Putnam, 1996).

The Islamic Calendar

Also based on the moon, the Islamic calendar dates from Mohammed's flight from Mecca, the Hegira, in 622 A.D. The year has only 354 days so that its New Year moves with respect to the seasons. It makes a full cycle every 32½ years. The twelve Islamic months are:

Muharram	Rabi II	Rajab	Shawwal
Safar	Jumada I	Shaban	Zulkadah
Rabi I	Jumada II	Ramadan	Zulhijjah

Muharram 1 is the New Year. The months begin with the sighting of the new moon.

In leap years, an extra day is added to the last month, making 355 days. Leap years are 2, 5, 7, 10, 13, 16, 18, 21, 24, 26, and 29 in a cycle of 30 years. The year 1420 (April 1999–April 2000) is the 10th in the cycle so it will have 355 days. This method of counting makes the Islamic lunar calendar almost an exact match for the solar year. While other lunar calendars add in extra days (intercalation), the Koran forbids this.

The Chinese Calendar

One of the oldest calendars still used, the Chinese lunar calendar is said to have been invented by Emperor Huangdi in 2637 B.C. By 350 B.C., the Chinese were able to calculate the solar year. Years are counted in cycles of 60. The years within each cycle are divided into repeating 12-year cycles. Each of these 12 years is named after an animal, as described in Chapter 4. The year 2000 in the Gregorian calendar is the year of the dragon, the 17th year in the 78th cycle. The Chinese New Year starts at the second new moon after the beginning of winter. Another important celebration in the Chinese calendar is the Moon Festival in mid-autumn. Share *Moon Festival* by Ching Yeung Russell, illustrated by Christopher Zhong-Yuan Zhang (Boyd Mills, 1997), in which she recalls the joys of family and tradition when she was a child in China.

The Aztec Calendar

The Aztecs flourished in the Valley of Mexico from 1215 to 1521. Although they had no horses and no wheels, they possessed sophisticated astronomical knowledge and built a vast, powerful nation. Because the Spanish conquest destroyed most of their culture, we know very little about them. They counted using a base 20 system. The Aztecs had two calendars, adopted from the Mayans. One was for sacred or ritual purposes and had 20 days that combined with the numbers 1–13 to yield 260 days. The day names and numbers told a person's fortune.

The Aztec day signs.

Aztec Day Signs

1. Crocodile	11. Monkey
2. Wind	12. Grass
3. House	13. Reed
4. Lizard	14. Ocelot
5. Serpent	15. Eagle
6. Death's Head	16. Vulture
7. Deer	17. Motion
8. Rabbit	18. Flint knife
9. Water	19. Rain
10. Dog	20. Flower

The other calendar represented the solar year and had 18 months of 20 days each to make 360 days. To this were added five empty or unlucky days to complete the year. Children born during this time received names meaning worthless, will never amount to anything. The two calendars meshed every 52 years, which was a time of celebration.

How Music Came to the World, retold by Hal Ober and illustrated by Carol Ober (Houghton, 1994) is a source of pictures and other information on the Aztecs and their calendar.

Other Calendars of the World

Students can explore other calendars, such as the Native American year of moons. *Thirteen Moons on Turtle's Back: A Native American Year of Moons,* by Joseph Bruchac and Jonathan London, illustrated by Thomas Locker (Philomel 1992) is an excellent introduction with poems to represent the traditions of different native groups.

Students can also investigate the Hindu, Assyrian, and Persian calendars.

REFLECTIONS

We have presented information in this chapter to encourage you to begin your teaching for multicultural understanding immediately. With the help of these activities and resources, you can introduce diversity into any curriculum and any classroom. But we believe that multicultural teaching means more than just occasional celebrations. As you read the entries for each month, you will note opportunities to mention the contributions of varied groups throughout the year. In addition, calendar-based discussions of people, issues, and events will lead to students' greater appreciation of their own cultural heritage as well as better understanding of others.

APPLICATIONS

1. Choose a holiday, such as St. Patrick's Day or Valentine's Day, that is often celebrated in popular culture. Use this as a base for a unit on multicultural understanding. Possible topics include how this holiday is celebrated in different regions or different countries, the origin of the customs associated with this holiday, and underlying themes that promote multicultural concepts.

Develop a bibliography of books and other resources to help you build your unit. Plan lessons that integrate writing, discussion, and thinking skills. Present your unit to the class.

2. Focus on birthdays. Find out how to say "Happy Birthday" in one hundred languages. How do people celebrate birthdays in different cultures? Make a list of ways to create a multiethnic atmosphere (food, music, decorations) in the classroom and to make the children feel special.

3. Choose a group (ethnic, religious, or regional) to be responsible for and research names, dates, events, and other kinds of information to include in a multicultural calendar. Try to find special holidays celebrated by this group, names of significant individuals, and important contributions by the group.

Where would you look for this information? What kind of information is most difficult to find? Why?

Prepare lessons to present this information to students.

EXPLORING FURTHER

Joyce Armstrong Carroll. (1993). *Books for Special Days: Integrated Teaching of Reading, Writing, Listening, Speaking, Viewing, and Thinking.* Jackdaws Series No. 4. Englewood, CO: Teacher Ideas Press.

Mary Ann Heltshe, & Audrey Burie Kirchner. (1991). *Multicultural Explorations: Joyous Journeys with Books.* Englewood, CO: Teacher Ideas Press.

John Kremer. (1996). *Celebrate Today!* Rocklin, CA: Prima.

Byrd Baylor. (1986). *I'm in Charge of Celebrations.* Illustrated by Peter Parnall. New York: Scribner's.

Lois Sinaiko Webb. (1995). *Holidays of the World Cookbook for Students.* Phoenix, AZ: Oryx.

Library of Congress. *Today in History.* www.loc.gov.

Hope Martin, Louise Bock, & Susan Guengerich. (1995). *Multicultural Math Fun: Holidays around the Year.* Portland, ME: J. Weston Walch.

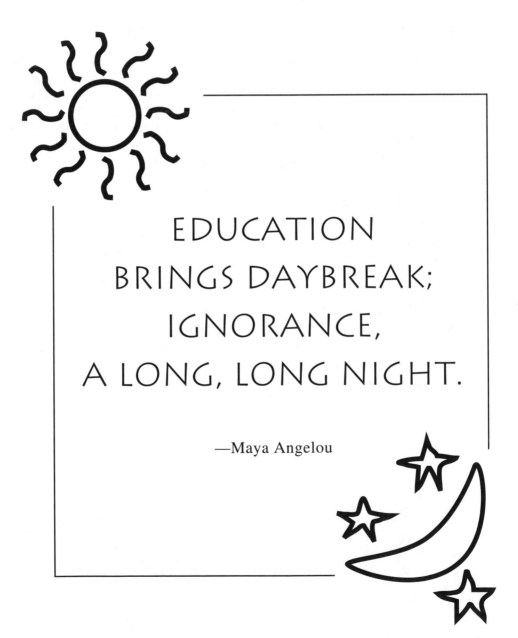

EDUCATION
BRINGS DAYBREAK;
IGNORANCE,
A LONG, LONG NIGHT.

—Maya Angelou

Part III

Reflecting on Multicultural Education

Now that we have completed our exploratory journey together, it is time to reflect on what we have learned about multicultural education. Because multicultural concepts are learned over a period of time, it is helpful to assess where we are today as we begin making plans for how we might continue our progress tomorrow.

In this chapter we acknowledge the problems and issues that we must surmount as we move forward, examining the pros and cons of the issues involved and preparing to face the dragon of controversy. We also summarize a number of promising practices that support multicultural teaching in the schools and in teacher education. In addition, we provide a checklist that may help you assess your development as a teacher of multicultural education.

After reading this chapter, you should be able to:

- Identify problems and issues that must be addressed if you are to carry out a successful multicultural education program.
- Describe progressive thinking and promising practices that support effective multicultural teaching.
- Evaluate the assumptions underlying multicultural education as presented in this text.

PROBLEMS AND ISSUES TO BE ADDRESSED

As a teacher, you will continue developing your multicultural knowledge base, and you will continue working toward the outcomes we have identified for student learning. However, the following problems and issues that may need to be addressed in your school or district as you work toward developing a full-fledged multicultural program that offers equity for all students:

Knowledge about Multicultural Education
Stereotypes, Prejudice, and the Dreaded R-Word
A Prescribed Curriculum

> Fear of Handling Controversy
> Communicating with Parents
> Censorship Efforts
> Homophobia's Impact on Schooling
> Misinformation about Student Language
> The "English Only" Movement
> Assessment, Testing, and the Effect of Bias
> Conservative Resistance to Multicultural Education
> The Relationship of Violence to Multicultural Education
> Reactions to Immigrants and Immigration

Knowledge about Multicultural Education

Prior to 1978, *multicultural education* was not even listed as a category in the *Education Index,* which indicates that few articles were being written in pedagogical journals about this topic. An entry for *Mexican Americans* first appeared in the 1963–1964 volume. At that time multiethnic topics were referred to as *Intergroup Education.* All references to blacks were entered under *Negroes* until 1978. References to Asian Americans were listed under *Orientals* until 1980. Only within the past decade do we find a substantial number of books and articles on multicultural education. This text was one of the first to address the topic in 1979.

Given the lag that typically occurs between the development of a theory and its impact on practice, these findings make it clear that we have not yet sufficiently emphasized teaching about cultural diversity in teacher education programs. Few classroom teachers and professors of teacher education today were educated to teach multicultural concepts. Members of the public educated years ago, too, still frequently use the melting-pot metaphor with well-meaning, but mistaken, intent and effects; and such terms as *culture* are often misused in textbooks and public dialogue.

Standards listed in 1987 by the National Council for Accreditation of Teacher Education (NCATE) include multicultural education. Teacher education programs are therefore now examined to see that multicultural concepts are present in class syllabi. The expected "multicultural perspective" is defined as

> . . . a recognition of (1) the social, political, and economic realities that individuals experience in culturally diverse and complex human encounters and (2) the importance of culture, race, sex and gender, ethnicity, religion, socioeconomic status, and exceptionalities in the education process.[1]

Teachers need to know accurate definitions, terminology, and concepts that can be shared with students at all levels of instruction. They need to know literature that will inform such instruction. They also need to accept the responsibility for teaching to enhance empathy in all classrooms.

The solution to this problem lies in both preservice and inservice staff development. This text is designed to add to the knowledge base for future teachers as well as those already in the field. Throughout the text we have presented numerous up-to-date references that you can explore to extend your knowledge base. We have also recommended experiences and activities that will enhance your ability to teach for diversity as you work with young learners.

Stereotypes, Prejudice, and the Dreaded R-Word

All of us grew up within a culture surrounded by beliefs and behaviors that we accepted without question. As young children, we usually associated with persons from the same culture and probably tended to consider our way of thinking and behaving as the "right" way to think or behave. Thus, stereotyped thinking may begin, and we may become prejudiced against those who think or behave differently.

Until recently, *race,* the dreaded R-word, has been avoided in both private and public discourse. Sweeping this word and its implications for society under the rug, however, will not eliminate *race* as a factor that affects our thinking, so we need to get the topic out on the table. As we approach the twenty-first century, for the first time, race is appearing frequently in the media. For example, in 1996, a majority of California voters, led by an outspoken African American member of the University of California Board of Regents, passed an anti-affirmative action proposition that resulted in an immediate drop in the numbers of people of color admitted to the California University System. This action was followed in such other states as Texas. In June, 1997, President Bill Clinton and others called for addressing issues related to racism. Addressing a college graduating class, Clinton stated: "We have torn down the barriers in our laws. Now we must break down the barriers in our lives, our minds, and our hearts." Representative Tony Layton presented a bill offering a public apology to all those whose ancestors were slaves before 1865. Such behaviors are clearly controversial and should result in more open discussion.

We can consciously change our thinking. Education, for example, informs us. As we encounter people from broader circles, we learn that thinking and behavior differ. Gradually, we learn to accept diverse thinking as a normal state of affairs. Mobility, television, the newspaper, literature—all serve to broaden our perspectives. If minds are open to new ideas, stereotyped thinking will be revised as teachers, students, and parents learn to accept differences and to realize that different does not connote "deficient" or "wrong."

Yet we continue to hear crude ethnic jokes or references in the speech of supposedly educated people. Children's rhymes and stories often contain stereotyped references children may or may not understand. Women, people of color, and the elderly continue to be discriminated against. We need to stand up for what we believe as we teach children how to think multiculturally.

A Prescribed Curriculum

Those who influence curriculum development are not always well informed. For example, former education secretary William Bennett, a highly literate man schooled in the classics, published a list of literature for K–8 classrooms in his report entitled *James Madison Elementary School: A Curriculum for American Students.*[2] He included only a few titles with multicultural content. In fact, of a total of 200 books listed by title, only 6% can be identified as multicultural. One title, *Sylvester and the Magic Pebble,* by William Steig, contains stereotypes of (1) a female housekeeper/wife/mother and (2) police portrayed as pigs. (Such a book could be recommended only as a basis for a lesson on how stereotyped thinking permeates our society.) At best, Bennett's list of publications reveals a lack of information, if not concern. It is clear that "multicultural representation" was not one of the criteria for the selection of these books.

We must select instructional materials that include a greater percentage of quality literature by and about members of different ethnic groups as well as the many identity groups that have special needs and concerns. We must also find time in the already burgeoning curriculum for multicultural education. Multicultural concepts belong in every classroom and should therefore be written into the objectives of every lesson. From self-esteem to immigration to the contributions of men and women of every race and religion to the history of the United States, lessons must reinforce the worth of every person who makes up our diverse population.

The curriculum is prescribed in many ways, for example:

Textbooks selected
Commercial tests used by school districts
State departments of education—course of study
Specialty organizations—NCTE, NMA, NAEYC, IRA
Critics, researchers, authors

You may wish to explore this topic in the following resources:

William Bennett. *James Madison High School* and *James Madison Elementary School*. U.S. Government, 1988.

E. D. Hirsch. *Cultural Literacy.* Houghton Mifflin, 1988.

Mary Ellen Van Camp, ed. *Testing.* Support for the Learning and Teaching of English, NCTE, December 1988.

Fear of Handling Controversy

Teachers and textbook publishers have a tendency to avoid topics that invite controversy in the classroom. Teachers feel uncomfortable with the expression of real emotion—fear, anger, or conflict. Publishers deliberately excise multicultural issues from reprinted materials. An example of the latter is noted in the reprinting of *Sound of Sunshine, Sound of Rain* by Florence Heide (Parents, 1970). The climax of this outstanding short novel, a racial confrontation that provides insight into the development of a major character, is deleted from both the reprint in a basal reader and the filmed version of this well-written book. Without this realistic scene, the quality of the author's work is diminished because the character development remains one-dimensional; and the students have missed an effective multicultural learning experience about humanity.

Dealing with real topics in the classroom adds vitality and stimulates student involvement in learning. Children who are confronting racism and dealing with the pain of conflict in their own lives benefit from classroom discussions that acknowledge the reality of what they face. Reading and discussion, for example, may suggest ways that others have found to deal with problems students encounter. Teachers need to seek ways of engaging students in multicultural topics even if these subjects may be controversial. Such literature as that cited throughout this text can help you present controversial issues and human feelings through a kind of simulation that is not threatening. Authors who include sensitive topics in well-written novels, dramas, or essays have created useful texts from which students can learn multicultural concepts. All educators share the responsibility for knowing and making skillful use of instructional options beyond the less inspiring textbook to support multicultural education.

Communicating with Parents

Teachers need to apprise parents of the expected learning outcomes students are working toward in their classrooms. Parents also need to become directly involved in their children's learning, providing encouraging support for school-initiated learning. On occasion, you will have a parent who objects to the content of the curriculum you are presenting or to a specific classroom activity. This opposition might center on multicultural content or activities. For example, many parents object to a curriculum that works toward developing self-esteem, which they equate as "teaching values." It is wise to discuss such an objection with your principal to determine proper handling of the matter and to obtain administrative support for your decisions. The principal should be able to clarify any legal aspect to be considered as well as to suggest appropriate interpersonal tactics. The law demands, for example, that we respect parental religious beliefs. As with all planning, our concern should remain student-centered as we attempt to avoid making a child feel ill at ease as a result of this parent-school interaction.

Censorship Efforts

Censorship may involve parental objections, discussed above, but censorship is such a complex and frequent concern that it deserves special attention. This topic could well be the subject of staff development within your district or a discussion for your school staff, including the principal. For example, you can determine together just how to handle requests to eliminate books from a reading list or from the school library. Having a procedure in place is very helpful for all staff members.

You might begin by obtaining material from various professional organizations. Many groups have an organizational stance that they will share with you. They may also suggest procedures and provide sample forms that are useful. Such information also provides the authority of a large, respected professional group to support your school practices. For example, the National Council of Teachers of English (NCTE) will give you one free copy of its position statement *Censorship: Don't Let It Become an Issue in Your Schools,* written by its Committee on Bias and Censorship in the Elementary School and published in 1978. It will also provide one free copy of a newer statement related to nonprint media, *Guidelines for Dealing with Censorship of Nonprint Materials,* published in 1993. Address requests to NCTE, 1111 Kenyon Rd., Urbana, IL 61801. (You might also request a copy of their latest catalog, which lists other helpful teaching materials.)

A subtler kind of censorship is the result of teachers' prioritization of what is presented in the curriculum. Teachers often appear uninterested in multicultural education. Given a choice in selecting workshops at a conference, they tend to choose topics that fit the mainline curriculum—for example, ideas for teaching reading or motivating student writing. It is difficult to know how to overcome this passive resistance.

As long as multicultural education remains a kind of "fringe" area of study, it has little chance of impacting student thinking. We know that we can only hope to integrate multicultural concepts and attitudes across the "real" curriculum. Until multicultural goals and objectives are specifically listed within the elementary and middle school curricula with clear expectations that they will be achieved, teachers will not give them the attention they deserve.

Homophobia's Impact on Schooling

The broad issue of human rights in contemporary society includes awareness of homosexuality, gay rights, and lesbianism. These topics are frequently in the newspapers and on television, so they cannot be ignored. Whatever your personal stance, you need to be prepared to deal with questions from students and/or parents. You may also be involved in decision making at the school or district level regarding faculty hiring or firing, the purchase of instructional materials, and curriculum planning. This controversial topic requires discussion at all levels within the school district.

Questions in this area often also relate to censorship, as many school districts have discovered. For example, when New York City adopted a multicultural program entitled *The Rainbow Curriculum,* which included materials related to homosexual lifestyles, parents demanded that children's literature titles dealing with this topic be removed from the library. They also questioned inviting lesbian parents to the classroom or any similar recognition that a child had same-sex parents. Imagine how children who have same-sex parents feel when the school district appears to support the homophobia found in society as a whole.

As has been true with any controversial topic in children's literature, for example, death, titles presenting homosexual lifestyles are gradually appearing. Note that this topic is not brand new. You may wish to examine the following:

Frances Hanckel. *A Way of Life: A Young Person's Introduction Into What It Means to Be Gay.* Lothrop, 1979.

John Donovan. *I'll Get There; It Better Be Worth the Trip.* Harper, 1969.

Rudy Galindo with Eric Marcus. *The Autobiography of Rudy Galindo.* Pocket Books, 1997.

Norma Klein. *Now That I Know.* Bantam, 1988.

George Shannon. *Unlived Affections.* Harper, 1989.

See also the discussion of families in Chapter 5.

Misinformation about Student Language and Bilingual Instruction

Often educators are misinformed about how best to help students improve their use of the English language, which most deem necessary for advancement within the United States. The Oakland (CA) School Board, for example, made headlines in late 1996 by declaring that African American students, who comprise 53% of their K-12 population of 52,300, use unique language patterns derived from West African languages. Furthermore, they termed this vernacular *ebonics,* a coined word based on "ebony" and "phonics," and stated that teachers were to use ebonics to help students learn. In addition, they made the mistake of stating that ebonics was "genetically based." Shocked educators across the country spoke up vehemently, as did such African American notables as Jesse Jackson and Maya Angelou. Secretary of Education Reilly quickly made it clear that Black English was not a separate language that would entitle the Oakland School District to bilingual funding. William Labov, expert researcher on use of the black vernacular in inner cities, clarified that Black English is learned and that students using it could learn standard English, thus becoming bidialectal. Thus, although these school board members clearly wanted to help their African American students, an obvious lack of information turned their well-meant efforts into an embarrassment. (They later revised their resolution, correcting the errors that had been made.)

The problem of how to teach students to use standard English effectively is not new. In 1976, the National Council of Teachers of English published a statement entitled: "Students' Right to Their Own Language" in which they concluded that students' oral language should be accepted by the schools without evaluation. (See Chapter 8 for text.) A child's home language constitutes part of each student's prior knowledge on which teachers can base further development, including the learning of standard English, if appropriate. The teacher's acceptance and respect for the child's language serves to support each student's self-esteem.

Is there only one way to teach children who are not proficient in English? The controversy focusing on bilingual instruction is being addressed by Californians in 1998 as they vote on a bill that permits schools to use "whatever method that works" to help native speakers of languages other than English learn English. The results of such instruction is to be evaluated to determine continued funding by the state. These resources provide additional background:

Kenji Hakuta, Chair; National Research Council. *Improving Schooling for Language-Minority Children: A Research Agenda.* National Academy Press, 1997. 483-page report; $55 from the Academy, 2101 Constitution Avenue NW, Washington DC 20418.

William Labov. "The Ebonics Controversy." National Public Radio, January 21, 1997. (Transcripts available)

The "English Only" Movement

As mentioned in Chapter 1, the "English only" movement became a national concern in the 1980s, led by S. I. Hayakawa, then Senator from California. A number of states jumped on this bandwagon, declaring English the official state language. Today there is an active national organization that seeks to extend this effort. NCTE discusses the drawbacks of this policy in its position statement *The National Language Policy: A Position Statement from the Conference on College Composition and Communication* (one copy free from NCTE, 1111 Kenyon Rd., Urbana, IL 61801).

The English-only movement runs counter to efforts to support instruction in children's native languages. Current research recommends that a child learn to read and write in the native language first while English is being acquired. Such professional organizations as Teachers of English to Speakers of Other Languages (TESOL) bring thousands of teachers together at annual conferences to address the complex issues involved. They publish a newsletter and varied instructional materials to support bilingual education. Inquire about their publication list: 1600 Cameron St., Alexandria, VA 22314. NCTE offers a free position statement on this topic, *TESOL and Bilingual Education,* prepared by the Committee on Issues in ESL and Bilingual Education. Teachers at all levels should be well informed regarding issues related to language development and literacy instruction because the issue is far from dead. In 1998, "English for Our Children," an initiative by California State Representative Unz, again attempts to discontinue bilingual education.

Assessment, Testing, and the Effect of Bias

All methods of assessment are being critiqued on the basis of equity. To provide for diverse learning styles, students need to experience varied methods of assessing mastery. A new assessment strategy that is receiving much attention is portfolio assessment, a method that is highly individualized.

More pertinent to this textbook is the concern about cultural bias in tests. Test authors are being asked to review all tests to determine whether they contain cultural bias. Are there underlying assumptions about common knowledge that place some students at a disadvantage?

The American Association for Higher Education (1 Dupont Circle, Washington, DC 20036) has published the following excellent summary of assessment practices, "Principles of Good Practice for Assessing Student Learning":

1. **The assessment of student learning begins with educational values.**
   Assessment is not an end in itself but a vehicle for educational improvement. Its effective practice, then, begins with and enacts a vision of the kinds of learning we most value for students and strive to help them achieve. Educational values should drive not only *what* we choose to assess but also *how* we do so. Where questions about educational mission and values are skipped over, assessment threatens to be an exercise in measuring what's easy, rather than a process of improving what we really care about.

2. **Assessment is most effective when it reflects an understanding of learning as multidimensional, integrated, and revealed in performance over time.**
   Learning is a complex process. It entails not only what students know but what they can do with what they know; it involves not only knowledge and abilities but values, attitudes, and habits of mind that affect both academic success and performance beyond the classroom. Assessment should reflect these understandings by employing a diverse array of methods, including those that call for actual performance, using them over time so as to reveal change, growth, and increasing degrees of integration. Such an approach aims for a more complete and accurate picture of learning, and therefore firmer bases for improving our students' educational experience.

3. **Assessment works best when the programs it seeks to improve have clear, explicitly stated purposes.**
   Assessment is a goal-oriented process. It entails comparing educational performance with educational purposes and expectations—these derived from the institution's mission, from faculty intentions in program and course design, and from knowledge

of students' own goals. Where program purposes lack specificity or agreement, assessment as a process pushes a campus toward clarity about where to aim and what standards to apply; assessment also prompts attention to where and how program goals will be taught and learned. Clear, shared, implementable goals are the cornerstone for assessment that is focused and useful.

4. **Assessment requires attention to outcomes but also and equally to the experiences that lead to those outcomes.**

Information about outcomes is of high importance; where students "end up" matters greatly. But to improve outcomes, we need to know about student experience along the way—about the curricula, teaching, and kind of student effort that lead to particular outcomes. Assessment can help us understand which students learn best under what conditions; with such knowledge comes the capacity to improve the whole of their learning.

5. **Assessment works best when it is ongoing, not episodic.**

Assessment is a process whose power is cumulative. Though isolated, "one-shot" assessment can be better than none, improvement is best fostered when assessment entails a linked series of activities undertaken over time. This may mean tracking the progress of individual students, or of cohorts of students; it may mean collecting the same examples of student performance or using the same instrument semester after semester. The point is to monitor progress toward intended goals in a spirit of continuous improvement. Along the way, the assessment process itself should be evaluated and refined in light of emerging insights.

6. **Assessment fosters wider improvement when representatives from across the educational community are involved.**

Student learning is a campus-wide responsibility, and assessment is a way of enacting that responsibility. Thus, while assessment efforts may start small, the aim over time is to involve people from across the educational community. Faculty play an especially important role, but assessment's questions can't be fully addressed without participation by student-affairs educators, librarians, administrators, and students. Assessment may also involve individuals from beyond the campus (alumni/ae, trustees, employers) whose experience can enrich the sense of appropriate aims and standards for learning. Thus understood, assessment is not a task for small groups of experts but a collaborative activity; its aim is wider, better-informed attention to student learning by all parties with a stake in its improvement.

7. **Assessment makes a difference when it begins with issues of use and illuminates questions that people really care about.**

Assessment recognizes the value of information in the process of improvement. But to be useful, information must be connected to issues or questions that people really care about. This implies assessment approaches that produce evidence that relevant parties will find credible, suggestive, and applicable to decisions that need to be made. It means thinking in advance about how the information will be used, and by whom. The point of assessment is not to gather data and return "results"; it is a process that starts with the questions of decision makers, that involves them in the gathering and interpreting of data, and that informs and helps guide continuous improvement.

8. **Assessment is most likely to lead to improvement when it is part of a larger set of conditions that promote change.**
   Assessment alone changes little. Its greatest contribution comes on campuses where the quality of teaching and learning is visibly valued and worked at. On such campuses, the push to improve educational performance is a visible and primary goal of leadership; improving the quality of undergraduate education is central to the institution's planning, budgeting, and personnel decisions. On such campuses, information about learning outcomes is seen as an integral part of decision making, and avidly sought.

9. **Through assessment, educators meet responsibilities to students and to the public.**
   There is a compelling public stake in education. As educators, we have a responsibility to the publics that support or depend on us to provide information about the ways in which our students meet goals and expectations. But that responsibility goes beyond the reporting of such information; our deeper obligation—to ourselves, our students, and society—is to improve. Those to whom educators are accountable have a corresponding obligation to support such attempts at improvement.

Conservative Resistance to Multicultural Education

Related to the expressed concerns about censorship and the handling of controversial topics is the recognition that certain individuals and groups resist or actively combat multicultural education, because they do not believe that this emphasis is appropriate in our schools. They argue for assimilation into the so-called majority culture and the use of English as the only language in the United States. They bemoan the use of culturally sensitive terminology for groups and tag such efforts as "political correctness," a term that has acquired strong negative connotations in the media.

Daniel Boorstin, Pulitzer Prize–winning historian and former librarian of Congress, states: "The menace to America today is in the emphasis on what separates us rather than on what brings us together—the separations of race, or religious practice, of origins, of language."[3] He sees the idea of a "hyphenated American" as "un-American" and will not use such terms as African American, stating that we are all Americans. He does not support bilingual teaching, citing his own Jewish heritage as an example of appropriate assimilation in the new world. Author of numerous texts on the American experience through history, he advocates an emphasis on community rather than diversity, and he favors accommodating immigrants as an aspect of American humanism. If such a respected, prominent writer and thinker speaks against multicultural approaches in education and the celebration of diversity, just think of the numbers of lesser-known people who share this viewpoint!

Objections often come from religious groups who rely on "freedom of religion" to support their objections to practices in the schools. You might like to read the January 1994 issue of The Association of Supervision and Curriculum Development's journal, *Educational Leadership,* which presents ten articles explicating aspects of this contemporary issue under the title "Public Schools and the Christian Fundamentalists." This issue is also explored in a special report, *Church, State, and the Religious Right,* published by Americans United for Separation of Church & State, 8120 Fenton Street, Silver Spring, MD 20910.

Those who disagree with multicultural approaches to education will never totally disappear from our society despite our best efforts. As teachers, you must be aware of such opposing viewpoints and prepare to combat criticism of sound theories and practices that the schools are trying to implement. You need to have a clear understanding of your stance and the rationale for including multicultural education in the schools in order to argue persuasively.

The Relationship of Violence to Multicultural Education

Children of all ages are exposed to violence in their lives. More than one-third of the first and second graders in our nation's capital have seen dead bodies. Forty-five percent report that they have witnessed muggings, and thirty-one percent report having witnessed shootings.[4] Recently, the National Medical Association, comprising 16,000 black doctors, addressed "violence reduction in the African American community." The association's president, Dr. Leonard Lawrence, stated "We've really got to teach our young people that there are alternative ways of problem solving" and noted that "there is some value in being disciplined," being in charge of one's behavior. Lawrence advocated teaching students "the positive aspects of discipline at a very early age, teaching them how to achieve, how to learn, how to interact with other people." He also encouraged adults to spend time with young people, to serve as models and mentors to boys and girls growing up under difficult circumstances.[5]

Violence and abuse touch all of our lives. People of all national origins and cultural backgrounds cause violence and abuse, and all are at some time the victims of such attacks on human rights, even if only indirectly. Teaching for diversity addresses concerns that may help bring violence under control. Teaching students "how to get along," for example, stresses self-esteem, empathy, and equity, which should help alleviate the same conditions that lead to stereotyping and discrimination as well as violence and abuse. Thus, as we work toward achieving one goal, we will also be working toward achieving the second.

Working with students at risk, discussed in some detail in Chapter 2, should also help to reduce violence and abuse, particularly in relation to adolescents. We need to address the problems that follow from having young people who drop out of school, especially males, on the street with nothing constructive to do. The long summer school vacation may also prove to be a problem if students have nothing to occupy them and do not have supervision during those months.

Reaction to Immigration and Immigrants

"The people of North America," wrote Senator Daniel Patrick Moynihan, "are the descendants of one of the greatest migrations in history. And that migration is not over. Koreans, Vietnamese, Nicaraguans, Cubans, and many others are heading for the shores of North America in large numbers. This mix of cultures shapes every aspect of our lives. To understand ourselves, we must know something about our diverse ethnic ancestry. Nothing so defines the North American nations as the motto on the Great Seal of the United States: *E Pluribus Unum—Out of Many, One.*"[6]

Toward the end of the twentieth century the topic of immigration has become the center of controversy particularly in such Mexican border states as California and Texas. In California, a state that houses a high percentage of illegal Mexican immigrants, a bill was passed to limit the rights of immigrants, including denying medical care and the children's right to attend the public schools. Although the bill was struck down as unconstitutional, the sentiments continue to exist.

Forgetting that almost all of us are the children of immigrants, many U.S. citizens are calling for closing the United States to immigration. The media attempt to treat the controversy fairly by featuring the contributions of various cultural groups to local communities and to the nation as a whole. This sensitive issue, which has no easy solution, requires careful study. Presented as a theme for investigation, it offers a special challenge for young people to address, as noted in Chapter 4.

Recap

Teachers must recognize the controversial nature of issues related to multicultural education. Each of us has to reflect on the rationale for what we teach and how we provide for the good of each learner in our classrooms. We need to be prepared to discuss issues that will almost certainly arise throughout a teaching career. Once we acknowledge the existence of the issues presented in this section, we can address them and strive to find solutions. Multicultural education can become a reality.

PROGRESSIVE THINKING AND PROMISING PRACTICES

Today we see visible efforts to deal with issues related to multicultural education. However, a difference of opinion remains. We need to support progressive thinking and to recognize exemplary practices that can be replicated across the country.

Self-Esteem—The Bottom Line

Humanistic educators wrote of self-image and self-concept in the 1960s, and affective education became a goal for many teachers.[7] Benjamin Bloom recognized both cognitive and affective domains in writing objectives for education.[8] Concern for the student as the center of the curriculum was expressed by such theoreticians as James Moffett in the first edition of *The Student-Centered Curriculum*.[9]

Currently there is renewed interest in the student's role in the learning process. We talk of student self-esteem as the foundation for learning; we recognize that all students need a sense of worth—an "I can" attitude—if they are to strive to achieve. We are concerned about the classroom climate as we try to build an attitude of trust between student and teacher. We try to let students know that making mistakes is an essential part of real learning, so that they will dare to take risks as they brainstorm and solve problems together. We need citizens who have genuine self-esteem, for they are the people who can reach out confidently to others with empathy and caring. Self-esteem undergirds the effort to save at-risk students—a topic of national concern that we discuss later in this section.

You may wish to explore this topic in the following resources:

Jack Canfield and Harold Wells. *100 Ways to Enhance Self-concepts in the Classroom,* 2nd ed. Prentice-Hall, 1996.

Matthew McKay and Patrick Fanning. *Self-Esteem.* St. Martin's, 1987.

Eileen Tway, ed. *Reading Ladders for Human Relations,* 6th ed. National Council of Teachers of English, 1981.

Writing "Thinking"

Focus on the writing process, as advocated by National Writing Project consultant-teachers across the country for the past decade, is closely tied to the development of thinking skills. Thinking leads to writing as one way of expressing ideas, and the process of writing these ideas extends thinking. Thus, the writing of "thinking" is a generative process that engages students in dealing with real issues and concerns. Students who have self-esteem express their ideas confidently, and their successful writing supports the growth of self-esteem, which is another interlocking learning process that should be in any classroom.

You may wish to explore this topic further in the following resources:

Julie Jensen, ed. *Composing and Comprehending.* ERIC Clearinghouse on Reading and Communications Skills, 1984.

Judith Langer and Arthur Applebee. *How Writing Shapes Thinking: A Study of Teaching and Learning.* National Council of Teachers of English, Research Report No. 22, 1987.

Carol Olson. *Thinking/Writing: Fostering Critical Thinking Skills through Writing.* University of California at Irvine, 1984.

James Squire, ed. *The Dynamics of Language Learning.* National Conference on Research in English, 1987.

Iris M. Tiedt. *Writing: From Topic to Evaluation.* Allyn and Bacon, 1989.

Iris M. Tiedt et al. *Teaching Thinking in K–12 Classrooms.* Allyn and Bacon, 1989.

Literature-Based Reading Instruction

A developing trend is the use of literature or trade books to support instruction in all subject areas. The use of library books instead of the usual textbook humanizes the curriculum and lends a vitality to learning that has not heretofore been present. Studies point out that the usual history textbook, for example, presents a sterile summary of events compared to a well-written trade book.[10] Furthermore, literature (including nonfiction, narrative prose, and poetry) sets historical events in a rich context that may more effectively engage student interest in learning. Students who read Scott O'Dell's novel, *Sarah Bishop,* for example, will have an affective knowledge of the War for Independence that is not produced by the sterile prose of most history textbooks for young adults.

Use of literature presumes that we will dismiss the necessity to "cover a textbook" in favor of guiding students to choose selections that provide different perspectives of the same period of history or the geography of a country. This approach also presupposes a different way of teaching—employing discovery methods that lead students to question and to think as they analyze, evaluate, and reflect. This approach presupposes, too, a confident teacher who can facilitate student learning and who does not need to lean on textbooks that provide questions at the end of each chapter and an answer key to ease the task of grading. We need a way of teaching that leads students to construct their own meaning based on knowledge gathered from varied sources. Literature study offers such a way, a way that also engages students in a humanistic experience that may lead to the empathy we are attempting to achieve through multicultural education.

Whole-language instruction, a popular theory of teaching in the elementary school, uses literature for instruction and the development of literacy skills. Based on sound theory, a whole-language program encourages students to use both oral and written language, real language for real purposes. This approach includes listening to many stories read aloud and also reading many books. As they write and read, children also learn to connect sounds (phonemes) and symbols (graphemes), popularly termed "phonics," as they work with words in context. They respond to the stories they hear through active discussions, acting out, retelling; through literature they learn varied content about many interesting topics. They also begin to author books themselves, putting their books on the shelf beside those of other writers. Above all, they learn to enjoy reading and writing. Resources include:

Anne Haas Dyson and Celia Genish, eds. *The Need for Story: Cultural Diversity in Classroom and Community.* National Counil of Teachers of English, 1994.

Kenneth Goodman. *What's Whole about Whole Language?* Heineman, 1989.

Janet Hickman et al. *Children's Literature in the Classroom: Extending Charlotte's Web.* Christopher-Gordon, 1993.

Heidi Mills et al. *Looking Closely: Exploring the Role of Phonics in One Whole Language Classroom.* National Council of Teachers of English, 1992.

Marilou Sorensen and Barbara Lehman. *Teaching with Children's Books: Paths to Literature-Based Instruction.* National Council of Teachers of English, 1995.

Zena Sutherland et al. *Children and Books.* Scott Foresman, 1992.

The Professionalization of Teaching

Increasingly, attention is being placed on the quality of teaching and the professionalization of teaching as a respected career. A 1988 nationwide study by the Association of Supervision and Curriculum Development identified the following teacher-related issues as being of concern:

1. Inconsistency of teacher certification requirements and the overuse of "alternative" or "emergency" teaching certificates.
2. Limited criteria for teacher evaluation.
3. Loss of self-esteem for teachers leading to low morale.
4. Low salaries negating efforts to attract best teachers.
5. Lack of preparation in instructional skills and classroom management.
6. Shortage of highly skilled teachers and gradual reduction of persons choosing teaching as a career.
7. Inadequate staff development for teaching roles and responsibilities.
8. Lack of preparation time to handle numerous tasks required of teachers.

Respondents to the same survey recommended emphasis on the following to improve the quality of instruction and to provide a more professional role for teachers at all levels:

- Empowerment: Teachers need more control and autonomy in the classroom and in determining what is taught in general.
- Recruitment: We need to work to attract top-quality people to teaching as a career.
- Retention: We also need to work to retain top-quality teachers in the field.
- Roles: Teachers need support as they assume new roles, for example, in management of the inclusive classroom.
- Training: Teachers need more professional staff development opportunities.[11]

The establishment of The National Board of Teaching represents a positive effort to upgrade the status and ability of teachers in the field. Funded by the Carnegie Foundation and grounded in the work of Lee Shulman, the board provides a performance-based test as a basis for national certification as a master teacher. It is expected that many top teachers will opt to acquire this national recognition.

Site-based management is another positive approach to involving teachers in decision making about how education is carried out at the local level. Although not an easy process to initiate, some principals and their staffs are committed to the necessary study and effort required. The emphasis is on collaboration rather than top-down direction; everyone needs to be informed. Such promising practices add to a sense of empowerment for teachers involved.

Activism results from teacher empowerment as teachers become advocates for school change. Informed teachers are needed to take a position and speak on children's behalf. Ask yourself what you truly believe about teaching. What do you have to say about teaching to provide equity for diverse learners?

True empowerment of the teacher comes from within. It is not something that an external task force can fund or a legislature can enforce. We all, however, have a responsibility to nurture this sense of empowerment, which is akin to self-esteem and self-confidence. The teacher who has this sense of power is best able to teach multiculturally, addressing controversy with equanimity and sharing leadership with young learners in the classroom.

Teacher education can empower novice teachers by providing them with basic knowledge in the foundations, liberal studies, and pedagogy, including multicultural education. Such teachers have confidence in their knowledge base, but above all they know how to apply this knowledge in the classroom. Furthermore, the teacher who possesses a sense of empowerment is best able to nurture that same feeling in students.

You may wish to explore this topic further in the following resources:

James A. Banks and Cherry Banks. *Multicultural Education: Issues and Perspectives,* 2nd ed. Allyn and Bacon, 1997.

Louis Harris. *The Second Year: New Teachers' Expectations and Ideals, A Survey of New Teachers Who Completed Their Second Year of Teaching in Public Schools in 1992.* Metropolitan Life Insurance Co., 1992.

Bruce Joyce et al. *The Self-Renewing School.* Association of Supervision and Curriculum Development, 1993.

Seymour B. Sarason. *The Case for Change: Rethinking the Preparation of Educators.* Jossey-Bass, 1993.

Schools as Centers of Inquiry

Gradually, teachers are recognizing that direct, teacher-dominated instruction is not as effective as discovery methods that engage students in inquiry. We need to consider the goals of education in terms of student learning, the expected outcomes that we identify. The testing of student achievement should then reflect what we really mean to teach. The evaluation of teacher performance should in turn reflect our expectations for student learning.

In direct instruction the teacher typically lectures, perhaps addressing questions to individual students one by one; only a small percentage of students are actively involved at any one time, and there is little student interaction. This is the quiet, orderly classroom; learning follows predictable lines and is easily evaluated. In this type of teaching, the teacher generates the questions, and the kind of question asked has one correct answer, which of course the teacher knows. This has been the traditional mode of instruction for many years.

When inquiry approaches are used, however, the students generate questions to which they need to know the answers. There is self-motivation as each one works 100% of the class time on a self-selected problem or project. Metacognitive approaches guide students to awareness of the thinking processes in which they are engaged. They talk and write to express thinking and test their ideas against the thinking of other students in pairs or small groups. They accept ownership for the learning that is going on because they selected a topic in which they have an interest. Far from abdicating their role, teachers plan extensively in order to set up discovery learning situations; often they plan directly with students. They facilitate and support the learning process and serve as resource persons.

Evaluation of progress is part of the inquiry—a process shared by teacher and student. In this kind of classroom students have an opportunity to learn more than is presented in a single textbook, and they naturally develop self-esteem. Thus, what they learn is both cognitive and affective, but it may not always be easily measured by tests used by school districts. Because such approaches are more sensitive to individual student needs, they fit with the outcomes we have identified for multicultural education. They also show promise in supporting the at-risk students, an identified group that needs special attention in our schools.

Explore this topic further through the following resources:

Kenneth Goodman et al. *Report Card on Basal Readers.* National Council of Teachers of English, 1988.

Robert J. Marzano et al., eds. *Dimensions of Thinking: A Framework for Curriculum and Instruction.* Association for Supervision and Curriculum Development, 1988.

James Moffett and Betty Jean Wagner. *The Student-Centered Curriculum,* 3rd ed. Houghton Mifflin, 1996.

Reflection (Thinking), an Essential Aspect of Learning

Opportunities for thinking of all kinds, but especially reflection, need to be integrated throughout instruction at all levels. The child is a thinker from birth, an active learner observing what is happening in the world, asking questions as a way of learning, processing information. The child's acquisition of language is an example of the amazing discovery process in action as the newborn human gradually abstracts the complexities of a grammar system from language heard in the environment. Constructing hypotheses and developing theories about how the language works, children test these hypotheses by communicating. Never afraid of making errors, children talk, talk, talk, trying out what they have learned.

Only recently have we recognized the need to relate what we know about the infant's acquisition of speech to the later acquisition of literacy abilities. While acknowledging the limitations of this way of learning more complex content and skills, we realize that learner-generated questioning and the construction of hypotheses are natural and essential aspects of thinking and learning that we need to continue to encourage. This approach has much to offer multicultural education, too, as children probe into new areas of study.

Teachers are stimulated by the challenge of teaching thinking skills. Engaging students in thinking activities encourages the students to generate the questions rather than the teacher. This kind of student-centered instruction can involve learners in problem solving and interacting with other students as they study concepts related to racism, stereotyping, and prejudice. Multicultural literature offers an opportunity to explore a wide variety of thought-provoking topics. Analysis, synthesis, and evaluation are the kind of advanced thinking skills even the youngest students can employ when led by a competent teacher.

You may wish to explore this topic further in the following resources:

Beau F. Jones et al., eds. *Strategies for Teaching and Learning: Cognitive Instruction in the Content Areas.* Association of Supervision and Curriculum Development, 1987.

Iris M. Tiedt et al. *Reading/Thinking/Writing: A Holistic Language and Literacy Program for the K–8 Classroom.* Allyn and Bacon, 1989.

Iris M. Tiedt et al. *Teaching Thinking in K–12 Classrooms.* Allyn and Bacon, 1989.

S. R. Yussen and M. C. Smith, eds. *Reading across the Life Span.* Springer-Verlag, 1993.

Early Childhood Education

We have long known that attitudes and values are firmly rooted in what is learned during a child's early years. What is not learned at this time, furthermore, constitutes a great loss that may never be overcome. Although we now recognize and can work to correct it, children who do not have good learning opportunities during these early years enter kindergarten and first grade with a handicap.

Early childhood intervention instruction for children may alleviate any discrepancy an individual child may have. Such projects as Head Start and other organized preschool programs strive to build a strong experiential and knowledge base before children enter the formal school system, so that children are better prepared for success in formal schooling from the outset.

As we are making special efforts to prepare children to enter school, we are also rethinking the concept of "readiness." Rather than making the student "ready" for literacy instruction, for example, we are now considering how the school can better meet the needs of each individual child. This fits with our emphasis in this text on teaching for diversity to provide equitable education that accommodates individual learning styles and abilities.

The ungraded primary is not a new idea, but it has come into its own in many contemporary schools that recognize the importance of individualizing instruction. In an ungraded structure, the emphasis is on achieving specific outcomes rather than moving through the grades. We know that some children require more time (and some less) to achieve the basic foundation for learning on which upper-grade teachers can build. Giving children more time without branding them "failures" by "holding them back" increases children's success rate and their sense of self-esteem. Thus, they have a much better chance of success throughout their elementary school years.

Vivian Paley, an experienced kindergarten teacher in New Orleans, New York City, and Chicago's Laboratory School, focused on the ethics of play with young children. To avoid exclusionary attitudes and behaviors, she established this rule: "You can't say you can't play." Children quickly learned to accept the rule as fair, although many discussions ensued related to its implications. Paley notes that in her early years of teaching she tried to ignore children's unfairness, hoping it would work itself out. It was only when she was almost sixty years old that she undertook to assume a more active leadership role as a teacher. She has written a number of books about her experiences, including *You Can't Say You Can't Play* (Harvard University Press, 1992). As she states optimistically, "If every kindergarten in the country were to promote this idea and it would continue year by year by year, in twenty years, when everybody got out of college, we would have a nicer world."[12]

You may wish to explore this topic further in the following resources:

Hillary Clinton. *It Takes a Village and Other Lessons Children Teach Us.* Simon & Schuster, 1996.

Eugene E. Garcia et al, eds. *Meeting the Challenge of Linguistic and Cultural Diversity in Early Childhood Education.* Yearbook in Early Childhood Education, Volume 6. Teachers College, 1995.

V. Hildebrand. *Introduction to Early Childhood Education.* Macmillan, 1986.

B. Spodel et al. *Foundations of Early Childhood Education.* Prentice-Hall, 1987.

Early Childhood Education Network—Contact S. M. Childs, Teaneck Public Schools, One Merrison St., Teaneck, NJ 07666.

Young Children, journal of the National Association for the Education of Young Children (NAFYC), 1834 Connecticut Avenue, NW, Washington, DC 20008.

Dimension, journal published quarterly by Southern Association on Children under Six (SACUS), Box 5403, Brady Station, Little Rock, AR 72215.

Growing Concern for At-Risk Students

Within the past decade, various studies have pointed out that the United States faces an economic crisis. In the next century we will not have the educated work force that we need in order to compete in the world. The reason is clear: A high percentage of our students are dropping out of school long before graduating from high school. Instead of a trained work force, we will have a welfare-dependent segment of society that does not contribute to the nation's economy. Instead, these uneducated young people will drain the national income.

School districts and whole communities are addressing the problem of these at-risk students. This group includes the hundreds of thousands of young girls who become pregnant each year, the young adolescents on the streets involved in drugs and crime, and the little children who come into our schools with limited knowledge and experience. Multicultural education, with its emphasis on self-esteem, empathy, and equity, offers a hope of reaching these students before they drop out of school and out of mainstream society.

James Comer stresses the need for emphasizing relationship issues and the social condition—"interaction between teacher and student, between parent and student, between parent and teacher." In carrying out his School Development Program, he argues for providing support for "the kind of development that all children need." He also emphasizes the need to recognize the influence of poverty, which is an alarming reality in our large cities."[13] The Children's Defense Fund reports that the percentage of children under eighteen living in poverty is over 40% in Detroit, Laredo, New Orleans, Flint, Miami, Hartford, Gary, Cleveland, Atlanta, and Dayton. What is appalling is that the percentage of children living in poverty in the United States, the "land of plenty," is more than double that of Canada, Britain, France, the Netherlands, Sweden, and West Germany.[14] We need to continue efforts to support children who are in our schools.

You may wish to explore this topic further in the following resources:

Association for Supervision and Curriculum Development, 1250 N. Pitt St., Alexandria, VA 22314. Audiocassette series: five tapes by educators from large urban school districts describing how they are handling the problem of at-risk students.

Robert D. Barr and William H. Parrett. *Hope at Last for At-Risk Youth.* Allyn and Bacon, 1995.

James S. Coleman. "Families and Schools." *Educational Researcher,* August/September, 1987: 32–38.

James Comer. "Dr. James Comer's Plan for Ensuring the Future." *Black Issues in Higher Education.* May 20, 1993, pp. 42–47. See also his books: *Beyond Black and White, Black Child Care, School Power,* and *Maggie's American Dream.*

Dianne W. Hayes. "Learning in Poverty: Children in Crisis." *Black Issues in Higher Education.* June 17, 1993, pp. 21–25.

M. Lee Manning and Leroy G. Baruth. *Students at Risk.* Allyn and Bacon, 1995.

Relating International, Global, and Multicultural Issues

Global and international issues are directly related to multicultural education at the world level of interaction. Americans need to learn how to operate in a rapidly changing world scene. U.S. foreign policies must change, and the citizens of this democracy must understand and support such change. Professor Richard Gardner outlines global issues in a 1992 report sponsored by the United National Development Programme (UNDP). He sees the following as being threats to the welfare of the world, including the United States:

1. Environmental degradation: Lack of emphasis on environmental concerns in the United States, saving the planet.
2. Energy productivity: U.S. failure to deal with the energy problem; the limits of natural resources.
3. Population growth: Failure to lead efforts to control population explosion; problems related to hunger and poverty.
4. People on the move: Handling of refugee and immigration problems, particularly in terms of human rights.
5. Humanitarian crises: Intervention in other countries to assure human rights; what is our responsibility and our role.
6. Drugs: More effort put into controlling the demand for drugs rather than focusing on the supplier; the United States is the big consumer.[15]

Students might well discuss any of these issues, generating questions about U.S. policy and how it might be changed. It is interesting to consider, too, the factors that prevent such changes from taking place. Any one of these concerns offers an opportunity to seek out information and to become involved in effecting change in your community.

An executive speaking for the international division of a large conglomerate includes the following among the projected corporate needs for the year 2000:

Employees who are not predominantly ethnocentric in their view of the world.

People who are able to work and live abroad effectively, who are comfortable with expatriation and repatriation and have the potential for linguistic success for studying foreign languages.

Employees who understand that the United States is competing on an even playing field in the next century . . . that the competition is as good as, often better than, that offered by U.S. organizations.

Employees who are willing to take risks—to try and maybe have setbacks, but who can get up, learn from adversity and try again. . . .

Employees who do not rely on English only sources of information. . . .[16]

This statement supports the need for educating students to live in a multicultural world. It extends the empathy we are trying to achieve among persons living in the United States to the global village that we share. Children who are brought up with limited perspectives of the world will be handicapped, unable to move beyond the narrow environs in which they were raised.

You may wish to explore this topic further in the following resources:

James Banks and Cherry Banks, *Multicultural Education: Issues and Perspectives.* Allyn and Bacon, 1997

Carnegie Endowment National Commission Report. *Changing Our Ways.* Brookings Institute, 1992. (Order from the Institute, Box 029, Washington, DC 10042 for $12.95, including shipping.)

Paulo Freire and Donaldo Macedo. *Literacy: Reading the Word and the World.* Bergin and Garvey, 1987.

June Jordan. *On Call: Political Essays.* South End Press, 1987.

M. Trow. "Comparative Reflections on Leadership in Higher Education." *Journal of Education,* 20: pp. 143–59.

M. Tsukada. "A Factual Overview of Education in Japan and the United States." In W. K. Cummings et al., ed. *Educational Policies in Crisis: Japanese and American Perspectives.* Praeger, 1986.

Technology and Interactive Learning

During the past decade, educators have been encouraged to utilize computers at all levels to stimulate learning. Computer companies have donated equipment, and local experts have contributed time to set up computer centers. Even the President and Vice President have been directly engaged in "wiring" schools across the nation so that elementary and secondary school students will have access to the latest technology.

However, one of the most important aspects of promoting the use of technology in education is teacher preparation. Professional development within the school districts is needed if teachers are to use computers to the fullest advantage. (See Chapter 3 for a list of Internet programs that are recommended to support multicultural education.) Additional resources include:

Carnegie Endowment National Commission Report. *Changing Our Ways.* Washington DC: Brookings Institute, 1992. (Order from the Institute, Box 029, Washington DC 10042 for $12.95, including shipping.)

Recap

As we consider multicultural education, it is important to note progressive thinking and practices that stand out as exemplary. Across the country, teachers and school districts are making sincere efforts to reach multicultural goals from different perspectives. Grounded in the principle of achieving self-esteem for all students and leading to understanding of others, these programs may address the needs of preschool children or adolescent at-risk students; they may be directed toward preparing the teacher; or they may deal directly with selection of content or methods of delivering the curriculum. Increasing support can be identified for practices that support multicultural education.

REVIEWING THE STUDY OF MULTICULTURAL TEACHING

In this book we have presented a philosophy of teaching that is grounded in humanity and a sincere desire to make the world a better place in which to live. We believe that education, particularly in the early years, offers the only route to the empathy for others that is necessary to achieve cooperative planning and harmonious living in an interdependent world. It is our belief that multicultural education is subsumed in the meaning of democracy as we aim to carry it out in the United States. We hope to educate teachers who will bear this message.

Multicultural teaching is a broad topic that cannot be taught in one single course. Therefore, we have presented multicultural studies as a spiraling curriculum comprising concepts and understandings that evolve over years of schooling. Threading its way through all instruction, multicultural education is a lifelong endeavor. For the purposes of review and assessment, we list again here the assumptions on which we have based our presentation, presented in Chapter 1. As we revisit these assumptions, we will consider the implications of each one in terms of practice. Use this self-assessment as you plan for your professional development as a multicultural teacher.

Where are you in your development as a multicultural teacher? In which areas do you feel the most need for additional study? It is important to remember that multicultural education will continue for all of us throughout our lives. We all have much to learn about "getting along" with others.

Assumptions Underlying Multicultural Teaching

MULTICULTURAL EDUCATION: THEORY AND PRACTICE

Well prepared	Adequate	Needs study	
			1. The United States is a multiculture, a society comprising many diverse cultures. All of living, including schooling, involves contact between different cultures and is, therefore, multicultural. No one culture can be considered more American than any other.
			2. The United States is gradually moving away from its expressed goal of assimilation of making everyone alike (the melting-pot metaphor) toward recognizing and appreciating the diversity in our society (the "tossed salad," or mosaic, metaphor). Educators play a role in disseminating this knowledge and acting on its implications.
			3. Multicultural education is too complex and pervasive a topic to be encompassed in a single course for teacher educators. All of education must reflect multicultural awareness. Curricula for grades K–8 must be designed to teach content about our multiculture and to provide equity for all learners in all subjects.
			4. We should not pretend or even aim to be creating teaching materials that are bias-free. Instead, we should guide students to recognize the biases from which they and all people operate.
			5. We need to clarify our use of such terms as *culture, ethnicity,* and *race.* We also need to be aware of accepted labels for groups of people within our population, speaking out against insensitive usage whenever appropriate.

Well prepared	Adequate	Needs study	
			6. Although every child grows up within a given culture, he or she is shaped over the years by additional influences, such as education and personal interactions with others. Education can guide students to become more aware of and appreciative of their individual cultures, their heritage. Children can also learn to avoid ethnocentrism by being open to the cultural ideas of others.
			7. All children enter school with a store of prior knowledge, closely aligned with their individual cultural backgrounds, on which teachers can build.
			8. Education can guide all students to become more aware and appreciative of the many cultures that people contributed to what is now the United States. Diversity should be viewed as a strength, not as disunity.
			9. Teachers need to be aware of their own cultural backgrounds and biases. They need to be aware of how these biases might influence their expectations of students and how they interact with others. Open dialogue with students will acknowledge these cultural influences as common to us all. Both teachers and students can learn together about different ideas and ways of thinking.
			10. Multicultural teaching is exciting because it is grounded in reality. Through active, constructivist learning strategies, students can become directly involved in their learning. At the same time, teachers may find such multicultural approaches more difficult because they may include controversy and emotion. Since discussions do not usually result in identification of "right answers," resulting ambiguity may cause students to feel unsettled.
			11. Multicultural education, global studies, and internationalization of the curriculum are related in their focus on human concerns. Thus, a study of universal needs suggests topics that overlap so that the three are not completely separate areas to be added to the school curriculum.
			12. Multicultural education deals with values and attitudes as well as knowledge. We can guide students to be aware of their own thinking and that of others. We guide them to make choices based on expressed reasoning, problem solving, and decision making. Because changes in values and attitudes and the development of empathy take time, assessing such changes quickly is not possible.

REFLECTIONS

Education can empower, and teachers are the enabling agents who can make it happen. In this chapter, we have reflected with you on the beliefs that we have shared in this book, restating what we believe about teaching. We have also recognized problems and issues that may impede multicultural teaching and have identified ways in which education for understanding might realistically come about. We have concluded on a positive note with a discussion of progressive thinking and promising practices that are already in effect. We hope that you will find support for your endeavors to implement multicultural education in your classrooms.

Now that we have come full cycle in our study of multicultural education, we are reminded of the words of the noted author Aldous Huxley, which appeared in an interview in the *New York Times* in 1926:

> So the journey is over and I am back again, richer by much experience and poorer by many exploded convictions, many perished certainties. For conviction and certainties are too often the concomitants of ignorance . . . I set out on my travels knowing, or thinking I knew, how men should live, how be governed, how educated, what they should believe. I had my views on every activity of life. Now, on my return, I find myself without any of these pleasing certainties . . . The better you understand the significance of any question, the more difficult it becomes to answer it. Those who attach a high importance to their own opinion should stay at home. When one is traveling, convictions are mislaid as easily as spectacles, but unlike spectacles, they are not easily replaced.[17]

As we reflect on our journey, consider how your thinking has changed. What convictions have you lost along the way?

APPLICATIONS

1. Begin a clipping file of multicultural issues that appear in your local newspaper for a period of at least a month. Write a summary statement about multicultural concerns in your local area; these may reflect national or worldwide concerns.

2. Focus on one obstacle to the implementation of multicultural education enumerated in this chapter. Discuss this problem in a CLG. Share your group's thinking with the full class.

3. Begin interviewing local educators to identify one exemplary practice related to multicultural education in your area. Write a review of this idea or program and attempt to obtain newspaper coverage for this outstanding instructional practice.

4. Write a letter to the editor of your local newspaper, pointing out the accomplishments of one minority group in your community.

ENDNOTES

1. National Council for Accreditation of Teacher Education. *Standards, Procedures, and Policies for the Accreditation of Professional Teacher Education Units.* NCATE, 1987.
2. William Bennett. *James Madison Elementary School: A Curriculum for American Students.* U.S. Government Printing Office, 1988.
3. Daniel Boorstin. Speech at Moorhead State University, April 17, 1993.
4. Bob Herbert. "Children the Victims of Violence." *The Forum* newspaper, Fargo, ND. August 21, 1993, p. A4.

5. Leonard Lawrence. Speech to the National Medical Association, December, 1992.

6. Anne Galicich. *The German Americans.* Chelsea House, 1992, p. 11.

7. Arthur Combs. Chair of the Committee, ASCD Yearbook, *Perceiving, Behaving, Becoming.* ASCD, 1962. Mario Fantini and Gerald Weinstein. *The Disadvantaged.* Harper, 1968. William Glasser. *Schools without Failure.* Harper, 1969.

8. Benjamin Bloom. *All Our Children Learning: A Primer for Parents, Teachers and Other Educators.* McGraw, 1981.

9. James Moffett and Betty Jean Wagner. *Student-Centered Language Arts and Reading Curriculum, K–13,* 3rd ed. Houghton Mifflin, 1996.

10. The Bradley Commission. *Reforming the History Curriculum.* The Commission, 1989.

11. ASCD, Survey, 1988.

12. Mary Beth Marklein. "Learning to Play by New Rules: Teacher Adds Ethics of Play to Preschool Curriculum." *National Retired Teachers Association Bulletin.* September, 1993, p. 24.

13. James Comer. *Black Issues,* October, 1992.

14. Carnegie Endowment National Commission. *Changing Our Ways.* Brookings Institute, 1992. (Report available for $12.95, including shipping, from Box 029, Washington, DC 10042.)

15. Richard Gardner. *Global Issues,* United National Development Programme, 1992.

16. Michael Copeland. International Divisions, Procter & Gamble Company. Letter to Dr. Leon Boothe, president, Northern Kentucky University.

17. Aldous Huxley. "Interview." *New York Times.* September 17, 1926.

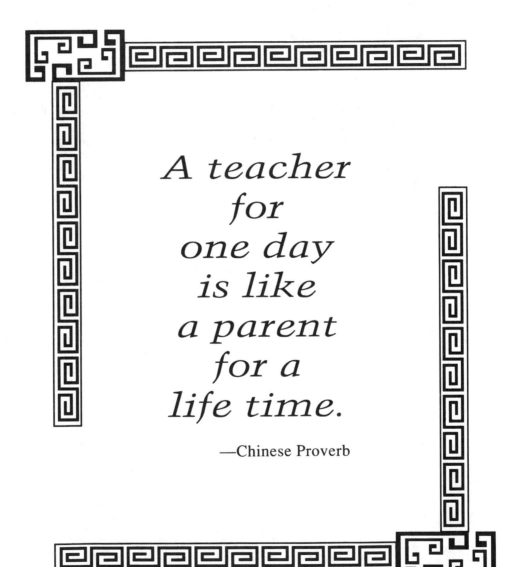

*A teacher
for
one day
is like
a parent
for a
life time.*

—Chinese Proverb

Appendix

Developing Your Multicultural Knowledge Base: Recommended Readings and Resources

As you work with information presented in the ten chapters of *Multicultural Teaching,* you will find these extensive lists of books helpful as you develop units of study. After you have completed this textbook, the lists will prove invaluable to you to support your teaching in any K–8 classroom.

While using this detailed list of resources, you will want to continue expanding the list in areas that particularly interest you. For example, if you plan a broad study of Japan and Japanese Americans, you will want to explore *Japanese Education Today,* a publication from the U.S. Department of Education. Note that most resources listed in the preceding chapters are not included in the Appendix.

MULTICULTURAL UNDERSTANDINGS: INTERGROUP RELATIONS, ETHNIC STUDIES, GLOBAL EDUCATION

The books listed here will extend your knowledge and understanding about the diverse cultures and groups that make up the population of the United States. At the same time, you will become aware of the universal concerns that transcend national borders.

James A. Banks. *Multiethnic Education: Theory and Practice.* 3rd ed. Allyn and Bacon, 1993.

James A. Banks. *Teaching Strategies for Ethnic Studies.* 6th ed. Allyn and Bacon, 1997. A good overview with many suggestions for the adult reader; suggests books that will provide information about specific ethnic groups.

Christine Bennett. *Comprehensive Multicultural Education: Theory and Practice.* 4th ed. Allyn and Bacon, 1999.

California State Dept. of Education. *Studies of Immersion Education: A Collection for U.S. Educators.* The Department, 1984.

Robert A. Carlson. *The Quest for Conformity: Americanization through Education.* Wiley, 1975. Explains hostility toward nonconformity; gives historical perspective.

H. T. Collins and S. B. Zakariya, eds. *Getting Started in Global Education.* NAESP, 1982. Good overview of this viewpoint.

Arthur Combs. *A Personal Approach to Teaching: Beliefs That Make a Difference.* Allyn and Bacon, 1992.

Francesco Cordasco, ed. *American Ethnic Groups: The European Heritage.* Arno, 1980.

CIBC Racism and Sexism Resource Center for Educators. *Human and Anti-Human Values in Children's Books: Guidelines for the Future.* The Council, 1996. Analyzes over 200 books and explores hidden messages transmitted to young readers.

Leonard Davidman. *Teaching with a Multicultural Perspecitve.* Longman, 1994.

Henry Ferguson. *Manual for Multicultural Education,* Intercultural Press, 1987.

Angela Grunsell. *Let's Talk about "Racism."* Gloucester, 1991.

J. Joseph Huthmacher. *A Nation of Newcomers: Ethnic Minority Groups in American History.* Dell, 1981.

Minnesota Humanities Commission. *Braided Lives.* The Commission, 1991.

Joan Morrison and Charlotte Zabusky. *American Mosaic: The Immigrant Experience in the Words of Those Who Lived It.* Dutton, 1981. Oral history.

Thomas Sowell, *Race and Culture.* Basic Books, 1994.

Stephen Thernstrom et al. *Encyclopedia of American Ethnic Groups.* Harvard University Press, 1980.

Background Information about the World

If you are near a large city, visit the embassies of specific countries. If not, you can write on school stationery to request free information.

Africa

Ghana: Press Attaché, Embassy of Ghana, 2460 16th St., NW., Washington, DC 20009.

Tunisia: Embassy of Tunisia, 2408 Massachusetts Ave., NW., Washington, DC 20008.

Union of South Africa: Information Service of South Africa, 655 Madison Ave., New York, NY 10021.

Asia, Middle East, and the Pacific

Australia: Australian News and Information Bureau, 636 Fifth Ave., New York, NY 10020.

Burma: Embassy of the Union of Burma, 2300 S St., NW., Washington, DC 20008.

China: Embassy of the Republic of China, 552 National Press Building, Washington, DC 20004.

India: Information Service of India, 2107 Massachusetts Ave., NW., Washington, DC 20008.

Indonesia: Embassy of the Republic of Indonesia, 2020 Massachusetts Ave., NW., Washington, DC 20006.

Iraq: Embassy of the Republic of Iraq, 1801 P St., NW., Washington, DC 20036.

Israel: Consul General of Israel, 105 Montgomery St., San Francisco, CA 94104.

Japan: Information Section, Embassy of Japan, 2514 Massachusetts Ave., NW., Washington, DC 20008.

Jordan: Embassy of the Hashemite Kingdom of Jordan, 2319 Wyoming Ave., NW., Washington, DC 20008.

Korea: Embassy of Korea, 1145 19th St., NW., Suite 312, Washington, DC 20036.

Malaysia: Embassy of Malaysia, 2401 Massachusetts Ave., NW., Washington, DC 20008.

New Zealand: New Zealand Embassy, 19 Observatory Circle, NW., Washington, DC 20008.

Pakistan: Embassy of Pakistan, 2315 Massachusetts Ave., NW., Washington, DC 20008.

Russia: Russian Embassy, 1706 18th St., NW., Washington DC 20009.

Sri Lanka: Embassy of Sri Lanka, 2148 Wyoming Ave., Washington, DC 20008.

Turkey: Turkey Tourism & Information Office, 500 Fifth Ave., New York, NY 10036.

Canada

Canadian Government Travel Bureau, Ottawa, Ontario, Canada K1A 0H6.

Alberta: Alberta Government Travel Bureau, 1629 Centennial Building, Edmonton, Alberta, Canada T5J 4L6.

British Columbia: Dept. of Travel Industry, Govt. of British Columbia, 1019 Wharf St., Victoria, British Columbia, Canada V8W 2Z2.

Greater Vancouver Visitors and Convention Bureau, 650 Burrard St., Vancouver, British Columbia, Canada V6C 2L2.

Manitoba: Manitoba Tourist Branch, Dept. of Tourism and Recreation, Winnipeg 1, Manitoba, Canada.

Yukon: Yukon Tourism, Travel and Information Branch, Govt. of the Yukon, Box 2703, Whitehorse, Yukon, Canada.

New Brunswick Tourism, Post Office Box 12345, Fredericton, New Brunswick, Canada E3B 5C3.

Ontario Travel, Queen's Park, Toronto, Ontario, Canada M7A 2E5.

Québec Tourisme, C.P. 979, Québec, Canada 83C ZW3.

Saskatchewan Tourism, 1919 Saskatchewan Drive, Regina, Saskatchewan, Canada S4P 3V7.

Europe

Denmark: Danish Information Office, 280 Park Ave., New York, NY 10017.

Finland: Embassy of Finland, 1900 24th St., NW., Washington, DC 20008.

France: French Government Tourist Office, 972 Fifth Ave., New York, NY 10021.

Germany: German Information Center, 410 Park Ave., New York, NY 10022.

Ireland: Irish International Airlines, 564 Fifth Ave., New York, NY 10036.

Italy: Italian Government Travel Office-ENIT, 630 Fifth Ave., New York, NY 10020.

Netherlands: Royal Netherlands Embassy, 4200 Linnean Ave., NW., Washington, DC 20008.

Norway: Norwegian Embassy Information Service, 825 Third Ave., New York, NY 10022.

Portugal: Casa de Portugal, Portuguese National Tourist Office, 570 Fifth Ave., New York, NY 10036.

Spain: Spanish Embassy, Cultural Relations Office, 1629 Columbia Rd., NW., Washington, DC 20009.

Switzerland: Swiss National Tourist Office, 661 Market St., San Francisco, CA 94105.

South America

Colombia: Information Services Staff, Foreign Agricultural Information Division, U.S. Dept. of Agriculture.

Ecuador: Embassy of Ecuador, 2535 15th St., NW., Washington, DC 20009.

Venezuela: Embassy of Venezuela, Institute of Information and Culture, 2437 California St., NW., Washington, DC 20008.

United States

Here is a list for requesting tourist information from the 50 states and the District of Columbia. Postcards are best for mail requests.

Alabama: Bureau of Tourism and Travel, Post Office Box 4309, Montgomery, AL 36103.

Alaska: Division of Tourism, Post Office Box 110801, Juneau, AK 99811.

Arizona: Office of Tourism, 1100 West Washington Street, Phoenix, AZ 85007.

Arkansas: Tourism Office, 1 Capitol Mall, Little Rock, AR 72201.

California: Office of Tourism, Post Office Box 9278, Van Nuys, CA 91409.

Colorado: Tourism Board, Post Office Box 38700, Denver, CO 80238.

Connecticut: Department of Economic Development, 865 Brook Street, Rocky Hill, CT 06067.

Delaware: Tourism Office, 99 Kings Highway, Box 1401, Dover, DE 19903.

District of Columbia: Convention and Visitors Association, 1212 New York Avenue, NW, Washington, DC 20005.

Florida: Division of Tourism, 126 West Van Buren Street, Tallahassee, FL 32399.

Georgia: Department of Industry and Trade, Box 1776, Atlanta, GA 30301.

Hawaii: Department of Tourism, 2270 Kalkaua Avenue, Suite 801, Honolulu, HI 96815.

Idaho: Department of Commerce, 700 West State Street, Boise, ID 83720.

Illinois: Bureau of Tourism, 100 West Randolph, Suite 3-400, Chicago, IL 60601.

Indiana: Division of Tourism, 1 North Capitol, Suite 700, Indianapolis, IN 46204.

Iowa: Department of Tourism, 200 East Grand, Des Moines, IA 50309.

Kansas: Travel and Tourism Division, 400 Southwest Eighth Street, Fifth floor, Topeka, KS 66603.

Kentucky: Department of Travel Development, 2200 Capital Plaza Tower, Frankfort, KY 40601.

Louisiana: Office of Tourism, Post Office Box 94291, L.O.T., Baton Rouge, LA 70804.

Maine: Office of Tourism, 189 State House Station 59, Augusta, ME 04333.

Maryland: Office of Tourism Development, 217 East Redwood Street, Baltimore, MD 21202.

Massachusetts: Office of Travel and Tourism, 100 Cambridge Street, 13th floor, Boston, MA 02202.

Michigan: Travel Bureau, Post Office Box 30226, Lansing, MI 48909.

Minnesota: Office of Tourism, 375 Jackson Street, 250 Skyway Level, St. Paul, MN 55101.

Mississippi: Department of Tourism, Post Office Box 22825, Jackson, MS 39205.

Missouri: Division of Tourism, Post Office Box 1055, Jefferson City, MO 65102.

Montana: Travel Montana, Room 259, Deer Lodge, MT 59722.

Nebraska: Division of Travel and Tourism, 301 Centennial Mall South, Room 88937, Lincoln, NE 68509.

Nevada: Commission on Tourism, Carson City, NV 89710.

New Hampshire: Office of Travel and Tourist Development, Post Office Box 856, Concord, NH 03301.

New Jersey: Division of Travel and Tourism, 20 West State Street, C.N. 826, Trenton, NJ 08625.

New Mexico: Tourism and Travel Division, Post Office Box 20003, Santa Fe, NM 87503.

New York: State Department of Economic Development, 1 Commerce Plaza, Albany, NY 12245.

North Carolina: Division of Travel and Tourism, 430 North Salisbury Street, Raleigh, NC 27603.

North Dakota: Parks and Tourism Department, Capitol Grounds, Bismarck, ND 58505.

Ohio: Division of Travel and Tourism, Post Office Box 1001, Columbus, OH 43266.

Oklahoma: Tourism and Recreation Department, 500 Will Rogers Building, Oklahoma City, OK 73105.

Oregon: Tourism Division, 775 Summer Street N.E., Salem, OR 97310.

Pennsylvania: Office of Travel Marketing, Post Office Box 61, Warrendale, PA 15086.

Rhode Island: Tourism Division, 7 Jackson Walkway, Providence, RI 02903.

South Carolina: Division of Tourism, Post Office Box 71, Room 902, Columbia, SC 29202.

South Dakota: Department of Tourism, 711 East Wells Avenue, Pierre, SD 57501.

Tennessee: Department of Tourism Development, Post Office Box 23170, Nashville, TN 37202.

Texas: Department of Commerce, Tourism Division, Post Office Box 12728, Austin, TX 78711.

Utah: Travel Council, Council Hall, Capitol Hill, Salt Lake City, UT 84114.

Vermont: Travel Division, 134 State Street, Montpelier, VT 05602.

Virginia: Division of Tourism, 1021 East Cary Street, Richmond, VA 23219.

Washington: State Tourism, Post Office Box 42513, Olympia, WA 98504.

West Virginia: Division of Tourism and Parks, 1900 Washington Street East, Building 6, Charleston, WV 25305.

Wisconsin: Division of Tourism Development, Post Office Box 7606, Madison, WI 53707.

Wyoming: Division of Tourism, I-25 at College Drive, Cheyenne, WY 82002.

Newsletters and Journals

Each month a number of newsletters and journals report promising practices related to multicultural education, lists of books, and other instructional materials of interest to teachers. Request sample copies and information about subscribing to those that have something to offer your staff.

The Booklist and Subscription Books Bulletin: A Guide to Current Books. American Library Association. 60 E. Huron St., Chicago, IL 60611. Request *Book Links*.

Booknotes. World Affairs Council of Northern California, 312 Sutter St., Suite 200, San Francisco, CA 94108.

The Bulletin. Council of Interracial Books for Children, CIBC Resource Center, Room 300, 1841 Broadway, New York, NY 10023.

Bulletin of the Center for Children's Books. University of Chicago Press, Box 37005, Chicago, IL 60637. Reviews new books and makes recommendations about purchasing.

Canadian Ethnic Studies. The University of Calgary, Calgary, Alberta, Canada.

Civil Rights Digest. United States Commission on Civil Rights, 1121 Vermont Ave., NW, Washington, DC 20425.

Colloquy. School Program, World Affairs Council, 312 Sutter St., San Francisco, CA 94108. Excellent source of up-to-date information and publication lists.

Education and Society. Anti-Defamation League, 823 United Nations Plaza, New York, NY 10017.

Explorations in Ethnic Studies. Journal of the National Assn. of Interdisciplinary Ethnic Studies, California State Polytechnic University, 3801 W. Temple Ave., Pomona, CA 91768.

The Horn Book Magazine. Park Square Bld., Boston, MA 02116. Good articles; lists information about new books and authors.

Integrated Education. Integrated Education Associates, School of Education, University of Massachusetts, Amherst, MA 01003.

Journal of Comparative Cultures. National Bilingual Education Assn., 9332 Vista Bonita, Cypress, CA 90630.

Journal of Ethnic Studies. Western Washington State University, Bellingham, WA 98225.

Journal of the National Association for Bilingual Education. 1201 16th St., NW., Washington, DC 20036.

Kirkus Reviews. 200 Park Ave. S, New York, NY 10003 (Bimonthly).

Language Arts (with membership in NCTE). 1111 Kenyon Rd., Urbana, IL 61801. Articles on all aspects of language instruction; reviews books for children and professional materials; often features authors with full-page photo.

Melus: The Multi-Ethnic Literature of the United States. Dept. of English, University of Southern California, Los Angeles, CA 90007.

Multicultural Education. National Assn. for Multicultural Education. Caddo Gap Publicationa, 3145 Geary Blvd. #275, San Francisco CA 94118.

NABE: Journal of National Association of Bilingual Educators. Alma Flor Ada, ed. Los Angeles Publishing Co., 40-22 23rd St., Long Island City, New York, NY 11101. Subscription free with membership, quarterly publication.

The Negro Educational Review. Box 2895, General Mail Center, Jacksonville, FL 32203.

School Library Journal. 1180 Avenue of the Americas, New York, NY 10036.

Social Education. National Council for the Social Studies, 3501 Newark St., NW., Washington, DC 20016.

TESOL Newsletter, TESOL Quarterly. Teachers of English to Speakers of Other Languages, 455 Nevits, Georgetown University, Washington, DC 20057.

STUDYING SPECIFIC GROUPS

As we work with students in the classroom, we can develop units of study focused on one specific group. At that time students can read fiction and nonfiction to learn more about one part of our American multiculture.

Included here are lists of books for adults, information for students, bibliographies of available materials, and sources of additional up-to-date information and resources. Although these lists are not exhaustive, they do provide titles to get you started. Always consult your local librarians and the library catalog to locate other materials. Also refer to such reference tools as *Children's Catalog, The High School Catalog, Education Index,* and

Reader's Guide to Periodical Literature to continue locating new books and articles that may help you.

Exploring the Backgrounds of Asian Americans

This section explores books and resources that provide information about Americans who have Chinese, Japanese, Korean, Filipino, or Vietnamese backgrounds. More information is listed in the following sections under specific groups.

General Resources

Don Nasanishi, ed. *Asians and the American Educational Process.* Oryx Press, 1982.

Franklin Odo. *In Movement: A Pictorial History of Asian America.* Visual Communications, 1977.

Linda Perrin. *Coming to America.* Delacorte, 1980.

Amy Tachiki et al., eds. *Roots: An Asian American Reader.* University of California at Los Angeles, 1971.

Periodicals

Amerasia Journal (irregular). Asian American Studies Center, 3232 Campbell Hall, UCLA, Los Angeles, CA 90024.

Asian American Review (irregular). Asian American Studies, 3407 Dwinelle Hall, Berkeley, CA 94720.

Bridge: An Asian American Perspective (quarterly). Box 477, Canal Station, New York, NY 10013.

Bulletin of Concerned Asian Scholars (quarterly). Box W, Charlemont, MA 01339.

Intercom (3–5 times a year). The Center for War/Peace Studies, 218 E. 18th St., New York, NY 10003. Articles on issues, resources, and guides for teachers on subjects related to Asia.

Additional Sources

Asia Society. 725 Park Avenue, New York, NY 10021.

Asian Writers' Project/Asian Media Project. *Sojourner.* Berkeley Unified School District.

UNICEF. *Children of Asia.* 331 E. 38th St., New York, NY 10016.

Visual Communications. Asian American Studies Central, 1601 Griffith Park Blvd., Los Angeles, CA 90026.

Exploring the Backgrounds of Chinese Americans

General Resources

China Books & Periodicals, Inc. 2929 Twenty-fourth Street, San Francisco, CA 94110. (Subscriptions to magazines published in China; English language).

China International Travel Service. 6 East Chang'an Avenue, Beijing, People's Republic of China.

East/West: The Chinese American Journal (weekly). 838 Grant Avenue, Suite 307, San Francisco, CA 94108.

U.S.–China Peoples Friendship Association. 50 Oak Street, San Francisco, CA 94102.

Teaching Materials

Center for Teaching about China. 407 So. Dearborn St., Suite 945, Chicago, IL 60605.

The China Project. Hoover Bldg., Stanford University, Stanford, CA 94305.

Ed Young and Hilary Beckett. *The Rooster's Horns.* World, 1978. (Directions for producing a puppet play.)

Fiction

Frank Chin. *The Chicken Coop Chinaman: The Year of the Dragon: Two Plays.* University of Washington, 1981.

Maxine Hong Kingston. *China Men.* Ballantine Books, 1980.

———. *The Woman Warrior: Memoirs of a Girlhood among Ghosts.* Vintage, 1976.

Books for Students

Fiction

Kathleen Chang. *The Iron Moonhunter.* Children's Book Press, 1977.

A. B. Chrisman. *Shen of the Sea: Chinese Stories for Children.* Dutton, 1968. Short stories.

M. DeJong. *The House of Sixty Fathers.* Harper and Row, 1956.

Demi. *Liang and the Magic Paintbrush.* Holt, 1980.

Eleanor Estes. *The Lost Umbrella of Kim Chu.* Atheneum, 1979.

M. Flack and K. Wiese. *The Story of Ping, A Duck Who Lived on a Houseboat on the Yangtze River.* Viking, 1933.

*T. Handforth. *Mei Li.* Doubleday, 1938.

*E. Lattimore. *Little Pear: The Story of a Little Chinese Boy.* Harcourt Brace Jovanovich, 1931.

E. Lewis. *Young Fu of the Upper Yangtze,* rev. ed. Holt, Rinehart and Winston, 1973.

R. L. McCune. *Pie-Biter.* Design Enterprises of San Francisco, 1983.

Leo Politi. *Mr. Fong's Shop.* Scribner's, 1979.

A. Ritchie. *The Treasure of Li-Po.* Harcourt Brace Jovanovich, 1949. Short stories.

Jay Williams. *Everyone Knows What a Dragon Looks Like.* Four Winds, 1976.

Jade Snow Wong. *Fifth Chinese Daughter.* Harper, 1945.

Laurence Yep. *Child of the Owl.* Harper, 1977.

Jane Yolen. *The Seeing Stick.* Crowell, 1977.

Nonfiction

Jack Chen. *The Chinese of America.* New York: Harper and Row, 1980.

Dorothy Dowdell. *The Chinese Helped Build America.* Messner, 1972.

Leonard Fisher. *The Great Wall of China.* Macmillan, 1986.

Jean Fritz. *China Homecoming.* Putnam, 1985.

Clarence Glick. *Sojourners and Settlers.* University of Hawaii, 1980.

Noel Gray. *Looking at China.* Lippincott, 1975.

Minfong Ho. *Maples in the Mist.* Lothrop, 1996.

Corrine Hoexter. *From Canton to California.* Four Winds, 1976.

Ellen Hsiao. *A Chinese Year.* Evans, 1970.

Pat Mauser. *A Bundle of Sticks.* Atheneum, 1982.

Ruthanne Lum McCunn. *An Illustrated History of the Chinese in America.* Design Enterprises of San Francisco, 1979.

Milton Meltzer. *The Chinese Americans.* Crowell, 1980.

Joe Molnar. *A Chinese-American Child Tells His Story.* Watts, 1973.

Victor Nee and Brett D. Nee, eds. *Longtime Californians: A Documentary Study of an American Chinatown.* Pantheon, 1972.

J. R. Roberson. *China from Manchu to Mao.* Atheneum, 1980.

Bonnie Shemie. *Houses of China.* Tundra Books, 1996.

Stan Steiner. *Fusang: The Chinese Who Built America.* Harper, 1979.

Betty Lee Sung. *An Album of Chinese Americans.* Watts, 1977.

———. *The Chinese in America.* Macmillan, 1972.

Ed Young. *High on a Hill: A Book of Chinese Riddles.* World, 1980.

Folklore

*Claire Bishop. *The Five Chinese Brothers.* Coward, 1938.

Frances Carpenter. *Tales of a Chinese Grandmother.* Doubleday, 1937.

Hou-tien Cheng. *Six Chinese Brothers.* Holt, 1979.

Marilee Heyer. *The Weaving of a Dream.* Viking, 1986.

Lotta Hume. *Favorite Children's Stories from China and Tibet.* Tuttle, 1962.

Carol Kendall and Yao-wen Li. *Sweet and Sour: Tales from China.* Seabury, 1982.

Jeanne Lee. *Legend of the Li River.* Holt, 1983.

———. *Toad Is the Uncle of Heaven.* Holt, 1985.

Ai-Ling Louie. *Yeh-Shen: A Cinderella Story from China.* Philomel, 1982.

Neil Philip, ed. *The Spring of Butterflies and Other Folktales of China's Minority Peoples.* Lothrop, 1986.

Catherine Sadler. *Treasure Mountain: Folktales from Southern China.* Atheneum, 1982.

Diane Wolkstein. *White Wave: A Chinese Tale.* Crowell, 1982.

*Jane Yolen. *The Emperor and the Kite.* World, 1957.

Ed Young. *The Terrible Nung Gwama: A Chinese Tale.* Philomel, 1978.

Diane Wokstein. *White Wave: A Chinese Tale.* Harcourt, 1996.

Nathan Zimelman. *I Will Tell You of Peach Stone.* Lothrop, 1976.

Feenie Ziner. *Cricket Boy: A Chinese Tale Retold.* Doubleday, 1977.

Exploring the Backgrounds of Japanese Americans

General Resources

Japan Chronicle. The Pacific and Asian Affairs Council, Pacific House, 2004 University Ave., Honolulu, HI 96822.

Japan External Trade Organization (JETRO). 360 Post St., Suite 501, San Francisco, CA 94108.

Japan Information Service. 1737 Post St., Suites 4–5, San Francisco, CA 94115.

Japanese American Citizenship League. 224 So. San Pedro St., Room 506, Los Angeles, CA 90012.

Japanese American Curriculum Project. Box 367, San Mateo, CA 94401.

Nichi Bei Times (daily). 2211 Bush St., San Francisco, CA 94119 (in Japanese and English).

Social Studies Development Center. Indiana University, 2805 E. 10th St., Bloomington, IN 47405.

Stanford Program on International and Cross-Cultural Education: The Japan Project. Stanford University, Stanford, CA 94305.

Books for Adults

Frank Gibney. *Japan: The Fragile Superpower.* New American Library, 1985.

Akemi Kikumura. *Through Harsh Winters: The Life of a Japanese Immigrant Woman.* Chandler, 1981.

Joy Kogawa. *Obasan: A Novel.* Godine, 1982.

Gene Levine and Robert Rhodes. *The Japanese American Community: A Three-Generation Study.* Praeger, 1981.

Edwin Reishauer. *The Japanese.* Harvard, 1977.

Thomas Rohlen. *Japan's High Schools.* University of California, 1983.

Jared Taylor. *Shadows of the Rising Sun.* Morrow, 1983.

United States Department of Education. *Japanese Education Today.* U.S. Government Printing Office, 1987.

Robert Wilson and Bill Hosokawa. *East to Africa: A History of the Japanese in the United States.* Morrow, 1980.

Books for Students

Fiction

Pearl Buck. *The Big Wave.* Day, 1948 (new edition 1973).

Hadley Irwin. *Kim/Kimi.* Macmillan, 1987.

*Tony Johnston. *Fishing Sunday.* Morrow, 1996.

Tetsuko Kuroyanagi. *Totto-Chan.* Harper, 1982.

Katherine Paterson. *The Master Puppeteer.* Crowell, 1976.

————. *Of Nightingales That Weep.* Crowell, 1974.

*Leo Politi. *Mieko.* Golden Gates, 1969.

Allen Say. *The Inn-keeper's Apprentice.* Harper, 1982.

*Yoshiko Uchida. *The Birthday Visitor.* Scribner's, 1975.

————. *The Best Bad Thing.* Atheneum, 1983.

————. *The Happiest Ending.* Atheneum, 1985.

————. *Journey Home.* Atheneum, 1978.

Yoko Kawashima Watkins. *So Far from the Bamboo Grove.* Lothrop, 1986.

Taro Yashima. *The Golden Footprints.* World, 1960.

————. *A Jar of Dreams.* Atheneum, 1981.

————. *Umbrella.* Viking, 1958.

Nonfiction

*Edith Battles. *What Does the Rooster Say, Yoshio?* Whitman, 1978.

Maisie Conrat and Richard Conrat. *Executive Order 9066: The Internment of 110,000 Japanese Americans.* California Historical Society, 1972.

Jane Dallinger. *Swallowtail Butterflies.* Lerner, 1983 (originally published in Japan).

Daniel Davis. *Behind Barbed Wire.* Dutton, 1982.

Dorothy Dowdell. *The Japanese Helped Build America.* Messner, 1970.

Sam Epstein. *A Year of Japanese Festivals.* Garrard, 1974.

Budd Fukei. *The Japanese American Story.* Dillon, 1976.

Jane Goodsell. *Daniel Inouye.* Crowell, 1977.

Jeanne Wakatsuki Houston and James Houston. *Farewell to Manzanar.* Houghton Mifflin, 1973.

Estelle Ishigo. *Lone Heart Mountain.* Japanese American Curriculum Project.

Takeo Kaneshiro. *Internees War Relocation Center Memoirs and Diaries.* Vantage Press, 1976.

Noel Leathers. *The Japanese in America.* Lerner, 1967.

Toshi Maruki. *Hiroshima No Pika.* Lothrop, 1982.

Robert Masters. *Japan in Pictures.* Sterling, 1978.

Dennis Ogawa. *Jan Ken Po.* Japanese American Research Center, 1973.

Robert San Souci. *The Samurai's Daughter.* Dial, 1992.

Allen Say. *The Bicycle Man.* Parnassus, 1982.

Shizuye Takashima. *A Child in Prison Camp.* Tundra Brooks, 1971.

Tobi Tobias. *Isamu Noguchi: The Life of a Sculptor.* Crowell, 1974.

*Taro Yashima. *The Village Tree.* Viking, 1953.

Folklore

Joanne Algarin. *Japanese Folk Literature: A Core Collection and Reference Guide.* Bowker, 1982.

Virginia Haviland. *Favorite Fairy Tales Told in Japan.* Little, 1967.

Margaret Hodges. *The Wave.* Houghton, 1964.

Jane Hori Ike. *The Japanese Fairy Tale.* Warne, 1982.

Nancy Luenn. *The Dragon Kite.* Harcourt, 1982.

Gerald McDermott. *The Stonecutter.* Viking, 1975.

Arlene Mosel. *The Funny Little Woman.* Dutton, 1972.

Patricia Newton. *The Five Sparrows.* Atheneum, 1982.

*Michelle Nikly. *The Emperor's Plum Tree.* Greenwillow, 1982.

*Allen Say. *Once under the Cherry Blossom Tree.* Harper, 1974.

Yoshiko Uchida. *The Magic Listening Cap.* Harcourt, 1955.

*Taro Yashima. *Seashore Story.* Viking, 1967.

Poetry

Virginia Olsen Baron, ed. *The Seasons of Time; Tanka Poetry of Ancient Japan.* Dial, 1968.

Harry Behn, comp. *Cricket Songs: Japanese Haiku.* Harcourt Brace Jovanovich, 1964.

———. *More Cricket Songs: Japanese Haiku.* Harcourt Brace Jovanovich, 1971.

Sylvia Cassidy, comp. *Birds, Frogs, and Moonlight: Haiku.* Doubleday, 1967.

Richard Lewis, ed. *In a Spring Garden.* Dial, 1965. (Also on film; Weston Woods.)

———. *The Moment of Wonder: A Collection of Chinese and Japanese Poetry.* Dial, 1964.

Exploring the Backgrounds of Korean Americans

Books for Students

Fiction

Elisabet McHugh. *Raising a Mother Isn't Easy.* Greenwillow, 1983.

Nonfiction

Sylvia McNair. *Korea.* Children's Press, 1986.

Wayne Patterson. *The Koreans in America.* Lerner, 1977.

Folklore

Oki S. Han. *Kongi and Potgi: A Cinderella Story from Korea.* Dial, 1996.

So-un Kim. *The Story Bag: A Collection of Korean Folktales.* Tuttle, 1955.

Kathleen Seros. *Sun and Moon: Fairy Tales from Korea.* Holly, 1982.

Exploring the Backgrounds of Filipino Americans

General Resources
Periodicals

Filipino American Herald (monthly). 508 Maynard Avenue, Seattle, WA 98108.

Philippines Mail. Filipino American Media of California, Box 1783, Salinas, CA 93901.

Books for Adults

Carlos Bulosan. *America Is in the Heart.* University of Washington, 1973.

Hyung-chan Kim and Cynthia Mejia, eds. *The Filipinos in America.* Oceana Publications, 1976.

Teresita Laygo, ed. *Well of Time: Eighteen Short Stories from Philippine Contemporary Literature.* American Bilingual Center, 1977.

Alfredo Muñoz. *The Filipinos in America.* Mountainview Press, 1971.

Luis Teodoro. *Out of This Struggle: The Filipinos in Hawaii, 1906–1981.* The University of Hawaii, 1981.

Books for Students
Fiction

*Janet Bartosiak. *A Dog for Ramón.* Dial, 1966.

Carlos Bulosan. *The Laughter of My Father.* Harcourt, 1942.

Al Robles. *Looking for Ifugao Mountain.* Children's Book Press, 1977.

Nonfiction

Manuel Buaken. *I Have Lived with the American People.* Caxton, 1948.

John Nance. *The Land and People of the Philippines.* Lippincott, 1977.

Luis Taruc. *Born of the People.* International Publishers, 1953.

Folklore

Jose Aruego. *A Crocodile's Tale: A Philippine Folk Story.* Scholastic, 1975.

Elizabeth Sechrist. *Once in the First Times: Folk Tales from the Philippines.* Macrae, 1969.

Exploring the Backgrounds of Vietnamese Americans

General Resources

Duong Thanh Binh. *A Handbook for Teachers of Vietnamese Students: Hints for Dealing with Cultural Differences in Schools.* Center for Applied Linguistics, 1975.

Tam Thi Dang Wei. *Vietnamese Refugee Students: A Handbook for School Personnel.* National Assessment and Dissemination Center for Bilingual/Bicultural Education, 1980.

Books for Adults

Charles Anderson. *Vietnam: The Other War.* Presidio Press, 1982.

Frances Fitzgerald. *Fire in the Lake: The Vietnamese and the Americans in Vietnam.* Vintage, 1972.

Bruce Grant, ed. *The Boat People.* Penguin, 1979.

Gail P. Kelly. *From Vietnam to America: A Chronicle of Vietnamese Immigration to the United States.* Westview, 1977.

Stephen Wright. *Meditations In Green.* Scribner's, 1983 (fiction).

Books for Students

Fiction

Rosemary Breckler. *Sweet Dried Apples: A Vietnamese Wartime Childhood.* Houghton Mifflin, 1996.

Tricia Brown. *Lee Ann: The Story of a Vietnamese Girl.* G. P. Putnam's Sons, 1991.

Marylois Dunn. *The Absolutely Perfect Horse.* Harper, 1983.

Katherine Paterson. *Park's Quest.* Dutton, 1988.

Nonfiction

Janet Bode. *New Kids on the Block: Oral Histories of Immigrant Teens.* Franklin Watts, 1989.

Edward F. Dolan. *America after Vietnam: Legacies of a Hated War.* Franklin Watts, 1989.

Mace Goldfarb. *Fighters, Refugees, Immigrants: A Story of the Hmong.* Carolrhoda, 1982.

Peter Goldman and Tony Fuller. *What Vietnam Did to Us.* Morrow, 1983.

James Haskins. *The New Americans: Vietnamese Boat People.* Enslow, 1980.

Don Lawson. *An Album of the Vietnam War.* Watts, 1986.

Robert Mason. *Chickenhawk.* Viking, 1983.

Huynh Quang Nhuong. *The Land I Lost: Adventures of a Boy in Vietnam.* Harper, 1982.

Jon Nielson. *Artist in South Vietnam.* Messner, 1969.

Tim Page. *Tim Page's Vietnam.* Knopf, 1983.

Marc Talbert. *The Purple Heart.* Harper, 1992.

Lynda Van Devanter. *Home before Morning: The Story of an Army Nurse in Vietnam.* Beaufort, 1983.

Folklore

Mark Taylor. *The Fisherman and the Goblin.* Golden Gate, 1971.

L. D. Vuong. *The Brocaded Slipper and Other Vietnamese Tales.* Addison-Wesley, 1982.

Exploring the Backgrounds of Black/African Americans

General Resources

James Banks and Cherry Banks. *March toward Freedom: A History of Black Americans.* Fearon, 1978.

John H. Franklin. *From Slavery to Freedom: A History of Black Americans.* Vintage, 1980.

Alex Haley. *Roots: The Saga of an American Family.* Doubleday, 1976.

Vincent Harding. *There Is a River: The Black Struggle for Freedom in America.* Harcourt, 1981.

W. A. Low and Virgil Clift, eds. *Encyclopedia of Black America.* McGraw-Hill, 1981.

Nelson Mandela. *The Struggle Is My Life.* Pathfinder, 1986.

Rudine Sims. *Shadow and Substance: Afro-American Experience in Contemporary Children's Fiction.* National Council of Teachers of Engish, 1982.

Geneva Smitherman. *Talkin and Testifyin: The Language of Black America.* Houghton Mifflin, 1977.

Periodicals

Africana Library Journal: A Quarterly Bibliography and Resource Guide. 101 Fifth Ave., New York, NY 10003. Evaluations of books on Africa published throughout the world.

The Black Scholar, P.O. Box 908, Sausalito, CA 94965. Valuable book review section.

Crisis. Organization of the National Association for the Advancement of Colored People. The Crisis Publishing Co., 1790 Broadway, New York, NY 10019.

Ebony. Johnson Publishing Co., 1820 S. Michigan Ave., Chicago, IL 60616.

Freedomways. Quarterly Review of the Negro Freedom Movement. Freedomway Associates, 799 Broadway, New York, NY 10013.

Jet. Johnson Publishing Co., 1820 S. Michigan Ave., Chicago, IL 60616.

Journal of Black Studies. 275 S. Beverly Dr., Beverly Hills, CA 90210.

The Journal of Negro History. Published quarterly by the Association for the Study of Negro Life and History, 1538 Ninth Street, NW., Washington, DC 20001. Contains scholarly articles on Negro culture and history, book reviews, important documents.

Negro-American Literature Forum for School and University Teachers. Indiana State University, Terre Haute, IN 47809.

Negro Heritage. P.O. Box 1057, Washington, DC 20013.

Negro History Bulletin. The Association for the Study of Negro Life and History, Inc., 1538 Ninth Street, NW., Washington, DC 20001.

Sepia. Sepia Publishing Co., 1220 Harding St., Fort Worth, TX 76102.

Books for Students

Fiction

C. S. Adler. *Always and Forever Friends.* Clarion, 1988.

Nana H. Agle. *Maple Street.* Seabury, 1970.

Martha Alexander. *Bobo's Dream.* Dial, 1970.

William H. Armstrong. *Sounder.* Harper, 1969.

Simi Bedford. *Yoruba Girl Dancing.* Viking, 1992.

Kathleen Benson. *Joseph on the Subway Trains.* Addison-Wesley, 1981.

Clayton Bess. *Story for a Black Night.* Houghton Mifflin, 1982.

Candy Dawson Boyd. *Circle of Gold.* Scholastic, 1984.

Clyde Bulla. *Charlie's House.* Crowell, 1983.

*Jeannette Caines. *Abby.* Harper, 1973.

*———. *Just Us Women.* Harper, 1982.

Ann Cameron. *More Stories Julian Tells.* Knopf, 1986.

———. *The Stories Julian Tells.* Pantheon, 1981.

Alice Childress. *A Hero Ain't Nothin' but a Sandwich.* Coward, 1973.

Bess Clayton. *Story for a Black Night.* Houghton, 1982.

*Lucille Clifton. *Amifica.* Dutton, 1977.

———. *The Lucky Stone.* Delacorte, 1979.

———. *My Friend Jacob.* Dutton, 1980.

———. *Three Wishes.* Viking, 1976.

Barbara Cohen. *Thank You, Jackie Robinson.* Lothrop, 1974.

James Collier. *Jump Ship to Freedom.* Delacorte, 1981.

Olivia Coolidge. *Come by Here.* Houghton, 1970.

*Pat Cummings. *Jimmy Lee Did It.* Lothrop, 1985.

Beth Engel. *Big Words.* Dutton, 1982.

Nancy Farmer. *The Ear, the Eye, and the Arm.* Orchard, 1994.

*Tom Feelings and Eloise Greenfield. *Daydreams.* Dial, 1981.

Louise Fitzhugh. *Nobody's Family Is Going to Change.* Farrar, 1974.

Paula Fox. *How Many Miles to Babylon?* White, 1967.

*D. Freeman. *Corduroy.* Viking, 1968.

Jean Fritz. *Brady.* Coward, 1960.

Lorenz Graham. *North Town (and other titles).* Crowell, 1965.

Bette Greene. *Get On out of Here, Philip Hall.* Dial, 1981.

———. *Philip Hall Likes Me, I Reckon Maybe.* Dial, 1974.

*Eloise Greenfield. *Grandmamma's Joy.* Collins, 1980.

———. *Me and Nessie.* Crowell, 1975.

———. *Sister.* Crowell, 1974.

———. *Talk about a Family.* Lippincott, 1978.

Virginia Hamilton. *Arilla Sun Down.* Greenwillow, 1976.

———. *M. C. Higgins the Great.* Macmillan, 1974.

———. *The Magical Adventures of Pretty Pearl.* Harper, 1983.

———. *The Time-Ago Tales of Jahdu.* Macmillan, 1969. Short stories.

———. *Zeely.* Macmillan. 1967.

Sarah Hayes. *Happy Christmas, Gemma.* Lothrop, 1986.

William Hooks. *Circle of Fire.* Atheneum, 1982.

Lila Hopkins. *Eating Crow.* Watts, 1988.

Kristin Hunter. *Soul Brothers and Sister Lou.* Scribner's, 1968.

Belinda Hurmence. *A Girl Called Boy.* Clarion, 1982.

Hadley Irwin. *I Be Somebody.* Atheneum. 1984.

June Jordan. *Kimakao's Story.* Houghton, 1982.

———. *New Life: New Room.* Crowell, 1975.

Elaine Konigsburg. *Jennifer, Hecate, Macbeth, William McKinley, and Me, Elizabeth.* Atheneum, 1967.

Jill Krementz. *Sweet Pea: A Black Girl Growing up in the Rural South.* Harcourt, 1969.

Julius Lester. *This Strange New Feeling.* Dial, 1982.

*Joan Lexau. *Benjie.* Dial, 1964.

*———. *I Should Have Stayed in Bed.* Harper, 1965.

*———. *Me Day.* Dial, 1971.

*Lessie Little and Eloise Greenfield. *I Can Do It Myself.* Crowell, 1978.

*Sharon Bell Mathis. *The Hundred Penny Box.* Viking, 1976.

———. *Teacup Full of Roses.* Viking, 1972.

Walter Myers. *Mojo and the Russians.* Viking, 1977.

Ann Petry. *Tituba of Salem Village.* Crowell, 1964.

*Anita Riggio, *Secret Signs Along the Underground Railroad.* Boyd Mills, 1997.

Harriette Robinet. *Ride the Red Cycle.* Houghton, 1980.

———. *Washington City Is Burning.* Atheneum, 1996.

John Rosenburg. *William Parker: Rebel Without Rights.* Millbrook, 1996.

Ouida Sebestyen. *Words by Heart.* Little, 1979.

John Shearer. *I Wish I Had an Afro.* Cowles. 1970.

Louisa Shotwell. *Roosevelt Grady.* Collins, 1963.

Alfred Slote. *Jake.* Lippincott, 1971.

John Steptoe. *Marcia.* Viking, 1976.

———. *Train Ride.* Harper, 1971.

———. *Uptown.* Harper, 1970.

Eleanor Tate. *Just an Overnight Guest.* Dial, 1980.

Mildred Taylor. *Let the Circle Be Unbroken.* Dial, 1981.

————. *Song of the Trees.* Dial, 1975.

Theodore Taylor. *The Cay.* Doubleday, 1969.

Ianthe Thomas. *Hi, Mrs. Mallory.* Harper, 1979.

*————. *Walk Home Tired, Billy Jenkins.* Harper, 1974.

*————. *Willie Blows a Mean Horn.* Harper, 1981.

Janice Udry. *What Mary Jo Shared.* Whitman, 1966.

Cynthia Voight. *Come a Stranger.* Atheneum, 1986.

Jane Wagner. *J. T.* Dell, 1971.

Mildred Walter. *The Girl on the Outside.* Lothrop, 1982.

Karen Whiteside. *Brother Mouky and the Falling Sun.* Harper, 1980.

Brenda Wilkinson. *Not Separate, Not Equal.* Harper, 1987.

Vera Williams. *Cherries and Cherry Pits.* Greenwillow, 1986.

Jeanette Winter. *Follow the Drinking Gourd.* Knopf, 1998.

Nonfiction

Ashley Bryan. *I'm Going to Sing: Black American Spirituals.* Vol. 2. Atheneum, 1982.

H. Buckmaster. *Flight to Freedom.* Crowell, 1958.

Burke Davis. *Black Heroes of the American Revolution.* Harcourt, 1976.

Eloise Greenfield. *Childtimes: A Three Generation Memoir.* Crowell, 1979.

James Haskins. *Black Theater in America.* Crowell, 1982.

Jesse Jackson. *Blacks in America.* Messner, 1973.

Julius Lester. *To Be a Slave.* Dial, 1968.

Milton Meltzer. *All Times, All Peoples: A World History of Slavery.* Harper, 1980.

————. *The Truth about the Ku Klux Klan.* Watts, 1982.

Christine Price. *Dance on the Dusty Earth.* Scribner's, 1982.

Roger Rosen and Patra McSharry, eds. *Apartheid: Calibrations of Color.* Icarus World Issues Series. Rosen Publishing Group, 1991.

Conrad Stein. *Kenya.* Children's Press, 1985.

Charles Sullivan, ed. *Children of Promise: African-American Literature and Art for Young People.* Harry Abrams, 1991.

Courtni Wright. *Journey to Freedom: A Story of the Underground Railroad.* Holiday, 1994.

Karen Zeinert. *The Amistad Slave Revolt and American Abolition.* Linnet, 1997.

Biography

David Adler. *Martin Luther King: Free at Last.* Holiday, 1986.

*Aliki. *A Week Is a Flower: The Life of George Washington Carver.* Prentice-Hall, 1965.

Caroline Arnold. *Pelé: The King of Soccer.* Watts, 1992.

Roland Bertol. *Charles Drew.* Crowell, 1970.

Arna Bontemps. *Fredrick Douglass: Slave—Fighter—Freeman.* Knopf, 1959.

Susan Brownmiller. *Shirley Chisholm.* Doubleday, 1970.

A' Lelia P. Bundles. *Madam C. J. Walker.* Chelsea, 1991.

James Collier. *Louis Armstrong: An American Success Story.* Macmillan, 1985.

Jean Cornell. *Louis Armstrong, Ambassador Satchmo.* Garrard, 1979.

Ossie Davis. *Langston: A Play.* Delacorte, 1982.

Esther Douty. *Charlotte Forten: Free Black Teacher.* Garrard, 1971.

Ophelia Egypt. *James Weldon Johnson.* Crowell, 1974.

Mark Evans. *Scott Joplin and the Ragtime Years.* Dodd, 1976.

Doris Faber. *The Assassination of Martin Luther King, Jr.* Watts, 1978.

*Tom Feelings. *Black Pilgrimage.* Lothrop, 1972.

H. Felton. *Edward Rose: Negro Trail Blazer.* Dodd, 1967.

———. *Mumbet: The Story of Elizabeth Freeman.* Dodd, 1970.

Franklin Folsom. *The Life and Legends of George McJunkin, Black Cowboy.* Nelson, 1973.

Florence Freedman. *Two Tickets to Freedom: The True Story of Ellen and William Craft, Fugitive Slaves.* Simon and Schuster, 1971.

Miriam Fuller. *Phillis Wheatley: America's First Black Poet(ess).* Garrard, 1971.

Berry Gordy. *Movin' Up.* Harper, 1979.

Shirley Graham. *Booker T. Washington.* Messner, 1955.

Eloise Greenfield. *Paul Robeson.* Crowell, 1975.

———. *Rosa Parks.* Crowell, 1973.

——— and Lessie Jones Little. *Childtimes: A Three-Generation Memoir.* Crowell, 1982.

Virginia Hamilton. *Paul Robeson: The Life and Times of a Free Black Man.* Harper, 1974.

———. *W. E. B. Du Bois.* Crowell, 1972.

Richard Hardwick. *Charles Richard Drew.* Scribner's, 1967.

James Haskins. *From Lew Alcindor to Kareem Abdul Jabbar.* Lothrop, 1972.

———. *I'm Gonna Make You Love Me: The Story of Diana Ross.* Dial, 1980.

———. *Katherine Dunham.* Coward, 1982.

———. *The Life and Time of Martin Luther King, Jr.* Lothrop, 1977.

———. *One More River to Cross: The Stories of Twelve Black Americans.* Scholastic, 1992.

———. *A Piece of the Power: Four Black Mayors.* Dial, 1972.

———. *Shirley Chisholm.* Dial, 1975.

Robert Hayden. *Eight Black American Inventors.* Addison-Wesley, 1972.

———, ed. *Kaleidoscope: Poems by American Negro Poets.* Harcourt, 1967.

————. *Seven Black Scientists.* Addison-Wesley, 1970.

Hettie Jones. *Big Star Fallin' Mama: Five Women in Black Music.* Viking, 1974.

June Jordan. *Fannie Lou Hamer.* Crowell, 1972.

————. *Harriet and the Runaway Book: The Story of Harriet Beecher Stowe.* Harper, 1977.

Mervyn Kaufman. *Jessie Owens.* Crowell, 1973.

Bill Libby. *Joe Louis, The Brown Bomber.* Lothrop, 1980.

————. *The Reggie Jackson Story.* Lothrop, 1979.

Aletha Lindstrom. *Sojourner Truth.* Messner, 1980.

Robert Lipsyte. *Free to Be Muhammad Ali.* Harper, 1978.

Polly Longsworth. *Charlotte Forten: Black and Free.* Crowell, 1970.

Sharon Bell Mathis. *Ray Charles.* Crowell, 1973.

Ann McGovern. *Runaway Slave: The Story of Harriet Tubman.* Four Winds, 1965.

Patricia McKissack. *Mary McLeod Bethune: A Great American Educator.* Childrens, 1985.

Milton Meltzer. *Langston Hughes.* Crowell, 1968.

Howard Meyer. *Colonel of the Black Regiment: The Life of Thomas Wentworth Higginson.* Norton, 1967.

Elizabeth Montgomery. *Duke Ellington: King of Jazz.* Garrard, 1972.

————. *William C. Handy: Father of the Blues.* Garrard, 1968.

Carman Moore. *Somebody's Angel Child: The Story of Bessie Smith.* Crowell, 1970.

Elizabeth Myers. *Langston Hughes.* Garrard, 1970.

Corinne Naden. *Ronald McNair* (Black American of Achievement). Chelsea, 1991.

Shirlee Newman. *Marian Anderson.* Westminster, 1966.

Victoria Ortiz. *Sojourner Truth.* Lippincott, 1974.

Steve Otfinowski. *Marian Wright: Defender of Children's Rights.* Blackbirdy Rosen, 1991.

Rosa Parks. *Rosa Parks: My Story.* Dial, 1992.

Diane Patrick. *Coretta Scott King.* Franklin Watts, 1991.

Lillie Patterson. *Benjamin Banneker.* Abington, 1978.

————. *Sure Hands, Strong Heart: The Life of Daniel Hale Williams.* Abington, 1981.

Kathilyn S. Probosz. *Alvin Ailey.* Bantam, 1991.

Charlemae Rollins. *Famous American Negro Poets.* Dodd, 1965.

Pearle Schulz. *Paul Laurence Dunbar.* Garrard, 1974.

*Alan Schroeder. *Satchmo's Blues.* Doubleday, 1996. (Fictionalized)

Katherine S. Talmadge. *The Life of Charles Drew.* Twenty-First Century Books (Holt), 1992.

Midge Turk. *Gordon Parks.* Crowell, 1971.

Elizabeth Van Steenwyk. *Ida B. Wells-Barnett: Woman of Courage.* Franklin Watts, 1992.

Alice Walker. *Langston Hughes, American Poet.* Crowell, 1974.

John A. Williams. *The Most Native of Sons.* Doubleday, 1970.

Diane Wolkstein. *The Cool Ride in the Sky.* Knopf, 1973.

Elizabeth Yates. *Amos Fortune: Free Man.* Dutton, 1950.

Bernice E. Young. *Harlem: The Story of a Changing Community.* Messner, 1972.

Folklore

Verna Aardema. *Behind the Back of the Mountain.* Dial, 1973.

*———. *Bimwili & the Zimibi; A Tale from Zanzibar.* Dial, 1985.

*———. *Bringing the Rain to Kapiti Plain.* Dial, 1981.

———. *The Lonely Lioness and the Ostrich Chicks; A Masai Tale.* Knopf, 1996.

———. *Oh, Kojo! How Could You?* Dutton, 1984.

———. *Tales from the Story Hat.* Coward, 1960.

Joyce Arkhurst. *The Adventure of Spider; West African Tales.* Little, 1964.

Ashley Bryan. *The Adventures of Aku.* Atheneum, 1976.

Harold Courlander. *Beat the Story Drum, Pum, Pum.* Atheneum, 1980.

———. *The Crest and the Hide and Other African Stories. . . .*Coward, 1982.

———. *The King's Drum.* Harcourt, 1962.

———. *Olade the Hunter.* Harcourt, 1968.

Elphinstone Dayrell. *Why the Sun and the Moon Live in the Sky.* Houghton, 1968.

Mary Joan Gerson. *Why the Sky Is Far Away.* Harcourt, 1974.

Linda Ghan. *Muhla, The Fair One.* Nu Age Editions, 1991.

Ann Grifalconi. *The Village of Round and Square Houses.* Little, 1986.

Gail Haley. *A Story, A Story.* Atheneum, 1970.

Robert Ingpen and Barbara Hayes. *Folktales and Fables of the Middle East and Africa.* Chelsea, 1994.

*Ezra Jack Keats. *John Henry.* Pantheon, 1965.

Julius Lester. *The Knee-High Man.* Dial, 1972.

Joan Lexau. *Crocodile and Hens.* Harper, 1969.

Van Dyke Parks. *Jump! The Adventures of Brer Rabbit.* Harcourt, 1986.

Adjai Robinson. *Singing Tales of Africa.* Scribner's, 1974.

Peter Seeger. *Abiyoyo.* Macmillan, 1986.

Philip Sherlock. *Anansi, the Spider Man.* Crowell, 1954. (Also on film; Weston Woods.)

Poetry

Arnold Adoff, ed. *My Black Me: A Big Book of Poetry.* Dutton, 1974.

Ama Bontemps. *Golden Slippers. An Anthology. . . .* Harper, 1941.

Gwendolyn Brooks. *Bronzeville Boys and Girls.* Harper, 1956.

Paul Dunbar. *Greet the Dawn*. Atheneum, 1978.

*Nikki Giovanni. *Spin a Soft Black Song*. Hill and Wang, 1971.

Eloise Greenfield. *Daydreamers*. Dial, 1981.

Nikki Grimes. *Something on My Mind*. Dial, 1978.

Langston Hughes. *Don't You Turn Back*. Knopf, 1970.

June Jordan. *Who Look at Me?* Crowell, 1969.

Exploring the Backgrounds of Latinos/Hispanics

The largest group in this category is Americans with Mexican backgrounds. However, we also need to be aware of such other groups as Puerto Ricans and Cubans.

General Resources

Patricia Beilke and Frank Sciara. *Selecting Materials for and about Hispanic and East Asian Children and Young People*. Shoestring, 1986.

Milton Meltzer. *The Hispanic Americans*. Crowell, 1982. (For students also.) National Hispanic University, 225 East 14th Street, Oakland, CA 94606.

Febe Orozco. "A Bibliography of Hispanic Literature." *English Journal* (November 1982).

Isabel Schon. *Basic Collection of Children's Books in Spanish*. Scarecrow, 1986.

———. *Books in Spanish for Children and Young Adults*. Scarecrow, 1985.

Shirley Wagoner. "Mexican-Americans in Children's Literature Since 1970." *The Reading Teacher* (December 1982).

Exploring the Backgrounds of Mexican Americans/Chicanos

General Resources

Rodolfo Acuña. *Occupied America: A History of Chicanos*. Harper, 1981.

Rudolfo Anaya. *Bless Me Última*. Tonatiuh, 1972.

Livie Duran and Bernard Russell, eds. *Introduction to Chicano Studies*. Macmillan, 1982.

Matt Meier and Feliciano Rivera, eds. *Dictionary of Mexican American History*. Greenwood Press, 1981.

Margarita Melville, ed. *Twice a Minority: Mexican American Women*. Mosby, 1980.

Isabel Schon. *A Bicultural Heritage: Themes for the Exploration of Mexican and Mexican-American Culture in Books for Children and Adolescents*. Scarecrow, 1978.

James Vigil. *From Indian to Chicanos: A Sociocultural History*. Mosby, 1980.

Periodicals

Aztlán: International Journal of Chicano Studies Research. Campbell Hall, Rm. 3122, University of California, Los Angeles, CA 90024.

Bronze. 1560 34th Avenue, Oakland, CA 94601.

Carta editorial. P.O. Box 54624, Terminal Annex, Los Angeles, CA 90054.

Chicano Student Movement. P.O. Box 31322, Los Angeles, CA 90031.

Compass. 1209 Egypt Street, Houston, TX 77009. (Free)

El gallo. 1265 Cherokee Street, Denver, CO 80204.

El grito del norte. Rt. 2, Box 5, Española, NM 87532.

El hispanoamericano. 630 Ninth Street, Sacramento, CA 95825.

Inside Eastside. P.O. Box 63273, Los Angeles, CA 90063.

Lado. 1306 N. Western Avenue, Chicago, IL 60622.

El malcriado. P.O. Box 130, Delano, CA 93215.

Mexican American Sun. 319 North Soto St., Los Angeles, CA 90033.

La opinión. 1426 S. Main Street, Los Angeles, CA 90015.

La prensa libre. 2973 Sacramento Street, Berkeley, CA 94702.

Proyecto Leer Bulletin, 1736 Columbia Road, NW., St. 107, Washington, DC 20009.

La raza. 2445 Gates Street, Los Angeles, CA 90031.

Times of the Americas. P.O. Box 1173, Coral Gables, FL 33134.

La verdad. P.O. Box 13156, San Diego, CA 92113.

Books for Students

Fiction

Patricia Beatty. *Lupita Mañana.* Morrow, 1982.

*Harry Behn. *The Two Uncles of Pablo.* Harcourt Brace Jovanovich, 1959.

Rose Blue. *We Are Chicanos.* Watts, 1974.

Clyde Robert Bulla. *The Poppy Seeds.* Crowell, 1955.

*Eve Bunting. *Going Home,* HarperCollins, 1996.

Hila Colman. *Chicano Girl.* Morrow, 1973.

Ed Foster. *Tejanos.* Hill and Wang, 1970.

Marian Garthwaite. *Tomás and the Red-Haired Angel.* Messner, 1966.

Maurine Gee. *Chicano Amiga.* Morrow, 1972.

Dorothy Hamilton. *Anita's Choice.* Herald, 1971.

Kathryn Hitte and William B. Hayes. *Mexican Soup.* Parents', 1970.

Evelyn S. Lampman. *Go Up the Road Slowly.* Atheneum, 1972.

Claudia Mills. *Luisa's American Dream.* Four Winds, 1981.

*Pat Mora. *Agua, Agua, Agua.* Goodyear, 1994.

———. *The Race of Toad and Deer.* Orchard, 1995.

———. *Tomás and the Library Lady.* Knopf, 1997.

Iris Noble. *Tingambatu: Adventure in Archaeology.* Messner, 1983.

James Norman. *Charro: Mexican Horseman.* Putnam, 1970.

Scott O'Dell. *The Black Pearl.* Houghton Mifflin, 1967.

———. *Carlotta.* Houghton, 1977.

———. *The King's Fifth.* Houghton Mifflin, 1966.

Helen Rand Parish. *Estebánico.* Viking, 1974.

Paula Paul. *You Can Hear a Magpie Smile.* Nelson, 1980.

*Leo Politi. *Juanita.* Scribner's, 1948.

*———. *Pedro, the Angel of Olvera Street.* Scribner's, 1946.

*———. *Three Stalks of Corn.* Scribner's, 1978.

Barbara Ritchie. *Ramón Makes a Trade: Los Cambios de Ramón.* Parnassus, 1959.

Jessie Ruiz. *El gran Cesar.* Education Consulting, 1973.

Nancy Smith. *Josie's Handful of Quietness.* Abingdon, 1975

*Barbara Todd. *Juan Patricio.* Putnam, 1972.

Elizabeth Borton de Treviño. *Nacar, the White Deer.* Farrar, Straus, and Giroux, 1963.

Dorothy Witton. *Crossroads for Chela.* Messner, 1956.

Biography

Bernadine Bailey. *Famous Latin American Liberators.* Dodd, Mead, 1960.

Mark Day. *Forty Acres: César Chávez and the Farm Workers.* Praeger, 1971.

Ruth Franchere. *César Chávez.* Cromwell, 1970.

Robert Jackson. *Supermax: The Lee Treviño Story.* Walck, 1973.

W. J. Jacobs. *Hernando Cortés.* Watts, 1974.

Albert Marrin. *Aztecs and Spaniards: Cortés and the Conquest of Mexico.* Atheneum, 1986.

Ronald Syme. *Juárez: The Founder of Modern Mexico.* Morrow, 1972.

Florence White. *César Chávez: Man of Courage.* Garrard, 1973.

Folklore

John Bierhorst, ed. *The Hungry Woman: Myths and Legends of the Aztecs.* Morrow, 1984.

B. Traven. *The Creation of the Sun and the Moon.* Hill and Wang, 1968.

Poetry

Richard Lewis, ed. *Still Waters of the Air: Poems by Three Modern Spanish Poets.* Dial, 1970.

Pat Mora. *Confetti: Poems for Children.* Lee and Low, 1996.

Alastair Reid and Anthony Kerrigan. *Mother Goose in Spanish/Poesías de la Madre Oca.* Crowell, 1968.

Gary Soto, *Neighborhood Odes.* Harcourt, 1992.

Exploring the Backgrounds of Puerto Ricans

General Resources

Kenneth Aran et al. *Puerto Rican History and Culture: A Study Guide and Curriculum Outline.* United Federation of Teachers, 1990.

Patricia Beilke and Frank Sciara. *Selecting Materials for and about Hispanic and East Asian Children and Young People.* Shoestring, 1986.

Books for Adults

María Theresa Babin and Stan Steiner, eds. *Borinquen: An Anthology of Puerto Rican Literature.* Vintage, 1974.

Joseph Fitzpatrick. *Puerto Rican Americans: The Meaning of Migration to the Mainland.* Prentice-Hall, 1971.

Clifford Haubert. *Puerto Rico and Puerto Ricans: A Study of Puerto Rican History and Immigration in the United States.* Hippocrene Books, 1974.

Karl Wagenheim. *Cuentos: An Anthology of Short Stories from Puerto Rico.* Shocken Books, 1978.

Books for Students

Fiction

Pura Belpré. *Santiago.* Warne, 1969.

Rose Blue. *I Am Here: Yo Estoy Aquí.* Watts, 1971.

Nardi Campion. *Casa Means Home.* Holt, 1970.

Arthur Getz. *Tar Beach.* Dial, 1979.

Gloria Gonzalez. *Gaucho.* Knopf, 1977.

Lynn Hall. *Danza!* Scribner's, 1981.

Myron Levoy. *A Shadow like a Leopard.* Harper, 1981.

Nicholasa Mohr. *Felita.* Dial, 1979.

———. *Nilda.* Harper, 1973.

Louisa Shotwell. *Magdalena.* Viking, 1971.

Piri Thomas. *Stories from El Barrio.* Knopf, 1978.

Sandra Weiner. *They Call Me Jack: The Story of a Boy from Puerto Rico.* Pantheon, 1973.

Nonfiction

*Antonio J. Colorado. *The First Book of Puerto Rico.* Watts, 1978.

Morton Golding. *A Short History of Puerto Rico.* Watts, 1978.

Barry Levine. *Benjy Lopez: A Picaresque Tale of Emigration and Return.* Basic Books, 1980.

Robin McKown. *The Image of Puerto Rico: Its History and Its People: On the Island—On the Mainland.* McGraw, 1973.

Joe Molnar. *Elizabeth: A Puerto Rican-American Child Tells Her Story.* Watts, 1974.

Lila Perl. *Puerto Rico: Island between Two Worlds.* Morrow, 1979.

Geraldo Rivera. *Puerto Rico: Island of Contrasts.* Parents, 1973.

Julia Singer. *We All Come from Puerto Rico Too.* Atheneum, 1977.

Morris Weeks, Jr. *Hello, Puerto Rico.* Grosset, 1972.

Biography

Paul Allyn. *The Picture Life of Herman Badilla.* Watts, 1972.

Alfredo Matilla and Ivan Silen, eds. *The Puerto Rican Poets: Los Poétas Puertorriqueños.* Bantam, 1972.

Clarke Newlon. *Famous Puerto Ricans.* Dodd, 1975.

Philip Sterling and Maria Brau. *The Quiet Rebels.* Doubleday, 1968.

Folklore

Ricardo Alegría. *The Three Wishes.* Harcourt, 1969.

Pura Belpré. *Dance of the Animals.* Warne, 1972.

——— ——. *Once in Puerto Rico.* Warne, 1973.

———. *The Rainbow-Colored Horse.* Warne, 1978.

———. *The Tiger and the Rabbit.* Lippincott, 1965.

Exploring the Backgrounds of Cuban Americans

General Resources

Esther Gonzales. *Annotated Bibliography on Cubans in the United States 1960–1976.* Florida International University, 1977.

Books for Adults

Geoffrey Fox. *Working-Class Emigrés from Cuba.* R. E. Research Associates, 1979.

Irving Horowitz. *Cuban Communism.* Transaction, 1984.

William Mackey and Von Beebe. *Bilingual Schools for a Bicultural Community.* Newburg House, 1977.

Rafael Probías and Lourdes Casal. *The Cuban Minority in the U.S.* Florida Atlantic University, 1973.

Eleanor M. Rogg. *The Assimilation of Cuban Exiles: The Role of Community and Class.* Aberdeen, 1974.

Hugh Thomas. *The Cuban Revolution.* Westview, 1984.

Books for Students

Margaretta Curtin. *Cubanita in a New Land: Cuban Children of Miami.* Miami Press, 1974.

Virginia Ortiz. *The Land and People of Cuba.* Lippincott, 1973.

Lorin Philipson and Rafael Llerena. *Freedom Flights.* Random, 1980.

Exploring the Backgrounds of Native Americans

General Resources

Russell Barsh and James Henderson. *The Road: Indian Tribes and Political Liberty*. University of California, 1980.

Dee Brown. *Bury My Heart at Wounded Knee*. Holt, 1970.

Robert Burnette and John Koster. *The Road to Wounded Knee*. Bantam, 1974.

Mary Gloyne Byler. *American Indian Authors for Young Readers*. Association on American Indian Affairs, 432 Park Ave., South, New York, NY 10016. An annotated bibliography.

The Council on Interracial Books for Children. *Chronicles of American Indian Protest*. A collection of documents recounting the American Indian's struggle for survival. Offers supplemental reading assignments for classes.

John Lane Deer and Richard Erdoes. *Lame Deer, Seeker of Visions*. Washington Square, 1984.

Vine Deloria, Jr. *Custer Died for Your Sins*. Avon, 1970.

———. *God Is Red*. Laurel, 1979.

David Edmunds, ed. *American Indian Leaders: Studies in Diversity*. University of Nebraska Press, 1980.

Zane Grey. *The Vanishing American*. Washington Square, 1984.

Barbara Graymont. *The Iroquois in the American Revolution*. Syracuse U. Press, 1972.

Jamake Highwater. *The Primal Mind*. Harper, 1981.

Alvin Josephy, Jr. *Now That the Buffalo's Gone*. Knopf, 1981.

Francis Paul Prucha. *American Indian Policy in the Formative Years*. University of Nebraska Press, 1962. Trade and Intercourse Acts, 1790–1834.

William Sturtevant, ed. *Handbook of North American Indians*. U.S. Government, 1981.

Dale Van Every. *Disinherited*. Morrow, 1966. Removal of the Cherokee.

Alan Velie. *American Indian Literature*. Harper, 1980.

Frank Waters. *The Man Who Killed the Deer*. Swallow, 1970.

Edmund Wilson. *Apologies to the Iroquois*. Vintage, 1959. Historical and contemporary problems.

Periodicals

AAIA. 432 Park Ave., New York, NY 10016. General and legislative information; newsletter.

Akwesasne Notes. Mohawk Nation via Roosevelt Town, NY 13683. Indian paper; current events and activities. Donation, publishes calendar.

American Indian Culture and Research Journal. 3220 Campbell Hall, University of California, Los Angeles CA 90004.

American Indian Media Directory. American Indian Press Association, Room, 206, 1346 Connecticut Ave., NW., Washington, D.C. 20036. Listing press, radio, TV/video, film, theater.

Warpath. United Native Americans, Inc. Box 26149, San Francisco, CA 94126.

Wassaja. American Indian Historical Society, 1451 Masonic Ave., San Francisco, CA 94117. Monthly newspaper; significant events.

Additional Sources

Alaska Rural School Project. Univ. of Alaska, College, AK 99701.

American Indian Education Handbook. California State Dept. of Education, 1982.

Bibliography of Nonprint Instructional Materials on the American Indian. Instructional Development Program for the Institute of Indian Services and Research, Brigham Young University. Brigham Young University Printing Service, Provo, Utah 84601, 1972.

Navajo Curriculum Center. Rough Rock Demonstration School, Rough Rock, AZ.

Navajo Social Studies Project. College of Education. The University of New Mexico, Albuquerque, NM 87106.

Senate Committee on Labor and Public Welfare, Washington, DC.

South Central Regional Ed. Lab. Corp., 408 National Old Line Bldg., Little Rock, AR 72201.

Books for Students

Fiction

Olaf Baker. *Where the Buffaloes Begin.* Warne, 1981.

Byrd Baylor. *When Clay Sings.* Scribner's, 1972.

Denton Bedford. *Tsali.* Indian Historian Press, 1972.

Jospeh Bruchac. *Eagle Song.* Dial, 1997.

Clyde Bulla. *Conquista!* Crowell, 1978.

Patricia Calvert. *The Hour of the Wolf.* Scribner's, 1983.

Elizabeth Cleaver. *The Enchanted Caribou.* Atheneum, 1985.

Belle Coate. *Mak.* Parnassus, 1982.

Alice Dagliesh. *The Courage of Sarah Noble.* Scribner's, 1954.

Ann Dixon. *How Raven Brought Light to People.* MacMillan, 1992.

T. A. Dyer. *A Way of His Own.* Houghton, 1981.

Dale Fife. *Ride the Crooked Wind.* Coward, 1973.

Jean Craighead George. *The Talking Earth.* Harper, 1983.

Paul Goble. *Lone Bull's Horse Raid.* Bradbury, 1973.

*———. *Red Hawk's Account of Custer's Last Battle.* Pantheon, 1970.

Danita Haller. *Not Just Any Ring.* Knopf, 1982.

James Houston. *Eagle Mask.* Harcourt, 1966.

———. *Ghost Paddle.* Harcourt, 1966.

Ruth Karen. *Feathered Serpent: The Rise and Fall of the Aztecs.* Four Winds, 1982.

Kathleen Kudlinski. *Night Bird: A Story of the Seminole Indians.* Viking, 1993.

D'Arcy McNickle. *The Surrounded.* University of New Mexico, 1978.

———. *Wind from an Enemy Sky.* Harper, 1978.

Scott O'Dell. *The Amethyst Ring.* Houghton Mifflin, 1983.

———. *Sing Down the Moon.* Houghton Mifflin, 1970.

———. *Streams to the River, River to the Sea: A Novel of Sacagawea.* Harper, 1986.

Harry Paige. *Johnny Stands.* Warne, 1982.

Virginia Driving Hawk Sneve. *Betrayed.* Holiday House, 1974.

Elizabeth Speare. *The Sign of the Beaver.* Houghton Mifflin, 1983.

Hyemeyohsts Storm. *Seven Arrows.* Harper, 1972.

*Betty Waterton. *A Salmon for Simon.* Atheneum, 1981.

Gloria Whelan. *The Indian School.* HarperCollins, 1996.

Bernard Wolf. *Tinker and the Medicine Man: The Story of a Navajo Boy of Monument Valley.* Random House, 1973.

Nonfiction

Aline Amon. *The Earth Is Sore; Native Americans on Nature.* Atheneum, 1981.

Virginia Irving Armstrong, ed. *I Have Spoken.* Sage Books, 1971.

Brent Ashabranner. *Morning Star, Black Sun: The Northern Cheyenne Indians and America's Energy Crisis.* Dodd, 1982.

———. *Children of the Maya; A Guatemalan Indian Odyssey.* Dodd, 1986.

White Deer Autumn. *Ceremony In the Circle of Life.* Carnival, 1982.

Paul D. Bailey. *Ghost Dance Messiah.* Westernlore, 1970.

Gordon C. Baldwin. *The Apache Indians: Raiders of the Southwest.* Four Winds, 1978.

Byrd Baylor. *Before You Came This Way.* Dutton, 1969.

Alex W. Bealer. *Only the Names Remain: The Cherokee and the Trail of Tears.* Little, Brown, 1996.

John Bierhorst, ed. *A Cry from the Earth: Music of the North American Indians.* Four Winds, 1978.

———. *In the Trail of the Wind; American Indian Poems and Ritual Orations.* Farrar, Straus and Giroux, 1971.

Sonia Bleeker. *The Maya.* Morrow, 1961.

———. *The Navajo: Herders, Weavers and Silversmiths.* Morrow, 1958.

———. *The Sioux Indians: Hunters and Warriors of the Plains.* Morrow, 1962.

Ann Nolan Clark. *Circle of Seasons.* Farrar, Straus and Giroux, 1970. Describes ceremonies of the Pueblo Indians.

Kate Connell. *These Lands Are Ours: Tecumseh's Fight for the Old Northwest,* Steck-Vaughn, 1993.

Chief Eagle Dallas. *Winter Count.* Golden Bell, 1968.

Janet D'Amato. *Algonquian and Iroquois Crafts for You to Make.* Messner, 1979.

Vine Deloria. *Indians of the Pacific Northwest.* Doubleday, 1977.

Charles A. Eastman. *Indian Boyhood.* Dover, 1971.

Amy Ehrlich. *Wounded Knee: An Indian History of the American West.* Holt, Rinehart and Winston, 1974.

Richard Erdoes. *The Pueblo Indians.* Young Readers' Indian Library, 1967.

———. *The Native Americans: Navajos.* Sterling, 1978.

———. *The Rain Dance People: The Pueblo Indians.* Knopf, 1976.

Norma Farber. *Mercy Short.* Dutton, 1982.

Franklin Folsom. *Red Power on the Rio Grande: The Nature of the American Revolution of 1680.* Follett, 1973.

Grant Foreman. *Indian Removal* University of Oklahoma Press, 1932.

Frieda Gates. *North American Indian Masks: Craft and Legend.* Walker, 1982.

Miriam Gurko. *Indian America: The Black Hawk War.* Crowell, 1970.

Mary Sayre Haverstock. *Indian Gallery.* Four Winds, 1973. A biography of George Catlin.

Wilma P. Hays. *Foods the Indians Gave Us.* Washburn, 1973.

Robert Hofsinde. *Indian Arts.* Morrow, 1971.

W. Ben Hunt. *The Complete Book of Indian Crafts and Lore.* Golden, 1976.

Indian Culture Series. Montana Reading Publications, Level 4, Stapleton Building, Billings, MT 59101. Series written and illustrated by Indian children for Indians.

Johanna Johnston. *The Indians and the Strangers.* Dodd, Mead, 1972.

Alvin Josephy. *The Nez Percé Indians and the Opening of the Northwest.* Yale University Press, 1965.

William Loren Katz. *Early America, 1492–1812.* Watts, 1974.

Theodora Kroeber. *Ishi: Last of His Tribe.* Parnassus, 1964.

Oliver La Farge. *The American Indian.* Golden, 1960.

Richard Lytle. *People of the Dawn.* Atheneum, 1980.

N. Scott Momaday. *The Way to Rainy Mountain.* Ballantine, 1970. A poetic mixture of retellings of Kiowa tales, stories for the history of the Kiowa, and the author's memories of his grandmother.

Dorothy Morrison. *Chief Sarah. Sarah Winnemucca's Fight for Indian Rights.* Atheneum, 1980.

Hermina Poatgieter. *Indian Legacy.* Messner, 1981.

Sally Sheppard. *Indians of the Eastern Woodlands.* Watts, 1975.

Nancy Simon. *American Indian Habitats.* McKay, 1978.

Virginia Sneve. *The Cherokees.* Holiday, 1996.

William O. Steele. *Talking Bones*. Harper, 1978.

Craig Kev Strete. *When Grandfather Journeys into Winter*. Greenwillow, 1979.

Helen H. Tanner. *The Ojibwa*. Chelsea House, 1992.

Olivia Vlahos. *New World Beginnings, Indian Cultures in the Americas*. Viking, 1970.

Betsy Warren. *Indians Who Lived in Texas*. Steck, 1970.

Charlotte Yue. *The Pueblo*. Houghton Mifflin, 1986.

Biography

Ingri d'Aulaire and Edgar P. d'Aulaire. *Pocahontas*. Doubleday, 1946.

Victor Boesen. *Edward S. Curtis, Photographer of the North American Indian*. Coward, 1977.

Clyde Bulla. *Pocahontas and the Strangers*. Cromwell, 1971.

Margaret Crary. *Susette La Flesche: Voice of the Omaha Indians*. Hawthorne, 1973.

Russell Davis and Brent Ashabranner. *Chief Joseph, War Chief of the Nez Percé*. McGraw-Hill, 1962.

Mary Gardner. *Mary Jemison: Seneca Captive*. Harcourt, 1966.

Marion E. Gridley. *American Indian Women*. Hawthorne, 1974. Describes the lives of 19 women ranging over a period of 300 years.

Janet Klausnen. *Sequoyah's Gift: A Portrait of the Cherokee Leader*. HarperCollins, 1993.

Lois Lenski. *Indian Captive: The Story of Mary Jemison*. Lippincott, 1941.

Peter Pitseolak. *Peter Pitseolak's Escape from Death*. Delacorte, 1978.

C. Fayne Porter. *Our Indian Heritage: Profiles of 12 Great Leaders*. Chilton, 1964.

William Steele. *The Wilderness Tattoo: A Narrative of Juan Ortiz*. Harcourt, 1972.

Ronald Syme. *Osceola: Seminole Leader*. Morrow, 1976.

Tobi Tobias. *Maria Tallchief*. Cromwell, 1970.

Charles Morrow Wilson. *Gerónimo*. Dillon, 1973.

Edgar Wyatt. *Cochise, Apache Warrior and Statesman*. McGraw-Hill, 1973.

Folklore

John Bierhorst, ed. *Lightning Inside You and Other Native American Riddles*. Morrow, 1992.

Byrd Baylor. *A God on Every Mountain Top*. Scribner's, 1981.

———. *Moon Song*. Scribner's, 1982.

Natalia Belting. *Our Fathers Had Powerful Songs*. Dutton, 1974.

———. *Whirlwind Is a Ghost Dancing*. Dutton, 1974.

Elizabeth Cleaver. *The Enchanted Caribou*. Atheneum, 1985.

Edward Curtis. *The Girl Who Married a Ghost*. Four Winds, 1978.

Tomie DePaola. *The Legend of the Bluebonnet*. Putnam, 1983.

———. *The Legend of the Indian Paintbrush,* Putnam, 1988.

Dorothy DeWit, ed. *The Talking Stone: An Anthology of Native American Tales and Legends.* Greenwillow, 1979.

*Paul Goble. *The Great Race of the Birds and Animals.* Bradbury, 1985.

————and Dorothy Goble. *The Gift of the Sacred Dog.* Bradbury, 1980.

George Grinnell. *The Whistling Skeleton, American Indian Tales of the Supernatural.* Four Winds, 1982.

Christie Harris. *Mouse Woman and the Mischief-Makers.* Atheneum, 1977.

————. *Once More upon a Totem.* Atheneum, 1982.

Jamake Highwater. *Anpao: An American Indian Odyssey.* Lippincott, 1977.

Ken Kesey. *The Sea Lion: A Story of the Sea Cliff People.* Viking, 1991.

Ekkehart Malotki. *The Mouse Couple: A Hopi Folktale.* Northland, 1988.

*Penny Pollock. *The Turkey Girl.* Little Brown, 1996.

Gail Robinson *Raven the Trickster: Legends of the North American Indians.* Atheneum, 1982.

Ann Siberell. *Whale in the Sky.* Dutton, 1982.

Janet Stevens. *Coyote Steals the Blanket; A Ute Tale.* Holiday, 1993.

Harriet P. Taylor. *Coyote and the Laughing Butterflies.* Macmillan, 1995.

William Toye. *The Fire Stealer.* Oxford, 1980.

Judith Ullom, comp. *Folklore of the North American Indians: An Annotated Bibligraphy.* Library of Congress, 1969.

Sheron Williams. *And in the Beginning . . .* Atheneum, 1992.

Rosebud Yellow Robe. *Tonweya and the Eagles and Other Lakota Indian Tales.* Dial, 1978.

Poetry

Aline Amon. *The Earth Is Sore: Native Americans on Nature.* Atheneum, 1981.

*Jamake Highwater. *Moonsong Lullaby.* Lothrop, 1981.

James Houston. *Songs of the Dream People.* Atheneum, 1972. Chants and images from the Indians and Eskimos of North America.

Henry Wadsworth Longfellow. *The Song of Hiawatha.* Dutton, 1960.

Ramaho Navajo Students. *Reflections on Illusion—Reality.* Pine Hill Media Center, 1981.

Nancy Wood. *War Cry on a Prayer Feather.* Colorado Centennial Commission, 1991.

Exploring the Backgrounds of Jewish Americans

General Resources

Nathan Belth. *A Promise to Keep: A Narrative of the American Encounter with Anti-Semitism.* New York Times, 1979.

Max Dimont. *The Jews in America: The Roots, History and Destiny of American Jews.* Simon and Schuster, 1978.

Irving Howe. *World of Our Fathers: The Journey of the East European Jews to America and the Life They Found and Made.* Simon and Schuster, 1976.

——— and Kenneth Libo. *How We Lived: A Documentary History of Immigrant Jews in America, 1880–1930.* Richard Marek, 1979.

Anita L. Lebeson. *Pilgrim People: A History of the Jews in America from 1492 to 1974.* Minerva Press, 1975.

Milton Meltzer. *Never to Forget: The Jews of the Holocaust.* Harper, 1976.

———. *Taking Root: Jewish Immigrants in America.* Farrar, 1976.

Chain Potok. *The Chosen.* Simon and Schuster. 1967.

Jerome Rothenberg, ed. *A Big Jewish Book: Poems and Other Visions of the Jews from Tribal Times to the Present.* Doubleday, 1978.

Books for Students

Fiction

Lynne Reid Banks. *One More River.* Morrow, 1992.

Tamar Bergman. *The Boy from over There.* Houghton, 1988.

Marge Blaine. *Dvora's Journey.* Holt, 1979.

Miriam Chaiken. *Finders Weepers.* Harper, 1980.

———. *Yossi Asks the Angels for Help.* Harper, 1985.

Eth Clifford. *The Remembering Box.* Houghton Mifflin, 1985.

Barbara Cohen. *Bitter Herbs and Honey.* Lothrop, 1976.

———. *The Carp in the Bathtub.* Lothrop, 1972.

Gloria Goldreich. *Lori.* Holt, 1976.

———. *Season of Discovery.* Nelson, 1976.

———. *A Treasury of Jewish Literature.* Holt, 1982.

Bette Greene. *Summer of My German Soldier.* Dial, 1973.

Johanna Hurwitz. *Once I Was a Plum Tree.* Morrow, 1980.

Robert Lehrman. *The Store That Mama Built.* Macmillan, 1992.

Sonia Levitin. *Journey to America.* Atheneum, 1970.

———. *A Sound to Remember.* Harcourt, 1976.

Harry Mazer. *The Last Mission: A Novel.* Delacorte, 1979.

Marietta Moskin. *Waiting for Mama.* Coward, 1975.

I. L. Peretz. *The Case against the Wind and Other Stories.* Macmillan, 1975.

*Mildred Phillips. *The Sign on Mendel's Window.* Macmillan, 1985.

Shalom Rabinowitz. *Holiday Tales of Sholom Aleichem.* Scribner's, 1979.

Lois Ruby. *Two Truths in My Pocket.* Viking, 1982.

Carol Snyder. *Ike and Mama and the Block Wedding.* Coward, 1979.

Fannie Steinberg. *Birthday in Kishenev.* Jewish Publication Society, 1976.

Nonfiction

Chana Abells. *The Children We Remember.* Kav-Ben Copies, 1983.

*David Adler. *A Picture Book of Hanukkah.* Holiday, 1982.

Joanne E. Bernstein. *Dmitry: A Young Soviet Immigrant.* Ticknor and Fields, 1981.

Deborah Brodie. *Stories My Grandfather Should Have Told Me.* Hebrew Publishers, 1977.

Miriam Chaikin. *Ask Another Question: The Story and Meaning of Passover.* Clarion, 1985.

————. *Sound the Shofar; The Story and Meaning of Rosh Hashanah and Yom Kippur.* Clarion, 1986.

Hila Coleman. *Rachel's Legacy.* Morrow, 1978.

Norman Finkelstein. *Remember Not to Forget.* Watts, 1985.

Milton Meltzer, ed. *The Jewish Americans: A History in Their Own Words 1650–1950.* Crowell, 1982.

Bert Merter. *Bar Mitzvah, Bat Mitzvah: How Jewish Boys & Girls Come of Age.* Houghton, 1984.

Claire A. Nivola. *Elisabeth.* Farrar, Straus, 1997.

Susan Purdy. *Jewish Holiday Cookbook.* Watts, 1979.

Johanna Reiss. *The Upstairs Room.* Crowell, 1972.

Ellen N. Stern. *Embattled Justice: The Story of Louis Dembitz Brandeis.* Jewish Publication Society, 1971. (Biography)

Folklore

Barbara Cohen. *Yussel's Prayer.* Lothrop, 1981.

Florence Freedman. *Brothers; A Hebrew Legend.* Harper, 1985.

Marilyn Hirsh. *Could Anything Be Worse? A Yiddish Tale.* Holiday, 1974.

Jose Patterson. *Angels, Prophets, Rabbis and Kings from the Stories of the Jewish People.* Illustrated by Claire Bushe. Peter Bedrick, 1991.

Uri Shulevitz. *The Magician.* Macmillan, 1973.

Isaac B. Singer. *The Golem.* Farrar, 1982.

————. *Zlateh, the Goat, and Other Stories.* Harper, 1966.

Margot Zemach. *It Could Always Be Worse: A Yiddish Folk Tale Retold.* Farrar, 1976.

Exploring Additional National Origins

In addition to the more detailed lists of books for children for important minority groups presented in the preceding pages, here are recommended books about specific countries or areas of the world.

Australia, New Zealand, and Tasmania

*Pamela Allen. *Who Sank the Boat?* Coward, 1983.

Patricia Beatty. *Jonathan Down Under.* Morrow, 1982.

Kate Darian-Smith. *Exploration into Australia.* Simon & Schuster, 1996.

National Geographic Society. *Amazing Animals of Australia.* The Society, 1984.

Ruth Park. *Playing Beatie Bow.* Atheneum, 1982.

Joyce Powzyk. *Tasmania, A Wildlife Journey.* Lothrop, 1987.

Marilyn Sachs. *Call Me Ruth.* Doubleday, 1982.

Patricia Wrightson. *A Little Fear.* Mc Elderry, 1983.

———. *The Nargun and the Stars.* McElderry, 1974.

Austria

Carol Greene. *Austria.* Children's Press, 1986.

Brazil

Ted Lewin. *Amazon Boy.* Simon & Schuster, 1993. See: "Reading the World: Brazil" in *Booklinks,* May, 1997.

Britain

Joan Aiken. *The Shadow Guests.* Delacorte, 1980.

Rachel Anderson. *The Poacher's Son.* Oxford, 1983.

Louise Borden. *The Little Ships: The Heroic Rescue at Dunkirk in World War II.* McElderry, 1997.

Mitsumasa Anno. *Anno's Britain.* Philomel, 1982.

Shirley Blumenthal. *Coming to America: Immigrants from the British Isles.* Delacorte, 1980.

Nancy Bond. *Country of Broken Stone.* Atheneum, 1980.

John Branfield. *The Fox in White.* Atheneum, 1982.

Susan Cooper. *The Selkie Girl.* McElderry, 1986.

Alan Hamilton. *Queen Elizabeth II.* Hamilton Hamish, 1983.

Barbara Hill. *Cooking the English Way.* Lerner, 1982.

Penelope Lively. *Fanny's Sister.* Dutton, 1980.

Richard Mabey. *Oak and Company.* Greenwillow, 1983.

Michelle Magorian. *Good Night, Mr. Tom.* Harper, 1982.

Alison Morgan. *Paul's Kite.* Atheneum, 1982.

Rosemary Sutcliff. *Frontier Wolf.* Dutton, 1981.

———. *Song for a Dark Queen.* Crowell, 1982.

Canada

W. D Valgardson. *Sarah and the People of Sand River.* Douglas & McIntyre/Publishers Group West, 1996.

Caribbean

Jonathan London. *The Village Basket Weaver.* Dutton, 1996.

Egypt

Polly S. Brook. *Cleopatra, Goddess of Egypt, Enemy of Rome.* Harper Collins, 1995.

Florence Heide and Judith Gilliland. *The Day of Ahmed's Secret.* Lothrop, 1990.

Norma Katan. *Hieroglyphs: The Writing of Ancient Egypt.* Atheneum, 1981.

Elizabeth Mann. *The Great Pyramid.* Mikaya Press, 1997.

*Lise Maniche. *The Prince Who Knew His Fate.* Philomel, 1982.

France

Walter Buehr. *The French Explorers in America.* Putnam, 1961.

Vivian Grey. *The Chemist Who Lost His Head: The Story of Antoine Lavoisier.* Coward, 1983.

Virginia Haviland. *Favorite Fairy Tales Told in France.* Little, 1959.

Virginia Kunz. *The French in America.* Lerner, 1966.

Germany

Margot Benary-Isbert. *The Ark.* Harcourt, 1953.

Lee Cooper. *Fun with German.* Little, 1965.

T. Degens. *Freya on the Wall.* Harcourt, 1997.

———. *The Visit.* Viking, 1982.

Robert Goldston. *The Life and Death of Nazi Germany.* Bobbs, 1967.

Evert Hartman. *War without Friends.* Crown, 1982.

Ilse Koehn. *My Childhood in Nazi Germany,* Greenwillow, 1972.

Hans Richter. *Friedrich.* Holt, 1970.

Greece

Isaac Asimov. *The Greeks: A Great Adventure.* Houghton, 1965.

Nina Bawden. *The Real Plato Jones.* Clarion, 1993.

Julie Delton. *My Uncle Nikos.* Crowell, 1983.

Margaret Hodges. *The Avenger.* Scribner's, 1982.

Norma Johnston. *The Days of the Dragon's Seed.* Atheneum, 1983.

Jonathan Rutland. *See Inside an Ancient Greek Town.* Warwick, 1979.

Janet Van Duyn. *The Greeks: Their Legacy.* McGraw, 1972.

Jill P. Walsh. *Children of the Fox.* Farrar, 1978.

Jane Yolen. *The Boy Who Had Wings.* Crowell, 1974.

India and Pakistan (Sri Lanka)

Lloyd Alexander. *The Iron Ring.* Dutton, 1997.

*Marsha Arnold. *Heat of a Tiger.* Dial, 1995.

Anni Axworthy. *Anni's India Diary.* Whispering Coyote Press, 1992.

*Ruskin Bond. *Cherry Tree.* Boyd's Mills, 1991.

*Marcia Brown. *Once a Mouse: A Fable Cut in Wood.* Atheneum, 1991.

Catherine Chambers. *Sikh.* Children's Press, 1996.

David Cummings. *India.* Thomason Learning, 1995.

Demi. *Buddha.* Holt, 1996.

———. *One Grain of Rice.* Scholastic, 1997.

*Arthur Dorros. *Elephant Families.* HarperCollins, 1994.

Leonard E. Fischer. *Gandhi.* Atheneum, 1995.

Anita Ganeri. *India.* Dillon, 1993.

———. *What Do We Know about Hinduism?* Peter Bedrick, 1996.

Rumer Godden. *The Valiant Chatti-Maker.* Viking, 1983.

*Jim Haskins. *Count Your Way through India.* Carolrhoda, 1989.

Madhur Jaffrey. *Seasons of Splendour: Tales, Myths, and Legends of India.* Atheneum, 1985.

*Aleph Kamal. *The Bird Who Was an Elephant.* Lippincott, 1989.

Dilip Kadodewala. *Hinduism.* Thomson Learning, 1995.

Sharon Kaur. *Food in India.* Rourke, 1989.

*Ted Lewin. *The Sacred River.* Clarion, 1995.

*———. *Tiger Trek.* Simon & Schuster, 1990.

Maryana Mayer. *The Golden Swan.* Bantam, 1990

Vijay Madavan. *Cooking the Indian Way.* Lerner, 1985.

Caroline Ness. *The Ocean of Story.* Lothrop, 1996.

F. W. Rawding. *Gandhi and the Struggle for India's Independence.* Lerner, 1982.

Susan Roth. *Buddha.* Doubleday, 1994.

Jerry Schmidt. *In the Village of the Elephants.* Walker, 1994.

John Severance. *Ghandi: Great Soul.* Clarion, 1997

Aaron Shepard. *Savitri: A Tale of Ancient India.* Whitman, 1992.

*Jessica Souhami. *Rama and The Demon King.* DK Ink, 1997.

Radhika Srinivasan. *India.* Marshall Cavendish, 1990

*Rabindranath Tagore. *Amal and the Letter from the King.* Boyd's Mills, 1992.

*————. *Paper Boats.* Caroline House, 1992.

Madhu B. Wangu. *Hinduism: World Religions.* Facts on File, 1991.

Indonesia

Alice Terada. *The Magic Crocodile and Other Folktales from Indonesia.* University of Hawaii Press, 1994.

Ireland

Karen Bransom. *Streets of Gold.* Putnam, 1981.

Patricia Giff. *The Gift of the Pirate Queen.* Delacorte, 1982.

James Johnson. *The Irish in America.* Lerner, 1976.

Sondra Langford. *Red Bird of Ireland.* Atheneum, 1983.

Joan L. Nixon. *The Gift.* Macmillan, 1983.

Catherine Sefton. *Island of the Strangers.* Harcourt, 1985.

Mary Tannen. *The Lost Legend of Finn.* Knopf, 1982.

Margaret Wetterer. *The Giant's Apprentice.* Atheneum, 1982.

Italy

Elisa Bartone and Ted Lewin. *American Too.* Lothrop, 1996.

Penrose Colyer. *I Can Read Italian: My First English-Italian Word Book.* Watts, 1983.

*Tomie De Paola. *Big Anthony and the Magic Ring.* Harcourt, 1979.

Ronald Grossman. *The Italians in America.* Lerner, 1966.

Erik Haugaard. *The Little Fishes.* Houghton, 1967.

Virginia Haviland. *Favorite Fairy Tales Told in Italy.* Little, 1965.

Middle East

Aramco World Magazine. 1800 Augusta Dr., Suite 300, Houston, TX 77057. Wonderful photography and informative articles; request free subscription.

Sally Bahdis. *Sitti and the Cats.* Roberts Rinehart, 1993.

Robert Ingpen and Barbara Hayes. *Folk Tales and Fables of the Middle East and Africa,* Chelsea House, 1994.

Barbara Cohen and Bahija Lovejoy. *Seven Daughters and Seven Sons.* Atheneum, 1982.

Russell Davis and Brent Ashabranner. *Ten Thousand Desert Swords.* Little, Brown, 1960.

*Florence Heide and Judith Gilliland. *Sami and the Time of Troubles.* Clarion, 1992.

L. E. Leipold. *Folktales of Arabia.* Denison, 1973.

Arthur Scholey, comp. *The Discontented Dervishes and Other Persian Tales.* Deutsch, 1982.

*Virginia A. Tashjian. *Three Apples Fell from Heaven.* Little, Brown, 1971.

*Barbara K. Walker. *The Courage of Kazan.* Crowell, 1970. Well-written story; beautiful illustrations.

Peru

Gillian Cross. *Born of the Sun.* Holiday, 1984.

Emilie Lepthien. *Peru: Enchantment of the World Series.* Children's Press, 1992.

Poland

Sollace Hotze, *Summer Endings.* Clarion, 1991.

Anne Pellowski. *Winding Valley Farm: Annie's Story.* Philomel, 1982.

Christine Szambelan-Stravinsky. *Dark Hour of Noon.* Lippincott, 1983.

Portugal

Esther Cross. *Portugal.* Children's Press, 1986.

Russia and Other Former Soviet Republics

E. M. Almedingen. *Land of Muscovy: The History of Early Russia.* Farrar, 1972.

Bonnie Carey. *Baba Yaga's Geese and Other Russian Stories.* Indiana University Press, 1973.

Kornei Chukovsky. *The Silver Crest: My Russian Boyhood.* Holt, 1976.

Barbara Cohen. *Molly's Pilgrim.* Lothrop, 1983.

Guy Daniels. *Ivan the Fool and Other Tales of Leo Tolstory,* tr. by the author. Macmillan, 1966.

Karen Hesse. *Letters from Rifka.* Holt, 1992.

Kathryn Lasky. *The Night Journey.* Warne, 1981.

Albert Likhanov, translated by Richard Lourie. *Shadows across the Sun.* Harper, 1983.

Claire R. Murphy. *Friendship across Arctic Waters: Alaskan Cub Scouts Visit Their Soviet Neighbors.* Photographs by Charles Mason. Dutton, 1991.

James Riordan. *Tales from Tartary.* Viking, 1977.

Uri Shulevitz. *Soldier and Tsar in the Forest.* Farrar, 1972.

Ernest Small. *Baba Yaga.* Houghton Mifflin, 1966.

Alke Zei. *The Sound of the Dragon's Feet.* Dutton, 1979.

Scandinavia

Ulla Andersen. *We Live in Denmark.* Watts, 1984.

Peter Asbjørnsen. *East of the Sun and West of the Moon.* Doubleday, 1977.

James Bowman. *Tales from A Finnish Tupa.* Whitman, 1936.

Patricia Coombs. *The Magic Pot.* Lothrop, 1977.

Mary Hatch. *13 Danish Tales.* Harcourt, 1947.

Virginia Haviland. *Favorite Fairy Tales Told in Denmark.* Little, 1971.

———. *Favorite Fairy Tales Told in Norway.* Little, 1961.

———. *Favorite Fairy Tales Told in Sweden.* Little, 1966.

Martin Hintz. *Sweden.* Children's Press, 1985.

Anita Lobel. *King Rooster, Queen Hen.* Greenwillow, 1975.

*———. *The Pancake.* Greenwillow, 1978.

Sylvia Munsen. *Cooking the Norwegian Way.* Lerner, 1982.

Elsa Olenius, comp. *Great Swedish Fairy Tales.* Delacorte, 1973.

Joan Sandin. *The Long Way to a New Land.* Harper, 1981.

Otto Svend. *The Giant Fish and Other Stories.* Larousse, 1983.

Thailand

Minfong Ho. *Hush! A Thai Lullaby.* Orchard Books, 1996.

Astrid Lindgren. *Noy Lives in Thailand.* Macmillan, 1967.

Judith Spiegelman. *Galong, River Boy of Thailand.* Messner, 1970.

Venezuela

Helen Croucher, *Jaguar.* Scholastic, 1997.

United States

In addition to the books listed below under special regions, here are a few additional resources that will be helpful.

Amy Cohn. *From Sea to Shining Sea.* Scholastic, 1993.

Kathryn Cusick and Faye Morrison. *Golden Poppies: An Annotated Bibliography of California Historical Fiction and Non-Fiction for Young Readers.* Shoestring, 1986.

Elva Harman and Anna Milligan. *Reading for Young People: The Southwest.* American Library Association, 1982.

Barbara Immroth. *Texas in Children's Books: An Annotated Bibliography.* Shoestring, 1986.

Appalachia

Ann Isaac. *Swamp Angel.* Dutton, 1994.

George Ella Lyon. *Borrowed Children.* Watts, 1988.

Doris B. Smith. *Return to Bitter Creek: A Novel.* Viking, 1986.

Ethel F. Smothers. *Down in the Piney Woods.* Knopf, 1992.

Cajun (Acadia and Louisiana)

Berthe Amoss. *The Loup Garou.* Pelican, 1979.

John Bergeron. *Cajun Folklore.* Bergeron, 1980.

Muriel Fontenot Blackwell. *The Secret Dream.* Broadman, 1981.

Elaine C. Crump. *Chinaberry Beads.* Pelican, 1978 (poetry).

*Alice Durio. *Cajun Columbus.* Pelican, 1975.

Tim Edler. *The Adventures of Crawfish-Man.* Little Cajun Books, 1979.

———. *Dark Gator, Villain of the Atchafalaya.* Little Cajun Books, 1980.

*Mary Alice Fontenot. *Clovis and E. Escargot.* Acadiana, 1979.

———. *Clovis Crawfish and the Singing Cigales.* Pelican, 1981.

Lois Lenski. *Bayou Suzette.* Lippincott, 1943.

*James Rice. *Cajun Alphabet.* Pelican, 1976.

———. *Gaston Goes to Mardi Gras.* Pelican, 1977.

George Smith. *Bayou Boy and the Wolf Dog.* Quality Books, 1973

Isadore L. Sonnier. *Cajun Boy.* Exposition Press, 1980.

Robert Tallant. *Evangeline and the Acadians.* Random, 1957.

*Trosclair. *Cajun Night before Christmas.* Pelican. 1974.

EXPLORING SPECIAL IDENTITY GROUPS

Although many identity groups could be included, we have selected only three major groups: (1) the aged, (2) people with disabilities, and (3) women and girls.

Aging and the Aged

Jeannie Baker. *Grandmother.* Deutsch, 1978.

Anne E. Baldwin. *Sunflowers for Tina.* Four Winds, 1978.

Jennifer Bartoli. *Nona.* Harvey, 1975.

Gunnel Beckman. *That Early Spring.* Viking, 1977.

Rose Blue. *Grandma Didn't Wave Back.* Watts, 1972.

Pearl Buck. *The Beach Tree.* John Day, 1955.

Robert Burch. *Two That Were Tough.* Viking, 1976.

———. *The House of Wings.* Viking, 1972.

Betsy Byars. *Trouble River.* Viking, 1969.

Kay Chorao. *Lester's Overnight.* Dutton, 1977.

Vera Cleaver. *Queen of Hearts.* Lippincott, 1978.

——— and Bill Cleaver. *The Whys and Wherefores of Litta Belle Lee.* Atheneum, 1974.

Eth Clifford. *The Rocking Chair Rebellion.* Houghton Mifflin, 1978.

Helen Constant. *The Gift.* Knopf, 1983.

Barbara Corcoran. *The Faraway Island.* Atheneum, 1977.

Tomie de Paola. *Now One Foot, Now the Other.* Putnam and Sons, 1981.

———. *Watch Out for the Chicken Feet in Your Soup.* Prentice Hall, 1974.

Norma Farber. *How Does It Feel to Be Old?* Dutton, 1979.

Patricia Lee Gauch. *Grandpa and Me.* Coward, 1972.

Rumer Goden. *The Fairy Doll.* Viking, 1956.

M. B. Goffstein. *Fish for Supper.* Dial, 1976.

Susan Goldman. *Grandma Is Somebody Special.* Whitman, 1978.

———. *Grandpa and Me Together.* Whitman, 1979.

Bob Graham. *Rose Meets Mr. Wintergarten.* Candlewick Press, 1992.

Phyllis Green. *Mildred Murphy, How Does Your Garden Grow?* Dell, 1977.

Constance Greene. *The Unmaking of Rabbit.* Dell, 1972.

Lucille Heins. *My Very Special Friend.* Judson, 1974.

Kevin Henkes. *Grandpa & Bo.* Greenwillow, 1986.

Charlotte Herman. *Our Snowman Had Olive Eyes.* Dutton, 1977.

Russell Hoban. *How Tom Beat Captain Najork and His Hired Sportsman.* Atheneum, 1974.

Edith T. Hurd. *I Dance in My Red Pajamas.* Harper and Row, 1982.

Johanna Hurwitz. *Roz and Ozzie.* Morrow, 1992.

Louise A. Jackson. *Grandpa Had a Windmill, Grandma Had a Churn.* Parent, 1977.

Dayal K. Khalsa. *Tales of a Gambling Grandma.* Potter, 1986.

Barbara Kirk. *Grandpa, Me, & Our House in the Tree.* MacMillan, 1976.

Eleanor J. Lapp. *The Mice Came in Early This Year.* Whitman, 1976.

Kathryn Lasky. *I Have Four Names for My Grandfather.* Little, Brown, 1976.

———. *My Island Grandma.* Warne, 1979.

Joan Lexau. *Benjie on His Own.* Dial, 1970.

Jan Loof. *My Grandpa Is a Pirate.* Harper, 1968.

Max Lundgren. *Matt's Grandfather.* Putnam, 1972.

Norma Fox Mazer. *A Figure of Speech.* Delacourt, 1973.

J. F. Mearian. *Someone Slightly Different.* Dial, 1980.

Miska Miles. *Annie and the Old One.* Little, Brown, 1971.

Claudia Mills. *Gus and Grandpa.* Farrar, Stauss, 1997.

Elaine Moore. *Grandma's House.* Lothrop, Lee and Shepard, 1985.

Evaline Ness. *Josefina February.* Scribner's, 1963.

Shirley P. Newman. *Tell Me, Grandpa; Tell Me, Grandma.* Houghton, 1979.

Steven Palay. *I Love My Grandma.* Raintree, 1977.

Melinda Pollowitz. *Cinnamon Cane.* Harper and Row, 1977.

Fran Pratt. *Understanding Aging.* Conant School, 1982.

Dorka Raynor. *Grandparents around the World.* Whitman, 1977.

Eleanor Schick. *Peter and Mr. Brandon.* Macmillan, 1974.

David M. Schwartz. *Supergrandpa.* Lothrop, 1991.

Ruth Sonneborn. *I Love Gram.* Viking, 1971.

Tobi Tobias. *Jane Wishing.* Viking, 1977.

Janice May Udry. *Mary Jo's Grandmother.* Whitman, 1970.

Susan Varley. *Badger's Parting Gifts.* Lothrop, Lee and Shepard, 1994.

Barbara Williams. *Kevin's Grandma.* Dutton, 1975.

Elizabeth Winthrop. *Walking Away.* Harper and Row, 1973.

Sally Wittman. *A Special Trade.* Harper and Row, 1978.

Charlotte Zolotow. *I Know a Lady.* Greenwillow, 1984.

———. *My Grandson Lew.* Harper, 1974.

People with Disabilities

General Resources

Joanne E. Bernstein and Bryna J. Fireside. *Special Parents, Special Children.* Whitman, 1991.

Tricia Brown. *Someone Special, Just like You.* Holt, 1984. Photographs.

*Mary Ellen Powers. *Our Teacher's in a Wheelchair.* Whitman, 1986.

Ron Roy. *Move Over, Wheelchairs Coming Through: Seven Young People in Wheelchairs Talk about Their Lives.* Clarion, 1985.

Blindness/Problems with Eyesight

Lynn Hall. *The Soul of the Silver Dog.* Harcourt, 1992.

Florence Heide. *Sound of Sunshine, Sound of Rain.* Parents', 1972.

Madeleine L'Engle. *The Young Unicorns.* Farrar, Straus, 1968.

Ramona Maher. *The Blind Boy and the Loon and Other Eskimo Myths.* Day, 1969.

Sharon Mathis. *Listen for the Fig Tree.* Viking, 1974.

*Ellen Raskin. *Spectacles.* Atheneum, 1978.

Theodore Taylor. *The Cay.* Doubleday, 1969.

William Thomas. *The New Boy Is Blind.* Thomas, 1980.

Brain Damage

Daniel Keyes. *Flowers for Algernon.* Harcourt, 1966.

Kim Platt. *Hey, Dummy.* Dell, 1971.

C. L. Rinaldo. *Dark Dreams.* Harper, 1974.

Cerebral Palsy

*Joan Fassler. *Howie Helps Himself.* Whitman, 1975.

Jean Little. *Mine for Keeps.* Little, 1962.

Jan Slepian. *The Alfred Summer.* Macmillan, 1980.

Deafness

Elaine Costello. *Signing: How to Speak with Your Hands.* Bantam, 1983.

Meindert DeJong. *Journey from Peppermint Street.* Harper, 1968.

Judith Greenberg. *What Is the Sign for Friend?* Lothrop, 1985.

Ellen Howard. *The Cellar.* Atheneum, 1992.

Edna Levine. *Lisa and Her Soundless World.* Human Sciences Press, 1974.

Mary Riskind. *Apple Is My Sign.* Houghton, 1981.

Eleanor Spence. *The Nothing Place.* Harper, 1972.

Lou Walker. *Amy: The Story of a Deaf Child.* Lodestar, 1985.

Maia Wojciechowska. *A Single Light.* Bantam, 1968.

Dwarfism

M. E. Kerr. *Little Little.* Harper, 1981.

Susan Kuklin. *Thinking Big; The Story of a Young Dwarf.* Lothrop, 1986.

Emotional Problems/Mental Illness

Eve Bunting. *One More Flight.* Warne, 1976.

Carol Carrick. *Stay Away from Simon.* Clarion, 1985.

Joanne Greenberg. (Hannah Green). *I Never Promised You a Rose Garden.* Holt, 1964.

Virginia Hamilton. *The Planet of Junior Brown.* Macmillan, 1971.

Deborah Hautizig. *Second Star to the Right.* Greenwillow, 1981.

Florence Heide. *Secret Dreamer, Secret Dreams.* Lippincott, 1978.

M. E. Kerr. *Dinky Hocker Shoots Smack!* Dell, 1972.

Norma Klein. *It's Not What You Expect.* Pantheon, 1973.

Phyllis Naylor. *The Keeper.* Atheneum, 1986.

John Newfeld. *Lisa, Bright and Dark.* Phillips, 1969.

Zibby O'Neal. *The Language of Goldfish.* Viking, 1980.

Virginia Sorensen. *Miracles on Maple Hill.* Harcourt, 1956.

Patricia Windsor. *The Summer Before.* Harper, 1973.

Learning Disabled

*Joe Lasker. *He's My Brother.* Whitman, 1974.

Marilyn Levinson. *And Don't Bring Jeremy.* Holt, 1985.

Missing Limbs

Cynthia Voigt. *Izzy, Willy-Nilly.* Atheneum, 1986.

Orthopedic Impairment

Harold Courlander. *The Son of the Leopard.* Crown, 1974.

Marguerite DeAngeli. *The Door in the Wall.* Doubleday, 1949.

Meindert DeJong. *The Wheel on the School.* Harper, 1954.

Ester Forbes. *Johnny Tremain.* Houghton, 1971.

Russell Freedman. *Franklin Delano Roosevelt.* Clarion Books, 1991.

Patricia Lee Gauch. *This Time, Tempe Wick?* Putnam, 1992.

Isabelle Holland. *Heads You Win, Tails I Lose.* Lippincott, 1973.

Irene Hunt. *No Promise in the Wind.* Follett, 1970.

Mollie Hunter. *The Stronghold.* Harper, 1974.

Katherine Paterson. *Of Nightingales That Weep.* Crowell, 1974.

Bonnie Turner. *The Haunted Igloo.* Houghton Mifflin, 1991.

Retardation

Frank Bonham. *Mystery of the Fat Cat.* Dutton, 1968.

Betsy Byars. *Summer of the Swans.* Viking, 1970.

Vera Cleaver and Bill Cleaver. *Me, Too.* Lippincott, 1973.

Lucille Clifton. *My Friend Jacob.* Dutton, 1980.

Barthe DeClements. *6th Grade Can Really Kill You.* Viking, 1985.

Gerda Klein. *The Blue Rose.* Hill, 1974.

Shyness

Muriel Blaustein. *Jim Chimp's Story.* Simon and Schuster, 1992.

Speech Impediments

Rebecca Caudill. *A Certain Small Shepherd.* Holt, 1965.

Julia Cunningham. *Burnish Me Bright.* Pantheon, 1970.

Joan Fassler. *Don't Worry, Dear.* Human Sciences, 1971.

Marguerite Henry. *King of the Wind.* Rand, 1948.

Breaking Down Stereotypes of Women

Primary Grades

Arlene Alda. *Sonya's Mommy Works.* Simon, 1982. A photographic essay of a contemporary family in which mother has a career.

Norma Klein. *Girls Can Be Anything.* Dutton, 1973. Marina lets her kindergarten pal, Adam, know that "girls can be anything."

Mercer Mayer. *Liza Lou and the Yeller Belly Swamp.* Four Winds, 1976. How Liza Lou outwits the swamp devil.

Eve Merrian. *Mommies at Work.* Scholastic, 1973. Picture book showing all kinds of mommies at all kinds of jobs.

Amy Schwartz. *Bea and Mr. Jones.* Puffin, 1982. A kindergartner and her father change places.

John Steptoe. *Daddy Is a Monster . . . Sometimes.* Lippincott, 1980. Story of a single, loving parent and his two children.

———. *My Special Best Words.* Viking, 1974. A delightful picture book about Bweela, age three, Javaka, age one, and their father.

Middle Grades

Karen Ackerman, *When Mama Retires.* Knopf, 1992.

Sally Hobart Alexander. *Maggie's Whopper.* Macmillan, 1992.

Sue Alexander. *Nadia the Willful.* Pantheon, 1983. Nadia, daughter of Sheik Tarik, deals with her brother's death.

Caroline Bauer. *My Mom Travels a Lot.* Warne, 1982. Story about good and bad situations caused by mother's many absences from home.

Eve Bunting. *Summer Wheels.* Harcourt, 1992.

Vera and Bill Cleaver. *Hazel Rye.* Lippincott, 1983. The struggles between an eleven-year-old girl and her father.

B. Cole. *Princess Smartypants.* Putnam, 1986.

Mary Jett-Simpson. "Girls Are Not Dodo Birds! Exploring Gender Equity Issues in the Language Arts Classroom." *Language Arts.* 70:104–108. Feb., 1992.

Nancy Kline. *Elizabeth Blackwell: A Doctor's Triumph.* Conari Press, 1997.

Madeline L'Engle. *A Wrinkle in Time.* Ariel, 1962.

Ogden Nash. *The Adventures of Isabel.* Illustrated by James Marshall. Little, Brown, 1991.

Tamora Pierce. *Alanna, The First Adventure.* Atheneum, 1983. Lord Alan's twin daughter, Alanna, and son, Thom, trade places. Alanna trains to be a knight, and Thom trains to be a sorcerer.

Doreen Rappaport. *Living Dangerously: American Women Who Risk Their Lives.* Harper, 1991.

Barbara Robinson. *The Best Christmas Pageant Ever.* Harper, 1972. Story of family of six children who wreak havoc on the town's annual Christmas pageant.

Phyllis Root. *The Listening Silence.* Harper, 1992.

Cynthia Voight. *Homecoming.* Atheneum, 1981. Dicey, a thirteen-year-old girl, cares for her brothers and sisters after they are abandoned. See also *Dicey's Song, The Calandar Papers,* and *Solitary Blue* by the same author.

Young Adults

Carol Brink. *Caddie Woodlawn.* Macmillan, 1970. Caddie, who lives in the Wisconsin frontier, is an adventurous tomboy who resists accepting her sex role.

Barbara Cohen. *Seven Daughters and Seven Sons.* Atheneum, 1982. Buran of Baghdad disguises herself as a boy to help her family.

Norma Klein. *Give and Take.* Viking, 1985. The summer before Spence enters college provides unexpected experiences with women.

———. *Mom, the Wolf Man and Me.* Pantheon, 1972. Brett's unmarried mother decides to marry without asking her daughter's permission.

Norma Fox Mazer. *Dear Bill, Remember Me?* Delacorte, 1977. Collection of eight short stories in which young girls break away from conventional female role.

Robin McKinley. *The Blue Sword.* Greenwillow, 1983. Harry, a teenage girl, exhibits courage in this story of magic and fantasy.

Marilyn Sachs. *Call Me Ruth.* Doubleday, 1982. Rifka (Ruth) and her mother, Faigel, are Russian immigrants. Ruth is torn between the old and new ways.

Index